Party Politics

IVAN HINDERAKER
UNIVERSITY OF CALIFORNIA
AT LOS ANGELES

Party Politics

Henry Holt and Company   NEW YORK

To Birk and Mark

Preface

This book has two purposes. The first is to describe the American political system and the character and functions of its two major parties — Democratic and Republican. The second is to distill from lessons of American political history and from findings of contemporary research the variables that appear to be most influential in determining which side in an election contest will win or lose. Out of the development of both of these related themes it is my hope that the reader, whether he agrees with my conclusions or not, will arrive at a better understanding of American party politics.

To those publishers who have granted permission to reprint passages from their books and cartoons, to the many authors from whose works I have drawn, and to all those who have helped in the preparation of the manuscript I wish to acknowledge my thanks.

Los Angeles, Calif.   I. H.
March 1, 1956

Acknowledgments

I am grateful to the following cartoonists (and their publishers) who have so aptly " hit the nail on the head " with so very few words:

American Meat Institute, 52

Jim Berryman, *The Washington Evening Star,* 527

Brett, *The Miami Herald,* 525

Jacob Burck, *Chicago Sun-Times,* 408

Conrad, *The Denver Post,* 388

Whitney Darrow, Jr., *The New Yorker,* 467, 513

Ben Day. From a collection of cartoons in the Library of the University of California at Los Angeles, 8

Robert Day, *The New Yorker,* 203, 451

Richard Decker, *The New Yorker,* 436

Democratic National Committee, 560, 561

Herblock, *The Washington Post,* 35, 148, 350, 601

Helen E. Hokinson, *The New Yorker,* 119

Interlandi, *The Des Moines Register and Tribune,* 104, 376

Justus, *The Minneapolis Star,* 235, 424, 567, 666

R. A. Lewis, *The Milwaukee Journal,* 198, 226

John T. McCutcheon, *Chicago Tribune,* 77

Thomas Nast, *Harper's Weekly,* 316, 317, 477

Eldon Pletcher, *The Sioux City Journal,* 627

Newton Pratt, *The Sacramento Bee,* 8, 69, 164, 178, 379, 509

Bruce Russell, *The Los Angeles Times,* 43

Yardley, *The Baltimore Sun,* 542

Contents

PART ONE

Introduction

INTRODUCTION

The major party and the pressure group are the organized institutions through which most individuals collectively participate in the American political process. For a relatively insignificant proportion of the electorate there is also the alternative of the minor party.

Though the distinctions between major parties, pressure groups, and minor parties are not always clear, in general they are different in the following respects. The major party is primarily interested in developing an appeal broad enough to capture the offices of government and only secondarily is it concerned with specific governmental programs. Conversely, the pressure group has as its foremost end the influencing of governmental policies in the areas of the pressure group's interest. Though the pressure group too may engage in public election activity, the purpose is not the winning of elections as such but rather to obtain access to elected public officials who, by their official actions, can help or hurt the pressure group in its efforts to gain what it wants from government.

The objectives of minor parties fall somewhere between those of the major parties and pressure groups with some minor parties more like the former and others more like the latter.

Part One places the major party, the pressure group, and the minor party into relationship with one another and all three institutions into relationship with the government they either want to run or influence. Before proceeding to develop the functions and characteristics of these institutions, however, it is first necessary to introduce the men who make the American political system work — the politicans. Here is the subject of the first chapter.

The Politician

Lincoln's strength is of a peculiar kind. It is not aggressive so much as passive and among passive things it is like the strength not so much of a stone buttress as of a wire cable. It is strength swaying to every influence, yielding on this side and on that to popular needs, yet tenaciously and inflexibly bound to carry its great end; and probably by no other kind of strength could our national ship have been drawn safely thus far during the tossings and tempests which beset her way. Surrounded by all sorts of conflicting claims, by traitors, by half-hearted timid men, by Border State men and free State men, by radical Abolitionists and Conservatives, he has listened to all, weighed the words of all, waited, observed, yielded now here and now there, but in the main kept one inflexible, honest purpose, and drawn the national ship through.

Harriet Beecher Stowe [1]

All Americans can pay their respects as they lift eyes up the full height of the Washington Monument, as they stand in hushed stillness in the Lincoln Memorial or across the Potomac in the Jefferson Memorial, or as they gaze off above the treetops at Mount Rushmore in the Black Hills of South Dakota where the sculptured head of Theodore Roosevelt is placed alongside the busts of these three of his predecessors in the office of the President of the United States. These and some few others are the great American statesmen. Yet the monuments didn't get where they are, nor did the men for whom

----

[1] *Watchman and Reflector,* January, 1864. Quoted by Wilfred E. Binkley, *American Political Parties* (New York: Alfred A. Knopf, 1949), p. 240.

the monuments were erected get into public office and leave outstand-
ing records as Presidents because they were *not* politicians. Each man
made the record that produced the monument for precisely the opposite reason. He was a master politician.

What do we think about real live politicians? That is quite another matter. The popular stereotype is not flattering. Politicians, the
stereotype suggests, are fat from living out of the public trough,
spineless because they refuse or have to be pushed into taking stands
on controversial issues, opportunistic because they have no principles,
selfish because they have no conception of the higher public interest,
shameless because they are willing to be photographed kissing anything from a race horse to an infant in arms, and corrupt because no
man can long seek and hold public office without becoming a tool of
the devil.

When George Gallup's National Institute of Public Opinion in
1944 asked its now famous and since-repeated question — " If you
have a son would you like to see him go into politics as a life work
when he gets out of school? " only 30 percent of his sample said
" Yes," and 70 percent said " No." When those who indicated they
would like to see their sons enter politics were asked to give reasons
for their position, the largest classifiable group (22 percent) said,
" Need clean-minded men in politics to supplant crooks in there
now; need higher type; need men of character and education."
Thirty percent of those who answered in the negative thought, " Politics are too crooked, unethical, corrupt, rotten . . . ; no honest politicians." Another 16 percent of those answering " No " felt, " Temptations and influences too great; even good men become crooked;
would be led astray by bad influences; many politicians are cor-
rupted." [2]

What are the reasons for this stereotype of the politician? There
has been proved corruption, both Democratic and Republican brand.
Both parties and their politicians have sometimes used unethical tactics. Politicians have called other politicians names and have im-
pugned their motives, and the effects of name-calling and motive
questioning linger on. People seek scapegoats on which to blame
their difficulties, and politicians are handy targets, especially those
who happened to be in office when the troubles started. Or people

[2] From Hadley Cantril (ed.), *Public Opinion 1936–1946* (Princeton:
Princeton University Press, 1951), p. 534.

wish to satisfy ego drives in order to be " better," and politicians in all their caricatured degeneracy are easy to feel superior to. These are some of the more common explanations. Though they may in part help answer the question, they do not constitute the whole answer.

One of the most important reasons for the tendency to lump politicians into a " low-life " category, regardless of whether they are very good or very bad or somewhere in between, stems from a failure, an inability, or an unwillingness to understand a few basic facts about our system of government. First, it cannot work without the politician. Second, the politician has to operate within a system which imposes certain requirements with which he must to some degree conform in order to politically serve and survive.

THE POLITICIAN AND HIS FUNCTIONS

Who are the politicians? The first thought may be of some political boss like Thomas Joseph Pendergast of Kansas City, Missouri, a man who never ran for office but exercised more power in his territory than any who did. By dispensing jobs and social services of a sort, controlling ballot boxes, and maintaining a tightly disciplined organization, he was able to pick mayors, governors, and United States Senators. He controlled city and state contracts and, on the side, made himself personally wealthy through his cement and liquor businesses. Here was a man who literally had a stranglehold over the affairs of his city and state, and because of this fact, a man with more than just a little influence in national politics.

Massachusetts had its Curley; Pennsylvania, its long succession of " big " Republican bosses; Tennessee, its Crump; Illinois, its Kellys and Nashs. Nor does the roll call of the old-time bosses stop with the names of these men. Others using similar techniques rose to political power in most of the major cities of the land. Their philosophies represented some variation of the theme of the once notorious Tammany Hall's George Washington Plunkitt — " There's an honest graft, and I'm an example of how it works. I might sum up the whole thing by sayin': ' I seen my opportunities and I took 'em.' " [3] Some of these men went to jail for " seein' and takin' " and some didn't, but all contributed to the stereotype of the politician.

---

[3] W. L. Riordon, *Plunkitt of Tammany Hall* (New York: McClure, Phillips and Company, 1905) , p. 3.

If not a city boss, perhaps the first thought that comes to mind at the mention of the word " politician " is a public official who was either convicted of violating the law or one on whose political activities enough doubt was cast to leave the public with the feeling that he should have been convicted. For a time in 1947, Democratic Congressman Andrew J. May of Kentucky, long chairman of the House Military Affairs Committee, occupied the headlines when he was indicted and convicted of bribery and conspiracy. So did Republican Congressman J. Parnell Thomas of New Jersey, nationally known as chairman of the House Un-American Activities Committee. In 1949 he too was indicted and convicted of conspiring to defraud through salary kick-backs from persons on his office staff.

In 1951 Democratic National Committee Chairman William M. Boyle resigned under fire for " selling political influence." In 1953, because of charges that he had previously exercised improper influence in connection with public buildings in Kansas, Republican National Chairman Wesley Roberts also resigned under a similar barrage of criticism. Whether one wants to go back to Teapot Dome or further, or only to the more recent Bureau of Internal Revenue disclosures of 1951 or the New York race track scandals of 1953, there will be current news and big black headlines about politicians who have not or who seem not to have lived up to their calling as what T. V. Smith terms " secular priests of our common faith in one another."

At the same time the public hears much less of the politicians who are not breaking the law, not taking liberties with the spirit of the law, or not being accused of either. The term " politician " thus comes to be associated with all that is disreputable or shady in public life, but no one word has evolved to round out the other half of a dichotomy. " Statesman " is not such a term. It is a title earned by a very few. Only out of death, passage of time, and from sympathetic historians are the reputations of men who were politicians elevated to the mythical pinnacle of statesmanship.

We refer to men running for public or political party office as " candidates "; to party officials as " party officers," or by their respective party title such as " state chairman "; to members of legislative bodies as " representatives " or " senators," or by their legislative position titles such as " speaker "; and to elected officeholders in executive branches of government by such titles as " president " or " governor." These designations do serve an important purpose, but they do not fill the need for what all those occupying such positions have in common. Neither do such titles account for the many who, though they hold no official party or public position, perform political functions just as surely as those who are party or public officials or candidates for public office.

POLITICIANS

Even more deficient for the purposes of definition is a classification which attempts to use "good politician" to distinguish from "bad politician." The political function is, in itself, neither good nor bad. Politicians, as they perform political functions, can be either good or bad or some degree of either, depending upon who, whether it be a court or a voter, is making the value judgment and depending upon the standards against which the judgment is being made.

Artemus Ward, when he remarked to Abraham Lincoln, " I am no politician, and my other habits are good," made interesting popular humor but not good scholarly sense. A few similar examples of usages that have distorted the meaning of other terms related to

AND " POLITICIANS "

" politician " reinforce the point. Popularly, the word " propagandist " tends to be associated with one who either illegally or unethically mass communicates, or in an even more extreme interpretation, with anyone who communicates a message to which the person making the judgment is opposed. If the propagandist is on your side, he is a " public relations man " engaged in respectable " educating." Likewise with the term " lobbyist." One who engages in illegal or unethical influencing of legislators tends to be associated with that title, or perhaps one who merely lobbies for a point of view on an issue different from that which the person making the judgment holds. If the lobbyist is on your side, the tendency is to find some other title like " legislative advocate " with which to describe his activities. So also with the " political machine " (bad) as distinguished from the " political organization " (better, if not good) . Yet divorced from their propagandistic content, the terms " propagandist," " lobbyist " or " political machine " are and should be just as neutral as politician.

Who, then, is the politician? For the purposes of this study of *Party Politics*, the politician is one who runs for or holds elective public office, one who runs for or holds elective political party office, or one who is actively associated with candidates, elected public office-holders, political parties, or independent organizations in their attempts to influence the outcome of elections for public office.

The dangers of over-simplification and arbitrary delimitation in such a definition are immediately apparent. Ruled out is the universally broad interpretation that anyone engaged in influencing any other person or persons is a politician. Also ruled out are all the individuals who contest for position and power in the multitude of organizations which are not primarily concerned with contesting in elections for public offices. Neither does the definition include those who man the public offices or one party's offices in authoritarian states. Rather, the definition is designed for the democratic-representative system of government, and central to the definition is the concept of free elections to determine who shall hold elective public office. The politician seeks actively to win and hold elective public office, either for himself or for someone whom he supports.

The function of the politician is not only to conduct the affairs of government. Dictators also govern. His function is rather a combination of two principal functions — governing when in office and attempting to obtain or maintain power through the winning of popular support. Each element must be placed in relationship with the other. They are inseparably interrelated, and the politician always has to be working at mobilizing the voters in majority or plurality quantity, whichever is necessary, in order to win election or re-election to public office.

In his role of building popular support, the politician offers an alternative which the voter may accept or reject. At the same time, and whether the politician so intends or not, he also interests and educates the citizens in public affairs. In his role of governing, if given an opportunity to govern, the politician provides a peaceful means through which the conflicts of a democratic society can be mediated. His duty here is " to find through the art of compromise a way of life in which nobody will escape some share of common burdens and in which everybody will get some share of the benefits of life which we together create." [4]

Two eloquently written passages, the first by Chester C. Maxey, President of Whitman College, and the second by Frederick M. Davenport, himself a former Congressman and throughout his life a practicing politician, cut through to the heart of the politician's function. Both are quoted at length:

> When it is tried to picture democracy without politicians, the imagination balks. Popular rule supposedly is accomplished by the force of public opinion expressing and exerting itself in definite ways and to definite ends. But when one considers the dynamics of public opinion, he sees the hand of the politician necessarily ever at work. Large masses of people . . . do not move spontaneously and universally in self-determined directions. Like the waters of the sea, they are inert and incapable of self-propulsion. Collective intelligence and collective will independent of the individual humans constituting the collectivity simply do not exist; hence, public opinion cannot be self-starting and self-guiding. In order to think and act with any degree of cohesion and common purpose the vast populations of modern states must be activated and confined to a few major channels of response to activation. Stimulation alone is not enough; there must be stimulation to patterns of thought and action which are so few and so readily understandable that the individual particles of the great human mass may effectively group themselves for common behavior. Here is where the politicians perform a highly useful social function. They supply not only the necessary stimulation but also the indispensable canalization whereby the multi-scrambled ideas and motivations of the millions may be converted into corporate decisions and action. This renders possible the thing called democratic government, and the politicians are the catalyzers of the democratic process. [5]

---

[4] T. V. Smith, *The Legislative Way of Life* (Fulton, Mo.: Westminster College, 1940), p. 55.

[5] Chester C. Maxey, "A Plea for the Politician," *The Western Political Quarterly* (September, 1948), Vol. I, No. 3, p. 277. Reprinted by permission of *The Western Political Quarterly*.

The able and useful type of politician is the man who persuades people to behave like rational human beings when they are in danger of milling around like muddle-headed cattle, something that now and then happens in the best-regulated democracies. He understands the management of the gregarious instinct in mankind. He has a peculiar sensitivity to the mental, and particularly to the emotional, processes of the popular mind. He knows how to mellow and mollify, if anybody can, the pressure groups, such as the newspapers, the financiers, the labor leaders, the veterans, the farmers. His is the task in a modern democracy of moulding these disparate and often hostile interests into something like mutual understanding. It is his business to refine and combine the two kinds of energies which are ever fighting for the mastery in a democracy — the ignorance, the folly, the envy, the passion, the prejudice and the self-interest on the one hand, and the virtue, the kindliness and the idealism of the masses of the people on the other.[6]

THE POLITICIAN: HIS ENVIRONMENT

If some politicians sometimes and other politicians most of the time fall or seem to fall short of a theoretically ideal performance of their function, the cause may lie either with the man and his own standards or in the institutional framework within which he must operate. This section is an examination of the pressures imposed on the man by the system.

The confession of an anonymous Congressman is in point. Why did he run for office the first time? Because he felt the incumbent in his district was such a fence straddler and engaged in so many foolish publicity antics that the voters deserved something better. Mr. Anonymous defeated the incumbent.

Did the new Congressman act much differently? The answer, he confesses, was in the negative. Though he did give himself the benefit of the doubt by feeling that he was more forthright and that his efforts for publicity were in better taste, he found himself saying and doing things in a manner not substantially different from his predecessor. Once the anonymous Congressman settled himself in his House of Representatives office in Washington, decided he liked being a Congressman, and began to think about his next election cam-

---

[6] Frederick M. Davenport, " The Magnitude of the Task of the Politician," *Harvard Business Review* (July, 1933) , Vol. 11. No. 4, p. 470. Reprinted by permission of the *Harvard Business Review*.

paign only two years hence, he began to understand much more clearly some things about the political system which only started to be apparent during his campaign.[7]

More votes than his opponent had put him into public office. He would have to win more votes than his future opponents to stay in office. Winning votes would be a factor which he would have to take into consideration in everything he did as long as he remained in public office. Before running for office the anonymous Congressman had thought of campaigning as being separate from and incidental to governing. Now he had become fully aware of the inseparability of the two functions.

Combining the arts of political leadership and winning votes, however, is no simple achievement. Furthermore, if the importance of the combined process and its dynamics are not understood, even the most able politician can often be made to appear to be a very foolish or evil man, even though he is acting intelligently and is motivated by high ideals.

If the only issues in politics were sin and motherhood, the politician would have few problems. He would oppose the former and favor the latter. But these are not the issues, even though some desperately try to make them so. The real issues are by their very nature controversial. On some issues on which opinion crystallizes and splits his constituency into two approximately equally balanced and intensely feeling opinion groups, the politician, if he can, may find it necessary to straddle the fence. On other issues which lend themselves to compromise, he must try to find the most acceptable common ground and stand on it, even at the risk of making all sides a little unhappy. On still other issues, the resolution of which may be postponed, the politician may be forced to withhold a commitment until the last possible moment in the hope that somehow the problem will solve itself or events will make decision easier at a later date. In any constituency there will also be issues on which the vast majority take a strong position on one side. Here, even though the politician may personally disagree, he may find it necessary to put aside his own feelings for a more basic consideration — to stay in office and thus be able to provide the leadership he can for the other policies in which he believes.

As an opinion leader, the politician worthy of his title dare not

---

[7] Adapted from an anonymous Congressman's " confession."

lose touch with his constituency by getting too far ahead of it. If he does, he risks putting himself out on an issue limb so far that the branch is too weak to hold him up. Politics is the art of the possible. The successful politician knows when and on what to compromise, and when and on what to stand firm. He has his finger on the public pulse and knows how to translate the pulse beats into the kind of words and actions which can produce political results. He knows how to attract, lead, and hold public attention.

In his second campaign for the Illinois State Legislature, Abraham Lincoln made this pledge:

> If elected I shall consider the whole people of Sangamon County as my constituents, as well as those that supported me. While acting as their representative I shall be governed by their will on all such subjects upon which I have the means of knowing what their will is, and upon all others I shall do what my own judgment teaches me will best advance their interests.[8]

Though this statement of the young Lincoln appears to overlook the function of leadership, it does in essence show an understanding of an aspect of politics without which political leadership is impossible — a basic respect for public opinion and the power of public opinion. What Lincoln here leaves unsaid, but what his total political record represents, is the mark of the highest order of political ability, namely, that he succeeded in leading though he seemed to follow.

Fence straddling, compromise, postponement, and sensitivity to the opinions of the electorate represent neither corruption nor immorality. Nor are they the marks of weak and vacillating men. The environment of the democratic-representative system is such that no man can be a successful politician without being skilled in these arts. An examination of the electorate, as viewed from the vantage point of the politician, shows why this statement is true.

Four words and a phrase, suggests George A. Graham, dominate the lives of the vast majority of the American people in their relation to their government — specialist, organization, loyalty, pressure, and " I am not a politician." In our highly complex society we tend to know about and be interested more and more in our own specialties and less and less in the whole broad field of public affairs. We are organized into thousands of specialized organizations. Our primary loyalty,

---

[8] Quoted by Smith, *op. cit.,* p. 86.

except in times of national crisis like war, tends to lie with the specialized organizations to which we belong. Through the specialized
organizations we focus intense pressures on those who govern to
adopt policies which we regard as furthering our own and immediate
objectives. All the while we insist, " I am not a politician," and proceed to leave to others the business of being candidates for public
office, holding public office, or working in political parties. By dis-
avowing politics in the broader public sense, we find it easier to in-
tensify our loyalty to our specialized organizations and to go ahead
to press our demands on those who are the politicians.[9]

If the many interest groups were just passively interested in governmental policy, the politician's problem would not be the complicated one it is. He might, immediately and forthrightly, without giving the matter a second thought, take whichever position on an issue
he felt best combined his concept of the public interest with what he
felt to be the opinion in his constituency. But pressure groups are
not passive by nature or intent, and their leaders, some subtly and
others not so subtly, do their best to wield their weapons of votes and
campaign contributions where both will hurt if the politician does
not do what they want him to do.

From the time he begins to campaign or help others campaign
for public office, the politician is immediately made aware of the
pressure groups. Perhaps because he is a member of one group and
an opposition group feels its chances for sympathetic treatment would
be low should he be elected, the opposition group may file one of its
members to run against him. Inevitably he will receive questionnaires
from a multitude of pressure groups asking for his opinion on issues
about which each is most concerned. One day he may have the representatives of the Women's Christian Temperance Union call on
him in an attempt to size him up, and the next day there is likely to
be a delegation from the associated brewers. To make sure he knows
why the groups of which he himself is a member are supporting him,
perhaps he will be informed that they can wholeheartedly back his
aspirations for public office because they know he will be their friend
when they have elected him.

Always the representatives of the interest groups will in some
manner or another let him know how many members, by generous

    [9] From George A. Graham, *Morality in American Politics* (New York:
Random House, 1952) , pp. 253–259.

computation, they have. Always also the group leaders will imply that theirs is a powerful and unified organization which can deliver a block of votes either for or against him depending upon whether or not he can see fit to react favorably to what the group wants.

The candidate and his organization will also need money with which to buy newspaper ads, mailings, placards, billboards, and radio and television time. Though the amounts necessary have never been small, campaign costs have skyrocketed in recent years with the advent of the new mass media of communication. Congressman Martin Dies (D), Texas, estimates that where a good Congressional campaign could be staged on $7,500 in 1930, today at the same relative effectiveness level, the cost will mount to from $25,000 to $50,000. If one runs for the United States Senate in Texas, Dies estimates, he will need at least $500,000.[10] Congressman Dies' figures are not out of line with comparable costs for comparable campaigns in other states. If the candidate's object is the White House, the money necessary is measured in millions instead of hundreds of thousands or thousands of dollars.

From where does such money come? Mass drives for many little contributions for political campaigns have been notably unsuccessful. That means that the amounts have to be raised from big contributors, either individuals or pressure groups. Generally it is the latter, and if large contributions come from individuals, they are almost always from persons with strong pressure group ties.

The campaign of the candidate for public office will also need precinct workers to make grass-roots contacts. Some volunteer workers the candidate will attract himself. Some he might take on as paid employees, but this makes it necessary to raise more money. Some other workers may be mobilized from among the membership of supporting pressure groups, but here as with contributions, the implication of the pressure group is that its contribution of man-hours also comes for a price. Where funds and election workers are mobilized by the candidate's political party, the group pressures, though more diffuse and indirect, nevertheless still operate, if not directly on the candidate, then indirectly through the party to the candidate.

Not only the politician's political life is at stake and vulnerable, however. Most politicians are not full-time politicians and carry on their political activity as incidental to their business. Pressures can

---

[10] *Saturday Evening Post* (October 30, 1954), Vol. 227, No. 18, p. 138.

be applied on a politician's business too, and the type of pressure is illustrated in the words of one first-term state legislator who gives his reasons for not seeking re-election:

> I'm in business. I have to make enough out of it to live well because my first responsibility is to my wife and children. But every time I cast a vote on a major issue, I lost customers. One side or another would boycott my store and take their trade elsewhere. I couldn't stand that for long. Soon I would have had the whole town against me. Nor could I cast an independent vote in the legislature if I had to think each time of the impact on the cash register at home. I decided that the only solution was to withdraw from politics.[11]

These are some of the stimuli which quickly make the politician conscious of the role of organized pressure groups and unorganized interests in the American political system and of the delicate nature of his relationships as a politician to them. If he is elected to public office, and for as long as he remains in public life, this is one of the political facts of life which the politician must take into account.

All politicians, if they are to have staying power, have to commit themselves in some degree to some combination of pressure groups. If the combination is strong, the politician's power base is on the way to becoming strong. But just as commitments are necessary, so are overcommitments dangerous. To overcommit to one or a few pressure groups is to risk the loss of the votes of members of still other groups — except where the latter may regard the commitment moderate enough to feel they too will have an opportunity to gain a fair hearing for their case at another time. The politician's commitment problem is further complicated by the fact that there are an indeterminable large number of voters who, though they have pressure group connections, do not feel them strongly enough to counterbalance other factors which might influence the way in which they vote.

To this point in the development of the politician's environment, the analysis has centered on the organization of the electorate as it relates to winning electoral support. Other elements of the environment, the politician's political party and the election system in which he must operate are the subjects of subsequent chapters of this book. One more environmental conditioning factor, however, deserves attention here — the nature of public office and the require-

---

[11] Richard L. Neuberger, *Adventures in Politics* (New York: Oxford University Press, 1952), p. 66. The first-term state legislator was not Mr. Neuberger.

ments which each office imposes on its occupant. The legislative system tends to produce legislative politicians of one mold; the environment of the elected public executive, another type.

First, take the problem of the legislator. Why does he tend to appear at best as an able specialist in some one field of governmental activity and at worst as a petty provincial politician? Only for a brief time in the early history of Congress were all introduced measures debated first on the floor where the whole house made policy decisions before the bills were sent to committee for polishing. The press of legislative business soon made it necessary to establish standing committees and to refer newly introduced bills to them for detailed study and policy recommendation. The standing committee system has since become the general practice in American legislative bodies. Here is where the bulk of legislative business is done. Here is where, if a member is to gain distinction and the public attention which goes with distinction, both will have to be earned. Though he might prefer to be a generalist concerned with the broad questions of all public policy, he is forced in the direction of specialization.

The demands of the dominant interests of his district supplement the standing committee system in producing a specialist-type of legislative politician. If the representative comes from a predominantly agricultural district, for example, he is expected to get himself on the agricultural committee and on committee issues and on house issues to " vote his district." If his opponents at home can show that he has not been both tireless and effective in the advancement of the " district's interests," he will have political consequences to pay.

Why is it that many of the men who rise to positions of legislative power often appear neither able nor representative of the entire community which the legislative body serves? In large part it is because committee assignments in Congress, at least for the choice committees, are based on seniority, and elevation up the committee ladder to the powerful chairmanship or to the number-one minority position is the result of seniority. Or, in state legislatures where the seniority rule is not always rigidly followed, top committee positions will tend to go to those who were strategic men in electing the presiding officer. Here too, ability or outlook is not generally the controlling consideration.

Why does it seem that the legislator is often not much more than an errand boy for his constituents, spending large portions of his time in obtaining information for them or making contacts for constituents having business with departments of the executive branch? It is because constituents expect such service, and the legislator has seen what has happened politically to those of his colleagues who neglected their letter writing or agency contacting. Why is the typical legislator an accomplished logroller, trading votes with other members, often regardless of the individual merits of the issue? It is because the legislator soon learns that most of his fellow legislators logroll, and that in order to get his legislation through he has to make trades or deals with his colleagues who also have bills they want passed.

Why does misconduct on the part of a legislator generally go unpunished by the house of which he is a member? In part it is because legislators regard such punishment as a dangerous weapon which could be used for political purposes, in part because they will want future votes or other support from the man who might have earned punishment, and in part a group feeling that one member should not question the motives or actions of fellow members. Why do legislators often appear to have little or no regard for party lines in their voting? Partially it is because their parties are so weak they either have no party line or are not in a position to give the legislator enough help to protect him from the pressure groups which would be offended by a vote against them.

This is not to say that the legislative system and all or most of its products are bad. Neither is it to say both the system and its products cannot be improved. It is rather to indicate some of the significant factors which operate in the system to produce the kind of legislative politicians it does.

Where the political environment to which the legislator finds himself subjected tends to make him a specialist or " local politician," that of the elected executive produces the opposite effect. The President or a governor has as his constituency not just one portion of the community but the entire community. Where the legislator may have only to consider the more homogeneous combination of power groups in his restricted area, the political sights of the elected executive must be more broadly directed to the whole and more heterogeneous city, state, or country.

The elected executive's responsibility to the voters is more direct than that of his legislative counterparts. Though he can pass the blame for an action or a failure to act to the legislature, nevertheless, he and his positions are exposed and in public view. He and only he, in the final analysis, is held responsible for what he and his executive establishment say and do.

Responding to his different environment, the successful executive politician tends to be a distinct type as is the legislative politician another type. When a " typical " legislator moves on to serve as an elected executive, he often surprises his former house-mates by the markedly different political coloration which he assumes. If the " typical " executive type later serves in a legislative body, he too will have to adapt to the quite different situation if he is to fit in his new place. Likewise, the political party politician is of still a different political breed.

Environment is not the only factor tending to make the politician what he is. It is, however, a very important one. Often it is controlling, and never can it be disregarded. The extent to which the institutional environment does control or not depends upon the man, his abilities, his qualities of character, his standards and his conception of what constitutes the public interest.

THE POLITICIAN: HIS STANDARDS

He who would sit in judgment on the moral quality of a politician's words and deeds should first construct a realistic set of standards against which judgment may be made. To take the politician out of his environment and to place him in a vacuum tube without reference to the limitations — both human and institutional — under which popular government is conducted is to examine something which does not exist. Too often we tend to idealize a dead Abraham Lincoln into " an alabaster saint who never could have done what Lincoln did because he would not have played politics with Lincoln's calculating cleverness." [12] At the same time we tend to heap on the live politician, " playing politics " and trying to do it " with Lincoln's calculating cleverness," little but reproach — the same kind of reproach Lincoln himself got while he was yet among the living.

Realistic standards do not destroy idealism. Realism is the solid foundation under the road which must be traveled if ideals are to be implemented. Nor does realism carry the implication that there are no standards, but rather realism gives standards meaning.

The first standard to which the politician should be expected to

---

[12] Maxey, *op. cit.,* p. 276.

adhere is the prevailing level of morality of the community of which he is a part. Stealing, lying, corruption, lawbreaking — these are expected and realistically so, to lie outside the politician's code. His code of integrity should be one of the highest. For those who do not measure up, the shorter the route out of politics the better. But is this enough? Even Boss Thomas Pendergast could say: ". . . I have never broken my word. The biggest mistake a man can make is failing to keep his word. Sometimes I've been sorry I made a promise but I've always kept it. I'm just an ordinary fellow that was able to keep his word." [13]

Inherent in the concept of democratic-representative government is another set of standards meeting the test of realism by which the politician should be expected to be judged. Manipulators of the people in dictatorships may carry " the end justifies the means " philosophy to its extreme by pounding home the big lie, killing, seducing, brainwashing, and a whole assortment of techniques not tolerable in a representative democracy. The democratic-representative politician must respect the importance of keeping the channel of free elections open. He must confine himself to the presentation of his case through persuasion. He must, in short, live by the democratic-representative " rules of the game." If disregard of more and more " rules of the game " became general practice among politicians, there is some point below which political morality could no further fall without destroying the democratic-representative process and plunging the people into the clutches of dictatorship.

A third standard, though one surrounded by much controversy and one most difficult to apply, is that the politician should function as an interpreter of the public interest. One school of thought would deny the existence of such a standard separate from the sum total of private interests. Individuals and groups, they reason, pursue their private objectives, pressures on government are built up, the politicians in public office make their decisions in response to the pressures felt by them, and the result is the best attainable public policy. In such a system, the politician does not have to worry about a public interest. His only concern is that he properly gauge the power of the different private groups in order to retain or strengthen his base of political support.

---

[13] Ralph Coghlan, " Boss Pendergast," *The Forum* (February, 1937) , Vol. 97, No. 2, p. 70.

A second school of thought takes sharp issue both with this concept of the way the American system now works and with so mechanical an interpretation of the politician's function. Those who hold to this latter view would describe the public interest as an " aggregate of common interests, including the common interest in seeing that there is fair play among private interests." [14] Here there is real concern that the disruptive effects of " pressure group war " can do significant damage to the unifying fabric of the community. Pressure groups should themselves moderate their claims on government out of regard for the other elements of the community. If they do not, then it is the politician's responsibility to make the painful decisions which can produce moderation. E. E. Schattschneider asserts: " The function of politicians is now very largely to explain to people why they must make greater and greater sacrifices." [15]

Is it too much to ask of the politician that he be willing to be guided, if not by the somewhat vague term " public interest," by what United States Senator Ralph E. Flanders (R), Vermont, calls " long-range selfish interests " instead of " short-sighted selfish interests "? [16] In theory it is not too much to ask, but the difficulty of the standard lies in how it shall be interpreted in specific cases. For that there is no universally applicable answer. Each person as he judges a politician will, after looking at the problem through the politician's eyes as well as his own, have to come to a conclusion based on his own conception of " *long-range* selfish interests."

The standards by which a politician is guided are but a direct reflection of the standards which the community expects of him. Low standards in the community will be reflected in low standards of campaigning and public officeholding, and the converse is also true. If the individual citizen is unwilling to judge the politician on his whole record rather than how far he gave in to specific demands of that citizen or his pressure groups, then it is difficult if not impossible for the politician to think in broad and public instead of narrow and private terms. If the public does not call the politician to task for taking liberties with the spirit of democratic-representative " rules of

---

[14] E. E. Schattschneider, " Political Parties and the Public Interest," *The Annals of the American Academy of Political and Social Science* (March, 1952), Vol. 280, p. 22.

[15] *Ibid.*, p. 23.

[16] From Howard R. Bowen, " How Public Spirited is American Business? " *The Annals* . . . (March, 1952), Vol. 280, p. 89.

the game," then there will always be those who will say " anything goes " and who will pull down others with them. If the public standards of personal morality are low, then those of the politician are likely to be lower than they should otherwise be.

Those who are students of the history of political morality in the United States see a distinct improvement in the standards of political life. Today, as never before, the public conscience finds expression through a system of mass media of communication which throws a spotlight on anything and everything that politicians do. The fact that newspaper headlines, the radio loudspeaker and the television screen are reporting political wrongdoing is not a sign that politicians as a group have warranted the stereotype which has evolved about them. Rather the publicity is a sign that the popular control system is working, that there are standards, and that a few who have not respected the standards are being called to account.

The stereotype of the politician is wrong and harmful and should be erased. Contempt is not the reward which politicians as a group should receive, but respect — a respect based on understanding the importance of the politician to the functioning of government and the party system, on understanding the environment in which the politician has to function, and on crediting him for being public-minded enough to engage in political activity instead of leaving the job to others.

For those who have wanted to become politicians but have not as yet dared to take the step because of the calling's ill-repute, F. S. Oliver's clarion challenge to the would-be politician should help set the thinking straight:

> Politics is the most hazardous of all professions. There is not another in which a man can hope to do so much good to his fellow creatures, neither is there any in which by a mere loss of nerve he may do such widespread harm, nor is there another in which he may so easily lose his own soul, nor is there another in which a positive and strict veracity is so difficult. But danger is the inseparable companion of honor. With all the temptations and degradations that beset it, politics is still the noblest career that any man can choose.[17]

---

[17] F. S. Oliver, *Politics and Politicians* (London: Macmillan Company, Limited, 1934) , p. 82. Quotation printed as adapted by Davenport, *op. cit.,* p. 477.

CHAPTER TWO

The Major Party

By taking the name "Republican," the Jeffersonians hoped to pin on their rivals the imputation of being unrepublican. But the Federalists were republicans, although not Democrats. By taking the name Democrats, the majority faction of the Republican party hoped to pin on its foes the imputation of being undemocratic and by the time of the first election of Andrew Jackson, to be deemed "undemocratic" was almost as fatal in American politics as it is to-day. By taking the name "Whig," the opponents of Jackson hoped to get attributed to themselves some of the aura of revolutionary patriotism that clung about the honoured name. And when it was necessary to find some common name for the old Whigs, "Free Soil" Democrats, desponding "Know Nothings" who were forced into common action by the introduction of the Kansas-Nebraska Bill in 1854, it was soon realized that a mere negative and, possibly, too concrete title like "Anti-Nebraska," would not do and the coalition fell back on the sacred name "Republicans," to show that they, not the slavery-favouring Democrats, were the true heirs of Jefferson. The new party soon became proud, almost inordinately proud of its new and increasingly meaningless name. Since 1868, the two major parties have remained the Democratic and the Republican, the latter, on the whole, preferring to forget its salad days when it tried to take over the assets of the Jeffersonians. And the fact that all Republicans claim to be democrats and all Democrats to be republicans, makes the confusion of party names nearly complete.

D. W. Brogan [1]

----

[1] *Politics in America* (New York: Harper and Brothers, 1954), pp. 46–47. Reprinted by permission of Harper and Brothers.

Democratic-representative government as we know it today is the product of a long and slow evolution up from monarchical authoritarianism. First it was necessary to pry the parliament away from the tight grip of the king and to make the king subject to the parliament rather than its overlord. Next came a gradual expansion of the electorate to which the parliament was responsible. When the electorate reached a size unmanageable without organization and simplification of alternatives, political parties developed to fill the need. Such was the pattern emerging in Britain when the framers of the United States Constitution applied themselves to the task of drafting our fundamental law.

Those sitting in the Constitutional Convention, however, wanted no truck with political parties. The mere fact that a party system was developing in Britain did not mean there should be one in the new United States. Nowhere in the Constitution does one find any mention of political parties. Presidents, United States Senators and Congressmen, the framers seemed to believe, could be chosen without them. As late as the end of Washington's second term as President he was warning in his Farewell Address against the " baneful effects of the spirit of party."

Those who drew up the Constitution recognized that inevitably there would be issues on which individuals and groups would disagree, to be sure, but the opposing arguments should not, as the framers saw it, be advanced by permanent organizations contending for political power. Rather, it was hoped, groups would form on the different sides of an issue, and after the question was settled, those groups would disappear to be replaced by other group patterns as new issues arose. Permanent political parties, it was felt, would split the nation into factions; the splitting, in turn, would do irreparable damage to national unity.

Only James Madison, embroiled in the fight over ratification of the Constitution in New York State, has left written evidence that some of those who wrote that " most perfect document " foresaw the development of political parties, whether they wanted them to come or not. The Constitution, he argued in the classic tenth paper of *The Federalist,* would temper and control political factions. These were his words:

> A landed interest, a manufacturing interest, a mercantile interest, a monied interest, with many lesser interests, grow up of necessity in civilized nations, and divide them into different classes, actuated by

different sentiments and views. The regulation of these various and interfering interests forms the principal task of modern legislation, and involves the spirit of party and faction in the necessary and ordinary operations of government.

Political parties were not long in forming. Figuratively, that happened before the ink with which the Constitution was written had time to dry. In the ratification campaign there were the Federalists pressing for adoption and the Anti-Federalists against adoption. In Washington's first administration Hamilton built a Federalist party of sorts. By 1800 Jefferson had established a Republican party truly national in scope and with the beginnings of a grass-roots type of organization characteristic of our parties today. Only for a brief period from the middle 1810's until the middle 1820's, in the so-called one-party " era of good feeling," were the hopes of the framers of the Constitution — that there be no contending political parties — even remotely realized. Party warfare began again in the last half of the 1820's, and party warfare has been with us since.

The political party system which has developed in the United States is doubly unique. First, it has, except for the brief one-party era, been a two-party system. Only Britain and some British Commonwealth nations are similar to the United States in this respect. Far more numerous than two-party systems are the multi-party arrangements of other representative democracies or the one-party arrangements of authoritarian states.

Ours is a two-party system because the two major parties, Democratic and Republican, are the only ones which have a reasonable prospect of capturing control of the government. Both winner and loser receive relatively equal proportions of popular Presidential votes. Between the two major parties and all the minor parties is a power differential so great that, to compare the major and minor party is like setting an Indian burial mound alongside Pike's Peak.

Built into the American system are controls which keep the defeated major party far out of reach of all others. The losing major party will always win at least some seats to enable it to keep a hold in the Congress. The sectional nature of American politics and alternating terms of office (House, two years; Senate, six years; President, four years) help produce this effect. Though the Democrats have been more fortunate than Republicans with always the Solid South upon which to fall back, Republicans too have had their sectional footholds and have some carefully drawn " safe " districts. The defeated major party retains its major party status for still another reason. As the winning major party loses support because it cannot live up to the expectations of all who supported it and because it has to make decisions which alienate groups of voters, those who break off from the major party in office can only go to the major out-party if they would have their opposition votes count. The minor party is no alternative except for the man who would throw away his power by casting a protest vote.

Multi-party systems are those in which there are three or more political parties, no one or two of which have a chance to win a majority of the votes of the electorate. The distinction between multi- and two-party systems, it should be noted, is not based on numbers of parties alone. Even a two-party system may have three or more parties. From time to time in the United States, if a voter does not want to vote Democratic or Republican, his variety of choice has run the gamut from Socialist to Prohibition to Christian Nationalist to Vegetarian to Independent Progressive and, at one time, to Communist party. Multi-party systems are generally prevalent in countries with parliamentary systems of government.

The second reason for the uniqueness of the American party system is the character of the two major parties. Edmund Burke defined political parties as bodies of men united for promoting the national interest according to some particular principle upon which they were all agreed. Burke's definition is not a realistic one for American major parties, but political parties in most other countries, particularly in multi-party systems, can in part be described in Burkian terms. Though both Democrats and Republicans claim to be both " party-principled " and " all agreed," the study of American party history does not support such major-party propaganda.

The American major party is decentralized and lacking in party principles to the point where foreign observers, after comparing the American variety with what they have at home, wonder how the Democratic or Republican parties even warrant the title " political party." Foreigners are used to parties which are centralized because party leadership has the tools with which to discipline the membership and is inclined to use those tools. Foreign observers are also accustomed to parties which either have some core of long-term basic principle, or parties which at least enunciate programs in campaigns and then, if elected and controlling a majority in the parliament, can deliver what they have promised.

The following passage from Englishman D. W. Brogan's *Politics in America* sharply outlines the contrast which he finds in the United States:

> . . . [T]he present American party system . . . makes it difficult to pin responsibility on the " party in power " and almost impossible to pin responsibility on the party not " in power." Indeed, it is sometimes argued that being " in power " in the nation, merely means that the President is head of the Democratic or Republican " party " but that no definite meaning can be attached to the word " party." Thus a voter who is a loyal Republican may vote for the presidential candidate and for the Republican candidates for the Senate and the House with no assurance that he is electing federal officers who have anything in common save the party name. The Senator, the Representative may oppose a great part of the President's programme and for its success, he may have to depend on Democratic members of the Congress. The case may be still worse in the case of the election of state party officers. Their ambitions, needs, probable line of action may be opposed to the views, needs and programme of the national federal party. A party " victory " may, in fact, be a defeat, if party victory is interpreted as meaning the victory of a legislative or administrative programme.[2]

American major parties, again, are concerned primarily with winning elections, and only secondarily with controlling governmental policy. They are big, clumsy, compromising, and platform robbing. They are unstable and lacking in cohesion. They are flexible and always searching for the issue combination which can develop the broadest electable appeal.

What makes the American major parties what they are? What are the alternatives to the existing party arrangement? Why must the parties operate as they do?

THE PROBLEM OF MAJOR PARTY ORGANIZATION [3]

Three possible types of major party organization might be identified to bring the problem of major party organization into focus. The first two show what the American major party is not, and the third shows what the major party is. First, there is the unitary or cen-

---

[2] Page 87. Reprinted by permission of Harper and Brothers.
[3] See E. E. Schattschneider, *Party Government* (New York: Farrar and Rinehart, 1942).

tralized British type of party controlled from the top. This is the pattern toward which the long-defunct Federalist party of George Washington and Alexander Hamilton was groping. The British parties and the Federalists are, however, hardly comparable. Where the Conservative and Labour parties have a structure which reaches down to the grass roots, the Federalists, because they opposed organized parties as a matter of principle, never did succeed in sinking their roots down to the bottom of the electorate. The Federalist party was in reality a group of like-minded legislators and executives held briefly together in support of Alexander Hamilton's program, but operating without an organized popular foundation. When confronted by the Jeffersonian Republican party, which was based on state and local organizations, the Federalists were badly handicapped in the resulting competition.

Second, there is the type of party where local, state, and national components function as parts of a theoretically democratic organization in which policies are initiated or at least approved at the precinct level and then are implemented at the higher levels. This, suggests E. E. Schattschneider in his *Party Government,* is what we generally think the American major parties are, though, in fact, they are not. Any similarity between type two in theory and the American major parties in practice is coincidental.

Third is the decentralized party where power is held by those who dominate local organizations. If they or their faction do not control the state party machinery, they will not recognize the state central committee, and both local and state units of the major parties oppose development of strong power in the national organizational units of their parties. The Democratic and Republican parties are more or less loose coalitions of local and state units. Organizationally, the major party is little more unified than a confederation.

To find the most important factor in answer to the question of why decentralization is, organizationally, the single most significant characteristic of the American major party, it is necessary to return to the definition of a major party. It is an organized group concerned primarily with winning elections. With that as the principal objective, one can expect to find the major party adapting its structure to most effectively enable it to win elections. This is what has happened, and the environment of the election pattern in the United States is the most important key to understanding why the major parties have developed organizationally as they have.

Major party organizations tend to be strongest at the local level, next strongest at the state level, and weakest on the national level. A view of the federal pattern of elections furnishes one explanation for such a distribution of party power. For only one year out of four and for only the offices of President and Vice President of the United States are there truly national elections. Excluding the territories such as Alaska and Hawaii, 96 United States Senators, 48 governors, numerous other state executive branch officials such as attorneys general and secretaries of state, and a handful of the 435 Congressmen (where the seat is filled by at-large elections) are chosen by the electorates of entire states. Otherwise all of the thousands of other public officers holding party designation offices and the thousands that are nonpartisan are selected from constituencies within and smaller than the states.

Though the qualitative importance of national and state elections may be greater to the major party, the weight of quantity of offices at stake is greatest at the substate level. Add to this the custom that Congressmen be residents of the districts from which they seek office and the general state legal requirements that candidates for other offices be residents in the districts in which they run. These factors tend toward an intraparty decentralizing kind of power dynamics.

Sectional factors in American politics also operate toward the same result. Each of the major geographical areas of the country such as the South or Pacific West have characteristics which distinguish them from other areas, and this fact has political consequences. Take, for example, the problem which sectionalism imposes when civil rights legislation is the issue. What would be politically acceptable for a candidate running for an office in a Los Angeles district with a heavy concentration of Negro voters would be quite unacceptable in most sections of the South. The politician quickly gets the point. If he is in a national organ of the party, he will think twice about attempting to set and impose a national party policy which would wipe his party's candidates out in either one section or another. Even subsectional differences within a state limit the state party units in the policy-establishing function.

The effects of sectionalism, like the effects of the pattern of elections of the federal system, tend to result in the national party leaving the state units of the party to largely shift for themselves on the positions they take on issues. Likewise, the tendency also is for state party organs to be passive in the position-determining sense. Nor are the local units much interested in issues as such. Policy determination, except where Presidents and governors provide party program leadership, is left largely to the party's elected officials functioning as individuals.

The fact that the election process at all three levels of government is divided into two parts — the primary stage in which the party chooses its nominees and the general election in which the voters select the candidates they want to hold public office — also has its impact on the organization of the major parties. Those in the party who can control the nominating process can control the party. The nominee is the front for the party in the general election campaign, and should he win, it will be he who makes the record for which the party will be held responsible.

Because each of the major parties are coalitions of different interest groups and because the character of the party's nominees is so critical to interest-group access to governmental decision-making power points, one finds within each of the major parties a continuing struggle between factions which want the party to select the nominee of their choice. The most substantial major party activity between elections is, therefore, that which leads up to nominee selection. This, in turn, tends to draw attention away from platform-making and to result in an organization designed primarily for picking nominees and, if there is time left, for rationalizing for propaganda purposes what the party's office holders are doing.

Yet even nominee selection is no longer a function over which major party organizations have direct control. The party convention device for naming nominees has been supplanted by some type of direct primary election in every state except Connecticut. With few exceptions, the voters and not an organ of the party select a political party's nominee.

In states with closed primaries only those affiliated with a party may participate in that party's primary, but some dozen states remove nominee selection still another step from the hands of the official party organizations. In nine open-primary states the voters are not required to register their party affiliation, but may vote in the primary of whatever party they desire on primary election day. The state of Washington with its wide-open primary does not even restrict the voter to an either/or decision for one party or another but permits him to jump from party to party for the different offices.

California allows candidates for nominations to cross-file into the primary elections of all parties on the ballot, and in the past, large numbers of Democrats have become nominees of both the Democratic and Republican parties; and Republicans, the nominees of both their party and the Democrats. The movement to devise primary election laws to weaken political party organizations did not stop with these devices. Minnesota and Nebraska elect their state legislators without party designation. At the local level throughout the country nonpartisan officers are the exception rather than the rule.

Although a very few states now allow the political party to make preprimary endorsements and to have the party convention's choice indicated on the ballot or, as in Iowa and South Dakota, postprimary conventions may pick the nominee in case no candidate gets a required percentage of the primary vote, for all practical purposes the political party organization is left to extralegal and informal devices in its attempts to control the state and local nominee selection process. The environment of the American pattern of elections not only tends to produce major parties with greatest strength in the local units and least in the national unit, but also tends to insure that not even the local party organizations shall be very strong.

Effects of the pattern of elections in the United States, and secondarily sectionalism, have done more than influence the organization and determine the strength of the major political parties. They have been among the principal reasons for the evolution and maintenance of the two-party system itself.

Article II, Section 1 of the Constitution, as amended by the Twelfth Amendment, setting up the Electoral College procedure for electing Presidents, provides " the person having the greatest number of votes shall be the President, if such number be a majority of the whole number of electors appointed." If no person has an absolute majority, the choice is made by the House of Representatives from the top three candidates. If the House elects, the winner shall still need a majority of all the state House delegations, each such delegation casting one vote.

This language leaves little room for the candidate of a minor party. Further, it places a red stop signal before groups within either major party which might like to break away from their major party affiliation and try to " go it alone." For a major party to split deeply is almost certainly to give the victory, as in 1912, to the opposition major party. Mobilizing absolute majorities leaves room for only two big and powerful contestants because only if there are two such parties can either party, or indirectly the voter through either party, have a reasonable prospect of success. To refuse to compromise far enough to win required absolute majorities is to refuse power.

Secondly, American legislative bodies are almost without exception picked through the single-member district plan rather than the multi-member district which characterizes the legislator-selecting process of most multi-party countries. In the single-member district system only one man is elected from each constituency, and unless a minor party itself becomes major in a district, its candidate has little chance. Also, for a party to win control of a legislative body, it must have strength widely scattered over at least enough districts so that it has a chance to win a majority of them. When both factors are combined with the sectional nature of American politics as it tends to prevent the out major party from slipping to minor party status, a two-party system is the logical result.

Are the two-party system and the major parties as presently constituted necessarily the best instruments of government for the United States? In reply to the former — the two-party system — there is general agreement that the answer is affirmative. In respect to the desirability of the latter, however, there is much controversy. Objections may be classified into two principal types: first, that the moderate though significant differences between the two major parties are so confused and ill-defined as to be unintelligible to the electorate; and second, that a governmental system depending so strongly upon single elected chief executives is a threat to the system's long-term stability.

THE PROBLEM OF PARTY PRINCIPLES

Standard catalogues of political party functions read as follows: Political parties should provide alternative choices on political issues for the voter. They should interest and educate. They should serve as an intermediary between the citizen and his government, thus humanizing that relationship. They should serve as a rallying point around which groups may form to attempt to capture the offices of government. They should govern and give the voter someone to hold responsible if the policies and acts of government are not to his liking. They — the out-party — should provide an opposition check to

the party in power. They should give unity to government to bridge
the gap created by the separation of powers and federal systems. They
should serve as innovators of public policy by raising new issues and
advocating new policies. The parties should serve as a vehicle through
which the public interest can be safeguarded against the pressures
created by private groups in their efforts to influence governmental
policy.

Experience has shown that the raising of new issues and advocating of new policies is left almost entirely to minor parties. Seldom
does a national election turn on an issue on which the two major
parties are clearly divided. The fight for woman suffrage may be used
as an illustration. For some fifty years before woman suffrage was
finally achieved, minor parties had been demanding it, and alliances
of pressure groups formed on both sides to forcefully proclaim their
positions. Both the Democratic and Republican parties postponed
their decision and straddled the fence. Only when the demand became so widespread and generally agreed upon that it could not be
ignored, did the major parties choose sides. Then both jumped at
the same time and in the same direction. So it has been with popular
election of United States Senators, the income tax, regulation of
business, and most of the other major policy decisions which represented sharp breaks from previous and established policy.

Political parties do serve as humanizing intermediaries between
government and the people, but as a party function this is becoming
less and less important. Perhaps the highest point of " intermediating " in a party sense were the services performed, oftentimes on a
low ethical plane, by the organizations of the old-time political bosses.
Most of the " intermediating " of today goes not through the party
organizations, but is performed by politicians as individual candidates or officeholders.

With the exception of whatever bridging of the gap between the
separate yet checked-and-balanced branches of government and between the national and state elements of the federal system is done by
the parties, all the other functions listed above are either directly or
indirectly intertwined with the party's business of winning elections.
The parties do not think of themselves as providing alternatives for
the sake of providing alternatives, but in terms of what kind of positions will win votes. The strategicians of both major parties generally
come to conclusions which differ only in small degree.

Nor do the major parties interest and educate for the sake of interesting and educating, but to win votes. They do attempt to serve as rallying points around which groups may congregate to capture government, but in this function, again, the primary object is the same. In the process of governing, too, the principal motivation is the kind of record which will win the kind of support which will in

'JUST A MINUTE, BUSTER'

turn keep the in-party in office. Neither do the major parties consciously provide an opposition for opposition's sake, but rather to enhance the possibilities of a return to power.

The problem of party principles may be brought more sharply into focus by a summary examination of Republican problems in policy formation during the era of New Deal. Democratic administrations since 1933 had produced some domestic and foreign affairs programs which unquestionably had been accepted by the great majority of the American people. Social security was here to stay. The right of labor to organize and bargain collectively was no longer a legitimate subject for political debate. The federal government was committed to the utilization of all its resources to eliminate or moderate boom and bust extremes of the business cycle. Collective security rather than a philosophy of isolationism was the major underlying assumption behind our relationships with the other countries of the world.

Did Republican " party principles " preclude Republicans from accepting and acting upon the basis of these facts? Obviously not. Neither of the two major parties have nor should the opposition allow either to have a monopoly on the best ways of solving current problems. Aside from the bipartisan standards of integrity, respect for democratic-representative process and a philosophy which includes a concept of the public interest, the fewer the imagined permanent political " party principles," the better for the future of the party. Parties, as with politicians, need to be flexible enough to adapt to the times and to stay in tune with the people. Only if they can do both will they be given an opportunity to lead in the directions the people will consent to follow.

What, during this period, were so-called " Republican principles "? High tariffs? With what a Republican Congressman Richard Simpson of Pennsylvania might hold, a Republican Charles Taft of Ohio would take sharp issue. Because a party once advocated protectionism is no reason that that party should continue to be a high-tariff party regardless of the world economic situation in which the United States might find itself. Because some Republicans fought the establishment of a social security system, should that mean the party is or should be forever dedicated to block improvement of the social security system? Because Congressional Republicans had traditionally been more hostile to Presidential leadership than Democrats, should that mean that when the Republicans returned to the White House in 1952 they should discard their biggest advantage over the Democrats by refusing to recognize the leadership position and possibilities of President Eisenhower? Was economy in government such an established Republican principle that whenever the party is in office it should reduce taxes regardless of the requirements of national security and the level of the national debt? What should happen when the " principle " of a balanced budget conflicts with the " principle " of reducing taxes? Is free enterprise a Republican principle which would bar a Republican administration from taking necessary steps to avert depression or inflation, or dictate the repeal of legislation to safeguard the consumer from impure foods and drugs?

The able party politician looks closely at the arguments of those who will tolerate no compromise on issues or those who cloak their positions on issues with the flag of " party principles." As the party politician probes behind the protective covering of such an argument, he finds not " party principles " but only proposed methods that individuals or groups would use to solve current governmental problems. The able party politician's test is not whether the position should be judged against some " party principle." Rather the test is the proposal's political, economic, moral, and social soundness.

He who tolerates no position which conflicts with his concept of " party principles " is one who would force his major party to throw away the flexibility it needs to survive. If his position cannot stand on its own merits and if many support it on " party principle " grounds, the party leadership should begin to worry. If such a position is accepted as the basis for official party words and actions, at that point that party is no longer politically healthy.

Both major parties have at some time or another since the Civil War been on all sides of most of the significant issues of American politics. Though at any one time there have usually been some differences between the positions of the two major parties, those differences have been only of degree, and most often they are differences of small instead of large degree. This is because both major parties are similar in organization, because the problems of each period seldom lend themselves to two radically different types of common-sense solution, and because each major party sees approximately the same pattern as it surveys the sources from which it must earn votes in order to win.

ALTERNATIVES?

Alternatives to the two-party system would have to be one of two types, either a one-party or a multi-party system. Alternatives to the presently constituted major parties operating within a two-party system also lend themselves to classification into two categories. One of these would have the Democrats and Republicans realigned into two definite and distinguishable conservative and progressive parties. The other would attempt to change the structural characteristics of the

Democratic and Republican parties from their existing loose coalition status into centralized organizations with the national unit of party government powerful enough to control President, party members in Congress, and party policies.

One-Party System? Stalin's Russia, Hitler's Germany, Mussolini's Italy, Franco's Spain, Peron's Argentina, Mao's China — these are or have been some of the nations with one-party systems. All are authoritarian dictatorships. The highly centralized single political party in each is an instrument of the dictator, not a vehicle for either the expression of popular choice or for holding responsible those who govern. To some, an " ordered " totalitarian system with its monolithic party may have its attractions, but these some are not the vast majority of the people of the United States.

Could the United States have a one-party system without having an authoritarian dictatorship? Though for approximately a decade from 1816 to 1824 this country did have such a system, several factors suggest it will not happen again. The Federalists, holding a Washingtonian philosophy deploring the " baneful effects of faction," had no example to follow and not enough time in which to disengage themselves from the Hamiltonian longing for monarchy to understand the rapidly changing early American political environment. Both major parties today are democratic in outlook and grounded in the political realities which 150 years of experience have taught.

Though both major parties, at one time or another, may temporarily have appeared to be " going under " because they were not flexible enough to adapt to a new set of political circumstances, yet sooner or later adapt they have. If neither major party has at times seemed to fill popular needs, rashes of minor parties have sprung up over the body politic to force the major parties back into their appointed roles. If a major party became so politically insensitive it persisted in mistaking the voices of small and vocal extremist minorities for the voice of a majority of the American electorate, a new major party would tend to form to fill the breach. Given the nature of democratic society today, organized political parties, grouped either in a two- or multi-party arrangement, are an inevitable consequence.

It is true that several of the American states are known as " oneparty " states, but here the term " one-party " is used in a different sense. " One-party state " has meant that one party has been very successful in winning offices while its opposition has been notably unsuccessful. Though organized opposition may have been feeble, however, it could and sometimes did exist.

Even " one-party " politics in this sense in the states has, during the past two decades, shown a marked tendency to decrease. The once safe Republican bastions of strength ranging from little Maine to big Pennsylvania now boast virile Democratic parties which no Republican dare overlook or ignore. Though the same trend has not yet penetrated to Republican advantage by making significant in-roads on Democratic state and local strength in the Solid South, yet in Presidential elections the once iron-cast " one-party " status in the southern states appears to be melting. The trend in state and national politics suggests the United States will not become a " one-party " country in the forseeable future.

Multi-Party System? For those who demand that their political parties stand on a narrow set of permanent party principles, a multi-party system may seem to be the logical answer. If in the two-party system there are only two parties with a reasonable prospect of winning, both have to be big and unwieldy; if there are many parties with approximately similar chances of success, any group of individuals can form a tightly disciplined little party of their own just big enough to win some legislative seats. The latter type of party can afford to dedicate itself to its own immediate and closely defined policy objectives. Where the major party in a two-party system must compromise to hold many different elements within its coalition; the small party is more homogeneous and has to compromise little if at all. Both external and internal pressures on the leaders in a major party push those leaders into a posture of fence straddling and toward a middle-road position; pressures on the leader in a small party are in the opposite direction.

The big party needs to be flexible; the small does not have to bother itself with flexibility because its objectives seldom change or require adaptation to changing trends and events. Where the big party has to try to steal the most successful platform planks of the opposition in order to also attempt to appeal to the whole broad political middle, the small party hardly ever need be accused of platform-robbing. For those who like their political problems and parties simple with still a chance at some election winning, a party in a multi-party system may seem to be the answer. For those whose sense of order is violated by having to register a vote for what seems to be tweedledum or tweedledee, the multi-party system offers a clear and unfrustrating solution. However, the advantages of the multi-party system generally stop at this point.

Though many small and " principled " parties may give the voter a sense of order lacking in a two-party system when he marks his ballot, the effect of a multi-party system tends to create disorder when the many parties, no one of which has a majority, attempt to conduct the business of government. If no one party controls a majority of the legislative body, majorities can only be constructed out of coalitions of the elected representatives of several parties. Look to the example of governmental instability in France to note some of the more extreme consequences. Deadlock, or a state of affairs close to deadlock, is the handicap. Premiers and governments rise and fall with dangerous regularity. The effective conduct of foreign affairs is always difficult and sometimes impossible. Solutions to serious domestic problems generally can never quite be brought down out of the future tense to be applied in the present.

For the purposes of illustration, assume the structure of government of the United States and its election system were changed from one which now encourages a two-party system to one which would foster a multi-party system. United States Senator Joseph McCarthy (R) , Wisconsin, would have long ago left the Republican party and gone off in another direction followed by his supporters. From the opposite end of the Republican party, Senator Wayne Morse of Oregon would have preceded McCarthy, and perhaps would already have appropriated the title " Constitutional Conservatives." Assume further that more fractionation took place on the Republican side, and that the different elements of the Democratic party also splintered off from their present allegiance. Each of the new parties could then concentrate on its own pet objective. Each would no longer have an incentive to build a moderate program capable of enlisting nation-wide support. Instead, their bases of power could be either sectional, class, religious, or ideological, and each could shout its message at the top of its voice to its own particular supporters.

No one of the parties would be likely ever to command an absolute majority in the Congress. Neither would the Presidential nominee of any party be likely to win a majority of votes in the Electoral College. If the Presidential vote-counting system remained, Presidents would be selected from among the top three candidates by some kind of coalition of parties in the House. If the United States shifted to a cabinet system, government would have to be conducted by a coalition of parties. Perhaps, under such an arrangement, the voter might be more satisfied that his party reflected his particular viewpoint. In this sense he might be less frustrated. But the obstacles standing in the way of the effective operation of his national government would produce frustrations of an infinitely more serious sort. Even theoretically, a multi-party system for the United States would at best be a poor alternative.

Two Ideologically Realigned Major Parties? Few critics of the present-day ideological character, or lack of character, or the Democratic and Republican parties would advocate either one-party or multiparty systems as substitutes for the two-party system. A two-party structure is recognized as having demonstrable advantages. However, might not the major parties more effectively perform their functions of providing alternatives, clarifying issues and responsibility for the voter if they were realigned into sharply distinguishable conservative and progressive parties between which the conservative voter and the progressive voter could make an intelligent selection?

Throughout American history, it is said, the political contest has been between a humanistic majority of the people versus a dominant economic minority. It has been contended that the Democratic party has best stood for the former; the Republican party, the latter. Yet, because both major parties succeed in making themselves look so much alike, their true nature is not readily apparent. Only when one party assumes a definitely conservative character and the other a progressive character, the argument continues, will elections take on meaning and the voter be able to register intelligent choices.[4]

How " definitely conservative " should the Republican party become; how " definitely progressive," the Democratic party? Here is the obstacle which the realigner finds between the statement of theory and its practical implementation. If " dynamic conservatism " is popular, the Democrats do not want to allow Republicans uncontested claim to a good thing, whatever the title represents. Rather, Democrats will try to show that it is they who are in fact the " real " mod-

---

4 See Max Lerner, " The Outlook for a Party Realignment," *The Virginia Quarterly Review* (Spring, 1949), Vol. 25, No. 2, pp. 179–193. For an opposing view, see Oren Root, " Do We Need a Political Realignment? " *Commonweal* (April 15, 1949), Vol. 30, No. 1, pp. 6–8.

erate conservatives and at the same time try to push the popular mind's conception of Republicanism off the right end of the conservative scale toward an identification of the Republican party with reaction. If " forward-looking progressivism " is popular, Republicans will, in turn, claim that they are the " true " moderate progressives while the Democrats are in fact wild radicals. The lifeline of each major party is anchored somewhere in the political-middle of the period, and each party does its best to pull itself in and at the same time to try to push the other out. To ask either major party to become " definitely " anything unless the opposition major party can " definitely " become substantially the same thing is to ask the major parties to throw out the first article of their catechisms on political strategy.

The American political system has operated, except for the Civil War issue, in a manner in which the serious opinion splits on issues have taken place largely *within* the major parties and not *between* them. This has had two significant stabilizing effects — one stabilizing the major parties themselves and the other stabilizing the American political system. First, in the case of the major party, because each is by nature a broad coalition, neither can " fly " off toward either political extremity of conservatism or progressivism without disintegrating. To remove the healthy pull of Republican moderate progressives from the Republican party and of the Democratic moderate conservatives from the Democratic party would invite greater extremism. Party history has shown that the outside forces that pressure the broad-based major parties to hold together tend to be stronger than the inside centrifugal forces which would exert pressure to force them apart.

Second, if the moderating balance wheels within each of the major parties were removed, in place of two moderate major parties facing each other as is the case now, election contests would be fought between extremes. Campaigns would tend to become less restrained. When elections turned out the in-party, the prospect would be a violent shift of governmental policies toward either the left or the right instead of a moderate transition from the policies of the old in-party to the policies of the new in-party. Today the losing party takes its defeat with admirable grace, wires congratulations to the winner, moves peaceably out of office, analyzes its mistakes and shortcomings. and begins to plan for the next election. If the two major parties represented extremes, the incumbent party defeated in an election might feel it had so many " principles " at stake that the national welfare could not stand letting the out-party assume office. A democratic-representative government can thrive in a moderate and stable political climate; in a climate of extremes, it cannot.

Relays as They Should Be Relayed

If both Democratic and Republican parties moved to extremes of right and left, it is not likely the two extreme parties could satisfy the needs of the electorate. Between the two poles two new major parties might develop, or the system might be forced into some kind of multi-party pattern. If one major party moved to an extreme and the other did not, the political future of the party which did the moving would be at stake.

Advocates of sharp ideological realignment generally lend themselves to classification into one of three groups. First, there are those who are Democrats who would expect their party to stay moderate and lay out the " welcome mat " to all refugee moderate Republicans. The Republican party could, then, never win another national election. Second, there are those of both major parties who, because of their devotion to " party principles " as they interpret them, have lost sight of the kind of platform and kinds of candidates required to win Presidential elections and Congressional majorities. Third, there are those who, asserting no partisan motivation, feel that the Democratic and Republican parties are too much alike, that this is not as it should be and that realignment would correct the deficiency. The whole sweep of American political party history suggests that the third group is being less than realistic, both in the end it seeks (if that end be a realignment of the major parties on an ideological basis) and in the means by which the end would be achieved.

Two Centralized Major Parties? Where the realigners would sharpen the ideological conflict between the major parties, another group of critics puts its emphasis on a type of centralized and disciplined internal major party organization patterned after political parties as they exist in Great Britain. This objective, it is felt, might be accomplished without creating two ideologically extremist parties with the consequent liabilities of extremism. To illustrate the possibility the Conservative and Labour parties are cited as examples — each centralized and yet each moderate in program.

The argument for major party centralization may be roughly summarized as follows. Because the Democratic and Republican parties are decentralized coalitions of state and local party organizations and lacking in both national machinery and unity, they are not able to organize their members in the executive and legislative branches so that they support a program in line with a meaningful party platform. Party responsibility to the voters is virtually nonexistent. This is bad because the domestic and foreign relations problems of today are so serious and complicated they cannot be solved by piecemeal or haphazard actions. What is needed are parties which can submit comprehensive programs to the voters, and parties which can translate popular mandates into governmental action.

Here are some of the more important proposals for centralizing the major parties as outlined in the American Political Science Association Committee on Political Parties' 1950 report, *Toward a More Responsible Two-Party System*.[5] First, a representative national party council of approximately fifty members should be established to prepare preliminary drafts of platforms to be submitted to the party conventions, to recommend the persons the conventions should endorse for seats in the Congress, to discuss candidates for the Presidential nomination and perhaps perform a preliminary screening of such candidates, and to interpret the party's position on problems which develop between national conventions.

Second, national conventions should meet at least every two years, and the number of convention delegates should be restricted to a small enough figure to ensure actual deliberation on issues. Third, the character of the national committee should be changed. At present its members reflect the views of the dominant elements in the state parties because the members of the national committee are picked by each state party or its delegation to the national convention, and the choices are automatically ratified by the convention. The convention should not bow to state delegations on this matter, but should rather pick national committee members who reflect the views of a majority of the national convention.

Fourth, the national party platforms should be binding, and if there is doubt about any of their provisions, interpreted by the party council. Fifth, Congressional organization and procedure should be reformed to dispense with the seniority rule and the filibuster as practiced in the Senate. Party caucuses should be used for deciding positions on issues, and such decisions should be binding. The national units of the party should participate in selecting party leadership in the Senate and House, and relationships between the party leaders in the two houses of Congress and the executive should be institutionalized.

Though the American Political Science Association committee makes numerous other recommendations, those cited above are adequate to a general understanding of how the committee would try to implement its desire for a " more responsible two-party system." The committee would have " those who identify themselves as Republicans or Democrats to think in terms of support of . . . program, rather than in terms of personalities, patronage and local matters."

---

[5] Supplement to the *American Political Science Review* (September, 1950), Vol. 44, No. 3, Pt. 2.

d seek to limit the power of pressure groups " which are best
d if the individual legislator and administrative official are
defenseless in the face of their special pressure " by having the
s defend their legislators and administrators from such pressures.

If the parties are not centralized and membership is not disciplined, *Toward a More Responsible Two-Party System* foresees the
following grave consequences:

> *Four* of these *dangers warrant special emphasis. The first danger is
> that the inadequacy of the party system in sustaining well-considered
> programs and providing broad public support for them may lead to
> grave consequences in an explosive era. The second danger is that the
> American people may go too far for the safety of constitutional gov-
> ernment in compensating for this inadequacy by shifting excessive
> responsibility to the President. The third danger is that with growing
> public cynicism and continuing proof of the ineffectiveness of the
> party system the nation may eventually witness the disintegration of
> the two major parties. The fourth danger is that the incapacity of the
> two parties for consistent action based on meaningful programs may
> rally support for extremist parties poles apart, each fanatically bent
> on imposing on the country its particular panacea.*[6]

The report of the Committee on Political Parties immediately
incurred a barrage of countercriticism directed at the desirability of
the committee's objectives, the committee's interpretation of what
would happen should its recommendations be adopted, and at lack
of realism in the methods by which the committee would achieve its
reforms.[7] Arguments of the " anti-report " school of thought among
political scientists can be summarized as follows:

(1) The United States two-party system and the two major
parties have developed into their present form to fill the particular

---

[6] *Ibid.,* p. 92. Reprinted by permission.

[7] See T. William Goodman, " How Much Political Party Centralization
Do We Want? " *Journal of Politics* (November, 1951), Vol. 13, pp. 536–561;
Norton E. Long, " Party Government in the United States," *ibid.* (May, 1951),
pp. 187–214; Austin Ranney, " Toward a More Responsible Two-Party System:
A Commentary," *American Political Science Review* (June, 1951), Vol. 45, pp.
488–499; Julius Turner, " Responsible Parties: A Dissent from the Floor," *ibid.*
(March, 1951), pp. 143–152; Murray S. Stedman, Jr., and Herbert Sonthoff,
" Party Responsibility — A Critical Inquiry," *Western Political Quarterly* (September, 1951), Vol. 4, No. 3, pp. 454–468. See also Malcolm Moos, *Politics, Presidents and Coattails* (Baltimore: The Johns Hopkins Press, 1952), Chap. 6.

needs of politics in this country. It is doubtful that the character of the major parties can be changed without substantially altering the constitutional framework of the American system. To entertain hopes of transplanting a British party to the political soil of the United States is to overlook the differences between politics in Britain and this country.

The British party pattern developed in a country where the people were committed to the idea of majority rule. Though Americans may think they worship at the altar of majority rule, in reality this is not true. When United States Senator John W. Bricker (R) , Ohio, told the 1952 Republican National Convention during the heated Eisenhower-Taft fight that ours was not a system based on majority rule, he received a round of boos. Bricker was right, though he made a tactical error in saying what he did when he did.

The framers of the Constitution set out to devise ways and means of tempering or thwarting unrestricted majority rule. Majority rule implies a majority of all the people of a country. Yet the Constitution established a federal system, allocating some powers to the national government and reserving others to the states. The framers did not contemplate a national majority with power to enforce its will on all matters upon the states. Majority rule also implies a legislative supremacy unrestricted by Presidential or judicial veto. The Constitution separated and checked-and-balanced the three branches of government. The Bill of Rights is another of the obstacles to majority rule. National majorities may not tamper with the rights of the first ten amendments as interpreted by the courts to safeguard the rights of individuals from government invasion. Ours is a *government by consensus* and *not by majority*. It is sympathetic to the political desires and problems of minorities. Centralized and disciplined political parties are possible only in majority-rule systems.

(2) State and local units have long controlled the Democratic and Republican parties, intentionally keeping the national organizations weak so that party policies in the various sections of the country can be adapted to local needs and local political psychology. The power of state and local groups to determine what shall be party policy in their respective areas is vital to their continued existence. This power is guarded jealously, and with cause. If a central body of the party set policy and could enforce discipline, and if the national policy of a party did not fit the climate of opinion in the constituency, the state and local units would face the dismal prospect of repeated

defeats. Implementation of the American Political Science Association Political Parties Committee report would tend to increase the number of " one-party " states and areas.

(3) The Republican and Democratic parties do not fall as far short of performing the functions of clarification of the issues and responsibility as the committee report implies. Platforms of the major parties do provide alternatives of degree and, on some issues, different positions. Furthermore, studies of voting records in Congress reveal a fairly high index of party voting. Failure to fully execute the program of the majority party does not indicate confusion of issues or lack of party responsibility. It stems from the fact that the Presidential candidate, his party in Congress, and the national conventions, all represent different electorates. The most helpful and the soundest proposals of the committee report are those which seek to make these different constituencies for the different offices similar, such as recommendations that House terms coincide with Presidential terms and that the features of the Electoral College vote-counting procedure be changed to eliminate the " pivot state factor " in Presidential election campaigns.

(4) Centralized " bossism " in centralized parties might be even more objectionable than the localized variety. There is no assurance that the proposed type of major parties would be any more democratic than the present major parties. Further, if each major party were tightly controlled by a " national party oligarchy " and the possibility of one party's control of Congress and the other's control of the White House were not removed, the President-Congress relation might become so rigid that a frozen solid deadlock would result.

(5) The commitee report reveals its authors are in reality opposed to both the separation of powers and the federal system principles written into the Constitution. The report would attempt to reform the American system by grafting onto the Presidential form of government selected characteristics of the parliamentary form without the protections of the latter, and it would discard the protective features of the existing Presidential form of government. Presidential irresponsibility could not only be continued, it could now be hidden behind a façade of enforced agreement only appearing to be " party responsibility."

The major party's primary concern is not with reforming or remaking either the two-party system or itself. Neither is it the major party's primary concern to be responsible. The problem of the major party as viewed from within the major party, is much more immediate — How to win in the political system as it now exists? Perhaps, after proceeding through the complete study of party politics, one will have to conclude that in merely " doing what comes naturally " by fighting to build and hold enough popular support to win elections, the major parties are performing a function which should take second position to none other. The individual should withhold his final decision until he is ready to make it. All the remaining parts of this book will touch directly or indirectly on the questions raised in this section.

CHAPTER THREE

The Pressure Group

Shoe manufacturers want a higher tariff.
Farmers want parity prices.
The merchant marine wants subsidies.
So do the airlines.
The silver bloc wants 71 cents an ounce, and would take $1.00.
Teachers want federal aid.
Unions want the closed shop.
Dairymen want a prohibitive tax on oleomargarine.
Railways want to weaken the waterways and the bus lines.
Cattlemen want Argentine beef plainly labeled not fit to eat.
Insurance men do not want too much social security.
Medical men want to scuttle socialized medicine.
Coal operators want hydroelectric projects halted.
Drug men would like food and drug reformers quietly chloroformed
* — which would not displease publishers either.*
The aluminum interests want no nonsense at all about competitors
* getting hold of new government plants.*

One could continue the list until it became a saga. The objective behind these wants is usually a direct subsidy for the interest itself, or a hand grenade for a competitor. Practically all the labors of the economic pressure groups revolve around these twin goals. Observe, however, that such goals are often in violent conflict as among the several groups. This is no harmony chorus.   Stuart Chase [1]

---

[1] *Democracy Under Pressure* (New York: The Twentieth Century Fund, 1945) , p. 23. Reprinted by permission of The Twentieth Century Fund.

Before society became a highly complicated and interwoven complex of specialties, it was possible for only the small farmer and his immediate family to produce a steak. His sons and dogs looked after the cattle. Though he probably owed money, his financing was simple. He had no commercial fertilizers. He used horses and muscle instead of power machinery. The cattle fed off the pasture. He was his own veterinarian. He cut his own wood and made his own rail fences. He shipped little of his product. He was his own butcher and meat packer. But times have changed, and the " How many people does it take to produce a steak? " advertisement of the American Meat Institute, reproduced as Figure 1 on page 52 dramatically tells part of the story of that change.

Twenty specialties, according to the American Meat Institute, contribute directly to the steak-producing process. If the advertising agency which prepared the ad had not been trying to design a neat and easy-to-look-at magazine page, more directly contributing specialties could have been included. If one were to try to include indirectly contributing specialties, the total list would run into the hundreds. Except for the blacksmith who is fast disappearing in his once familiar form and perhaps the cowboy, the specialties are organized into pressure groups, all of which seek more or less to influence governmental policy as it relates to the interests of their particular specialty.

The banker can belong to such organizations [2] as the American Bankers' Association, Independent Bankers' Association, or National Savings and Loan League. For the fertilizer producer, there is the National Fertilizer Association; for the oil refiner, the American Petroleum Institute or Independent Petroleum Association of America; for the steelworker, the United Steelworkers of America; for the brewer, the Small Brewer's Association, and for the brewery worker, the Brewery Workers' International Union; for the sugar refiner, the American Sugar Cane League, U. S. Beet Sugar Association, or U. S. Cuban Sugar Council; for the lumberman, the National Lumber Manufacturers' Association; for the feed dealer, the Grain and Feed Dealers' National Association; for the truck driver, the International Brotherhood of Teamsters, and for his boss, the American Trucking Association; for the meat packer, the National Independent Meat Packers' Association, Western States Meat Packers' Association or

---

[2] Following organizations all have Congressionally registered lobbyists.

Figure 1

How many people does it take to produce a steak?

When you plank the cash on the counter for a slice of sirloin, some of it may represent *your own pay* for the part *you* played in getting that steak to your table.

We'll make ourselves clear. It takes a lot of people to help produce that steak in this mid-20th-century economy of ours.

The people we've put in the picture above, for instance. And many, many others. Though you may not realize it, some product you, yourself, help make or sell or service may play a part in producing steaks.

1. **The cowboy** or range hand who looks after the cattle.

2. **The banker** who finances land, herd and equipment.

3. **The chemist** who makes insecticides, serums and fertilizers.

4. **The oil refiner** who provides the fuel for the power machinery so many ranchers use.

5. **The steelmaker** who provides a multitude of items, from fencing and branding irons to filing cabinets.

6. **The brewer**
7. **The sugar refiner**
8. **The cotton ginner**
9. **The flour miller**
} who furnish some of the by-products used to make the livestock feeds with which ranchers and feeders supplement grass.

10. **The veterinary** who looks after the health of the cattle.

11. **The blacksmith** who shoes the horses and repairs ranch machinery.

12. **The airplane pilot** who sprays ranges and fields, destroying pests.

13. **The lumberman** who provides the wood for corrals and barns and pens.

14. **The windmiller** who makes the machinery that keeps man-made ranch water holes working.

15. **The feeder** who takes lean range cattle and puts about 25% more beef on them by intensive feeding.

16. **The truck driver**
17. **The railroader**
} who haul cattle to market and meat to you.

18. **The stockyards man** who provides "room and board" for the livestock, and the **commission man** who is sales agent for the producer.

19. **The meat packer** who processes and distributes the beef.

20. **The retailer** who is the final link between all these people . . . and *you.*

American Meat Institute

Headquarters, Chicago • *Members throughout the U. S.*

52

Eastern Meat Packers' Association; for the wholesaler, the U. S. Wholesale Grocers Association, and for the retailer, the American Retail Federation. These organizations only touch the surface of the real number of pressure groups involved in just this one steak-producing process.

When the members of any of these groups need medical attention, they will come in contact with other persons who are members of the American Nurses Association, American Dental Association, American Medical Association, American Optometric Association, or American Hospital Association. Their ice cream may be produced by a member of the International Association of Ice Cream Manufacturers. For their oleomargarine manufacturers, there is the National Association of Margarine Manufacturers; for their ice, the National Association of Ice Industries; for their laundry, the American Institute of Laundering; for their infants' diapers, the National Institute of Diaper Services; for the man from whom they buy a soft drink when visiting a western park, the Western Conference of Park Concessionaires. Lobbyists registered with the Congress work for organizations ranging from Republic Steel Corporation to the Vitrified China Association to the American League for an Undivided Ireland.

Pressure groups attempting to influence government have been a fixture in American politics since the very beginning, only today there are more of them and they are bigger, better organized, more effective, and in general more powerful. Nor are pressure groups indigenous to America. In some form and in varying degrees of strength, depending upon the degree of specialization in societies, they do exist everywhere in nontotalitarian countries. In each, they tend to develop techniques most suitably adapted to the governmental system in which they must operate.

Why the proliferation of pressure groups in the United States? The most important reason is that they have a legitimate and necessary function to perform. In the earlier simple societies it was comparatively easy for a representative elected from a single-member geographical district to represent his constituency in its totality. Division of labor was elemental. Loyalty to the whole community came ahead of loyalty to special-interest organizations. As the full impact of the industrial revolution came to be felt, the nature of the community changed. Now a trucker, for example, would find a strong pull away from his sense of community affiliation because he was identified with other truckers with closely similar problems and interests in

other communities. Also, as the old type of community unity tended
to disintegrate under the multiplication of specialties, it became
more difficult and later impossible for the legislator and governmental executive to represent the many differing elements in his district without help. The pressure group arose to fill the need.

Partly as a result of pressure group demands, governments took
on more functions. Increasing governmental functions as they affected
unorganized interests in the community tended to, in turn, give rise
to the organization of still more new groups. During periods of war,
the national government has encouraged groups of specialties to organize in order to have a more effective means for reaching the members of some particular public. Once organized and with a group
bureaucracy installed, the group continues to function even when
the original purpose for organization is gone with the end of war.
Bureaucracies find other objectives around which memberships can
be rallied and for which they can pressure government.

One more reason for interest groups on the scale which they exist
today should be added. Large organizations with hundreds of thousands or millions of members scattered over wide geographical areas
would not have been possible if the only means of communication
among the leaders and among the members was face-to-face contact.
The revolution in communication which produced the new mass
media and the revolution in transportation which produced the fast
train and airplane make face-to-face contact among leaders always
possible and face-to-face contact among the membership unnecessary.

Sociologically, because man is a social animal seeking both self-
expression and security, and because he cannot satisfy all of these
needs alone, group organization is an inherent part of society. In
some groups, such as those with a philanthropic object, self-expression
tends to be most important. In other groups, particularly those of
economic motivation, security tends to be the most important. But
regardless of which of the two drives is primary, any group seeks to
attain its object by trying to control the environment in which it finds
itself — either by attempting to impose restraints to force competition out of its area as in the case of two labor unions engaged in a
jurisdictional fight to see which shall be the bargaining agent, or by
attempting to neutralize or make friendly the environment through
the propaganda which the group puts out.[3]

---

[3] From Earl Latham, " The Group Basis of Politics: Notes for a Theory,"
American Political Science Review (June, 1952), Vol. 46, No. 2, pp. 385–387.

The resulting social milieu has been ably described by Professor Earl Latham of Amherst College:

> All of these [restraints, neutralizing and making friends] are methods by which the environment in which groups dwell is made safe and predictable to them, and, therefore secure. And because the relations of people are myriad and shifting, subject to cycles of deterioration and decay, because the environment itself changes with each passing hour, there is a ceaseless struggle on the part of groups to dominate, neutralize or conciliate that part of the environment that presses in upon them most closely. In this struggle, there is an observable balance of influence in favor of organized groups in their dealings with the unorganized, and in favor of the best and most efficiently organized in their dealings with the less efficiently organized. Strong tend to take advantage of the weak. . . . Or, to put it another way, organization represents concentrated power, and concentrated power can exercise a dominating influence when it encounters power which is diffused and not concentrated, and therefore weaker.[4]

The particular concern of the political scientist is how strong organized groups interact with and act upon government and what is the effect of the interaction process. Are pressure groups becoming so strong and are they using their power in such a manner as to constitute a threat to our concept of democratic-representative government? What are the tools in the pressure group's public relations kit? Where and how do pressure groups touch the major political parties? What are the standards against which pressure group power may be judged?

ELEMENTS OF PRESSURE GROUP POWER

Pressure group power does not vary directly with the size of the group's membership, the skill of its leaders, its status in society, its resources, its organizational structure, or any other single characteristic. Rather, degree of power is determined by many different factors, no one of which stands alone and none of which have meaning unless they are related to the purpose of the pressure group and the environment in which it must function. For purposes of illustration, the most important elements of pressure group power will be threaded into an examination of one of the most unusual, best-organized and

---

[4] *Ibid.*, p. 387. Reprinted by permission of *The American Political Science Review.*

strongest pressure groups the United States has known — the Anti-Saloon League.[5]

Objective. The Anti-Saloon League began as a single-purpose organization with that single purpose a moral one — " get rid of the saloons." " Ten Nights in a Barroom " may be a theme for risque barn theaters today, but in the days of the League it was no joke. Few of those who indulged in alcoholic beverages or were not opposed to those who did indulge, could feel much love for the typical " disease, destitution, and depravity causing " saloon of that period. Not until the Anti-Saloon League was already powerful did it branch out from its anti-saloon concentration into, first, local option, and then to the broader purpose of legal prohibition. There was only one issue on which its members and fellow travelers had to agree.

Other things being equal, a single-purpose pressure group or one whose objectives are clustered about a single purpose is likely to be more effective than a broad-purpose organization. The greater the number of points on which agreement is sought, the more difficult it is to hold an organization together for the advancement of its broad program. Further, an economic purpose if it can be at least partly obscured by moral or patriotic overtones, will fall on more fertile ears than one which is solely economic.

At the opposite extreme from the Anti-Saloon League are such vaguely defined groups as consumers and white-collar workers. Though consumer associations have tried to organize the former and labor unions the latter, organization has been notable only by its very weak and local character or complete absence. Until the members of either group can attain a stronger feeling of identity and begin to interact on the basis of the problems they share in common with other individuals in the same group, efforts to organize will continue to be as unsuccessful as they have been in the past.

Status. The Anti-Saloon League was built on a foundation of Protestant churches with its local agents the ministers of those churches.

---

[5] The Anti-Saloon League, founded as a national organization in 1895, was the major generating force behind local option legislation in the states and eventually national prohibition. It was at the height of its strength at the time of the passage of the 18th Amendment. After that it declined in power, and since the repeal of prohibition in 1933, it has not been a significant national pressure group. See Peter H. Odegard, *Pressure Politics: The Story of the Anti-Saloon League* (New York: Columbia University Press, 1928).

The churches already had the kind of status in their communities and nationally that ensured at least a respectful hearing for the League's message. Arrayed on the other side were the then low-status brewers and distillers who, if they were able to present their case, would have to do it behind closed doors and not in public. In more contemporary terms, for an example of the lowest level of status, there is the American Communist party. Anything it endorses is likely to have received the " kiss of death."

Status or prestige of some organizations can be so high that the organization does not need to formally ask the governmental official to do what it wants. If it makes its wishes known, even in a round-about way, its desires find a way of taking the form of governmental action. High-status organizations find it easy to strike up alliances with other organizations for a joint effort to achieve common objectives. Likewise, high-status organizations are likely to be those which have the largest financial resources and those which find it easier to raise more money when and if they need it.

Membership. The members of the Anti-Saloon League, in addition to being united on a narrowly defined and simple moral issue of "good versus evil," were many in number and geographically distributed over the entire United States. Particularly were their concentrations high in rural areas. An organization with such membership characteristics is in an ideal position to swing great weight in legislative bodies.

If an organization has a substantial number of voters in every state legislative district and every Congressional district, it can apply pressure on the legislator where it hurts the most — his prospects of re-election. Disregarding political party affiliation of candidates, personality, or general positions on other issues, the League made the man's record or campaign position on the League's platform the test. If the candidate did not measure up, the League precinct organization (composed of every available man, woman, and child and instructed to contact every house in every block) went out against him. If he did pass the muster, and only if he did, would this power be on his side.

Though the League's greatest proportion of members was found in rural areas, this did not impose the degree of handicap in legislative influence which limits other organizations whose greatest concentrations are in the cities. American state legislatures, apportioned as they are on an area as well as a population basis, give rural areas a greater proportion of seats than the rural areas deserve on the basis of their percentage of state population. In the United States House of Representatives, though its representation is based solely on population, there is still distortion of the same kind because rural-controlled state legislatures, in apportioning Congressional districts, want it that way. The United States Senate with two Senators from each state, regardless of population, is dominated by the smaller states.

Pressure groups with membership concentrated in city areas are, in turn, in a more advantageous position if they want to influence the President of the United States and if those concentrations are in the large and doubtful pivot states like New York, California, and Illinois. States or combinations of a few states such as these are often decisive in Presidential elections.

One more important membership factor should be mentioned — that of overlapping memberships. Few persons belong to only one pressure group. Severe strain can be placed on one group's unity when a member finds that one or more other groups to which he belongs are in conflict with the first group. If he has to make a decision, possibly he might take the crisp course of decision for one side or the other, or what is more likely, he might become passive under the force of the cross-pressures. To the Anti-Saloon League, the problem of overlapping memberships was minor at most. To erase the saloon, to be for local option, or later to be for national prohibition resulted in relatively few overlapping-membership conflicts for the type of person who was active in the Anti-Saloon League.

Organizational Structure. The Anti-Saloon League appeared at first glance to be a loosely federated type of organization, but if one looked beyond the black and impersonal lines of the organization chart, he found control so strongly vested in the national unit that the opposition " liquor interests " were wont to claim the League's structure " might well excite the envious approval of an oriental despot." Real power rested with its general superintendent, national executive committee, and its full-time paid professional employees. Each state too had its own board of directors, executive committee, general superintendent, and paid staff, but the state organizations were definitely controlled by and did not control the national organization.

Generally, a unitary rather than a federal type of structure enables the organization to act more effectively. Membership in the former is in the national unit, and power is concentrated there. In federally organized pressure groups membership is usually either in a state organization or in some functional subunit such as the American Federation of Labor's craft unions. Power in the federal type is divided, some resting in the state or functional subunit and some, depending upon how much the state or functional subunits will give up, in the national body. The Democratic and Republican parties are examples of how weak national units of federal organizations can become. Few federally organized pressure groups are able to achieve the unity of operation characteristic of the League.

Leadership. The Anti-Saloon League's leaders were able strategists and functioned in a type of organization which made strong leadership possible. That these individuals were able strategists is borne out by their willingness to compromise to attain one step of their objective at a time. An organization with a single moral purpose is one of the most difficult to keep in constant touch with political reality. The temptation to crusade immediately for the maximum objective (prohibition, in the case of the League) always exists because it is " right " and regardless of whether the soil has been prepared for the propaganda seeds or not. In starting first against the saloon, then when the time was right branching out to local option, and finally to prohibition, the League's leaders were revealing a degree of flexibility and understanding which was a major factor in their success.

Even if leaders are able, however, they need a type of organizational environment in which they are given the freedom to make the kind of decisions which the political situation requires. The League was such an organization. Its funds came from monthly subscriptions from individuals, solicited through the participating Protestant churches. Though representatives of the affiliated churches sat on League boards of directors, they left most policy decisions to the professional leaders. Another factor which contributed to freedom of operation for the leaders lay in the fact that funds came in small amounts from many people rather than from one or a few very large contributors. The League's leadership did not have to, as leaders of many groups do, mold its words and actions to fit the whims of one or a few large contributors.

Every organization will have its active minority, namely, the relatively small group of leaders which in fact control. Robert Michels in his *Political Parties: A Sociological Study of the Oligarchical*

Tendencies of Modern Democracies,[6] found this to be so even in what he felt were the most democratically motivated organizations he could find to study — European democratic-socialist parties. The nature of organization itself demands that officers and bureaucracy shall spend more time in the affairs of the group than rank and file members. Once in office, especially if salaried office, there is the tendency to want to stay, and custom and other pressures function on the members to make them want their leaders to remain. Leadership takes time, and only a few can economically afford to devote much time to their group associations. Some persons have talents which enable them to lead while others do not. Factors such as these operate to create and sustain an organization's active minority.

The question is not whether there shall be an active minority, but rather it is what kind of leadership shall the active minority provide? If the men who occupy the positions of leadership maintain two-way channels of internal communication to keep the membership satisfied and as united as possible, and at the same time keep themselves informed, if the leaders are flexible enough to constantly adapt to changing external events and if they are able strategists in winning external support, the pressure group has added another element which will affect the degree of power it can generate. Leadership and organizational structure, membership, status, objective — all of these are elements upon which the pressure group's external relations will depend.

PRESSURE GROUP PUBLIC RELATIONS

The object of the public relations function is to control the environment in order to insure maximum security and maximum opportunity for achieving group objectives. The public relations process itself consists of attempting to impose restraints on the environment by destroying or reducing competing groups to impotency, of attempting to neutralize groups which cannot be won over as friends, and of attempting to make friends whenever that is possible. If unrestrained, this " group war " could only result in violence and disorder, but pressure groups as well as the rest of a democratic-representative society are governed by " rules of the game " which make certain types of conduct unacceptable. Those who flagrantly disregard

---

[6] (Glencoe, Ill.: The Free Press, 1915).

the " rules of the game " place themselves in the position of doing more harm than good. Every standard definition of public relations, specifically or by implication includes, in addition to the function of persuasion, the function of trying to identify the objectives of the propagandizing group with the " rules of the game " and the broader public interest.

No longer do organizations hold to the philosophy of " the public be damned." Every organization, pressure group or otherwise, recognizes that in public opinion there is power — the power of votes and their influence on public officeholders and political parties, the power of buyers, the power of stock purchasers, and the power of potential members. Organizations substantially dependent upon public good will, and few there are which do not lend themselves to such classification, start from the premise that they operate in a buyers' market. Public opinion analysis has itself become an important specialization. After the opinion researchers make their rounds, the results are studied, the decisions are made and then people and groups are flattered, cajoled, entertained, educated, and lobbied.

When the decision as to objective has been made, the remainder of the public relations process may be classified into the following steps: first, analyzing the publics to determine from which support is essential and to determine how best to approach each public in the support-winning attempt; second, selecting the medium or media of communication, either a mass medium like radio or a particular medium like a personal contact, in order to most effectively get the message across; third, deciding how to use the medium, such as the decision of whether to use advertising, publicity, a combination of both, or perhaps a certain kind of personal contact; and fourth, maintaining a continuing evaluation of the effectiveness of the public relations programs being followed.

If the pressure group is a large business corporation, the main outlines of its public relations operation will appear broadly as outlined below. Analyzing the publics upon which it is dependent results in the identification of such groups as employees, stockholders, competitors, communities in which units of the corporation are located, and government. Our particular concern is with governmental relations, but programs instituted for all the other groups are related to governmental relations.

With employees, not only does the corporation want smooth labor-management relations, but it hopes that employees who have a financial stake in the company will also exert their influence as voters and as constituents of elected public officials toward governmental policies on which both labor and management of the same company can agree would best further the joint objectives of both. With stockholders, not only does the corporation want its stock to be in demand, but it tends to prefer a wide distribution of ownership in the hope that stockholders who also have a financial stake will exert their influence with government toward common company-stockholder objectives. Company-dealer, company-competitor, and company-community activity based upon common objectives in each relationship can also have their effect on government. In the case of the company-competitor combination, the result is the now familiar national trade association — a holding company of sorts, employing specialists in lobbying and communication to bring the concerted pressure of many companies to bear on those who are legislators, elected public executives, and governmental administrators.

Governmental relations in an earlier period consisted largely of backstage working to get " the right man " elected to legislative office, keeping him on " the right track " for as long as he was in office, and staying out of public view. Methods were often crude, so crude that Walt Whitman, in one of the milder passages of his period on the subject of lobbying, could write, " bawling office-holders . . . kept editors . . . bribers, compromisers, lobbiers, spongers."

Governmental relations today in the era of " the new lobby " as distinguished from the era of " the old lobby " are quite different. First, there are many more pressure groups and many more lobbyists, and no one of them holds the power which once rested in the hands of " wicked old Sam Ward, King of the Lobby," of the 1860's and 1870's. Second, with legislative delegation of wide discretionary powers to agencies of the executive branch of government, the present-day lobbyist is an administrative as well as a legislative lobbyist. Third, pressure groups have come to realize that if they are to be successful on the legislative or administrative fronts, it is necessary to build public good will and to marshal popular support which will in turn make itself felt on public officials by getting them to think that what the pressure group desires is what the people want. Fourth, the lobbying function is not only a pressure-developing machine, but also one which provides a not inconsiderable service in educating and informing public officials and their electorates.

The lobbyists of the pressure groups, many of them former legislators or governmental administrators selected for their contacts, for their knowledge of the workings of government, and for their understanding of the forces which determine public opinion, are generally able and high-quality types of people. It is they, working with friendly legislators and executives, who can apply the gentle touch; and working with those not so friendly, a touch which may include an appropriate amount of pressure. It is they who appear for and present the case of their pressure group before legislative committee or administrative board hearings. It is they who co-ordinate the pressure group's propaganda output with the legislative or administrative " situation." When necessary, it is they who become the group diplomats who mobilize whole alliances of pressure groups for or against some bill or governmental policy.

Though the legislator and administrator may at times resent the power of pressure groups and the mental torment which they sometimes impose on the mind when it is engaged in decision making, the legislator and administrator cannot live without them. The relationship is reciprocal, and each party has something which the other wants. For both the legislator and administrator, there is technical information, political advice, and the pressure group's channel of communication. Fortunate is the politician who can win praise in the pressure group's publications. Studies show that the trade paper is read more carefully and assimilated more thoroughly than any other kind of printed word. Likewise, the pressure group's internal media of communication provide a service for the governmental administrator whose function is one which, if it is to be properly administered, depends upon whether the members of the groups most affected understand what is being done, why it is being done, and what is expected of them. And for the politician, again, there is still the matter of contributions for the financing of his next campaign.

Granted that pressure groups are necessary, is there some point in the development of their power beyond which the tolerances of structure and spirit of a democratic-representative system of government can no longer stretch? Some are of the opinion that such a point has nearly or already been reached and that democracy is in jeopardy. Others take a more sanguine view. The question is the subject of the concluding section of this chapter. Before proceeding to it, it is necessary to examine the relationship between pressure groups and the major political parties as each is used or consents to be used by the other.

PRESSURE GROUPS AND THE MAJOR PARTIES [7]

Pressure groups work both through major parties and around them. If the party organizations are strong and party membership is disciplined as in Britain, pressure group attempts to influence government must of necessity be centered on those who control the parties. British Conservative and Labour party leaders select their respective party's nominees for each House of Commons constituency, draft the platform on which the party goes to the people, and control the policies of government and opposition after elections.

The American major party, as has been noted, presents quite a different picture. Nominee selection is decentralized and to varying degrees removed from the hands of party organs. National party platforms drafted when the party does not have one of its own in the White House are a product of state and local party organization and pressure group influences as both play upon the assembled platform committees of the national conventions. Even if the party does have the Presidency, the platform product may not in all respects resemble what it would have been should the President himself have done the drafting. Party nominees do not necessarily support the whole platform, and on occasion a Presidential candidate publicly repudiates parts with which he does not agree.

Except as provided by a chief executive, there is no single party program for governing. Legislators may go one way and the President the other, or should most of a President's majority in Congress follow him in most respects, always there will be factions either dragging their feet or in open disagreement. If the Congress or one house thereof is controlled by the opposition party, there is even less central direction of governmental program.

Where in the British system access to those who make governmental decisions in major part hinges on access to those who control the majority party, in America the pattern of access is diffused. Should the question be one of national governmental policy, if the pressure group loses in one house of Congress, it may succeed in the next to at least force a compromise. If it fails in both houses, it may win a Presidential veto. Failing that, all is still not necessarily lost — there is the administrative agency which will be charged with administering

---

[7] See David B. Truman, *The Governmental Process* (New York: Alfred A. Knopf, 1951), Chaps. 9 and 10.

the program or enforcing the law, and as a last resort there is the court system with its sometimes seemingly endless possibilities for delay. In the United States those who sit in the different seats of power in the major parties are only one of several different sets of power points to which the pressure group may direct attention if it is to affect governmental policy.

With this as background, what are the ways in which the pressure groups and major political parties come in contact with one another? There are several. Pressure groups may seek to have their own members join and work up to positions of power within the major parties. They may try to influence what the major party platforms have to say on the subject of their special interest. They may attempt to play an active role in the nomination and general election process.

The pressure group enters each of these relationships as a specialist interested in what it can do to mold governmental policy in its particular field or fields of interest. The political party enters, on the other hand, knowing that it needs a power base composed of many organized pressure groups and other unorganized but identifiable groups making up the electorate. If the political party overcommits to any one pressure group, it knows that the consequences can be measured in terms of loss of support from others. The party also knows most pressure groups are attempting to maintain relations with both major parties at the same time.

Infiltration of the Democratic and Republican parties by the pressure groups is the least complicated of the three types of party-pressure group contact. Rare indeed is the political party organization which is not ready to welcome the new recruit. Always there is need for more precinct workers, envelope sealers and placard putter-uppers (for the placards of your party), and placard tearer-downers (for the placards of the opposition). If the recruit is willing to give a little of his time and energy, he immediately becomes a member in good standing. If he can also apply intelligence and initiative, he can rise quickly in the organization. Furthermore, if his special interest and daily occupation is in such fields as insurance, the law, real estate, dentistry, or any other of a long list, he can develop his own business and enter upon a new social life at the same time as he attempts to look after the interests of his pressure group within the major party of his choice. To the infiltrator accrues still another benefit — as he gains more and more power in a political party he tends to become increasingly important to the pressure group or groups of which he is also a member. If his party activity results someday in his election to public office, his pressure group position is still further enhanced.

The infiltration process does not work in only the pressure group-to-party direction, but also the other way. As the infiltrator becomes more active in party affairs, he gains an education in the realities of party politics, and in his party role his pressure group loyalties must take second position behind his party loyalty. Though he still works for his pressure group objectives, now he begins to understand why the broad-based major party cannot accede to his pressure group's every demand.

Party platform-influencing is the second type of pressure group-major party contact. Here the pressure group, if it has access to the platform committees, may succeed in writing the plank which most directly affects its interests. If not that, and if the group is an important one, it will obtain a hearing before a subcommittee of the platform committee. Though the resultant party platforms, ambiguous as they are likely to be, may not have profound effect on future governmental policies, several purposes are served by pressure group platform-making participation.

For the pressure group, there is the opportunity to see how each of the major parties will react to its demands. If there is substantial danger that one of the major parties would deny access if its candidates were elected, what happened in the platform-preparation might put the pressure group on warning. If it was treated better by the opposition major party convention, perhaps the pressure group will use its experience as a basis for committing itself further than it otherwise would in the subsequent campaign. Also for the pressure group, participation in platform-formation offers an opportunity for publicity. Pressure group leaders can show their members that they are attending to business, and if the issue is important enough, the group's position might gain the kind of general publicity which would enable them to present their message through nation-wide news channels. In the third place, if a favorable platform plank has been adopted — and both major parties will go as far as they can to so please the major pressure groups — the elected officeholders can later be reminded of the " pledges " made by their party convention.

For the major parties, the platform-making process is one of several ways in which the party attempts to build its coalition of supporting groups for the forthcoming campaign. During the campaign the platform serves the purpose of a propaganda device, not used much for its general effect but cut up into parts for dissemination to the groups interested in the subject matter of specific planks. Another party purpose served is to give an indication of the balance of power among the several factions at a nominating convention. From the opening prayer until nominations are made, party politicians are looking for every sign which might show how close nomination contests will go when the final vote is taken. How the controversial platform questions are settled is one of those signs.

More important than either infiltration or platform-influencing are a pressure group's contacts with the major parties in primary and general elections. Because the major parties are weak in everything but the business of winning elections and because the party organizations themselves are not constructed to control the operation of government after election, the most effective pressure group activity is often carried on during campaign season. If the man elected is himself a pressure group leader he will tend to become both public official and inside-lobbyist for his pressure group when in office. This applies not only to businessmen turned politician, but also to educators, legionnaires, or any other members of pressure groups. When elected to office, the officeholder may feel a new and broader responsibility because of that office and a duty to represent all the people of his constituency, but the eyes through which he as legislator or elected executive see are still the same eyes he had before holding public office.

If the man elected is not a pressure group leader, the next best access to him is through some pressure group leader who is his close friend, who is of the public official's party, who contributed to his campaign, who helped other ways in his nomination and election, and whose judgment the public officer trusts. Only if the pressure group functions in campaigns, perhaps openly or perhaps secretly, can this kind of access be built. The rewards of nomination and election activity can be great. The dangers of such activity are also great.

As a matter of general policy, most pressure groups avoid permanent identification with either major party. Though there are exceptions, as with some of the labor organizations which maintain solid Democratic party ties and some business organizations which are just as solidly Republican, election activity is usually in behalf of individual candidates in specific elections. To do otherwise is to risk having no access at all or to impose strains on the unity of the pressure group's membership. Some pressure groups carry their caution to the extreme of betting on every potential winner, even if it means some kind of support for two or more candidates for the same office.

When labor organizations are openly Democratic or business organizations openly Republican, the step is taken because each group feels its access would be so limited should the other party gain office that identification is worth the chance. Where parties are weak, such pressure groups have actually moved into a party to such an extent that in some areas they have become the local party unit — running it, financing it, furnishing the bulk of precinct workers, and for the *quid pro quo,* using it for their own purposes.

What are the results of pressure group-political party relations? Stuart Chase states one view:

> With Congressman Doaks looking for the high sign as to how he shall vote from the American Farm Bureau Federation man, from the American Federation of Labor man, from the National Association of Manufacturers' lobbyist — and getting pretty cross eyed in the process — we have about stopped counting on him to represent the whole community. Who does look out for us? There are two answers: we ourselves and the President of the United States.[8]

Note that Chase does not include political parties. The same author continues:

> With the Big Three — business, labor, agriculture — all organized in an impressive way, the typical Congressman has his troubles. In a clash, whom will he support? Here is the Hon. Clarence Cannon of Missouri, apparently requested by William Green of the AF of L to vote for the subsidy bill. Mr. Cannon searches his heart and comes up with this classic reaction: " I have always followed Mr. Green on labor bills. But this is not a labor bill. This is a farm bill. On this bill I follow the farm leaders." Just when Mr. Cannon follows the welfare of the United States is not revealed.[9]

Few legislators would be surprised to hear Congressman Cannon's statement coming from one of their number. Legislators would recognize a double dilemma in the above quotations. One of these is the feeling of being pulled apart between the force of the American

---

[8] *Op. cit.,* p. 105.
[9] *Ibid.,* p. 19. Reprinted by permission of The Twentieth Century Fund.

Farm Bureau Federation going one way and the American Federation of Labor going the other, and if the legislator's district is an approximately even balance between farm and industrial population, that feeling would be one of acute pain. The legislator would be condemned if he did and condemned if he did not — unless he wanted to and could find a compromise or could " duck the vote."

Wee, The People

The second dilemma is one without horns, but consists rather of a question to which there is no definitive answer: What is in the public interest? If the legislator himself is to make the decision, public interest would have to evolve from a combination of his own personal thought patterns, his response to pressures from the more powerful groups in his district, and what he felt to be solid information which had sifted down from the claims and counterclaims of the American Federation of Labor and American Farm Bureau Federation representations. If the legislator were to look elsewhere for definition of public interest on an issue, his two possible sources of aid would be the President of the United States or his political party. If the President is of the legislator's party, he could follow both President and party at the same time. If not, he might try to follow party only to find that his party had no party-wide decipherable position. Or if the leadership of his party in his house did take a stand and that conflicted with the stand of the President, then how should he decide? If the legislator has been a legislator for long, he will know that the President's concept of public interest or his party's concept will also be conditioned by the somewhat different pressure group forces which play on them.

Is there no escape from pressure groups for elected public officials? The answer is negative. Although no public official should sign over his power of action to a pressure group neither can he arrive at a "public-interest" or "long-range selfish" view of the public interest without the help of pressure groups. Does that mean that each major pressure group dictates public policy in its area of specialty? Not necessarily. There are controls within the American system which tend to prevent any one pressure group or any complex of pressure groups from domination of government, even without centralized major parties with strong disciplinary weapons for use against their legislators and elected executives.

PRESSURE GROUPS ARE NOT RUINING DEMOCRACY

Lawrence H. Chamberlain, in his systematic study of the origin of ninety major pieces of federal legislation in the fields of business, tariff, labor, national defense, agriculture, federal credit, banking and currency, immigration, conservation, and railroads from 1890 to 1940, came to this conclusion:

> Of the ninety major laws studied, approximately twenty per cent fall to the credit of the President; roughly forty per cent were chiefly the product of Congress; about thirty per cent fall into the joint presidential-congressional category; and slightly less than ten per cent are identified as primarily the handiwork of external pressure groups.[10]

---

[10] *The President, Congress and Legislation* (New York: Columbia University Press, 1946), p. 453. In general, Chamberlain found pressure group "handiwork" most clearly shown in tariff legislation.

The pressure groups' 10 percent included one labor act in 1926, one national resources act in 1924, one railroad act in 1903, and four tariff acts — 1890, 1897, 1922, and 1930.

Though Chamberlain's work did not cover defeated legislation where defeat might be said to be primarily the result of pressure group activity, nor can any such study measure precisely the influence of pressure groups on President, Congress, or joint President-Congress legislation credits, the findings are nonetheless significant. Though pressure groups are often thought to be able to move heaven and earth (an idea not often discouraged by pressure group leaders), pressure group power does not approach such a magnitude as to destroy the American system. Power they do have, but either because of it or in spite of it, a product at least implying some broad concept of public interest from both President and Congress is discernible.

Presidential influence was preponderant in such well-known pieces of legislation as the Emergency Banking Act of 1933, the Securities and Exchange Act of 1934, six major national defense acts, and the Reciprocal Trade Agreements Act of 1934. Congressional influence was preponderant in such legislation as the Norris-LaGuardia Act of 1932, the Soil Conservation Act of 1936, the Federal Reserve Act of 1913, the Clayton Act of 1914 and the National Labor Relations Act of 1935.[11] Certainly there will be those who will disagree and hold that some of these laws were not in the public interest and there will be others who will hold that there should have been more of the same, but most can agree that the Presidents and Congresses of the period have not abandoned the American people to be devoured by the "pressure group wolves."

Few pressure groups attain the power of the Anti-Saloon League, and it flourished on the American scene for only a relatively short period of time. Pressure group power is limited by factors internal to the pressure group organization and external in the system in which they must function. Internally, though a pressure group might have financial resources, it might not have the proper membership characteristics; though it might have skilled leaders, it might not have the best organizational structure; though it might have status, it might not be united in objective. Few meet the ideal effectiveness operating standards on all counts. Within pressure groups, as within legislatures, the process of compromise and concession to mem-

---

[11] *Ibid.*, pp. 450–452.

bers with overlapping interests in other groups is constantly at work.

Externally, there are other checks. First, the demands of one organized group may conflict with those of another, or if there is no organized opposition, perhaps a specific issue will produce one. Second, ours is a separation of powers and federally diffused power system, and to capture one branch of government does not mean capture of the other branches, nor to capture one state does not mean capturing the remaining forty-seven. Third, sectional forces in American politics may function as a check on the national pressure group, or subsectional forces within states, as a check on state pressure groups. Fourth, the single-member district system of electing legislators tends to produce representatives who owe responsibility to a variety of organized and unorganized groups. Fifth, " rules of the game " standards of conduct set up outside limits which no pressure group may long and consistently safely exceed. Sixth, there is an *esprit des corps* among elected public officeholders and nonelective administrators which has its own ways of taking care of those among themselves who do not live up to the prevailing concept of public trust. Seventh, lobby-regulation legislation on the national level and in many of the states, though hardly effective as enforcement measures, does require registration and does produce some publicity for lobby activity and monies spent for such activity. Eighth, as pressure groups have grown larger, so has government, and the latter does have the power and often exerts it to maintain the upper hand. Ninth, since Theodore Roosevelt the Presidency has developed to a new leadership position in the formulation and statement of national policies, and the same trend is evident in the office of governor in most states. Tenth, the major political parties as they now exist, do provide, though perhaps not as effectively as they should or many would hope they could, a check on pressure groups.

Though none of these factors standing alone might be an adequate safeguard and though each might not always operate or operate quickly enough, in their sum-total effect there is counterbalancing power of adequate strength. As long as the channels of communication remain open, they will continue to perform their control functions.

CHAPTER FOUR

The Minor Party

We arraign the Republican and Democratic Parties as false to the standards reared by their founders; as faithless to the principles of the illustrious leaders of the past to whom they do homage with the lips; as recreant to the " higher law," which is as inflexible in political affairs as in personal life; and as no longer embodying the aspirations of the American people, or inviting the confidence of enlightened, progressive patriotism. Their protest against the admission of " moral issues " into politics is a confession of their own moral degeneracy. . . . Each accuses the other of extravagance in congressional appropriations, and both are alike guilty; each protests when out of power against the infraction of the civil-service laws, and each when in power violates those laws in letter and spirit; each professes fealty to the interests of the toiling masses, but both covertly truckle to the money power in their administration of public affairs. Even the tariff issue . . . is no longer treated by them as an issue upon great and divergent principles of government, but is a mere catering to different sectional and class interests. . . . The competition of both the parties for the vote of the slums, and their assiduous courting of the liquor power and subserviency to the money power, has resulted in placing those powers in the position of practical arbiters of the destinies of the nation. We renew our protest against these perilous tendencies, and invite all citizens to join us in the upbuilding of a party . . . that prefers temporary defeat to an abandonment of the claims of justice, sobriety, personal rights and the protection of American homes.

Recognizing and declaring that prohibition of the liquor traffic has become the dominant issue in national politics, we invite to full party

73

fellowship all those who on this one dominant issue are with us agreed, in the full belief that this party can and will remove sectional differences, promote national unity, and insure the best welfare of our entire land.

From the Prohibition Party Platform of 1892 [1]

In the introductory quotation the Prohibition party of 1892 was calling upon citizens of the United States to discard their major party affiliation and their sectional political interests to redeem America by supporting the Prohibition party. Such feelings of frustration at the limitation of choice afforded by the two-party system and such hopes for a new major party to implement solutions to problems of the day have been expressed time and again in language related to the context of almost any period of American politics. Sometimes the words are more politically realistic and sometimes less realistic, but always there is the same reoccurring theme.

Similar thoughts were expressed by Anti-Masonites of the 1820's, who were aroused to form a political party because of the strange disappearance in 1826 of one William Morgan who had " revealed the secrets of Masonry." Or perhaps the words of protest are those of one of the inflation-cursed bread rioters of New York City during the panic of 1837 as he turned to the Locofoco (Equal Rights) party with its demand for a return to hard money. Or in the 1840's or 1850's he may have been a Liberty party man dissatisfied because neither Democrats nor Whigs would admit that the depression of 1837 had been imposed by a "spendthrift, slaveholding South upon a frugal, industrious, and unsuspecting, free-labor North." [2] He could have been a Know-Nothing (Native American Party), convinced that mass immigration was the major evil of the body politic, or a Free-Soiler with his battle-cry of " Free Soil, Free Speech, Free Labor, and Free Men." In the 1880's or 1890's, the writer may have been a Greenbacker, Prohibitionist, Anti-Monopolist or Populist; or in 1948, an Independent Progressive or Dixiecrat.

Of those movements which do result in a minor party organization, some are like a match flaring for a few moments hardly noticed

---

[1] Major and minor party platforms from 1840 through 1924 may be found in Kirk H. Porter, *National Party Platforms* (New York: The Macmillan Company, 1924).

[2] Wilfred E. Binkley, *American Political Parties* (New York: Alfred A. Knopf, 1949), p. 183.

then to go out, be thrown away, and forgotten. A few, however, do produce a larger imprint. Of the latter, some like the Prohibition party may continue to survive to use their minor party position as a propaganda vehicle even though the party has no prospect of electoral success. Others will enjoy temporary election successes within a limited geographical area in proportion to their willingness to broaden appeal and in proportion to the failure of the major parties.

Perhaps the typical minor party's finest hour is on that dismal day when all seems lost as either or both of the major parties sits up and takes notice of the support which the minor party has generated and begins to swallow up the minor party's platform and perhaps its organization and some of its leaders. The extent that the swallowing-up process makes a major party alter its direction to make sure of holding a new element the minor party brings to it, is generally the final test of the degree of success of the minor party movement.

The Anti-Masonic party was absorbed by the Whigs, but before disappearing it did educate both those in secret societies and outside of them on some of the implications of secret organization in a democratic system. And before the Anti-Masons faded away, they did leave to all future parties the example of the first national nominating convention. Locofocos were gathered into the Democratic party, but at a price which has led historians to suggest that the transaction was a Locofoco absorption of Democrats except in name. Know-Nothings became so strong they took over the Whig major party and appeared to be on the way toward becoming the Democrats' major long-term antagonists. Then the Know-Nothings waned and were gulped up, along with earlier Liberty party men, Free Soilers, and others, into the Republican party. From the Free Soilers the Republican party took nothing less than almost their entire platform. Most of the Populists eventually became Democrats, and many of the Peoples' party platform planks found their way into both Democratic and Republican party platforms.

The dynamics of minor party-major party relations are not complete without showing also the workings of a variety of minor party known as the " splinter party." Here we have an organizational phenomenon which sprouts out of temporary unresolvable discord between the factions of a major party. The splinterers are in fact secessionists, but they usually wait until their major party holds its national convention before taking the drastic step. Not liking what the major party produces either in platform or nominations or both, and not having enough power to make the major party over into their own image, the losers stalk out, generally not to join the opposition major party, but to try to organize quickly a new party to contest for votes.

In 1948 Henry A. Wallace tried to entice out of the Democratic party those who might have felt that President Harry S. Truman was not liberal enough, and Governor Strom Thurmond of South Carolina and the Dixiecrats took their walk because Truman was too liberal. The Man from Independence won in spite of the defections. In 1896 when Democrats risked making the campaign turn on one issue which stood out above all others — soft-money Democracy versus hard-money Republicanism — both major parties splintered. Hard-money Democrats went for McKinley; soft-money Republicans, for Bryan.

In 1872 there was the Liberal Republican bolt which resulted in the nomination of Horace Greeley to do battle with Ulysses S. Grant. In 1912 there were the Theodore Roosevelt Progressives; and in 1924, the Robert M. LaFollette, Sr., Progressives. Only in 1912 did the new party significantly influence the outcome of the presidential election. Then the Bull Moose outpolled the regular William Howard Taft Republican ticket to throw the election to Woodrow Wilson.

After losing the election, the " splinter party " tends to dissolve quickly. Most of its members once again hear the call of their old major party tie. Some others use their new-found independence and experience of major party irregularity as a bridge on which to walk across to join the opposition party.

In addition to the minor party with a " splinter " purpose, others might be classified as *single-purpose* like the Prohibition or Greenback parties; still others as *sectional* such as the Farmer-Labor party of Minnesota in the 1930's and the American Labor party of New York; still others as *class* parties such as the Socialists. In a category all of its own there is the Communist party, a part of an apparatus directed from the Kremlin and dedicated to overthrowing the governmental system which it would use in its attempt to rise to power.

The number and strength of minor parties varies from time to time and place to place. In 1952 the minor parties' voices were so feeble only scattered sounds from them could be heard over the Eisenhower-Stevenson debate. In 1948 with Dewey, Truman, Thurmond,

and Wallace and major competition so diffused, occasionally attention also went to the Socialist party with its venerable Norman
Thomas running for the last time, and the Socialist Labor, Prohibition, Greenback and Christian Nationalist parties. The minor parties
have an ebb and flow in state elections too, but those sectional minor
parties which have developed significant strength have generally been
found in states with weak major parties such as Minnesota and Wisconsin, or in those states like New York in which the major parties

A THIRD PARTY VIEW OF A PRESIDENTIAL CAMPAIGN (1912)

The *Chicago Tribune's* famous cartoonist, the late John T. McCutcheon, drew
this cartoon, titled " The Challenge," after the Bull Moose Party nominated
Theodore Roosevelt. The *Tribune* campaigned for Roosevelt, and so, incidentally, did Harold Ickes.

are so evenly balanced that a strong minor party may be decisive in
throwing the state election result or the Presidential contest one way
or the other.

One of the foremost minor-party scholars, historian John D.
Hicks, finds it difficult to generalize a theory of origin for minor
parties. The first assumption is that they are depression-spawned, but
this, he finds, is not consistent with the record. More likely, he concludes, minor parties " have come about as the natural by-products
of our diverse sectional interests." Hicks concludes:

Major parties must command support in every section, and must
manage somehow to collect everywhere the maximum number of

votes. That one man's meat is another man's poison has frequently been true as between the various sections of the United States. When, therefore, a certain policy is meat to the industrial East, for example, but poison to the agricultural West, such a policy must be rejected by a major party — particularly if it is the governing party — or disguised, or evaded. Let a whole section begin to feel that its interests are being permanently discriminated against by both old parties, and the time for a plain-spoken third party, organized mainly along sectional lines, is about ripe.[3]

Minor parties in the United States appear to be on the decline. One of the major reasons lies in the direct primary system which permits a candidate of almost any stripe of party regularity or irregularity to win and continue to win a major party nomination. This, in turn, permits an accommodation of sectional pressures not possible before the advent of the direct primary. It is interesting to note that the last Presidential election in which a minor party determined the outcome was in 1912 when the direct primary movement in the states was just reaching the height of its momentum. All other cases where minor parties were or have appeared to be decisive in Presidential elections occurred in the 1800's — 1844, 1848, and 1884. In an average Presidential election minor parties receive approximately 5 percent of the popular vote. Though in 1924 they did go up to a high of 16.5 percent, in 1952 minor party nominees in total won less than .05 percent of the popular Presidential vote. Never as strong in Congressional as Presidential contests, minor parties in recent years have had only one or two United States House of Representatives seats.

What, then, are the alternatives for a group interested in translating group principles into governmental action? One is that the members as individuals might work within the major parties. If the object is the accomplishment of a set of group objectives, this first alternative has only limited usefulness. Another alternative is to organize into a pressure group which might operate around the major parties, or both around and through them whenever the latter is possible. This is the alternative which, if the number of groups selecting it is any criterion, promises the greatest rewards.

A third possibility is to form a minor party whose purpose will

---

[3] "The Third Party Tradition in American Politics," *The Mississippi Valley Historical Review* (June, 1933), Vol. 20, No. 1, pp. 27–28. Reprinted by permission of *The Mississippi Valley Historical Review*.

be primarily to propagandize as a party rather than as a pressure group, but without the right to hope to win Presidential elections or seats in Congress and with only limited hopes of accomplishing more on the electoral fronts in the states. Staring those who select this alternative in the face, however, is the somewhat humiliating (to a minor party man) function which students of American politics ascribe to minor parties. Minor parties permit their members to " blow off steam " without damaging the fabric of the whole political system! To the dedicated minor party leader, the last thing he wants to contemplate as an end product of his labors is " blowing off steam."

Fourth in the list of alternatives for the group interested in a principle or set of principles is the formation of a minor party in the hope it will displace an existing major party. If this is the object, the group's leaders should take a long, cold and hard look at the obstacles. There is no better tool through which the minor party leader set on replacing a major party can size up the enormity and almost impossibility of the task he has set than Paul H. Douglas' *The Coming of a New Party*, written in 1932.[4] In this book, first, the minor party man will recognize his own sense of frustration with the major parties as his only practical alternatives on election day. In it also, he will see carefully constructed the brick walls through which he must pick his way on the route to his objective. With the benefit of some twenty-five years of hindsight, he will also note the lack of political reality in means through which Douglas suggested a minor party might make itself major. The section which follows outlines the argument of *The Coming of a New Party*. It will be followed by a critical analysis of the book.

" THE COMING OF A NEW PARTY "

The Setting. For a decade before 1932 farmers had been slowly sinking into deeper depression. In 1929 the stock market crashed bringing economic America to its knees. Everyone interested enough to care, whether he was of the Socialist party or the United States Chamber of Commerce, recognized that something was wrong and went searching for ways and means by which the wrong might be righted.

Douglas, looking to the lot of the salaried or wage worker, felt

---

[4] New York: Whittlesey House of McGraw-Hill Book Company, Inc., 1932.

labor's need was for greater security through social insurance and protective legislation. To get these things, he felt, labor needed more effective organization and would have to enter politics. It should be borne in mind that 1932 was three years before the Wagner Labor Relations Act and that act's subsequent stimulation of organized labor's jump from some 5 million to 14 million members. Neither, at the time, was the right to organize and bargain collectively generally accepted as a right.

Farm prices had fallen to rock-bottom lows, and farm mortgage foreclosures had multiplied. The farmer's lot, Douglas felt, could be improved if tariffs on manufactured goods were reduced and if part of the farmer's tax burden was shifted onto those segments of the community more able to pay. For the average economically hard-up citizen-consumer, Douglas wanted to reduce power rates, prevent deflation, and redesign the tax structure.

These were the interests and these the objectives around which Douglas would build a new political party. So drastic a step was necessary, he felt, because neither the Democratic or Republican parties, controlled as they were by " big business," would recognize the needs of the remainder of society. How little Douglas expected from Franklin D. Roosevelt is revealed in the following statement:

> It is a sobering thought that twenty years ago many progressives were pinning similar hopes on Woodrow Wilson. Wilson, with all respects to Governor Roosevelt, was a far keener thinker and a more determined fighter than the latter. Seldom indeed has the presidency seen a more skilled or more resolute party leader. And yet after eight years of office President Wilson retired with the Democratic party as cancerous as ever in its composition and as conservative in its policies. If such was the fate of Wilson, how can we hope for better things from Franklin Roosevelt? [5]

Here, then, was the setting. Following is a condensation of the book.

The Case for Working Within the Major Parties. The obstacles which tend to make Americans think they have to work within the Democratic and Republican parties are not to be underestimated. Strong sentimental attractions exercise a hold on many to bind them to one of the major parties. The major parties possess political organizations reaching down to the precinct level " to get out the vote,

---

[5] Douglas, *op. cit.*, p. 171.

distribute propaganda, and grant petty favors which bind the recipients more closely to them."

Working against a minor party are other factors. One is the assumption that if progressives take their leave of the major parties, the latter will be more reactionary than they were in the first place. There are the difficulties faced by a minor party man when he asks a major party legislator to support a program. " Why should I help you," will be the answer, " since even if I do, you will still run a candidate against me? " Also, with direct primary laws, labor and progressive forces seem to have greater opportunities for successful working within the major parties, and thus formation of new parties is discouraged.

The political structure of the American system imposes other obstacles. First, there is the federal system. Because labor and progressive forces must largely look to the 48 states for legislation, it is almost impossible to have a unified minor party policy such as that of European labor parties. The latter work inside centralized or unitary states. Second, we have a presidential or separation of powers system instead of a cabinet form of government. In the United States the chief governmental executives do not depend for continuance in office on a legislative majority. Rather the executives are directly elected by the people for fixed terms. Under the cabinet systems which do depend on legislative majorities for continuance in power, small parties can exercise great weight if they are several and are in a balance of power situation. This cannot occur in the United States.

Third, there is the single-member district system of electing legislators which discourages voters from supporting a minor party lest the worst major party win. " So clumsy is our electoral system that large groups of voters feel themselves estopped from expressing their real choice and fancy themselves condemned to an almost perpetual support of an unsatisfactory second best." [6] Without proportional representation minor parties find it difficult to grow. Fourth, there is the Supreme Court's power of judicial review. The court is dominated by the holders of property and a philosophy of status quo. It is small wonder that many have given up the political contest in despair. Fifth, Democrats and Republicans have tightened state legal requirements to make it more difficult for minor parties to get on the ballot — another cause for despair.

---

[6] Douglas, op. cit., p. 134.

" For all these reasons, therefore, it has been commonly believed that those who favor a separate and progressive farmer-labor party are too few to make any real dent upon American life." The obstacles against a minor party's becoming a major party can, however, be overcome. For many reasons it is impossible for progressives to work satisfactorily within either of the major parties.[7]

The Case for Not Working Within the Major Parties. Those who would " bore from within " the major parties underestimate two things. First, there is the massive " strength of political corruption and the dominance of the capitalistic class in both of the two old parties." Second, the major parties, either because they are corrupt or their programs are watered-down, " cannot have the power to move the blood of the great masses of the people whose support is essential if the progressive cause is to triumph." [8]

In the Republican party of 1932, from Maine through New Hampshire, Massachusetts, Connecticut, New York, Pennsylvania, Ohio, Illinois, Minnesota, Montana, Colorado, Arizona, and California, there is either outright corruption or the Republican party leadership is clearly tied to dominant business interests. Inside the national Republican party, the combined strength of such progressives as Norris, Borah, and Cousens and the forces behind them is weak and insignificant.[9]

Nor would it be desirable to try to take over the Democratic party, even though it might be for sale at a relatively cheap price.

> Fundamentally the Democratic party is a discordant combination of Southerners and of the immigrants of our Northern cities. The former are native, Protestant, dry, and conservative; the latter are largely of foreign stock, Catholic, and wet. The two sections of the party differ, therefore, in temperament and policies and they find agreement between them difficult if not impossible.[10]

The Democrats of the South are as much the representatives of property and business as northern Republicans, and the former have the principles of Jeffersonian individualism and states' rights on which to base their rationalizations. Southern Democratic leaders often turn the attention of poor whites and factory workers from their real needs by incitement of racial prejudice.

---

[7] Douglas, *op. cit.*, p. 123.   [9] *Ibid.*, pp. 140–150.
[8] *Ibid.*, p. 139.   [10] *Ibid.*, p. 151.

Democratic state parties are a dismal combination of the James M. Curleys of Massachusetts, Tammany Hall and Mayor Walker of New York, a nonexistent Democratic party in Pennsylvania likely playing ball with the Republicans, the hopeless state of the Democracy in Illinois with its " Bath-house John " Caughlin and " Hinky-Dink " Kenna, and the St. Louis and Kansas City machines of Missouri. State Democratic parties have not hesitated to nominate reactionaries; and John J. Raskob, former head of General Motors and a close associate of the Duponts, is chairman of the Democratic National Committee. Raskob has the Democratic party in financial debt to him, and additional money required for campaigns will have to come from capitalistic interests. " Mr. Raskob's frank policy seems indeed to make the Democratic party another Republican party which will openly compete with the latter for the favor of big business." [11] Furthermore, Democrats have made no real efforts toward tariff reduction, and they have vied with Secretary of the Treasury Andrew Mellon to reduce upper-bracket income taxes.[12]

Should the progressives join forces with Franklin D. Roosevelt? The answer is negative because no matter how rightly motivated and how Roosevelt might try, the Democratic party would still remain " the Democratic party " — " only a sweeping and wholesale transformation can make the Northern wing of the party approach the outer limits of decency." Standing in the way, however, will be the almost compelling pressure on a Democratic President to recognize the local Democratic machines, and Roosevelt has himself been " extremely reluctant to offend Tammany even when great principles were at stake." [13]

> There is nothing that liberals need to rid themselves of more than the infantile notion that a president can by himself greatly change things. He is dependent upon the politically organized forces of the country for the adoption of a legislative program and for his own renomination and re-election. As long as the corruptionists and conservatives are the only groups which have the wit to possess real organizational strength, a president or governor will be compelled either to let them alone or help them have their way.[14]

---

[11] *Ibid.*, p. 165.
[12] For survey of Democratic party of 1932, *ibid.*, pp. 150–167.
[13] *Ibid.*, p. 169.
[14] *Ibid.*, p. 171.

To " bore from within " will, for still other reasons, be less than adequate for the progressive cause. In so doing, enthusiasm that comes from being intimately associated with a movement is dampened. With a new party workers and farmers and liberals will have something they can be enthusiastic about, and no longer will they be politically without a home.

For progressives to confine their activity to raiding the primary elections of the major parties will be to continually be caught up in dilemma after dilemma. What does an organized bloc within one of the major parties do if it loses the primary? If it supports the unsatisfactory winner, the cause is compromised away. If it bolts after the primary, it is open to charges of hypocrisy and will have a difficult time paying for an expensive general election campaign on top of an expensive primary campaign.

Even though progressives should win both a state primary and general election, their troubles would just be beginning. Should they support the national Presidential candidate of the major party they succeeded in capturing at the state level? To do so would tend to weaken the whole movement. To not do so invites trouble with the national party organization and reprisals should the Presidential nominee of that major party get into the White House. It is virtually impossible for state major party leaders to maintain their positions in one of the major parties if they are not " regular " in Presidential campaigns.

A further difficulty arises because, if progressives are " boring from within," they will select the best major party in their state. Progressives in one state might pick the Democratic party and those in another, the Republican party. Then in Presidential election campaigns they will be split between the two major parties and cancel each other out of influence.

If progressives play a trading game with major party political machines, disastrous results can occur. If the machine helps them attain something of what they want, then the machine is credited and is helped in its struggle to perpetuate itself in power. Or perhaps progressives assist the machine and then receive nothing in return when one of their own leaders sells out the cause. Or, if progressives are elected to office under a major party label, it is easier for them to backslide on their progressive ideals and attachments. Here are the temptations dangled before the eyes of the potential progressive backslider:

A liberal or radical who is elected to office as a member of an old party is obviously subject to many insidious temptations to betray the group which elected him. He is forced in some degree to affiliate with the party politicians that surround him. He is exposed to the blandishments of the social lobby of the wealthy. This type of temptation is peculiarly strong in Washington and frequently robs Senatorial Samsons of their radical virility. Moreover, not having a firm and cohesive group behind him, he tends always to be in a very precarious position and is in great danger of being unhorsed and denied a renomination. Yet nearly everyone who has tasted public office wishes to continue in it. Consequently, unless he is a man of unusual principle, he will look for allies from other and from frequently contradictory sources. He thus tends to become " a compromiser and trimmer, and the virtue gradually passes out of him." [15]

If progressives have their own party, there will be fewer defections from the movement. Behind the members is their own party organization. There is the party platform to show the way. If those members who are elected to public office are faithful, they will be renominated and helped. Advocacy of the progressive cause is thus more coherent, continuous, and stable.

The Difficulty of Replacing a Major Party Is Exaggerated. " These difficulties, while real, need not be fatal, and certainly they are not as great as would attend an effort to clean the Augean stables of either of the two old parties and to make them instruments for fulfilling the real interests of the people." [16] Sentimental attachments to the two major parties will disappear as the movement raises new issues and provides a base to which new loyalties may be attracted. The success of the Farmer-Labor party in Minnesota is an illustration.

A new party is not necessarily foreclosed from attaining major party status. Half of the 48 states are now " one-party " — " one-party " Democratic in the South, and " one-party " Republican in the New England states, Pennsylvania, Michigan, Iowa, North Dakota, and Oregon. In these states the new party would not be a third party but a second party. Only a new party in these states can break down their " one-party " structure because either of the old major parties, depending upon the state, is unacceptable as an alternative.

In the politically doubtful states, the new party would for a

---

[15] Douglas, *op. cit.*, pp. 188–189.   [16] *Ibid.*, p. 192.

time have to be a minor party, but historic reasons for the intensely individualistic attitude of Americans toward property and government are disappearing and because neither major party will recognize this fact, a new party can ride on the trend. If such a new party were enthusiastically supported by those classes which stood to gain from a new order, the Democratic party would soon disintegrate. As the new party grew, conservatives of the Democrats and Republicans would join forces and throw sops to the progressives to try to stop their disattachment. But the movement would continue, and with the American love of being on the winning side, soon " great swarms of voters " would flock to it. Although the Democratic machines of Boston, New York, Chicago, and Kansas City would resist longer, they too would eventually fall.

> . . . [I]f my analysis is correct, this old order is rapidly passing and the changing conditions of life must inevitably create a new attitude of mind. Increasing numbers of the farmers, the industrial workers, and even the middle classes will see that they can collectively improve their lot. As this occurs, the structure of the old parties will, because of their affiliations, almost inevitably prove incapable of satisfying the interests and aspirations of the workers and another party will come forward.[17]

Although what has happened to minor parties in the past (except the Republican party) will not bar the rise of a new major party, lessons can be learned from minor party mistakes. Patient planning and deeply penetrating organization will be necessary instead of the too often impetuous last-minute rush at the sound of a political fire alarm. The new party should be more careful than some have been to guard against Communist party infiltration. The new party should be more careful than some have been to keep itself honest by refusing membership to those of questionable character, and should have the right to question members on their official conduct and to expel those who violate the party's code of conduct. The new party should work for a system of proportional representation for electing membership of legislatures. The new party should not go to the " progressive " Democrats and Republicans, but should be so strong that they will come to it. The new party should not split over the wet-dry issue, but both wets and drys should fit in harness together for the accomplishment of the greater common cause.

---

[17] Douglas, *op. cit.,* p. 198.

Membership should be based on dues, thus furnishing mass small contributions instead of being compelled, as the major parties are, to pay in patronage or " cash at the public expense." The new party's name should be either Peoples' party with the advantage of an appeal which might attract white-collar workers, or Farmer-Labor party with the advantage of being more concrete. In some of the industrial states it might be called " Labor party." Farmer and worker should not organize separately to scatter their effect, but join together. Although their interests might seem different, in fact there will be much on which they can agree. Farmers can concede social insurance and protective labor legislation to urban workers, and the latter can concede reduced tariffs and taxes to the farmer. Both will be interested in reducing power rates and in an extension of such social securities as education and public health.

What should be the new party's relation to the Socialist party? People tend to be prejudiced against the name " socialist," and except in areas where the Socialist party is strong, there should be a new organizational base with which the Socialists could go along. As to the type of candidates, better it would be to pick a Norman Thomas who would be one to fully subscribe to the platform and one who would give his life-long allegiance than to select a LaFollette or Wheeler who might not stay attached.

" THE COMING OF A NEW PARTY " — A CRITIQUE

The United States Senator Paul H. Douglas (D) , Illinois, of the middle 1950's would not today write as did the Paul H. Douglas in 1932. The times, the state of economic health, the major parties, the power of Presidents, and the outlook of those who man the institutions of government have undergone a remarkable transformation in the past twenty years. And though Douglas continues to be a man of high moral character and determination to do what is right as he sees that right, he no longer holds the honest " political realist " in contempt. He has observed with his own eyes and himself experienced the political realities which must be recognized and mastered preliminary to the accomplishment of political results.

Though Senator Douglas is not today of the opinion that the American economy is as strong as it should be, he would not hold to the socialist ideal of nationalization of the major production and distribution functions of the economic system. Douglas is one who can today see the advantages in the capitalistic system and work to improve what he feels to be its defects in order, in turn, to improve the capitalistic system's operation. He may even accept the thesis that here in the United States we are witnessing the evolution of a revolutionary capitalism — a revolutionary capitalism based on a broad distribution of the national wealth and high general consumer buying power — which is achieving or on the way to achieving the ends sought by the doctrinaire European socialist.

Today the right of labor to organize and bargain collectively is a generally accepted right. Labor is organized in strength massive enough to hold its own with business and the farmer. There has been protective labor legislation, and social security systems have been instituted. Farm prices are underwritten by the federal government, and tariffs on manufactured commodities have been reduced. Income tax laws are based on the " ability-to-pay " theory. Both major parties are committed to throwing all the resources of the federal government behind efforts to eliminate boom and bust extremes of the business cycle. In some areas there is public power, and everywhere power producers are under strict regulation.

These are the kinds of programs economist Paul H. Douglas of 1932 was seeking. Though all of the items are to some extent subjects of controversy, few there are today who dare advocate outright repeal of any one of them. The degree of each (How far to go?) will always be a matter for political debate, but Senator Douglas in taking his position knows that the question is one of degree and not one on which the politically responsible opposition is challenging the fundamental philosophy of the program.

These results have not been produced by some minor or new party, but by the major parties working within the two-party system. The case for working within the major parties is stronger than the Douglas of 1932 made it appear. The case for not working within the major parties is weaker than he made it appear. The difficulties facing a group that seeks to replace a major party are not exaggerated.

The Case for Working Within the Major Parties Appraised. Take first the theory that if progressives leave their major parties the latter will be more reactionary than they had been in the first place. The Douglas of 1932 noted the theory and then dismissed it on the ground that the major parties were so corrupt and unable to inspire enthusi-

asm that progressives could not use them anyway. He did not, however, refute the theory as such, nor did he state the broader question
— What happens when any large group, whether it be progressive or
conservative, drops out of a major party?

Major parties are coalitions of many different groups of voters.
These groups may be economically motivated, religiously motivated,
or otherwise idealistically motivated. If such a group represents
enough power within a major party, it will be able to make its influence felt in the kind of party platforms adopted, kind of candidates,
and kind of governmental records made when that party controls a
public office. Clearly remove any such strong element so the major
party knows that whatever it does the element cannot be won back
and you have a new power base. Because the power base is new, the
major party will now try to adjust itself to maximize the recognition
it can give to the elements of its new pressure pattern. It no longer
has to consider the seceded group. Remove a conservative wing, and
a major party will tend to become more progressive; remove a progressive wing, and it will tend to become more conservative. Each
wing acts as a counterbalance to the others only so long as it stays a
wing and does not remove itself from the party.

The Douglas of 1932 assumed the Democratic party would fade
away. In 1932 it was just at the threshold of the first long era of Democratic supremacy since the pre-Civil War days of Jacksonian Democracy. If Douglas had not made such an assumption, the only alternative would have been a multi-party system, and in his stated desires
for such devices as proportional representation, Douglas appears to
regard a multi-party arrangement for the United States as preferable
to the two major parties. Yet this is to overlook the fact that a multi-
party United States, as presently organized, is almost an impossibility.

Take secondly the difficulties faced by a minor party man when
he asks a major party legislator to support some program in which he
is interested. If the request is on an uncontroversial matter, most
legislators will provide what assistance they can, even if they know
there is little or no hope of winning support. But noncontroversial
matters are seldom important matters. If the request were controversial, immediately the legislator has to, as do the major parties, look
to his power base. If the most powerful group in his constituency, for
example, asks for one thing and the minor party petitioner asks for
another, there is little doubt as to how most legislators will vote. In
this relationship the minor party man is left without bargaining

power. If the group is interested in legislation and if it ignores this problem, it is not being politically realistic.

If the assumption is that the minor party will eventually become a major party, two questions might be asked. What is to happen to the interests of the minor party before it becomes major? The prospect is enough to discourage even the most unrealistic group leader as he ponders the implications of minor party isolation. What is to happen to the group's interests if the minor party never becomes major? The second question, after a look at the odds against prospects of success, is enough to stop most groups which might contemplate a minor party. Only if a group has no access initially might it have nothing to lose by a minor party venture.

The Coming of a New Party also sets up the obstacles of the federal system, the separation of powers system, the single-member district system of electing legislators, and state laws designed to make it difficult for a minor party to get on the ballot. These are formidable obstacles and not to be dismissed lightly. Yet, after showing how European unitary and cabinet forms of government and proportional voting systems encourage minor parties, the Douglas of 1932 does not go on to discuss the practicability of changing the American system to one which would make possible the type of party system he desires. To develop in detail the tactics by which a minor party might try to become major without first outlining the steps necessary to remove the almost insurmountable obstacles of the system is to put the cart before the horse with the possibilities excellent that you will never reach home.

The Case for Not Working Within the Major Parties Appraised. Consider the proposition that those groups which would " bore from within " are wasting their time because of the political corruption of the two major parties and their domination by the " capitalistic class." The Paul Douglas of 1932 was rightly stirred to wrath over the corruption he saw in the major parties, but he allowed those evidences of corruption to bring himself to a conclusion which could not anticipate the wonders cleansing agents of the future might perform. The old-time political boss of 1932 with his methods of 1932 is not much in evidence in the 1950's. Social security laws lessened the importance of his little favors; civil service laws dried up many of his sources of patronage and tightened standards of governmental administration dried up many of his sources of graft; Hatch acts took the appointees he recommended for government jobs out of politics; the Bureau of Internal Revenue and the courts put him in jail for income tax evasion; and the increasing abilities of Presidents to provide party leadership softened his once iron-clad grip on his home territory. All these, either singly or in combination, had their effect. Though political bosses continue on the scene and always will be, certainly both major parties are " within the outer bounds of decency."

Perhaps the Douglas of 1932 did assess with accuracy the hold which " big business " had on both major parties and the purposes for which the dominant economic groups used the major parties. Organized labor then was still relatively weak in the pressure it could focus on the major parties, and the farm groups had no clear objective toward which to apply the power they had. Today the pattern has changed. The farm groups do know what they want and are in a position of approximately equal strength in both major parties to exert influence. Though organized labor is considerably stronger in Democratic councils, its influence is not to be discounted in the Republican party. Though the business community is stronger in the Republican party, it is no negligible influence among Democrats. Each of these groups is, in turn, divided into subgroups which are by no means always in agreement. Neither major party is owned by nor can it be manipulated solely for the objectives of any one group to the exclusion of the others.

The Douglas of 1932 also made certain assumptions about the issue of the " capitalistic class " which no longer are valid. Advantages of capitalism versus the advantages of state socialism are no longer a subject for debate. True it is that even the post office system is socialism so that America is not purely capitalistic, but it is predominantly so in both theory and practice. Democrats, Republicans, farmers, workers, and businessmen proceed from and no longer question this assumption. The voices of anticapitalism are not being listened to, and the kind of new party envisioned by the Douglas of 1932 would be dismissed as idle dreaming if put into today's setting. Even the once sure way to winning applause from the political-speaking platform — to cry out against " big business and Wall Street " — no longer raises the hackles of political audiences as it once did. " Big business," partly because it has been forced and partly because it now recognizes its dependence on public opinion and consumer purchasing power, has had to broaden its sights to critically examine its relationship to the rest of the community.

Nor has the Democrats' North-South split been as paralyzing on the party as the Douglas of 1932 predicted it would be. Though that party surely has its northern-wing versus southern-wing problems, at least in crisis the Democrats were able to function in a relatively co-herent manner, and they were able to hold enough together to domi-nate the national government from 1933 to 1952. Indications, at least before the segregation fight, were for a lessening of North-South Democratic party tensions — not because either wing was surrender-ing to the other, but because interests did not seem as far apart and because each was learning better to know and understand the other.

The major parties, yes even the Democratic party evolving out of the Democratic party of 1932 which Douglas felt had no function to perform, have both served legitimate functions and have re-sponded to popular needs. No doubt they could have been more re-sponsive, but there is no way of knowing whether that is so or not. " Boring from within " is not a waste of time for any group in either of the major parties.

A second major point made by Douglas in his case for not work-ing within the major parties was that because both the major parties were corrupt and dominated by the " capitalistic class " they would not have the power to " move the blood of the great masses of the people whose support is essential if the progressive cause is to tri-umph." Inability to arouse enthusiasm was predicated on the degree of corruption and capitalistic domination which Douglas saw and felt would continue. One need only point to the enthusiasm which sustained the Democratic party for twenty years with a program con-taining most of what the Douglas of 1932 wanted, and to the enthu-siasm for the Eisenhower of 1952 running on a platform which made no sharp break from the philosophic foundation of the immediate New Deal past. In the latter case, part of the " moving of the blood " was motivated by another factor Douglas would have found it hard to anticipate in 1932 — " clean corruption out of government! "

Let us examine Douglas' assumption about the inability of the President to implement his program, to be relatively free of the domi-nation of state and local organizations in his actions, and to exercise any influence over the integrity level of the state and local machines. Since 1932 the principal charge against Presidents has not been that they were mere puppets being manipulated from below, but rather that their latitude of leadership opportunity had become so broad there was danger of dictatorship. It is true Presidents do have to take state and local party organizations into account, but generally the latter are most interested in federal patronage. With over 90 percent of the federal government employees under civil service, there is no longer much patronage to be had.

The President is more and more becoming chief legislator in that it is he who states party program objectives and at the same time he is increasingly becoming party chief in the sense that the units of his party are under greater compulsions to make themselves over into his image. If ever " boring from within " the major parties with the object to influence a major party President was a fruitless activity for a group interested in governmental policy, it no longer is. The President does have power, provided he has the ability to exercise it, and to gain access to him can today be one of the most productive activities to which a group can devote its energies and resources.

A fourth group of objections which *The Coming of a New Party* makes against " boring from within " centers around the dilemmas which will be caused by participating in the direct primaries of the major parties. If the " boring " group loses in the primary, what shall it do? Should it support the winner or bolt? The answer, if the group intends to continue in the major party, is generally the former. The faction with which the group was aligned lost the primary election because it could not develop enough support to win, but instead of seceding, the group is generally better off in supporting to some degree its major party nominee, even if the group cannot be enthusiastic about him. If the group does not support the nominee and the nominee wins, access to him is likely to suffer; if the group does support its major party nominee, it stays in good graces within the party and can work to develop enough popular support to try to win the next primary election. Similar considerations apply to the question of what a group should do if its faction does win both primary and general elections in a state and then is faced with the alternative of supporting or not supporting that major party's Presidential nominee.

In a sense these may be dilemmas, as Douglas suggests, but seldom is the group called upon to make a decision between the pure white of " all right " on one side and the pure black of " all wrong " on the other. Most groups can make " grey " decisions, even if they are sometimes difficult. Here is one of the prices which a group concerned with influencing governmental policy and working within the major parties must pay.

There is also the Douglas-posed dilemma resulting when the

members of a group in some areas " bore within " the Democratic party and members in another area choose the Republican party. Then in Presidential election campaigns the group will be split between the two major parties and cancel itself out. Often the process does work this way, but there is more than one side to the argument. In return for splitting in the general election by being on both sides, the group may, like a common stock buyer, hedge against the possibility of a big loss. Now the group may have access regardless of which side wins. To maintain access at all costs is generally regarded as the most conservatively wise choice by most group leaders. Only if the possibilities of access within one of the two major parties are so low as to give the group little choice, will it employ the all-or-nothing tactic.

Take fifth the analysis made by the Douglas of 1932 of the results of " playing the game " with the major party organizations. If the party machine helps the group achieve its objectives and gets credit for that help, then the group is helping the party organization perpetuate itself. When confronted with this choice, the group interested in controlling governmental policy has to decide whether it wants governmental programs more than getting rid of the party machine, or, whether destroying the machine comes first. If the latter is the primary objective, then every effort should be made to destroy. Until the power of the party machine has slipped, however, the group's access for the programs it would like to have made governmental policy is likely to suffer.

The Douglas of 1932 was of the opinion that if progressives are elected to office under a major party label, it is easier for them to backslide than it would be if they were elected from a new progressive party. It is true that any member of a group that becomes a major party man or comes in intimate contact with major party men will probably have a broader outlook than before. But generally the two alternatives are either to have a chance with a major party or no chance with a minor party. The risk of " backsliding " is one the group has to take. Douglas writes in 1932 as though a progressive is contaminated by every contact with the compromising major party politicians, and especially so for the progressive who is elected to office as a major party nominee and " surrounded by ' compromiser ' and ' trimmer ' party politicians with whom he is forced to some degree to affiliate." United States Senator Paul H. Douglas (D) , Illinois, could not and would not so write today. After a man has himself campaigned as a major party nominee and held public office, he is likely to subscribe to the following passage from T. V. Smith:

> True, when seen from the shining cliffs of perfection the legislative process of compromise appears shoddy indeed. But when seen from some concentration camp of the only alternative way of life, the compromises of legislation appear but another name for what we call civilization and even revere as Christian forbearance.[18]

The Difficulties of Replacing a Major Party Are Not Exaggerated. The Paul Douglas of 1932 held that while the obstacles facing a minor party's elevation to major party status were significant, nevertheless, they would not be as great as the obstacles standing in the way of " an effort to clean the Augean stables of either of the two old parties and to make them instruments for fulfilling the real interests of the people." Such a statement was not valid in 1932, and it is much less so today.

Though Douglas recognized the sentimental attachments of many of the electorate to the two major parties, he felt, as the new party gained strength, raised new issues, and provided a base to which new loyalties could be attached, that the sentiments would shift. Had he then had available the results of political behavior studies which have been made in recent years, this problem would not have been dismissed as lightly as it was. It is estimated that up to a huge 85 percent of the electorate maintain partisan consistency from one Presidential election to the next. " Realistic " politicians operate from this kind of an assumption when they try to place their major emphasis on getting out to vote their own partisans and the relatively small percentage of voters who are considered doubtful or independent and inclined to switch-voting.

The Coming of a New Party also makes the prospects of the party Douglas proposed seem relatively easy as the roll call of the states is called. Simplest would be the problem of the " one-party " South and Republican New England, Pennsylvania, Michigan, Iowa, North Dakota, and Oregon. Here, because there was only one party of significant strength, the new party could rise because it would be the second major party in the state. Few there were even in 1932 who could agree with this estimate. Prevailing opinion has always been

---

[18] *The Legislative Way of Life* (Chicago: The University of Chicago Press, 1940) , p. 92.

that a new party would be handicapped for much the same reasons that the weak major party in each of these states was handicapped. Developments in these states since 1932 no longer make the " one-party state " as satisfactory a descriptive term as it once was. Except in the South, all of the mentioned states have two vigorous major parties, and perhaps the South too is cracking. From the " one-party " states the Douglas of 1932 then moved on to the doubtful states, and through sweeping generalizations soon had " great swarms of voters " flocking to the new party in them.

Some of *The Coming of a New Party's* advice to a minor party was sound. Patient planning and a solid organizational structure are obviously better than spur-of-the-moment activity and weak organization. The warning to guard against Communist-party infiltration was likewise well put, and if it had been read and heeded by such as the Elmer A. Benson wing of the Minnesota Farmer-Labor party of the 1930's, that party and some other movements like it might have been spared some of the disastrous defeats they were administered at the polls.

Admonition to the new party to keep itself honest was fitting, only the means proposed left much to be detailed. Would each potential member have to pass a party court before he were admitted? Would members stay members if some of their number were called to account before a party court to determine whether or not they should be expelled? No party in the United States except the Communist party has been able to enforce such discipline, and when attempts have been made, moral questions become hopelessly intertwined in party factional in-fighting.

It is one thing to say that legislators should be elected by a system of proportional representation, and quite another to put proportional representation into constitutions. Except for a few municipal governments, the single-member district is almost the universal American practice. It is also one thing to advise a new progressive party not to go to " progressive " Democrats and Republicans but rather make the latter come to the new party, and it is quite another to be strong enough to exude such party magnetism. It is one thing to ask " wet " progressives and " dry " progressives to fit in harness together without trying to make the new party responsive to their wet or dry wishes, but it is quite another to get the dedicated " wet " or " dry " to see the matter in such a subdued light. It is one thing to hope for a party financed on membership dues, and another to build a large and strong party if dues are required.

It is one thing to ask the farmer and urban laborer to work together in a " principled " as distinguished from a major party, and it is another to get the two groups to do it. The farm wing will be charging that the party's name is " farmer-LABOR "; and the labor wing, that it is " FARMER-labor." This is not to say the two groups cannot work together in a third party, but it is to suggest that seldom does such a nonmajor party combination last long.

In the final analysis, perhaps the declining strength of the never-strong American Socialist party is one of the best indications of what would have happened had *The Coming of a New Party* led to the organization of the minor party proposed. Such a group would hardly have had the time to hold its first convention before it would have discovered most of what it wanted in the New Deal. If it would then have taken the next step to adopt a purely state socialistic program, it would have found that the Socialist party already was in the field. Though one can never say a new party of the future cannot arise to replace a major party, no such set of conditions which might produce that result is now in sight. To create a minor party in the hope it will become a major party is not a practical alternative for the group interested in influencing governmental policy.

PART TWO

Major Party Organization

▍ INTRODUCTION

American major parties are structurally weak, highly decentralized, and non-" party-principled " organizations. While Part One introduced these characteristics and suggested some of the reasons for them, Part Two is an examination of major party organization in detail.

Two additional introductory points should be made. (1) The primary purpose in the discussion of state and local election machinery in *Party Politics* is to examine that election machinery as it influences the pattern of major party organization and politics. This is the reason that the chapter on state and local election machinery is considered in this Part. (2) Major party organization outside government cannot be adequately understood without placing it into relationship with party organization inside government in the executive and legislative branches. The concern in Part Two is, therefore, not just with the party outside government. Rather it is to develop an overall view of party organization.

CHAPTER FIVE

State and Local Election Machinery

By the time you get this letter the folks over the nations will be march-
ing on the polls to cast their vote, and as I sit here thinking of all the fun
I am going to miss on next Tuesday, and what a Fight it is going to be
getting those folks out, some will have to be paid and some will not,
others might have to get hit on the nose, and still others will not, I can
just sit here on Tuesday next and say well they are at it, Boy and the
money will be flying around, and when Sevan (7) O'Clock arrives and the
polls are supposed to be closed, trying to squeeze some more in the polling
place, and the side that thinks they are in the lead trying to keep them
out, and the side that feels as though they might need a few more to pull
the old Fight out of the fire, well who can say that a feeling like that does
not tear at the heart strings, what a play that game is, then when the Day
is done, and you can get a few of the other side's Girls and go drink some
good Beer and tell the doings of the Day till well into the Wee Hours of
the next Wednesday, there is really no Ill feelings about politics when
one stops to think of it, and after all Professor who is hurt by a little
Fighting here and there, I believe always in the saying that to the victor
belong the spoils, Monday night going to the Ward headquarters and the
Committeemen getting their money, and any last minute orders what to
do, then waiting on the fireing line for the day to start and like every
other battle, the loser saying well if I had done this or that thing it might
have been different.

"Famous" Fogarty [1]

----

[1] Philadelphia ward executive "Famous" Fogarty's letter, written from
jail, was published in T. J. Salter, "Letters from Men in Action," *National*
Municipal Review (September, 1937), Vol. 26, No. 9, pp. 417–418. Reprinted by
permission.

Dictatorships may be distinguished from democracies in several respects. In the dictatorship the individual person is more or less the means to the end of the state; in the democracy, the individual tends to be an end in himself. The one system tends to hold the dignity and privacy of the human being in low respect; the other, in high respect. In the dictatorship, government-by-law tends to mean government by those who sit in the seats of power and whose word is the law; in democracies, though the institutions of government need to be manned by men and the laws interpreted by them, government-by-law tends to mean that there is law above both the governors and the governed. The dictatorship tends to be a monolithic type of society in which all the organized segments must subject themselves to the control of the dictator or be forced underground; the democracy tends to be a multi-group type of society with freedom to organize into many different kinds of groups, each working for its own particular set of objectives.

In the dictatorship there is no free-election channel up through which the citizens may control their government and through which minorities may someday become majorities and attain governmental power. Democracies, on the other hand, do prize political freedom and maintain a free-election system through which the popular will may be expressed. These are some of the distinctions between dictatorships and democracies. They are not to be applied in their pure or absolute form, but rather are distinctions of degree. If any one may be singled out as a more basic symptom of the quality of a democracy than the rest, it is the freedom of elections. Without such freedom all of the other qualities of democratic-representative government which we hold so dear might soon be destroyed.

Herman Finer has drawn the alternative to the system which makes provision for peaceful turnover of those who govern:

> The miserable, fearful subjects of a dictatorship are . . . entrapped in the bitter margin between fawning self-debasement and the hazards and blind extremity of revolution, revolution not even for the major purpose of changing the nature of the state but merely to change the personnel of an administration. Yes: perhaps for a time their material welfare is better than it was before; and perhaps there is a promise of better things for the future: but now and for any foreseeable and attainable time, there reigns the *angst* of a human mind and conscience writhing in the straight-jacket of alien values. The medicinal principle which a dictatorship like all other political systems con-

tains is not the one which can be used as a daily diet, or, being used, can promise health: for it is either internal disruption of the dictatorial group or its overthrow in wholesale and protracted murder. Its medicine is brutality, even if heroic brutality, and brutality is poison.[2]

Was " Famous " Fogarty philosophically viewing the election process in this light when from the confinement of his jail cell he penned his one-sentence ode to election-Tuesday? Probably not, but neither do most whose business is not political philosophy. Showing through every clause that should have terminated a sentence is his love of the game of politics and the thrill of racing down each election-day " political home-stretch." He was in politics for his own reasons, and perhaps he was not conscious of all of them. Others may be in politics for the love of power, for the love of associating with those with power, for a livelihood, for achieving the economic and social objectives of the groups to which they belong, because they feel they want to make a contribution to a larger welfare than their own, or just " for the fun of it." Fogarty's words and the thoughts of most Americans participating in activity leading up to elections and in elections themselves, whatever the motive for participation may be, however, are not those which flow from the brains of authoritarian mentalities.

Though perhaps slowly, crudely, or unconsciously, the importance which political philosophy places on the election process as a tool for making democratic-representative government possible has been recognized. The process has not always met standards which we feel it should have met, or perhaps it still falls short of our ideal; yet the prevailing American spirit has been one which has produced movement in the direction of universal adult suffrage and of developing election machinery which does give the individual freedom of choice and which generally gives the voter a right to feel that his " X " marks will be honestly counted.

" Famous " Fogarty's tactics might not sound quite right, but his sentiments, regardless of whether they sprang from a " gaming " or a political-theory base, were compatible with democratic spirit. He was a cog in a political party machine which wanted to win elections. The party machine of his day operated under fewer of the restraints

---

[2] Herman Finer, *The Theory and Practice of Modern Government* (New York: Henry Holt and Company, 1949) , p. 951.

which are today imposed by law on election-day activities, nominee selection, and party organization. In an earlier day Fogarty would have had even more latitude to exercise his political ingenuity. A modern-day party politician may take fewer liberties with the elec-

The Register & Tribune Syndicate

*"Gad, When I Think Of The Power The People Have . . .
It Just Isn't Fair . . ."*

tion machinery and its spirit than could Fogarty. It is to this evolution that this chapter on state and local elections is devoted.

The discussion will be developed in three parts. First is the expansion of the electorate from narrow property-holding limits to one of universal adult suffrage. Here will be found the answer to the question, " Who may vote? " Second is the movement culminating in the Australian ballot and the ever tightening of loopholes through which the integrity of the election system might be drained away. Third will come the efforts of the states to improve on the party nominee-selecting process.

All of these developments are significant to political parties and the manner in which they must generally conduct themselves. Through them one may begin to understand some of the " rules of the game " within the bounds of which the parties are expected to stay. Each change in suffrage requirements or primary and general election laws has consequences which may upset intraparty, interparty, or professional-versus-amateur politician power patterns.

WHO MAY VOTE?

When governments are classified into dictatorships and democracies, the number of people participating in governing constitutes one basis of classification. In the dictatorship the number is relatively small; in democracies it is a high percentage of the total possible electorate. But even in a democracy all the people cannot vote and are not eligible for office. At what percentage point, then, does a democracy become a " democracy "? To that question no simple answer exists, and the standards which might be set in mid-twentieth century may not be the same as applied in 1800. In the latter year, in fact, it is not difficult to conclude that the size of the United States electorate in relation to the total adult population was not sufficient to meet the test.

Early in New England colonial history there had been religious qualifications for voting and holding office. General throughout the colonies were real-property qualifications, and only slowly did they give way to, first a minimum personal-property qualification and then to a minimum taxpaying qualification.

The Constitutional Convention avoided the question of suffrage, leaving it to the states to decide who should vote and who could hold office. If the framers of the Constitution had inserted a voter qualification provision, however, there is little doubt it would have been similar to those which prevailed in the states at that time.

A rough index of the proportion of adults permitted to vote during the founding period of the United States was developed by Charles Beard in his studies of the contest over ratification of the Constitution. He estimated that not over 25 percent of the adult males voted — some 160,000 out of a total population of 4 million. Of those who did vote, approximately 60,000 opposed ratification.[3]

---

[3] Charles A. Beard, *An Economic Interpretation of the Constitution of the United States* (New York: The Macmillan Company, 1921), Chap. 9.

The 60,000 were inland farmers whose number was soon to multiply as more and more immigrants and " low-status " and unenfranchised residents of the established coastal communities sought better fortune in the West. Here were the people who in 1800 were the nucleus of Jefferson's Republican party and were set on overthrowing the Federalists' ideal of rule by the rich and well-born.

By 1828 the property qualifications had almost disappeared. Newly enfranchised eastern workers combined with the more numerous western farmers to elect the rough and ready Andrew Jackson to the Presidency. By 1850 most of the states with tax qualifications had also repealed those restrictions. The United States was the first major nation to attain full white adult manhood suffrage.

Opposing adult manhood suffrage had been those who looked upon the product of the frontier as uncouth or barbaric or worse, and upon the unpropertied of the cities as a menace to the established social, religious, and political institutions. But the forward march of democracy would not be denied. There were no social classes on the frontier. All men were economically and socially equal, and the frontiersman fiercely held there should be political equality too. He had learned when Hamilton sent the army out to put down armed rebellion against the Whiskey Tax that force was not the road to success. Instead, with the weight of ever increasing numbers to offset the slower growing coastal communities, the West could be the strongest element in a group combination which could capture the national government and have it adopt programs which the " common man " of that day saw as in his interest. With the expansion of the suffrage and Jackson came the political campaign pitched to the great masses of people. Such has been the nature of campaigns ever since.

In the period since the mid-nineteenth century, three suffrage problems remained for settlement. The first came about because of the politically upsetting effect of immigration as coastal states' populations swelled. The second was whether the newly free Negro was to have the right to vote and hold office. And the third was what to do about women — whether to keep them in the home all the time or to allow them to participate in government affairs.

The Immigrant. From Ireland alone, over a million immigrants entered the United States in the decade from 1845 to 1855. In the year 1851 over 600,000 foreigners set foot on American shores. Wilfred E. Binkley has described what happened as a result:

New Orleans was almost swamped with new arrivals. Europe was un-
loading its almshouses, asylums, hospitals, and prisons on America. . . . [O]nly the sturdiest ever reached the frontiers. The larger
river cities " acted as a filter for the scum," who clogged city almshouses, jails, and hospitals and infested the streets with pickpockets,
thieves, and beggars. These were normally Whig cities, but not only
were the Whigs, as the heavier taxpayers, burdened by supporting
the immigrants, but they were about to be outvoted by the foreigners
regimented under the management of the Democratic ward heelers.[4]

New York and New England too had their assimilation problems.

With Whigs vacillating between trying to win the votes of the
foreign born and taking a dim view of the new challenge to their
possibilities for power, the Know-Nothing party organized with its
principal purpose a frontal attack on the menace. When the politically
inept Winfield Scott, Whig candidate for President in 1852, was
ploughed under by the Democrats, Whigs blamed the foreign-born
vote and many Whigs began working with the Know-Nothings to
forever bar foreign-born citizens from holding public office and to
require twenty-one years of residence in the United States before
they could become naturalized.

Three significant political effects resulted from the impact of
this mass immigration on the eastern states and the large cities everywhere. (1) Connecticut and Massachusetts adopted the first literacy
tests in which voters were asked to be able to write their names and
be able to read the Constitution before gaining the right to vote. Eighteen states now have literacy tests of one type or another. (2) There
was the larger political effect on the composition of the major parties
of that time. " Scarcely any factor," writes Binkley, " played a greater
part in the breakup of old party alignments in the fifties than the
astonishing mid-century influx of aliens." [5] (3) Until immigration
slowed down and the passage of generations slowly worked the foreign
born up from a low of poverty and little education, the city party
machines of both parties (the Democrats having the larger share)
had voters of some degree of political helplessness to manipulate.

In the vastly different political circumstances of the western
states and territories, the immigrant found a heaven of sorts by comparison with the hell of the eastern cities of the 1850's. Western terri-

---

[4] Wilfred E. Binkley, *American Political Parties* (New York: Alfred A.
Knopf, 1949) , p. 188.

[5] *Ibid.,* p. 187.

tories seeking enough population to qualify as states and western states in search of manpower with which to develop themselves, welcomed the immigrant. Starting with Wisconsin in 1848, fifteen states permitted the alien to vote as soon as he had filed his declaration of intention to become a citizen. Some of these states took the right to vote away in the early 1900's, and the resurgence of nativism during World War I erased the rest.

The Negro. The " problem " of the foreign born and their relationship to the electorate no longer comprises a problem, except as the political parties and candidates lay their strategies for capturing the votes of the different nationality background groups. The emancipated Negro and his relationship to the electorate, however, is still a problem. It is so both for the Negro who wants to vote and hold office and for the conscience of America, one of the philosophical foundations of which is the modern interpretation of: " We hold these truths to be self-evident, that all men are created equal, that they are endowed by their Creator with certain unalienable Rights, that among these are Life, Liberty and the pursuit of Happiness."

Is the Negro in the electorate or outside it? Until recent years the answer has been " the outside." Today the Negro has begun to develop a potential of political power such as the foreign born have always had. No Presidential candidate, for example, can ignore the " Negro vote " in the large and doubtful pivot states. America stands on trial before the black peoples of Africa and the yellow peoples of the Orient, and they are watching in this era of cold war to see if the American way has room for colors other than white. Other factors are setting in motion changes in the economic and political character of the South, and even there the Negro's participation in the electoral process seems on the way to fuller general realization. The story of the long fight for Negro suffrage has been a sad one with excesses of commission and sins of omission on the part of both North and South. It, like no other, lays bare both the bad and the good in what might figuratively be called the American soul.

Before passions that led to the Civil War came to a head, some southern states did permit the free Negro to vote, but few were the places where he had such right. Nor was Negro suffrage, at least for the immediate period after the Civil War, a part of the Lincoln reconstruction program. Whether for political advantage to the Republican party or for idealistic reasons it was the Radical Republicans who forced the issue at a time when history shows neither the Negro nor the white were prepared to meet it.

The Thirteenth Amendment in 1865 terminated slavery, and it was followed three years later by the Fourteenth Amendment. The latter indirectly attempted to give the Negro the vote by providing that a state which abridged the right to vote for any other reason than participation in rebellion or other crime should have its United States House of Representatives seats " reduced in the proportion which the number of such male citizens shall bear to the whole number of male citizens twenty-one years of age in such State." This section of the Fourteenth Amendment has never been used.

In the Reconstruction Act of 1867, Negro suffrage was provided for in the choosing of delegates to the constitution-drafting conventions of several southern states. Finally, in 1870 came the Fifteenth Amendment: " The right of citizens of the United States to vote shall not be denied or abridged by the United States or by any State on account of race, color, or previous condition of servitude." But as soon as the brief interlude of " carpetbagger " domination was ended and southern whites regained control, the Solid Democratic South was born and the Negro was no more a part of the electorates of the southern states than he had been before the Civil War.

By a combination of intimidation and laws, the Negro was kept in his state of political subjection. Provisions of the Fifteenth Amendment did not apply to private individuals, but only to the federal and state governments. Thus private individuals, whether organized into the Ku Klux Klan or using more subtle methods, could frighten the Negro away from the polls. Nor did the Fifteenth Amendment, as interpreted by the United States Supreme Court, apply unless it could be shown that the state governments were discriminating *on account of* race, color, or previous condition of servitude.

Within the letter of the law, then, southern state legislatures could gerrymander legislative districts to minimize the effect of Negro voters. High residence requirements were imposed on the theory that the Negro more than the white was a transient. Poll tax laws were passed on the theory that the Negro could least afford to pay and would be more apt to lose his poll tax receipt before election day. The franchise was denied those convicted of a long list of minor crimes such as wife-beating and vagrancy on the theory that the Negro would be more likely to commit them and be convicted than the white. Literacy tests and property tests were designed to remove the Negro further from the electorate, and should he still find his way to the polls, there was always the discretion of the election board which might be applied toward the same end.

In addition, for the poor white who might himself be caught by the poll tax, or educational or property qualifications, there were " grandfather clauses " which provided that any man who had served in the armies of the North or South during the Civil War or any man descended from such a person should have the right to vote. And to make sure that the general election would have little meaning if the Negro voter should somehow get that far, there was the " white primary." With the South " one-party " Democratic, all the critical choices were made in the Democratic party primary elections.

Though the United States Supreme Court invalidated the Oklahoma " grandfather clause " in 1915,[6] by that late date the decision was not of much significance. More important as a legal remedy for the Negro was the case of Smith v. Allwright in 1944 [7] which took the position that the Texas primary was an integral part of the election machinery and thus the " white primary " was in violation of the Fifteenth Amendment.

Some of the southern states accepted the spirit of the latter decision, and some began devising other means of circumvention of it. The general election requirements which still tend to discriminate against the Negro remain. The southern Negro himself tends to be apathetic. Although Negro participation in primaries and general elections has recently increased, there is still a long road to travel before the United States can say it has universal adult suffrage.

What have been the political effects of debarring the southern Negro from the suffrage? They have been many, and a few of the more important ones deserve mention here. Because the Negro who would have tended to vote Republican had no right to do so, the Republican party has never been a truly national party. Republican organizations in the southern states have been little more than patronage machines. The Democratic party organizations in the South, without benefit of opposition, have been weak in an organizational sense and highly personalized and factionalized. Because it has been safely Democratic, the South has received little attention in Presidential campaigns as candidates have preferred to concentrate their time and efforts on politically doubtful areas. Southerners have seldom

---

[6] Guinn v. United States, 238 US347 (1915).   [7] 321 US649 (1944).

been given places on the national ticket of the Democratic party. At least until recently, that has not been necessary. In Presidential elections the Solid Democratic South has consistently given the Democratic nominee for President its electoral votes. Likewise, the Democratic party has been assured of Democratic House and Senate delegations from the southern states. Because of the " one-party " character of the South, general elections have meant little and the real decisions are made in the Democratic primaries.

If the Negro is in fact within the electorate, one set of political consequences will follow; if he is not, another set of consequences tends to govern. Those parties and public officeholders who have felt it to their advantage that the past situation should remain have usually opposed change; those who have felt they may gain advantages by a change have tended to work for changes. Whether to admit or not to admit a group to the electorate is a question which generally turns on what is expedient for the groups holding political power. It has been so in the past, and the political squabble between the Democrats and Republicans over the admission of Alaska and Hawaii is an example of the " expediency theory " operating in the present. Not even the decision to admit women to the electorate turned on " natural rights," which many feel should be the criterion for adult participation in government.

Women. With the addition of adult women to the electorate by the passage of the Nineteenth Amendment in 1920, the third major suffrage problem since the passing of tax qualifications had been solved, but again the solution was not easily reached. Women suffragettes had to fight every step of the way from their 1848 " Declaration of Sentiments " against man who " has usurped the prerogative of Jehovah " until the final success some eighty years later. They tried to add " sex " to the " race, color or previous condition of servitude " clause of the Fifteenth Amendment, but failed. Kansas in 1861 was the first state to allow women to vote on all school questions. In 1869 the territory of Wyoming granted full adult suffrage, and in 1890, upon admission to the union, Wyoming became the first state with such an electorate. By 1914 eleven western states had followed suit.

Between 1914 and 1920 in the drive for the constitutional amendment, the political parties, Congresses, and President Wilson were put under a kind of pressure which was to prove irresistible. Using as their power base the states in which they already had the vote, women suffragettes made a significant impact on Congressional elections in those states. When in 1916 the two major parties would go only as far as to favor woman suffrage *by state action,* activity shifted to a new intensity of propaganda and agitation. Picketing, petitioning, obstructing traffic, hunger striking, and posing as martyrs became the order of the day and produced reams of publicity. Opponents — the " liquor interests " who feared women would bring prohibition with them, business interests who feared the " labor vote " would double, the unorganized and weary husband who could not bear the prospect of finding his wife out " politicking " when he returned home after a hard day at work — could no longer hold their lines. Women took part in the 1920 elections which landslided Warren G. Harding into the White House, and have been voting and officeholding along with men since. Whether woman suffrage has wrought any significant political effects is still and probably will always be a matter of debate.

Summary. The electorate is today legally composed of all citizens over the age of 21, with the following qualifications: in Georgia and Kentucky the age limit has been reduced to 18; all states have residence requirements of generally one year's residence in the state, 60 to 90 days in the county and 30 days in the voting precinct; five southern states use poll tax qualifications; eighteen states have some kind of literacy test; and all states have some limitation on such classifications as the institutionalized mentally ill and criminals.

ELECTIONS IN GENERAL

What are the procedures through which the voter can select the candidates he wants to hold the different public offices? The procedures in the United States have gone through a long and continuing improvement. Only by showing the main outlines of their development can present practices and the reasons for them be understood, and only out of such a survey can the reader find the reasons behind the detailed statutes regulating political parties which are characteristic of most state election codes of laws today.

Ballots. During early colonial times voting was neither secret nor by ballot. Votes were registered at community meetings, either by general voice vote or by roll call. Nor were the first ballots of the standardized and publicly printed type. At first any piece of paper which the voter could find on his person or borrow from his neighbor would do. Next in the progression, political parties or candidates concluded they might win more votes if they printed and then distributed ballots with their names on them at the entrance to the polls on election day. The different parties or candidates chose their own color, size, and shape of paper. Although by the 1880's some states had begun to regulate ballots, the printing of ballots continued to be a private function.

Lax election procedures left ample opportunity for those who would abuse the system, particularly in the manner in which the politically unsophisticated foreign-born or uneducated citizen could be used by political party machines. Because party ballots were distinctive in color, size, or shape, it was easy to see how an individual voted. The lack of secrecy tended to encourage bribery and intimidation. The scarcity of laws regulating conduct of elections made it relatively easy for a person to cast a ballot in someone else's name, to go from polling place to polling place voting again and again, to create disorder and in the ensuing scuffle to stuff unnoticed the ballot box, or for election judges to perform fraudulent vote counts. These were the kinds of abuses, practiced with particular flagrancy in the large cities, which led just before 1900 to the first major election-conduct reform in American history — the Australian ballot.

Taking its name from the country where it originated, the Australian ballot met several needs for increasing the integrity of United States elections. First, no longer would political parties or candidates be allowed to print ballots which could be used in voting. This the state would do, and only election officials could hand them out to each individual voter. Second, the ballots had to be marked in secret, folded, and deposited in the ballot box. Because all were alike and because no identification markings were permitted without disqualifying the ballot, how a person voted was his own secret. Third, only the names of officially certified party nominees would be printed on the ballot. This, in turn, necessitated laws which defined political parties and established procedures of nominee certification to the official in charge of ballot printing.

Two principal variations of the Australian ballot are employed in this country. One, the *office-group* type, was the form of the first general state Australian ballot law as enacted by Massachusetts in 1888. It is employed by some eighteen states. Following is a simple illustration for California (a composite of 1952 and 1954), omitting minor parties, of the office-group ballot result:

FOR PRESIDENTIAL ELECTORS

(vote for one pair of candidates)

Office-Group I

Adlai E. Stevenson John J. Sparkman	Democratic
Dwight D. Eisenhower Richard M. Nixon	Republican

FOR UNITED STATES SENATOR

(vote for one)

Office-Group II

Thomas H. Kuchel	Republican
Samuel W. Yorty	Democratic

FOR GOVERNOR

(vote for one)

Office-Group III

Richard P. Graves	Democratic
Goodwin J. Knight	Republican

Some of the office-group ballot states like California rotate the order of the names in each office block. Other states either place them in alphabetical order or in an order based on the proportion of the total vote received by the political parties in the last preceding general election.

The year after the passage of the Massachusetts act, while three other states copied Massachusetts, Indiana established the second major type — the *party-column* ballot. A simple drawing, using the same offices and names as in the office-group illustration above, will give the idea of what a California ballot in 1952–1954 composite form might have looked like had that state adopted the Indiana pattern as have twenty-five states. The party-column example, also omitting minor parties, is on page 115. In some of the party-column states the placement of the parties is alphabetical, in others it is based on relative party strength, and in still others the determination is left to the discretion of the officer charged with printing the ballots.

Differences between the office-group and party-column types of ballots should be noted. In the former it is impossible to vote a straight party ticket without searching out the party affiliation of the candidates in each office-group. Split-ticket voting is thus encouraged. On party-column ballots, the voter can mark an " X " in the circle

Party Column I	Party Column II

For Straight Ticket
  Mark (X) Within This Circle   ◯

DEMOCRATIC	**REPUBLICAN**
For Presidential Electors Adlai E. Stevenson John J. Sparkman	*For Presidential Electors* Dwight D. Eisenhower Richard M. Nixon
For United States Senator Samuel W. Yorty	*For United States Senator* Thomas H. Kuchel
For Governor Richard P. Graves	*For Governor* Goodwin J. Knight

provided for straight ticket voting and by making the one mark, vote for all of that party's candidates. If the voter using the party-column type wants to practice split-ticket voting, he may still place a check in the circle of the party which has the most candidates of his choice and then he will have to place individual marks behind the names of the candidates from opposition parties for which he desires to vote, or he may disregard the straight ticket circle entirely. Note also the party emblems at the very top of each column of the party-column type. Many, though not all of the party-column states, allow the use of such emblems. One will not find them on the office-group ballot.

Except for South Carolina which has never adopted the Australian system, the remaining states represent some minor variation from the two main ballot types. Pennsylvania, for example, has an office-group arrangement but also has straight-ticket circles. Still others use the party-column type but do not have straight-ticket circles.

The form of the ballot has political implications. If a large number of voters cannot read or write the English language or know little or nothing about politics, the emblem on the party-column ballot may be the only means which a party machine has of making the voter understand what it is the machine wants him to do. Urban party politicians have based almost entire propaganda campaigns on that one elemental symbol — vote right and put an " X " in the circle under the Donkey, or vote for the Elephant, or whatever are the party symbols used. Even the relatively well-informed voter is often at a loss when he is faced with the typical long ballot requiring him to make decisions on offices or candidates which he has never heard of. Professional party politicians, therefore, tend to favor the party-column type ballot in the hope that a popular and well-known top part of the ticket will carry through the relative unknowns who are the party's candidates for the more minor offices. Professional party politicians also prefer a ballot which discourages split-ticket voting. The extent to which the voters mobilized by a party split their tickets away from that party is the degree of " inefficiency " of the organization.

V. O. Key, in his *Politics, Parties and Pressure Groups,* has cited two excellent examples of the kind of study to which politicians subject ballot forms and why such study is necessary. In 1941 the Republican state administration in Delaware split that state's party-column ballot into two parts for Presidential election years — one part for the Presidential contest and another for the state contests. What was the reason for the change? It was not an academic one. Rather, Delaware Republicans feared that the popularity of Franklin D. Roosevelt running at the top of the Democratic column in 1944 would take strength away from the Republican slate for state offices because many voters attracted by Roosevelt might check the Democratic straight-ticket circle, while with a split party-column ballot Roosevelt voters who tended to be Republican in state politics would find it easier to vote for Republican state candidates. In 1948, however, the shoe was on the other foot. Dewey and Warren carried Delaware convincingly but their strength did not reflect in proportion on the Republican state slate. Similarly, the proposal for a ballot change in Ohio in 1949 from the party-column to the office-group type was based on the theory that United States Senator Robert A. Taft might gain an additional 100,000 votes in the 1950 election if he were not in a party column opposite to that of Ohio's popular Democratic Governor Frank J. Lausche.[8]

Registration. Having examined the types of ballots in use in the states and having noted the steps taken to insure a secret vote, it is desirable to consider voter registration devices designed to attempt

---

[8] From V. O. Key, Jr. (New York: Thomas Y. Crowell Company, 1952), p. 654.

to make sure that only the qualified voter may receive a ballot. In the small rural community, election judges know personally all who would be qualified to vote. Informally they determine who has that right, and in the rare case of a challenge, informally they make their decision. Populous urban areas, however, present a more difficult problem. " Rural procedures " in the cities soon broke down and states generally have enacted voter registration laws, if not state-wide in application they at least apply to voters in urban areas.

To register, the qualified member of the electorate is required to show that he is entitled to vote and then, if his evidence is satisfactory, his name is placed on the registration list for the precinct in which he lives. When the potential voter, in areas where there are registration systems, comes to the polls his name will be checked against the registration list. If his name is there and if he is not challenged, he will be given his ballot and sent to a voting booth. When he has voted, the fact will be noted on the list. Except where registration lists are themselves faulty or fraudulent or the election judges are corrupt, those who would try to vote even though not qualified or those who would try to vote more than once find it difficult to succeed in their object.

For the political parties, the precinct list is one of the first tools which the new recruit to a party organization is taught to use. If registration is not by party, he will have to make out with the list as best he can. If registration is by party, it is possible with a little study to determine the size of the job which lies ahead. Should the recruit be a Democrat, for example, he will nurse his Democratic registrants along to keep them firm in the Democratic faith and he will make sure they get to the polls on election day. When he talks to Republicans, he knows that fact ahead of the conversation and can govern himself accordingly. Soon he judges some to be hopeless in their opposition and worth no further effort on his part. Others he may find shaky in their Republican allegiance, and these he can work on provided his registered Democrats and the urging of unregistered Democrats to register do not consume all of his available time.

The precinct worker will early discover that the lists which he obtains from his register of voters are to some degree inaccurate. Some on the list will have moved away from the precinct, and other eligibles, still unregistered, will have moved in. Some will have died. Some will have allowed their registrations to lapse. The problem of out-of-date registration lists is not the party precinct workers' alone.

In the *permanent* type of registration systems used in a majority of the states registrars of voters are constantly engaged in examining death notices, checking lists of those who have not voted frequently enough to keep their permanent registration active, and studying any other available source of information to keep their registration lists accurate.

Other states may have *periodic* registration systems under which the voter may be required to annually, biannually, or quadrennially re-register in order to stay eligible. The periodic registration system is designed to assure a more currently accurate list, but the administrative problems posed and the difficulties involved in getting persons to re-register generally make it the more difficult to operate. Under the periodic registration type the task of the party worker in keeping his registrants from disqualifying themselves is a more difficult one.

Election officials. Registration control, the Australian ballot, and detailed regulations as to how the ballots should be handed to the voter and how they should be deposited in the ballot box are only some of the steps which have been taken to make elections more honest. Because of the importance of having qualified election judges and clerks, some states require election officials to pass a simple merit test before they may be appointed. Instructions, written or otherwise delivered, go to election officials previous to election day to acquaint them in detail with the manner in which they are supposed to function in administering the election and in counting the votes. Some states specify that election officials for each precinct be bipartisanly chosen so one party cannot " stack " the precinct panel with persons who are exclusively of that party.

In the selection of election officials, whether there is a bipartisan requirement or not, the party has one minor source of patronage in each precinct for those who would value and need the one day's salary. In states where law does not require that polling places be located in public buildings, another minor source of patronage is the rent payment which goes to the person whose property is designated as the polling place.

In areas with strong party systems each party, in checking up on the other, may furnish an extralegal pressure to keep the conduct of the election clean. Poll watchers may be designated to stand by to watch the administration of the election during voting hours, and they or relief crews may go on to the night shift to also watch the ballot counting.

The checks which one party places on the election-day activities of the other and legislation to improve the ballot, election administration and vote counting, however, were still not enough to make the election process approach the degree of integrity which reform elements at the turn of the century thought it should. If both major parties had corrupt machines dominating party nominations, the voter in even an honest general election was left with two products of

"Which one is it that favors the garden for the Library?"

corruption from which to choose. Now the main emphasis of those who would improve the election system turned to the manner in which the parties should be permitted to select their nominees. The result was a supplanting of the state nominating convention by direct primary elections, and as part of this development, the political parties were soon to find themselves limited in both party organization and functions by an even greater mass of detailed legislation.

NOMINATING CANDIDATES

Perhaps the most important function of political parties in the United States, if their functions can be weighted, is that of nominating candidates to stand for office in general elections. In this country the number of elected officials runs into the several hundreds of thousands. For "one-party" areas like the Solid Democratic South, the primary election is in fact decisive and thus the real election. The same evaluation of importance of political party functions does not hold in other countries where fewer public officials are elected by popular vote, where the only public election is the general election, and where the party function of governing may be more important than nominee selection.

In spite of the importance of the primary stage of the election process in the United States, states did not seriously begin to regulate it until the early 1900's. Until that time the political parties were regarded as voluntary private associations. Today the parties are not so considered, but have become, instead, agents of state government.

By Caucus. The American nominee-selecting process has gone through several phases. At first there were no organized groups concerned with nominating candidates for offices, and nominations were made by individuals at meetings assembled for the purpose of electing officers. As differing interest groups reached the organization stage, it was soon apparent that the group which had made preliminary decisions before the general meeting and had planned strategy for implementing those decisions at the meeting was likely to be more successful than the groups which had not. Formalization of the *caucus* — a group assembled to decide on a course of action ahead of time when the whole body of citizens would make their public decisions — followed. It was but a simple next step for all the members of a state legislature of one party to meet and in secret to pick the nominees for state offices for their party. By 1800 the *legislative caucus* was the principal state party nominating device. At the national level and in the form of the *Congressional caucus,* it was the method from 1800 through 1824 by which the national parties chose their candidates for the offices of President and Vice President of the United States.

The legislative caucus and its Congressional counterpart did not function for a long period of time. They tended to be unrepresentative of an entire political party since each legislative district could elect only one legislator and he could be of only one party. Caucus decisions were made in secret, and this did not seem compatible with the greater emphasis being placed on democracy. A party's legislators might pick one who most met their specifications though he might not be the type which the party rank and file would have nominated had the selection power been vested in them. For reasons such as these, with the unrepresentative character of the legislative caucus the most significant objection, political parties moved toward the convention system.

By Convention. One of the factors important in the delegation of nomination functions to a legislative caucus had been the great difficulty of assembling delegates together in one state-wide meeting. For the county party, however, transportation problems were not nearly so acute. Early in the 1800's Jeffersonian Republicans began to use county conventions, composed of delegates chosen at party meetings in the townships, for making nominations for county offices. Even the Federalists, who opposed party organization as such, were later driven to copy the practice.

Could the convention also be used at the state level? Despite travel difficulties, the parties soon found that it could. In some states the first move in this direction was the *mixed legislative caucus* where delegates were chosen from the districts in which a party was not represented in the state legislature. The mixed caucus gave way to the *mixed convention* in which the party's legislators were entitled to participate only when there was no delegate present from their legislative district. Mixed conventions, in turn, were supplanted by the pure *delegate convention,* seating only those who had been chosen by county party conventions or, in other cases, those who had been chosen in township meetings. In other states the move to the convention from the legislative caucus was direct and without the intermediate mixed-caucus and mixed-convention steps. By the time of the Presidency of Andrew Jackson the state convention was the general practice for state party nominations and, in some states, for selecting Presidential electors.

The state party convention represented the entire active membership of the parties. It was flexible enough to permit compromise and to make possible the construction of balanced party candidate slates to appeal to the different segments of the electorate. It served the additional need of providing a place where party platforms could be prepared and ratified. Until the mid-nineteenth century influx of immigration and the rise of powerful and often unscrupulous party bosses, the delegate conventions worked well in the states.

Decline of the party convention as a nominating device, from the post-Civil War period until the advent of the direct primary, was a direct result of the manner in which the system was abused. Because state legislatures left the political parties almost entirely unregulated, unsavory practices developed. The faction in control of the party might call the caucus or primary at which delegates to the county convention were to be chosen on such short notice that few other than the members of the controlling group could attend. Perhaps a delegate-choosing caucus or primary would be held in such a disreputable place that " respectable " party members could not bring themselves to participate. Perhaps there would be " goon " squads of party toughs to intimidate or to stuff ballot boxes.

Should the machine fail to dominate delegate selection, it might try to bribe or frighten those who had been chosen to sit in the county convention. If that failed, the machine was still not beaten. Its fight could be shifted to the convention itself. The credentials of the anti-machine delegates could be challenged and others friendly to the machine seated instead. If the delegate-selection process was corrupt, the county conventions would be corrupt; if the county conventions were corrupt, the state conventions would be corrupt. The circle was a vicious one, and when tied to the reasons why a machine wanted to control party nominees — patronage, spoils, public contracts, public utility franchises, vice protection — it is little wonder that public demand for a change should develop.

The depths to which a county convention could sink is revealed in a roll call of delegates to an 1896 Cook County (Chicago) party convention in 1896. Of the 723 delegates, the discoverable occupations and personal records were in part as follows: [9] saloonkeepers, 265; political employees, 148; ex-burglars, pickpockets, and other jailbirds, 130; no occupation, 71; tried for murder, 17; keepers of houses of ill-fame, 2; lawyers, farmers, business and professional men, and so forth, 92.

Two possible alternative courses of action were open to those who would improve the manner in which the political parties selected their nominees. One was to regulate the party convention system. Several states in the last half of the nineteenth century passed laws establishing convention procedures to be followed, but many of these were optional with the party. They called for adequate notice of conventions, set the time and place of meeting, the procedure for

---

[9] From William Anderson and Edward W. Weidner, *American Government,* 4th ed. (New York: Henry Holt and Company, 1953) , p. 436.

selecting delegates, qualifications of those entitled to participate in delegate selection, the number of delegates entitled to attend, and the procedure for electing officers and conducting business. This type of legislation, however, was not extensively used, and by the 1890's, those who were for reform thought much more of the alternative of abolishing the whole state party convention system and substituting for it direct primary elections.

By Direct Primary. The first state-wide mandatory direct primary was enacted by Wisconsin in 1903 at the urging of Governor Robert M. LaFollette, Sr. Between 1903 and 1917 all but four states followed the Wisconsin example. Today only Connecticut has no direct primary but still employs the convention — now regulated — as the political party nominating device.

A general description of the direct primary follows. Primaries, like general elections, are conducted by the state and at state expense. Parties entitled to be included on the primary ballots are those which poll some minimum of the total vote at the last preceding general election. A candidate, to have his name placed on the ballot, must secure some number of signatures on his nominating petition and pay a relatively small filing fee. In a *closed primary* only party members who are so registered or who indicate their party affiliation at the polls may vote in a party's primary. In an *open primary* system the voter is given either one consolidated ballot which contains separate columns for all the parties or separate ballots for each party, but the voter may, when he gets into the voting booth, decide in which party's primary he will vote. Many, but not all, direct primary laws require that members of the county or local party committees also be elected by the voters in the primary election.

Although only Connecticut has no direct primary, other states still allow the political parties to use conventions for purposes other than platform drafting. In a few states, mostly in the South, the direct primary or convention is optional with the party. In some, like New York, party conventions are used to nominate some state-wide offices while the direct primary is used for other offices. In Iowa, if no candidate in the direct primary receives 35 percent of the vote, the appropriate party convention may pick the nominee. South Dakota has a similar *postprimary convention* provision. Colorado, Utah, Rhode Island, and New Mexico provide for *preprimary conventions* and indicate the results of the convention's voting on the primary election ballot. In still other states, extralegal party organizations, such as California's Democratic Council and Republican Assembly, make endorsements before the primary and publicize their choices. In Minnesota and Nebraska *nonpartisan primaries* are used to select members of the state legislature, and nonpartisan primaries are generally in use for local, school, and judicial offices.

Two major issues related to the strength of political party organization grow out of the nomination stage of the election process. Should direct primary legislation be repealed and the parties allowed to return to the convention system? If the answer to this question should be in the negative, or not a practical possibility, should the direct primary be of the closed or the open type?

From the first use of the direct primary by the Democratic party in Crawford County, Pennsylvania, in 1842 until the Progressive Movement during the first 15 years of the 1900's, the direct primary was consistently opposed by the so-called Old Guard and tended to be favored by the so-called New Guard forces in both major parties. There was good reason for such an alignment. The Old Guard was in control of the party organization, and with an unregulated convention system Old Guardists were dislodged only with extreme difficulty. Only through the channel of the party organization could New Guardists rise to party power and nomination for elective office. If New Guardists would not change their ways or thinking they were not likely to get very far. Robert M. LaFollette, in the midst of his fight against the Wisconsin Old Guard Republican machine of the 1890's, put his indictment of the convention system and stated his alternative in the following very forcefully stated and frequently quoted passage:

> Conventions have been and will continue to be prostituted to the services of corrupt organization. They answer no purpose further than to give respectable form to political robbery. Abolish the caucus and convention. Go back to the first principles of democracy; go back to the people. Substitute . . . a primary election — held under the sanction of laws which prevail at general elections — where the citizen may cast his vote directly to nominate the candidates of the party. . . . Then every citizen will share equally in the nomination. . . .[10]

---

[10] Robert M. LaFollette, *Autobiography* (Madison, Wis.: The Robert M. LaFollette Company, 1913) , p. 197.

Viewing the issue from the vantage point of the present instead of the days when the abuses of the unregulated convention system were at their height, no longer is the question cast into the all-good versus all-evil dichotomy as once it seemed to be. The state of Connecticut's example shows that a properly regulated convention system can work and be responsive to the will of the rank and file of party members. Nor has the direct primary destroyed political machines, though it has made it more difficult for a party oligarchy to control its party. If the first consideration is strong party organization, undoubtedly the convention system would be preferable. But strong party organization does not seem to be a controlling objective in the minds of most persons today, and no trend toward the substitution of the convention system for the direct primary is in sight.

Perhaps the most helpful and practical alternative is to combine advantages of the direct primary with some of the advantages of the convention through the device of the official preprimary endorsing convention. Here the party has an opportunity to put itself on record behind candidates it feels would best represent the party as nominees. At the same time the party leadership is forced to be more directly responsive to the party rank and file.

Perhaps the main reason why the movement toward preprimary endorsing conventions has not proceeded at a faster rate is the delicate political situation which exists within a party before its official nominees are selected in the primary election. Those who pick the losing faction are likely to find themselves on the outside in the next reshuffling of personnel in the party hierarchy. Thus the tendency is not to want to make pre-primary commitments. Only in a system where cross-filling is the practice, as in California, is the " intelligent " party forced to make a preprimary decision.[11] If it does not concentrate on one candidate for each office and if the opposition party does so concentrate, the party's votes will likely be split with the possibility that the cross-filed opposition candidate may win both major party primaries.

Distinguishing between the closed and open primary, the principal point of difference relates to the concept of party membership. In the open primary the voter need not decide his party affiliation until he actually votes. At worst, under the open primary, a party is

---

[11] Legally the official party organizations may not endorse before the primary. Extra legal party organizations like the Democratic Council and Republican Assembly, however, do make such endorsements.

left wide open to " raiding " by the opposition bent on nominating the worst candidates in order that the opposition may more easily defeat them in the general election. However, open primary " raiding " does not always work that way. To raid is possible only when there is no contest in a party's primary. Furthermore, to have the party's voters purposely vote in the primary of the opposition for the weakest candidates implies that the party is well enough organized to be able to instruct and mobilize its members to perform the act. More often, when " raiding " takes place, the raiders are not organized but rather are drawn to the opposition primary by a particularly important contest and in support of the strongest and most popular of the candidates.

Obviously the concept of party membership in an open primary system is more loose than in a closed primary system, but even a closed primary can be raided. In closed primary states which require voters to register by party affiliation, the political parties are as protected from raiding as they can be. Then, to raid, it is necessary to change registration. In other closed primary states the voter may be asked before he is handed his ballot to swear or affirm that he belongs to a party because he has voted for it in the past or because he intends to vote for it. Though here the voter does need to make a public commitment, there is generally much latitude for him to change his mind from election to election.

Party leaders in closed primary states tend to favor closed primaries and if, again, the principal objective is strong party organizations, the closed primary tends to contribute more to that end than the open primary. Opinion among party leaders in open primary states tends to split with those seeking to strengthen the tools with which the party oligarchy may control favoring the closed primary, and those desiring a more " fluid " kind of politics in favor of the open primary. In either closed or open primary states there is always more or less a tendency not to want to change the system unless the party or group have been unsuccessful with the system as it presently exists.

CHAPTER SIX

State and Local Party Organization

But it is the clear understanding of the political machine that is generally lacking and this is the vital thing. Lack of an accurate and clear conception of the party machine, its factors and functions, its methods and scope, means hopeless and helpless political bewilderment. The voter who has not that has nothing upon which to base political knowledge and can acquire none that is sound or worthwhile. He is like a small child in the dark.

It is literally amazing how extremely little the average man and woman who vote know about these things and how completely they fail to grasp the vital importance of knowing about them. Even among some of those who are themselves cogs in the wheels, there is confusion of thought and ignorance of the realities of which they form part.

The general idea of a political organization is that it is sinister and somewhat secret association of men who run politics, live by graft, and are headed by a boss who is a very vicious fellow indeed. As to how the machine operates, who belong to it, how they get in, what they get out of it, what they do, how they do it, what are its uses, what are its effects, what power it possesses, and where are its vulnerable spots, they have only the haziest notion.

The truth is that political organizations are absolutely essential to the conduct of the government — city, state, or national. This is a government by parties. Parties can no more be held together and made to function without organization than any great business could be run

without organization. Without organization there would be no parties.
Without parties there would be no government.

Frank R. Kent [1]

It is hardly surprising that few have a thorough understanding of state and local party organization. In each state there is some kind of maze of state and county central committees; city, ward, and precinct committees; village and township committees; and Congressional district, state senatorial district, and assembly district committees. Some of the committees are provided for by law, and others are the creations of candidates for public office. Some are so large in size that deliberation is impossible, and some are small and workable. In one state might be found a hierarchy with a virtual dictator installed at the top, and in other states there may be little or no communication between different levels of organization or between different party units at the same level. In some cases local party committees might work for the election of the entire party ticket, and in others for only the party's candidates for local office. Types of party organization in politically doubtful states are usually different from types of organization in the safe or " one-party " states, and within the latter, the strong party will present one picture and the weak party another.

Behind the formal organization of the parties will be found the even more important and personalized web of informal human relationships which need to be understood if the party organization chart is to have meaning. Though formal organization changes only slowly, informal organization is in a state of constant flux. Some party functions may be detailed in state statutes, and others may be specified in party constitutions or be the result of unwritten party customs. In addition to the party organizations outside the legislature, there are the " legislative parties " with their own and generally independent organizations. In spite of complicating factors such as these, however, it is possible through generalization to develop the main outlines of state and local party organization.

Five other introductory points should be made. First, as noted in Chapter Two, in a real sense it may be said that there are no permanent national political party organizations in the United States. A

---

[1] *The Great Game of Politics* (New York: Doubleday, Doran and Company, 1933), pp. 343–344. Reprinted by permission of Doubleday and Company.

strong President might temporarily make his party appear to be a national party, but seldom is even this minimum achieved. The American major parties resemble, instead, confederations of forty-eight state parties. Second, as noted in Chapter Five, state and local party organizations are no longer private and voluntary associations. Rather they are creatures of the states, and much of the important data on organization and function will be found in the election laws of the several states. Though not every state has adopted the Australian ballot and though not every state has a direct primary election, all states do regulate their political parties. The general tendency is to regulate in detail.

Third, party organizations are built around the electoral units of the states. At the bottom is the precinct committee or committeeman serving the party for the smallest election administration units made up of from 250 to 600 voters. In urban areas, immediately above the precinct level, there is generally to be found a ward committee or committeeman in charge of party precinct activities within each district which elects a city councilman. Should city council members be elected in nonpartisan elections, instead of a ward organization, perhaps the party will substitute the assembly district as the intermediate level between precinct and county. At the county level, with its county elective offices to be filled, there will be a county party chairman and a county committee. For Congressional districts, where they encompass several counties, some states provide for Congressional district committees and Congressional district chairmen. At the top level of state and local party organization will be found the state central committee and state chairman.

The pattern of party organization in rural areas below the state level is similar, except for this general distinction. Because populations are smaller the number of party organizational units tends to be fewer and they tend to cover larger geographical areas. In many rural counties the base party unit is the county committee.

Fourth, generally it is possible to draw a horizontal line on the state and local party organization chart between the county committees and chairmen and the state central committees and their chairmen. This line can be used to indicate that the state central committee does not often exercise much if any control over county party activities. County committees generally go their own way, cooperating with the state organization of the party when it suits the county's fancy or interest and not doing so when it does not.

Fifth, in every state and local party organization and on each level of such organization there will be at least one political machine. A machine is a faction of the party organized under the leadership of one or a few persons with the principal object of gaining or maintaining control of the party organization. Such machines are not peculiar to politics, but are found in any type of organization. The question is not shall there be machines, but what kind of tactics may they employ and to what ends should they use their power.

Our examination of state and local party organization will be developed, first, through a study of local party organization; second, state party organization; and third, party organization *inside* the state government. These sections will be followed by a fourth to introduce the question of the possibility or desirability of more centralized state parties.

LOCAL PARTY ORGANIZATION

The Party at the Precinct Level. Frank R. Kent's *The Great Game of Politics,* published first in 1923, begins in this way:

> No clear idea of a party organization can be had unless you start from the bottom.
>
> To discuss Presidential politics without understanding precinct politics is an absurdity. It is like trying to solve a problem in trigonometry without having studied arithmetic.
>
> The election precinct is the smallest political division. . . . [s]o is the precinct executive the smallest unit in the party machine. While he is the smallest he is also, by long odds, the most vital. . . . He is the bone and sinew of the machine. He is its foundation and the real source of its strength. If he does not function, the machine decays. If he quits, the machine dies.
>
> He is the actual connecting link between the people and the organization, and he is the only connecting link — the only man in the machine who has any point of direct contact with the voters, who knows anything about them, who has any real influence with them. All that the boss has in the way of power comes from the precinct executives. All that the machine has in the way of substance and solidity, he gives it. Without him there is no machine. He is the indispensable cog in the wheel.[2]

---

[2] *Op. cit.,* pp. 1–2. Reprinted by permission of Doubleday and Company.

Certainly this was an accurate estimate of the importance of the precinct executive through the last half of the nineteenth century and
up through the 1920's.

Then, except for newspaper publicity and advertising and mass
meetings, the only method by which candidates could directly contact
voters was through personally ringing doorbells, and since this was
generally impossible, candidates always needed the indirect contacts
which only the precinct executive could furnish. In those days it
was imperative that there be a continuously functioning party unit
at the person-to-person level. Nor were party positions on issues, no
matter how popular they might be, enough to enable the precinct
executive to win the allegiance of the voters. The successful precinct
executive developed a much stronger party-voter tie through his person by bestowing favors in order to win personal gratitude to win
votes.

The power of a precinct executive's part of the total " machine
vote " might roughly be calculated in the following manner:

1. himself, wife, grown children, parents and in-laws, perhaps some
   brothers and sisters — at least five sure votes;
2. selection of three paid election officials who also had " family
   votes " — at least 15 sure votes;
3. designation of a polling place (rented by the county) with another
   " family vote " — at least five sure votes;
4. judicious distribution of campaign funds allotted to his precinct —
   at least ten sure votes or more if the precinct executive didn't want
   to use part of the money for personal expenses;
5. persons living in his precinct and having city or county jobs by
   virtue of the precinct executive's recommendation to the ward
   executive — at least 35 sure votes;
   TOTAL: at minimum some 65 votes and enough to generally
          carry his precinct in any primary election and per-
          haps enough to swing the general election.[3]

Frank Kent estimated that Tammany Hall at its height could generally muster a " machine vote " of from 350,000 to 400,000.[4]

But the efficient precinct executive did not stop with his 65 " all-
weather " votes. " There's only one way to hold a district," said District Leader George Washington Plunkitt of Tammany Hall, " you
must study human nature and act accordin'." Political clubs spon-

---

[3] From Kent, *op. cit.*, Chapter 4.   [4] *Ibid.*, p. 23.

soring dances, glee clubs, baseball teams, and a wide variety of social activities were maintained. Poor families were helped. Plunkitt and his precinct executives would follow the fire engines, and if a family were burned out, would find them a place to live, buy clothes for them, and tide them over their misfortune. Jobs, both public and private, were found. Persons were bailed out of jail, and lenient justice might be arranged. Voter registration fees were paid. And, from Plunkitt, again:

> And the children — the little roses of the district! Do I forget them? Oh, no! They know me, every one of them, and they know that a sight of Uncle George and candy means the same thing. Some of them are the best kind of vote-getters. I'll tell you a case. Last year a little Eleventh Avenue rosebud whose father is a Republican, caught hold of his whiskers on election day and said she wouldn't let go till he'd promise to vote for me. And she didn't.[5]

The precinct executive in some areas attempts to use similar techniques today, but his job of ingratiation with his voters is a more difficult one. Radio, television, and the many other amusement and social outlets have developed in competition. Economic prosperity and social security systems have lessened the need for the political machine's brand of social security. Merit systems have taken away some of the patronage. Election-law regulation has restricted election-day activities. The political literacy level has risen, and political issues have taken on a new importance. Alfred E. Smith, describing the New York political system through which he had risen to become Governor of New York and Democratic Presidential nominee, in 1935 saw the change coming:

> . . . the younger generation now coming into power . . . are not going to be so easily led by the old-time political methods. . . . I feel very strongly that consideration will in the future be given for service to the whole city by the political party rather than the ability of the district leader to hold his forces by personal favor. . . . Both of the major political parties lose their power when the great masses of the people become dissatisfied with their administration, and in that event I do not believe that the power or influence of the district leader [and his organization] can avert political disaster.[6]

---

[5] W. L. Riordan, *Plunkitt of Tammany Hall* (New York: McClure, Phillips and Company, 1905), p. 53.

[6] Alfred E. Smith, *The Citizen and His Government* (New York: Harper and Brothers, 1935), p. 19.

There are other reasons why the importance of the precinct executive has declined. No longer is the position the only entrance through which a person must enter a political party organization preliminary to the long climb up each rung of the machine's advancement ladder. With the public opinion poll as a tool for determining opinion on political subjects and for measuring the quality of a party's or candidate's appeal, the precinct executive has ceased to be the sole source of information for party leaders to know how things are going at the grass roots. No longer is he the principal channel for propaganda. In most areas the function of precinct executive is not the full-time avocation it once was. Laws debarring public employees make it difficult for one to hold public office and to serve as a precinct executive at the same time, and even without such statutes, low-paying public jobs are not as attractive by comparison with the income advantages which are more general in private employment.

The precinct executive, precinct chairman, or precinct committee, provided the party has enough members to fill the committee positions, is still an important " cog in the wheel " of party organization. If anyone in the party is to establish personal contacts with the voters, the precinct executive will have to be the man. The parties do need precinct workers for registering voters, for intensive campaigning, and for getting out the vote. A good record in one's precinct can be used as a springboard to higher party or public position.

No longer, however, is the precinct executive " indispensable." If he were, then both major parties would have faded away. A majority of the voting precincts in the United States today do not have precinct executives, to say nothing about precinct committees.

The Party at the Ward Level. Next step up from the precinct executive in the local party hierarchy is the ward executive or ward committee and chairman. If the party is not organized on a ward basis, perhaps the area of jurisdiction is an assembly district. It was often at this level that the old-time political club developed as a tool for the ward executive and his precinct executives. It is here where the modern adaptations of political clubs are to be found — Young Democrats, Young Republicans, Democratic clubs, Republican clubs. If there is no precinct organization, in the cities the ward organization acts as the base party unit.

While organization in each precinct may no longer be indispensable, there is a reason, in addition to the function of campaigning, why some kind of ward organization does tend to be necessary. Here is the electoral unit at which the party begins to make nominations for some public offices. Perhaps it is a city councilman and a state assemblyman, and perhaps working jointly with other wards, there is a share in selecting the man who will be the organization's choice for a state senate or United States House of Representatives seat. If the ward party unit is a part of a close-knit political machine and not of the committee type, it will be the ward executive's recommendation for city councilman and assemblyman from his ward that the city boss will accept. If a ward executive is more powerful than the other executives in a state senate district or Congressional district, he is likely to have the controlling voice in choosing the men who will have machine backing for those offices in the primary election.

Where the committee type of organization prevails, the ward chairman's choice will have to meet with the committee's approval, and the result may sometimes be a product more satisfactory from the standpoint of a broader public interest. In a few states, with California a notable example, formalized procedures have been established for the calling of a " fact-finding committee " in a district in which a public office is vacant for the specific purpose of endorsing a candidate in the primary election.

In a city where a party is well organized and does have its voting precincts manned with party workers, the ward executive will usually be an ex-precinct executive who could deliver more votes than the other precinct executives of the ward. Because the precinct executives will be responsible to the ward executive, it will be the latter who appoints the former. If the political machine is kept oiled with ample patronage, the ward leader will tend to hold a better public job than the precinct executives. Through his hands will pass the campaign funds for the precinct executives below him. His tenure in his position of ward executive will be assured as long as he can deliver the machine vote. Frank Kent estimated the average ward executive had about 1,300 sure votes which he could swing — almost " one fourth of all the voters entitled to vote [in primaries] and approximately three fourths of those who do vote [in primaries.]" [7]

The Party at the City or County Level. It is at the city-wide level of party organization, or the county level in a rural political organiza-

---

[7] Kent, *op. cit.,* p. 37.

tion, where one finds the typical political " boss." If he is strong, the boss might also control or share largely in the control of the state party organization, but the city or county is the power base from which he operates. When party power is not concentrated in the hands of a single boss, it frequently is diffused with several persons — some perhaps holding official party positions and some with no public or party position — sharing in party control. Always, however, there will be a boss or bosses of some kind directing the party machinery.

The typical professional city boss started as an assistant to a precinct executive, and then became a precinct executive himself. From there he expanded his power and moved on to become a ward executive, and then to the still higher post of district leader. As one of the strongest district leaders, he became the boss's assistant and when his boss died or retired, he himself became boss; or by another route, he may have split with the boss and gone on to defeat him in the city primary election and moved to the top in this manner.

For many of such professional bosses, their political activity is nothing but a business and the party organization is used to that end. The boss selects the machine's candidates for city-wide elective office and ratifies the choices of the ward executives or other district executives for elective offices from districts within the city with an eye to securing the kind of candidate who will, if nominated and elected, always be responsive to the machine that put him in office. By virtue of his control of public offices, the boss finds numerous possibilities to support himself and his machine at the public expense. If there is no merit system, he has patronage and can force political assessments from those whose public jobs are dependent on his recommendation. Even with merit systems he may succeed in devising ways and means of circumventing them.

If the boss's machine is powerful, private groups will come to him with financial support in return for favorable public policies. Or, because of the boss's power, he may be able to go to private groups or business organizations and threaten trouble if they do not cooperate with him. He may be in league with gambling or vice interests. He may use the police force, the licensing board, or the building inspector's office to harass his opponents. He may control the courts. If a professional boss is strong and the opposition machine is weak, he may " buy out " the other side; or if both party machines are strong, he may establish " working relations " with the opposition.

But these are not the only kinds of city or county bosses. Even when the more flagrant practices of some bosses tended to make the title " boss " one of opprobrium, there were bosses who were not ready to sell out to the highest bidder and did hold power in their own right and tried to use it to what they regarded as legitimate and honest purposes. Though the equivalents of some of the more disreputable of the old-time political bosses still ply their trades in some jurisdictions with only a modernization of the old techniques, political machines have tended to become more respectable.

The time when city-wide and state-wide issues run competition with favor-bestowing as a vote winning technique on the precinct level has arrived. The latter technique is still important, but it is much less so than it once was. Today it is more necessary to have " clean " and able candidates running for the important offices, and such candidates are generally of a type which will not be as subservient to the narrow interests of the political machine once they get into office. Adlai Stevensons, Thomas Deweys, and Paul Douglases are more and more being selected by political machines for the broader popular support which they can develop.

Now, if the boss no longer has patronage as the principal cement with which to bind his organization, he must be more careful to properly balance his tickets with members of the different interest and ethnic groups on which he depends for votes. Instead of handing out dollar bills, he must try to reward the groups with the type of legislation and governmental policies that they want. Instead of relying upon the " shady " contributions of the underworld, the machine itself must attempt to " stay clean " and cultivate legitimate business, labor, or other respectable sources of income.

In areas where the strong party machine type of organization has broken down, the " bosses " who run the party may appear in different form. Perhaps a labor organization or combination of business organizations is the dominant element, and its leaders may control whatever party organization exists. Or, perhaps there is no single party organization worthy of the title, but instead there are several competing organizations clustered around the principal personalities contesting for public office and whatever advantages control over a party name can give.

Rare indeed is the political organization that operates as pure democratic theory would suggest it should with precinct caucuses selecting precinct committee members, a chairman, and delegates to the ward committee; with ward conventions selecting a chairman, committee members, and delegates to the city or county committee; and so on up the party hierarchy. The important policy and personnel decisions are usually made by the ward executives at that level and by the city or county bosses at their level. If selection of the different committees is by primary election, so few voters vote on party offices that the choices of the party leaders generally are ratified.

Formally, county party organization will appear in general as detailed here. There will be a county committee, and often it will be chosen by the party voters in a primary election. In some states county committeemen and committeewomen are named by party nominees for public office; in others precinct or ward committees choose representatives to sit on the county committee; and in still others procedures are established for a county convention with delegates to that convention empowered to name the county committee members. The county chairman will, in turn, be selected by the county committee, and generally he will be the choice of the boss or the complex of bosses actually in control of the party machine. In counties with one large city it will be the city party leaders who are in a position to procure the county chairmanship for their man.

Since the county committee is not *under* the state central committee in the sense that the county committee is responsible to it, the county committee is generally not in the same sense *over* the city party organizations within its geographical boundaries. In rural areas or in urban areas where there are no strong city party machines, the county chairman may control patronage within the county. He will also attempt to effect whatever campaign co-ordinating that is possible and will have at least some part in determining the character of the party slate of candidates for the primary election. If the county chairman is powerful in his own right or represents those who are powerful, he can make his job a significant one. If he is neither, the county chairman is just a man filling an office established by state law but, politically, accomplishing relatively little. For many county chairmen almost the only claim to distinction is the fact that they serve on their party's state central committee.

STATE PARTY ORGANIZATION

Each major party has a state central committee and a state chairman in each of the forty-eight states. The committees range in size from small working groups to California's more than 600 members. The manner of choosing state central committees varies widely from state to state. California's method of choice is one of the most involved, directly or indirectly combining most of the selection system characteristics of the other states. There all the party's state elected executives and legislators and United States Senators and Congressmen or nominees for those offices are members. If there is no man from the party in one of these offices and if the opposition successfully cross-filed and stole the nomination, then the officers of the state central committee may appoint persons to fill the vacancy. Second, party officeholders or nominees or appointees may each in turn appoint three additional associate members of the state central committee. Third, all county chairmen are members of the state central committee. The full state central committee is much too large for deliberation, and even the executive committee, which is appointed by the state chairman, usually numbers over 100 members. Therefore, it too can hardly be a working group.

By comparison with California, election procedure in most other states is relatively simple. A set number of members of the state central committee may be chosen by each Congressional district committee or in Congressional district primary elections. The state committee may be composed of county chairmen or Congressional district chairmen, or the entire membership may be selected by the state party conventions.

At the head of the state central committee will be a chairman, chosen either by the state central committee or by the party's nominee for governor. If the choice is by state committee, again the figure of a state party boss (other than the governor) may dictate the choice. The state boss is likely to be the most powerful large city boss or perhaps he may be a United States Senator who has over the years become the boss of his state's whole party machinery. Generally, the man who is state chairman is not himself the boss, but rather has been picked by those who hold the real power.

Functions of the state central committee vary. The committee constitutes the governing body of the party between state party conventions. In some states, mostly southern, if the direct primary or convention methods of nominating are optional, the state central committee will make the choice. In some states it is empowered to set the date of the primary election. If there is a state-wide co-ordinated party campaign, the officers of the state committee may direct it or hire the professional campaign managers who do. Usually state patronage clears through the committee if its relations with the governor are amenable. Federal patronage may clear through it if it maintains good relations with the senior United States Senator from that state and of that party. If there are no United States Senators from one of the parties of a state and that party controls the White House, perhaps the White House working through the national committee chairman will make the state chairman its patronage-clearing point.

Unless set by law, the state central committee establishes the dates for state and local party conventions. Except where candidates raise their own campaign funds, it is the chief state-wide campaign fund collector and campaign fund distributor. Functions such as these give the state central committee, and particularly its officers, enough power so that no party faction wants another faction to gain control. No city boss can feel that his position is consolidated unless he or he in combination with other bosses controls the state central committee. Nor can any governor know that one of his flanks is not vulnerable and exposed without similar central committee control. If the governor and the city or county bosses are not working together, or if the bosses are split, spirited fights often take place over selection of state central committee members and the state chairman. If the chairman is able and is of your wing of the party, he can be of much help; if he is able and is of another wing of the party, he can do much damage.

An illustration of the political stakes involved in state central committee control and of the kind of intraparty in-fighting which can flare around the method of selection and methods of operation of a state central committee is to be found in Minnesota politics during the period from 1936 through 1938 when Harold E. Stassen was seeking his first nomination for the office of governor of Minnesota. For the third consecutive state election, Minnesota Republicans had been roundly defeated in 1936. To rebuild the Minnesota Republican party for the 1938 campaign and to stop, if possible, what appeared to be a desire of some of the leaders of the Republican State Central Committee to fuse with the antiadministration wing of the Farmer-Labor party, a group of young Republicans led by Stassen began a campaign to dislodge the Republican Old Guard from its control of the State Central Committee.

Ringing declarations calling for the establishment in Minnesota of a Republican party from which would be " excluded those selfish interests which seek to use wealth or extensive corporate holdings as the key to improper influence " were issued. Young Republican League conventions passed resolutions demanding Republican action. One of the Republican Congressional nominees defeated in the 1936 election began his own assault. When the Executive Committee of the Republican State Central Committee turned down his plan for reorganization of party machinery, he charged that they were a " group of political barnacles that had been clinging to the Republican party since the Hoover regime." Their obstruction, he added, was " . . . simply a post-mortem on Minnesota Republicans at which they dissected the body, pronounced it dead, embalmed it and set no date for the resurrection. If the usual procedure is followed, an attempt . . . will be started about the day before the next election." [8]

Noting the dissatisfaction, the Executive Committee decided to call a meeting of the State Central Committee — then made up of representatives of Republican nominees for state offices — and to invite county chairmen and chairwomen to consider the reorganization question. The combined group met on June 29, 1937, and had presented to them a new constitution which would make county chairmen and chairwomen members of the State Central Committee. By a unanimous vote it was agreed to hold a special Republican convention in the fall to submit a new constitution to the membership of the party. The Executive Committee was to set the time and place, and a special committee was to redraft the proposed constitution.

On October 8 the Executive Committee met, and for a time the June 29 State Central Committee minutes could not be found. Then followed a debate over whether the instructions for a fall convention were mandatory. When finally the minutes were located, the instructions were shown to be mandatory, but now a convention was opposed on the grounds that there would not be sufficient time to call a convention, that the proposed constitution would be contrary to state law, and that delegates to such a convention would be " handpicked " and " they'll take this organization away from you and do things you don't want to." After a long debate, by a 19 to 2 vote, it was decided to call a fall convention, but the time, place, and manner of delegate selection was left to a special committee under the chairmanship of the State Central Committee chairman.

---

[8] *St. Paul Pioneer Press,* May 10, 1937.

On October 27 the secretary of the Republican State Central Committee announced another meeting of the Executive Committee for November 5. This action was being taken, he said, at the suggestion of the committee appointed to arrange the fall convention. Furthermore, there was no money in the party treasury with which to finance such a convention!

On November 5 the anticonvention group on the Executive Committee estimated that a convention would cost a very large amount of money, and argued that it could not be raised. Pro-convention forces ridiculed both the estimate and the argument and charged delaying tactics. Stassen, there by virtue of a proxie, urged action and warned that party workers wanted activity. Then the first arrangements committee was discharged and a new one appointed, and to allay Old Guard fear that the Stassen forces would use such a convention to seek party endorsement of Stassen for governor, a motion, seconded by Stassen, was passed to recommend to the convention that it not endorse candidates.

Finally on November 17 from the new arrangements committee, after Stassen had personally raised the necessary money but not from the " usual party sources," a defiant call was issued to a December 15 winter convention. On the latter date the convention met, and the new constitution was passed by an overwhelming majority. Now the Old Guard shifted to attempting to postpone the selection of new officers. On January 15, 1938, the new State Central Committee met to consider the question, and the Old Guard officers stayed in control. Wrote one of the political columnists of the Republican *Minneapolis Journal:* " The Old Guard is still the Old Guard; any successful attempt at change in state leadership must first involve considerable change in county chairmanships." [9]

Behind the intraparty conflict over the State Central Committee was the Stassen candidacy for the Republican nomination for governor. Stassen had been campaigning since October 1937, and throughout his speeches he stressed the need for " revitalizing " the Republican party. " Let us make that party a sound, liberal party responsive to the just demands of those who labor. . . . Let us keep that party away from Wall Street and in tune with Main Street. Let us keep that party out of the control of professional lobbyists." [10] The Republican Old Guard did not want to be " revitalized " nor did they want as

---

[9] January 17, 1938.   [10] *Ibid.,* March 8, 1938.

the Republican nominee for the state's highest office one who would try to revitalize. The Old Guard fought its battle from their position of strength within the Republican State Central Committee. Stassen fought through his growing strength with the voters who would be entitled to participate in Minnesota's open primary.

On February 18, 1938, the Executive Committee again became a battleground. A motion to call a preprimary endorsing convention similar to that used by the Farmer-Labor party was voted down by a 15 to 10 vote. Most of the minority were Stassen supporters, and all of the majority were regarded as either working openly or quietly for "the candidate of the Old Guard." The vote was regarded as an Old Guard victory, and Stassen-supporting Republican organizations censored the Executive Committee and accused it of breaking faith with the rank and file by failing to carry out the intent of the new party constitution.

On April 18 a Minneapolis Republican attorney filed suit against the officers of the State Central Committee for an injunction to prevent the holding of party caucuses for the next state convention which had been scheduled for June 27, one week after the primary election. The grounds for the suit was the charge that the new Republican constitution violated Minnesota election laws. But the caucuses were held, and in some cases turnouts were so large and feelings so intense that special corps of policemen were necessary to preserve order.

Harold E. Stassen, aged 31, won the Republican nomination for governor in the primary election, and with the victory he won the Republican organization. On June 27 the Executive Committee acceded to his request to postpone the state convention until September 2. A July State Central Committee meeting was headlined in the newspapers: "GOP Chiefs Meet To Do As Stassen Asks." Stassen's slate of State Central Committee officers was installed. On September 2 the Republican state convention enacted a platform that led political reporter Joseph H. Ball (later to be a Stassen appointee to the United States Senate) to write: "Two years ago, half of the planks in it would never even have gotten out of committee." [11]

The Stassen forces would not have succeeded in capturing the machinery of the Minnesota Republican party had the convention system still been in use. Perhaps they might not have won in a closed primary system, because it is estimated that the Democratic and

---

[11] *St. Paul Pioneer Press,* September 5, 1938.

Farmer-Labor " raiding vote " in the Republican primary in 1938 was very high. This is the kind of political situation the party machine fears, and when the New Guard gains control of state party machinery and eventually itself becomes an Old Guard for a new New Guard to shoot at, the kind of situation that now the new Old Guard also fears.

Here is a specific case study of the type of power struggle which goes on around a state central committee and its officers. Sometimes the struggle is less intense and perhaps sometimes it gets more intense, but it always continues because the political stakes are high. To learn what faction or factions control a party's state central committee is one of the quickest and simplest ways of assessing that party's state-wide internal balance of political power.

PARTY ORGANIZATION INSIDE GOVERNMENT

To this point in the examination of state and local party organization, the primary concern has been with the party *outside* of government. The party organs from the precinct level to the state central committee have as their primary functions the selection of candidates for nomination, getting those candidates nominated, and then electing them to public office. If the election is won, then it is incumbent on the party to do its best to operate the government. Now the emphasis must shift to the party *inside* government — the party's members in the legislative branch and their organization and the party's members in the elective positions of the executive branch of government.

For an example of an " outside-government " party which maintains control over an " inside-government " party, the organization of the powerful city boss can best serve the purpose. Not only does such a boss have his district leaders, ward executives, and their precinct executives working for him, but also the public officeholders who have won election with the help of the machine. Get a " Muldoon " — one who will " vote right " and " stay hitched " [12] — elected, and then the boss is in a position to win from government whatever patronage and favors it has in its power to bestow. Though the boss's most important job is to get his men nominated in order to control his party organization, his second most necessary objective

---

[12] Kent, *op. cit.,* p. 58.

is those public offices. If there are long periods of patronage and spoils drought, boss, machine, and party are likely to wither away.

If the boss is a city boss, his targets are the city council, the mayoralty, and numerous other elective city officers. If he is both a city and county boss, he also wants the county board of supervisors and such elective officials as the county sheriff. If, in turn, he is a state boss, his targets include the state legislature, the governorship, and elective state officials. " Think of it," wrote Frank Kent in 1923, " the city councils which pass the ordinances for the cities and regulate city taxes, and the state legislatures, which fix taxes for the state and pass all state laws, are largely composed in every city and every state of men personally chosen by one or the other of the party machine executives — and chosen by him primarily for the purpose of ' delivering ' his vote when needed. What this really means is that they vote the way the boss wants when they get the word." [13]

This is not the pattern of party-government relations advocated by those who desire stronger party government in the United States. Rather, the boss type of governmental control might, if the bosses hold no official positions, be termed irresponsible party government. Responsible party government, on the other hand, implies there should be a democratic party organization responsive to the rank and file of party membership and a party capable of implementing its platforms if elected to hold control of the institutions of government. Such a responsible party should be motivated by program and not by patronage and spoils. It should provide alternatives, and above all it should be responsible in that the electorate can hold it to account for its record in office.

Responsible parties of this type do not exist in the states today. Either there is the irresponsible machine boss who has the power but gets it in the wrong way and uses it for the wrong ends, or there are party organizations which are too weak to control elected executives and legislators. Thus they are unable to deliver on the platform planks the party might advocate. At the state level of government, even the able and powerful state boss finds it more difficult to control government than is the case in a city or county. Because many city and county governments now elect their public officials without party designation while state officers are almost without exception partisan, and because the problem of party responsibility at the state level is

[13] *Ibid.,* p. 55.

more important to an understanding of the character of the American major parties, attention for the remainder of this section will be focused on party-government relations at the state level.

Although party government in the United States Senate and House of Representatives, certainly by comparison with British party organization standards in the House of Commons, is weak, party government in state legislatures tends to be even weaker. There are scattered studies of party organization in some of the state legislatures, but only the American Political Science Association Committee on American Legislature's *American State Legislatures,* published in 1954, presents a systematic attempt to generalize on this subject.[14] Its findings may be summarized as follows.

In estimating the degree of party cohesion in state legislatures, in only 17 states was it regarded as strong; in 11, moderately strong or strong only occasionally; and in 20, weak or nonexistent. Pressure politics was judged to be a more important factor than party politics in 24 states, in 14 the two factors were balanced, and in only 7 state legislatures were party considerations more important than pressure group considerations. Only in 15 states were state-wide issues considered more important than local issues.[15] Even in organizing the legislative houses, according to the study, the majority party acts effectively as a party to select party members for leadership positions in only some 28 state senates and 29 assemblies. In 11 senates and 10 assemblies party organization for this purpose was found to be weak or nonexistent.[16]

---

[14] Belle Zeller, ed., (New York: Thomas Y. Crowell Company, 1954), Chap. 12. Malcolm E. Jewell, "Party Voting in American State Legislatures," *The American Political Science Review* (September, 1955), Vol. 49, pp. 773–791, includes the legislatures of Massachusetts, New York, Pennsylvania, Ohio, Illinois, Washington, Missouri and Colorado. Two of Jewell's conclusions deserve special note: (1) "In many of the American states with a strong two-party system, during sessions when party balance in the legislature is not one-sided, partisan considerations influence to a significant degree the legislative voting on issues about which there is some measure of disagreement"; and (2) "The degree of party voting appears to be significantly higher in those two-party states which are larger and more urban. In these states more than in rural states the Democratic party represents the big-city, metropolitan areas, and the Republican party the smaller cities and rural districts." See also W. Duane Lockard, "Legislative Politics in Connecticut," *ibid.* (March, 1954), Vol. 48, pp. 166–173; William J. Keefe, "Parties, Partisanship, and Public Policy in the Pennsylvania Legislature," *ibid.* (June, 1954), Vol. 48, pp. 450–464; and Keefe, "Party Government and Lawmaking in the Illinois General Assembly," *Northwestern University Law Review* (March, 1952), Vol. 47, pp. 55–71.

[15] Zeller, *op. cit.,* p. 193.   [16] *Ibid.,* p. 194.

For only half of the senates and assemblies are majority party caucuses used for important purposes, and in only 15 states do minority party caucuses amount to much. Formal party steering or policy committees are found in only a dozen state legislatures.[17] In 29 states the assistance of the majority party was regarded as a significant factor in advancing the governor's legislative program, and in 19 states the governor's leadership was classified as weak.[18] Taken as individual items, these data may not appear to have great meaning, but their sum-total effect is to indicate that, in general, political parties are not able nor organized inside government to control both governor and legislature and thus to control governmental policy.

When the states are classified into safe Democratic or Republican, relatively safe for either party, or doubtful with an approximately even balance between the parties in the legislature, a more specific type of generalization is possible.[19] Of the 18 " one-party " states, Democrats controlled 11 southern states, Arizona, and Oklahoma; and Republicans, Kansas, Maine, North Dakota, South Dakota, and Vermont. Here the minority party does not count, and the legislatures tend to split into permanent factions resembling almost two different parties, or into shifting factions. Leadership is not party leadership, but factional leadership. Often the governor may be of one faction and the legislature is controlled by another, or perhaps one house might be controlled by one faction and the other by another.[20]

Of the 9 states in which one party tended to be stronger than the other but where the minority party held a significant number of seats in the legislature (Republican — Iowa, New Hampshire, New Jersey, Oregon, Wisconsin; Democratic — Kentucky, Maryland, New Mexico, West Virginia), majority party unity tended to be relatively stronger than in " one-party " states, but there was still considerable factionalism within the majority party. In all 9 of these states for the period 1949–1951 both houses of the state legislature and the governorship were controlled by the same party.[21]

The remaining 19 of the 48 states, excepting Minnesota and Nebraska where the legislatures are nonpartisan, were classified for the

---

[17] Zeller, *op. cit.*, p. 195.
[18] *Ibid.*, p. 198.
[19] For the bienniums of 1949–1951 and 1951–1953. See *ibid.*, pp. 199–210.
[20] *Ibid.*, pp. 207–210.
[21] *Ibid.*, pp. 206–207.

period as " two-party " in the sense that both parties' strength in the
two houses of the legislature in each state was quite evenly balanced.
Here party cohesion of both major parties reaches its highest point
in legislative party organization. Most significant fact for the concept
of party government about these states, however, was that only in 4
of the 19 during 1949–1951, and in only 7 during 1951–1953 were
both houses of the legislature and the governor's office controlled by
the same political party.[22]

If there is to be party government, the majority party must be
able to build a bridge over the separated and checked-and-balanced
legislative and executive branches of government. In the " one-party "
states dominant party factionalism tends to undermine the possibility
of constructing the bridge. In the doubtful states where parties are
more highly organized, the fact of even party balance tends to result
in election results which split control of the two houses of the legislature and the governor's office among the two major parties. Party
bridging-of-the-gap thus becomes difficult, if not impossible in these
states. Inspection of party and legislature, writes V. O. Key, " reveals
that in a goodly proportion of American states the mechanism of government does not permit party government in the usual sense but
puts teeth into the doctrine of checks and balances by, in effect, assigning different branches of government to different parties." [23]

Political pressures on the governor's office tend to be different
from those on the legislature, and pressures on one house of the legislature may be different from those on the other. Governors are responsible to a state-wide electorate — one in which urban voters will
always cast a large proportion to the total vote. Governors, to be
elected and re-elected have to design their program for the whole
state, but particularly for the cities.

In the state legislatures, however, rural areas tend to be over-
represented and urban areas underrepresented. Generally, the seats
in state senates are apportioned to counties or on some other area
instead of population basis. California has the most extreme example
with Los Angeles County's over 5 million inhabitants having one
state senator while the three mountain counties of Alpine (241),
Inyo (2,118) and Mono (11,658) also share one state senator. Even
in the lower houses of state legislatures which are based on popula-

---

[22] *Ibid.,* pp. 203–206.
[23] V. O. Key, Jr., *Politics, Parties, and Pressure Groups* (New York:
Thomas Y. Crowell Company, 1952), p. 326.

tion, the manner in which assembly seats are apportioned tends to overweight the vote power of the rural voter in relation to the vote power of the urban voter. Because there is no effective means for compelling state legislatures to construct districts equal in population

"I Have The Same Trouble"

for houses which are supposed to be based on population, city districts can be made to include more people than rural districts.

Rural areas tend to be conservative on matters of interest to city populations, and vice versa. With rural influence dominating in at least one house of the state legislature and with huge city majorities electing the governor, the differences in constituencies of the two branches of state government are immediately apparent. Often the prevailing pattern of political party strength in the states has been one in which Democrats tend to be stronger in urban areas and Republicans stronger in rural areas. Assume for purposes of illustration, that such a pattern prevails in a state. Then, if a Republican governor is replaced by a Democrat, often neither house of the legislature follows the trend. Or, if the house based on population does respond to the gubernatorial trend, generally the county-based senate will not do so. Combined with this is the fact that most state senates elect only a proportion of their membership every two years. The possibility of the new governor's party controlling both executive and legislative branches of the state government is still further removed.

If political party considerations override urban-rural factors in a reapportionment, or if the former overlap the latter, another type of exaggeration of differences between the constituencies of governor and legislature follows. The party in control of the legislature at the time legislative districts are reapportioned tends to make its own districts safe and small and those of the opposition safe and large. Or, even if the districts are relatively equal in population, often the mere location of district boundary lines is enough to enable the observer to predict with a high degree of accuracy the number of Democrats and Republicans who will be elected. As a result, it is possible for the party in control to make itself stronger in the legislature than it would have been had the minority party done the reapportioning. Conversely, until the next reapportionment, the minority party's strength in the legislature will be weaker because it did not preside at the last reapportionment.

Because legislators of the majority party draw their district lines to enhance their chances of re-election by making their districts safer and because in concentrating their opponent's strength to also produce safe opposition districts, legislators may feel themselves freer to be more extreme Democrats or Republicans than they might otherwise dare to be. Doubtful legislative districts, on the other hand, tend to produce legislators who are more moderate in their Republicanism or Democracy. In a doubtful state, the governor, responsible to the whole state for his election, does not have a safe district. He will thus tend to be a party moderate rather than a party extremist. When a high proportion of legislators are " safe " and the governor is " not safe," gubernatorial party leadership is difficult.

Should party government on the state level be largely ineffective or nonexistent, that weakness itself has a compound effect. If the party can give the legislator no party line to follow or has little assistance for the legislator who does follow a party line at the risk of alienating important pressure group elements in his district, the legislator has of necessity to think primarily in terms of his constituency as he himself interprets it.

If a local party boss is the most powerful force behind a legislator's nomination and election, the latter will tend to give all or a large part of his allegiance to that local boss. If there is no single boss and party organization is weak in his district, the legislator is on his own — building his own power base with the interest groups on whose support he depends, raising most if not all the funds necessary for his campaign and conducting the campaigns with his own devices.

The following passage from T. V. Smith's *The Legislative Way of Life,* describing the thoughts which press in on a legislator as he makes party-versus-district decisions, is an ideal example of the problem confronting the governor when he attempts to provide party leadership. It should be noted in introducing the quotation that T. V. Smith is writing of a personal experience which occurred when he was a member of the Illinois State Senate, and it should also be noted that Illinois political parties are more highly organized than the parties of most states. Here is the passage:

> When I first ran for the legislature, I declared that I would work against forms of taxation that bear more heavily upon those least able to pay. Such a commitment during the election was destined to bear fruit that was personally bitter for me, and that shortly. Public relief was just then coming to be the heavy burden which it has since remained. The governor of my state had been driven to a sales tax as his chief reliance for relief funds. Among the early bills upon which I as a new legislator had to vote was a proposal to continue and substantially increase this tax on sales. . . .

> The governor, an honorable man, was not only my party leader, but was a man whom I had supported and who in turn had supported me. Indeed, he had of his own generosity enabled me to get the party nomination, when party elements in my own district would have kept, and but for him could have kept, me from the race. To make the personal matter as bad as possible, I must add that I was the governor's official representative in the Senate, since his home was in my district.

> His tax measure was hard pressed. He, of course, expected me to support it, as a party leader might. Indeed, he asked me to support it, as a hard-pressed man would. To make bad matters worse, it

turned out that the measure lacked one vote commanding enough support to pass. The relief situation made it imperative to have funds at once, and there was no other way to get immediate funds. The sales tax *had* to pass, and only one vote was required! I held the vote. The governor needed it. I thought it best to vote no. It was a *tough* spot, a spot in which any person in the legislature may get caught. . . .

That vote taught me that life in the legislature is not altogether one of ease. I made enemies that day who have not forgotten. Had I not committed myself during the campaign against this form of taxation, I should hardly have paid so great a price for so short-lived a virtue. . . . The process of getting elected has its own influence upon the way one lives after being elected.[24]

MORE CENTRALIZED STATE PARTIES?

The report of the American Political Science Association Committee on Political Parties suggests that there is a real need for a reexamination of the purposes and functions of state and local party organization. The present system with its multiplicity of conventions and committees lends itself to boss rule, and prominent members of the parties often, therefore, refuse to serve on party committees. State parties are not able to formulate meaningful programs " to guide their representatives and to inform the voters," and city and county party organizations are even more deficient in this respect. There should, the report continues, be a reorientation of party leaders " from preoccupation with patronage and control of offices to interest in local, state, regional and national policies." [25]

That many state political parties are organizational monstrosities cannot be denied. They were not designed to be organizationally efficient, and perhaps the very purpose behind legislation establishing state parties was just the opposite — to keep the parties inefficient as a means of tempering the power of political bosses. Can state par-

---

[24] (Chicago: The University of Chicago Press, 1940), pp. 56–59. Published under The John Findley Green Foundation lecture series and delivered at Westminster College, Fulton, Missouri. Reprinted by permission of Westminster College.

[25] Committee on Political Parties of the American Political Science Association, *Toward a More Responsible Two-Party System*, published as a supplement to *The American Political Science Review* (September, 1950), Vol. 44, No. 3. Pt. 2, pp. 44–45.

ties be reorganized and reoriented without bringing back a more powerful type of political boss? Though the objective may be a desirable one, it is not likely soon to be attained.

As long as there is political patronage, it is in the very nature of political leaders and party followers to be interested in getting it. As long as political parties continue to be primarily interested in winning elections, their " interest in local, state, regional and national policies " will tend to be placed in a position of secondary importance. To expect otherwise is to ask that the character of American major state parties be something which it is not. Though political issues are more important in state politics today than they once were, no party other than a minor party or one which in essence tends to become a pressure group can afford to forget that its first business is vote-winning. Party leaders are oriented to this system in which they must operate, otherwise they could not and would not have become party leaders. Their " reorientation " will take place only when and if the system changes first.

American state and local parties have either been dominated by a boss or a combination of a few bosses, or they have been parties in which power is highly diffused. Experience in this country has not shown that there can be centralized state major parties and at the same time major parties which are truly democratic in their operation. Given the nature of the system, the nature of the parties and the nature of the American politician who tends to place high value on individual independence, the only realistic hope for state party government lies in the ability of the governor to provide leadership and to use the weapons available to him to attempt to keep his party members in the legislature in line.

The governor, however, is not as responsible to his party as he is responsible to his state-wide electorate. The party thus becomes a device, and often it is a clumsy device, limited in its functions to helping its nominees to be elected to office. The party organization itself is not and cannot be capable of directing the operation of government. Only the governor can do that. If he is not politically able, governmental policies will be a result of a complex pattern of governor-senate-assembly relations where one branch or house may lead at one time and another at another time.

Nor is there any indication on the part of governors and legislators that they would want political parties strong enough to control governmental policy. For the governor, this would cut down the flexibility which he now has to construct an appeal to the broad base of the electorate on which his election to or continuance in office depends. The legislator's flexibility to adapt himself to his district would also be severely limited. Those active in political party organizations are not a mirror of either the governor's or a legislator's constituency. Active party members are only a very small segment of the electorate and therefore represent only a limited group's opinion. The more doctrinaire a party becomes in the stands it takes on issues, the more dangerous is that party to the electoral success of its nominees and public officeholders, and the more aloof will they tend to hold themselves from it.

Legislators pass and governors sign legislation under which state and local parties must function. Neither are likely to attempt to establish state party systems which would substantially limit their political maneuverability. Though legislation has been and is continuously being enacted to attempt to limit the excesses of political bossism, the character of state parties cannot be expected to undergo marked changes.

Governors over the period of the past fifty years have greatly strengthened their leadership positions, a movement which legislatures have tended to resist. If the states are to move closer to an ideal of party government, it will be through the further enhancement of the office of governor.

CHAPTER SEVEN

National Party Organization: The National Convention

" Once more," the special correspondent of The Times *(of London) cabled from Chicago on Sunday, " those who have confidence in the United States have the laugh on those who believe the worst of it." The American political system, so revered in its own country, has never lacked critics on this side of the Atlantic. . . . The free-for-all of an American election, designed to enable the people to choose whomsoever they will, has many times seemed only to put clowns, and worse than clowns, in high places. . . . But on the great occasions, on the supreme issues, it has the habit of doing the right thing; and if it does the right thing only at the eleventh hour, after many prophecies of disaster, it does the right thing handsomely. . . . Europeans, viewing the clumsy chaos of the nominating conventions, . . . yet resulting in the nomination of two such admirable teams as General Eisenhower and Senator Nixon, Governor Stevenson and Senator Sparkman, will be moved once more to reflect that God moves in a mysterious way his wonders to perform. . . .*

Most European political systems, confronted with a position of spiritual stalemate like this, could do little about it; preferment in politics is a matter of climbing the ladder, and when there is a vacancy at the top, the choice is limited to two or three familiar — possibly far too familiar — figures. The great strength of the American system, for all its turbulence, is that the long arm of the people's choice can go deep into the barrel and pull out the best men available — in the present case, a man who has never played a part in Federal politics, and a man who has never held elective office at all. . . .

154

*In either of these hands, the leadership of the free world is safe.
Those of us who have no votes, but whose lives and liberties yet depend
upon the policies of the United States, can settle back to watch the show
with the comfortable knowledge that we shall be able to cheer the winner
in all sincerity, whoever he may be. . . .*

The Economist, *August 2, 1952.*[1]

Political party organization may be divided into three more or
less distinct categories. First are the party delegate conventions which
assemble in election years to draft party platforms and, where permitted, to nominate party candidates for public office. Second are the
party committees to which, at least in theory, is left the conduct of
party affairs between conventions. Third is the party in government
— the party organizations in legislative bodies and in the executive
branch. On the national level of party government, the national conventions perform the first type of function, and it is they who are
the subject of this chapter. The national committees, party organizations in Congress, and the President as party chief will be considered
in the two chapters which follow.

Those who drafted the Constitution left to the Presidential electors of the several states the functions of nominating and electing the
President and Vice President of the United States. It was expected
that many states would have a favorite son, that seldom would one
man gain a majority of votes in the electoral college, and that the
choice of President and Vice President would often revert to the
House of Representatives. The framers did not foresee the development of national political parties, nominating their party candidates
for the two offices and able to dominate the selection of electors in
the several states. How little anticipated was the political party is
evident from the original Constitution's provision that the man with
the highest number of electoral votes be the President and the man
with the next highest number the Vice President.

The rise of political parties quickly rendered obsolete part of
the Constitution's Presidential nomination and election procedure.
By 1800 the Jeffersonian Republicans had so organized their party's

---

[1] Pages 265–266. Quoted by Paul T. David, Malcolm Moos, and Ralph M.
Goldman, *Presidential Nominating Politics in 1952: The National Story* (Balti-
more: The Johns Hopkins Press, 1954) , p. 232. Reprinted by permission of *The
Economist.*

electors that both Thomas Jefferson as candidate for President, and Aaron Burr, as candidate for Vice President, received the same number of electoral votes. Only because Hamilton came to the aid of Jefferson in preference to the "dangerous" Burr by persuading "lame-duck" House Federalists to vote for Jefferson, was the latter's election as chief executive assured. With the passage in September, 1804 of the Twelfth Amendment, requiring electors to vote separately for a President and Vice President, party tickets for the two offices could safely be constructed without the possibility that the wrong man might be chosen President. The Twelfth Amendment also tended to insure the election of a President and Vice President from the same party.

From Jefferson's nomination for a second term in 1804 until the late 1820's, the Congressional caucus became the formal device through which party nominations for President and Vice President were made. In a day when the only means of transportation was the horse and party members in both houses of Congress were already assembled in one place, the development was a logical one. Individual electors in each state were not in a position to make a sound choice based on national political considerations. Nor, if there was to be a party ticket, could the matter be left to unco-ordinated state selection processes. Somewhere there had to be a national party organ to make the nominations, and only in the party in Congress did such a unit — the Congressional caucus — exist.

Convenience was not the only factor to commend the Congressional party caucus. Here were the party's ablest politicians — men who knew personally the candidates for nomination; men who, if they stayed in office, would have to be responsible to their party for their choice; and men who were more likely to be national in outlook than their less traveled and politically educated party officers and members in their home states. The President would have to work with Congress, and the Congressional caucus might more successfully than some other nominating group select persons for the Presidency who would be congenial to the Congress. Here, for the time, was the most logical Presidential nominating device.

In 1808 the Republican Congressional caucus, at the urging of retiring President Jefferson, picked James Madison as its Presidential nominee. Protests already were being voiced against the system. Sidney Hyman in his *The American President* quotes a pro-Monroe Republican Congressman from Virginia:

I cannot consent, either in an individual or representative capacity, to countenance, by my presence, the midnight intrigues of any set of men who may arrogate to themselves the right, which belongs only to the people, of selecting proper persons to fill the important offices of President and Vice President. Nor do I suppose that the honest people of the United States can much longer suffer, in silence, so direct and palpable an invasion upon the most important and sacred right belonging exclusively to them.[2]

But Monroe's turn with the Congressional caucus was to come.

If in 1808 the power of the Republican Congressional caucus was a " direct and palpable invasion upon the most important and sacred right " of the people, in 1816 when Monroe was the Presidential nominee, that body's power in the Presidential selection process had doubled. Because the Federalist party was so weak that its nominee had almost no chance of election, the Republican caucus was in fact both nominating and, for all practical purposes, selecting the next President of the United States. In 1820 all Congressmen and Senators were invited to the Republican caucus, and Monroe again in effect gained re-election as a result of the caucus decision. Only after Monroe's second term did the " honest people of the United States " refuse to longer " suffer " under the power of " King Caucus." The catalytic agent in producing the change from the caucus to the convention system of making Presidential and Vice Presidential nominations was not Monroe, but Andrew Jackson.

Only some 25 percent of the Republicans in Congress participated in the 1824 Congressional caucus which accepted President Monroe's choice as his successor for the Presidential nomination — Secretary of the Treasury William H. Crawford. In competition with Crawford were Jackson, John Quincy Adams, and Henry Clay, and when for the first time popular vote totals in Presidential elections were published, Jackson was listed with the most popular votes. Jackson also received the highest number of electoral votes, but he did not have a majority and thus the House made the decision. Adams, with the help of Clay, was elected President. Clay became the Secretary of State, and Jackson supporters began a four-year campaign to undermine the Congressional caucus in preparation for the campaign of 1828.

The caucus, it was charged, had become a tool of a Congressional

---

[2] (New York: Harper and Brothers, 1954) , p. 132.

oligarchy. It was unrepresentative. The will of the people had been flouted by the House. The power of nominating candidates for the offices of President and Vice President should be closer to the people. So discredited had the Congressional caucus become by 1828 that it was used by neither of the two new political parties emerging out of the Republican one-party era. Both Jackson and John Quincy Adams were nominated by state legislatures — a transitional step to the 1832 national conventions of National Republicans and Democrats. Where in 1828 the inadequacies of the horse as a means of fast transport had seemed to debar national party conventions, by 1832 new iron horses and railroad tracks had removed what had once been the biggest barrier to national party conventions.

The quadrennial national conventions have been a fixture of American politics ever since. At their worst they have warranted the ridicule of an H. L. Mencken:

> It is instructive to observe these great men at the solemn business of selecting a First Chief for the greatest free Republic ever seen on earth. One hears, in their speeches, such imbecilities. . . . One sees them at close range, sweating, belching, munching peanuts, chasing fleas. They parade idiotically, carrying dingy flags and macerating one another's corns. They crowd the aisles, swapping gossip, most of it untrue. They devour hot dogs. They rush out to the speakeasies. They rush back to yell, fume and vote.

> The average delegate never knows what is going on. The hall is in dreadful confusion, and the speeches from the platform are mainly irrelevant and unintelligible. The real business of a national convention is done down under the stage, in dark and smelly rooms, or in hotel suites miles away. Presently a State boss fights his way out to his delegation on the floor, and tells his slaves what is to be voted on, and how they are to vote.[3]

At their best, the national conventions have many times over earned the accolade of *The Economist* printed as the introductory quotation for this chapter. Even the conventions of which Mencken wrote in 1932 produced such results as Franklin D. Roosevelt and Herbert Hoover. From " sweating, belching, peanut munching, gossip swapping " delegates and " bosses emerging from dark rooms under the stage " have also come such men as Woodrow Wilson, Charles

---

[3] *Making a President* (New York: Alfred A. Knopf, 1932), pp. 28–29. Reprinted by permission of Alfred A. Knopf.

Evans Hughes, Theodore Roosevelt, William McKinley, William Jennings Bryan, Grover Cleveland and Abraham Lincoln.

THE DELEGATES [4]

In the first national conventions the new voice of party democracy was not always as representative as it should have been. Jackson managers, intent on securing the Democratic nomination for Martin Van Buren of New York in 1836, were able to secure a unanimous vote for their man from a convention packed with federal job-holders and so irregularly apportioned among the twenty-two states and two territories represented that two thirds of the total convention delegates came from Virginia, New Jersey, Maryland, and Pennsylvania. From critics of the new national nominating procedure " there was a cry that the old caucus system had been revived in a worse form than the original, in that timeservers had replaced legislators as the main actors." So " informal " were procedures that when a Tennessean in Baltimore learned there were no delegates from his state, he was admitted to the floor and voted Tennessee's 15 votes for Van Buren — 15 votes from an anti-Van Buren state which had no delegation present.[5]

From the time of the formation of the Republican party until 1916, both major parties allotted to each state two national convention votes for each United States Senator and Congressman. For the Democratic party such a uniform system of apportionment worked satisfactorily. For the Republican party, frozen out of any chance to win states in the Democratic Solid South, it did not.

What happened at the Republican National Convention of 1912 which nominated William Howard Taft, largely because he had the solid backing of southern state Republican federal patronage machines, finally forced Republicans to produce a more representative national convention. In the states which had held Republican Presidential preference primaries, Roosevelt won nine and Taft only one. With Taft's nomination, Roosevelt Progressives bolted their party. In the Wilson victory of 1912 — a Democratic victory only by the grace of the Republican split — Roosevelt ran far ahead of Taft. If Republican national conventions were to approximate Republican

---

[4] Principal source for this section was David, Moos, and Goldman, *op cit.,* Chap. 5.

[5] From Hyman, *op. cit.,* pp. 143–144.

party strength in the states, some kind of discriminatory bonus system of convention vote apportionment was needed.

In 1916 Republican delegates were apportioned four at large to each state and one for each Congressional district. In addition, for each Congressional district in which the Republican nominee for President had received 7,500 votes in the last Presidential election, the state would gain an additional delegate. Under the 1916 rule, as compared with the 1912 rule, for example, a southern Democratic " one-party " state with five Congressmen was now entitled to only nine delegates where before it had fourteen. In subsequent years Republicans have raised even higher the party-support test for national convention delegate apportionment to the states.

In 1952 Republicans allotted no convention votes to Congressional districts in which the Republican vote for President in 1948 had been below 1,000. If a Congressional district had cast between 1,000 and 10,000 votes for the Republican ticket in 1948, then it would get one delegate, and only if the vote had been over 10,000 would the state party be entitled to two delegates for each Congressional district. Furthermore, if a state had been carried by Dewey in 1948 or had recently elected a Republican United States Senator or governor, it was entitled to six bonus delegates. For the 1956 Republican National Convention, the delegate apportionment scheme was slightly altered again. Instead of the 1,000 Republican Presidential-vote minimum before a Congressional district would be entitled to one delegate, the figure was raised to 2,000. Only if a Congressional district comprises the entire state do Republicans automatically award two convention votes for that House seat.

For the 1952 Democratic National Convention delegates were apportioned to the states as follows: two convention votes for each United States Senator and Congressman, and four bonus votes for those states which the Democratic Presidential nominee had carried in the preceding Presidential election. The Democratic move to the bonus system came first in 1944 when a bonus of two was set, and at the 1948 convention (for 1952) when it was increased to four. On November 19, 1955 the Democratic National Committee, operating under authority granted to it by the 1952 Democratic National Convention, further expanded its bonus incentives. Four extra convention votes for 1956 were also apportioned to states which had elected a Democratic governor or a Democratic United States Senator since 1952. In computing Democratic national convention votes for each state for 1956, however, it is necessary to note also that the Democratic National Committee also provided that no state should have less than its 1952 vote strength regardless of the application of the apportionment formula.

For purposes of summarizing the Democratic and Republican national convention apportionment rules in force for 1956 conventions, California will be entitled to the following delegations:

I. For the Democrats
   4 votes at large for two United States Senators
   o votes at large because no Congressmen are elected at large
  60 votes for California's 30 Congressional districts
   o bonus votes because California did not go for Stevenson in 1952 nor has it elected a Democratic governor or Senator since 1952
   4 votes because California did go for Truman in 1948 and thus had the bonus in 1952
  ___
  68 California votes in the Democratic National Convention of 1956

II. For the Republicans
   4 votes at large for two United States Senators
   o votes at large because no California Congressmen are elected at large
  60 votes for California's 30 Congressional districts, each of which gave Eisenhower more than 10,000 votes in 1952
   6 bonus votes for any one of the following three reasons:
       (1) California's electoral votes went to Eisenhower in 1952;
       (2) California elected a Republican United States Senator in 1954;
       (3) California elected a Republican governor in 1954
  ___
  70 California votes in the Republican National Convention of 1956

Though Republican national conventions will seat only full-vote delegates, Democrats admit oversize delegations and permit their members to cast fractions of one vote. For the Democratic National Convention of 1956 there can be a maximum of 2,744 delegates and 1,372 votes, and a maximum of 1,896 alternates. For the Republican National Convention of 1956, 1,323 delegates and the same number of alternates are authorized.

Though it might be said that each state has its own particular method of chosing delegates to the Democratic and Republican national conventions because no state's procedure is exactly like another, it is possible to roughly distinguish two main types of procedure — the Presidential primary and the convention system. Some states combine both primary and convention, selecting a portion of their delegates with one device and another portion with the other. In a few cases neither a primary or convention is used, and delegates may be selected by state central committees.

In 1952 fourteen states had Presidential primaries for both major parties. Only two of the fourteen, California and South Dakota, elected at-large and Congressional district delegates on a consolidated ballot by state-wide vote. New Hampshire, Massachusetts, New Jersey, West Virginia, Ohio, Wisconsin, Nebraska, and Oregon elected delegates-at-large by state-wide primary vote and Congressional district delegates by Congressional district primary votes. In New York, Pennsylvania, Illinois, and Minnesota at-large delegates were selected by state party conventions or committees and Congressional district delegates by Congressional district primaries. In Alabama, Florida, and the District of Columbia primary elections were used only by the Democratic party in 1952.[6]

How complicated is the attempt to generalize about even the states using the Presidential primary is further revealed when these states are classified according to the degree by which the state tries to relate the delegate-selection process to particular candidates for the Presidential nominations. In Wisconsin, Minnesota, South Dakota, and California in 1952 the voter could, by making a single mark on his ballot, vote for his choice for Presidential nominee and a slate of delegates favoring that nominee. At the opposite extreme are six Presidential primary states — New York, Pennsylvania, West Virginia, Alabama, Illinois, and Nebraska — in which candidates for delegate run only on their own name and may not have their preference for Presidential nominees indicated on the ballot. In an intermediate classification, Florida, New Hampshire, Massachusetts, and New Jersey have candidates for national convention delegate positions with their nominee preferences noted on the ballot, and in separate squares there is also the opportunity for the voter to vote directly on the candidates for their party Presidential nomination whose names have been entered in that state.

---

[6] From David, Moos, and Goldman, *op. cit.*, p. 162.

The Presidential primary may be used both to choose national convention delegates and to indicate the relative strength of the several candidates for each party's Presidential nomination. Some of the systems serve the former purpose well. In the words of the authors of the American Political Science Association research project which studied Presidential nominating politics in 1952:

> All of the primaries produced delegations that were seated without any questions being raised as to their credentials. Most of the delegations produced in primaries were reasonably representative groups that in the end were probably able to give expression to the will of their constituencies, even when there was some reason to suspect that their constituents might have been burdened by afterthoughts between the scattered dates of the primaries and the actual holding of the national conventions.[7]

Not as much can be said for the reliability of Presidential preference primaries as indices of actual strength of candidates for Presidential nominations. In few states are the names of all active candidates for party Presidential nomination on the ballot, and seldom is there a head-on contest between principal contenders. A disastrous defeat in a state primary might well upset a candidate's careful build-up to his national convention. If a state has a favorite son, few are the other candidates who will permit their names to be filed in opposition in his state.

In 1952 Stevenson took no part in state Presidential preference primaries. In 1944 neither did Dewey, and in 1940 neither did Willkie. Yet all were eventually nominated. In 1952 the ground swell of popular support evident for General Eisenhower in such primaries as those of New Hampshire and Minnesota, the latter by write-in voting, was an essentially accurate measure of his popularity, and helped Eisenhower managers engineer their candidate successfully past the candidacy of Robert A. Taft. Dewey in 1948 was likewise helped, particularly by his victory in Oregon over Harold E. Stassen.

In only a very few of the Presidential preference primary states where voting for Presidential candidates is possible is an attempt made to bind the delegates from the state to the popular primary election choice. There is good reason for this. Perhaps by national convention time, the candidate winning a state's vote is not a realistic contender

---

[7] Ibid., p. 185.

for the nomination, or he may not have been a realistic choice at the time of the primary. After the first national convention ballot, a state delegation cannot and should not be inflexibly bound to a decision which no longer may have meaning. About all instructions to a delegation can mean is that the delegation support the state's popular

Man Of The Hour

choice as long as he has a chance — a very elastic requirement at its unenforceable best.

Should all or a majority of the states employ Presidential preference primaries and bind their state delegations to the decision, the national convention would tend to lose its flexibility. Clumsy though the national conventions may be, " that long arm of the people's choice," in the words of *The Economist*, " can go deep into the barrel and pull out the best men available." Had they been forced through an unpredictable mill of Presidential preference primaries and been faced with the inevitable prospect of serious fights in most of the states, perhaps neither Eisenhower nor Stevenson would have consented to be candidates for their respective nominations in 1952.

Delegates, yes even state bosses, generally are good judges of the qualities which make a man an electable Presidential nominee. The major parties tend to resist a system which would bind the national convention to a Presidential nominee who might temporarily be in the public spotlight, but one who may have neither the qualities of a good candidate nor exhibit promise as a successful President of the United States.

This is not to suggest that the existing Presidential preference primaries do not perform a useful function. They do. First comes the New Hampshire primary; then follow the primaries of Minnesota, Wisconsin, Illinois, New Jersey, Massachusetts, Pennsylvania, Maryland, Indiana — and so on through the pre-national convention season. A very rough pattern of relative candidate strength sometimes does develop through the series of primaries, and when it does, a national convention is put on warning against what might otherwise be a tendency to nominate a " party regular " and " safe " man without broad appeal. The existing primaries also give to the candidates who are not a part of the inner party circle an opportunity to exhibit their wares and to attempt to create a demand for their services. Sometimes in such primaries real intraparty divisions on domestic or foreign policy issues come into the open to make the rank and file of the party more aware of the stakes they have in the different candidates for nomination and in time for the rank and file to create popular pressures on those who will make the final decision.

Approximately one third of the delegates to Democratic and Republican national conventions are chosen in primaries; the remainder are elected by state party conventions or by state central committees. Again, state laws in the nonprimary states are a jungle of variations. Generally the convention process begins with the precinct party organization selecting delegates to a county convention which, in turn, selects delegates to Congressional district conventions where Congressional district delegates to the national convention are elected. The Congressional district conventions may then select delegates to the state convention where at-large delegates to the national convention are picked. Here, as in states with Presidential primaries, there is opportunity, if the rank-and-file party member sees fit to use it, for participating in the Presidential nominating process.

Or, perhaps delegates to the state party convention are selected by county or local party committees, as occurred in Rhode Island, Michigan, North Dakota, Montana, Wyoming, and Idaho in 1952. In states such as these, or in those where state central committees choose national convention delegates, rank-and-file party members have little opportunity to influence the final national convention result. In 1952 the Georgia, Arkansas, Louisiana, and Arizona Democratic state committees chose national convention delegates, and in Arizona and Florida the Republican national convention delegations were selected in the same way.

CONVENTION PRELIMINARIES

Before the national convention delegate-selection process begins, the national committee will have decided upon the convention site. Other things being equal, the city which has an adequate convention hall and which bids the highest guarantee for financing a national convention is the one selected. But sometimes other things are not equal, and the choice of convention site may hinge on political factors. With Alfred E. Smith, a wet and a Catholic, in 1928 the apparent Democratic nominee, Democrats journeyed to Houston, Texas, in the southern land of drys and Protestants. In 1956 a major reason for Republican selection of San Francisco, in addition to the Golden Gate city's salubrious summer climate, was the desire to make Republican decisions in a moderate political environment. At the time Republicans chose San Francisco, the coals of the McCarthy controversy were still warm, and Chicago, the most likely alternate, was one of the centers of McCarthy strength. Also, moderate Republicans, as they contemplated Chicago's bid for 1956, could not forget the vitriolic attacks of the *Chicago Tribune* when Eisenhower was nominated in 1952.

At the time the national committee selects the convention city, it also designates the time when the convention shall meet. In the past Republicans have generally convened during June. Democrats, except for three occasions in the last half of the nineteenth century, have met shortly after the Republican National Convention. In 1956, both in the order of the Democratic and Republican conventions and the months of meeting, past patterns were altered. Campaigns in the age of television have become so expensive and the new medium is so well adapted to permitting a candidate to present his case in a shorter period of time that logic and problems of finance have dictated shorter national campaigns. Republicans in 1956 set their national convention for August 20, as late as deadlines for placing Presidential and Vice Presidential nominees' names on all the states' ballots permitted. Democrats, who have had the advantage of the last national convention word for many years, met in Chicago on August 13.

With the site and date settled, the national committee issues its call, notifying the state and territorial parties of the pending national convention, of the number of delegates apportioned to each state, and of the general rules under which delegates are to be selected, if not provided otherwise in state law. The state delegations are then chosen, advance agents of the national committee finally move to the convention city to make sure all is ready, delegates at the appointed time converge on the convention city, and once again a national convention is about to start.

ORGANIZATION AND PROCEDURE

When the convention first convenes, the chairman of the party's national committee serves as presiding officer. He will call the convention to order. The national anthem will be sung to the accompaniment of the convention hall organ and a powerful voiced soprano or baritone. The convention chaplain will lead in prayer. The call will be read by the secretary of the national committee. The mayor of the convention city will throw open the arms of civic hospitality. Perhaps the governor of the convention state, if he is of that party or a not too " reprehensible " member of the opposition, will be called upon to wax on the glories of his state. The national chairman will then attempt to produce the first real convention flames of partisan enthusiasm in his opening address. Whether he succeeds in this objective or not, he will also submit to the assembled delegates the national committee's recommendation for temporary chairman. The convention will almost always approve the recommendation by acclamation.

In the evening of the first day the temporary chairman or keynoter is given the opportunity to rise to what should be the highest oratorical heights of the convention as he issues his call to arms. For the party convention of the party out of power, in the words of Sidney Hyman, the keynote is a part of a process of " symbolic mayhem performed in ritualistic dances. Incense is burned and celestial bells are struck. An elaborate jingle of verbal insults is aimed at the President and those close to him. The broadest flourish comes at the moment when the keynote speaker rises before the nominating convention. . . . First he whets his axe on the grindstone of several thousand fire-spouting words. Then, while his audience shouts its ecstasy, he chops off the head of the President." [8] Or, for the party in power, the 1944 theme of Democratic keynoter Robert S. Kerr of Oklahoma would have a familiar ring to any hypothetical man fortunate or unfortunate enough to have heard all in-party national convention keynotes:

> We have stormed the beaches of poverty and discouragement and fear, and seen the hearts of the people filled with new life, lifted with new hope and buoyant with superb confidence. We have overrun the ramparts of special privilege and reaction and planted the banner of Democratic liberalism high on the hill of human progress. Let our opponents, who have grown fat in a prosperity they could not build for themselves, do their worst. Under our great Commander in Chief we will not retreat! We will not falter in mid-passage! We will win! [9]

Except for the mayor of the convention city and perhaps the secretary of the national committee, every one of these participants from chaplain to keynoter will have been chosen to some degree for reasons not unrelated to the political position and problems of the party. The chaplain is likely to be one who has to some extent identified himself with the party. For Republicans, he will be a Protestant; for Democrats, he may be a Catholic. In any event, he will not come from a small-in-membership religious sect but from one of the larger church bodies. And for the remaining major church groups, clergymen from each may be called upon to offer the opening prayer at subsequent sessions.

Nor will quality of voice and technique necessarily control in the designation of convention song leaders and soloists. Some may be big names in the entertainment field who, by their participation, it is hoped, may induce apolitical music fans to support that party. Over the course of several convention sessions musicians from major social or racial groups will have been in the national party spotlight long

---

[8] Hyman, *op. cit.,* p. 84.

[9] Quoted by Hugh A. Bone, *American Politics and the Party System* (New York: McGraw Hill Book Company, 1955), p. 424.

enough for the members of their groups to know that one of their own had played a national convention role.

The national chairman of the party in power comes to the national convention as first the agent of the President who chose him and only secondarily as a national party official. The national chairman of the party out of power is the national committee's apostle of party unity serving out his last days as party chairman before being replaced by the campaign manager of the successful candidate for the party's Presidential nomination. Keynoters for both parties are in a position similar to that of the out-party national chairman. They too will be replaced soon — the next morning, in fact, by the permanent convention chairman. They too are supposed to keynote for the whole party, and they too are expected to state only the minimum positions on which the vast majority of the party is united.

Generally the keynoter will be one who is not himself a candidate for Presidential or Vice Presidential nomination, or one who is not a serious contender. He will also probably be one who has not committed himself to any of the contesting candidates. The possibility always exists that a keynoter could put on a performance such as William Jennings Bryan did in his " Cross of Gold " keynote at the 1896 Democratic National Convention and stampede the convention into nominating himself or the candidate he might support. Unless the national convention is to renominate an incumbent President, the national committee attempts to pick a neutral keynote speaker.

In addition to his neutrality, the keynoter should possess a combination of other qualities. He should be a lively speaker. A national convention gets off to a dull start if he is not. He should be partisan in a party sense. He should in his person serve some political purpose. Perhaps that purpose is to enable the party to give a favorable impression of itself on some point which it fears it has been " misrepresented " to the public. An example of this kind of availability might be the selection of Governor Harold E. Stassen of Minnesota to keynote the 1940 Republican National Convention. Of Stassen's selection, Raymond Clapper wrote: " Governor Stassen, a young, vigorous, new figure . . . inclined toward a moderate liberal course, and immensely popular in Minnesota . . . is exactly the personality to dramatize the rejuvenation which Republicans think they are undergoing." [10]

---

[10] *St. Paul Pioneer Press,* April 19, 1940.

Perhaps the party is in low spirits and needs a " grand old man " of the party to attempt to readjust perspectives or soften with humor intraparty tensions. Such was the role appointed for Alben Barkley at the Democratic National Convention of 1948. Or, perhaps an extremist wing of the party needs pacifying without major concessions being made, and a party takes the risk of giving the hero of such a wing its keynote spot. Such was a reason for General MacArthur's selection as Republican keynoter in 1952.

If not at the first session, then on the second day of the convention, the chairman of each state and territorial delegation will be asked to submit his list of the persons from his state or territory to serve on the four standing committees of the convention — credentials, permanent organization, rules, and platform and resolutions. These recommendations will later be ratified by official convention action. General practice is to seat one person from each delegation on each of the first three committees, and one man and one woman from each delegation on the platform committee. And as the committees are hard at their work, on the convention floor there is a parade of party speakers — Senators, governors, Congressmen.

In normal order of business, the first of the four convention committees to report is the credentials committee. After examining the credentials of the several delegations, the committee will recommend to the whole convention who should or who should not be seated and thus be entitled to participate in convention business. Generally there are few contests, and the report is quickly adopted by those delegates who have been certified on the temporary roll of delegates as prepared by the national committee. If such is the case, the convention moves next to the report of the committee on permanent organization containing that committee's recommendations for permanent officers of the convention. If contests over the seating of some state delegations are long and the credentials committee report is delayed, however, Republicans proceed to permanent organization as a first order of business.

When there is a close contest over the Presidential nomination and should a significant number of delegate seats be contested, what happens at the credentials-determining stage of the convention may well settle who the nominee will be. The classic illustration occurred in the Republican National Convention of 1912. With the race between President Taft and Theodore Roosevelt promising to be very close, the Taft-controlled Republican National Committee, in preparing its temporary roll of delegates, settled every dispute between the two contending sides in favor of Taft supporters. If Roosevelt had been able to have seated some fifty disputed delegates pledged to him — and by most nonpartisan observers it was felt they rightfully should have been seated — Roosevelt could have controlled the convention. Yet by virtue of their majority of delegates on the temporary roll, Taft forces were able on every disputed delegation to keep the Roosevelt partisans out.

For the Republicans the parallel at the credentials approving stage between the conventions of 1912 and 1952 was striking. When in 1952 the customary motion was made to adopt the rules of the previous national convention until the report of the committee on rules could be received and acted upon, Governor Arthur B. Langlie of Washington — leaning to Eisenhower — offered a substitute motion. It would bar delegations from Georgia, Louisiana, and Texas, which had been placed on the temporary roll by the Robert A. Taft controlled national committee, from voting in convention or committee until the whole convention had decided whether to seat the Taft or the Eisenhower delegations from those states. The Langlie resolution carried by a 658 to 548 vote.

More interesting than the proceedings on the floor of the Republican National Convention of 1952 on its second day were the televised hearings of the credentials committee. That committee recommended upholding the national committee's recommendation to seat the pro-Taft delegation from Georgia (17 convention votes). Taft forces surprisingly conceded the Louisiana dispute to the Eisenhower delegation from that state (13 votes). On Texas, the committee voted to seat 22 Taft and 16 Eisenhower delegates.

Action now shifted to the convention floor, and one of the most dramatic moments of the convention followed — the debate between United States Senator Everett Dirksen of Illinois for the Taft side of the Georgia delegation dispute and Washington State Senator Donald Eastvold for the Eisenhower groups. By a 601 to 531 vote, the pro-Eisenhower delegation was seated. The recommendation of the credentials committee on Louisiana delegates was accepted, and before the committee's recommendation on Texas delegates came to a vote, Taft forces defaulted and a 38-man Eisenhower delegation from Texas was seated. On the Langlie resolution and the Georgia delegation contest, Taft's candidacy had suffered severe setbacks. For Taft another roll-call defeat on the Texas delegation issue would have been to risk irreparable damage by helping Eisenhower partisans create the illusion of an Eisenhower bandwagon before delegates straining to be on the winning side.

If the 1952 Republican battle over credentials was hectic, that of the Democratic National Convention of that year was even more so. Nor did the Democratic fight terminate early in the convention, but it continued through and into the Presidential nominating proceedings. In an attempt to prevent another Dixiecrat revolt of 1948, United States Senator Blair Moody of Michigan, chairman of the rules committee, on the first day of the convention secured passage of a " loyalty oath " resolution which read in part:

> No delegate shall be seated unless he shall give assurance to the Credentials Committee that he will exert every honorable means available to him . . . to provide that the nominees of the convention for President and Vice President, through their name or the names of the electors pledged to them, appear on the election ballot under the heading, name or designation of the Democratic party.[11]

Much of the 1952 Democratic convention debate concerned the question of whether the Virginia, South Carolina, and Louisiana delegations had submitted satisfactory oaths. Finally, as nominations were being made, the issue could no longer be postponed. After a roll call so disordered that the correct vote was not determined until the official proceedings appeared a year later, and after it had seemed that the convention would refuse to permit the three state delegations to participate, they were accepted. For a credentials fight to drag on through much of an entire convention was most unusual. The Democratic credentials disputes were not, however, decisive in swinging the Presidential nomination to one candidate or another.

After the reports of the credentials committee and of the committee on permanent organization have been acted upon, the convention next proceeds to the report of the committee on rules. Its recommendations may include temporary rules for the particular convention, or rules of a more permanent nature.

Such matters as order of business, apportionment of delegates for future conventions, or convention procedure are within the jurisdiction of the committee on rules. The principal activity of the Democratic rules committee in 1952 was the Moody " loyalty oath " resolu-

---

[11] Quoted by David, Moos, and Goldman, *op. cit.,* p. 125.

tion. It did not, however, recommend a permanent rule on the subject to the convention.

Where Democratic national conventions " proceed on a sort of common law basis handed down in lore quadrennially compiled in Clarence Cannon's *Democratic Manual*," [12] Republican national conventions are more formal in considering and adopting rules. In 1952 rules committee recommendations adopted by the Republican convention included making the Langlie resolution a permanent convention rule, regulating the manner of calling precinct and county conventions, changing the procedure by which contests over delegations should be heard by the national committee when it prepares the temporary roll of convention delegates, and adding Republican state chairmen to the national committee for such states as gave the Republican Presidential nominee their electoral votes at the last Presidential election, those having a majority of Republicans over Democrats from their state in Congress, or having a Republican governor.[13]

THE PLATFORM

From the Democratic platform of 1952:

> For twenty years, under the dedicated guidance of Franklin Delano Roosevelt and Harry S. Truman, our country has moved steadily along the road which has led the United States of America to world leadership in the cause of freedom.

From the Republican platform of 1952:

> We assert that during the last twenty years, leaders of the Government of the United States under successive Democratic Administrations, and especially under the present Administration, have failed to perform . . . basic duties; but, on the contrary, that they have evaded them, flouted them, and by a long succession of vicious acts, so undermined the foundations of our Republic as to threaten its existence.

From the Democrats, again:

> An objective appraisal of the past record clearly demonstrates that the Democratic Party has been the chosen American instrument to

---

[12] *Ibid.*, p. 86.   [13] See *ibid.*, pp. 86–90.

achieve prosperity, build a stronger democracy, erect the structure of world peace, and continue on the path of progress.

From the Republicans, again:

For twenty years the Administration has praised free enterprise while actually wrecking it. . . . We charge that they work unceasingly to achieve their goal of national socialism. . . . The present Administration, in seven years, has squandered the unprecedented power and prestige which were ours at the close of World War II.

From the Democrats, again:

Democratic policies and programs rescued American agriculture from the consequences of blight, drought, flood and storm, from oppressive and indiscriminate foreclosures, and from the ruinous conditions brought about by the bungling incompetence and neglect of the preceding twelve years of Republican mal-administration.

From the Republicans, again:

We charge the present Administration with seeking to destroy the farmers' freedom.

From the Democrats, again:

Under the guidance, protection, and help of Almighty God we shall succeed in bringing to the people of this Nation a better and more rewarding life, and to the peoples of the entire world, new hope and a lasting, honorable peace.

From the Republicans, again:

. . . [T]he Republican Party stands confident that it expresses the hopes of the citizens of America and certain that it points out with integrity a road upon which free men may march into a new day — a new and better day — in which shall be fulfilled the decent aspirations of our people for peace, for solvency and for the fulfillment of our best welfare, under the guidance of Divine Providence.

Such are the products of national convention platform-making processes. Though platforms do contain declarations more definite than these excerpts from the 1952 platforms, in general the quotations are not unrepresentative of the whole documents. Exaggeration is the order of the day. The platforms are generally too long to be serviceable as campaign documents, and too long or regarded as too meaningless to be read by many. It is the character, record, and state-

ments of the Presidential nominee and not the party platforms by
which the parties are judged in Presidential campaign years. Nevertheless, more actual committee working time is spent on the platform
than any other convention activity, and more leading Senators, Congressmen, and other party leaders serve on the platform committee
than on any other committee.

A week or two ahead of the national convention, a subcommittee
of the full platform and resolutions committee will meet in the convention city to conduct hearings. Before such a group, or later before
such subcommittees as are set up on civil rights, foreign affairs, labor,
and other important political issue areas, will appear the representatives of major and minor pressure groups. Each spokesman will seek
to have the party draft a plank in the field of its interest in compli-
ance with its demands. Many of the platform committee members
will have their own ideas or bring the ideas of their state party leaders
as to what should be included in the platform. Perhaps a subcommittee will have a distinguished consultant working with it, as did John
Foster Dulles with the 1952 Republican subcommittee on foreign
relations.

When all the data have been gathered and all those who are to
be heard have been given their opportunity to speak, the subcommittee writes its part of the platform. Some subcommittees will find little
disagreement among their members, and their job will be done
quickly. Others, such as is always the case with civil rights subcommittees with both northern and southern members on them, will
draft and compromise until the pressures of the convention demand
that they conclude their labors. The subcommittee report goes to the
full platform and resolutions committee, and the recommendations
are either accepted or further compromised. This is standard operating procedure for the party which does not have a President. For the
party that does control the Presidency, usually it is he who determines
what shall go into the planks on which he has strong opinions. The
committee recommendation then goes to the convention floor where
sometimes the entire platform may be adopted with no debate, but
where at other times an issue might split a convention down to its
very foundations.

The most famous recent floor fight over a highly controversial
platform plank took place in the 1948 Democratic National Convention on the issue of civil rights. As the plank emerged from the platform and resolutions committee, its compromised character was ac-

ceptable to neither the more extreme " civil rights " northerners nor " states rights " southerners. Substitutes proposed by the latter group were voted down by the convention. " Civil rights " forces, led by Hubert H. Humphrey of Minnesota, offered a specific civil rights program and indorsed President Truman's civil rights policies. This resolution, when forced to a vote, narrowly gained passage. As a result, part of the Alabama delegation and all of the Mississippi delegation left the convention.

In essence the conflict was between two sectional groups, each representing what it felt was the necessary and proper position of the party on this issue in its section. Here in action was one of the major forces tending to make United States major parties as broad-based and compromising as they are. Seldom do national conventions get so " out of control " that party unity is risked in floor fights over platform planks. Nomination battles enough are yet to come.

The report of the American Political Science Association's Committee on Political Parties, *Toward a More Responsible Two-Party System,* made several recommendations for improving platform-making procedures.[14] First, national platforms should be formulated every two years instead of every four years. With party leaders, however, sometimes every four years seems too often. At the two-year midpoint between Presidential elections, the parties tend to resist going officially on record. The Congressmen and Senators up for re-election then prefer the freedom of their own platforms and do not want to be bound to any potentially embarrassing national party policy, particularly when there is no possibility of any help from a Presidential nominee.

Second, local party meetings, it was also recommended, should be held regularly " for the discussion and consideration of platform proposals." Yet local party clubs which confine themselves to the academics of public issues generally do not last long. Such local party activity is also generally discouraged by legislators and elected executives who would rather have large and social-activity motivated clubs which can supply precinct workers in quantity in campaigns and which can rationalize and propagandize for the policies which the party's legislators and elected executives establish. A party club tenaciously trying to hold party candidates for public office to the club's conception of what should be party program can severely limit the

---

[14] P. 56.

candidate's ability to develop broad appeal to win votes from the opposition party as well as from his own.

Third, the Committee on Political Parties recommended that state party conventions should withhold platform declarations until after the national platform has been adopted, that the state conventions should attempt to confine their platform planks to state and local matters, that the national platforms should " emphasize general party principles and national issues," and that state parties should consider national platforms binding on them. If the American major parties were national parties, this might be the manner in which the platform-making and platform-interpreting process would work. But the major parties are not national parties. Sectional and subsectional pressures in politics, though they may appear to be decreasing in force, are still strong. Consider, for example, the continuing conflict over civil rights questions, particularly within the Democratic party, and attempt to visualize southern states accepting a strong national civil rights plank. Or, take as examples the 1952 campaign issue of returning tidelands to the states, or public versus private power development, or other questions with real sectional alignments.

Fourth, it is recommended that the parties prepare their preliminary platform drafts in advance of their national conventions. As the report notes, both parties now have their platform committees or subcommittees thereof meeting before their national conventions. Republicans have occasionally established independent pre-convention platform study or policy commissions. This fourth recommendation is most likely to gain acceptance by the party out of power searching for a way to get back into power. Whenever such a committee attempts to be a policy committee by stating what in its opinion its party stands for, however, it runs into trouble and repudiation. For the party in power, its President and his program are party policy.

NOMINATIONS

After the adoption of the platform, the national convention is ready to transact its main business — the selection of its nominee for the office of President of the United States. Nominating procedure begins with the alphabetical call of the roll of states, Alabama coming first. Alabama, because it has been a " safe " Democratic state, will not have a serious contender for the Presidential nomination in either Democratic or Republican national conventions. Practice has been for the Alabama delegation to either pass or, more often, yield to the state delegation of the man who has been selected to make the nominating speech for the candidate which the Alabama delegation favors. In the 1952 Republican National Convention Alabama yielded to Illinois, and so United States Senator Everett Dirksen's nomination

Smoke Filled Room

of Senator Robert A. Taft came before the nominations of California's Earl Warren, Eisenhower, and MacArthur. In the 1952 Democratic National Convention Alabama yielded to Georgia, whose Senator Walter George nominated his fellow Georgian, Senator Richard Russell. Alaska yielded to Tennessee for Senator Estes Kefauver's nomination, and so on until all candidates had been nominated.

After each oratorically impassioned nominating speech concludes with the name of the man who can save the party, the United States, and the world comes the traditional demonstration. At the signal, delegate supporters leap to their feet and the doors to the convention floor are thrown open to nondelegate supporters who can be mobilized to bring the demonstration up to respectable size. With the organ blaring, noise machines whirling, and demonstrators yelling and holding high their signs, the march around the convention floor proceeds. Each side has dreamed a " Walter Mitty " dream that its candidates name will arouse such a spark of enthusiasm that the entire convention, in spite of the fact that it contains supporters of other candidates, will rise and demonstrate for hours, carried away by the impelling logic of supporting that side's candidate. Demonstrations, however, don't often produce that result, and after the first few minutes cannot even maintain good theatrical effect.

When order has been restored after each demonstration, a series of seconding speeches will follow. Though they are shorter than the nominating speech, their theme is the same. And, as the nominator has been chosen for his strategic position in one of the large state delegations or because by the honor accorded to him he might swing over some critical and doubtful delegation, those picked to make seconding speeches are named for similar reasons.

When the roll call of states for placing candidate's names for nomination before the convention is concluded, the balloting ensues. In both Democratic and Republican conventions a majority of all the delegates is needed to nominate. Though Republicans have always operated under such a rule, Democrats have not. Until the Democratic convention of 1940, the Democratic party had required two-thirds majorities to nominate, with the result that more ballots were usually necessary at Democratic conventions than at Republican conventions. In 1924, for example, Davis was not nominated until the 103rd ballot.

Principal support for the two-thirds rule came from southern Democrats. Through the requirement, they were in a position to almost always force the nomination of one who would be an acceptable compromise to the delegations from the Solid Democratic South. When the two-thirds rule was abolished at the 1936 Democratic convention, southerners acquiesced in the change — for a price. In return, they got a bonus rule similar to the one which had been adopted by the Republicans. Four additional delegates would be added to the Democratic delegation from each state that had given its electoral votes to the Democratic nominee in the preceding Presidential election.

Democratic and Republican voting procedures differ in one respect today. If a state delegation comes to a Democratic national convention instructed to operate under a " unit rule," in which the entire delegation's vote is to be cast as the majority of that delegation decide, the convention will not recognize split voting from such a delegation. Republican national conventions always accept split delegation voting regardless of the instructions under which a state delegation may be operating.

If a party's President is a candidate for renomination, usually he will carry on the first ballot. If an active pre-convention contest has taken place, not infrequently the winner is selected also on the first ballot. So it was with Eisenhower's nomination in 1952. At the conclusion of the first ballot roll call, Eisenhower had 595 votes, Taft 500, Warren 81, Stassen 20, and MacArthur 10. To win, 614 were necessary, and before the vote could be announced, Minnesota switched from Stassen to Eisenhower and the resulting stampede culminated in a joint motion by Senator William Knowland of California (for Warren) and Senator John Bricker of Ohio (for Taft) to make the vote unanimous.

Stevenson won his 1952 nomination on the third ballot. On the first, Kefauver led with 340, and he was followed by Stevenson with 273, Russell 268, Harriman 123½, Kerr, 65, and Barkley 48½. Principal development of the second ballot was the shift of Kerr's 65 votes, and over-all Stevenson had picked up 50 additional votes and Barkley 30. Kefauver now had 362½ and Stevenson 324½. Before the third ballot, Harriman of New York announced for Stevenson, and as soon as the third ballot began the Democratic stampede of 1952 was on.

Anticlimactic to the nomination of the party's Presidential candidate is the selection of his running mate. Balloting for the Vice Presidential nomination is largely a formality — to ratify the choice of the head of the ticket. Where one set of " availability " factors applies in choosing the Presidential nominee (to be discussed in Chapter Seventeen), another set almost entirely dependent on the characteristics of the Presidential nominee's political appeal comes into play.

Always an attempt is made to " balance the ticket," both in terms of geography and shades of political philosophy within the party. And if possible, both nominees should be from large and doubtful pivot states whose electoral votes may be decisive in November. Eisenhower came from New York and his nomination campaign was engineered by the Dewey organization; Nixon come from California, and was a man calculated to appeal to a degree to conservative Republicans who might feel strained to support an Eisenhower candidacy. If Republicans had nominated Taft for the Vice Presidency in 1952, it would have been because it was felt an even stronger counterbalance to Eisenhower was necessary to hold the party together. Stevenson came from the pivot state of Illinois, and Sparkman from Alabama. Though Alabama is no pivot state, it was felt southern Democrats needed a special form of political bait, and Sparkman appeared to be most acceptable to both northern and southern wings of the party. Dewey of New York and Warren of California, and Truman of Missouri and Barkley of Kentucky were the two tickets in 1948; Dewey and Bricker of Ohio, and Roosevelt and Truman, in 1944; Willkie of New York and McNary of Oregon, and Roosevelt and Henry Wallace of Iowa, in 1940 — these combinations are typical of the pattern.

On occasion, the Vice Presidential nominee may be one who was instrumental in making possible victory for the Presidential nominee. Such was the case with John Nance Garner of Texas in 1932. Roosevelt's nomination was put over on the fourth ballot in that year when Garner, backed by the Texas and California delegations, swung to Roosevelt and brought with him the two states' combined total of 90 votes — enough to overcome Roosevelt's 88-vote deficiency on the third ballot.

As a device for nominating Presidential and Vice Presidential candidates, it is generally agreed that the national convention has served the parties well. As a platform-making organization, however, the convention receives a lower mark. The differing relative abilities of national conventions to perform these two types of functions is but another indication of the principal purpose of the major party — to nominate a ticket which can win the election. Elections are not won on platforms nor are they often won by parties which dissipate their strength by heavy intraparty platform fighting.

Several proposals for substituting a national direct primary for selection of Presidential nominees have been offered in recent years. Proponents of such plans argue that only in this way can the power of nomination be taken away from state party bosses, that the rank-and-file party voter is more properly motivated to do a better job of nominee selection, and that more satisfactory Presidential nominations will be the result. National Presidential primaries would, in the opinion of defenders of the national convention system, be undesirable for the following reasons: first, they would weaken and split the parties too greatly; second, they would make it impossible for the parties to take into account sectional and other factors requiring compromise; third, they would render co-ordination of Presidential and Vice Presidential nominee selection difficult; fourth, they would require intensive primary campaigns reaching into all the states; and fifth, they would make some other means of preparing a party platform necessary. Because these arguments and the general question of national convention versus national primaries are so directly related to an over-all appraisal of the major parties, their discussion in detail is left to Chapter Twenty-three of this book.

CHAPTER EIGHT

National Party Organization: National Committee and Party in Congress

----

We have much to learn from the English on this matter of political organization in a democracy. For over the course of many years they have forged a system of party government in the full sense of the term. The system serves three cardinal purposes. It unites the various branches of the government in order to carry out the will of a popular majority. It staves off the thrusts for power of minority groups. And as recent events have made clear, it offers the voters a genuine choice between two fairly distinct programs. . . .

The difference between the British system and ours is not, of course, one of personality, but one of basic political organization. There the party is supreme. Its role in national life is so meaningful and decisive that most Englishmen vote in terms of the party program and record, rather than on the basis of the personality, salesmanship, and promises of the individual candidate. . . .

And the victor at the polls discovers that the party ties are even firmer once he has taken his place in the House of Commons. Often, in the words of Winston Churchill, he " becomes a silent drudge, tramping at intervals through lobbies to record his vote, and wondering why he comes to Westminster at all." . . . He may have fought hard for his point of view within the party councils, but once the party has made up its mind on an important matter, he is expected to go along. . . .

How to explain the contrast between party domination of the legislative in Britain and the constant disruption of party lines in Congress? The answer, in part, lies in the greater homogeneity of the British people that permits a more cohesive political structure. But that is not the whole answer, for Britain too has her sectional rivalries that cut across parties, her special interests that would use either party in their quest for influence. The main reason for that contrast is the organization of political power in Britain as compared with America.

James MacGregor Burns [1]

The introductory quotation from James MacGregor Burns' *Congress on Trial* has summarized the effect of organization of political power in Britain. In that country " the party is supreme." Whichever party wins a majority of seats in the House of Commons is in a position to enact its program. For pressure groups, access to the national government can come only through the political party leaders. Legislators find themselves bound to their party's line.

For the causes behind these effects one must look to the British system of government and to the manner in which British political parties are organized. A brief examination of both the system and the national organizations of the parties produced by the system can do much to enable one to better understand American national party organization.

Britain has a unitary form of government with all legal power centralized in the national government, as distinguished from the federal form as found in the United States where some powers are delegated to the national government and others reserved to the states. British political parties outside the Parliament are also centralized. Where American party organization on the national level can only be understood after an examination of the Democratic and Republican parties which has begun at the bottom level and worked upward, the procedure for studying the British party is to start from the opposite direction — from the top.

At the apex of the British party is the central office. Under the direction of the party chairman, the central office supervises all outside-Parliament party activity. It collects national party funds, maintains elaborate research units, issues national party propaganda, ad-

---

[1] *Congress on Trial* (New York: Harper and Brothers, 1949), pp. 36–39. Reprinted by permission of Harper and Brothers.

ministers party schools, and secures political speakers for local party associations. Party central offices also operate regional offices to provide on-the-spot assistance to local party associations and to supervise the activities of those associations. In each local association there is a full-time professional party agent who in effect owes his final responsibility to the central office. Furthermore, though the local associations do collect money from membership and candidate contributions, the amounts locally collected are not enough to finance the bulk of local party activity. Because the local associations must look to the central office for much of their money, because central office personnel supervise local association activity, and because of the valuable services performed by the central office, there is little temptation for the local association to step out of line with national party policy.

When it comes time for the selection of party candidates to stand in a general election for a House of Commons seat, the central office's decision as to whom the local association's candidate shall be tends to be decisive. Often the man selected as party candidate does not himself live in the constituency from which he seeks office, but rather is put there by the central office. If a man's election is considered essential by the party, he will be designated to run for office in a " safe " party constituency, and if he is not as important, the district selected for him will tend to be not as " safe." Though a local association may try to influence selection of its candidate and usually the process is one of cooperation, the local association seldom will protest long if it is over-ruled by the central office. Never will a local association strike out on its own because the central office can always undermine those who would try.

During campaigns the central office supervises the candidates who have been selected by the party. If a candidate so conducts himself as to appear to be prejudicial to the party cause, the final decision on his actions will rest with the central office. Should a candidate openly depart from the party line, he can be replaced and so starved of money and services and so disgraced before the party's voters as to render his election impossible.

Before proceeding to British party organization inside the Parliament, it is first necessary to note another characteristic of the British form of government. It is not a separation of powers system with a president and congress separately elected and a senate exercising a veto over a house, a president exercising a veto over congress, a supreme court in a position to veto both a president and congress, and all three branches checked and balanced against one another. Instead of the presidential form, Britain has a cabinet system. The Prime Minister is the leader of the majority party in the House of Commons and also the chief executive. The members of the Cabinet are both of the Commons majority party and heads of the executive departments. Neither can the House of Lords veto acts of the Commons, nor is there a supreme court with the power of judicial review.

The majority party in the House of Commons is thus in a position to put into effect the kind of governmental policies it has promised the voters it would, provided the majority party holds together. As the central office has weapons with which local associations and constituency candidates can be disciplined, so do the leaders of the majority parliamentary party have the means of enforcing discipline over their members of Parliament. If the threat of being shorn of the party label at the next general election does not induce the members to comply with party caucus decisions, there is the further threat of a dissolution of the House of Commons — a dissolution to call for an immediate election to see whom the voters will support in the dispute. This " ultimate weapon " tends to produce party legislative discipline if other means should not.

After a party candidate has been elected to the Commons, he becomes a part of his parliamentary party. Meetings of its caucus will be held to discuss party positions on important issues and to relate those positions to the platform on which the party campaigned in the last general election. Though most of the decisions tend to be made by the Prime Minister and Cabinet when his party is in a majority and by the minority leaders when his party is not in power, the rank-and-file Commons party member may express himself in caucus and occasionally the decisions of party leaders might be reversed or modified. Whatever the party caucus decision, however, it is considered binding once it has been made.

By contrast with the British party, American party institutions at the national level are weak indeed. Instead of a central office with strong power extending down to the very bottom of the party, there are the Democratic and Republican national committees with their few functions and little or no power over state and local party organizations. National committee members are delegates from the " sovereign " state parties, and national committee chairmen tend to be the agents of party Presidential nominees. Separate from the national committee, and separate from each other, are the Congressional and

Senatorial campaign committees. Although both campaign committees are a part of each party organization in each house of Congress, they are not used as party discipline-enforcing units to hold a party's legislators in line. The general purpose party organizations in House and Senate are weak and their powers are widely diffused into the hands of many different party power points. Lastly, on the national level of American political party organization, there is the President acting in his role as political party chief — sometimes succeeding to a degree, and sometimes failing.

Our study of American national party organization in this chapter is divided into, first, a section on the national committee; second, a section on Congressional and Senatorial campaign committees; and third, a section on party organization in Congress.

THE NATIONAL COMMITTEE

Both Democratic and Republican national committees are agencies established by and operating under the instructions of the respective national party conventions. Prior to 1952 the methods of selecting members of the two major party national committees were similar. Each of the states, territories, and possessions of the United States were entitled to one national committeeman and one committeewoman — the committeewomen being added after the adoption of the Nineteenth Amendment. By action of the Republican National Convention of 1952, to the Republican National Committee were added state Republican party chairmen for each state which meets one of the following tests: first, that the state was carried by the Republican nominee for President in the last Presidential election; second, that the state has a Republican governor; or third, that the state's delegation in Congress has a majority of Republicans.

For the Republican party to take such a step while Democrats did not, there is a logical explanation. In large part, the Republican action was a reflection of the sectional character of the party as opposed to the national character of the Democratic party. Mississippi's Republican organization, if such it can be called, had as much representation before 1952 on the Republican National Committee as did safe Republican states like Vermont or doubtful pivot states like New York. Catalyzing the change in composition of the Republican National Committee, was the Eisenhower-Taft contest for the Republican nomination for President in Chicago in 1952. Eisenhower was supported by almost all the Republican governors and won the nomination, but Taft forces were in control of the Republican National Committee. Under the new arrangement the states on which the Republican party must depend in order to win Presidential elections and Congressional majorities possess a greater voice in national committee affairs.

The American Political Science Association Committee on Political Parties would have both major parties further change the composition of their national committees to have the members more accurately " reflect the actual strength of the party within the areas they represent." Applying a unit principle of representation, the Committee on Political Parties suggests that each state's representatives on the national committees be entitled to cast votes which are weighted in relation to the proportion of the total party vote which comes from each state. Under the plan, for example, the votes of New York national committee members would count for much more than those of the members from a small state like Nevada. Such weighting of votes, it is felt, would tend to make the national committee more truly representative, would induce state parties to greater effort in turning out the vote and would develop a stronger sense of responsibility within the national committees.[2]

In theory national committeemen and committeewomen are elected by the national convention. In practice, however, the selection is left to the several state parties. A very few states designate their national committeemen and committeewomen in the state primary election in Presidential election years. In other states they are picked by the state central committee, by state party conventions, or by the state's delegation to the national convention. Whatever the method of state party choice, its selections are almost always ratified by the national convention. Republican state chairmen, who are ex-officio members of the Republican National Committee by virtue of the positions which they hold, are seated as soon as the National Committee satisfies itself that one of the three standards listed above has been met. Because of the manner in which members of the national committees are selected, those members tend to think of themselves more as representatives of their state parties than as national party officials.

---

[2] Committee on Political Parties of the American Political Science Association, *Toward A More Responsible Two-Party System*, published as a supplement to *The American Political Science Review* (September, 1950), Vol. 44, No. 3, Pt. 2, p. 39.

The Committee on Political Parties would have the national conventions use the authority they already have to take a more active part in selecting national committeemen and committeewomen. The national conventions, it is suggested, should then choose for national committee membership the type of party members from each state who would support the convention's statements of party policy and its choices of party candidates.[3] How such a plan would operate might best be illustrated with the Democratic National Convention of 1952. It will be recalled that some southern Democratic state organizations at that time were threatening to bolt the party to support Dwight D. Eisenhower, the Republican nominee for President, and that a fight occurred on the floor of the convention over the issue of whether a " loyalty oath " to support the convention actions should be required before permitting state delegations to participate in making convention decisions. The Committee on Political Parties proposal would, in effect, have the convention apply the " loyalty oath " principle to the selecting of national committeemen and committeewomen.

For the same reasons why the Democratic National Convention of 1952 did not impose a " loyalty oath " for participation in the decisions of the convention, it is hardly likely that either major party will react favorably to the application of the same principle in election of national committee members. The major party combinations are composed of so many different kinds of state party elements, the task of holding them all together is such a delicate one, and the margin of victory in Presidential elections is generally so close that neither major party national convention dares risk the alienation of significant segments of its potential support by imposition of " loyalty oath " discipline. Attempts of Democratic party leaders since 1952 to placate the antagonisms engendered by the " loyalty oath " controversy of that year indicate the controlling importance of all of these political considerations.

Likewise, the type of representation on the national committee is not likely to be substantially altered in the direction of making the national committee " truly representative " of the party. Though the large states control enough convention votes to accomplish such a change, several factors lead one to the conclusion that large state votes would not be cast for this purpose. First, the psychology of federal parties as distinguished from national parties is still too strong. Sec-

---

[3] *Ibid.,* p. 39.

ond, the primary business of a national convention is to nominate the party's candidate for President. The convention is composed of groups attempting to secure the nomination for their man. No candidate for a nomination and the groups backing him are likely to risk the possibility of losing votes from the smaller delegations which would oppose substantial reconstitution of the plan of representation on which the national committee is based.

Third, the functions of the national committees as such are not important enough to make a big fight over the issue. It is the national chairman who is the key figure, and it is he who wields much of the committee's power. National chairmen, however, are not in fact chosen by their national committees unless their party is out of office and a choice has to be made between Presidential elections. At all other times, the national chairman is chosen by the party's Presidential nominee or the President and the choice is ratified by the national committee. The national chairman owes primary responsibility not to the members of the national committee but to the man who selected him.

What are the qualities for which a Presidential nominee looks when he designates his choice for national committee chairman? Foremost is the ability to manage the Presidential election campaign, and generally the national chairman will be the person who has run the nominee's campaign for nomination. Thomas Dewey's Herbert Brownell, Franklin Roosevelt's James Farley, William McKinley's Mark Hanna — these linkings of names show the prevailing pattern.

If the party's nominee is successful, the national chairman who conducted the campaign will tend to be retained in his party office and, as the agent of the President, becomes chief federal patronage dispenser. Until recent years it has also been the practice of Presidents to name the chairman of the national committee to the Cabinet position of Postmaster General. This practice has given the party chairman an official position in the administration and a public office salary. The Post Office Department was the logical choice because it had a large number of patronage jobs within it and was the kind of department in which the nonpatronage decisions required of its head were not likely to have political consequences that might alienate any of the wings of the party.

If the party's nominee for the Presidency is defeated, the national chairman who conducted the unsuccessful campaign resigns relatively soon after the election. Only in such a situation does a national committee itself pick the new chairman, and the man selected will tend to be the choice of the party group in control of the national committee. Such a group will tend to use the opportunity to get a chairman favorable to its choice for the next Presidential nomination. When no one element of the party is strong enough to control, the national chairman will be a compromise choice and will for his tenure in office find his most important job that of trying to hold the party together. In neither case is the national committee chairman the real party leader. For the party controlling the Presidency, national party leadership has to come from the President. The party without one of its own in the White House has no single party head.

In the office of the national committee, but functioning under the direction of the national chairman, one will find large professional and full-time staffs. Republicans had approximately 100 such employees over 1953 and 1954, while the Democratic national committee staff for the same period ranged from 50 to 60. In Presidential election campaigns sizable additions of temporary staff workers are added.

Each national party headquarters maintains a research unit to compile lists of and analyze the sins of the opposition and its own accomplishments, and to conduct a continuing evaluation of the party's prospects. The results of research are made available to the President, Senators, and Congressmen of the party, and to state and local units which know the value of research and want to use such data. Since Charles Michelson as Democratic National Committee publicity director so effectively undermined the position of the Hoover Administration in the public mind and helped set the stage for Democratic victory in 1932, both Democrats and Republicans have come to the conclusion they cannot get along without permanent and professional publicity or public relations divisions. Through these units vast amounts of propaganda flow. Principally the party message is issued to the media of communication through press releases or ghost-written into speeches for party notables. In recent years the Democrats have successfully established a monthly magazine, *The Democratic Digest,* and both parties are experimenting with the motion picture and its adaptation for television use. National committee staff specialists are also maintained for youth and women's activities and for contacts with nationality and occupational groups.

Arrangements for national conventions are another function of the national committees. The national committee selects the convention city, sets the dates of the convention, issues the call, and chooses the keynoter and other temporary officers of the convention. If during the course of a Presidential campaign either the Presidential or Vice Presidential nominee should withdraw or die, the national committee would be the agency for deciding what procedure to follow in naming a new nominee. And overlapping all the functions which have been enumerated, there is the national committee's function of working with the state party organizations. A national chairman may largely run his national committee, but he has to depend upon the national committeeman and committeewoman for smooth working relationships with each state party. Here is where, as the national committee presently operates, the national committeemen and committeewomen make their greatest contributions to the successful working of their party organization.

More important, for purposes of comparing American major parties with British parties, are functions which the national committees do not perform. Where the central offices of the Conservative and Labour parties participate in selecting candidates for House of Commons constituencies, contribute substantially to their campaigns, and supervise the conduct of the campaigns, the primary business of the Democratic and Republican national committees is only one of these — campaigning to elect Presidents. Selection of Presidential and Vice Presidential nominees is the business of the national conventions. Selection of a party's nominees for seats in Congress is left in most states to the voters voting in primary elections, with the state party organizations often not officially committed to any candidate before the primary. After party nominees for the United States Senate and House of Representatives have been chosen, then the Congressional and Senatorial campaign committees begin to operate in an attempt to elect as many from their party to their house as possible. The objective of each such committee is to win a majority of seats in its house, thus securing control of the organization of that house.

CONGRESSIONAL AND SENATORIAL CAMPAIGN COMMITTEES

The first Congressional campaign committee was established by Republicans in Congress in 1866. It resulted from the following developments. Through the administrations of President Lincoln Republicans in Congress were infuriated time and again by the manner in which Lincoln would act, even on matters clearly given to the Congress by the Constitution, and then submit his action later to Congress for ratification. Though the Constitution gave Congress power to raise and support armies and to make rules for the military forces, Lincoln did both by executive proclamation. Despite the Constitutional provision that no money be drawn from the Treasury unless appropriated by Congress, Lincoln ordered a large sum paid to private citizens for the purchase of military supplies.

When Radical Republicans protested that the President was subordinate to Congress, Lincoln replied by stating that he did not think Congress was the whole government of the United States. Bending to abolitionist pressures for compensated emancipation legislation, Lincoln sent Congress his bill and threatened to veto any other act. When Congress complied with his request, he sent to the Capitol the veto message he would have used if his terms had not been met. The Emancipation Proclamation was issued while Congress was not in session. Lincoln himself suspended the right of *habeas corpus* through a broad interpretation of his powers as commander in chief.

President Lincoln, ignoring the Congress, proclaimed in 1863 his own policy of amnesty and reconstruction. Furious Radical Republicans passed their own harsh reconstruction resolution, and Lincoln vetoed it. Here was the principal campaign issue of 1864, and Lincoln was re-elected in spite of the open opposition of many of the most influential Republicans in Congress. After Lincoln's assassination in 1865, when President Andrew Johnson had made clear he intended to continue Lincoln's policies, Radical Republicans in Congress set about finding ways and means of taking direct action against the President — ways and means which subsequently led to the attempted impeachment of President Johnson in 1868 which failed by only one Senate vote.[4]

In 1866 President Johnson controlled the Republican National Committee, and Congressional Republicans feared the powers of the national committee would be used against them in the Congressional elections of that year. At issue was the question: "Shall the President or Congress reconstruct? "[5] To assist Republican Congressmen in their campaigns the Republican Congressional Campaign Committee was organized. At the time, it competed with the Republican Na-

[4] From Wilfred E. Binkley, *President and Congress* (New York: Alfred A. Knopf, 1947) , Chap. 6.
[5] *Ibid.*, p. 251.

tional Committee. The device worked successfully in the elections of 1866 and Republicans continued to use it. In the 1870's the Democrats also organized their own Congressional campaign committee. Both Democratic and Republican committees were made up of one Congressman for every state which had one or more representatives of that party, plus a smaller group of Senators of that party.

After the passage of the Seventeenth Amendment providing for popular election of United States Senators instead of election by state legislatures, Senate members of the Congressional campaign committees withdrew. The Congressional campaign committees became House campaign organs. Senate Republicans (1916) and Democrats (1918) established their own Senatorial campaign committees.

Presently, the Republican Congressional Campaign Committee consists of one representative from each state with Republican representation in the House. The membership of the Democratic Congressional Campaign Committee is determined in the same way, though there is also provision to add an additional committeeman for any state which has no Democrats in the House and a committeewoman for each of the 48 states. Members are nominated by their state party delegations in the House, and the choice is ratified by the party caucus.

Senatorial Democratic and Republican campaign committees average eight or nine members in size. Senate Republicans permit appointment by the chairman of the Republican caucus while Senate Democrats vest the power in the Democratic floor leader. Appointments are made only after consultation with those senators of the party who are up for election during the two-year term of Senate campaign committee office. In practice no party member up for reelection serves during the term in which he must return to his state for a new six-year lease on Senate life.

Though the first Congressional campaign committee was established to ensure a Congressional campaign organization as distinguished from the national committee, today in both parties Congressional and Senatorial campaign committees generally cooperate closely with their respective national committees. Two reasons explain the cooperative mood. Most of the money for the operation of the Senatorial and Congressional campaign committees and for distribution to party candidates for Senate and House comes from the national committees. Furthermore, in Presidential election years the fortunes of so many Congressional nominees are so tied up with their party's Presidential nominee that close working relations are almost a matter of necessity. The Congressional committees, however, are in no sense under the national committees.

Congressional and Senatorial campaign committees carry on independent research. They also utilize the data and research facilities of their national committees. They prepare speeches, maintain facilities for the preparation of radio and television programs which the Senator or Congressman can have broadcast in his home state or district, and send field representatives to the states to talk with local party leaders and to size up state and local prospects. All these activities are pointed toward those Tuesdays after the first Mondays of November in those even-numbered years.

Because the seats of perhaps 300 House members are usually safely Democratic or Republican, the Congressional campaign committees waste little work or money in such districts. Rather, they concentrate on the approximately 100 doubtful Congressional districts, and doubly concentrate on the some 30 to 40 districts in which Democratic and Republican party strength is divided on an almost 50–50 balance. For the Senatorial campaign committees, the concentration is even more pin-pointed. Only one third (32) of the Senate seats are regularly up for election every two years. Some of these will be safe for one party or the other. It is the remainder which receive Senatorial campaign committee attention. Because the Solid Democratic South gives Democrats a wide margin of safe seats over Republican safe seats, the work of the Republican Senatorial and Congressional campaign committees is more costly and time and activity consuming than that of the Democratic Senatorial and Congressional committees. (See Chapter Sixteen for a detailed analysis of each major party's problem in winning Congressional majorities.)

The Senatorial and Congressional campaign committees are not party-disciplining organizations, assisting candidates in the primary election or withholding assistance in general election campaigns because the Senator or Congressman in question has not been a faithful adherent of whatever party line is established by his President or Senate or House party leaders. It is true that the committees sometimes do involve themselves secretly in behalf of a candidate before the primary election. In California, for example, if a Congressional candidate does not receive help in the primary election, he may be beyond assistance after the primary if the opposition candidate successfully cross-files and wins both major party nominations. No member or officer of a Senatorial or Congressional campaign committee is likely, however, to be willing to admit to pre-primary activity. The theory is that until the nominee has been selected, neither House nor Senate campaign committees should commit themselves. If they do, it is felt the result would be bitter intraparty strife.

As discipline against a party's members of Congress does not come from the Congressional or Senatorial campaign committees which are in charge of distributing nationally collected funds for Congressional campaigns, neither is much more party disciplinary power vested in the regular House and Senate party organizations. In the following section these organizations will be examined to show the reasons for this.

PARTY ORGANIZATION IN CONGRESS

The Caucus. At the base of the Democratic and Republican party organizations in both houses of Congress is the caucus. Caucuses as used by the parties in Congress differ in two significant respects from those employed by the Conservative and Labour parties in the House of Commons. The British party requires adherence to the party line for membership in its caucus. The caucuses in Congress tend to permit any house member to participate provided *he says* he is a member of the party in whose caucus he wants to sit. Where the British party parliamentary caucuses are used to arrive at party positions on issues to which the member is then bound, the caucuses in Congress seldom take positions on issues and when they do, the members of the caucus do not necessarily consider such decisions binding.

The membership tests imposed by Congressional party caucuses are highly flexible. Only in very rare cases have individuals been excluded from a caucus in which they wanted to participate, and no consistent pattern of reasons for exclusions may be formulated from those few cases. If any standard for membership has evolved, it may be the requirement that a member of the Congressional party should have supported the Presidential nominee of his party in the preceding Presidential election. Even in this there has been no real consistency. Though the Republican supporters of La Follette's Progressive party in 1924 were temporarily read out of the Republican party by House and Senate caucuses, in the following Congress when their votes were needed for Republican majorities, they were invited back in. Such well-known Republican Senatorial " bolters " as George Norris, Joseph Ball, and Hiram Johnson still remained as Senate Republican caucus members in good standing during the Franklin Roosevelt administrations. The Senate Republican organization needed every vote it could get, and it could not be particular about the party regularity of its caucus members. During and after the Presidential elections of 1940 and 1944, it sometimes appeared that to be considered a " good " Congressional Republican it was necessary to openly oppose or quietly " sulk-out " the Willkie and Dewey campaigns.[6]

Anti-New Deal Democrats in Congress from 1938 through 1952 were strong enough, when allied with Republicans, to block many of the domestic proposals of Democratic Presidents. Yet to read anti-New Deal Democrats out of Senate and House Democratic organizations would have been to emasculate the Democratic Congressional party organizations. Although in 1938, President Roosevelt went around his party in Congress to urge the people of several states to defeat powerful Democratic Congressional opponents in primary elections, his " purge " attempt was a failure.

In a Senate Republican caucus one may find a William Langer of North Dakota sitting next to a Joseph McCarthy of Wisconsin; in a Senate Democratic caucus, a Theodore Bilbo of Mississippi next to a Herbert Lehman of New York; in a House Republican caucus, a Carroll Reece of Tennessee next to a Jacob Javits of New York; in a House Democratic caucus, a John Rankin of Mississippi next to a James Roosevelt of California. If the political parties outside the Congress often seem a strange assortment of political bedfellows, the party caucuses in Congress seem even more so. Here the members have long voting records which can be placed alongside one another. Two Congressmen may have the same party label, but often their voting records when viewed in their totality would not suggest that fact. This is the kind of stuff of which a party caucus is made. The very heterogeneity of each Congressional caucus membership imposes limits on the functions which the caucus can perform.

The Democratic caucus in the House has gone as far as any Congressional party caucus to attempt to bind its members to caucus decisions. Its rules provide that a two-thirds caucus vote of the full Democratic membership of the House shall bind all members of the caucus *unless*, first, the question involves a construction of the Con-

---

[6] See Clarence A. Berdahl, " Some Notes on Party Membership in Congress, I," *American Political Science Review* (April, 1949), Vol. 43, No. 2, pp. 309–321; and for Part II of the article, *ibid.* (June, 1949), No. 3, pp. 492–508.

stitution; second, the member has made contrary pledges in his campaign for office; or third, the member has received contrary instructions by resolution or platform from his nominating authority. Even if the two-thirds vote to bind was attainable and the Democratic House caucus made many issue decisions, the loopholes through

The Milwaukee Journal

Ike's Second 'Battle Of The Bulge'

which a member could escape those decisions are wide ones. Republicans, to get away from the implication that their caucuses are binding, call their caucuses " conferences."

The purpose of the Congressional party caucus is, as a party, to decide on a course of action before questions come up for resolution on the floor of the house. By making a secret and preliminary decision the party will be spared intraparty public fighting on the floor. Unified on a course of action, the theory of the caucus continues, the party will have a better chance to have the whole house adopt the policies it wants. In Congress the caucuses work in this manner on questions of organization, but almost never on other issues.

In the House, each party caucus will nominate its candidate for Speaker; and in the Senate, its candidate for President Pro Tempore. Who shall occupy the positions of party floor leader, party whip, and who shall be party policy or steering committee members are determined by majorities of the respective party caucuses. Caucuses also formally pick their nominees for standing committee memberships and committee chairmen. However, they do not perform this latter function for party political reasons. Instead, each caucus has some kind of committee on committees which selects the party's standing committee slate according to an almost absolute seniority formula. The caucus automatically ratifies those recommendations.

Though there have been occasions when a party caucus has deprived one of its members of the committee assignments to which he might be entitled by virtue of his seniority, the practice is exceptional. Once a member of Congress becomes a member of a standing committee and continues to be re-elected, he can continue to serve on his committee and at the same time climb a ladder on which his advancement to the chairmanship hinges only on his staying power and having his party in control at the right time. Whether he works with his house party majority on issues or not is beside the point.

When bills and resolutions are introduced in Congress, they are referred to a standing committee for detailed study and action. Here is the first major legislative stage through which legislation must pass. Even though a majority of the majority party or a majority of the house might favor passage, it is extremely difficult to discharge from a standing committee any bill which the committee does not approve. The standing committee and its chairman are able to say whether the party and house shall have a chance to vote on the matter.

Caucus party discipline might in part be enforceable if standing committee assignments and chairmanships were granted only to those who were in accord in policy matters with a majority of a party caucus. Committee assignments and committee chairmanships, again, are not so used. Most members of Congress feel that without the seniority rule, the Congressional parties would be paralyzed because of the intraparty battles which would rage in a nonseniority selection procedure. The majority of a party caucus could use its Congressional or Senatorial campaign committee's distribution of funds for election campaigns as disciplinary leverage or have its campaign committee enter primary election contests against a party maverick, but this is not done either.

Another source of caucus disciplinary power might appear to be Congressional patronage which includes several hundred Capitol jobs ranging from elevator operator to Senate and House chaplain classifications. Congressional patronage, when placed under a closer scrutiny, however, is so minute that even if the caucus patronage committees did try to use jobs to get the party member in line, the effect would be negligible. At most a Senator of the majority party is likely to have perhaps two Capitol policemen and an elevator operator, and in the House Congressional patronage for each member of the majority is even thinner. " Two policemen and an elevator operator " do not represent disciplinary power. Especially is this true when Senators and Congressmen often give their appointments to persons living in Washington, D. C., and not from their home states or districts.

Why is there almost no caucus-imposed party discipline in Congress? The answer is simple. Most members of Congress do not want such discipline. Party government may be fine in theory, but each legislator wants to maintain his own freedom of action to make his own decisions as he thinks they should be made. Illustrative of the American legislator's psychology on this point was a debate during one of the panels on political parties at the American Political Science Association national convention in 1949. United States Senator Paul H. Douglas (D), Illinois, and some five political scientists comprised the panel. Most of the political scientists argued for binding caucus decisions, while Senator Douglas took the position that, though he wanted stronger parties, he did not want to blindly commit himself to whatever might be any future Senate Democratic caucus decision. Many members of Congress feel they at least in part owe their election to their ability to convince the voters that they are fighting or are relatively independent of " party machines." Short of a wholesale turnover of the tradition of individual independence which American legislators cherish, and a nationalization of political issues, the Congressional party caucuses cannot and will not be fitted into the mold of the British parliamentary party caucus.

Congressional Procedure and Party Organization in Congress. Procedure in the British Parliament is adapted to making it possible for the majority of the majority party to control every power point through which a piece of legislation must proceed from its origin to final passage. All important measures originate in the executive departments and move through the Cabinet and Prime Minister to the floor of the House of Commons. There, the whole House makes its policy decision. If the House of Lords does not approve, it can at most hold up general bills for one year and special categories of priority bills such as appropriations for 30 days. The bill then becomes a law.

Only some of the measures introduced in either chamber of the American Congress originate in the executive branch of government. Others may originate from pressure groups, individual members, or Congressional committees. Should the bill come from the President, he, like the pressure groups, must find a member of Congress to introduce it. On its introduction, the bill will be sent to the appropriate standing committee whose members and chairman, and not the full majority of the house, will determine whether the bill shall or shall not be recommended to the floor for passage.

In the House, most important legislation will next have to go for a special order to the Rules Committee, whose members also hold their positions by virtue of the seniority system. If the Rules Committee grants a special order, it will also set the time when the House will consider the measure, state the conditions under which amendments may be offered, and allot the time to be allowed for debate. Only if the bill gets this far, will the full House for the first time have an opportunity to act.

If the House approves, the bill goes to its Senate introduction and is then referred to a Senate standing committee. Should it survive this stage, the next step will be consideration on the Senate floor under rules permitting unlimited debate. If a group of Senators is numerous and well-organized enough to conduct an effective filibuster, the legislation may be talked to death even though a majority of Senators favor its passage. If the Senate passes the bill with amendments and the House does not concur in those amendments, a conference committee, not necessarily representative of the majorities in both houses, will be appointed to compromise Senate and House differences. If a conference committee does agree, its report must either be accepted or rejected in full by the respective majorities of the two houses.

In the British Parliament the majority of the majority party has control of a bill at every step of the legislative process; in the American Congress, at only a few stages can the majority party control. How might Congressional procedures be adapted to facilitate party government in the House and Senate? One set of recommendations would make standing committees and their chairmen an integral part of the party organizations by abolishing or modifying the seniority rule. Another would have the Senate establish a cloture rule by which debate could effectively be cut off, thus making the filibuster impossible. Still another would have a party leadership committee, selected by the entire party membership and responsible to it, assume the responsibility for scheduling of legislative business, thus taking that power in the House away from the Rules Committee.

As noted in the previous section on the party caucus, neither party in Congress has shown any disposition to depart from or modify to any significant degree the seniority rule. In recent years only one of several attempts to reduce the power of the House Rules Committee was successful, and it only for the life of one two-year Congress. In 1949, after a decade during which conservative and generally southern Democratic members of the House Rules Committee joined with conservative Republican members to block or harass Democratic administration domestic proposals, Democratic leaders secured the passage of the " 21-day rule " to make it easy to discharge legislation awaiting special order action in the Rules Committee. Under the rule a standing committee chairman could call up for House action any bill on which the Rules Committee had reported adversely or any bill which it had held up for more than 21 days. Though the " 21-day rule " served its purpose for several important measures during the Eighty-first Congress, in 1951 it was repealed. Since 1953 the Republican majority members of the House Rules Committee have worked so closely with the Eisenhower Administration leaders that their scheduling powers have not presented " obstruction " problems.

How strong is the Senate's desire for the right of unlimited debate is illustrated in the development and interpretation of its ineffective cloture rule. After a century with no check on debate, during the World War I emergency the Senate adopted the following rule (Rule 22) : (1) if sixteen senators filed a motion to stop debate on " any pending measure," the question of cloture would have to be put to the Senate; (2) if two thirds of those present and voting agreed to shut off debate, each Senator would be allowed one more hour; (3) the " pending measure " would then be brought to a vote with two thirds of those present and voting required for passage. Interpretations of the rule further narrowed its effectiveness. When in 1946 opponents of fair employment practices legislation began a filibuster on a motion to amend the Senate *Journal,* Rule 22 was held

not to apply. Two years later another precedent of interpretation was established — the rule did not apply to a filibuster on a motion to bring up a measure, but only to a measure after it had become a " pending measure."

After the 1948 elections a bipartisan group of Democratic and Republican senators proposed that Rule 22 be changed to permit cloture on any business before the Senate. Southern Democrats filibustered on the motion to bring up the measure, and even though Vice President Alben W. Barkley ruled cloture did apply, his ruling was not upheld by the Senate. The filibuster continued, and to return the Senate to its other important business, Rule 22 was changed to provide (1) that now an absolute two-thirds majority of the Senate would be required instead of two thirds of those present and voting; (2) that there could be no limitation of debate on changes in the rules; and (3) that now cloture could be applied both to pending measures and motions to consider a measure. Another move to achieve an effective cloture rule in the first days of the Eighty-third Congress (1953) was overwhelmingly defeated.

These are the major procedural obstacles to party government in the Senate and the House. The failure of the caucus to serve as an institution of party government, except on organizational matters, has already been noted. With such limitations as background, one may now proceed to the party leadership positions in House and Senate.

Speaker, Floor Leader, Whip, Policy Committee. In the United States House of Representatives the Speaker is the presiding officer of the House and at the same time the leader of the majority party. Although seniority is not decisive in his selection, he will usually be one of the senior members of his party, and therefore a representative from a " safe " district. Generally he rises to his position through an apprenticeship as his party's floor leader, and once a man has the speakership, the practice is for the party to re-elect him for as long as he is a member and whenever his party controls the organization of the House.

For some years prior to 1910, the Speaker in fact ran his party in the House. He had the right of arbitrary recognition, and used that right for disciplinary purposes. Unless a member was recognized by the Speaker, he had no way of participating in the business of the House and thus no way of gaining recognition and obtaining for his district the type of legislation which might help his re-election prospects. The Speaker appointed the chairman and members of the standing committees, and this right he too used for disciplinary effect. He was the chairman of the Rules Committee, and with his party's majority on that committee, controlled all scheduling of legislation to be considered. Through the Speaker's control of the chairmen of the Ways and Means and Appropriations committees, he had financial leverage over the individual member. During the period from 1890 to 1909 the House of Representatives came closer to party government in the British sense than either house of Congress had before or has since.

In 1909, however, the House rebelled. Democrats and western progressive Republicans combined forces against Republican Speaker Joseph Cannon to effect rules changes designed to diffuse the powers held by the presiding officer. A consent calendar procedure was instituted to make possible the passage of noncontroversial measures without the necessity of gaining recognition from the Speaker. For the same purpose, a Calendar Wednesday rule was adopted to make it possible for standing committee chairmen to call up measures they and their committees wanted. In short order, the Speaker was forbidden the right to serve on the Rules Committee, and taken also from him was his power to appoint standing committee members and chairmen. The Speaker is still the most powerful House and party figure, but he is no longer a one-man oligarchy. Now his chief stock-in-trade must of necessity be his skill in persuasion, skill in exchanging little favors for votes when his party needs them most, and whatever parliamentary skills he can apply to his party's advantage.

The presiding officer of the Senate, the Vice President, is not a member of that body and is not considered his party's Senatorial leader. Some leadership he may be able to accomplish for his President, but only if he is a highly skilled politician and can tread softly to avoid being charged with " interfering" in his Senate party's affairs. Next highest in Senate rank is the President Pro Tempore, nominated by the majority party caucus and elected by the Senate. But the President Pro Tempore is not the majority party's leader in the Senate either. Rather the position goes to a senior party member. It is largely honorary except for the fact that the holder of the office is third in the line of Presidential succession after the Vice President and Speaker.

As the Speaker is the leader of the majority party in the House, the floor leader tends to be the strongest officer of the House minority party and of both Senate parties. Unlike the Speaker, however, he has no formal powers with which to command in exercising leadership. Rather his success is dependent on an ability to earn respect, confidence, and cooperation in the interest of the common party cause. It is he who manages debate on the floor in somewhat the sense of a quarterback calling the signals for a football team. When speakers on behalf of the party's position on an issue are arranged, their selection is made through the office of the floor leader. He is a co-ordinator in that he has to attempt to tie together all elements of the party in his house as represented in the policy committee, standing committee chairmen, or minority leaders and the organization of the party whip and his assistants.

If a critical vote is due, it is the responsibility of the floor leader, working through his principal assistant, the whip, to mobilize his forces. He must get the party rank and file in the house to go along with a program, and get them to the floor at a time when their votes can be made to count. He has also the responsibility of knowing what the rank and file are thinking about the issues — in other words, the " temper of the house." A floor leader does not have to be and is not necessarily the most intelligent member of his party in his house. He does not have to know more about some special field of legislation than anyone else. Both abilities, it is true, may help, but more important than both is a high order of political ability — knowing how to bargain, when to compromise and when to be firm, sound grounding in the intricacies of legislative procedure, an ability to provide the kind of incentive to the other members of the party team to get them pulling roughly in the same direction even though some do not want to do so.

In one sense, floor leadership positions are rewarding in terms of recognition and the opportunity to serve the party. But there is some bitter to go with the sweet. The job is often difficult and thankless, and sometimes politically dangerous. Always there are the pressures of the individual members wanting to go off in one direction because of personal desires or what each interprets as the needs of his district. These the floor leader must seek to minimize on the few big issues on which the party leadership takes a position. Also, the American legislator prides himself on his independence. This motivation the floor leader must respect and yet try to channel into the party cause. Perhaps harder still is the resolution of the conflict when the

floor leader himself wants to be independent and yet finds it necessary to subordinate his own inclinations to the party program.

The political dangers inherent in the position of floor leader
flow from his identification with a national party program which
might be a political liability in his home state or district. Ernest Mc-
Farland, of Arizona, majority floor leader in the Eighty-second Congress, was defeated for re-election in 1952 and his Eighty-first Congress
predecessor, Scott Lucas, of Illinois, met the same fate in 1950. Some
have attributed both defeats to the fact that both Senators were majority leaders at a time when President Truman's popularity was low.
The difficulty for each lay in his identification with the President.
At least McFarland's sacrifice on the altar of Presidential support was
an unwilling one. Through his 1952 Arizona campaign, he repeatedly
tried to assure the voters that even if he was Democratic floor leader,
he did not go along with everything President Truman did or said.

The Speaker and his party's floor leader and the House minority
floor leader have the advisory assistance of steering or policy committees for policy and strategy planning. In the House these advisory
bodies, chosen by the respective caucuses, include several standing
committee chairmen, representatives from the major geographical
sections of the country, the floor leader and whip, and the Speaker, if
the party has one. House Republicans call their leadership advisory
committee a policy committee, and Democrats call theirs a steering
committee. Though different in name, the functions of the two are
essentially similar. Both operate informally and without the aid of
permanent professional staffs. Both are relatively inactive.

Senate Democrats and Republicans have in the past ten years
also organized policy committees, and both maintain permanent
staffs. The Republican Policy Committee of 24 members is chosen by
the Republican Conference for two-year terms. The Democratic Policy Committee of 9 members is chosen by the Democratic floor
leader. Although the policy committees do provide a forum where
party policy and tactics may be discussed and where decisions may
be reached, they are not " party government " agencies. Neither attempt to bind their party membership to conform to the positions
taken by the policy committee, and whenever an issue is highly controversial, the policy committees tend to avoid making party-splitting
decisions.

Offices of Senate Democratic leadership are somewhat more integrated and thus better adapted to providing leadership than are those

of Senate Republicans. Where Republicans vest the chairmanship of their caucus in one man, the chairmanship of their policy committee in another, and their floor leadership in a third, Democrats combine all three into the hands of their floor leader.

In general, it may be said that party leadership is considerably diffused among several different party committees and leaders in each house, and that the committees and leaders of a party often work at cross-purposes. Nor is there assurance that party policy (if there is one) in one house will be the same on an issue as party policy of the same party in the other house. Both Democrats and Republicans have resisted establishment of joint Senate-House policy committees.

THE CONGRESSIONAL PARTY IN ACTION:
A BRIEF CASE STUDY

The first bill introduced in the House in the Eighty-third Congress (January, 1953), HR 1, provided in part for an immediate individual income tax reduction. It was referred to the Ways and Means Committee, of which Daniel A. Reed (R), New York, HR 1's author, was chairman. The Ways and Means Committee reported the bill favorably to the House, and asked the Rules Committee to grant a special order which would prohibit consideration on the House floor of any amendments which might not be acceptable to the Ways and Means Committee. The Rules Committee refused and quietly bottled up the measure because President Eisenhower and Republican leaders in Senate and House — not including Mr. Reed — had decided the only responsible course was to balance the budget before cutting taxes.

One of the principal arguments used by Republican Chairman Reed was that individual income taxes should be reduced immediately because the excess profits tax on corporations was due to expire on June 30, 1953. If corporations were to be allowed a reduction, should not individual taxpayers be entitled to a similar tax advantage at the same time? Representative Reed answered his own question in the affirmative. The Republican Administration said no, and asked that the excess profits tax be extended for a period of six months.

Although House Republican leaders were sure they had enough votes to pass an excess profits tax extension on the floor of the House, they had first to get the measure through Reed's Ways and Means Committee before the House would have an opportunity to vote. Mr.

Reed stood solidly blocking the way for the President's proposal. Reed was tying up excess profits tax extension in the same way the Rules Committee had pigeonholed his HR 1.

President Eisenhower and House Republican leaders used every means of persuasion on Representative Reed. Persuasion failed. Strategy conferences on what would be the best means of forcing the measure out of the Ways and Means Committee followed. Assuming the Committee would not take favorable action, only two courses were available to the House Republican leadership, and both were hazardous at best. The most obvious alternative would have been to attempt to discharge the Ways and Means Committee (take the bill away from it). To succeed it would be necessary to get 218, an absolute majority, of the 435 House members to sign a discharge petition before the measure could be brought to the floor. Members, even if they favored the excess profits tax extension, would be reluctant to be responsible for by-passing the Ways and Means Committee, or any standing committee, for that matter. If committees are by-passed often, House business would become hopelessly tangled. The fact that signing a discharge petition might mean incurring the wrath of the powerful Mr. Reed was an additional deterrent. And for Democrats there was still another incentive for refusing to sign a discharge petition — not wanting to help the Republicans out of an embarrassing position.

The second alternative, and the course of action decided upon, was one so seldom used that there were less than half a dozen precedents parliamentarians could rely upon. It was to have the Rules Committee discharge the Ways and Means Committee. Though the Rules Committee on the basis of precedent did have the power to perform such an act, the announcement of this plan of action produced an uproar. Representative John McCormack of Massachusetts, Democratic whip, announced House Democrats would vote against such a procedure on the ground that it would represent a detour around traditional procedure. Many Republicans also had their doubts about a practice which would permit their party's House leadership to by-pass a standing committee decision.

The showdown vote that was expected to come — a vote which might have been negative — did not materialize. Instead the Republican House leadership backed down from the threat of using Rules Committee power after obtaining assurances from Mr. Reed that he would call a meeting of the Ways and Means Committee and after assurances from the Republican members of the committee that they would report out a satisfactory excess profits tax extension even if Reed continued his opposition. The Ways and Means Committee did so act, and finally the Republican Administration's proposal passed Congress.

For President Eisenhower and House Republican leaders success was attained only after a campaign on which they went all-out to achieve their point. But there was more than prestige involved. If the efforts of the Republican leadership had failed, Democrats in the Congressional elections of 1954 could have hammered with the charge that Republicans reduced corporation taxes before individual income taxes — a political barrel over which Speaker Joseph Martin and House Republican floor leader Charles Halleck did not want their party stretched.

In this case the majority party leaders triumphed. Without a major effort, in many other cases, majority party leaders may be defeated. On a few occasions, particularly in the Senate, though a majority of the members of the President's party may follow his recommendation, perhaps the floor leader himself is not in concert with the White House wing of his party. Because the Congressional parties are not organized to provide party leadership and the national committees are even less organized for that purpose, the function is left mostly to the President — provided the party is fortunate enough to have the Presidency.

CHAPTER NINE

National Party Organization: The President

Congress is a heterogeneous group of individuals responsible to local machines and special interests; the president represents an over-all constituency whose mass verdicts often differ from the dictates of pure localism. To reconcile these two political patterns the president needs some means for controlling local party organizations. If a direct line can be established between the national headquarters of the party and the local political workers who do the daily work of politics, the president's chances of getting dependable support in Congress are greatly increased. Unless the president can offer substantial help in fighting local political battles, he cannot demand support from the congressmen from these localities. Since politicians must please the dominant elements in their districts, the chief executive must become a factor in local politics. He may accomplish this in part by the general prestige he enjoys; this is, however, a transitory influence and not likely to maintain the loyalty of the machines throughout his term. The president can often enhance his local strength through the use of patronage, but support won in this way is no more enduring than human gratitude nor is it stronger than the expectation of further favor.

We have created a position of great power but have made the full realization of that power dependent upon influence rather than legal authority. Hence if our president is to be effective, he must be a politician as well as a statesman. He must consider the political expedience of contemplated actions as well as their consistency with his concept of the public interest.

The element of contingency in our system is inherent in the uncertainty of party programs and party discipline. We are apparently willing to give popular support to a president while at the same time rejecting some of his most cherished measures. The president is titular head of the nation, chief legislator, and chief representative, as well as chief executive; we do not necessarily support him in all roles at the same time.

Pendleton Herring [1]

Excluding Dwight D. Eisenhower whose record as President is not complete and Harry S. Truman whose record history has not yet had time to place in perspective, some seven, more or less, Presidents have been honored with the title of " strong President." The seven are George Washington, Thomas Jefferson, Andrew Jackson, Abraham Lincoln, Theodore Roosevelt, Woodrow Wilson, and Franklin D. Roosevelt. Why single out these Presidents? Though no one man conducted himself in office exactly like another, it is possible to note several characteristics which they had in common.

Each understood the importance of Presidential leadership and possessed the political abilities to develop something of the potential inherent in the office. Each either took part in the establishment of a new party or injected a new vitality into an old party to raise its performance level considerably above what it had been before he became chief executive. Each had a hold on the imagination of the rank and file of his party and went beyond to capture the loyalty and affection of large sections of the American electorate. Each, at least through his first term of office, led his party in Congress and with the aid of broad popular support was able to secure passage of much of the Presidential program, or as in the case of Lincoln, was able to out-maneuver Congress.

Perhaps Polk, Cleveland, and McKinley should be added to the ranks of " strong " Presidents, or if not, placed in a " moderately strong " category. Some would also add to this group Monroe, Taylor, Hayes, Benjamin Harrison, and William Howard Taft. Wherever the line is drawn, however, John Adams, Madison, Van Buren, John Quincy Adams, William Henry Harrison, Tyler, Fillmore, Pierce, Buchanan, Johnson, Grant, Garfield, Arthur, Harding, Coolidge, and Hoover tend always to be classed as " weak " Presidents.

---

[1] *Presidential Leadership* (New York: Rinehart and Company, 1940), pp. 2–3. Reprinted by permission of Rinehart and Company, Inc.

The " weak " Presidents in general, though their intentions may have been just as good as the intentions of the " strong " Presidents, did not possess a high political ability. They took a more narrow view of the functions of their office. They were either unable to build popular support, or did not see the necessity for doing so. They tended to appeal only to their party or some faction of their party instead of developing a broad all-party power base. They were dominated by or unable to lead their Congresses. True, they may have been confronted with great problems, hostile parties, or hostile Congresses. Yet so were the " strong " Presidents, but the members of the latter group succeeded in spite of the obstacles while the " weak " Presidents fell victims of the circumstances in which they found themselves.

John Adams was unable to work a miracle to stop or delay the dissolution of the Federalist party, but who can say that if the Federalists had had a Thomas Jefferson the party might not have survived. Calvin Coolidge, by a policy of purposeful drift, unwittingly set the stage for the debacle of the Hoover Administration. Perhaps, if the Republican party had had the Theodore Roosevelt of 1900 to 1908 in office in the 1920's, the excesses which led to the great depression of the 1930's might not have happened. Even as late as the Hoover Administration, who is to say that with a master politician in the Presidency the Republicans could not have successfully salvaged their position instead of allowing Democrats to enforce a 20-year period of electoral defeat? John Quincy Adams and Madison were so politically inept in the Presidency during their terms that they never got out from under the thumb of Congress. Grant and Harding so failed to grasp the elements of leadership that their administrations were led to disgrace by the corruption of subordinates for which they as Presidents bore the ultimate responsibility. William Howard Taft allowed a strong Republican combination to disintegrate.

With " strong " Presidents, political parties have prospered. Without them, although a party may have potentially sound economic, foreign policy, and emotional bases of support, it can only stagger from one election to the next, flounder through undistinguished administrations, and win only because the opposition party is an even less desirable alternative. Political parties need " strong " and dynamic Presidents to simplify the issues, to provide a symbol around which potential groups and sectional allies can attach themselves, to reach out to attract votes from independents and opposition, and to adapt the party organization and its program to the needs of the times. A party's United States Senators and Congressmen are not organized to perform these functions, nor if they were so organized, could they perform all of them; neither can the party's governors or rank and file members. Top party leadership, if there is to be party leadership, must come from its President or Presidential nominee. No other single man is as vital to the present and future of any party.

EVOLUTION OF THE PRESIDENCY [2]

Chief executives got off to a bad start in America. The colonial governor, when he acted as an agent of the king and as one who looked out first for the interests of Britain, was something less than popular. Many were hated. Colonial assemblies, on the other hand, did represent the colony's citizens who were qualified to vote. Legislatures were liked and respected. After the Declaration of Independence the new state constitutions established governments with strong legislatures and very weak executives.

By 1787 when the framers of the Constitution met in Philadelphia, however, there had been a reaction against legislative supremacy. Some of the state legislatures had written into law agrarian demands for inflation and legislatures were, in the minds of business groups, too responsive to antibusiness pressures. The delegates to the Constitutional Convention had also taken note of the inability of the Articles of Confederation Congress to function adequately without executive leadership. Furthermore, some of the Founding Fathers had read widely and been exposed to the thesis that the best way to prevent abuse of governmental power was to split that power between different branches of government.

What came out of the deliberation at Philadelphia was a compromise between legislative supremacy and executive supremacy. Legislative powers were vested in Congress; executive powers, in the President. But this was not all that was done to diffuse power. The legislature and executive were both cross-checked and interrelated by an intricate system of checks and balances. The President would

---

[2] Historical development of Presidency in this section based principally on Wilfred E. Binkley, *President and Congress* (New York: Alfred A. Knopf, 1947).

be chief administrator, commander in chief of the armed forces, and head of state. Yet Congress could impeach the President, pass the laws for him to enforce, appropriate the money he could spend, and declare war. The Senate was given a ratification check on Presidential appointments and treaties. Congress would legislate, but the President was empowered to veto legislative acts, to send messages to Congress outlining his recommendations on questions of the day, and to call special sessions. Congress, again, by a two-thirds majority in each of the two houses, could override a Presidential veto.

These are the main Constitutional provisions on which relationships between Congress and the President have been built. The Constitution did not intend that the President should become the leader of his political party, or that there should be political parties. Nor was the intention that the President should become the " champion of the people." Rather, the President was to serve as a kind of moderator soothing out conflicts between Senate and House and enforcing the laws passed by Congress. To achieve this end, Presidents were not to be elected by popular vote, but rather by an electoral college procedure in which the leaders in public affairs in each of the states would be selected as electors to deliberate and register their choice. Because no one candidate would often be expected to win a majority of electoral votes, the choice of the President was expected to revert frequently to the House of Representatives.

At best, the statements of intent and instructions of the Constitution to future Presidents and Congresses were only of a broad and general character and left much room for interpretation and development. Working relations between the two branches of national government have had to develop out of specific applications which have been made of the constitutional provisions. To understand the role of the President as chief legislator and the related role of political party chief, it is necessary to outline the steps through which the Presidency and pattern of President-Congress relations have evolved.

George Washington, who had served as president of the Constitutional Convention, attempted to make the office of President of the United States what the framers of the Constitution had intended it to be. Though he did his best to hold himself above political conflict, however, someone had to plan and direct a national program. This function was assumed by Secretary of the Treasury Alexander Hamilton. Congress referred its problems, through Hamilton, to the executive departments for study and recommendation. The executive departments, through Hamilton, sent back drafted bills. So influential was America's first and last " prime minister " that most of the important measures of Washington's first term were Hamilton-inspired.

Jeffersonian Republicans, when they gained control of the House during Washington's second term, put into practice their legislative supremacy ideas by tearing down the pattern of executive-legislative relations that Hamilton had built. The House discontinued the practice of referring legislative business to the executive departments, and instead referred them to House committees. Department heads were investigated and heckled with endless questions about their conduct of office. From the time Hamilton's leadership was rendered ineffective and then impossible, the House spent most of its hours in leaderless confusion until Jefferson took office in 1800.

How would President Jefferson, a long-time advocate of legislative supremacy, provide leadership for a party which agreed with his philosophy and was noted chiefly for its ability to thwart the executive branch? Jefferson was a practical man, and understood that without his leadership nothing could be accomplished. He made his mark as one of the strongest Presidents in American history by leading his party's members in Congress through the device of the secret Congressional party caucus. Jefferson was substantially able to influence Congressional leadership appointments and Congressional program. Until the last year of his second term he held perhaps more solid support in Congress than any President who has come after him.

From 1800 until Jackson, Congress had the upper hand in relations with the executive branch. Where Jefferson had employed the caucus to lead, Congress now turned the caucus around and used it to control Presidential nominations and to dominate Presidents. Even within the executive branch the President was no longer regarded as the leader, but more as a temporary chairman presiding over a cabinet of permanent departmental secretaries.

In 1828 Andrew Jackson arrived on the scene, and the character of the Presidency and President-Congress relations again changed. Jackson was not beholden to Congress for his nomination, but rather to the people through a Democratic party which was for the first time in American history organized down to the grass roots in much the manner of parties of today. The new President, claiming a " mandate from the people," used the veto, Presidential messages, and other previously unexplored political facets of his position to re-establish the Presidency as a co-equal of the Congress. This was not achieved without a fight. Congressional anti-Jacksonians fought rear-guard actions at every step in their effort to return once again to an era of congressional supremacy. Jackson, to them, was a tyrant " King Andrew."

Yet even when Whigs did gain the White House in 1840 and 1848, Whig Presidents seemed to forget the Congressional-supremacy ideas they had appeared to hold before assuming the office. During the Tyler Whig Administration all but one of the cabinet resigned in an attempt to force the President to resign. When that did not work, Whigs sought unsuccessfully to impeach. Democrat Polk, from 1844 to 1848, was able to work with his party's majorities in the two houses of Congress and to get his program passed. From 1848 to 1852 the Whigs had their last chance, but Taylor and Fillmore too wanted to be Jackson-type Presidents rather than fit themselves into the Congressional Whig's conception of what the Presidency should be.

It is more than a little ironic that an ex-Congressional suprem-acy Whig, Abraham Lincoln, should have been the man who stretched the constitutional powers of the Presidency far beyond any chief executive. As a leader of Congress, Lincoln might be termed a failure, but as a leader of a people in a war crisis, he was a success. Many items of the Lincoln program did pass through normal Congressional proc-esses, but the things which he could not get Congress to do, Lincoln did by executive proclamation, relying sometimes on retroactive Con-gressional approval, or if it was not forthcoming, on his powers as commander in chief.

At the news of Lincoln's assassination many Congressional lead-ers found a new hope for the old Whig concept of President-Congress relations. Vice President Johnson as an ex-Senator would give the Congressional function the recognition, it was felt, that it deserved. When Johnson continued Lincoln's cabinet, Lincoln's policies, and Lincoln's type of President-Congress relations, Congressional suprem-acy Senators and Representatives were furious. After augmenting their strength in the Congressional elections of 1866, they moved to impeach Johnson. By the razor-thin margin of one Senate vote, Radi-cal Republicans almost succeeded where Whigs had failed. Had An-drew Johnson been impeached on political grounds, a precedent might have been established which would in the future have forced all Presidents, under the threat of political impeachment, into a secondary position behind Congress.

From Grant to Cleveland, with perhaps a few temporary exceptions, Presidents were not successful in focusing the spotlight of public attention on themselves. Here was a period of reaction from the Lincoln years. Through the organization of Congressional campaign committees, the Congressional parties were able to conduct their own campaigns for re-election independent of the presidentially controlled party national committees. The power of the President to name officers in the executive branch was severely restricted through the Senate's ability to enforce " senatorial courtesy " — requiring the President to clear with the senior Senator of his party before making an appointment from that Senator's state as a condition for Senate approval of the appointment. The most powerful economic groups of the time did not want " strong " Presidents functioning as " tribunals of the people " who might get out of control, but rather sought " safe " candidates who would be amenable to the wishes of the more controllable Congress. In some of the administrations of this period the President almost abdicated his leadership function to groups of the Congress working through him. Indicative of where national government power lay was the title of Woodrow Wilson's classic treatise on the national government published in 1885 — *Congressional Government*.

Beginning during the last decade of the nineteenth century, however, the character of the Presidency again underwent a profound change. Now the " weak " President tended to become an exception rather than the rule. Breaking out of a narrow President-Congress relationship pattern, the Presidents began again supplementing their direct approach to Senators and Congressmen by going directly to the people. Grover Cleveland was the first of the modern school. McKinley was much more successful than Cleveland, and Theodore Roosevelt proved himself to be the master of the new techniques of Presidential power for leading Congress and his party.

It was Theodore Roosevelt, a Republican, who started the twentieth-century series of political " deals " with his Square Deal. In foreign affairs he had his " big stick." He approached Congress as the leader of both his party and country, and until the end of his administrations he was able to secure passage of most of the legislation he sought. Taft tried to be a " strong " President in the new tradition, but failed. Wilson came with his New Freedom and also led his party and Congress until the last two years of his second term. Harding, Coolidge, and Hoover were the twentieth-century exceptions, and would have been more at home and more successful had they served in the 1870's and 1880's. Franklin D. Roosevelt made the New Deal a political household word. By his political abilities and, aided by economic and war crises, he was able to control Congress during his first term, and generally in the field of foreign affairs thereafter. He went on to break the third-term tradition and then to win a fourth election. Truman attempted to be a " strong " President and often succeeded, and Eisenhower, though he at first appeared to take the pre-1900 view of the Presidency, has also set out to make himself a " strong " President.

With foreign affairs becoming an increasingly important function of the national government, the center of attention is directed more and more at the President who is the chief foreign affairs officer of the country. Alexis de Tocqueville, writing in 1835, predicted this development: " If the existence of the Union were perpetually threatened, if its chief interests were in daily connection with those of other powerful nations, the executive department would assume an increased importance in proportion to the measures expected of it and to those which it would execute." [3] Today a President's ability in foreign affairs is based on the support which he can generate among the people, in his party, and in Congress. And for both foreign affairs and domestic support building, the revolution in mass media of communication has given the President tools which Presidents of an earlier day could never have dreamed would someday be available.

Congressional Republicans have tended to be more distrustful of " strong " Presidential leadership than Congressional Democrats, but today the Republican party is learning the lesson that without an able and " strong " President the party as well as the country cannot have the leadership it needs and deserves. Whether for Democrats or Republicans, the party's record is dependent on the record of its President.

OBSTACLES TO PRESIDENTIAL LEADERSHIP

Major parties both want and do not want " strong " Presidents. The wanting or not wanting depends on what part of a party one is

---

[3] Quoted by Sidney Hyman, *The American President* (New York: Harper and Brothers, 1954) , p. 5.

considering. If one considers the ordinary voter who identifies himself with a party but who has no party position or re-election to Congress at stake, then the tendency is to want a " strong " President. Party officials, with patronage and party recognition at stake, tend to split roughly into two groups. First are those who are recognized by their President as the party leaders in their area, and second are those who are not. The former tend to be willing to accept and follow Presidential leadership provided it is not strong enough to have a nationalizing effect on the balance of party organizational power. The latter will generally exhaust ingenuity in attempting to limit their President's power, even if that course means defeat in the general election. Similarly, a party's members in Congress lend themselves into rough classifications as pro-President and anti-President, depending in large part on whether the legislator's district or state is similar or different in interests to the electorate which elected the President.

Powerful interest groups also tend to divide on the subject of " strong " Presidential leadership. Those groups, such as labor organizations, which feel their greatest power lies with the large masses of voters in the large pivot states usually favor a " strong " President. Those whose programs might not have broad popular appeal, whose membership is evenly distributed in most of the Congressional districts, or whose principal resource is financial tend to prefer working with a national government in which the President is relatively weak and the Congress is strong. Generally, the opposition party for the time it is out of the Presidency will also be found arrayed against concentration of " dictatorial " power in the Presidential office, though when the party once again re-enters the White House, many of its elements may quickly switch to the " strong " President position. The principal reasons why these different groups tend to want or not want " strong " Presidents illustrate how great are the obstacles to effective Presidential leadership and how necessary it is for the chief executive to be an able politician if he is to lead successfully.

The President and State Party Bosses. The state party boss or bosses — or " leaders " if the term " bosses " carries an unsavory connotation — have to look in two directions for threats to the security of their position. It is necessary to keep always in good repair their power base within their state party organization. Second, the state bosses seek to prevent a concentration of party power at the national party level which might constitute a threat to their security. The

United States has not had national political bosses. An explanation for this phenomenon is that state bosses will not permit it. If there were a national boss, the state boss could not feel secure unless he were *the* national boss. Because a national party boss' power could only be built on a foundation of state bosses, the latter are in a position to see that control does not shift to a national party official or to some powerful individual operating without party position and in the background at the national level.

Another reason there is an absence of national party bosses is that whatever centralizing tendencies may exist within a party tend to center in the person of the President. If a President is " strong " in his own right, he is not as dependent on individual state bosses, and to the extent he is independent of them, to that degree may he succeed in making his party over in his own image. Here is the principal threat to state party bosses' political power. In a political party when it does not control the Presidency, the power of state bosses is unchallenged from above. In a political party with one of its own in the White House, there does exist that potential challenge from the President.

State party bosses attempt to insulate themselves from Presidential " free-wheeling " in several ways. One is to maintain control of the national conventions through which the Presidential nominee is selected. The state boss prefers to lead a state delegation to the national convention which is uncommitted to any of the major candidates for the nomination. Sometimes, if he has his own way, the delegation is an uninstructed one or travels to the national convention proclaiming its support of a " favorite son." Once at the national convention, if such a delegation operates under a unit rule where the total vote of the delegation will be cast as the majority of the delegation vote, the bargaining power of the state boss can be considerable. This he can use in an attempt to get the kind of nominee who would be most satisfactory to him. The popular hero capable of stampeding a convention as Willkie did in 1940 is not the kind of man desired by the state boss.

If a convention should be overwhelmed by a Willkie, sometimes some of the state bosses will sit out the campaign, preferring defeat to the prospect of having the leadership of the party slip to the kind of President they fear he might be. If a Willkie attempts to establish his own Willkie Clubs to parallel the party organizations in the states, the state party bosses will do their best to stamp out the new threat to state party control. If the party's prospects of victory appear to be close or impossible and if " safe " nominees without popular appeal are not realistic choices, the attempt is made to nominate the man who might best combine both appeal and safety qualities.

Should the party's Presidential nominee be a man with power in his own right and should he be elected, the bosses have another device to enhance their possibilities of access to the national administration and to protect their control over federal patronage in their states. That is the tool of " senatorial courtesy." If a state leader controls or is working with the senior Senator of his party from his state, or with the only Senator of his party from his state, federal patronage will be routed through him. As federal patronage decreases before the expansion of the federal civil service, however, the patronage power of the state party boss tends to decrease.

One of the principal reasons for Hatch Act provisions restricting the political activities of federal employees was to lessen the possibility that a President Roosevelt could build in the states his own political machine which might become a threat to Democratic Party leaders already in control in the states. Though the act did forestall the possibility of independent Presidential patronage machines at the state level, it also took from the state party leaders a large number of potential members of their own organizations.

In the struggle for power within the parties, a " strong " President able to capture the popular imagination by his presentation of national issues and by the manner in which he conducts his office presents state party leaders with another problem. For a President to build such popular support, it is necessary for him to attempt to take positions and make appointments satisfactory to a much broader constituency than that represented by his own party organization. The line of such a President's first responsibility runs directly to the voters, and particularly to voters in certain key states, and it runs only indirectly to state party leaders. Where a state leader may demand the appointment of 100-percent party-partisans, the public in general wants the best possible man. Where a state leader may demand that the President be 100-percent party-position as the state leader interprets that position, the general public cares not whether the President is 90-percent, 70-percent, or 20-percent " Democratic " or " Republican " as long as he succeeds in solving the problems of the time and meeting the needs of the people. In a sense, the problem of state party leaders is a dilemma between their desire for " weak " Presidents who will not constitute a threat to their state party control and their need for " strong " Presidents if the party is to be really successful in winning votes.

To this point in the examination of state party leader-President relations, state party leaders or bosses have been generalized into a single category which could lead to the assumption that all were alike and reacted in the same way. Such generalization is necessary to show the organizational pressures at work within a party, but unqualified it would be too broad. The relation between state leaders and their President will tend to vary from state to state, from time to time, and from personality type to personality type.

Where a state party has a " strong " governor and he is largely in control, the attitude is likely to be more sympathetic to a " strong " President than if a state has a " weak " governor and the governor is primarily a front for others who do actually control. For the party in a doubtful state where state elections may possibly hinge on the popularity of a party's President or the positions he takes on issues, a " strong " President will tend to be more acceptable than he would be to the leaders of a party in a " safe " state or one in which the President's policies are unpopular. When a state's party leaders are in the inner circle of a President's advisory corps, have his confidence, and are in a position to participate in policy formulation, the attitude toward a " strong " President will be different from that of state party leaders who do not have close access to the President. Factors such as these will determine the intensity of the state-national intraparty conflict over power. The seeds of potential rivalry, however, are always present.

The President and His Congressional Party. If a President and enough of his party's candidates for Senator and Congressman are elected with majorities in both houses of Congress, why is it often so hard for President and Congress to work together for the advancement of a common party program? Even though the same persons who vote for Senators and Congressmen also vote for President, the constituencies of the members of Congress and the President are quite different. Members of the House of Representatives come from 435 districts with widely varying political pressure patterns. Furthermore, though the representation in the House is based on population, the manner in which state legislatures tend to overrepresent rural voters and underrepresent urban voters produces a political complexion in the House which gives rural areas more weight than they have in Presidential elections. The Senate is representative of states, with two Senators from large and small states alike. The upper house of Congress distortion from the national pressure pattern is much greater than that of the lower house.

The President, chosen by the national electorate, finds focused on him the composite of pressures from the whole country. As he reacts to those pressures, the positions he takes will conflict with the desires of some states and Congressional districts. Take, for example, a Presidential decision to disperse defense plants from coastal areas to inland areas which a President might conclude is in the national interest. Immediately he is challenged by members of Congress of both parties from the coastal states which resist having potential defense contracts turned elsewhere. Or, if a President might decide that no section should have nationally subsidized low electric power rates at the expense of other sections, again the representatives of those states which are being subsidized will rise as one man in protest.

True that he is the only single object of the national pressure pattern, but the President must also have special consideration for the sectional allies of states which form the nucleus of his power base and for the large and doubtful pivot states which may prove decisive in the next Presidential election. Always a President must, before he makes a decision, weigh the consequences his actions will produce in New York, California, Illinois, and in the newly doubtful states of Pennsylvania and Michigan. If he has the alternative on an issue of pleasing New York at the expense of Nevada, Presidential politics dictates that Nevada will generally have to be the loser. Such are some of the complications which tend to produce intraparty tensions in Congress and intraparty tensions between a President and his party in Congress. If one party controls the White House and the other party controls one or both houses of Congress, the President-Congress friction level is likely to be much greater.

Other factors operate to make Presidential leadership over Congress difficult. A state may give its electoral votes to a Franklin D. Roosevelt Democrat or an Eisenhower Republican; it may at the same time elect anti-Roosevelt Democrats or anti-Eisenhower Republicans to Congress. Congressmen and particularly Senators who have received much public notice begin to see visions of themselves as future Presidents, and some chart their courses not so much in terms of building a party program in cooperation with the President but as

persons trying to advance their own political fortunes in preparation
for the higher honors they hope will come. Congressmen and, again,
particularly Senators, are traditionally anti-chief executive whenever
they think a President is encroaching on Congressional powers, and
often for that reason tend to resist Presidential leadership.

Standing committee chairmen in both houses are chosen under
the seniority rule. The effect has been to install men in committee
chairmanships who come from " safe " districts rather than those
from close and doubtful districts which more accurately reflect the
type of pressures which determine the outcome of Presidential elections. In the House almost every major piece of legislation must gain
the approval of the seniority-selected Rules Committee before it is
scheduled for floor consideration. In the Senate, any minority, as long
as it has enough members to run a long-term filibuster, can talk a bill
to death. In both houses, at numberless points in their complicated
parliamentary procedures, one man or a small group may succeed in
changing the character of a bill or ensure its defeat. Either house may
investigate the executive branch, harass it with demands for information, or actually involve itself in what should be day-to-day questions
of administrative determination.

A President, if he is to be successful in his role of chief legislator,
must overcome these actual or potential obstacles. They are formidable and also formidable are the power tools which even Congressmen of the President's party may see fit to use against him. " The Constitution joins the president and Congress for better or worse," writes
Pendleton Herring. " But there is no pledge to love, honor *and*
obey." [4] And from the same author: " Our president cannot afford the
luxury of fighting with Congress. The political life of our chief executive is so short and his effectiveness is so dependent upon Congressional support that a protracted battle, even though successful, is a
Pyrrhic victory at best." [5]

Presidential leadership of party organization outside Congress
and of party in Congress cannot be accomplished by " weak " Presidents, nor can leadership come from those who try to be strong but
have not the political finesse and abilities to be in fact " strong "
Presidents. The President has not been left as powerless or defenseless
in the contest for intraparty power as sometimes " weak " Presidents
have made it appear. He too has power tools which will enable him

---

[4] *Op. cit.,* p. 127.   [5] *Ibid.,* pp. 51–52.

to assume leadership — provided he knows what they are and how to use them.

THE ART OF PRESIDENTIAL LEADERSHIP

Presidents are not accepted as party leaders nor do they win passage for their legislative programs merely because they are nice and

The Milwaukee Journal

Lost, One Program, On Capitol Hill

likable fellows or solely through their ability at person-to-person intimate persuasion. These qualities help lay the groundwork for leadership, but neither one nor both are in themselves enough. The President must be able to generate political pressure on those whose support he needs.

Political pressure may take two general forms. One is the type through which a President would grant or withhold patronage or apply or not apply other sanctions on the party legislator or party official depending upon the degree of support which was given to the President. This first type of pressure can sometimes be used with telling effect, but it is not nearly as important as the power which accrues to a President from genuine and broad popular support. If a President is very popular with the rank and file of his party, state party leaders who might otherwise resist him are compelled to greater cooperation in order to retain their positions as state leaders. If the President and his program capture the imagination of the voters, Senators and Congressmen will hear the voices of the people who have the votes.

Politicians may respond to tact. They may respond to a personal appeal. They may respond to patronage or other actual or potential sanctions. But they have to respond to the political pressure put on them by an aroused constituency, whether that constituency be a Senator's state, a Congressman's district, a party convention, or a state central committee. Here is the one universal language that every politician understands, even if he knows no other.

Several of the Presidential leadership tools for dealing with Congress are derived from the language of the Constitution. There is the power of veto. Presidents before Jackson interpreted the veto power narrowly and tended to use it only to attempt to stop legislation deemed to be unconstitutional. Since the Jacksonian era it has become an accepted weapon for political purposes. More important as a Presidential leadership device than the veto itself is the Presidential threat of veto. By the latter the President may succeed in pressuring Congress to modify legislation into a form which would be acceptable to the White House. The threat of veto represents political power because the two-thirds majorities necessary in both houses to override a veto seldom can be mustered. At best, however, the veto and threat of veto can be used only sparingly, and the President does not have the power, as do some state governors, of vetoing specific items of a bill while approving the remainder of the bill.

The Constitution vests in the President the right to call special sessions of Congress. Threats of a special session, if the Presidential program is not passed, are not often effective. Nor do Presidents have the power, as do some governors, to limit a special session to the consideration of the items which are enumerated in the call. Unless there is a very real national emergency, Presidents generally prefer any respites they can get from the additional duties and harassments which attend Congressional sessions.

The Constitution also instructs the President to " from time to time give to the Congress information of the state of the Union, and recommend to their consideration such measures as he shall judge necessary and expedient." Each session of Congress, the President presents his State of the Union and Budget messages, the Economic Report, and special messages, but if they were heard only by the Congress, their effect would be relatively small.

Though the President may veto, Congress can override. Though the President may call special sessions, he cannot control what the Congress does once it assembles in special session. Though the President may recommend, Congress has no legal obligation to follow his advice. The authority specifically given to the President by the Constitution is not sufficient to enable him to become chief legislator. Influence with the general public and not authority over Congress is the key to Presidential power, and influence comes primarily through the extralegal and informal tools which are available to the President by virtue of the unique position he holds.

Focused in the office of President of the United States are potentialities for influence such as are found in no other single office in the democratic world. As chief of state and nonpartisan symbol of national unity, the President, if he is not too narrowly partisan in his political actions, can achieve a prestige which inevitably has profound political effect. As chief executive of the United States, and particularly as chief foreign affairs officer, the President can have centered on him the eyes not only of the people of this country but those of all the peoples of the world. As commander in chief in time of war crisis, the President becomes the rallying point of the nation's military effort. Broad popular support for the President by virtue of his performance of these functions, in turn, can enable him to strengthen his hold over his party, and both broad popular support and party support may be used as the foundation for Congressional influence. Basic to the whole power structure of the Presidency and to the performance level at which a President can function in these five roles is his ability to appeal to and win the people.

What are the ways in which a President may appeal directly to the people? He must be the " right " type of person for the " right " time — his personality and values being an expression of the spiritual and material needs of his age. Professor Eric F. Goldman has described well the quality in the following passage which is quoted at length:

Whatever their origins, all eight Presidents (the two Roosevelts, Washington, Jefferson, Jackson, Lincoln, Cleveland, and Wilson) who proved important moral leaders shared certain ways of carrying out their leadership. The essential technique, of course, was not to need any technique; the President had to be, in his own self, the morality incarnate — not all the values which made up the American credo, but the one which was foremost as an issue at the time. A good many Americans may well have doubted how much the stiff-backed George Washington was concerned with the economic and social strivings of farmers and mechanics, but the public could and did see in the architect of victory against the British Empire the new nation incarnate. If Grover Cleveland, who had paid a substitute to fight for him during the Civil War, was hardly a symbol of the Union, the immediate and continuing impression he left was one of burly honesty. Franklin Roosevelt's warmest admirers did not deny that he was quite capable of shrugging off political skulduggery, but to millions his very voice, rich and friendly, bespoke concern over ambitions frustrated by depression.

There is a story that a devoted follower of Jackson, asked whether his hero was going to Heaven, snorted in reply: " He will if he wants to." The successful moral leader has not only been the ideal incarnate; he has been or appeared to be, a man who could do something about it. In their most conscience-lashed moments, the American people, raised in a tradition of getting things done and getting them done quickly, have shown little interest in the ineffectual saint. With the exception of Washington, whose administrations closed just as political parties were forming, the moral leaders have been men who demonstrated that they could lead, manipulate, and if necessary, hammer their own political parties into line while simultaneously outwitting the opposition. They were all able to convince powerful segments of the population that they had foreseen the next curve in the road of history and were surely, adeptly preparing for it.

Once beyond these fundamentals, each exerted effective moral leadership in his own special way, with the aid of traits of mind and personality suitable to the age. At a time when dignity was akin to godliness, George Washington gave the idea of the Republic all the aloofness of his own impeccable serenity. In an era when the frontier was feeling its power but was a bit ashamed of its uncouthness, Jackson was Opportunity in a buckskin coat and a tall silk hat. Theodore Roosevelt, coming in the midst of the great expansion of communications, turned the White House into a spectacular advertising agency for reform. In the churchist early twentieth century, Wilson managed to make some of his most expedient political moves sound moral. And a generation later, when slickness was *de rigueur,* Franklin Roosevelt gave some of his most genuinely moral moves the glamour of seeming expedient.

Perhaps the most interesting additions to the arsenal of moral leadership were made by those notable innovators, Theodore and Franklin Roosevelt. As the twentieth century whirled ahead, with its farms and factories where the boss was as remote as a feudal lord, its shaking of family cohesion and of old, comforting standards, its harsh anonymity and impersonality, millions were feeling alone, frighteningly alone. Seeking some secure anchor, they turned back to religion or ahead to Freud or into and around a dozen movements. With the kind of moral leadership the Roosevelts gave, these people could turn, as no previous generation had been able to do, to the President of the United States. For the two Roosevelts permeated all of their leadership with the suggestion that they were not only some ideal incarnate, not simply able and colorful personalities, but fathers — fathers who would preserve essential American values with the personalized concern that a family expects from its head. " Steward of the nation." T. R. used to call the President in his more portentous moments. With a flick of the long cigarette holder, F. D. R. put it: " They want Poppa to tell them." [6]

In stating that the essential technique " was not to need any technique," Goldman is perhaps oversimplifying. Whether the " buckskin coat and a tall silk hat," the " long cigarette holder," or giving the impression of being men of action or of being able to see around " the next curve in the road of history " were conscious or unconscious, they were still techniques. The important point, however, remains, namely, that the man to reach the heights of popular appeal needs to express or appear to express the most pressing needs of the people at his point in time.

There is a more contemporary example. In their own way, President Eisenhower's personality and background fit into the foremost need of the 1950's — peace if possible, but military strength to defend ourselves if necessary. Here is a man of peace who has had a lifetime career as a man of war! Here is a man who, because of his global

---

[6] " The Presidency as Moral Leadership," *The Annals of the American Academy of Political and Social Science* (March, 1952), Vol. 280, pp. 42–44. Reprinted by permission of *The Annals.*

range of experiences and personal acquaintanceships with many of the political leaders of other countries, might be more successful than some other man in transforming intermittent cold and hot war into peace! But if war should come, who better would there be to direct the fight than the one-time Commander in Chief of the Allied Forces in Europe and our World War II hero!

A second way in which a President may appeal directly to the people is through the media of communication which are available to him because he is the President of the United States. If he personally presents a message to Congress, it will be carried on television, radio, and in the newspapers. When he wants to speak directly to the American people, again the facilities of television and radio are thrown open to him. Franklin Roosevelt's " My Friends " as it came into the homes and next to the firesides had a profound political effect, and because it was not during a political campaign, Republicans had no grounds for demanding equal time. The potentialities of television for Presidential leadership are even greater.

Through the White House press conference there is a weekly opportunity to make news. Vacation trips, " summit conferences," lighting the White House Christmas tree, kicking off a Red Cross drive, letters congratulating a couple on their golden wedding anniversary — these are some of the reasons why the President's picture, his words, and what are guessed to be his thoughts are every day before the American people. His daily doings, those of the First Lady, those of his dog if he has one, and those of his grandchildren will be reported and editorialized in detail.

Senators and Congressmen are in the news too. However, in general, the time or space devoted to any one of the 531 members of Congress is minute as compared with that given the President. If the President is able effectively to project himself and his program over the media available to him, he can reach down into the Senators' states and Congressmen's districts and make his voice, traveling via the people in those states and districts, heard in the halls of Congress. Also listening to measure the intensity of the relayed messages are political party leaders, with those of the President's party using their reading to re-examine their relationship to him and with those of the opposition party using their reading to determine whether damage has been done and whether a counterattack is desirable or necessary.

In infantry terms, direct communication with the people is a

President's "atomic cannon." What, now, are the smaller weapons in his arsenal designed for pin-point application of political pressure to the individual members of a President's party in Congress or to those in the state party organizations outside Congress?

Patronage is one such weapon. It was perhaps the principal reason why a potential House Democratic rebellion in 1933 against President Roosevelt's drastic economy bill could be squelched after this admonition was spoken by one of the Democratic leaders on the House floor: " When the *Congressional Record* goes to President Roosevelt's desk in the morning, he will look over the roll call we are about to take, and I warn you new Democrats to be careful where your names are found." [7]

Since Jefferson, Presidents have utilized patronage for leverage over their party. Lincoln used not only federal jobs, but also commissions in the army for the same effect. Stating the theory of patronage baldly, if a party member is " right," he gets his jobs; if he is " wrong," his jobs will go to some rival who is more willing to be " right."

Federal patronage, before the advent of civil service, was always available in quantity. Even after civil service the sources dried only slowly. Franklin D. Roosevelt, with the vast expansion of federal government agencies to meet the economic crisis and later the war crisis, was the beneficiary of what might be termed a patronage bonanza. Only since 1953 when President Eisenhower assumed office to find approximately 90 percent of federal employees under some form of civil service, has a substantial number of jobs not been available for the President to fill.

Two rules which have almost attained the status of principles of patronage dispensation should be stated. First, all patronage should not be passed out immediately after a President assumes office. When the jobs are gone, the political leverage which patronage brings is gone. Second, the President should be careful to use patronage as far as possible to strengthen his wing of his party. If he has delegated the job-dispensing function carelessly to one who represents a wing of the party different from that of the President, the latter may soon note a perceptible tendency for legislative votes and state party organizations to slip in a direction away from him and in the way that the job dispenser wants them to go.

---

[7] Herring, *op. cit.,* p. 59.

The President may choose his *Cabinet* for the political effect the members will have with different elements of the party organization, with Senators and Congressmen of his party, with geographical sections of the country and with the most powerful pressure groups. Ideal Cabinet members are persons who have political ability and political power in their own right, and who are also good administrators. If, however, a choice need be made between the politician and administrator, the former should get the first consideration. Day to day administration of a department can be handled by the administrators directly below the Cabinet level. For those positions, administrative competence and knowledge of the specialty area in which the department operates should control.

Abraham Lincoln's Cabinet is one of the best illustrations of how a President can enhance his position by wise Cabinet choices. Ulysses S. Grant's Cabinet is an example of how a President can undermine his position by poor selections. Lincoln attempted, in Carl Sandburg's words, to " combine the experience of Seward, the integrity of Chase, the popularity of Cameron; to hold the West with Bates, attract New England with Wells, please the Whigs through Smith and convince the Democrats through Blair." [8] Grant, on the other hand, a man who was not an effective politician and one who badly needed sound political advice, consulted with no one in making his appointments, and tended to pick personal friends without either political ability or political power. The Pennsylvanian he nominated for Secretary of Navy was known to neither of Pennsylvania's two Senators. Grant's nominee for Secretary of Treasury was a multimillionaire New York importer who frightened high-tariff Republicans.[9] Though several of Lincoln's Cabinet personally detested the President, he put up with that to gain the advantage of their political effect. Grant may have had a congenial Cabinet, but its members were of little political help, or it is perhaps more accurate to say they tended to be a hindrance.

A President's functions are primarily political. Cabinet members who thoroughly understand politics can assist the President by holding in line the party, geographic or economic groups from which they come, and by enabling the chief executive to delegate responsi-

---

[8] *Lincoln: The War Years,* Volume I (New York: Harcourt, Brace and Company, 1939) , p. 153. Quoted by Wilfred E. Binkley, *American Political Parties* (New York: Alfred A. Knopf, 1949) , p. 236.

[9] From *ibid.,* p. 293.

bility with confidence so he can concentrate on his top-level politics.
Department heads without political ability or power can keep a
President in hot political water and perhaps make it necessary for
him to handle their departmental political function as well as his
own.

A third small weapon at the disposal of the President is suggested
by his *daily appointment list*. To have the opportunity to visit with
the President, or better yet, to be asked to " consult with the President," is a high honor and not without its own political implication.
When Samuel Gompers as head of the American Federation of Labor
was frequently a guest of McKinley and later Theodore Roosevelt in
the White House, the following triple effect could be observed. Members of the American Federation of Labor could take pride in the fact
that their leader was being consulted by the highest officer of the
land. The publicity from such meetings helped Gompers maintain
his position with his union, and it helped the President attract both
Gompers and potential union member votes. It was not an accident
that McKinley and Theodore Roosevelt were able to build a Republican combination which included the eastern worker which, in turn,
prevented William Jennings Bryan from forging a western farmer-
eastern worker Democratic alliance.

The Congressman or Senator who " consults with the President "
will tend to be stronger at home because of the identification. Also,
the state or local party leader who is *persona non grata* to the President may get no invitations to the White House, no invitation to join
the President's entourage on his train as it travels through the leader's
state, or no invitation to sit on the platform when the President de-
livers an address in the state. If the popular appeal of the President
is strong, not to be asked to " consult with the President " when
others of your rank are so consulting can have its politically damaging effects.

A President may further influence state party leaders and party
members in Congress by the manner in which he *intervenes in primary and general election campaigns*. Intervention in general elections is a common practice and always the President is forced, in the
name of party unity, to some statement advocating the election of all
who run under his party label. More effective, however, are selective
and forceful endorsements of individual candidates of the President's
party. Here the chief executive may use his prestige by going out of
his way to show in some manner that he is strongly behind those

candidates of his party who have been or who promise to be his strongest supporters. If such men are elected or re-elected, they are likely to remain among those who are most loyal to the President.

Intervention in primary elections in his party is the most hazardous of the President's leadership tools. For a President to endorse one

" B—BUT, IT REALLY IS A WOLF "

of two or more candidates seeking nomination is to risk the enmity of those he passes over and the enmity of their supporters. It is also to risk resentment against Presidential interference in states or Congressional districts where he makes a pre-primary choice known. Franklin D. Roosevelt's " purge " attempt in 1938 will long stand as a warning to Presidents who contemplate public intervention in primary elections. The men Roosevelt opposed were able to turn his opposition to their candidacies into an advantage, and none of them were defeated.

The Roosevelt example, however, was Presidential intervention in primary elections in its clumsiest form, and should not necessarily keep a President from engaging in such leadership activity. Risk of backlash from " interference " in state party primaries can be minimized by the chief executive's being selective in the contests in which he takes a hand and by the chief executive's remaining in the background in his primary election operations. Little good is accomplished by attempting to defeat established Senators and Congressmen who control or largely control their state party organizations. Such Congressional opponents within the President's party must be lived with, and the President must do his best to get them on his side when he can or to neutralize their anti-President influence on issues when they cannot be won over. If an anti-President Senator or Congressman of the President's party is weak at home, the President may quietly be instrumental in inducing a strong candidate to run for the nomination. Or if the seat is held by the opposition party, the President may more easily, but still quietly, induce one from his own wing of the party to file for the office.

Principal argument against Presidential activity in primary campaigns is that such activity is damaging to party unity. The President, it is said, should do nothing to risk driving elements out of the party or to risk driving them into passivity for the party cause. Such an argument is valid, provided the party is already a winning combination. If the party does not represent a winning combination, to overstress unity is to invite the same fate as befell the Federalists. Solid unity in a party which is weak tends to prevent that party from expanding its appeal to take in enough other elements to enable it to be strong. There are times when a President neglects his opportunity to strengthen his own leadership position and the position of his party if he does not tactfully attempt to take a hand in securing the nomination of persons who will, when in Congress, assist in building the type of programs necessary for the party to win Presidential elections.

Part of a President's ability to use successfully the leadership tools at his command is dependent on the expectation that he will be a candidate for renomination and re-election. If he has announced that he will not be a candidate to succeed himself, some of the spotlights of public attention will shift from him to those who are candidates. In Congress his party will tend to break even further into factional groups, and now the focus of such factions will be toward potential Presidential candidates. State party leaders will begin to choose sides. Whatever patronage is available is only for the short remaining months of the President's term of office. In such a situation, Presidential influence tends to diminish. The Twenty-second (" two-term limit ") Amendment means greater difficulty for even the " strong " Presidents in their second terms of office.

When a man becomes President of the United States, what kind of a " President " shall he try to be? " As the seashells of 156,000,000 humming people raise a din in his ears, all the Presidents who have held his place before him lay a hand on his shoulders. They demand that he enlarge himself beyond his natural talents. They also demand that he tame his rebelliousness. One says, ' Thou shalt.' The other says, ' Thou shalt not.' One says, ' Be bold.' The other says, ' Be circumspect.' One says, ' The scrupulous respect for the law is the highest duty of every officer.' The other says, ' The higher duty is to save the country when it is in danger.' " [10] There is no set formula. The Presidency, while he occupies the office, will be what he makes it.

CONCLUSION

" Strong " Presidents are able to some degree to provide party and Congressional leadership; " weak " Presidents fail in both functions. Might it not be possible to institutionalize or formalize President-Congress and President-party relations to minimize the great contrast between the effectiveness of the two types of Presidents? Might not formalization of those relationships make the Presidency as an institution of government less dependent upon the abilities of the man who occupies the office? Might not formalization of those relationships make the President a more responsible chief executive?

Many suggestions to accomplish such a result have been advanced. Some would establish a joint President-Congress cabinet. Some would establish a national party council composed of party representatives from the executive branch, both houses of Congress, and other party organizations. Some would permit officials of the executive branch to participate on the floors of the two houses of Congress. Some of these proposals will be examined in Chapters Twenty-three and Twenty-four.

---

[10] Hyman, *op. cit.,* pp. 54–55.

PART THREE

Winning Elections:

PARTY HISTORY THREADED ON FOUR
THEMES

INTRODUCTION

In only one period of American political party history, for approximately fifteen to twenty years prior to the election of 1896, have the two American major political parties existing at the time been in a power position where each had as much chance as the other to capture the offices of the national government. First there was the brief period of Federalist supremacy from 1789 to 1800. It was followed by twenty-four years of Jeffersonian Republican party dominance. From 1828 to 1860 Jacksonian Democrats were substantially more successful than National Republicans and Whigs. From 1860 to 1932 Republicans were generally in control, and particularly was that party's strength greater than the Democratic opposition after 1896. From 1932 to 1952, the Democratic and Republican party positions were reversed from the immediately preceding period. Table 1 illustrates the supremacy phenomenon over the entire course of American political history.

Why has one of the two major parties of each era of party history tended to be supreme while the other is in effect a minority major party? The most obvious answer is that the supreme party was able to develop a broader base of popular support. Except for the transitory Federalist party, Jeffersonian Republicans, Jacksonian Democrats, Lincoln and Roosevelt Republicans, and Franklin D. Roosevelt Democrats were better able than their opposition to convince a larger number of people in the various sections of the country that they represented " peoples' parties " more dedicated to the best spiritual or material interests of more citizens eligible to vote than the opposition. Here is the simple yet major theme running through American political party history. Corollary to it are three minor themes, each in turn contributing to broad appeal.

First of the minor themes is the importance of political flexibil-

240

Table 1. Periods of American Political Party History Showing Which Major Party Was Supreme and Which Was the Minority Major Party for Each Period

(Note that in each era, the name of the supreme party is in capital letters and the name of the minority major party is in lower case. Note also that the name of the President who established or re-established his party as the supreme party after a period when it had been a minority major party is also in capital letters.)

President	Party	Presidential Election Years
WASHINGTON	FEDERALIST	1789
		1792
John Adams		1796
JEFFERSON	REPUBLICAN	1800
		1804
Madison		1808
		1812
Monroe		1816
		1820
J. Q. Adams		1824
JACKSON	DEMOCRATIC	1828
		1832
Van Buren		1836
*W. H. Harrison — Tyler	Whig	1840
Polk	DEMOCRATIC	1844
*Taylor — Fillmore	Whig	1848
Pierce	DEMOCRATIC	1852
Buchanan		1856
*LINCOLN —	REPUBLICAN	1860
Johnson		1864
Grant		1868
		1872
Hayes		1876
*Garfield — Arthur		1880
Cleveland	Democratic	1884
B. Harrison	REPUBLICAN	1888
Cleveland	Democratic	1892
*McKinley	REPUBLICAN	1896
— T. Roosevelt		1900
		1904
Taft		1908
Wilson	Democratic	1912
		1916
*Harding — Coolidge	REPUBLICAN	1920
		1924
Hoover		1928
*F. ROOSEVELT	DEMOCRATIC	1932
		1936
		1940
— Truman		1944
		1948
Eisenhower	Republican	1952

    * Died in office.

ity. Electorates are ever changing in character as are economic and social problems. If a party is to develop or maintain broad appeal, it must be flexible enough to continuously redesign its program and personality to the requirements of each transitional stage through which problems change and each stage through which the electorate passes. Though a party may at one time be broad enough in appeal to consistently win elections, inflexibility of organization and program paves the way for the opposition major party to come to power. Classic is the illustration of how the inflexible Federalist party was unable to adapt itself to its changing political environment.

A second minor theme is the importance of party unity. The major party with the greatest degree of internal cohesion, provided it also has broad appeal, will tend to be more effective than a less cohesive party. Unity itself is a contributing factor toward the production of broad appeal. A respectably united party at least gives the appearance of knowing what it is doing, and thus its leadership position and attractiveness to the electorate is enhanced. A united party is a more sparkling symbol than one rent continuously by deep and debilitating factionalism. The significance of this theme is nowhere more clearly discernible than the contrast between the Jacksonian Democratic party at the height of its power and the Whig party which was never able to pull itself together.

The third minor theme is the importance of Presidential leadership. The President or Presidential nominee is a major element in a party's appeal. If there is to be party unity, here is the source from which leadership toward unity must come. If there is to be flexibility, the President must be " strong " enough as a party leader to make possible the adaptation of the party to the new conditions of a new period. Where a Theodore Roosevelt can perform his functions in such a manner as to earn the title of master politician, a William Howard Taft, without the Roosevelt touch, may preside at his party's temporary and partial liquidation.

Broad appeal, flexibility, unity, and Presidential leadership are of prime importance to a major party and are the principal political lessons to be learned from American party history. Should they seem too elemental to warrant study, one need only examine the contemporary political scene in either major party to observe that even some practicing politicians in high party and public places are either not aware of the themes or do not regard them as significant. Also, one need not look far to find examples of men who have developed from poor politicians into able politicians because at some point in their development they began to understand the importance of the variations on these four themes and were able to make contemporary applications of them.

The able party politician is an artist in consciously or unconsciously being able to apply the political lessons of the past and his estimate of what will develop in the future to a realistic evaluation of the problems of the present. Though political settings of each period of party history may differ in degree one from another, the basic facts of political life have tended to remain constant throughout all the periods. From Federalists and Whigs there are negative lessons, and from Jeffersonian Republicans and Jacksonian Democrats there are some positive lessons to be learned. Democrats and Republicans since 1860 have, from one stage of their development to another, succeeded or not succeeded for some reasons which can be established and for other reasons which permit an " educated guess." Here are case studies which do have " bread and butter " significance for the practicing party politician of the 1950's, and validity for anyone who is to gain a basic understanding of party politics.

An attempt has been made in the four following chapters which comprise Part Three to examine the major parties for the nature of their appeal and for their quality of flexibility, unity, and Presidential leadership. All four characteristics are closely interrelated, and therefore overlapping between sections is inevitable. This form of organization has been chosen, however, because it makes possible the placing of greater emphasis on the importance of each characteristic as it relates to the degree of success of each major party in each period.

CHAPTER TEN

Federalists and Jeffersonian Republicans

On September 11, 1789, Alexander Hamilton took the oath of office as first Secretary of the Treasury. On March 22, 1790, Thomas Jefferson entered upon his duties as Secretary of State. By the summer of 1792, open warfare had broken out between these powerful members of the Cabinet. On August 23, 1792, President Washington wrote to Jefferson, and three days later to Hamilton, begging each of them for mutual forbearance lest their bitter quarrels " tare the Machine asunder " and disrupt the Union of the States. His appeal was in vain: Jefferson resigned his office December 31, 1793, and Hamilton . . . finally left office on January 31, 1795.

The great issues of policy, domestic and foreign, which occasioned this historic quarrel are well known. Jefferson cherished the ideal of an agricultural society; Hamilton a balanced economy calling for substantial development of manufactures, banking, corporations, and cities. Jefferson had an ardent faith in the masses; Hamilton had little. Jefferson favored little government and that mostly in the states and their smallest subdivisions; Hamilton needed a national government capable of energetic direction of the public economy to produce the balanced system he believed essential. Jefferson stood in principle for the predominance of popular legislative bodies; Hamilton expounded the theory and practice of executive leadership. In foreign affairs, Jefferson was attached to France and to the beneficent influence which he saw in the French Revolution, while Hamilton admired English institutions, feared the consequences of the Revolution, and believed that the interests of the United

States required above all the maintenance of good relations with Great Britain. These conflicts of policy in matters both domestic and foreign were fundamental, and fatal to effective collaboration.

Leonard D. White [1]

Out of the conflict between Alexander Hamilton and Thomas Jefferson, both members of President Washington's Cabinet, the first two American major parties evolved. Washington, following his

Figure 2. Electoral Votes for Federalist and Republican Candidates for President, 1789–1820

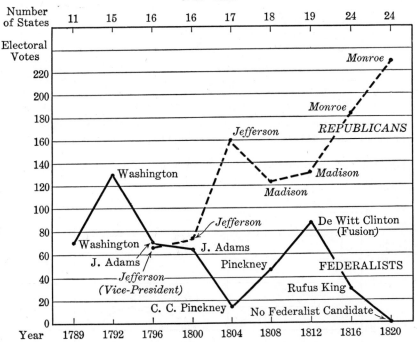

Notes: 1. Before the Twelfth Amendment, in effect for the first time in the Presidential election of 1804, the candidate with the most electoral votes, if he had an absolute majority, became President; and the second highest, Vice President.

2. During this period, in approximately half the states, Presidential electors were selected by state legislatures. Beginning in 1820, there was a shift to the "general ticket" popular election of Presidential electors, and by 1832, only South Carolina of the 24 states had its legislature selecting Presidential electors.

Source: U. S. Bureau of Census, *Historical Statistics of the United States, 1789–1945* (Washington, D.C.: Government Printing Office, 1949), p. 290.

---

[1] *The Federalists* (New York: The Macmillan Company, 1948), pp. 222–223. Reprinted by permission of The Macmillan Company.

Figure 3. Federalist and Republican Seats in the U. S. House of Representatives, 1789–1823

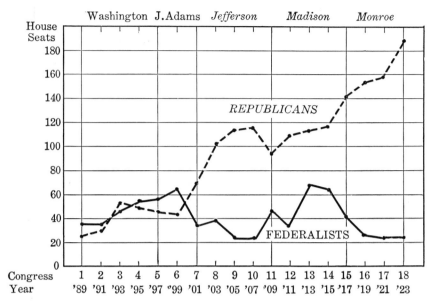

Source: U. S. Bureau of Census, *Historical Statistics of the United States, 1789–1945* (Washington, D.C.: Government Printing Office, 1949), p. 293.

Figure 4. Federalist and Republican Seats in the U. S. Senate, 1789–1823

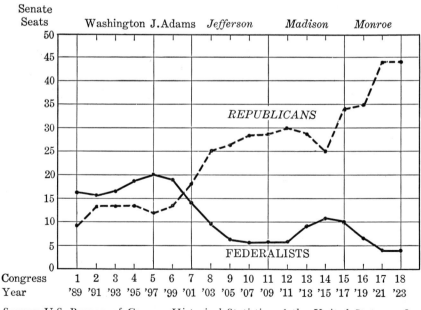

Source: U.S. Bureau of Census, *Historical Statistics of the United States, 1789–1945* (Washington, D.C.: Government Printing Office, 1949), p. 293.

theory that the President should remain above partisan conflict, did his best to hold himself aloof, but did not succeed. As questions were brought to a head, Presidential decisions were required. Generally the positions taken were in support of Hamilton or Hamiltonian objectives. The latter was the chief architect of the Federalist party program. Jefferson, Madison, Gallatin, and Monroe were the political and intellectual leaders of the Republican party, with Jefferson ranking first among the four.

Figure 2 shows in summary form the degree of electoral success achieved by the Federalists and Jeffersonian Republicans in Presidential elections; Figure 3, the degree of success in winning United States House of Representatives majorities; and Figure 4, the degree of success in winning Senate majorities. Even in the short decade of so-called Federalist " supremacy," the Republicans did capture control of the House for the 1793–1795 Third Congress, and in 1796 Jefferson came within three electoral votes of defeating John Adams for the Presidency (Adams 71, Jefferson 68). From this point Federalist fortunes, as the charts show, were on a decline which led to that party's virtual extinction by 1816. Republican successes, in contrast, came in such quantity that the party of Jefferson was, for a time, the only major party. Not until 1824 did Republicans split into the two wings out of which developed the Jacksonian Democratic party, on one side, and the National Republican party and later the Whig party on the other.

THE SETTING

Roots of economic conflict between groups making up the Federalist party and the Republican party are nowhere more sharply dramatized than in an event in Massachusetts in 1786 — Shays' Rebellion. Captain Daniel Shays and many veterans of the Revolutionary War like him had returned home to a mortgaged farm to find farm product prices low, taxes high, and the threat of foreclosure and debtors' prison very real. Those in control of Massachusetts politics in the 1780's — the propertied groups of the coastal towns — in addition to requiring property qualifications for voting and the right to serve in the state legislature, had apportioned representation in the upper house of the legislature according to taxes paid. As a result, the western farmer was underrepresented, and the workers of the coastal communities did not have the right to vote.

'Thus enthroned, the dominant interests proceeded to extract their pound of flesh,' writes Wilfred E. Binkley. " Not content with piling land taxes on debt-impoverished farmers, they superimposed a vicious poll tax that alone provided forty per cent of the state's revenues. Pathetic petitions came from farmers' meetings, protesting that in ' the state and county taxes, town and class taxes, the amount is equal to what our farms will rent for ' and ' many of our good inhabitants are now confined in gaol for debt and for taxes '; but all protests went unheeded by Governor and legislature." [2]

The embattled farmers finally resorted to unorganized use of force, breaking up sessions of courts at which demands of creditors or the state were being enforced against them. Then, organizing and enlisting the leadership of Shays, the farmers set out to seize the Springfield arsenal. Their objects were to abolish the Massachusetts State Senate, to move the capital inland away from Boston, to stimulate the sale of state lands, to reduce tax burdens, and to obtain inflation in order to ease the burden of debt. Shays' Rebellion was put down after Boston merchants raised enough money to send the state militia against the protesting farmers, but so frightened did the " established interests " of the community become that many of the demands were granted. Even more important, the incident catalyzed the movement which resulted in the meeting of the Constitutional Convention in 1878.[3]

Those rebelling farmers of 1786 in Massachusetts and others like them in similar economic circumstances were eventually to become Jeffersonian Republicans. The " Boston interests " and groups with similar economic stakes later became the heart of the Federalist combination. Of the latter, there was the creditor, frightened at the inflationary tendencies of the state legislatures. He wanted a strong central government to prevent inflation. There were the holders of Revolutionary War bonds and those engaged in war bond speculation. There was the Order of the Cincinnati, an organization of officers of the Revolutionary Army, and in the pockets of its members were promises of five years of extra pay. Congress' credit had, however, depreciated to the point of making the bonds and promises to pay almost worthless. A strong central government could establish sound credit.

---

[2] Wilfred E. Binkley, *American Political Parties* (New York: Alfred A. Knopf, 1949), pp. 12–13.
[3] From *ibid.*, pp. 12–14.

Speculators in western lands wanted a national army capable of policing their investments. Shipowners and shipbuilders wanted a navy to protect commerce on the high seas. Manufacturers and their employees wanted tariffs to help their infant industries. Southern planters looked for help against Indians in their push to the westward to open up new lands to replace acres already burned out. Merchants desired the elimination of tariff barriers between the states because economic warfare back and forth across state boundaries threatened to gradually strangle trade. A strong central government, it was felt, was necessary to accomplish these objectives.

Here were the principal economic forces which underlay the Constitution, worked for its ratification and later supported the Federalist program. The interests were those of the eastern seaboard. Within the seaboard, they were those of the larger towns; and within the towns, those of the economic and social " haves " as distinguished from the " have nots." The individual who tended to become a Federalist was likely to be a member of the long-established Congregational Church in New England or the state-supported Episcopal Church in the South. His ideal society tended to be of an aristocratic and stratified character. He liked the idea of a static society, all the better to maintain his position in it. When he looked out to the inland West, he saw the frontier populated with " barbarian agrarians " — a dangerous threat to the stability of his social, economic, political, and religious institutions.

Such apprehension was not without some cause. The agrarian had immigrated to this country from Europe to escape poverty, the degradation of a stratified social system, or to find religious freedom. If he were of native American stock, his economic and social status in the established coastal communities had been low. He looked beyond the hazards and inconveniences of the West toward a vision of something better for himself and his family. His creed was a militant democratic equalitarianism.

Most agrarians had had to buy their land from an " eastern speculator " who had arrived first, and they were in debt to creditors in eastern towns. While the creditor wanted deflation, the debtor wanted inflation. When the far-western farmer asked for help against the Indians, governors and legislatures were slow in responding or help never arrived. Underrepresented in the state legislatures, the agrarian bore more than his fair share of the tax burden. Likely to be a member of a dissenting Baptist, Presbyterian, or Methodist

" sect," the agrarian tended to resent being taxed to support a state church or to resist those who would and did attempt to enforce religious conformity upon him.

For a brief time the external threat of the British had brought the " eastern interests " and the " western interests " of the country together to fight the Revolutionary War through to victory. Then they parted again. Maintaining its hold on the agrarian's imagination from the war experience, however, were the bold phrases of the Declaration of Independence which he felt should apply just as much within America as they had against the British:

> We hold these truths to be self evident, that all men are created equal, that they are endowed by their Creator with certain unalienable Rights, that among these are Life, Liberty and the pursuit of Happiness. That to secure these rights, Governments are instituted among Men, deriving their just powers from the consent of the governed. That whenever any Form of Government becomes destructive of these ends, it is the Right of the People to alter or to abolish it, and to institute new Government. . . .

Western farmers were not delegates to the deliberations in Philadelphia in 1787. If they had been there, the result would have been different. A new form of centralization, the agrarian felt, would be no better than the old tyranny of Britain. To adopt such a form of government would be to abandon the ideals of the Revolutionary War. The states should retain their sovereignty and remain independent, and if a national government was to be vested with any real powers, such powers should be only in the field of foreign affairs.

The time was not yet for the voice of the West to be heard. Underrepresentation in the state legislatures carried over into similar underrepresentation in the state conventions set up to consider the question of ratifying the Constitution. As has been noted, the agrarian's potential ally, the worker of the coastal communities, did not yet have the right to vote. The new federal government, after the pro-Constitution forces compromised by promising a Bill of Rights, was established. The stage was then set for the development of the Federalist party program.

Before proceeding to the politics of the Federalists and Republicans, however, Census Bureau estimates of population characteristics of the 1790–1830 period deserve attention. Of the 3,929,214 inhabitants of the United States in 1790, only 5 percent or 201,655 lived in incorporated urban places of 2,500 or more people. By 1830, when the total population had reached 12,866,020, the percentage of urban to rural population was only 10 percent.[4] " In general it is safe to say that the Republicans from the beginning usually commanded a substantial popular majority. But there were large numbers who were not qualified to vote, and like all American majorities down to the present time, it was splintered and undisciplined." [5]

THE FEDERALISTS

Nature of Federalist Appeal. " Federalists accepted the philosophy of government for the people, but not government by the people. In their view, government could only be well conducted if it was in the hands of the superior part of mankind — superior in education, in economic standing, and in native ability." [6] John Adams, in his exchange of letters with his old antagonist, Jefferson, after both men had left political life, put it this way:

> You was well persuaded in your own mind that the nation would succeed in establishing a free republican government. I was well persuaded in mine, that a project of such a government, over five-and-twenty millions of people, when four-and-twenty millions and five hundred thousand of them could neither read nor write, was as unnatural, irrational, and impracticable as it would be over the elephants, lions, tigers, panthers, wolves, and bears, in the royal menagerie at Versailles.[7]

Such was the general Federalist philosophical premise about the nature and abilities of the common man.

Economically, the Federalists held that those in control of government were in the best position to determine what type of economy would best serve the needs of the infant United States and that the national government should adopt programs to accomplish their economic objectives. In a sense, the attitude was not dissimilar from some of the more advanced of the New Deal school of " economic planners " in the 1930's. The Federalists, however, wanted to round

---

[4] Statistics from *Historical Statistics of the United States 1789–1945: A Supplement to the Statistical Abstract of the United States* (Washington, D. C.: Government Printing Office, 1949) , p. 25.

[5] Stuart Gerry Brown, *The First Republicans* (Syracuse: Syracuse University Press, 1954) , p. 50.

[6] White, *op. cit.,* p. 508.

[7] Quoted by Brown, *op. cit.,* pp. 167–168.

out the American economy from one based primarily on agriculture to a " balanced agricultural-manufacturing-trading " society. Among the Federalists, Alexander Hamilton was the directing force behind the program designed to produce that result.

Hamilton's financial program was the master key to the Federalist position. The federal government should pay debts contracted with foreign creditors by pre-Constitution federation congresses; then it should pay face value on Revolutionary War bonds held by domestic creditors; next it should assume the debts of the states, most of which had been incurred in order to prosecute the Revolutionary War; and last a national bank should be established. Few disagreed with the first proposal, but the remaining three met with vigorous opposition.

Why, it was argued, should the federal government pay face value on government bonds when most of the bonds were in the hands of speculators who had acquired them at far below face value? Hamilton, however, prevailed. Just before the federal government obligated itself to repay at face value, speculators fanned out over the remote areas of the country buying up more bonds at large discounts from holders who were not aware of the impending action. The agrarian's contempt for the speculator was reinforced.

Only by an artful piece of logrolling did Hamilton gain Congressional approval for assumption of state debts. The national Capitol was first located in New York City. Hamilton won two Virginia representatives (Virginia had already paid up its debt) by agreeing to removal of the Capitol from New York to the banks of the Potomac. Pennsylvania's House delegation was in part swung into line when it was further agreed that Philadelphia should be the seat of government for a ten-year interim period in the move from New York to the District of Columbia.[8]

As a by-product to the establishment of sound credit, huge gains went into the pockets of security holders. They were happy and grateful to the Federalists. Agrarians, on the other hand, began to feel that the federal government was in league with the " speculator parasites," and they were frightened at the prospect of the new money power of the national government.

As the fourth main plank in the Hamilton financial program, a United States National Bank — a governmental agency in which

---

[8] From Binkley, *op. cit.,* pp. 38–39.

most of the stock was to be owned by private individuals and controlled by them through the holding of a majority of seats on the board of directors — was established. The purpose was to provide a nation-wide banking service, and incidentally at least, to tie the financial community even closer to the federal government. Men of money rushed to buy the stock, and the distrust of the agrarian with Federalist policies deepened.

Tariffs pleasing to manufacturers and those who worked in their establishments were passed, though they were not as high as Hamilton had asked. New England fishermen obtained subsidies to replace those previously paid by the British. Shipowners received preferential tonnage duties to compensate for the disadvantages of not being a part of the British Empire. " Hamilton," in the words of Binkley, " had perceived precisely the motivating means by which to unify the non-agrarian interests — the ' rich, the wellborn and the good ' — already the ruling class in their several communities." [9]

Federalists succeeded in establishing public credit. They did greatly help the shipbuilding industry, fisheries, and ocean-going commerce, but the time was not yet ripe for the industrial revolution which Hamilton had hoped to stimulate. Though Federalist plans had included internal improvements for harbors, roads, and canals, most of their accomplishments in this field were on harbor improvement, which particularly helped ocean-borne commerce. Roads and canals which might have attracted the farmer in need of farm-to-market means of transportation were neglected. Federalists did keep the new nation out of war at a time when peace was necessary for the new government to establish itself on a solid foundation.

Quality of Federalist Flexibility. In the early 1790's the business cycle had swung up to boom from the bust level of the middle 1780's, and the Federalist party cup seemed to be running over. But Hamilton's strength in achieving the results which he had produced was also his and his party's weakness. Rapid expansion of the frontier, organization of an opposition, and skillful opposition leadership had numbered the days during which the elements of the Federalist coalition, as it then existed, could continue to hold enough political power to control the national government. The Federalist party might have survived if it had had the ability to recognize the true nature of the

---

[9] *Ibid.*, p. 71.

rapidly changing political climate and the flexibility to adjust to change, but it was unable to adapt.

Hamilton in particular and the Federalists in general did not really understand the western frontier, the people who lived there, the common people who lived everywhere, and their potential political power. Instead, the Federalists acknowledged only the interests of New England as a section and the creditors, speculators, merchants, shippers, and shipbuilders. Federalist party members came from and represented these groups. The elements of the Federalist combination were rewarded and rewarded over again, but the emerging masses of western democracy were virtually ignored. The Federalists were never able to approach, to say nothing of win over, the new dynamic political forces that Thomas Jefferson organized into an opposition political party.

The story of Federalist insensitivity and inflexibility can be traced step by step. Agrarians had been frightened by each new item of Hamilton's financial program, but they were infuriated by Hamilton's whisky tax. To the West, whisky was considered a necessity, not only as a product for home consumption, but, more important, it was the means by which many farmers got their product to market. Without river transport or roads for carrying bulk grain, or if transportation was available it was too costly, conversion of grain into distilled spirits enabled the farmer to earn the cash required to buy necessities from the general store and to pay taxes. So vital to the economy of the West was whisky that it was even used in lieu of currency. Federalists could not have hit the western farmer in a more vital spot. Behind the whisky tax, the agrarian saw the hand of all those who would shift tax burdens onto him, or what was worse, who would deprive him of his means of livelihood. Armed revolt followed, and in 1794 the Hamilton-led United States Army was called out to put down the Whisky Rebellion.

Following Hamilton's leadership, Federalists used the rebellion in their political propaganda to show " that mobs of people were not to be trusted." A powerful central government was necessary, it was argued, to preserve order. Washington, using the same theme in his annual message on November 19, 1794, reflected on the rebellion and attacked " certain self-created societies " — Republican clubs — which had sympathized with the whisky rebels and had been attacking his administration.[10] Republicans responded with an increase

---

[10] From Brown, *op. cit.,* pp. 69–70.

in their opposition activity. The Whisky Rebellion, writes Stuart Gerry Brown, " was more than an incident. It proved the final guarantee that the two parties could never be united. . . . Federalist policies became more openly directed to the interest of the financial and commercial classes and more than ever devoted to the ascendance of the national authority over not only states but individuals. Republican cooperation became for the most part impossible. . . ." [11]

By the time of the Whisky Rebellion tension between the Federalist party and its opposition had already been rapidly increasing as a result of events in Europe. The French Revolution brought out, down to the very roots, the ideological cleavage between the two groups. Forces of social and economic position were horrified at the afterbirth of terror following the fall of the Bastille. The equalitarian, on the other hand, felt a strong bond of sympathy as he looked at an oversimplified picture of the Frenchman fighting to overthrow tyranny as Americans had done a few years before.

Then in 1793 France and Britain were at war, and important economic considerations were injected into American reactions. Trade with Britain largely supported the economy of New England and the coastal areas, but out on the frontier the farmer nursed a deep-seated anti-British grudge. He blamed England for inciting the Indians against him. His memory of the American Revolution had not been dimmed by the benefits of post-Revolutionary War trade. Pressures in the East tended to be for alliance on the side of England; those in the West were for helping France in her hour of need as she had helped us in ours. Washington embarked on a policy of neutrality.

As the Franco-English war progressed, Britain seized American ships. The channels of trade clogged. In an attempt to prevent involvement in another war, President Washington sent Secretary of State John Jay to London to negotiate differences, and at the same time dispatched James Monroe on a mission to France to quiet French suspicions of Jay's activities across the English Channel. Monroe, a Republican, was to be repudiated and to return home to write a book of condemnation of the administration. Jay brought back from London a treaty that alienated both the West and the South.

New England, backbone of the Federalist coalition, gained con-

---

[11] *Ibid.*, p. 70.

cessions in Jay's Treaty. Though western agrarians got nothing directly, unwittingly the Federalists presented the West with a new sectional ally of opposition to the party in power, namely, the South. Pre-Revolutionary War debts owed by southern planters to British creditors had long been a bone of contention between the two countries. Jay's Treaty agreed the debts should be paid in full and with interest. Southern planters had had pending, since the war, claims against the British for stolen slaves. Jay, an abolitionist, ignored these claims. The Secretary of State, not realizing that cotton was coming to be an item for export, agreed that the United States should not sell cotton abroad.[12] Jay's Treaty, stormed the South, ignored its interests in return for honoring those of New England.

By 1796 the Federalists were in serious political difficulty. Washington chose not to stand for a third term, and Vice President John Adams was the party's candidate for President. Only by a margin of three electoral votes was he elected over Jefferson, and the latter, the leader of the opposition, thus became Vice President. During the Adams Administration, while the Republicans were improving their organization for the elections of 1800, Adams proved both a weak leader and poor politician, and the Federalists split into two warring camps. Adams was on one side and Hamilton, since 1795 a private New York City lawyer but still actively trying to run the national government, was on the other. A major cause of Federalist intraparty dissension was the issue of whether the United States should go to war with France.

Between 1796 and 1798 an event in France had appeared to give the Federalists an opportunity to recoup power slipping away from them. After Jay's Treaty France had broken off diplomatic relations with the United States. When President Adams sent a representative to attempt to negotiate a restoration of relations, the French negotiators demanded a bribe preliminary to discussions on the subject. A wave of anti-French feeling swept America, and in part as a result, the pro-British Federalists increased Congressional majorities in the 1798 elections.

At this point Hamilton dreamed of a plan to win the West, but it was too late and the wrong kind of a proposal. If the United States went to war with France and won Florida and Louisiana, he reasoned, the Mississippi River could be opened as a transportation outlet for

---

[12] From Binkley, *op. cit.,* pp. 47–48.

the products of the frontier farmer. Hamilton's plan did not become a reality. Though the Federalists prepared for war, Adams suddenly decided not to fight. Hamilton turned on Adams, and the party split. Another result followed. Jeffersonian Republicans had been given a ready-made and politically effective issue for the elections of 1800 — the doubled spending of the Adams Administration for no apparent purpose.

Symptomatic of the political insensitivity of the Federalists, and also symptomatic of their philosophy toward individuals, were the Alien and Sedition Acts of 1798. Federalists by these acts attempted to suppress opposition rather than try to win it over to the Federalist point of view or to compromise the party's position sufficient to the development of a broader base of support. While Republicans wooed the naturalized voters, Federalists regarded the " foreign vote " as partly responsible for their party's slipping position. In the Alien Act they retaliated by upping residence requirements for naturalization from five to fourteen years, and empowered the President to deport any alien deemed by the President to be dangerous to the United States.

American critics of Federalist policies were attended to next with the Sedition Act. It made it a crime to organize or conspire to " oppose the government, to incite riots or insurrections against the the laws of Congress; or to publish false, scandalous, and malicious writings against the government, either House of Congress, or the President, with intent to bring them into contempt, to stir up sedition, or to aid or abet a foreign nation in hostile designs against the United States." Federalists sitting as judges interpreted the act broadly and applied it sternly, particularly against Republican newspaper editors.

With the Sedition Act, the very nature of the system of democratic-representative government established by the Constitution was being challenged. Republicans and a vast majority of the electorate disapproved, and the Federalist policy backfired to hasten the party's end. Madison and Jefferson led the Republican counterattack with the Virginia and Kentucky Resolutions, passed by the legislatures of those two states. If Congress could make it a criminal offense to criticize government, there could be no freedom of expression. These two states were issuing a call to the other states to join in declaring the Alien and Sedition Acts unconstitutional. Whether the Virginia and Kentucky Resolutions were the " bible " of the Republican campaign of 1800 or not, the Federalist insensitivity and inflexibility had given the people one more reason for ejecting Federalists from their positions of control of the federal government.

Quality of Federalist Unity. In one sense, for Washington's two terms, the Federalists were the most unified major party the United States has ever had. Without an organizational structure down through the states to the local levels of government and responsive to local and state pressures, the party was highly centralized with power vested in those Federalists who occupied positions in the federal government. Chief of these leaders was Secretary of the Treasury Alexander Hamilton. The centralization also was a major weakness of the party. Strong local and state units, if they had existed, might have moderated party policy into channels which could have made possible the development of a wide power base. The main fault of the Federalist program was not necessarily what the leaders of that party were attempting economically to accomplish, but rather flowed from the excesses to which Federalists were led because they did not take into account the necessity of broad popular support.

Perhaps it is unfair to judge the Federalist party by the same standards which are applied to other political parties. " Federalists never conceived of their group combination as constituting a political party, because they did not believe in such an institution" [13] The aristocracy should as a class rule, and the masses of people should know their place and follow! Organized political parties, they felt, would undermine that philosophy, and as Jeffersonian Republicans did organize, Federalists equated that activity with subversion. Though Republican organization did force Federalists to take countersteps in self-defense, what organization they did effect was based on the idea that the leaders governed the party. Because Republican organization had been so condemned, Federalists attempted to keep whatever organization they had a secret or to camouflage organized Federalist activity as nonpolitical and patriotic endeavor.

Washington, in his Farewell Address, warned his countrymen against " all combinations and associations under whatever plausible character " which " design to direct, control, counteract or awe the regular deliberation of the constituted authorities." Washington tried to keep both Hamilton and Jefferson and both Federalists and Re-

---

[13] Binkley, *op. cit.*, p. 49.

publicans working together in his administration. When Jay was in London negotiating Jay's Treaty and making Federalist foreign policy, Republican leader Monroe was in France making a Republican foreign policy. " Thus occurred the tragic paradox of two parallel American missions, charged with preserving the safety of the country, headed by leading figures of bitterly opposing parties, who held each other personally in contempt as to both character and policy." [14] Washington, though Federalists were dominant in his administration, gave the Republicans a platform within his administration from which to operate.

The Federalist party did not develop either broad appeal or a sound party organization. Prior to the Adams Administration, however, they were a highly unified group with leadership centering in the person of Hamilton. The latter's position was supported by the recognition which President Washington gave to him. With Adams as President, soon even Federalist unity was dissipated. Through 1795, after his resignation from the Cabinet, Hamilton, at Washington's request, was often called upon for advice. Hamilton frequently corresponded with the members of the Cabinet on domestic and foreign affairs policy questions, and with Federalist leaders in Congress on questions of policy and Congressional strategy. When Adams retained Washington's Cabinet, loyalties were split between the obligation to support the party's President and the *de facto* party leader who was now a private citizen.

Although the points at which friction came to the surface were several, the most revealing intraparty dissension involved the issue of Hamilton's rank in the army. Relations with France were strained, and Adams asked Washington to develop the armed forces to a state of readiness. Hamilton immediately made it known that if he could be inspector general, he would consent to serve as Washington's chief assistant. Though Adams had no intention of appointing him, after a long series of developments which led Adams to the conclusion that Washington might refuse to serve if Hamilton were not given the position he wanted, the commission was granted. The affair was significant, writes Leonard D. White, " because it illustrates how a struggle for political and military leadership disrupted the normal official obligations of Cabinet officers to their superior, the President. Pickering (Secretary of State), Wolcott (Secretary of the Treasury), and

---

[14] Brown, *op. cit.*, p. 106.

McHenry (Secretary of War) , all were driven into an equivocal position, caught between their duty to carry out the directions of the
President . . . and their personal and political loyalty to the principal personality of the Federalist party, who disputed the correctness
of the President's judgment — in a case involving his own military
ambitions." [15]

Conflict of loyalties progressively became more intense, and in
the Spring of 1800 Adams sacked two members of his Cabinet. On
May 5, as described by White, Adams charged McHenry with refusing
to appoint an Adams recommendation to a captaincy in the army,
with favoring Hamilton over Adams' choice as Washington's assistant
commander, with praising Washington and Hamilton in a report to
Congress, and with opposing Adams' 1798 mission to France. Mc-
Henry's resignation was demanded, and the next day was forthcoming.[16] Pickering, who had likewise incurred Adams' distrust, was also
asked to resign. When Pickering refused, Adams removed him within
a week of McHenry's ouster. Such was the state of unity in the Federalist party from which Adams sought re-election to the Presidency in
the year 1800.

Quality of Federalist Presidential Leadership. Since Washington
chose not to be a party leader but rather saw the Presidency as above
party, judgment on the quality of Federalist Presidential leadership
must be based primarily on the record of John Adams from 1796 to
1800. Adams, in his later exchange of letters with Jefferson, suggests
that the reason for his unpopularity had been his defense of a social
order ruled by those of social and economic aristocracy. Jefferson's
popularity, as Adams saw it, had flowed from the former's " steady
defence of democratic principles, and . . . invariable favorable opinion of the French Revolution." [17] Certainly this constitutes an over-
simplification of the reasons for Adams' generally poor record as
President.

After Jefferson's victory in 1800 — a victory made possible because Pennsylvania's electoral votes went to the Republican nominee
— Adams stated that the reason for his defeat had been the failure of
General Washington in 1798 to commission in the army Pennsylvania's Revolutionary War general-hero, Peter Muhlenberg. " And

---

[15] White, *op. cit.,* p. 247.
[16] From *ibid.,* p. 250.   [17] See Brown, *op. cit.,* p. 166.

what was the consequence? " later wrote Adams. " These two Muhlenbergs addressed the public with their names both in English and German, with invective against the administration and warm recommendations of Mr. Jefferson. . . . The Muhlenbergs turned the whole
body of the Germans, great numbers of the Irish, and many of the
English. . . ." [18] Though the Muhlenbergs may have been decisive
in swinging Pennsylvania and thus the election to Jefferson, this too
is an oversimplification.

When he came to office, the second President of the United States
might have been able to establish a base of power with a course of
action lying between the extremes of the Hamilton and Jefferson positions. This he did not have the political ability to accomplish. During the first part of his administration he followed a Hamiltonian direction and thus became identified with that portion of Federalism
which was most unacceptable to the emerging masses of western democracy. But, in return, Adams did not gain the support of Hamilton
or the majority of the Federalist party leaders.

When Adams changed direction by refusing to go on with a policy which would have led to war with France, he was put in the difficult position of having to explain away the " unexplainable " expenditures for arms. The Alien and Sedition Acts sealed his fate
— ensuring the fact that he could never win support from Republicans and driving away Federalists who had migrated inland from the
coastal communities and found themselves between Hamiltonianism
on the one hand and Jeffersonianism on the other.

Even with Pennsylvania lost to the Federalists in 1800, Adams
might have won New York. One seemingly minor but important
event — the arrest of one Jedediah Peck for circulating a petition for
repeal of the Alien and Sedition Acts and marching him 200 miles
across the state to New York City for trial just before the election —
furnishes one clue as to why Adams lost New York. " A hundred
missionaries stationed between New York and Cooperstown," wrote
a contemporary, " could not have done so much for the Republican
cause as this journey of Jedediah Peck from Otsego to the capital of
the state." [19] The year 1796 was the last in which politically critical
New York State gave its electoral votes to a Federalist.

President Adams, in short, was a leader who had allowed himself
to become so entrapped that he lost political following sufficient in

---

[18] Quoted by Binkley, *op. cit.,* p. 84.   [19] Quoted in *ibid.,* p. 83.

size to win Presidential elections. Though the Federalists could not yet know it, and though they looked forward to coming back from this defeat, in 1800 their party's sun was fast setting, never to rise again. Federalists themselves had been in part responsible for the turn of events. So had politically skillful Jeffersonian Republicans.

THE REPUBLICANS

Nature of Republican Appeal. To those who had believed all the charges hurled against Republicans in the campaign of 1800, Thomas Jefferson, the new President, would be an atheist leading a mob bent on the destruction of all the good things in American society. His First Inaugural Address, however, did not sound as though it had been prepared by a right-hand man of the devil. Though the Republican objectives were there, the tone was moderate.

In answer to the Alien and Sedition Acts Jefferson restated his concepts of freedom of speech and religion. The emphasis would be on state governments for domestic matters because the states were " the surest bulwarks against anti-republican tendencies," and on the national government in foreign affairs. Federalists had placed the national government first in all affairs. As if to recall the days of the Whisky Rebellion, the new President stated that, except in time of actual invasion, it would be the militia of the states and not the national army which would be relied upon if there were the threat of domestic disorder. There would be economy in government to ease tax burdens. Though he would give priority to agriculture, he did recognize commerce as its legitimate " handmaid."

The address showed that President Jefferson would not ignore New England and those who had opposed his candidacy. Nor would he try to suppress opposition. We are all republicans and all federalists! He would be the President of *all* the United States.

Jeffersonian Republicans did find a formula for American political power, and what Jefferson himself stood for was a good start. Here was a political theorist, yet a practical politician; a son of the frontier, yet a big planter; the man who wrote the Declaration of Independence and a symbol to democrats everywhere, yet a slaveholder; a religious freethinker, yet the idol of the dissenting fundamentalist religious sects of the frontier; a man who hated war, yet the leader of the frontiersman eager for war with Britain. Here was the first of America's master President-politicians,

Working with him were men such as James Madison, James Monroe, and Albert Gallatin. Together they had fought against Hamilton's financial program, against the Whisky Tax, against Jay's Treaty, and against the Alien and Sedition Acts. Most of these acts had been turned against the Federalists. Together these men had made a good start at organizing Republican party organizations in the several states. Now Jefferson was attempting, in his First Inaugural Address, to allay the fears of the Federalists that their interests would be disregarded as it had often appeared the Federalists themselves had disregarded the interests of the Republicans. So successful were the Jeffersonians in building broad appeal that as early as 1804 many Federalists had begun to leave their party to work in concert with Republicans.

Jeffersonian Republicans have been accused of " out-Federalizing " the Federalist party. This is hardly true. But partly through the conscious design of building broad appeal, partly because European wars had their effect on United States politics over half of the twenty-eight Republican years, and partly because Federalists moved into the Republican party and influenced its policies, much of the Republican program was substantially what moderate Federalists themselves could have been expected to enact had they continued in power.

Although there were pressures on Jefferson, as there are on any President who replaces one of the opposition party, to " clean house " and wipe the slate clean of the previous party's program, Jefferson moved cautiously. Only with respect to the Alien and Sedition Acts was there an immediate and sharp break from the past. In the first year of the Republican Administration the Federalist Alien Law was allowed to expire. In its place Jefferson persuaded the Congress to reduce the 14-year naturalization residence requirement for admission to citizenship to a mere declaration of the alien's intention that he wanted to become a citizen. The Sedition Act was repealed, and persons imprisoned for violations under the act were pardoned.

Republicans did not attempt to revoke the charter of the United States Bank, although in 1811 they let it expire. When the War of 1812 led to new problems of financing, a second United States Bank was chartered in 1816. Jay's Treaty remained in the law, as did New England fishermen's bounties. Republicans had ridiculed the idea of judicial review of legislative acts and did resent courts packed with Federalist judges, but they did not abolish or radically change the judiciary.

Federalists, in favor of maintaining a substantial interest-bearing debt, had hinted in 1800 that to elect Jefferson might mean having the federal government repudiate its obligations. Republicans did not repudiate. They retired the notes so rapidly that the country was almost debt-free when the War of 1812 sent the debt soaring again. Hamilton had wanted to establish a high tariff, and the Federalist Congress had given him only a compromised version for a moderately protective tariff structure. Republicans tended, at first, to leave the rates which had been set. But when European wars reduced foreign markets for agricultural produce and farmers and planters clamored for protection, the Republican party imposed in 1816 a high tariff program fully as protective as Alexander Hamilton had requested but had not received.

Two Federalist policies which Jefferson set out to change substantially, in addition to his move to decrease rapidly the Federal debt, related to taxes and the levels at which the military services should be maintained. While Federalists had been in power, Republicans had opposed a tax structure which they felt weighed too heavily on farmers. Most of the taxes were abolished prior to 1808. Republicans also set out to reduce the military forces. With the state militias available on call, what was the need of a large standing army? The army was reduced to a mere 2,500 men.[20] Navies, the Republicans reasoned, were little more than outright subsidies at the taxpayer's expense for ocean-going commerce. The navy was reduced to thirteen ships. When America become involved in the War of 1812, however, both the tax and armament policies had to be reversed — reversals that almost were not accomplished in time to prevent defeat at the hands of the British.

When the Federalists were in power, Republicans had opposed such actions as the establishment of the United States Bank on the ground that the Constitution did not delegate such powers to the federal government. Yet when Republicans themselves gained office, they could interpret the Constitution liberally enough to justify the purchase of the Louisiana Territory from France in 1803. The addition of Louisiana would strengthen the Republican party with its western and southern state bases of support and thus tend to weaken further the Federalist party. Now it was the Federalists instead of Republicans who were protesting too liberal construction of the Constitution.

---

[20] From Binkley, *op. cit.,* p. 87.

In the election of 1804 Jefferson won all but fourteen votes in the electoral college. By 1807 Republicans were in control even to the extent of occupying every governorship in " Federalist " New England except in Connecticut. Then came another European war, and its effects in America gave the Federalists their last opportunity to hope for a return to power.

France and England were fighting again. The British navy again began to seize American ships and impress American crews. Although the profits earned by shipowners were high enough to warrant the risks they took, Jefferson decided on an embargo in an attempt to enforce freedom of the seas. Exports dropped to almost nothing. New England and the tobacco-exporting South were caught in the grip of deep economic depression. Thinking the embargo could be enforced, Congress passed the Force Act which empowered agents of the federal government to take, without warrants, goods suspected to be enroute to a foreign market. At this, New England Republicans revolted and nominated George Clinton to oppose Jefferson's hand-picked choice as his successor, Secretary of State James Madison. Virginia proposed James Monroe. Undercurrents of other frictions within the Republican party came to the surface, and at the end of Jefferson's second term in 1808, for a time it appeared that the Republican party was about to explode as the Federalist party had done eight years before.

The election of James Madison as President did not solve the Republican problem. First he tried to compromise with the British. The reaction come in the Congressional elections of 1810 which brought Henry Clay and a " War Hawk " majority into the House of Representatives, and to their demands for war with England, Madison was forced to agree before he was renominated by the Congressional Republican caucus. In spite of Republican lack of preparedness and ineptness of leadership in the crisis leading to war, and in spite of the fact that General Andrew Jackson's victory at the Battle of New Orleans was about the only bright spot in an otherwise miserable War of 1812 record, the Republican party benefited politically. Federalists, making their last major mistake, had continued opposition to the war throughout the war. Republicans shouted " treason," and made the label stick. The Federalist party, though it did run candidates in 1816, never recovered.

Thus the United States entered the one era in which it had a one-party system. Madison served out his second term. James Monroe followed with two terms, and not until the John Quincy Adams Administration from 1824 to 1828 did two major parties re-emerge.

Quality of Republican Flexibility. The above discussion of the nature of Republican appeal has served the double purpose of revealing also the high quality of political flexibility which Jefferson brought to the office of President. This subject, however, deserves a brief further elaboration.

The "flexibility" attributes of Jefferson's political career are well summarized by Leonard D. White as he discusses the third President's relations with Congress:

> A combination of unforseeable circumstances contrived first to deny and then to affirm Republican doctrine on the relations that ought to exist in a democratic system between the legislative and executive branches of government. How tenuous both Republican and Federalist doctrine was, appeared during the eight years of Jefferson's administration. During these years Jefferson acted in contradiction to Republican theory at many points. He did not allow Congress that freedom of deliberation he had praised while in opposition, but dominated its movements and guided it to the course of action he deemed right. He did not subdue the executive power, but pushed it to an extreme in the enforcement of the embargo acts. He consciously cultivated institutions within the House, notably the caucus and the floor leader, to facilitate his wishes. He encouraged his able Secretary of the Treasury, Albert Gallatin, to intervene at any stage of legislative deliberation to ensure the " proper " consideration of administration policy. He did not restrain federal power, but acted on the theory of liberal construction. *Coerced by events, he adopted the Federalist position at crucial points, which proved his eminence as a statesman and his indifference to a narrow consistency of theoretical views, when faced with practical problems.*[21]

Here was a quality which permeated all of Jefferson's political acts, and when set alongside the inflexibility of a Hamilton, the contrast is marked indeed. Jefferson came to office as the head of a party which had cause to be aroused and to feel intensely its anger at Federalists in general and New England in particular. Jefferson, had he been of inflexible and doctrinaire political character, might have followed a course which could have made the Republican party as unacceptable and extreme in its own way as the Federalist party had been before it. Instead, he took the moderate Republican course and even the Federalist course if it seemed the best way in which to solve a

---

[21] *The Jeffersonians* (New York: The Macmillan Company, 1951), p. 131. Reprinted by permission of The Macmillan Company. Italics are the author's.

problem. He was eminently successful. The doctrinaire party leader can be a menace to his party and his country, no matter how brilliant he may be of mind; the flexible and able politician — if his motives are in the public interest — can make enduring contributions to both party and country.

As Jefferson and Hamilton present a bold contrast between one who possessed the characteristics of political flexibility and one who did not, so also does the contrast between two flexible politicians — Jefferson and his Vice President, Aaron Burr — illustrate political flexibility at its best and worst. With Burr, flexibility was a tool to be used for the personal ends of Mr. Burr. He had no significant philosophy of government or personal standards. His political flexibility was not a means to the accomplishment of great party and country ends.

As Burr did not have character, Jefferson did have it. Though the latter could and did compromise and turn direction when he felt the political situation demanded compromise and turning, running through the whole of the Jeffersonian Republican record is a respect for the individual and a devotion to the cause of freedom. Here was the Republican's great end. " But in the Republican scheme even freedom was to be only a condition. Beyond freedom the point was what a man did with it. The Republican wanted to improve upon it as the condition for a good life — not *the* good life. People, not *the* people, in a free republic could lead good lives, according to their many hopes and many dreams. Unity could be found in the honoring of multiplicity. Any other unity would soon or late be found to be tyrannical." [22] Everything else was but a means to the accomplishment of that objective.

Quality of Republican Unity and Presidential Leadership. From Jefferson through John Quincy Adams both the qualities of Republican unity and Presidential leadership varied greatly. Because both factors are, for the Republicans, so interrelated, they will be considered together.

When Jefferson assumed office, he led a party which had had experience only in opposing Federalists. Republicans, by temperament, were very individualistic. Rather than allow factional fighting in Congress to destroy his program and perhaps Republican prospects

---

[22] Brown, *op. cit.,* p. 172.

for winning elections, Jefferson assumed a forceful leadership role. Through his influence as President and as the accepted party leader, he was able to produce a substantial degree of party unity.

Jefferson named Congressional floor leaders, and they operated as agents of the administration. The caucus became an effective device for Presidential leadership. Jefferson himself took a hand in inducing able friends to run for Congress. Bills were drafted in the executive departments and accepted by Congress. Jefferson maintained close personal relationships with Representatives and Senators. Leading more than forcing, Jefferson successfully constructed a Republican organization in the national government which did bridge the gap between the executive and legislative branches.

The power which Jefferson wielded until the closing months of his second term may be illustrated by three episodes. The first was the purchase of the Louisiana Territory from France in 1803. As a member of the opposition during Federalist administrations, Jefferson had been a strict constructionist of the Constitution. The members of his party were still strict constructionists. Yet when the opportunity came to buy Louisiana, the President was able, without constitutional authority and admitting the fact, to engineer the transaction smoothly through the Congress. From the purchase, opposed by the Federalists, political benefits accruing to the Republicans were not inconsiderable, and the verdict of history has supported the soundness of the decision for the welfare of the country.

When Congressman John Randolph, a former Jefferson House floor leader and in 1806 chairman of the Ways and Means Committee, attempted to lead an open revolt against the President who, Randolph and his followers felt, was departing too far from Republican principles of strict construction, Jefferson handled the threat firmly and with dispatch. The House imposed a " gag " rule through which the long-winded Randolph could be effectively shut off. Randolph also soon found himself eased out of his committee chairmanship.

Another Jefferson-inspired measure, the Embargo of 1807, was unpopular with most of the members of Jefferson's Cabinet and Republicans in Congress. Yet here too, unfortunately for Jefferson and his party this time, the President prevailed without major difficulty. Republicans in Congress supported with legislation enforcement of the embargo in the face of mounting and intense opposition. " Even in January 1909," writes Leonard D. White, " Congress obediently accepted Jefferson's demand for more power at a time when it was evident that the policy was a failure in its external objects and a dangerous source of discord internally." [23]

The Embargo, however, was Jefferson's major political miscalculation. Just before he left office, his Republican majority in Congress split openly and wide in revolt and forced discontinuance of the policy. Now began, perhaps as a reaction to strong Presidential leadership which had been used to further a policy turned sour, a period of decline of the Presidency that was to last until Andrew Jackson. Without an effective opposition party, however, the Republican party was not forced to pay the political consequences which it might otherwise have suffered as a result.

Though James Madison had exhibited superior intellectual and political qualities when he worked with Jefferson in the statement of Republican philosophy, in opposition to the Federalist administrations and as Secretary of State in the Jefferson Cabinet, he proved to be one of the weakest of American Presidents. Nominated by the Republican Congressional caucus, he from the very first was also dominated by it. The Jefferson Embargo had left the Republican party confused, and the new President's task was to create a new unity. This he did not succeed in doing.

New England Republican farmers were ripe for Federalist plucking — provided the Federalist party had been able to perform the harvesting act. Southern Republicans wanted no more " Federalist compromising." Western Republicans, fearing they were running out of land, cast covetous eyes at Canada, and when England was reputed to be stirring up the Indians, war seemed to be the major subject on the western Republican mind. In the movement toward war, Henry Clay, elected to Congress and chosen Speaker of the House in 1811, was the real leader. Even after war was declared, Madison was somewhat like a chip being tossed about by ocean waves too big for him to comprehend or control. The President's organization of the armed forces and conduct of the war had been badly managed. " The army was unpaid, the Treasury was empty, the British fleet had captured, sunk, or bottled up our entire salt-water navy and had clamped down an airtight blockade on our Atlantic ports. The Capitol and Executive Mansion had been burned. . . . An expeditionary force of Wellington's presumably invincible peninsular veterans, equipped at the cost of a million pounds was known to be en route to New Orleans." [24]

---

[23] *The Jeffersonians*, p. 34.   [24] Binkley, *op. cit.*, p. 96.

Perhaps never in American history had circumstances been so favorable for an out-party wanting to return to office. But where were the Federalists? New England had refused to finance the " defense of America." It had refused to contribute men to add new " Republican states " out of Canadian territory. It had been flashing light signals from the New England coast to assist the blockade maintained by the British fleet. " Never were these luckless partisans to hear the last of the opprobrious epithet, the ' Blue Light ' Federalists." [25] At the very time news of Jackson's miraculous victory over the British at New Orleans reached Washington, entering the city from the opposite direction was a delegation from a Federalist Hartford Convention asking the federal government to meet certain demands as a price for support of the war effort. In the flush of national patriotism the ineptness of the Madison administrations had been forgotten and the Federalist party had now finally completed its own self-destruction.

For the remainder of the Republican period, Monroe proved to be a stronger President than Madison, but largely by choice he left Congress to transact its business in domestic affairs while he executed and administered the laws and achieved Presidential leadership in foreign affairs. John Quincy Adams came to office in 1824 under the cloud of election by the House, after Jackson had won a plurality in the electoral college. When Adams lost control of Congress in 1826, whatever influence Adams had had in his first two years of office was gone.

The approach of the second President Adams was almost Federalist in its economic orientation, though he and his followers claimed that they were the " true heirs " of Jefferson Republicanism. Andrew Jackson spoke now as the new voice of the new West, and he and his followers also maintained that they were the " true heirs " of Jefferson. The unnatural era of one party was over. A new period of American party politics with two new major parties was beginning.

---

[25] *Ibid.,* p. 95.

CHAPTER ELEVEN

Jacksonian Democrats and Whigs

- -

It was no accident that the Democratic party was focused in the presidency rather than Congress. Jacksonian Democracy originated as the personal following of one who symbolized the ideal of justice for the masses. He was represented as a champion of the under-dog and the Democratic party has always relied for its voting strength primarily upon the counties with poorer soils and the crowded wards of the great cities largely populated with recent immigrant stock. Quite naturally then these segments of American society see security by electing a national champion to the presidency which they conceive to be peculiarly their office.

To the well-to-do, however, Jackson was a demagogue, a preacher of social discontent, and the prosperous became the backbone of the opposition to Jackson. The dominant elements of the Whig party consisted of the great financial, commercial, and emerging industrial interests of the East, the more prosperous agrarians of the North and the great slaveholding planters of the South. These latter were obsessed with a phobia of a strong central government and when Jackson in 1832 let out his blast against the nullificationists these states righters allied themselves with the Whigs. Here then was a combination that never elected a president on a program but only through the stratagem of confusing issues by nominating the military heroes William Henry Harrison and Zachary Taylor.

Wilfred E. Binkley [1]

Generals turned politicians — Jackson, William Henry Harrison, Taylor, Scott, Frémont — figured in every Presidential election

[1] *President and Congress* (New York: Alfred A. Knopf, 1947), pp. 86–87. Reprinted under general permission policy of Alfred A. Knopf, Inc.

campaign from 1824 through 1856. Towering above them all was Andrew Jackson. The symbol of " Old Hickory " was a major element in
the adhesive binding together a winning combination of western
farmers, eastern workers, and, for a time, southern planters. The
Democratic party, of which Jackson was the first President, managed
to win control of the Presidency, except for two separated single four-
year terms, from 1828 until the Civil War. Democrats controlled the
House of Representatives for much of that period, and the Senate
for all but the Twenty-seventh and Twenty-eighth Congresses.

Figure 5. Electoral Votes for Democratic, National Republican, and Whig
         Candidates for President, 1824–1856

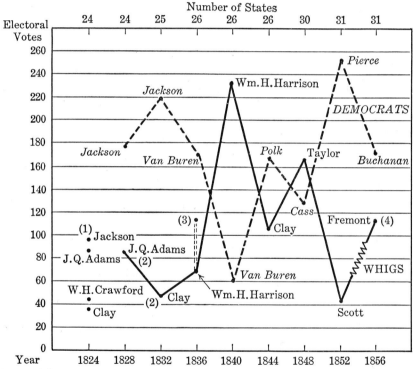

Notes: (1) In 1824 new party alignments were not distinct. Jackson had 99 electoral votes, Adams 84, Crawford 41, and Clay 37. The House chose Adams.

(2) John Quincy Adams in 1828 and Clay in 1832 were National Republicans.

(3) In 1836 Whigs were split with three tickets. Harrison had 73 electoral
votes, Hugh L. White 26, and Daniel Webster 14. W. P. Mangum, running as
an anti-Jackson candidate, had 11. Total of anti-Jackson votes was 113.

(4) By 1856, the Whig party had faded away. John C. Frémont was the first
Presidential nominee of the new Republican party.

Source: U. S. Bureau of Census, *Historical Statistics of the United States, 1789–
1945* (Washington, D.C.: Government Printing Office, 1949), pp. 289–290.

Three other generals were Whigs. William Henry Harrison ("Tippecanoe and Tyler Too"), capitalizing on the "Van Buren" depression of 1837, occupied the White House for a brief month before he died. Vice President John Tyler, who was in fact a Jeffersonian Democrat and had been placed on the ticket to corral Democratic votes, to the consternation of Whigs turned out to be just as Democratic in his sympathies as the party should have suspected he would be. After Henry ("If Only I Were a General") Clay's defeat in 1844, Whigs turned now to "Old Rough and Ready" Zachary Taylor, hero of the Mexican War. He too died in office, to be succeeded by Vice

Figure 6. Popular Votes for Democratic, National Republican, and Whig Candidates for President, 1824–1856

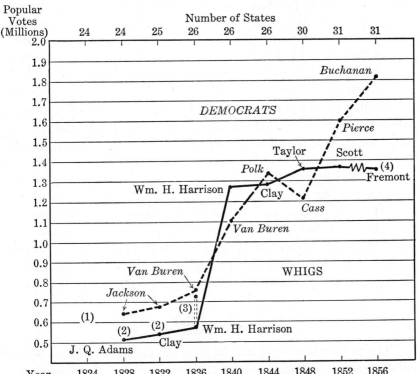

Notes: (1) In 1824, the first year popular vote totals were published, Jackson had 154,000, J. Q. Adams 109,000, Clay 47,136, and William H. Crawford 46,618. There was no party designation.

(2) Adams in 1828 and Clay in 1832 were National Republicans.

(3) Whig popular vote was split between Harrison 549,000, Hugh L. White 146,000, and Webster 41,000 (figures rounded). Total Whig vote was 735,651.

(4) Frémont was a Republican.

Source: U. S. Bureau of Census, *Historical Statistics of the United States, 1789–1945* (Washington, D.C.: Government Printing Office, 1949), pp. 289–290.

President Millard Fillmore. Whigs had not been happy with Taylor, nor were they satisfied with Fillmore. In 1852 the party for a third time turned to the military in the person of Winfield (" Old Fuss and Feathers ") Scott. The choice of Scott, one of the most inept of Presidential candidates, backfired even before election day. Fifth of the generals was John C. Frémont, " Pathfinder of the Rockies." He was the unsuccessful nominee of the new Republican party in 1856.

The story of what happened to the generals turned politician is a symptom of the relative positions and fortunes of the two major parties of the period. Until the early 1850's the Jacksonian Democratic party was a relatively solid and balanced combination holding a balance — though at times very narrow balance — of political power. The Whig party, it seemed, could gain office only by confusing the issues and with generals out in front. Even Providence seemed to be working on the side of the Democrats as both Whig general-Presidents died in office without being able to use the Presidency to consolidate gains and raise the Whig party just the little necessary to enable it to have consistently good prospects of capturing the national government. Finally, the Whig party was led to perhaps an unnecessarily early grave by a general whom Whigs must, in the campaign of 1852, have subconsciously asked God to remove from the scene if this were to be his approximate time to go. It was not the time for Winfield Scott, but was the time for the Whig party.

On examining Figures 5–8, one will note that all suggest that at no time after Jackson and before the breakup of the Whig party, were Whigs far behind Democrats. Perhaps if the Whigs had been able to increase their political effectiveness level in but small degree, the Whig and not the Democratic party might have been able to be the supreme party of a new era of party supremacy after Jackson.

THE SETTING

The political setting when Jackson was elected President in 1828 had changed greatly from that of the 1790's when Federalists were at the height of their power, and it had changed considerably from Jefferson's day. Where in 1790 only 5 percent of the population lived in the 24 incorporated places of 2,500 or more people, in 1850, 20 percent resided in the 236 places of 2,500 or more. Even at Jackson's time the dream of a rural-agricultural society was gone. Business was becoming an increasingly important part of the economy.

Moving rapidly westward also was the geographical center of

Figure 7. Democratic, National Republican, and Whig Seats in the U. S. House of Representatives, 1825–1859

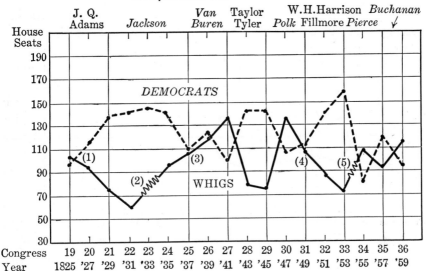

Notes: (1) In 19th and 20th Congresses, identification was " Jackson-men " and " Adams-men."

(2) In 21st and 22d Congresses, National Republicans were Democratic opposition. In 23d Congress, Anti-Masons had 53 and 60 members organized with neither party organization.

(3) In 25th Congress, Democrats had 108 and Whigs 107, and 24 unorganized members had balance of power.

(4) In 31st Congress, Democrats had 112 and Whigs 109, and nine unorganized members had balance of power.

(5) In 34th, 35th and 36th Congresses, Republicans were Democratic opposition. In 34th Congress, Republicans had 108 and Democrats 83, and 43 were unorganized; in 35th Congress, Democrats had 118 and Republicans 92, and 26 were unorganized; and in 36th Congress, Republicans had 114 and Democrats 92, and 31 were unorganized.

Source: U. S. Bureau of Census, *Historical Statistics of the United States, 1789–1945* (Washington, D.C.: Government Printing Office, 1949), p. 295.

United States population. Where in 1800 approximately 95 percent of the people lived east of the Appalachian Mountains, by 1828 that figure had gone down to about 70 percent. And with the westward movement came the admission of new states.

Federalist power had been developed out of the twelve states which had been admitted to the Union by 1789, and Rhode Island (1790) and Vermont (1791). Addition of two new western states (Kentucky 1792 and Tennessee 1796), though both became Republican, did not in itself change the balance of power leading to Jefferson's victory in 1800. Rather, the political shift came about because Jefferson was able to capture states which had once been Federalist. The

Figure 8. Democratic, National Republican, and Whig Seats in the U. S. Senate,
1825–1859

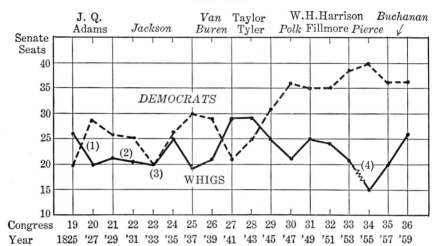

Notes: (1) In 19th and 20th Congresses identification was " Jackson-men " and
" Adams-men."

(2) In 21st, 22d, and 23d Congresses National Republicans were the Democratic party's opposition.

(3) In 23d Congress Democrats and National Republicans were tied, and
eight unorganized members held the balance of power.

(4) In 34th, 35th and 36th Congresses Republicans were Democratic party's
opposition.

Source: U. S. Bureau of the Census, *Historical Statistics of the United States,
1789–1945* (Washington, D.C.: Government Printing Office, 1949) , p. 293.

Republicans in being moderate in their Republicanism and often
Federalist in approach were merely responding to a power complex
in which New England was so strong that that section could not have
been ignored even if Jefferson had wanted to ignore it.

During the Republican period of control the center of political
power gravity shifted away from New England and in a westerly
southerly direction. Of the eight states admitted, four were in the
South (Louisiana 1812, Mississippi 1817, Alabama 1819, and Missouri 1821); three in the West (Ohio 1803, Indiana 1816, and
Illinois 1818) ; and only Maine (1820) was in New England. This
trend was precisely what New England Federalists had foreseen when,
as a condition for support in the War of 1812, the Hartford Convention had demanded constitutional amendments to require two-thirds
majorities in both houses of Congress for the admission of new states
and a plan of representation for the House based on a count of free
men instead of total population in the states.

While New England Federalists were failing in efforts to plug the hole in their political power dike by seeking means of stopping admission of new states in the West and South, another leak of serious proportions developed within eastern commercial and manufacturing communities. Immigrant foreigners swelled the population of the cities, and though the " foreign vote " and native American workers did not have the franchise by 1800, they had gained it by 1828. Here were potential allies of western farmers and southern planters against the men of commerce and industry in the East, provided the kind of leadership which could bind the three elements together could be found.

This is not to imply that the three sections of West, East, and South were not internally divided in political affiliation. There were conflicts within sections as well as between them. Also Southerners moved up into the western states and brought their southern orientation with them as they modified to their new environment. Easterners moved West and carried along their old ways of political thinking. Such were the divisions within sections that both Democrats and Whigs stood in relative balance to one another, with some states leaning one way and others to the other major party, until the crystallization of political opinion around the issue of slavery tended to force a realignment. W. Dean Burnham in analyzing county voting patterns of the Democratic-Whig period within the states concludes: " With a few notable exceptions the Democrats tended to carry the upland, interior, watershed, and frontier counties, while the Whigs tended to carry . . . the tidewater, the lake-shore, the sea-coast, the lowland, the river-bottom, and the well-settled counties." [2]

Strongest sectional element of Democratic strength was the West, and the hard core of the Democratic West was Jackson's own Scotch-Irish stock. Here, and among small farmers everywhere, one found the same debtor complex as in Jefferson's time, and the same demands for inflation. The farmer, if he had been foreclosed by the United States Bank as a result of the depression of 1819, felt much as had those who participated in Shays' Rebellion. " Money changers " in the East and the Bank received a large share of the blame.

The agrarian, particularly the Scotch-Irish, was still intensely anti-British. He still distrusted centralized religious authority and tended to belong to the same dissenting fundamentalist church

---

[2] *Presidential Ballots 1836–1892* (Baltimore: The Johns Hopkins Press, 1955), p. 19.

groups as had his generation before him. He was still an individualist and knew he was as good as the next man, whether for purposes of matching his physical strength or discharging the functions of a governmental office. With property qualifications for voting fast disappearing the agrarian found himself with a new political power.

States of the Ohio River valley were the chief source of Whig strength in the West. Kentucky and Tennessee were consistently Whig, even in the election of 1852 when Scott carried only four of the twenty-one states. Also in the Ohio valley, the southern portions of Illinois, Indiana, and Ohio tended to be Whig, and in each Presidential election prior to 1852, one or more of these states cast their electoral votes for the Whig nominee. Here was an area in which the economic interests were closely identifiable with those of the East to favor internal improvements for East-West trade and tariffs to pay for internal improvements and to protect manufactures and farm commodities.

Though it had expanded vastly in territory and population since 1800, the character of the West had changed less than that of the South and East. Both of the latter sections had begun to feel the full impact of the industrial revolution. For the South a substantial market for cotton had developed in England and was later to develop in New England. The invention of the cotton gin made possible large-scale cotton production, provided the planter had sufficient land and labor. Pressures were for expansion to the West, for more slaves, for federal government policies which would not interfere with the institution of slavery, and for a low tariff structure to facilitate trade with England. But in the South, as in the West, there were the smaller farmers whose political interest differed from those of the " big " farmer.

The East of the 1820's was the most radically changed of the three major sections of the country from Jefferson's time. Republican high protective tariffs had made factory investments more profitable than shipping, and at this very time immigration brought skilled mechanics, machines, and a swelling tide of laborers to work in factories. For the manufacturer, however, the sword of the industrial revolution had two-edged implications. Though manufacturing was stimulated, aliens soon to be citizens and armed with the right to vote presaged political competition.[3]

---

[3] See Charles A. Beard, *The American Party Battle* (New York: The Macmillan Company, 1929), pp. 57–61.

The East along with part of the West wanted high tariffs to help factories, jobs, and agriculture; the South, low tariffs to better ply English trade. The East and part of the West would both receive advantages by such internal improvements as roads, canals, and harbors — items which the South did not feel it needed and did not want to pay for in other sections of the country. In the West, and at least in the lower economic and social levels in the East, the conception of democracy and rights of the individual differed markedly from a South rapidly moving to an economy built on slave labor. The South and West both wanted the federal government to admit more new states; the East did not. South and West had a common bond in their distrust of eastern " monied interests."

Factors such as these suggest the very complicated problem confronting the so-called conservative and progressive wings of Jefferson Republicanism in the middle 1820's. How could an enduring political party be built out of the sectional, class, and emotional drives in all their bewildering complexity at this stage of American development? Democrats, measurably aided by the personality and political abilities of General Andrew Jackson, tried one approach; another was tried by National Republicans and later the Whig party, under the not always harmonious leadership of United States Senators Henry Clay of Kentucky, Daniel Webster of Massachusetts and sometimes John C. Calhoun of South Carolina.

NATURE OF DEMOCRATIC APPEAL

So different was the Democratic party appeal from 1828 to 1850 from that employed during the decade immediately prior to the Civil War that, though the party's name was the same, its character was so dissimilar from the first period to the second that in reality it was two parties. During the Jacksonian era the first commandment of Democrats was the Declaration of Independence and the party's godfather was Thomas Jefferson. After the party was captured by an alliance of big southern planters and eastern big businessmen, both the Declaration of Independence and Jeffersonian roots were passé.

Jacksonian Democracy assured the common man that the Democratic party was his personal vehicle to political power. Where Federalists had boasted of being the party of the rich and well-born, Jacksonians just as frankly proclaimed themselves as of and proud of the masses — masses banded together to turn out of office and out of power the forces of special privilege such as banks, monopolies, and aristocracy in general. Where Federalists and Republicans had developed a career government service, Jacksonians, with their philosophy of " to the victor belongs the spoils " and their faith in the ability of every man to discharge the functions of governmental office, substituted an outright patronage system.

On financial questions, the Democratic party followed the policies of early Jeffersonian theory, but Jackson went further in the application of the theory than had Republicans. Where Republicans had tried to pay off the national debt and had failed because of the obligations imposed by the War of 1812, Jackson, without new war obligations, achieved the objective. Where Jefferson had not revoked the charter of the United States Bank but waited until the charter expired, and where Republicans later themselves set up a second United States Bank, Jackson had no sooner settled himself in his office than he began to undermine the Bank — villain of debtor and hard-money Democrats alike. When in Jackson's first term the second Bank's charter expired and Congress passed an act to recharter, the President replied with a stinging veto message aimed at arousing the political passions of his followers against those in Congress who would so disregard the interests of the " poor " and favor the interests of the " rich." " Every man is equally entitled to protection by law," said the President's veto message, " but when the laws undertake to add to . . . natural and just advantages artificial distinctions . . . to make the rich richer and the potent more powerful, the humble members of society — the farmers, mechanics, and laborers — who have neither the time nor the means of securing like favors to themselves, have a right to complain. . . ." [4] Here was the first major issue of the Jackson Administration.

The second major issue flowed from the Tariff Act of 1832. Engineered through Congress by Henry Clay, the act established a moderately high protective level reflecting the desires of the East and those of the West who wanted revenue for building internal improvements. If Jackson refused to sign, as National-Republicans felt he would, he would be seriously damaged in both West and East. Jackson, however, did not veto the act, but chose instead to suffer the wrath of the low-tariff southern planter. That was not long in coming. South Carolina

----

[4] Quoted by Arthur M. Schlesinger, Jr., *The Age of Jackson* (Boston: Little, Brown and Company, 1946) , p. 90.

in November 1832, under the urging of John C. Calhoun, passed its Ordinance of Nullification which, claiming a precedent in the Virginia and Kentucky Resolutions, maintained that a state had the right to suspend an act of Congress if the state deemed the act unconstitutional.

President Jackson met the threat in his characteristically " head-on " style, and except for losing support among big southern planters, consolidated his position elsewhere. Nullification, he said, was disunion. If disunion were backed by force, it would become treason. The President, under the instructions of the Constitution, then, would be forced to put treason down by use of counterforce. Now added to Jackson's main theme of democracy was the symbol of " Jackson as the protector of the Union." South Carolina stood alone, in part perhaps, because Jackson had taken steps to win favor in Georgia and Alabama by clearing Indians out of the westward path of the expanding cotton planters.

Any party in power has to make decisions on questions which will drive away groups which originally supported it. Such groups in the Jackson Administrations were those who felt the President was assuming too much power, those who opposed the United States Bank veto, those who concluded Jackson had not done enough in the cause of internal improvements, those big southern planters alienated in the nullification controversy, and those who felt the army had too brutally swept Indians out of the path of southern land expansion. But as some groups are driven away, others are attracted or become more solid in their support. Jackson by 1832 had been in unquestioned control when he won 219 electoral votes to Henry Clay's (National Republican) 49. Jackson hand-picked as his successor Martin Van Buren of New York and, riding the Jackson wave, Van Buren in 1836 captured 170 electoral votes to the combined four-candidate opposition total of 112.

At the very time when ominous political clouds borne on a front of economic depression were about to pour out their storm, the extent of appeal which Jackson as a person brought to the Democratic party and his electoral combination is revealed in the acclaim accorded to him when he stepped down from the Presidency. The account of that event by Arthur M. Schlesinger, Jr., follows:

> The crowd which packed the East Lawn, their faces upturned in the noon sun, were profoundly silent. After the inaugural address the old General started slowly down the broad steps toward the carriage

below. As he descended the people yielded to their feelings; the pent-up flood of cheers and shouts broke forth; and they paid their long, last irresistible tribute to the man they loved. . . . Thomas Hart Benton, watching from a side window, felt himself stirred as never before. In later years he would recall many inaugurations, but compared to this they all seemed as pageants, " empty and soulless, brief to the view, unreal to the touch, and soon to vanish." This was reality, the living relation between a man and his people, distilled for a pause in the rhythm of events, rising for a moment of wild and scaring enthusiasm, then dying away into the chambers of memory.[5]

Perhaps even the appeal of Jackson could not have held up through a third 1836 to 1840 term of office. The policy of putting down the United States Bank had been followed by a flood of paper money from state banks, land and general speculation, and unrestrained boom. Jackson in 1836 warned of the consequences. On the floor of the Senate, Thomas Hart Benton of Missouri lamented:

> I did not join in putting down the Bank of the United States, to put up a wilderness of local banks. I did not join in putting down the paper currency of a national bank, to put up a national paper currency of a thousand local banks. I did not strike Caesar to make Anthony master of Rome. . . . The present bloat in the paper system cannot continue. . . . The revulsion will come. . . ." [6]

Within the Democratic party the new issue had already provoked a split more serious in its potential consequences than Jackson's reaction to nullification which had driven off the big southern planters. In the East the Locofoco hard-money movement, growing out of the worsening economic position of the worker as his wages lagged far behind the sharp inflationary trend, had begun to gain solid support as early as 1835. Van Buren was Locofoco in orientation. As the Jackson Administration moved to this position on money matters, the West began to slip in its Democratic allegiance. The choice of Van Buren as Jackson's successor tended to sharpen the nature of intraparty conflict. During much of Van Buren's Administration the country was in depression. The Democratic party combination which had swept Jackson into office was in bad repair. The deluge had come. Van Buren was linked to the " eastern bankers," and the Democratic party was charged with being responsible for the state of economic

---

[5] Arthur M. Schlesinger, Jr., *The Age of Jackson* (Boston: Little, Brown and Company, 1946), p. 215. Reprinted by permission of Little, Brown and Company.

[6] Quoted by *ibid.*, p. 129.

conditions. In 1840 Whig William Henry Harrison won 234 electoral votes to Van Buren's 60.

In the campaign of 1844 the principal issue revolved around a North-South conflict of interest which came to a head in the question of whether Texas should be annexed to the Union. If Texas were brought in, war with Mexico would be a certainty. Southern land expansionists wanted the new area at any cost, and the North had no enthusiasm for expanding the political power of the slavocracy, whether by peaceful or nonpeaceful means. When the Whig nominee, Henry Clay, sought to straddle the question, he was hurt in both North and South. Polk, on the other hand, evolved the ideal formula for the year of " manifest destiny " — " the reannexation of Texas and the reoccupation of Oregon." Here was something for the North too, and cast in the emotional overtones of " 54–40 or Fight! " Democrats managed to eke out a 38,367 plurality over Clay out of some 2,700,000 popular votes.

Once in office, however, President Polk found the harmonization of North and South an impossible problem. Oregon's northern boundary was compromised at 49 degrees without fighting for " 54–40." Tariff policy was in the direction of reduction of rates. Polk vetoed an important internal improvement bill. In general, northern Democrats and the North felt Polk had been too pro-southern.

In the next few years, the transition of the Democratic party into a southern-controlled party with important support coming also from eastern capitalism was complete. By 1856 that party was so different from what it had been in Jackson's day that the groups supporting Fremont and Buchanan could be classified in the following manner: " Fundamentally, the vote [Republican vote] was an achievement of farmers, native laborers, and little enterprisers. The economic royalists of the old Whigs, the captains of finance, industry, transportation, and commerce, by and large, had backed Buchanan." [7]

NATURE OF WHIG APPEAL

The Jacksonian Democratic appeal had been in fact Jeffersonian Republicanism applied in a form suitable to the political environment of a generation once removed from Jefferson. The lines between most of the features of the two programs were distinct. Whig appeal,

---

[7] Wilfred E. Binkley, *American Political Parties* (New York: Alfred A. Knopf, 1949), p. 221.

though it may superficially have appeared to be but an extension of the earlier Federalist program, was a new political commodity, and for the origins of that program, one must look to Henry Clay's ingenious " American System," developed as the Kentuckian sought to build a type of appeal which could place him in the office of President of the United States. Clay's orientation was not New England centered as Hamilton's had been, but rather western. His plan, calculated to win support from all sections, proceeded from a western base.

In 1824 as he for the first time sought the Presidency, Clay stated the objective which had evolved from a decade of his thinking about a solution to American economic problems. " Now our people present the spectacle of a vast assemblage of jealous rivals, all eagerly rushing to the seaboard, jostling each other on their way, to hurry off to glutted foreign markets the perishable produce of their labor." This was not as it should be. Instead, Clay would, by his American System, " transform these competitors into friends and mutual customers, and, by reciprocal exchange of their respective productions, to place the confederacy upon the most solid of all foundations, the basis of common interest." [8]

After the War of 1812, British manufacturers had " dumped " huge quantities of goods on the American market and sold by auction. America had moved into a cycle of depression. Manufacturers everywhere, even in the southern coastal states before large-scale cotton production became the dominant economic element in the South, clamored for protection. Merchants wanted protection, and so did the farmers of the West, particularly those of the Ohio valley. All these groups, with the exception of the South, would be advantaged by improved internal transportation facilities. Clay's program, then, was built on a protective tariff, with its most important byproduct, revenues which could be used for construction of internal improvements. Clay, as had Hamilton before him, was proposing a nationally directed kind of economic planning.

Unfortunately for Clay, by 1824 forces were at work which made his timing on the plan too late. By then the big cotton planters were solidly low tariff, and they never had felt they needed internal improvements because their river systems were adequate for transportation. New England shipping interests had never been enthusiastic about tariffs which cut down foreign trade, and Daniel Webster was opposed. Even for the West, though the objectives were desirable,

[8] Quoted by *ibid.,* p. 105.

" its appeal was to the intellect and not to the feelings. . . . Confronted by the dynamic personality of Old Hickory . . . the emo-
tion-starved pioneer lost interest in Clay's elaborate argument." [9]

In 1824 both Adams and Clay stood on the American System,
and when the former was selected by the House with Clay's assistance,
Adams set out to implement the plan. An inept politician, Adams
failed completely. Jacksonians captured both houses of Congress in
1826 and, in what has been termed a " four-year smear campaign,"
Adams was thoroughly discredited. Where Adams had served warning to all opponents of the American System by going all the way for
internal improvements and expansion of the national government at
national expense in his inaugural address and where by 1828 Adams'
position was well-known, Jackson entered the campaign of that year
under no such handicap. Aside from the fact that he was a hero, literally no one, perhaps not even Jackson, knew where he stood on the
issues of the day.

In the South he was regarded as low tariff, and in Pennsylvania
and the East as high tariff. In the West he was said to be pro-internal
improvement. Here was a slaveholder who the South was willing to
take a chance on, and a soldier the South thought might be a good
man to clear the way for southern land expansion. In the words of
Schlesinger:

> The new President's supporters in Congress had conspicuously failed
> to develop measures to meet the discontents which had toppled the
> previous administration. Their opposition to Adams and Clay had
> been confused and opportunistic, hiding a basic lack of ideas behind
> a smoke-screen of parliamentary obstruction and campaign invective.
> The campaign had reflected its shallowness. Hardly an issue of policy
> figures in the canvas, and, when Jackson triumphed, no one could
> be certain that his administration would not duplicate that of Madi-
> son or Monroe or even of Adams.[10]

Jackson had been in office but a short time when the South had
become restive, fearing its trust had been misplaced. To soothe the
southern planters, the President decided to make a token veto of
some minor internal improvement project, hoping that by his action
he would not alienate the West. Selected was the 20-mile Maysville
road in Clay's own Kentucky. National-Republicans attempted to
hold the action up as proof that Jackson was anti-internal improve-

---

[9] Binkley, *Parties*, p. 106.   [10] Schlesinger, *op. cit.*, p. 45.

ment. The Tariff of 1832, high enough in its protective features so as to invite a Presidential veto, was a Clay-led attempt to further clarify his point that Jackson was anti-American System. Jackson surprised the National-Republicans by signing.

Again in 1833 Clay attempted a new tactic designed to narrow Jackson's broad base of support, and conversely to establish one for National-Republicans. In response to western pressures to reduce the standard federal government sale price of $1.25 per acre for public land, Clay prepared the following answer. Land prices should be maintained at their existing level. This would please land speculators and investors, and eastern employers who did not want their labor supply enticed to the frontier. To offset western disappointment and at the same time gain support from East and South, Clay would have the proceeds from land sales allocated among the states in proportion to the number of electoral votes cast by each state. All states could be expected to rejoice at a windfall which might be used to build roads and canals, pay off debts already contracted for internal improvements, or to ease the state tax rates. Two other purposes would be accomplished, Clay suggested, by such an action. Since the United States Treasury would be drained, advocates of high tariffs would no longer have to be afraid of tariff reductions because revenues from this source would be needed to finance the operations of the federal government. Because the plan called for state and not federal development of internal improvements, the southern states would be free to use their allocations for whatever purpose they chose.[11]

Jackson was not outmaneuvered this time either. Where in 1832 he had defeated Clay's purpose by signing the Tariff Act, now he accomplished the Democratic purpose by vetoing the Distribution Plan of 1833. So complicated was the Clay plan, it could not be sold to a mass political market in competition with the simple and emotional Jacksonian appeal. For the same reason, Jackson's veto could not be successfully used against him to inflict major political damage.

After Jackson had alienated the big southern planter by his actions in the nullification controversy of 1832 and 1833, National-Republican leaders decided to attempt directly to make room for the "national"-hating states-rights South. The result was a change of name to Whig party. The new group assembled to do battle with Jackson in its first national convention in 1834.

---

[11] From Binkley, *Parties*, pp. 154–155.

Those who gathered to form the new party were the following. First, there were the National-Republicans — supporters of Adams, Clay, and the American System. Second, there were the Calhoun-led states rights nullifiers who were on what proved to be a temporary vacation from the Democratic party. Third, there were the Anti-Masons who had supported the candidacy of William Wirt for President in 1832 and, with their strength concentrated in the East, resembled National-Republicans in favoring higher tariffs and internal improvements. Fourth were Democrats such as United States Senator Hugh L. White, Jackson's former friend and fellow Tennessean, who for various reasons had broken away from the Democratic party.

So difficult was the problem of developing an appeal broad enough to solidify such a heterogeneous combination of groups, however, that Whigs were soon led away from Clay specifics and his intellectual approach to an adoption of Jacksonian emotionalism. With this type of appeal in 1840 and 1848, Whigs were successful, but even when they did gain power they were able to accomplish little in developing a broad support-winning program, and because their terms of power were so short, what was accomplished was quickly repealed by Democrats when the latter returned to control.

Not until the Compromise of 1850 were the Whigs in a position to develop an appeal both emotional and intellectual in content. After the Mexican War vast areas were added to the territories of the United States and fully half was below the Missouri Compromise line between slave area and free. The balance in the Senate was fifteen free states and fifteen slave states. California was clamoring for admittance. The South wanted more slave states, but no free states without a fair trade. The rising wave of abolitionist sentiment in the North demanded no more slave states under any circumstances. Under the leadership of Clay the Compromise of 1850 — admitting California as a free state, organizing the territory gained from Mexico without mention of slavery, and promising a new stringent fugitive slave act — passed the Congress. Whig President Taylor refused to sign, however, and not until his death and Fillmore's succession was the compromise passed.

In spite of what appeared to be Whig vacillation, the Compromise of 1850 was calculated to bring political advantage to the Whigs because finally, it seemed, the troublesome slavery question had been laid to rest. Whigs might now be the champions of Union. The country was prosperous. But the Whigs collapsed.

Whigs would have liked to restore the United States bank. They could not. Whigs wanted a sound currency, but could not get it either. Though the party passed legislation setting up subsidies for commercial enterprises, Democrats took office to repeal the laws. Whigs raised tariffs when in office. However, Democrats came back in to lower tariffs and finally to abandon the principle of protection. Whigs attempted to develop and use the United States navy as an arm for the expansion of trade, but Democrats held office over so much of the period that Whig policy had no opportunity to bear fruit. The Whig party had been mostly a failure, failing in the programs it appeared to want to implement, failing to successfully provide leadership when it did control the White House, and failing to so organize and develop itself as to consistently have good prospects of capturing the national government.

From 1840 until 1852 the Whig party had an excellent opportunity to establish itself on a foundation which might have meant the development of solid broad appeal. Lacking in unity and Presidential leadership, Whigs were unable to take advantage of the opportunities presented to them.

QUALITY OF DEMOCRATIC AND WHIG FLEXIBILITY

By 1828, the Adams men had become an identifiable faction within the Republican party which was to evolve into the National-Republican party (1828 and 1832), and then into the Whig party. Also by that year the Jackson men had become an identifiable opposition within the Republican party — an opposition which was to evolve into the Democratic party. Politicians had learned well one of the major lessons of the earlier Federalist-Republican period. Federalists had been politically inflexible; Republicans, flexible. Now the politicians who were attempting to build new national political parties were uniformly flexible in approach — in search of a formula which could develop for each the broadest possible base of support. Nor did the formula have to be one which was substantially intellectual in approach. Emotionalism and often outright demagoguery were put to use in campaigns as never before.

In 1800 in ten of the sixteen states Presidential electors were selected by the state legislatures. By 1824 eighteen of the twenty-four states provided for choosing Presidential electors by popular vote. By 1832 only South Carolina had not joined in the trend. Also in 1824, for the first time, total popular votes cast for the Presidential candidates were published. As the method of electing Presidential electors changed to place that function in the hands of the people, the nature of Presidential campaigns changed. First to grasp the significance of the new Presidential election environment were the partisans of Andrew Jackson.

John Quincy Adams, one who described himself as " a man of reserved, cold, austere and forbidding manners " [12] was a poor match for the colorful and warm personality of national hero General Andrew Jackson. The American System had its enemies as well as its friends, and was something concrete that could be argued against. Jackson, reputedly in favor of the American system, was a symbol who warmed the political heart of the masses of people and tended to make them forget their sectional and other differences. The circumstances under which Adams gained the White House — election by the House, though Jackson had been shown to be the leader in published popular votes and in electoral votes — provided the springboard from which Jacksonians embarked on their four-year campaign leading up to 1828. The will of the people had been disregarded! Because Clay had been appointed to the office of Secretary of State, the post from which men traditionally had moved up to the White House, Adams was accused of trying to take away from the American people their right to choose the next President. Adams, it was whispered, had a billiard table in the White House! Both houses of Congress from 1826 were controlled by the Jackson-men opposition intent on leaving no stone unturned in embarrassing the administration.

As Adams was being politically destroyed, the Jackson managers, led by Martin Van Buren, were clearing the anti-Adams field for Jackson's candidacy and building their sectional combination. W. H. Crawford, whose 1824 campaign had been managed by Van Buren, threw in his lot with Jackson and brought with him his southern support. John C. Calhoun was disposed of by offering him the Vice Presidency which was made to appear attractive enough to the ambitious Calhoun because, he was led to believe, Jackson at 61 was an old and a sick man. Bait for ex-Federalists took the form of " leaking " a letter which Jackson had written to President Monroe in 1816 urging appointment to the position of Secretary of War of a then well-known South Carolina Federalist.[13]

---

[12] Binkley, *Parties*, p. 109.   [13] From *ibid.*, pp. 115–118.

Such was the nature of the build-up for Jackson for 1828. Once in office, Old Hickory's dynamic personality, his personal political ability and the political abilities of the group of professional campaign managers with which he surrounded himself, were enough to consolidate gains and lay the foundation for the Democratic party. Throughout the Jackson administrations, political actions were, in a very un-Hamiltonian manner, always studied in relation to what would be their probable effect on the Jacksonian base of popular support.

By 1840 Whig managers had learned much from twelve years of Jacksonian Democratic party tactics and success, and now Whigs were to add embellishments of their own. Depression had created unrest, and the soil for Whig propaganda was thus well prepared. Old Guard Whigs had, after a struggle, been replaced by New Guard Whigs or old-guardsmen themselves had seen the futility of attempting to fight Jacksonianism on the old intellectual Whig terms. In key states like New York, Pennsylvania, and Massachusetts, Whigs set themselves up as the new champions of the people. Daniel Webster and Henry Clay, symbols for years of opposition to Jacksonian Democracy, were discarded, and in their place as the Whig nominee of 1840 was installed General William Henry Harrison, the highest running Whig in 1836.

When a Baltimore newspaper disparagingly referred to the Whig nominee as one who would be most happy if left in a log cabin with a barrel of hard cider, Whig leaders had found their 1840 campaign theme — a defense of log cabins and hard cider against the New York plutocrat, Van Buren, lounging in luxurious surroundings complete with a billiard table. Without a platform, the Whigs concentrated on an issueless campaign designed to make the elements of their combination forget any issues which might separate them.

Gone was the old Whig formalism and stuffiness, and in its place were the noisy parade and local gatherings with plenty to eat and hard cider to drink. Log cabin and cider barrel symbols were to be seen everywhere from parade floats to women's earrings. Lest Harrison attempt to talk issues and get into trouble, he was held to a minimum number of public appearances — figuratively, only enough to show that he was alive. His campaign managers made sure his every piece of correspondence was examined for its political implications. And as Democrats talked and wrote, one Orestes A. Brownson, a federal employee, published an article which Whigs were able to twist into making it appear that the Democratic party was for overthrowing free labor, property, and the church.

Here was " the new party of the common man," and so effective was the Whig campaign in stirring interest that over one million more voters trooped to the polls in 1840 than had in 1836 (see Figure 6). Though Harrison's margin of popular votes was very narrow (1,275,016 to Van Buren's 1,129,102), Whigs accomplished an electoral college landslide with 234 electoral votes to the Democrat's 60.

What had been the impact of the campaign on the individual voter? Schlesinger quotes one veteran of the Whig campaign of 1840 as saying: " So far as ideas entered into my support of the Whig candidate, I simply regarded him as a poor man, whose home was in a log cabin, and who would in some way help the people . . . while I was fully persuaded that Van Buren was not only a graceless aristocrat and a dandy, but a cunning conspirator, seeking the overthrow of the country's liberties." [14] The circumstances of the campaign of 1840 suggest that Whig success resulted in large part from the fact that many others like Schlesinger's one-man sample acted similarly for similar reasons.

Unable to consolidate gains from 1840 to 1844, the Whigs turned again to Clay. Running this time on a statement of old National-Republican aims and with victory apparently within his grasp, Clay attempted to fence-straddle on the one burning issue of the campaign — the annexation of Texas. Where in 1840 noncommitment had been an effective tactic, in 1844 the " Texas hedge " was not. Here was an issue that could not be dodged. By indecision Clay earned the distrust of both North and South in quantity sufficient to give Polk a narrow victory. In 1848 the Whigs, after Polk's generally pro-southern administration, came back to power. Again they were unable to consolidate gains, and with Scott in 1852 went down to their last defeat. By this time the Democratic party too was on its way to Civil War disintegration.

During the 1824 to 1860 period, the highest quality of Democratic flexibility was exhibited in the development and maintenance of Jackson's personal political power. He and his managers correctly assessed the political environment in which they found themselves, and exploited its possibilities. Once in power, Jackson maintained and strengthened his base of support. Though Whigs were on occa-

---

[14] Schlesinger, op. cit., p. 305.

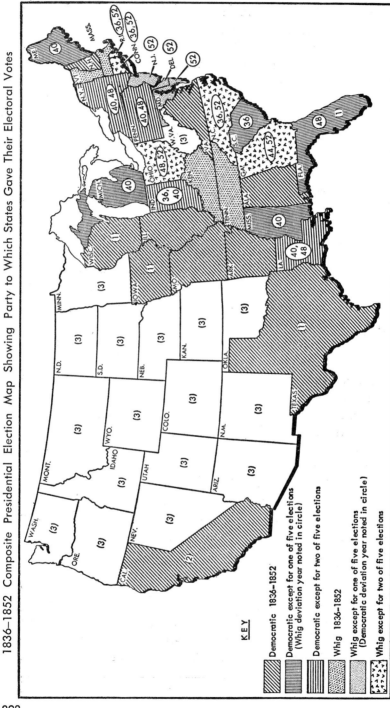

1836-1852 Composite Presidential Election Map Showing Party to Which States Gave Their Electoral Votes

KEY

Democratic 1836-1852

Democratic except for one of five elections (Whig deviation year noted in circle)

Democratic except for two of five elections

Whig 1836-1852

Whig except for one of five elections (Democratic deviation year noted in circle)

Whig except for two of five elections

Notes: (1) Voted in Presidential election for the first time in 1848. (2) Voted first in 1852. (3) Voted in no Presidential election over the period.

Source: W. Dean Burnham, *Presidential Ballots, 1836–1892* (Baltimore: The Johns Hopkins Press, 1955).

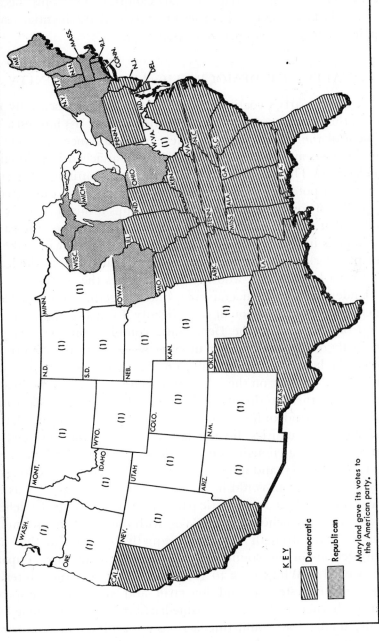

1856 Presidential Election Map Showing Party to Which States Gave Their Electoral Votes

KEY

Democratic

Republican

Maryland gave its votes to the American party.

Note: (1) Did not vote in 1856 Presidential election.

Source: W. Dean Burnham, *Presidential Ballots, 1836–1892* (Baltimore: The Johns Hopkins Press, 1955).

sion flexible enough to adapt to their campaign problems, because the party lacked essential qualities of unity and Presidential leadership, it was never able to realize its potential.

QUALITY OF DEMOCRATIC AND WHIG UNITY

A major party's coalition building function is essentially this. Within the nation are a complex of sectional and class interests. The problem of the major party is to develop an alliance of enough of those interests and to attract enough loosely attached individuals to win elections. This it can do by stating only the minimum objectives upon which potential elements of a potential alliance can agree. If the quality of common unity among the groups it might possibly win is so low that there is no statable minimum objective, then the party's only hope is in the development of a personality who will make the elements overlook their differences as they are attracted to the leader or " great white father " who in effect becomes the party.

Under Jackson, Democrats were drawn together both by a vague principle and the attraction of Old Hickory. Even after Jackson withdrew from leadership, the Democratic combination was made up principally of the small farmer in every section and the eastern city worker. At least they could unite on the theme of " the common man's party." Whigs, on the other hand, tended always to be in a position where the margin of victory could be attained only with a national hero, and unfortunately for the Whigs the luster of their Presidents' personalities did not last, either because they died too soon or lived long enough to be politically ripped apart by the warring Clay, Webster, and other minor Whig factions in the Congress.

Perhaps no man could have taken over the Whig party as Andrew Jackson did the Democratic party. Jackson's party had a definite center of gravity anchored in the West with the South in a secondary position. Whig strength was almost equally balanced in the three major sections of the country. Powerful indeed was the campaign drug needed if Whigs were to get protectionist easterner, internal-improvement westerner, and low-tariff and anti-internal-improvement southerner working in the same harness. Even when some kind of unity among those conflicting factions was achieved in Presidential campaigns, as soon as the party faced the cold light of the morning after in the next session of the Congress, the old disunity factors were again immediately at work.

Clay from the West, Webster from the East, and at times Calhoun from the South were the principal Whig competitors for leadership on the national government level. For two reasons they found it impossible to consistently work with each other. Each was expressing, even as he tried to construct a national program to use as a stepladder to the Presidency, the peculiar type of program which he saw as necessary for political success in his section of the country. In addition, each was personally ambitious for himself. Because there was no single party leader strong enough to get these men to work together in the name of the Whig party, they went their separate ways.

In part the Whig unity problem was aggravated because an accident of history placed all three of these able Senators in the same party at the same time. Because they were powerful intellects and speakers, their differences were newsworthy and tended to create in the public mind the picture of a party which did not know where it was going and would not know what to do once it arrived at its destination. Furthermore, Webster's standards of personal ethics permitted him to be very lax in the manner in which he earned money over and above his Congressional salary, and thus it was easier for Democrats to label the Whigs as " tools of the business interests." Clay tended to become a " defeated " perpetual candidate whose novelty had worn thin, one whose public position on too many issues was too clear, and one who had made too many enemies in the course of his Congressional career. Calhoun went back to the Democratic party.

The Whigs' hope for party unity and success lay in one of its general-of-the-armies nominees for the Presidency who, if elected, might like a Jefferson, Jackson, Lincoln, Theodore Roosevelt or Franklin Roosevelt have created a new *de facto* Whig party combination. That hope never materialized. What such a party leader might have done for the Whigs, however, is suggested by a comparison of Democratic and Whig popular votes in presidential elections from 1836 through 1852:

Year	Democrats	Whigs
1836	762,678	735,651 (three candidate total)
1840	1,129,102	1,275,016
1844	1,337,243	1,299,062
1848	1,220,544	1,360,099
1852	1,601,274	1,386,580

QUALITY OF DEMOCRATIC AND WHIG
PRESIDENTIAL LEADERSHIP

From Madison through John Quincy Adams, the Congressional caucus was used as a tool by Congress to dominate chief executives. Several factors made it possible for Andrew Jackson to reverse that trend and to re-establish the chief legislator and party chief roles as functions of the President's office. By Jackson's time, adult male white suffrage had arrived and the means of choosing Presidential electors in the states had shifted from election by state legislatures to popular election. Jackson had not been nominated by Congressional caucus nor did he owe his election to the House. The depression of the 1820's had created the widespread opinion among the economically less fortunate that the conservative wing of the Republican party, operating through the Congress, had deserted the people in order to sit at the same table with the economically more fortunate. In short, the common people were not fully able to politically express themselves and they were ready for a champion. Old Hickory, sensing the changed conditions, made himself into a " tribune of the people."

Throughout the Democratic versus National-Republican and Whig period, Democrats generally tended to exploit the new conception of the Presidency as an instrument of party warfare while the National-Republicans and Whigs stood violently opposed to " executive usurpation." If Federalist adherence to the principle that there should be no political party organizations was a major cause in the downfall of that first major party, the spurning of Presidential leadership was the single greatest operating deficiency of the Whigs. Jackson's rise and power made it clear that the people wanted a champion. Though Whigs were willing to adapt their campaign techniques to the lessons Democrats had taught them, the Whig party in Congress was never willing to go the next step to pick nominees who might be potentially strong Presidents or to allow Whig Presidents enough Congressional party backing to assume the role. On this particular party principle, the Whigs were as inflexible as Hamiltonian Federalists had been generally inflexible.

Whig attitudes toward chief executives were set by Congressional National-Republicans in their opposition to Jackson. The issue was clearly defined in the fight over Jackson's veto of legislation to recharter the second United States Bank. Jacksonians were antimonopoly; the United States Bank was, to them, a monopoly. Jacksonians were states rights in approach; the Bank could without the consent of states establish branch banks. Jacksonian debtors tended to favor inflation; the Bank was, to them, imposing deflation. Though the Federalist United States Supreme Court had in 1813 in McCulloch v. Maryland upheld the Bank's constitutionality, Jackson, when forced to make his decision, did so in part on the ground that the Bank was unconstitutional. The other branches of government too had the right to judge constitutionality questions — even the President! Regardless, the immediate question was whether the President should represent the " rich " or the " poor " in his official action. So completely did National-Republicans misjudge the political temper of the times that they encouraged widespread distribution of the veto message on the assumption it would hurt Jackson, and Clay made the veto his principal issue in the 1832 campaign.

His veto, Jackson felt, had been vindicated by re-election in 1832. While the United States Bank's charter still had three years to run, Jackson made plans to begin removing federal funds from it. When the Secretary of the Treasury refused, he was transferred. When Jackson's next Secretary of the Treasury also refused, he was removed. When finally Jackson moved Roger Taney from the office of Attorney General to the Treasury, Presidential policy was implemented, and from the Senate came a Clay-inspired resolution of censure against the chief executive. Jackson fought back against the " Senate oligarchy " which would hamper the " tribune of the people." Democratic state legislatures replaced Senators who had voted for the resolution, and Jackson emerged from the fight with a new Democratic majority in the Senate. In 1837 the Senate expunged the censure resolution from the record.

After the Whig party had elected Harrison in 1840, Congressional Whigs persisted in their Congressional supremacy attitude. Webster offered Harrison a Webster-prepared inaugural address. When Harrison went ahead to prepare his own inaugural message, Webster and Clay injected themselves into the process.[15] The product had Harrison denying that the Constitution intended the President to have a part of the legislative power. " And it is preposterous to suppose that a thought could be entertained for a moment that the President, placed at the capital, in the center of the country could better understand the wants and wishes of the people than their own

---

[15] From Binkley, *President and Congress*, p. 89.

immediate representatives who spend a part of every year among them . . . and (are) bound to them by the triple tie of interest, duty, and affection." [16]

Harrison perhaps learned more about the true nature of the Whig party in his one month as President than he had in his years as a Whig before election to the Presidency. Binkley writes: " Concerning the demands for patronage Harrison felt impelled to declare that Clay and Webster Whigs ' were bent upon seizing the reins of government ' and he is reported to have been driven to the point of saying frankly, ' Mr. Clay, you forget that I am President.' Ultimately he informed Clay that he would no longer deal with him except by letter." [17]

Tyler had a similar experience. Though he had resigned from the Senate in protest against " executive usurpation " and though he on first assuming office had shown an intention to take the traditional Whig view of a President's place, Tyler also soon found himself forced to the Jacksonian interpretation of the Presidency. When at Tyler's first Cabinet meeting, Webster went so far as to suggest that Cabinet action should be by majority vote with the President having only one vote, Tyler was driven to reply: " I am the President and I shall be held responsible for my administration." [18] When the Whig Administration carefully framed plans for a financial agency to replace the United States Bank without giving that agency the right to establish branches in the states — a plan in which Webster concurred — Clay redrafted the legislation in the Senate into the same kind of bank bill Jackson had vetoed. Tyler vetoed it. Another bill like the first was sent to the President. It too was vetoed.

Now, to attempt to get Tyler to resign to make way for the President Pro Tempore of the Senate, all but Webster of Tyler's Cabinet resigned. The Whig caucus denounced its President, and Whig party organizations let loose a torrent of abuse. But Tyler stood his ground. When another veto of a Whig high-tariff bill was administered, a House committee headed by John Quincy Adams drew up an impeachment resolution, which the House passed. Tyler's answer was not received for reading or publication by the House. Henry Clay resigned from the Senate to go home to Kentucky to await his party's call for 1844. Such was the state of the Whig party in its first four years of " controlling " the White House.

---

[16] From Binkley, *President and Congress,* p. 90.
[17] *Ibid.,* p. 89.   [18] *Ibid.,* p. 93.

Polk, with Democratic majorities in both houses of Congress for the first two years of his administration, accomplished most of his objectives, but lost in 1848 when his Democratic party badly split between northern and southern factions. In 1849 Whigs returned to the stage for what today seems the second act of tragic comedy. Taylor, as had Harrison and Tyler before him, began by stating Whig doctrine as to what should be his role as President. He, however, was not given a chance to become a party leader. Clay and Webster were in agreement, before Taylor took office, that he was a poor excuse for a President. Taylor, a southerner, soon exhibited enough independence of action to cause his repudiation by southern Whigs. Now, again, here was a Whig President standing astride the path of Henry Clay and the latter's last big plan for a Whig victory formula — the Compromise of 1850. Only a death in the White House and Fillmore's accession made the passage of the plan possible, but Fillmore too was rejected by 1852.

Had the American form of government been parliamentary in organization, the Whig party may have found its talents put to better use. But that party was in effect one operating under parliamentary theory in a Presidential system which was incompatible with the doctrine of Congressional supremacy. Whatever opportunity the Whigs had to enlarge their appeal to construct a solid winning combination was destroyed by doctrinaire application of this principle. Each Whig administration became a farce of confusion. Perhaps if Clay had won the Presidency in his prime, he like Jefferson would have devised a way to circumvent theory with the practical application of workable techniques. Whig fortunes did not permit that development to take place.

CHAPTER TWELVE

Republicans and Democrats, 1860 to 1932

The most successful of the opposition parties has been the Democratic Party since the loss of its earlier supremacy in national politics in 1860. Three times it has found a candidate capable of taking advantage of the mistakes and misfortunes of the party in power and driving its leaders from office. Compared with this record, that of the Whigs is poor and that of the Federalists after 1800 is pathetic. The stresses and strains of holding power disclosed the weaknesses of the Democratic combination of factions and prevented it under the leadership of Grover Cleveland and of Woodrow Wilson from preserving its ascendancy over the Republicans. Under Franklin D. Roosevelt's leadership the Democrats made more serious inroads upon the Republican sources of strength and, despite the mutual incompatibility between the rural Southern and the urban Northern factions, offered a more formidable challenge to the " ins " than at any time since the initial rise of Andrew Jackson. The presidential election of 1948 finally demonstrated that the Democratic Party had succeeded under the New Deal in exchanging roles with their Republican opponents.

The most successful of the " ins " up to the debacle of 1932 was the present Republican Party. Despite great vicissitudes of fortune and permanent exclusion from a large part of the South it managed to elect its presidential candidate at all but four of the campaigns between 1856 and 1932. It maintained its ascendancy, despite interludes of opposition triumph, more than twice as long as the Jacksonian Democrats. It produced few great Presidents, but could find many candidates capable of uniting its various

*factions and successfully exploiting the possibilities in the established
alignment of the major parties. Yet, when driven from power in 1932, it
was unable to regain control of the government in five successive elections,
a period of uninterrupted defeat exceeded only by that of the Democrats
following their downfall in 1860.*

Arthur N. Holcombe [1]

The era of Republican supremacy from 1860 to 1932 exceeds
by thirty years the life-span of any major " sun " party in United
States political history.[2] Federalists controlled the presidency for only
three four-year terms, and Jeffersonian Republicans for eight. Jacksonian Democrats were the " supreme " party from 1828 to 1860 and
over those years won six of the eight presidential elections. If the
Democratic era which was established by Franklin D. Roosevelt is
now over — an assumption which is not necessarily valid and which
only the outcome of future national elections can establish — Democrats were the " sun " party for the five 1932 to 1952 terms. The time
span from the Civil War to 1932 was 72 years and encompassed 18
presidential elections. Of the 18, Republicans won 14. Over the period, Republicans organized the Senate in 31 of the 36 Congresses,
and the House in 23 of the 36 Congresses.

Figure 9 contrasts the major party distribution of electoral votes
in presidential elections from 1860 through 1928; Figure 10, the
popular votes for the major party nominees for the same presidential
elections; Figure 11, the number of seats held by Democrats and Republicans in the House in each Congress; and Figure 12, the number
of Senate seats held by each major party in those 36 Congresses. In
summary, the figures suggest three relatively distinct political sub-
periods within the 72 years. The first, running up to 1876, was Republican, but with Democrats showing surprising strength in spite of
the Civil War and Republican waving of the " bloody shirt " of war
issues.

The second, from 1876 to 1896, is a period in which the two

---

[1] *Our More Perfect Union* (Cambridge, Mass.: Harvard University Press,
1950) , pp. 106–107. Reprinted by permission of Harvard University Press.

[2] " Sun party " is the term used by Samuel Lubell, *The Future of American
Politics* (New York: Harper and Brothers, 1952) , for the strongest or supreme
major party of any period of American political party history. The weaker of the
two major parties, or minority major party, in any period, Lubell calls the " moon
party."

Figure 9. Electoral Votes for Democratic and Republican Candidates for President, 1860–1928

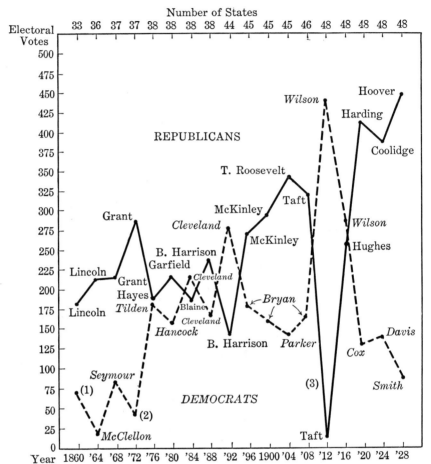

Notes: (1) In 1860 the highest ranking Democratic nominee, John C. Breckinridge, won 72 electoral votes. Stephen A. Douglas, another Democratic nominee, got 12; and John Bell, Constitutional Union Party, 39.

(2) In 1872 Horace Greeley, the Liberal-Republican party nominee, was supported by the Democratic party. He died during the campaign. The Democrat with the greatest number of electoral votes was Thomas A. Hendricks, Independent-Democrat, with 42.

(3) Theodore Roosevelt, Progressive Republican, received 88 electoral votes.

Source: U. S. Bureau of the Census, *Historical Statistics of the United States, 1789–1945* (Washington, D.C.: Government Printing Office, 1949), pp. 288–289.

Figure 10. Popular Votes for Democratic and Republican Candidates for President, 1860–1928

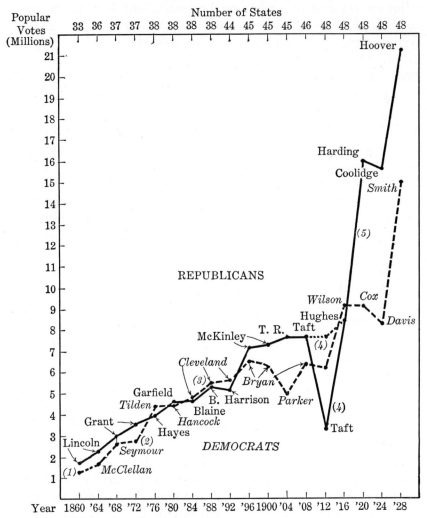

Notes: (1) John C. Breckinridge, Democrat, received 847,953 popular votes; Stephen A. Douglas, Democrat, 1,375,157; and John Bell, Constitutional Union Party, 590,631. Their total was 2,273,771 to Lincoln's 1,866,452.

(2) Horace Greeley, Liberal-Republican nominee supported by the Democrats, though he died during the campaign, received 2,834,125 popular votes.

(3) Though Cleveland won more popular votes than Benjamin Harrison in 1888, the latter had 233 electoral votes to Cleveland's 168.

(4) In 1912 Theodore Roosevelt's popular vote was 4,119,538. If the Taft and Roosevelt votes are added together, the Republican total if there had been no split would have been 7,604,518.

(5) The election of 1920 was the first in which women had the right to vote.

Source: U. S. Bureau of the Census, Historical Statistics of the United States, 1789–1945 (Washington, D.C.: Government Printing Office, 1949), pp. 288–289.

major parties were of almost equal strength, with Republicans more successful in Presidential elections and Democrats more successful in controlling the House of Representatives. Hayes won the disputed election of 1876 by only one electoral vote — 185 to 184, though Tilden had 4,300,590 popular votes to Hayes' 4,036,298. Garfield's 1880 popular vote plurality was only some 10,000 more than Hancock's out of some 9 million votes cast for the major party nominees. A difference of some 23,000 votes out of almost 10 million separated Cleveland and Blaine in 1884, and Cleveland's win in the electoral college came by virtue of his carrying New York by a plurality of slightly over 1,000 votes. In 1888 Benjamin Harrison was elected, though Cleveland received approximately 100,000 more popular votes out of the 11 million major party votes cast. In the nine Congresses from 1877 through 1893 Democrats organized the House seven times and the Senate twice.

The third subperiod ran from 1896 until 1932. Except for the Wilson interlude, made possible by the Taft-Theodore Roosevelt split in the Republican party, Republicans during these years were in undisputed control of the national government. It was not until 1896 that the power base of the Republican party came to represent a solid national majority.

THE SETTING

Through the pre-Civil War period the agricultural economies of West and South had contested for political power with the interests of business and commerce, particularly those of the East. Democrats sought to organize the former for political action; Whigs had tried to represent the latter and at the same time to develop an appeal broad enough to win national elections. The principal issues had been tariffs, internal improvements, the currency, and subsidies to business enterprises.

In the late 1840's the question of slavery was superimposed onto the others. The new issue was not strictly a question of the immorality or sin of human bondage. Rather, it was a complicated and interwoven mixture of politics, economics, and morals. Southerners controlled positions of leadership in both houses of Congress, Cabinets, the Supreme Court, and generally the policies of Presidents. More and more the North, including both West and East, came to the conclusion that the federal government was being run by and for the

South, and East and West began to feel they had more in common with one another than either section had interests in common with the South.

Where old river transportation routes had linked West and South, now railroads were an improvement on river boats, and railroads ran on an East-West axis. While once the West and South had seemed to agree on the desirability of low tariffs, now foreign markets for western agricultural products had dried up and the West and East could both feel affinity for more protection. The South had always opposed federally sponsored internal improvements, whereas the West and East had always been at least potential allies in behalf of federal development of roads, canals, and harbors.

The West and South had once been able to unite against the " money power " and hard-money attitudes of the East, but wildcat banks and the consequences had brought the westerner to a position where he did not see the eastern financier as quite the vicious character he had once seemed to be. Originally the West and South had been united against the East in pushing for westward expansion and the admission of new states; now West and South were locked in bitter competition to determine whether new territories should be slave or free. Such were the economic pressures tending to break down barriers between East and West. Politically, if the West wanted the power of the slavocracy checked, the objective could be accomplished only by working in some degree of political concert with the East.

Neither Democrats nor Whigs, split as they were between northern and southern wings, could bring themselves into line with the economic transformations taking place or into line with the growing northern demand for a more forthright position on the slavery question. Indicative of northern dissatisfaction with the two major parties was the appearance in the 1840's and 1850's of a rash of minor parties.

In 1840 and 1844 the Library party with James G. Birney was the means through which abolitionists could politically express themselves. Even it, however, presented an economic issue — that the southern slave economy had been responsible for the depression of 1837 — as well as a moral issue. In 1840 Birney had received 7,000 popular votes and in 1844, 62,000. By 1848 the minor party protest vote multiplied to 291,000 for Martin Van Buren as the candidate of the Free Soil party. Included here were Conscience Whigs who had

Figure 11. Democratic and Republican Seats in the U. S. House of Representatives, 1861–1931

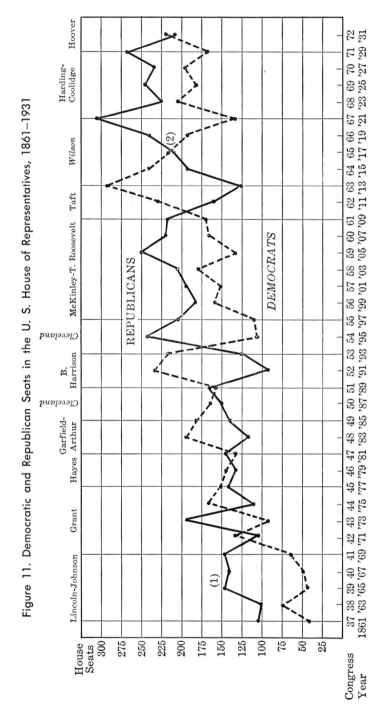

Notes: (1) In 1865 the Union party was the opposition to the Democratic party.
(2) In the 65th Congress the Democrats had 216 House seats and the Republicans 210. The balance of power was held by six unorganized members.

Source: U. S. Bureau of the Census, *Historical Statistics of the United States, 1789–1945* (Washington, D.C.: Government Printing Office, 1949), p. 293.

Figure 12. Democratic and Republican Seats in the U. S. Senate, 1861–1931

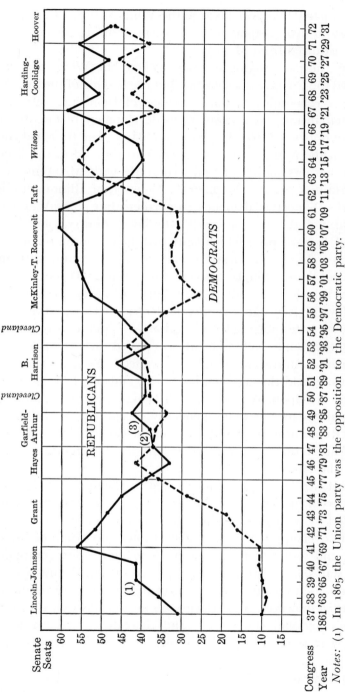

Notes: (1) In 1865 the Union party was the opposition to the Democratic party.
(2) In the 47th Congress the Republicans had 37 and the Democrats 37. The balance of power was held by one unorganized member.
(3) In the 48th Congress the Republicans had 38 seats and the Democrats 36. Two members were unorganized.

Source: U. S. Bureau of the Census, *Historical Statistics of the United States, 1789–1945* (Washington, D.C.: Government Printing Office, 1949), p. 293.

bolted their party that year because the Whig National Convention had refused to take a stand in favor of prohibiting slavery in the territories acquired from Mexico.

To lay the party-shattering issue to rest, the Whigs two years later offered the Compromise of 1850, but the halving of the Free Soil vote in 1852 rebounded to the advantage of Democrats instead of Whigs. Then, in 1854 events assured the development of a new northern party of opposition to the Democratic party. The time had come to decide on the route for a transcontinental railroad to the Pacific Coast. Southerners wanted a southern route with Memphis as its eastern terminus. Senator Stephen A. Douglas, of Illinois, leading the northern Democrats, demanded a northern line going West from Chicago through the unorganized Platte River country. Douglas got his railroad, but at a price which destroyed the Compromise of 1850. The Kansas-Nebraska Territory through which the transcontinental railroad would run, Douglas conceded to southern Democrats, was to be established to permit slavery until, when states would be formed, slave or free status would be determined by a vote of the people in each state applying for admission — " squatter sovereignty."

When the Kansas-Nebraska Bill was passed early in 1854, much of the North was outraged. Douglas was called a traitor. Indignation meetings were held throughout the North, and one of these in the schoolhouse at Ripon, Wisconsin, with Whigs, Democrats, and Free Soilers in attendance is today generally recognized as the one at which the Republican party was born. In the Congressional elections of 1854 Anti-Nebraska fusion slates landslided Democrats out of control of the House of Representatives.

Most of the Anti-Nebraskans elected to Congress in 1854 were also members of the Know-Nothing party — an organization of nativists appalled by the rising flood of immigration. They were workers afraid of an oversupplied labor market, Protestants afraid of Roman Catholics, and southerners who wanted no more immigrant-populated free states. For a brief time it appeared that the Know-Nothing party would rise to major party status in time to elect a President in 1856. In 1855, however, a pro-slavery resolution was forced through that party's national convention, and thereafter northern Know-Nothings were to become ready to join the Republican party, provided the inducements were right.

From 1854 to 1860 the developments were rapid leading to a realignment of political parties. Democrats and Whigs had been truly national parties with strength in every section, but now a party power pattern began to crystallize based on a North-South split. Republicans were to find all their strength concentrated in the North. Democrats were to find their northern power declining and their southern strength solid to the point of eventually producing the Solid Democratic South.

Politicians everywhere were startled at the remarkable showing of the Republican party in 1856 with the erratic Fremont as its nominee. Here was a party which had just held its first national convention in June of that year. Principally on the one platform plank which said that it was the right and duty of Congress to prohibit slavery in the territories. Republicans captured 42 percent of the two-party vote. The moderate antislavery position had now become respectable.

In 1857 the United States Supreme Court in the Dred Scott case declared that " once a slave always a slave " and voided the Missouri and 1850 compromises on the ground that slaves were property and as such the institution of slavery could not be excluded from the territories. Republicans took issue. In the same year the panic of 1857 occurred and damaged the incumbent Democratic party. John Brown, attempting to incite a slave revolt, raided Harper's Ferry, and was hung. *Uncle Tom's Cabin* became a best seller. Senator Charles Sumner of Massachusetts was beat up by Congressman Preston Brooks of South Carolina. Douglas split with Buchanan over the manner in which the administration was attempting to make Kansas a slave state. Tension within the Democratic party mounted, and when Douglas received the Democratic nomination in 1860, southern Democrats bolted and nominated Vice President John C. Breckinridge of Kentucky. Those who sought to preserve the union at all costs established the Constitutional Union party and nominated John Bell of Tennessee. Republicans nominated and elected Abraham Lincoln. South Carolina seceded on December 20, 1860, to be followed by the rest of the states which made up the Confederacy. The country was at war, and a new era in American party politics had begun.

NATURE OF REPUBLICAN APPEAL

How delicate is the problem of developing major party political appeal is well illustrated in the first efforts of the Republican party to determine what it as a party represented. In 1856 all that the heterogeneous conglomeration of nativists, prohibitionists, " wet " German immigrants, Free Soilers, conservative Whigs, radical aboli- tionists, workers, and unhappy Democrats could agree upon were the following planks. First, slavery should be excluded from the terri- tories. This was by far the most important element of the first Re- publican platform. Second, there should be a northern-route trans- continental railroad. Third, the federal government should sponsor other internal improvements. Because big business was aligned with Buchanan, Republicans could hit heavily at the Democrats as the enemies of the workers. Needing nativist support, however, the draft- ers of the Republican platform of 1856 dared not insert a homestead plank, nor did they dare take a stand on the tariff question for fear of driving away Democrats who might otherwise join the ranks.

Though Fremont captured 42 percent of the major party popular vote, Democrats in 1856 carried five of the 16 free states, including Illinois and Pennsylvania. Republicans had been shut out in the South. Clearly, if greater Republican strength was to be achieved, it had to come from these five still Democratic free states. By 1860 specific planks had been developed to attempt to lure all the northern states away from the Democrats.

There should be free homesteads for farmers, and for workers who wanted farms for themselves or their children — " Vote Yourself a Farm! " By this time Know-Nothings had little alternative but to support the Republican party. There should be a reversal of Demo- cratic low-tariff policies to attract the protectionist eastern manufac- turer. For 1860 Republicans needed protectionist eastern states more than those persons who might be attracted to the Democrats by low- tariff Democratic appeal. The rights of naturalized immigrants should be recognized as well as those of the native born. But most important for everyone in the North, the Republican party set itself up as the vehicle for all who would stop the expansion of the slave interests *into the territories.*

Such was the nature of the appeal that won for Lincoln the electoral votes of every northern state except New Jersey in the four-cornered contest for the Presidency in 1860. His victory was a triumph of western farmers and eastern workers. The eastern busi- ness community gave Lincoln little more support than that group had given Fremont in 1856. However this element was soon to fall into line behind the Lincoln Administration and by Grant's time was to assume a dominant role in Republican party councils.

Abraham Lincoln was not, strictly speaking, a Republican President. His was a Union party administration including, in addition to Republicans, the so-called " war " faction of the Democratic party which held secession to be treason. Lincoln in 1864 was renominated as a Union party man, and Andrew Johnson, a Democrat, was placed on the ticket to recognize the non-Republican element. So narrow was Lincoln's margin of control and so uncertain his base of popular support that, whether Republicans liked it or not, he often had to take his friends and the Republican party for granted and spread his rewards to peripheral groups in order to enlarge his support. Lincoln's Cabinet was constructed with an all-party and northern all-group appeal objective in mind. Federal patronage and commissions in the Union army were granted in the same manner. Similar all-party and all-group considerations ran through the governmental policies of the Lincoln Administration.

By his moderacy on the issue of slavery, the President sought to win border state slaveholders to his combination, and to hold workers who feared the consequence of a labor market in which ex-slaves might compete. The Emancipation Proclamation applied only to slaves in the Confederate states. Throughout, Lincoln's emphasis was placed on the broad and minimum object of successful prosecution of the war in order to preserve the union. Business and finance capitalism was weaned away from its Democratic ties by a high tariff and economic developments incidental to the war. The Union armies had to be supplied. The war had to be financed. Business boomed. Farmers in 1862 got their Homestead Act, and war prosperity reached them too. And above all there began to glow about Lincoln the symbol of the common and humble man who became President and was saving the Union.

Yet, the Union party with Lincoln at its head, with a Democratic Vice Presidential nominee, and with prosperity and the war finally going favorably, did not, as the election of 1864 showed, have a " supreme " party's power base. With a Democratic platform demanding an immediate end to the war, with General McClellan as Democratic nominee for President repudiating his party's platform, and without eleven of the states which were later to become solidly Democratic, Democrats still polled 45 percent of the major party vote. At this development the Radical Republicans, tending toward the abolitionist position, set out to insure Republican power in the South through the votes of the newly freed Negro. Still there was no Republican landslide. With the war hero General Grant as the Republican nominee and majorities for Grant in all the southern states permitted to vote for President in 1868 (Mississippi, Texas and Virginia had not yet qualified), Grant polled only 53 percent of the major party vote. In 1872 Democratic fortunes were tied to Horace Greeley, the nominee of the Liberal Republicans. Greeley died during the campaign, and Grant won re-election easily. More accurate as a reflection of the relative strength of the two major parties, however, was the disputed election of 1876.

The Republican party that Grant brought out of the Civil War period was not the same Republican party that Lincoln had taken in. Lincoln's party had been a farmer-worker party with Declaration of Independence overtones. Grant's party from 1868 was farmer-capitalist in nature with a declaration of independence to give the capitalist a free hand in the exploitation of America's natural resources. Lincoln came to office without the support of big business interests. Grant moved into the White House closely tied to the leaders of industry, commerce, and finance. As the Lincoln brand of Republicanism in 1860 had reflected the then dynamic forces in American politics, so did the Grant variety largely mirror the new dynamics of 1868.

The large-scale exploitation of United States natural resources had already begun. Seemingly limitless numbers of forests, mines, and other sources of wealth remained to be tapped. The capitalist, accumulating and investing the money to make such development possible, assumed a new respectability. Grant's problem, however, was not that he recognized the importance of the capitalist, but that trusting too much, he permitted the developers of the country too much free rein. The excesses which resulted severely damaged the Republican party at a time when it might otherwise have been building its strength.

The Republican party had saved the union, in the eyes of many, and to it accrued an enormous potential of patriotic and almost religious attraction. Coupled with that was Grant's own substantial prestige and a state of disorganization in the Democratic party created by those Democrats who continued to fight the Civil War. Western farmers were grateful for the farms they had been given. Yet the forces which Grant permitted to gain momentum tended to give his administrations and sometimes those Republican administrations of his pre-1896 successors the poor quality with which they are credited today.

Huge land grants to railroads placed the railroads and speculators between the best farm lands and those who would occupy and
farm them. Largely unregulated, the excesses of the railroads in everything from the manner in which they operated their elevators to the
charges for freight transportation drove many farmers into protest
movements and forced Republican state administrations to railroad
regulation. Business enterprise, expanding into a unified national
economy, combined into gigantic trusts with little concern for the
consumer or the methods it used against the weaker competitor. High
protective tariffs convinced the farmer that something was wrong
when he sold his product in an unprotected market while the manufactured products he had to buy were controlled at what the farmer
held to be an excessively high price level. Relatively hard-money policies angered the debtor farmers. The most aroused of them enrolled
in the Greenback and Populist parties.

In the Grant Administration the spoils system was an open invitation to the corruption which followed, as were the unscrupulous
" carpetbaggers " operating in the South. All these excesses furnished
ammunition for Democrats, minor parties, and disgusted Republicans. So odious was Grant Administration corruption that purity in
government became one of the principal issues in Presidential campaigns for some twenty years after.

From 1876 to 1896 both major parties were in relatively even
balance with the Republicans generally in control of the Senate,
Democrats the House, and Republicans the Presidency except for
the two Cleveland administrations. After federal troops had finally
left the South in 1877, the Republican party no longer had the alternative of seeking support in that section. It could only look to a combination of agrarians and eastern business interests. Until 1896, however, increasingly the power balance within the Republican party was
tipped in the direction of the latter, and thus the combination was
subjected to severe stress and strain.

It is necessary at this point to note also that the Democratic party
over the 1876 to 1892 period was hardly more satisfactory than the
Republican party as an outlet for western discontent. Southern and
border states gave Democrats about 70 percent of the electoral votes
that party needed to win a majority in the electoral college. For much
of the remaining 30 percent, Democrats looked to the Middle Atlantic states such as Delaware, New Jersey and New York. New Yorkers consistently became Democratic Presidential nominees, and the

Democratic party, like the Republican party, became responsive to the financial interests of the East, particularly to those of New York.

With both major parties compromising to hold the industrial and commercial East, the western farmer, protesting against high tariffs, monopolies, and hard money, turned elsewhere for groups through which he could politically express himself. Starting in the early 1870's, the Granger movement spread across the West and, though claiming to be non-political, it achieved substantial success in pressuring state legislatures to regulate railroads. From 1876 through 1884 the Greenback party attempted to organize agrarian discontent. It called for free coinage of silver, a graduated income tax, federal regulation of interstate transportation, and labor legislation. Then came the Farmers' Alliance, and it, in turn, was followed by the most serious threat of all to the major parties — the Populist party. In the Presidential election of 1892 Populists carried Colorado, Idaho, Kansas, and Nevada and won an electoral vote in North Dakota and another in Oregon. Populists captured over 1 million popular votes out of some 11 million total votes cast. The People's party platform, in addition to the Greenback planks listed above, demanded public ownership of railroad, telegraph, and telephone companies and postal savings banks, lowering of tariffs, and the initiative and referendum.

For a time the Populists appeared to be on the way to replacing the Democratic party as a major party. So loud was the voice of political protest that both major parties were forced to come to grips with issues they had sought to avoid. In 1896 the Democratic party responded by swallowing up the Populists' platform and nominating William Jennings Bryan. Republicans, likewise, readjusted their appeal, and a major political realignment took place. The end result was to give the Republican party a more solid base of support than it had ever had before.

Democrats in 1896 boldly cut themselves off from eastern capitalism in the hope that they could forge an alliance between the western farmer and eastern worker. The gamble proved disastrous. The latter tended to side with his boss, and McKinley and Theodore Roosevelt held the East and enough western states to establish a new era of Republican supremacy after the even balance of 1876 to 1896.

Where in Benjamin Harrison's time Republican policy had been to force labor into line for the employer, Theodore Roosevelt demanded that the employer negotiate with the employee. Also for the worker, there was prosperity and the "full dinner pail." Much of the Republican program came right out of the minor party platforms of the last quarter of the 1800's. An income tax amendment based on the ability to pay was placed in the Constitution. Meat inspection and pure food and drug acts set up safeguards for the consumer. The Hepburn Act provided for federal regulation of railroads. Instead of allowing unregulated exploitation of natural resources, conservation was the watchword of the new Republicanism.

McKinley and Theodore Roosevelt also began to lead the country toward a foreign policy of internationalism. A new pride at the influence of the United States swept the country, and behind that pride was also an economic side. Untapped world markets would now be made available for the products of American industry. Republicans did not fail to make the point that it was under Republican administrations that the new American power had expressed itself.

By 1908 Republican " supremacy " status had been soundly established as William Howard Taft rode into office as the designated choice of President Roosevelt. But all was not well within the Republican party. In part, because tariffs had been held high, the western wing of the party was restive. In accordance with the party's 1908 platform promise to the western farmer, Taft in 1909 called a special session of Congress to reduce tariffs. Before the special session was organized, western progressive Republicans under the leadership of Representative George Norris of Nebraska had combined with House Democrats to severely restrict the powers of Republican Speaker Joseph Cannon. Furthermore, the tariff enacted at that session, far from being what the West wanted, actually resulted in more advantageous types of protection for the East. Taft vacillated in his position on the act and pleased no one.

Having severely damaged himself with the West, Taft then attempted to out-do Roosevelt in trust busting. The President did not re-win the farmer, however, and out of the West flamed a strong Progressive Republican Movement. Now Taft had alienated the capitalist too. The final stroke of bitter fate hit the Taft Administration in the Ballinger-Pinchot controversy. It gave the impression that Taft was allied with " special interests " against those who would conserve the country's resources for the people. Taft's power base was gone. His renomination in 1912 by virtue of administration control of southern delegates to the Republican National Convention of that year resulted in the bolt of Roosevelt Progressives. Two terms of Democratic administrations followed.

In 1920 substantially the same power base that had been characteristic of the 1904 and 1908 elections returned a Republican administration to power. Two years before Republicans had captured
Congress, and when Wilson had brought the League of Nations

The Debut of the Elephant as the Republican Symbol

This very busy, complicated cartoon is significant because it represents the elephant in his
first appearance as the symbol of the Republican Party. The cartoon is by Thomas Nast. It
appeared in 1874 in Harper's Weekly as a warning to the Republicans against being stampeded
into nominating President Grant for a third term. The original caption under the cartoon read:
" The Third Term Panic ' An Ass, having put on the Lion's skin, roamed about in the Forest, and
amused himself by frightening all the foolish Animals he met with in his wanderings ' — Shake-
speare or Bacon." The Elephant, representing the heavy Republican vote, is pictured as about
to fall into a pit of troubles — third-term troubles — frightened by " Caesarism," by which is
meant the ambition of the faction of President Grant. (This description of the cartoon appeared
in the Los Angeles Times.)

Covenant to the Senate for ratification, it was turned down. The
American people, suffering from postwar disillusionment, wanted to
" return to normalcy." That was the prospect which Warren G.
Harding offered. So relaxed was Harding, however, that his liberali-
zation of public domain leasing policies immersed his administration
in the boiling political oil of Teapot Dome. The morally stern Cool-

idge was able to counteract the corruption and proceed through his administration under the slogan of " Keep Cool With Cal."

Republicans still showed their tender concern for the eastern capitalist element of the party. Income and inheritance taxes were

FIRST DEMOCRATIC JACKASS

Here is the donkey which Thomas Nast invented as the contemptuous symbol of the Democratic Party. The Democrats had attacked bitterly the late Edward M. Stanton, who had been Lincoln's Secretary of War. This was Nast's rebuke to them. The caption read: "A Live Jackass Kicking a Dead Lion. And such a Lion! and such a Jackass!" The cartoon appeared the first of many times in Harper's Weekly Jan. 15, 1870.

(This description of the cartoon appeared in the Los Angeles Times.)

lowered, the better to make money available for investments. Tariffs were restored to high levels, the better to give manufacturers a safely protected market. Money was ploughed into industry plant expansion far beyond the ability of the consumer to buy, and what was left went into a wild orgy of stock market speculation on Wall Street.

Meanwhile, the farmer had been in depression since the early 1920's, and Republicans could agree on no effective way of alleviating the farmer's distress. The deluge poured in on the Hoover Administration as the economy of the United States was brought to its knees, and Republican party strength crumbled like a house of cards.

During the 1920's the Republican party had been sitting on top of a political powder keg, but that party spent too much of its time admiring the view and not enough in finding out the nature of the foundation under what appeared to be a prospect of unlimited prosperity and Republican power. Nor were adequate precautions taken to make sure no matches got close enough to light the fuse which would set off an economic and political explosion. After the stock market crash of 1929 and the general depression had begun, Hoover seemed powerless to give the impression that he or his party recognized the gravity of the American problem or were capable of taking intelligent steps to solve it.

NATURE OF DEMOCRATIC APPEAL

The Democratic party's appeal from 1860 to 1932 also developed through several distinct phases. Civil War issues made almost any kind of a positive appeal impossible until 1876. From the latter date until 1896, with some qualifications toward the end of the period, Democratic strategy was similar to that of Republicans. In 1896 came a sharp break from the past with Bryanism, but Republicans were able to cut much of the ground out from under the Democratic party by their more moderate approach to reform and by stealing and implementing many of the Democrats' platform planks. Over the entire 1860 to 1932 period only during the first six years of the Wilson Administration did Democrats control the Presidency and both houses of Congress long enough to have an opportunity to translate into law a Democratic program. Even the legislation of those years and the personal appeal of Wilson, however, did not enable the party to capture away from Republicans significant elements of the latter's broad base of support.

Never has a major party suffered and yet survived under the impact of such a staggering set of difficulties as faced the Democratic party during the Civil War and reconstruction years. In 1860 that party had split into two sharply divided segments. When the South seceded, northern Democrats also found themselves divided between

" peace " and " war " factions. With the latter group largely working within the Union party combination during the war, the Peace Democrats went into the campaign of 1864 proclaiming that the war had been a failure and demanding peace at any price. Even before the election, however, the military tide had begun to turn and in the next year with the surrender of Lee, the Democratic platform of 1864 had been thoroughly discredited.

Then Democrats tied themselves to the moderate reconstruction policies of the Johnson Administration, but in the Congressional elections of 1866, Radical Republicans won large enough majorities to consistently over-ride Presidential vetoes. Democrats opposed the Thirteenth, Fourteenth, and Fifteenth Amendments, which Republicans represented as the political implementation of the principles for which the Union armies had fought. In 1868 the Democratic platform again condemned Negro suffrage. Democrats nominated a Vice Presidential candidate who was on record for demanding drastic action to overthrow the reconstruction program. When attempts were made to win over the recession-pressed farmer with an inflation plank, they were canceled out by the nomination for President of Horatio Seymour of New York, a hard money man. As McClellan had repudiated parts of the Democratic platform of 1864, so did Seymour in 1868.

In 1872 Democrats attempted to make Republican high tariffs the principal issue, and became involved in a campaign of support for arch-protectionist Horace Greeley. Greeley too was vulnerable to the " bloody-shirt " Republican tactic because he favored southern home rule and had signed Jefferson Davis' bail bond. Then Greeley died during the campaign, leaving the anti-Grant forces without any kind of a candidate on which they could unite. The Democratic party's attempt to join with Liberal Republicans in 1872 ended in dismal failure.

Developments of the next year, however, finally gave the Democrats their first real post-Civil War success. The panic of 1873 plunged the country into economic depression. Republicans were held responsible, and as a result of the Congressional elections of 1874, Democrats moved into control of the House for the first time since 1858. Still the Democrats could not make a clean break with Civil War issues. Though the platform of 1876 admitted that the Thirteenth, Fourteenth, and Fifteenth amendments were now generally accepted, activities of the Ku Klux Klan in the now emerging Solid

Democratic South plagued the party in the North. Principal issue between Tilden and Hayes was which of the two men could best reform the evils of the Grant administrations.

Tilden, though he won a narrow plurality of the popular vote, lost by one electoral vote in the disputed contest. For long-run Democratic prospects, however, the fact that it would be a Republican President who would withdraw federal troops from the South prevented Republicans from having a new reason in subsequent elections to be able to successfully wave again the " bloody shirt." Now began the period of even balance between the two major parties. Republicans attempted to maintain a western farmer-eastern capitalist alliance; Democrats, a South-eastern capitalist alliance. Since each party outdid the other in trying to win New York, neither party's appeal differed significantly from the other.

Cleveland in his first term seemed a little " unsafe " to the eastern capitalist, particularly when in 1887 he almost surely brought about his own defeat for re-election by straightforwardly coming out for a drastic reduction of tariffs. However, by his 1892–1896 term, Cleveland's general position was not dissimilar from that of both parties' Presidents for the period, oriented as they had been to New York business interests. Cleveland's support of the gold standard was solid, he employed federal troops against the Pullman strikers in 1894 fully as vigorously as Benjamin Harrison might have done, and after four years of New York City law practice, even Cleveland's position on the tariff seemed moderated during his second term.

Until 1896 both major parties had resisted adapting their appeals to the profound changes in American society which had come as a result of the industrial revolution after the Civil War. Then had come the panic of 1893. The Democratic party, if it had continued to temporize, may have found itself replaced by the Populists. Democrats in their adjustment, however, far overshot a moderate adaptation target. In 1896 they set out on a course which was to lead the Democratic party to defeat with Bryan in that year and again in 1900, and after a flirtation with a conservative sound-money candidate in 1904, back to Bryan and a fourth consecutive defeat in 1908.

Since the Greenback party there had been organized western farmer agitation for inflation. Western state silver-mining interests had joined in the assault on the gold standard. If only the gold standard were torn down, the arguments for the panacea concluded, the problems of America's economically unfortunate on the farms and in the cities would be solved. " You shall not press down upon the brow of labor this crown of thorns — You shall not crucify mankind upon a cross of gold." So concluded Bryan's keynote in 1896. The platform which was subsequently adopted threw caution to the winds and stated the idea just as strongly:

> Recognizing that the money question is paramount to all others at this time, we invite attention to the fact that the Federal Constitution named silver and gold together as the money metals of the United States, and that the first coinage law passed by Congress . . . made the silver dollar the monetary unit and admitted gold to free coinage at a ratio based upon the silver-dollar unit.

> We declare that the act of 1873 demonetizing silver without the knowledge or approval of the American people has resulted in the appreciation of gold and a corresponding fall in the prices of commodities produced by the people; a heavy increase in the burdens of taxation and of all debts, public and private; the enrichment of the money-lending class at home and abroad; the prostration of industry and impoverishment of the people.

> We are unalterably opposed to monometallism which has locked fast the prosperity of an industrial people in the paralysis of hard times. Gold monometallism is a British policy. . . . It is not only un-American but anti-American. . . .

> We demand the free and unlimited coinage of both silver and gold at the present legal ratio of 16 to 1. . . .

To make no mistake about the line Democrats were now drawing, the chairman of the Democratic National Committee stated the issue as he saw it: " Against the people in this campaign are arrayed the consolidated forces of wealth and corporate power. The classes which have grown fat by reason of federal legislation and the single gold standard have combined to fasten their fetters more firmly upon the people." [3]

Bryan won states which had been Populist in 1892 like Colorado, Idaho, Kansas, and Nevada, thus taking the wind out of the Populist party's sails, and he also won states like Nebraska, Montana, South Dakota, Washington, and Wyoming which had gone Republican in 1892. Bryan, however, lost states which had long been Democratic

---

[3] As quoted by Howard R. Penniman, *Sait's American Parties and Elections* (New York: Appleton-Century-Crofts, 1952), p. 206.

like New Jersey, Delaware, Kentucky, and Maryland, and others like Wisconsin, Illinois, and Indiana which had slipped from the Republicans in 1892. More critical was the fact that hitherto doubtful New York now turned convincingly to the Republicans. A major realignment of political strength which was to hold until the Republican split of 1912 had taken place. The prospect of an unknown radicalism had been too frightening. If Bryan was elected, many feared, credit would be destroyed and panic or even anarchy might follow. When McKinley and Theodore Roosevelt moderately but firmly moved in to the political center far enough to recognize and attempt to appease the forces of discontent, the Democrats' opportunity was gone. Democratic elements in the South, city boss ruled machines and some western farmers proved both difficult to manage and too weak, even when working together, to seriously challenge the Republican party.

In 1912 the Republican Progressives, in the words of their platform, " unhampered by tradition, uncorrupted by power, undismayed by the magnitude of the task," set out to provide " responsibility to the people " in place of " the deliberate betrayal of its trust by the Republican party " and " the fatal incapacity of the Democratic party to deal with the new issues of a new time." This competition within the Republican party split the Republican base of support and gave the Democratic party an opportunity through Wilson's leadership to demonstrate that the Democratic party was not necessarily as paralyzed as it had appeared to be.

The Democratic platform of 1912 demanded a downward revision of the tariff, and in 1913, for the first time since Buchanan's Administration, tariffs were significantly lowered and tailored to the farmer's desires. The platform struck out against private monopoly, and the Clayton Anti-Trust Act was passed and a Federal Trade Commission was established to break up monopolies, force competition, and enforce " fair trade " practices. The platform opposed a central national bank and " present methods of depositing government funds in a few favored banks, largely situated in or controlled by Wall Street, in return for political favors," and in 1916 the decentralized Federal Reserve System, under a board of governors appointed by the President, was set up. The platform applauded the adoption of the Income Tax Amendment to the Constitution, and by law the Wilson Administration imposed a sharply progressive income tax with high exemptions on the bottom end of the income scale.

This was the general tone of the Democratic appeal under Wilson's Presidency from 1913 to 1916. Yet popular though the President was and moderate though he was generally regarded, only barely did the Democrats return to power in 1916. World War I became the business of the second Wilson term of office, and when the President attempted to lead the United States away from its traditional policy against " entangling alliances " the country refused to be led. Harding in 1920 received an unprecedented 60 percent of the popular vote, and a Republican landslide re-established the Republican party on its pre-1912 power base.

QUALITY OF REPUBLICAN AND DEMOCRATIC FLEXIBILITY AND UNITY

Throughout the 1860 to 1932 period, both Republican and Democratic parties faced difficult problems in unifying the elements of their respective combinations. But, by comparison, the Democrats were in an infinitely more difficult position than Republicans. The western farmer, eastern capitalist, and at least many workers were always potentially combinable. A common ground for the South and East, however, was much more difficult to find. It is not surprising that the Republicans were dominant from 1860 to the Congressional elections of 1874, and then again from 1896 to the Congressional elections of 1910, and from 1920 to the Congressional elections of 1930. What is surprising, however, is the fact that the Republicans were not truly supreme over the entire seventy-two years.

That the Republican party did not live up to its potentialities may in large part be attributed to three reasons. Its quality of unity was not what it might have been, except for the McKinley-Theodore Roosevelt and Harding-Coolidge-Hoover periods. Even from 1920 to 1930, when Republican percentages of the total popular vote were higher than they had ever been, the seeds of disunity were growing and later helped make possible the era of Democratic supremacy which began in 1932. Failure to achieve a high degree of unity at all times during the period among the potentially combinable elements of the Republican party resulted, in turn, from the fact that the Republican party was not flexible enough nor did it often have the quality of Presidential leadership to live up to its very real opportunity to consistently chart a moderate broad-appeal course and thus establish and maintain a very substantial Republican supremacy.

Jeffersonian Republicans firmly developed their party's supremacy from the time Jefferson came to office in 1800, as did Franklin D. Roosevelt Democrats immediately after 1932. Jacksonian Democrats, though not as successful as either Jeffersonian Republicans or Roosevelt Democrats, accomplished a similar feat. Republicans, after the Civil War, had several opportunities to achieve what Jefferson and Jackson before them and Franklin D. Roosevelt after them did, but failed. Not until McKinley's first administration, some thirty-five years after Lincoln's election to the Presidency, were the Republican party's possibilities fully exploited.

In terms of political strategy, Lincoln tried to lead the Republican party along a road similar to that which Jefferson had taken the first Republican party. In Jefferson's time, extremists in his party would have, if unchecked, pursued a policy of vengeance against Federalist New England. This Jefferson did not permit himself or his party to do. Instead, he charted a moderate and practical political course aimed at winning over substantial numbers of Federalists to the Republican party. In this objective, Jefferson was successful, and in part for this reason, the Federalist party began a steady decline toward extinction.

By the end of Lincoln's first term, his administration had constructed a type of economic and patriotic appeal which could have served as the basis of a strong Republican West-East combination. By his moderate reconstruction policy Lincoln sought also to heal the wounds of the South, as Jefferson had healed those of New England. Had the Republican party consented to be led in Lincoln's direction, it is not outside the realm of conjecture that the strength of the Democratic party in the West and East, and even in the border states might have more sharply fallen off. Even if Lincoln could not have gone on to establish Republican strength in the states of the Confederacy, if the Democratic power base had been limited only to those states, Republicans would have been in unchallenged control for a long time to come.

Radical Republicans, attempting to force the South into a Republican mold, gambled heavily and lost heavily. After reconstruction, the states of the South went to the opposite extreme and their political emotions have been consistently and almost pathologically anti-Republican, except for 1928, when religion and prohibition were the exceptional issues, and for 1952. For similar reasons the border states also generally have gone Democratic.

1860–1892 Composite Presidential Election Map Showing Party to Which States Gave Their Electoral Votes

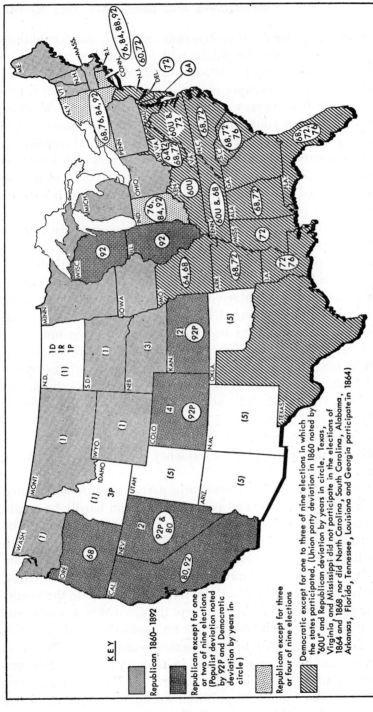

KEY

Republican 1860–1892

Republican except for one or two of nine elections (Populist deviation noted by 92P and Democratic deviation by years in circle)

Republican except for three or four of nine elections

Democratic except for one to three of nine elections in which the states participated. (Union party deviation in 1860 noted by "60U" and Republican deviation by years in circle. Texas, Virginia, and Mississippi did not participate in the elections of 1864 and 1868, nor did North Carolina, South Carolina, Alabama, Arkansas, Florida, Tennessee, Louisiana and Georgia participate in 1864)

Notes: (1) Voted in Presidential election for the first time in 1892. North Dakota's three electoral votes that year were split three ways, and Idaho went Populist.

(2) Voted first in 1864. (3) Voted first in 1868. (4) Voted first in 1876.

(5) Voted in no Presidential elections over period.

(6) New Jersey in 1860 gave the Republican party four electoral votes and the Democratic party three.

Source: W. Dean Burnham, *Presidential Ballots, 1836–1892* (Baltimore: The Johns Hopkins Press, 1955).

In spite of the harsh reconstruction tactics of the Republican party, that party's supremacy might still have been established in Presidential elections if the Grant administrations had been different from what they were. Corruption on the scale it was practiced, particularly from 1868 to 1872, was inexcusable for any political party. Widespread revulsion could only result. If Grant's opponents had not been very unlucky in the choice of their Presidential nominee in 1872, Democrats and Liberal-Republicans might very well have won control of the national government in that year. Grant had had an almost unparalleled opportunity to build within the North a strong Republican party power base. In that he failed.

Although the elements of the Democratic party constituted a much weaker potential power base than the elements which the Republican party could have exploited, Grant's administrations were followed by four " 50–50 " Presidential elections — a pattern of four elections in which the popular votes for President were split more evenly than in any other period in American history. The Liberal Republican defection in 1872 had been a symptom that much was very wrong within the Republican party. The Republican Mugwump defection in 1884 was more than a symptom. The Republican party nominated James G. Blaine who, in the Mugwumps' opinion, was tainted with a Grant Administration type of spoilism. This time it was likely that enough protesting Republican voters in New York's close election of that year went to Cleveland to narrowly give him New York and thus place in the Presidency the first Democrat since Buchanan.

The manner in which Democratic party strength maintained itself during the Civil War and reconstruction can hardly be attributed to positive qualities of Democratic appeal at that time. The party was split, inflexible, almost without leadership, and saddled with the liability of a powerful wing which persisted in inserting " principled " platform declarations which had the effect of driving off potential support in the North by refusing to concede the results of the war and then by refusing to accept the Civil War amendments to the Constitution which had become an established and generally accepted fact. Yet in 1864 the Democratic nominee for President polled 45 percent of the popular vote; in 1868, 47 percent; and from 1876 through 1888, approximately 50 percent. Furthermore, from 1876 to 1892, even though Republican Presidents might be in the White House, they seldom controlled the Congress. Two explanations for the continued maintenance of such Democratic strength appear valid. First, the prewar Democratic power base tended to overlap into the new era; and second and more important, the short-comings of the Republican party permitted the Democratic party to be stronger than it could otherwise have been. Here was a result for the Republican party quite different from that which Jefferson and Jackson had achieved for their parties.

In 1896 both major parties, as has been noted, shifted the nature of their appeal. As subsequent events were to show, Democrats in that year were too flexible. Somewhat on the scale which Radical Republicans had gambled and lost on their harsh reconstruction policy, now Democrats gambled and lost on free silver. Had the Populist platform been assimilated with discretion and the money position taken by the Democratic party been more equivocal and con-servative, perhaps the Democratic party might have been able to then create a second era of Democratic supremacy some forty years before it actually came with Franklin D. Roosevelt. Instead, in large part because Democrats temporarily priced themselves out of a large part of the political market, Republicans were permitted to triumph by more conservatively adapting to the new political environment.

For the first time since Lincoln, Republicans had in the Mc-Kinley and Mark Hanna team very skilled political leadership. Of McKinley, Speaker Joseph Cannon is reputed to have said, " he keeps his ears so close to the ground they get full of grasshoppers." [4] Though McKinley was a high-tariff man, he was not the old " moss-backed " arch reactionary that the present-day symbol of " Back to The Days of McKinley " would imply. Wilfred E. Binkley makes a strong case to show that neither McKinley nor Hanna were " enemies of labor " nor were they " reactionary capitalists." Binkley, in fact, suggests both were moderately progressive on political issues long before Theodore Roosevelt was converted to the cause of progressivism.[5] McKinley did not rise to Bryan's bait for class war with Bryan on the side which might potentially have more votes, but rather he and Roosevelt successfully campaigned propounding the proposition that farmers, workers, and capitalists could achieve more working to-gether than they could arrayed class against class.

---

[4] From Sidney Hyman, *The American President* (New York: Harper and Brothers, 1954), p. 176.
[5] See *American Political Parties* (New York: Alfred A. Knopf, 1949), pp. 324–336.

1896–1928 Composite Presidential Election Map Showing Party to Which States Gave Their Electoral Votes

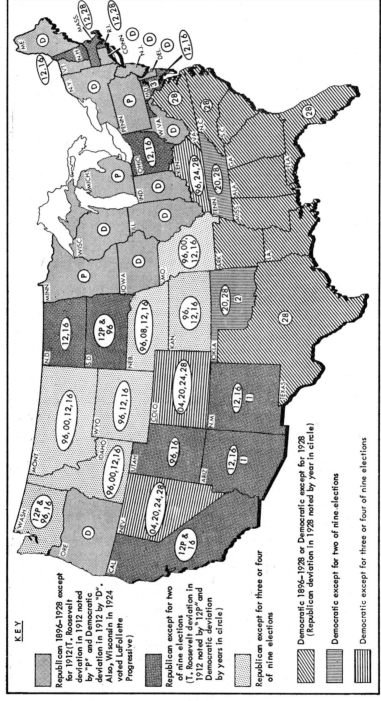

KEY

Republican 1896–1928 except for 1912(T. Roosevelt deviation in 1912 noted by "P" and Democratic deviation in 1912 by "D". Also, Wisconsin in 1924 voted LaFollette Progressive)

Republican except for two of nine elections (T. Roosevelt deviation in 1912 noted by "12P" and Democratic deviation by years in circle)

Republican except for three or four of nine elections

Democratic 1896–1928 or Democratic except for 1928 (Republican deviation in 1928 noted by year in circle)

Democratic except for two of nine elections

Democratic except for three or four of nine elections

Notes: (1) Voted in Presidential election for first time in 1912. (2) Voted first in 1908.

(3) Maryland's electoral votes were split in 1904 with seven Democratic and one Republican and in 1908 with six Democratic and one Republican and in 1908 with six Democratic and two Republican.

Source: Edgar E. Robinson, *The Presidential Vote, 1896–1932* (Stanford, Calif.: Stanford University Press, 1934) ; and *The World Almanac* (New York: World Telegram Corporation), p. 715 in 1913 edition and p. 914 in 1930 edition.

In 1896 McKinley received 51 percent of the popular vote for President and Bryan 46 percent; in 1900, McKinley won 52 percent to Bryan's 46 percent; in 1904, Roosevelt had 56 percent to Parker's 38 percent; and in 1908, Taft secured 52 percent to Bryan's 43 percent. Now the Republicans had developed a solid and consistently winning base of support. Also, the Republicans were firmly in control of Congress. After the Wilson interlude, Republican power became even stronger. Harding in 1920 got 60 percent of the popular vote for President and Cox only 34 percent; in 1924 Coolidge had 54 percent to Davis' 29 percent; in 1928 Hoover received 58 percent to Smith's 41 percent. In the last Presidential election of the Republican era of supremacy, Hoover won forty states, including Virginia, North Carolina, Florida, and Texas in the Solid Democratic South. In the Seventy-first Congress, which convened in 1929, exclusive of the South and border-state Democratic representatives, there were only 49 Democratic Congressmen and 13 Democratic Senators. Within the next four years, however, the relative power positions of the two major parties were to be completely reversed.

Even during the "good years" for Republicans, that party's combination brittlely shattered to pieces once in 1912 and suffered a significant crack twelve years later in the LaFollette excursion into the Progressive party of 1924. Over most of the period from 1896 until 1932 western Republicans were to some degree uneasy because Republican programs, particularly Republican tariffs, appeared to be too much designed to satisfy the eastern element which was in control of the party. The leadership of McKinley and Theodore Roosevelt had been adequate to hold West-East Republican internal differences to a minimum friction level, but during the Taft Administration the conflict could no longer be suppressed. Taft lost control of his party.

No political combination holds itself together through inherent built-in centripetal forces for a sustained period of time. Such a combination is given form and can maintain form only when it has adequate or inspired political leadership. This Taft was unable to provide. Yet even with Theodore Roosevelt unquestionably stronger with the voters than Taft in 1912, those in control of the Republican party preferred the party to go down to defeat, if go down it must, in order to keep Roosevelt out of control of the party machinery.

Less serious in its immediate consequences was LaFollette's break in 1924. Though Coolidge's percentage of the popular vote declined to 54 percent from Harding's 60 percent, the Democratic nominee in 1924 also received 5 percent less than the 1920 Democratic nominee. In Congress, however, Republicans two years later found they still needed the LaFollette Republicans in order to control. The Republican party could not get along without the "radical" western wing. The alliance of that party was a somewhat incongruous one, and its western half was hardly a satisfied partner. Depression-plagued farmers wanted federal government intervention to underwrite their sagging economy. This they did not get. On occasion only the Republican President with his veto power stood in their way. Farmers also wanted a revised and lowered tariff structure. This they did not get either. It was not hard for the western farmer to turn from the party of his traditional allegiance in the election of 1932. He had been psychologically prepared for the step over the course of many years.

Though Hoover was regarded as a mildly progressive candidate in 1928 and in a sense represented a concession by the Republican Old Guard to discontent within the party, Hoover's inflexibility, it later developed, made him a man with the worst kind of political temperament that Republicans could have found for the crisis produced by the 1929 crash. Hoover's inadequate political talents shattered the Republican party's broad base of support. In the words of V. O. Key, Jr.:

> Perhaps the puzzle of Hoover is to be explained by the fact that he was the first President who took his ideology seriously. The American political tradition had been pragmatic; we dealt with whatever came in whatever way seemed to be appropriate at the moment, using government as an instrumentality if need be. Hoover, however, adhered to principle; and his principles were those of reliance on private initiative, of abhorrence of governmental action, especially by the national government, and of individual responsibility.[6]

In the most devastating depression of American history, Hoover appeared to be idly standing by waiting for the storm to blow over, which it would not do. Governmental intervention, even federal governmental intervention, was needed. The Republican Administration appeared to be incapable of supplying it.

---

[6] *Politics, Parties, and Pressure Groups* (New York: Thomas Y. Crowell Company, 1953), p. 201.

For the Democrats, having once made the extreme commitment of 1896 to free silver and having suffered the political consequences of the action by giving Republicans an opportunity to capitalize on their new opportunity, there was relatively little that the party could do except try to exploit on the mistakes of the opposition. The elements of the Democrats' weak and inferior combination fought at each Democratic national convention, with the losers seldom happy at whatever degree of compromise was the result. Big city bosses carried with them such a bad name they tended to be a liability to the party outside the territories which they themselves controlled. There was little room for flexibility and the establishment of a level of party unity from which Democrats might have moved to attempt to take away from Republicans the latter's power base.

QUALITY OF REPUBLICAN AND DEMOCRATIC PRESIDENTIAL LEADERSHIP

Until McKinley and Theodore Roosevelt the Republican party did not develop an appeal broad enough to consistently capture control of the national government. It is not just a coincidence that the greatest Republican acquisitions of strength came during the administrations of the only two Republican Presidents from 1860 through 1932 who were successful as legislative leaders as well as chief executives. Lincoln literally circumvented Congress to accomplish many of his major objectives. Johnson was helpless in the face of a hostile Radical Republican Congressional majority that almost succeeded in impeaching him. Grant and Benjamin Harrison let Congressional leaders, not always in harmony among themselves, almost take over the functions of the Presidential office. Hayes and Garfield stood their ground in protecting the executive branch from legislative encroachment, but did not use their positions as Presidents to push substantive Republican legislative programs. Harding, Coolidge, and Hoover were so unsuccessful as leaders in legislation that they were in effect riding on the power base which McKinley and Theodore Roosevelt had built rather than making contributions of their own to the maintenance or broadening of that power base.

Commenting on Harding's pathetic attempts at legislative leadership and the bitter resistance with which they were met by Republicans in the Senate and House, Wilfred E. Binkley, in his *President and Congress*, writes:

So blind had Republican leadership become to the historical transformation of the presidency in the twentieth century, the fact that
it had become as never before the focal point of a major party's
strength, that they could not see how their emasculation of the great
office was impairing if not even dooming their party.[7]

What was that transformation of the Presidency that McKinley and
Theodore Roosevelt had wrought? The answer lies first in an examination of what the Presidency was not from 1865 to McKinley's first
term as President.

Reacting against Lincoln's very broad exercise of executive powers, Republicans in Congress, as they emerged out of the Union party,
determined to establish a Whig type of Congressional supremacy.
Johnson resisted, but had not the personal power to effectively do so.
Grant, with adequate personal power, did not choose to resist. Political novice that he was, the great Civil War general could not adapt
to his new role. Though leadership was expected from him, it was
not forthcoming. During his administrations the most influential Republican Senators were in control. They sought the spoils which
were in the President's power to bestow for the building up of their
own state machines, Grant gave them what they wanted, and without
applying adequate administrative controls, the Grant administrations left the one dominant impression of corruption.

Rutherford B. Hayes, by comparison with Grant was a relative
unknown and furthermore came to the office of President under the
cloud of the disputed election of 1876. But when the Senate set out to
continue its dominance over the chief executive, Hayes successfully
stamped out in practice his theory that the President and not Congress should run the executive establishment of the national government. Republican Senators tried to impose upon Hayes a Cabinet
composed of Senators and Senators' friends, generally spoilsman in
outlook. Hayes disregarded their offer and appointed some of the
most able men of his time, some of whom were civil service reformers, anti-Grant Republicans, and opponents of members of the Republican Senate oligarchy in their home states. When the Senate appeared to be on the way to refusing to confirm any of the Cabinet
appointments, Hayes went to the people and finally the pressure of
public opinion forced the Senate to confirm.

Bearding Republican Senate leader Roscoe Conkling of New

---

[7] (New York: Alfred A. Knopf, 1947), p. 218.

York in his own den, Hayes successfully removed several Conkling machine officials in the New York Custom House and appointed and won Senate confirmation for administrators of his own choosing. Garfield had to fight the same battle over the appointment of an anti-Conkling and anti-Grant Republican to the position of Collector of the Port of New York. After another prolonged battle, Garfield too was successful. Both New York Senators, Conkling and Platt, resigned to ask the New York Republican Legislature to re-elect them and show support for their position. When the New York Legislature refused, Garfield's victory was complete. For his stand against spoils, however, Garfield paid with the price of his life when he was shot down by a disappointed office-seeker. Preoccupation with President-Congress relations problems and morality in government ruled the day, and none of the Presidents of this period were able to move beyond them to conceive and follow through on comprehensive and coherent Presidential programs.

Chester A. Arthur, though he abandoned his earlier " spoilsman " approach to run a clean administration, got almost nothing from the Congress that he requested. Benjamin Harrison was Grant-like in his approach to the functions of his office, even to the extent of allowing free rein to Republican spoilsmen again. The one Democratic President of the period, Grover Cleveland, also abdicated the Presidential function of legislative leadership.

From 1865 until McKinley, to say that much of the time the national government was foundering in unorganized confusion is not an exaggeration. Although some of the Presidents sought to maintain the separation of powers system by operating as though the Presidency was a co-ordinate branch of the national government along with the Congress rather than subordinate to the Congress, even the most forceful of those Presidents went little beyond making recommendations to Congress. Seldom did the Presidents attempt to influence their party's members in Congress when the latter body was acting or not acting on Presidential recommendations. Often Congressmen and Senators were ignorant of Presidential positions on important questions. Nor until Speaker Thomas B. Reed in 1890 began to make a workable organization out of Republican party members in the House was either house of Congress effectively organized to provide leadership. It is little wonder that neither party could proceed effectively to develop a power base much stronger than the other.

With McKinley and Theodore Roosevelt came two Republican Presidents who had a new conception of the Presidency as the source of party integration of the executive and legislative branches of the national government — two Presidents who could make Republican Congressional party organizations responsive to White House leadership. Both men were more like Jefferson in the pattern of President-Congress relations they established than any other President from Madison through Cleveland. Jackson and Lincoln, it is true, had unquestionably earned the title of " strong Presidents," but each of these men was or was driven by the problem confronting him into being more of a " pressurer " of Congress than a leader in a cooperative process. McKinley and Theodore Roosevelt, until the latter's last two years of office, were the acknowledged leaders of their party, both inside and outside Congress. Both were able politicians with long records of political experience before assuming the Presidency. Both were powerful in their own right. Both found a formula for Congressional leadership. Both were aware of the main currents of political feeling in the United States and responded, each in his own way, to them. Both had a well-organized Republican House, with power centering in the Speaker, with which to work. Politically, both, and through them the Republican party, achieved success.

McKinley failed to win only one major objective while he was President — to avert war with Spain. It is rather ironical that out of the Spanish-American War of 1898, a war McKinley did not want, that he should gain the greatest increments to his prestige, and that out of his role as " President of the whole United States " in the war, McKinley should become the first of a succession of Presidents who have been leaders in world affairs. Theodore Roosevelt followed in the same tradition, as did Wilson, Franklin D. Roosevelt, Truman, and now Eisenhower. After McKinley an 1880-type President was a politically unthinkable type of President, even if the Republican party did have several of them.

What were the consequences of four twentieth-century Republican Presidents unable to provide Congressional leadership? The most obvious failure was the split of 1912 to make way for Wilson. The dire consequences to the Republican party after 1932 may not be traced directly to the failure of Harding, Coolidge, and Hoover as Presidential leaders; nonetheless, there is a relationship. Republicans in the campaign of 1920 had hit Wilson Democratic " executive autocracy " and Harding had pledged to restore " party government " in place of " Presidential government." Although Harding on occasion tried to provide leadership, Senate and House Republicans fiercely resisted it. With Coolidge, Republicans in Congress had no worry. He occasionally made his positions on legislative issues known, but never went beyond that point. On the issues on which he did take a stand, generally the Congress stood on precisely the opposite ground. Hoover, after gaining the feel of his office, did try to lead, but by that time Presidential initiative opportunities were lost and from 1930 to 1932 Republicans had lost control of Congress.

As the Harding-Coolidge-Hoover pattern of Presidential lack of leadership was a reaction against Wilson's opposite approach, so Franklin D. Roosevelt's concept of President-Congress relations was to be a violent reaction from his three Republican predecessors' abdication of the leadership function. Within the four years from 1932 to 1936, Roosevelt was to accomplish a re-establishment of the Democratic party power base on a scale which exceeded what McKinley and Theodore Roosevelt had done for the Republican party from 1896 to 1908.

CHAPTER THIRTEEN

Democrats and Republicans, 1932 to 1952

So the Democrats stole the Republicans' clothes, and this is always most embarrassing to the party which has gone bathing. Woodrow Wilson . . . and Franklin D. Roosevelt helped their party by seeing things about the new industrialism that Republicans refused to see. They out-nationalized the party of strong national government. The Republicans remained about where they were at the close of the Civil War, but time marches on. Theodore Roosevelt offered them a sublime opportunity to move with the times, but inertia and complacency proved too strong. In the 1920's the G.O.P. won what turned out to be a Pyrrhic victory. In blind opposition to Wilsonianism they turned the clock back to the days before Teddy Roosevelt, and thus placed a veto not merely on Wilson's New Freedom but on their own prophet's New Nationalism. Not only that, but they also repudiated their own best traditions in foreign policy in haste to win a fleeting triumph. Just because Wilson was an internationalist they became isolationists, although there was nothing in Republican traditions which committed them to this retrograde philosophy; in fact, it was Theodore Roosevelt who had again pioneered in constructing a doctrine of internationalism to suit the new age. How costly, indeed, was that 1920 victory. . . . It committed the party to laissez-faire *and isolationism at just the time when forces were preparing the graves of these venerable ideas. The Republicans fairly well sold their brains and souls for 12 years of power; it would be no unsuitable punishment if they had to pay for it with much more than twenty years of defeat. History insists inexorably on the expiation of sins.*

Roland N. Stromberg [1]

---

[1] *Republicanism Reappraised* (Washington, D. C.: Public Affairs Press, 1952), pp. 13–14. Reprinted by permission of The Public Affairs Press.

Imagine yourself waking in the middle of the night, shaking and covered with the cold sweat of a nightmare. When you had gone to sleep, you were happy and well-adapted to your environment. Then came the dream. Now you found yourself in a world different from that which you had known. Here you were not adapted and had no weapons with which to protect yourself. Then out of the corner of your left eye you saw moving up over the horizon of your subconscious an enemy. Your hurled at it the words and weapons which, from your experience, you were confident could stop its forward motion. This time they did not work. The enemy moved closer. Now you started to run back toward the world which you had always known, but though your legs were churning as rapidly as you could make them go, you did not move. The enemy was near. You yelled for help. Not a sound came from your mouth. The enemy pounced. Only then did you awaken to find with relief that you had only been dreaming.

The Republican party of modern times well knows the helpless feeling, only its experience was no dream. In 1928 that party had seemed on the threshold of a future of unlimited good fortune. Yet in the course of a few short years, the political environment had changed — a transformation from one political era to another, catalyzed by depression and consolidated by the New Deal. The enemy which came up out of the left horizon was Franklin D. Roosevelt. Republicans hurled words and deeds, the same words and deeds tested and proved through seventy years of American politics, but now the party's arrows bent as they left the bow or fizzled to the ground before reaching the target. The enemy, armed with his New Deal and followed by a seemingly endless mass of supporters, continued to advance toward and surround his victim.

Though the Republican party tried to run back to the political world it once had known and thought itself adapted to, it too was on a treadmill. It issued a call to arms to save all that was dear. The effect was as if no sound had issued from its spokesmen's mouths. In the 1920's "Return to Normalcy," "Keep Cool With Cal," and "Business is America's Business" had elected Republican Presidents and Republican majorities in both houses of Congress. Now the language was new and different and keyed to the theme of the "forgotten man." Part of the strange language was not in words at all, but rather consisted of alphabetical symbols that in themselves had profound meaning — WPA, PWA, NLRB, HOLC, REA, FDIC, RFC, OAA, SSA, FHA, AAA.

Figure 13. Party for Which 25 " Republican " or " Often Republican " States Before 1932 Cast Their Electoral Votes for President from 1888 through 1948

State	88	92	96	00	04	08	12	16	20	24	28	32	36	40	44	48
Mass.							D				D	D	D	D	D	D
R.I.							D				D	D	D	D	D	D
Minn.							P*					D	D	D	D	D
Ill.		D					D					D	D	D	D	D
Utah	#	#	D					D				D	D	D	D	D
W.Va.	D	D					D					D	D	D	D	D
Calif.		D					P*	D				D	D	D	D	D
Wash.		#	D				P*	D				D	D	D	D	D
Ore.							D					D	D	D	D	
N.Y.		D					D					D	D	D	D	
N.J.	D	D					D					D	D	D	D	
Wis.		D					D			L**		D	D	D		D
Wyo.	#		D				D	D				D	D	D		D
Ohio							D	D				D	D	D		D
N.M.	#	#	#	#	#	#	D	D					D	D	D	
Pa.							P*						D	D	D	
Mich.							P*					D	D		D	
Del.	D	D					D						D	D	D	
Conn.	D	D					D						D	D	D	
Ia.							D					D	D			D
S.D.	#		D				P*					D	D			D
Ind.		D					D					D	D			
Kan.		P***	D				D	D				D	D			
Neb.			D			D	D	D				D	D			
N.D.	#						D	D				D	D			

Notes: General — "Blank" means state's electoral votes were cast for Republican.

　　D — Electoral votes cast for Democrat.

　　P* — Electoral votes cast for Theodore Roosevelt Progressives.

　　L** — Electoral votes cast for Robert LaFollette Progressives.

　　P*** — Electoral votes cast for Populist.

　　# — State not yet participating in Presidential elections.

For seventy years the Republican party had, measured by its success in comparison with Democratic party success, been tuned more closely than the Democrats to the aspirations of America. In the 1930's it was *vice versa.* For those same seventy years the " front porch " of McKinley and the back platform of the campaign train had been the media of political communication. Now radio carried the voice of the master of the " fireside chat " across the nation, and Republicans had no leader who could match the performances of Franklin D. Roosevelt. Once Republicans in Congress had been regarded as towers of strength. Now the President of the United States

Figure 14. Electoral Votes for Democratic and Republican Candidates for President, 1932–1952

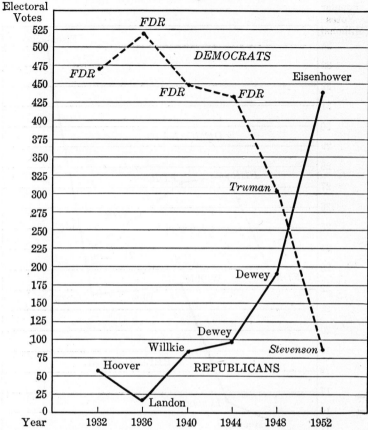

Source: For 1932 through 1944 elections, U.S. Bureau of Census, *Historical Statistics of the United States, 1789–1945* (Washington, D.C.: Government Printing Office, 1949), p. 288 and for 1948 and 1952, *Information Please Almanac 1955* (New York: The Macmillan Company, 1955), p. 283.

wielded so much influence that those who opposed him in Congress were condemned as obstructionists. Once the Republican party had been the " do-something " party. Now it was successfully labeled by the opposition as the " do-nothing " party. Once it had been the Republican party which was most effectively organized down to the grass roots. Now that organization looked puny and weak alongside the organization which James Farley had built.

Franklin D. Roosevelt's election in 1932 had not been just a fluke of an electorate's passing fancy. In the 1934 Congressional elections Democrats reversed a long-established trend when they in-

Figure 15. Popular Votes for Democratic and Republican Candidates for President, 1932–1952

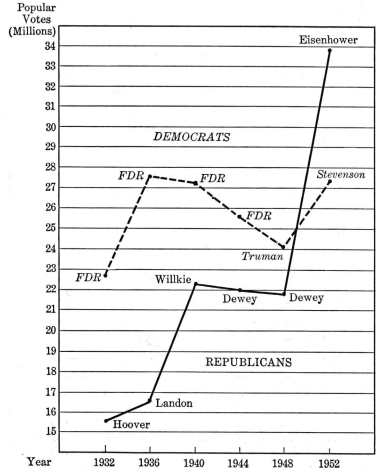

Source: The American Institute of Public Opinion, *The 1954 Pocket Almanac* (New York: Pocket Books, Inc., 1954), p. 145.

creased their in-party majorities in an off-Presidential election year. In 1936 the Democratic party won the most total landslide victory of modern American political history over an Alfred E. Landon who had made an all-out attack on the New Deal. Only little Maine and Vermont had stood by the man from Kansas. Democrats went on to win the White house again in 1940, 1944, and 1948. Only for the two years of the Eightieth Congress (1947–1948) did the Democrats fail to control both houses of Congress over the twenty-year period from 1932 to 1952.

How deep was the Democratic penetration of what had once been Republican or often Republican states is shown in Figure 13. Figure 14 graphs the extent of Democratic supremacy over the period by contrasting the number of electral votes cast for Democratic and Republican nominees in Presidential elections, and Figure 15, the extent of Democratic supremacy in winning popular votes. Likewise, Figure 16 contrasts the strength of the two major parties in the House, and Figure 17, the strength of the two major parties in the Senate.

THE SETTING

In March 1933 there were 14 million unemployed workers in the United States. Including families, that meant 30 to 40 million people directly affected by unemployment. Wages were sliding down, and at the sweat-shop lowest level the going rate was $5 or perhaps even less per week. Those without savings or credit could only turn to the soup lines.

Farm families, while they represented 22 percent of the population, were in 1932 earning only 7 percent of the national income — a drop of 8 percent since 1920. On March 4, 1933, wheat was 68 cents a bushel; beef, 5½ cents per pound; pork, 7¼ cents per pound. Farmers whose property was debt-free were relatively fortunate. They might be able to scrape along. For those who had mortgages with interest and principal payments, the farm market quotations meant potential disaster — their property might the next day become another statistic to add to the 10 percent of all farms in the United States which had been sold at public auction in the five-year period prior to 1932.

From June 1930 to June 1932 United States exports had declined from a $250 million annual value to $78 million. Manufacturing plants stood idle. The stock market continued down. Between 1921 and 1929, over 5,000 banks had failed, and between 1930 and 1932, 5,000 more closed their doors. Starting in the fall of 1931, banks all over the country had been subjected to panic runs. On October 31, 1932, Nevada declared a bank holiday. On February 4, 1933, Louisiana followed suit. On February 14 the action was taken in Michigan, and by March 1 in Alabama, California, Idaho, Kentucky, Mississippi, and Tennessee. On March 4 the Governor of New York closed the banks of that state, and in the next twenty-four hours all the remaining states took the same action. The entire banking system of

Figure 16. Democratic and Republican Seats in the U. S. House of Representatives, 1933–1955

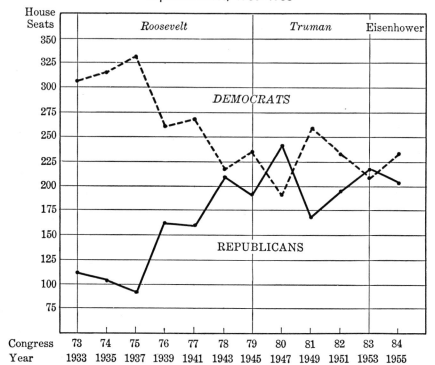

Source: For 73d through 79th Congresses, U. S. Bureau of Census, *Historical Statistics of the United States, 1789–1945* (Washington, D.C.: Government Printing Office, 1949), p. 293; for 80th through 84th Congresses, *Information Please Almanac 1955* (New York: The Macmillan Company, 1955), p. 29.

the United States had literally collapsed. Such was the nature of the American crisis when Herbert Hoover and Franklin D. Roosevelt rode up Pennsylvania Avenue to the Capitol for the latter's inauguration as President of the United States.

At today's level of employment and prosperity it is difficult to recapture the psychological scars which the economic crisis following the 1929 crash inflicted on individuals — psychological scars which had political implications. To better understand the soil in which Franklin D. Roosevelt planted the seeds of the New Deal, the following excerpt from an anonymous article, " Man Out of Work, by His Wife," in the July, 1930, issue of *Harpers Magazine* is quoted:

Then — crash! . . . " Sorry . . . your job is no good any more."

Figure 17. Democratic and Republican Seats in the U. S. Senate, 1933–1955

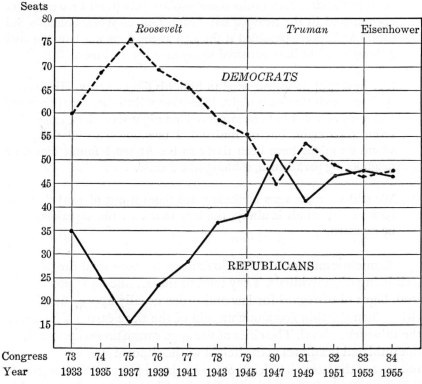

Senate
Seats

Congress   73   74   75   76   77   78   79   80   81   82   83   84
Year   1933 1935 1937 1939 1941 1943 1945 1947 1949 1951 1953 1955

Source: For 73d through 79th Congresses, U. S. Bureau of Census, *Historical Statistics of the United States, 1789–1945* (Washington, D.C.: Government Printing Office, 1949), p. 293; for 80th through 84th Congresses, *Information Please Almanac 1955* (New York: The Macmillan Company, 1955), p. 29.

I remember the sense of bewilderment and the all-gone feeling I had at the pit of my stomach at that time. It was as though the floor had suddenly floated out from under me.

I nursed [my husband] through a short physical illness that the shock and anger . . . had brought on.

As autumn wore on and so many bright prospects faded into thin air, while our precious bank account was painfully shrinking toward its last hundred, our mutual anxiety was sharpened into agony. We would find each other lying awake at night, tense with worry. . . . My own nerves were threadbare, and very often I gave way to fits of weeping when alone.

I knew, with every nerve quivering, that the "wolf at the door" proverb was a real, actual horror. . . . For the first time I have come to realize what is back of the commonplace paragraph I have so often encountered in the newspapers: "Man Out of Work Commits Suicide." And I have trembled if the step at the door was late, lest such a thought might have occurred to my own breadwinner.

[My husband] no longer tried to hide his despondency. His nervous state was such that each night, if he were a little late for supper and had not phoned, I became anxious. One night six o'clock came, then seven, then eight, but no husband. I telephoned to all the places where he might have been likely to be. At ten I found him on a neighboring park bench, sobbing like a child. . . .

We still bear the scars of those "five months out of work." In the back of our minds is always the fear that . . . the experience may be repeated.[2]

Economic and social crises do damage to more than the personal well-being of individuals. They tend to undermine legal processes as well. Signs of disregard for law and order usually appear first in the cities when the thin economic margin of the wage earner slips below the subsistence level. The cities of the 1930's were no exception. Some not unbiased headlines at the height of the sitdown strike controversy tell part of the story: "Critical Stage Declared Near in U. S. Strikes"; "Pickets Battle Police"; "1200 Rioting Taxi Strikers Run Wild in Chicago's Loop"; "Seven of Mob Shot Marching on CIO Office"; "Fifty Hurt When Angry Farmers Drive 1000 Strikers From Hershey Chocolate Factory." But disorder did not stop at city boundary lines. Farmers were spiking planks to stop other farmers' milk truck shipments which, even if the milk did successfully run the barricades, would bring little cash for the things the dairy farmer needed to buy. Other farmers menacingly draped noosed ropes from the haylofts of barns as warnings to anyone who would dare to bid on the home and land of a neighbor about to lose his property on the bidder's block at a mortgage foreclosure sale.

Here was economic catastrophe turning into dangerous social unrest — the same kind of unrest which had frightened the framers

---

[2] *Harpers Magazine* (July, 1930), Vol. 161, pp. 195–202. As quoted in Sebastian DeGrazia, *The Political Community* (Chicago: The University of Chicago Press, 1948), p. 124. Reprinted by permission of *Harper's Magazine*.

of the United States Constitution into establishing a strong central government when they did, the same kind that had preceded the election of Jackson in 1828, and the same kind which had forced both major parties to modify their character in the 1890's. Only now, in the 1930's, penetration of crisis reached more deeply into almost every segment of the community. How could the pressure be relieved. History showed two things would be necessary. First, an all-out effort had to be made to better economic conditions. Second, and just as important, those in positions of power and authority had to give the people the impression that they recognized the gravity of the people's plight and that they " cared."

Herbert Hoover had been able to do neither. He was so inflexibly dedicated to the principle that private enterprise and not government should solve the problems of the day that he could not bring himself to an imaginative and pragmatic formulation of the specifics of a program of governmental intervention — the only possible alternative given the nature of the crisis. Hoover, it is true, was in a difficult position. He had lost the press, a big proportion of the American people, and from 1930 he was faced with a Democratically controlled United States House of Representatives. If the President had had the ability to go to the people who were only waiting for Presidential leadership, however, any Democratic obstructionism in Congress could have been turned to Republican advantage.

Instead, Hoover allowed the Democratic party to make the symbols of the " Great Humanitarian " and the " Great Engineer " into boomerangs of mockery. His failure to successfully show that he " cared " permitted Democrats to blame him and the Republican party for dust storms, unemployment, farm foreclosures, and all the rest of the burdens of the times. Because of the Republican Administration's failure, Franklin D. Roosevelt was able to far exceed the accomplishments of the Wilson administrations by laying the foundations of a new and winning Democratic coalition, and in the doing, to usher in a new era of American party politics — an era of Democratic supremacy.

NATURE OF DEMOCRATIC APPEAL

Franklin D. Roosevelt, elected four times to the Presidency of the United States, was himself the core of much of the Democratic party appeal over the entire 1932 to 1952 period. Where the Hoover

Administration had failed to provide action on the scale demanded, until 1938 the Democratic party provided an abundance of domestic action. Perhaps even more important than Roosevelt Administration actions was the psychological effect created by the President in his relationship with the people. Roosevelt gave the appearance that he was one of the people and suffering with them. Here was a man, it was felt, who was trying to solve America's problems. People found it easy to identify themselves with the President who so convincingly began his speeches with " My Friends." Then at the very time the Democratic strength seemed to be slipping somewhat, international crisis intervened to give the incumbent major party a new lease on political life.

Franklin D. Roosevelt came to Washington on March 2, 1933. Conferences had already begun on steps to be taken in the most immediate crisis — the breakdown of the banking system. They continued while the new President in his inaugural address was telling the American people that the only thing they had " to fear was fear itself." The conference continued behind the new President's platform as he viewed the inaugural parade, and continued on through Sunday, March 5. Late that night the President closed all banks and called Congress into special session to meet on March 9. By midnight of March 9 the Emergency Banking Bill had been introduced, passed by both houses of Congress, and signed by the President with unprecedented Congressional speed. Starting in the middle of March, solvent banks were allowed to open. By the middle of April three fourths of the banks closed by Presidential order were again operating, and four months later over 90 percent of total bank deposits were available to depositors. A Federal Deposit Insurance Corporation program followed. New standards were required for bank management. Confidence in the banking system was restored.

Monetary reforms were set in motion to break the sharp deflationary trend. The Federal Reserve Board was given authority to increase or decrease credit as an economic control. The Securities Act of 1933 forbid securities in interstate commerce unless they were registered with the Federal Trade Commission, and penalties were set for falsely describing the character of stock issues. The 1934 Security and Exchange Act further aimed to curb certain stock-issuing practices and excessive stock market speculation. The Reconstruction Finance Corporation, established during the Hoover Administration, was given greater lending power and loans went to insurance companies, railroads and other businesses. The Home Owners Loan Act authorized over two billion dollars for the refinancing of homes. The Federal Farm Loan Act made available the same amount for the refinancing of farms. The Tennessee Valley Authority was set up to develop that area of the country and to provide a " yardstick " against which utility charges elsewhere could be measured. Public utility holding companies were subjected to regulation to prevent future Samuel Insulls from subjecting the country to repeat performances. The Railroad Relief Act attempted to help railroads further along the road to recovery.

Three billion dollars was authorized for the Public Works Administration to provide work for the unemployed. Works Progress Administration projects spread over the country. Civilian Conservation Corps camps were established. Emergency relief, through a whole series of acts, helped those who stood at the doorway to destitution. There was an Agricultural Adjustment Administration with subsidies to reduce farm production, and a National Recovery Administration to spread employment by shortening working hours and eliminating child labor, to increase consumer purchasing power, to prevent unfair competition, and to stimulate labor union organization. Such was the nature of the New Deal legislation designed to help solve the problems of the day. Much of it was quickly enacted and had often to be amended. The quantity of legislation was enormous. However, not all of the measures stayed on the statute books. Both the NRA and AAA, as well as a dozen other enactments of the period, were declared unconstitutional by the United States Supreme Court.

A second phase of New Deal legislation was largely designed to meet the objections of the Supreme Court to the NRA and AAA and yet accomplish the same objectives as had been intended in the original acts or to replace earlier legislation. One of the most important of these measures was the Social Security Act of 1935. It provided for an unemployment compensation system, for a national old-age and survivors insurance program to guarantee a minimum income to most wage earners and low-salaried workers who had reached the age of sixty-five, and for old-age assistance for the needy, aid to dependent children, aid to the blind, and public health services.

In a similar category is the National Labor Relations Act (Wagner Act) of the same year. It sought to guarantee labor's right to organize and bargain collectively. Employers were not to " interfere with, restrain or coerce " employees for union or bargaining activity, discriminate in hiring or firing against union members, or refuse to bargain collectively. To fill the gap created in the farm program by the voiding of the AAA, several acts were passed which resulted in soil conservation subsidy payments for the planting of soil-improving crops, in marketing quotas to restrict production, and in the establishment of parity programs. The Fair Labor Standards Act of 1938, among other things, set a minimum hourly wage and required time and a half for all hours over forty per week. The Hull Reciprocal Trade Agreements Act, also of 1938, once again put the Democrats on record for reduced tariff rates.

What was the political effect of the New Deal? *The New Dictionary of American History,* in its descriptions of the two major parties, sets up a dichotomy which, at least in the 1930's, perhaps represented popular opinion about the nature of the Democrats and Republicans. " Modern support of the [Democratic] party," it says, " has come from the farmer, labor, and the middle class." [3] The Republican party, according to *The New Dictionary of American History,* " is generally considered to represent the interests of ' Big Business ' and the upper middle class. Historically it has had an Isolationist foreign policy. Its domestic policy has contained high Tariff, hard money, and prohibition programs. It has also opposed government regulation of business, the Welfare State concept, government ownership of utilities, high taxes, and labor and social legislation." [4]

In addition to the Solid Democratic South, which Democrats could count on in the Presidential elections from 1932 through 1944, the Democratic party's appeal won also the support of the cities, and often the traditionally Republican farm states. Samuel Lubell in his *The Future of American Politics* [5] has related the statistics of population trends to the contest for political power between the two major parties to show why, in part, Democrats had developed a city power base even before 1932 and why the cities were tending to out-balance rural areas in political strength.

Between 1900 and 1914 some 13 million immigrants came to the United States, and a large proportion settled in the big cities to begin their upward struggle through economic want and social discrimina-

---

[3] Michael Martin and Leonard Gelber, *The New Dictionary of American History* (New York: Philosophical Library, 1952) , p. 171.

[4] *Ibid.,* p. 523.

[5] (New York: Harper and Brothers, 1952) .

tion. Their offspring were beginning to appear in the job market at the time of the 1929 stock market crash. Between Taft and Hoover the total number of people living in cities passed the number of those living in rural areas of the country — a trend which continues. Within the cities, birth rates among groups tending to vote Democratic exceeded the fertility of those tending to align themselves with the Republican party. Add to these developments the economic dislocation of the 1920's and 1930's, the New Deal's helping hand and the Republican inability to meet the crisis of economic adversity, and the explanation for the new distribution of political power between Democrats and Republicans stands out more clearly.[6]

From statistics showing the net major party plurality in Presidential elections in the twelve largest cities of the United States (New York, Chicago, Los Angeles, Philadelphia, Pittsburgh, Detroit, Cleveland, Baltimore, St. Louis, Boston, Milwaukee, and San Francisco — all cities large enough to often be critical in swinging their respective states from one party column to another), Lubell prepared the following tabulation:

Presidential Election Year	Net Party Plurality in 12 Largest Cities, by Party
1920	1,638,000 Republican
1924	1,252,000 Republican
1928	38,000 Democratic
1932	1,910,000 Democratic
1936	3,608,000 Democratic
1940	2,210,000 Democratic
1944	2,206,000 Democratic
1948	1,443,000 Democratic

Lubell's two conclusions from the data are, first, that the Republicans lost their city plurality in 1928, and not in 1932; and second, that the highest Democratic big-city plurality was obtained by the Democrats in 1936 *after* most of the New Deal legislation had been enacted into law, and not in 1932.[7] Here is the suggestion, then, that the depression alone is not a complete explanation of the new Democratic power.

Louis Bean, in examining the shift of major party strength from 1928 through 1936, has found the Democratic gain in House seats "strikingly paralleled by the jump in unemployment." For every

---

[6] From *ibid.*, pp. 28–41.   [7] *Ibid.*, pp. 34–35.

10 percent increase in unemployment, Democrats gained 16 percent of the total seats in the House. Or put in another way, for every additional million unemployed, Republicans lost fourteen seats.[8]

Democrats also made substantial inroads into Republican farm strength. All of the western farm states voted for Roosevelt in 1932

"And So You Have This Feeling of Being 'Not Wanted' "

and 1936. In 1940 Indiana (with native-son Wendell Willkie the Republican nominee), Iowa, North Dakota, South Dakota, Nebraska, Kansas, and Colorado returned to the Republican fold. In 1948 Wyoming, Wisconsin, and Ohio followed suit. Of great significance, however, is the fact that in 1948 Montana, Colorado, Ohio, and even Iowa went Democratic again.

[8] Louis H. Bean, *How to Predict Elections* (New York: Alfred A. Knopf, 1948), p. 24.

On that tense election eve of 1948, Republicans did not give up hope early in the evening when the election news from the big cities was bad. The farm vote was yet to be heard from. " Wait until the farm vote comes in! " When the farm returns were reported, however, they were not what was expected. The once strong, but often neglected " farm vote," bulwark of Republican power, continued the voting habits formed after the advent of the New Deal to offset Truman's loss of four southern states to the Dixiecrats. Why? Because memories of the 1920's and early 1930's were still fresh in mind when now the light flashed on as the farmer's wife opened the door of the electric refrigerator or the farmer backed his new car out of the garage. Could the Republicans be entrusted with another try at the helm of the national government? The farmer was not sure despite Republican assurances, and in his uncertainty he put off to the side thoughts which might have led him to vote for the party of his fathers. Instead, he voted the safe and conservative course — Democratic.

Just as politically startling as Democratic farm strength was the about-face of the " Negro vote " which, in a few pivot states, might be decisive in Presidential elections. Before Franklin D. Roosevelt it was Republican. Since 1932 it had shifted to Democratic. In spite of the fact that southern Democrats in Congress stood in the way of civil rights legislation, the Negro tended to look to Roosevelt, Mrs. Roosevelt, and Truman as persons who had personally been sympathetic to their minority problems. At the same time the Negroes' economic status had substantially improved. The Republican party, the party of Abraham Lincoln, and one unhampered by the need of making concessions to the southern wing, had not been able to hold the support of the Negro.

One major element of Democratic appeal for the latter half of the 1932 to 1952 period need be added. Though Franklin D. Roosevelt had not been an internationalist in some of his earlier actions as President, the rise of Hitler and related events abroad led him to change his opinion. America should become the " arsenal " of the democracies! The President made the fifty-destroyer deal with Britain and led the fights for lend lease and revision of the neutrality acts in the Congress. Generally he was supported by Congressional Democrats and opposed by Republicans. After December 7, 1941, with United States involvement in war a fact, the New Deal phase of the Roosevelt administrations was adjourned, and FDR became the nation's leader, first, in the prosecution of the war and second, in the preliminary steps for the establishment of peace.

In both the economic and military crises the President had assumed leadership and taken the initiative. The opposition party had generally tended to oppose him. Democratic appeal through both crises had been broad, and at least from 1932 through 1936 broad enough to make it appear that the Republican party would go the way of the Federalists and the Whigs.

NATURE OF REPUBLICAN APPEAL

Until 1937 the Republican party had little opportunity to develop any kind of an appeal. The shock of 1932 had left Republican confidence shattered. In Congress Democrats had such large majorities and were so surprisingly unified, Republican opposition availed little, and support for Democratic programs, when it was given, had little more advantageous political effect. Then had come the Landon defeat of 1936, with the Republican Presidential candidate engaged in a head-on conflict with the philosophy of the New Deal. Not until the next year with the " Roosevelt recession," widespread labor-management unrest, revelations of politics in the administration of relief programs, the failure of Roosevelt's court-packing and administrative reorganization plans, and southern opposition to the administration developing within the Democratic party — not until these developments was the Republican party once again able to hope to make significant inroads into Democratic strength. And when Republicans talked of the way in which they should proceed, they seemed to be speaking with two voices — one in the tradition of the Harding-Coolidge-Hoover school, and the other sounding as though it wanted to do what Theodore Roosevelt had done by adapting the most successful elements of Democratic appeal into an improved Republican package.

" Save America," pleaded Michigan's Republican United States Senator Arthur Vandenberg. Investigate the Tennessee Valley Authority — an " authoritarian state," and its " der fuehrer, David Lilienthal," said New Hampshire's Republican Senator Styles Bridges. Roosevelt maintains his position, suggested Republican Congressman James Wadsworth of New York, by bribing the American voting public. Herbert Hoover saw the New Deal's planned economy as an infection from the original stream of fascism. He proposed a trial two

years of " stop, look and listen." " Planned economists," charged Republic Steel Corporation's Tom Girdler, " are seeking to bring about
revolutionary changes — to alter our economic system, to undermine
our liberty and to destroy our system of private enterprise." The National Association of Manufacturers talked about tariffs for defenseless industry. Alfred P. Sloan, Jr., chairman of the board of General
Motors Corporation, early in 1937 made a statement which carried
the implication that the Republican party might also become a party
of protest if it chose to do so. Eighty cents of his every dollar in 1936,
he said, had gone to federal and state governments and charities.[9]

Mr. Sloan's protest may have raised a sympathetic response in
his club, but it was hardly the kind of protest with which the Republican party could rally the unemployed workers or bankrupt and
drought-parched farmers. For Senator Vandenberg to call upon the
people to " save America " from the Democrats had a hollow sound
to those who were convinced the Republican party did not care about
or want to understand the people while the Democratic party did.
To label the TVA as " authoritarian " made little more sense when
already people felt they saw constructive and democratically produced results flowing from dams and power plants to raise the living
standards of the Tennessee Valley. To hold that Roosevelt maintained his position by bribing the American people was to insult the
intelligence of millions of voters the Republicans needed if their
party was again to be successful. Regardless of what Herbert Hoover
said, the thought of the downhill economic skid during his administration was still too painful to make it possible for the Republican
ex-President to gain a hearing. Even if ears had been open, slogans
like " stop, look and listen," giving the implication that that was what
Hoover thought the American people should have done before the
New Deal was adopted, were hardly words to inspire political enthusiasm in the late 1930's.

While the leaders of business and industry had been valuable
prestige assets to the Republican party in the 1920's, now their names
and what they said tended to become a liability. Now even Republican newspapers in the farm belt could tell the National Association
of Manufacturers that if it wanted tariff subsidies for industry it

---

[9] Vandenburg, *Minneapolis Journal*, October 11, 1938; Wadsworth, *ibid.*,
August 27, 1938; Hoover, *ibid.*, April 1, 1938; Sloan, *ibid.*, July 1, 1937; Girdler,
ibid., June 5, 1938; Bridges, *St. Paul Pioneer Press*, March 10, 1938; N.A.M.,
Minneapolis Star, January 3, 1938.

should quit howling about subsidies to other groups — particularly farm groups. The words, advice, and sounds of the voices of old-time Republican leaders and many of their friends in the business world cried out as if from the past. A majority of the new political generation neither heard nor would have understood. The new political environment compelled the Republican party to develop a new appeal.

Shifts in the political climate had been evident far beyond the statistics of election returns. President Roosevelt's pressure on the United States Supreme Court forced the court to a reassessment of its position. As some of the justices had looked at their old philosophy, they did not like what they saw. Chief Justice Charles Evans Hughes, Republican Presidential nominee in 1916, led an Old Guard court to a New Guard position. District Attorney Thomas E. Dewey was prosecuting charges of grand larceny against Richard Whitney, the president of the New York Stock Exchange. The Stock Exchange barred Whitney for all time, adopted a drastically revised constitution and chose 31-year-old William McChesney Martin, Jr., as its new president.

Would the Republican Party be able to adapt to the new political environment? If it were to try, how? The skillful pen of Charles Michelson, Democratic National Committee publicity director, had, since 1930, painted the Republican party into the image of reaction. The skillful tongue of Franklin D. Roosevelt had assured the electorate that such a judgment was correct. The acts of many Republicans tended to reassure the American people that both Roosevelt and ghost-writer Michelson were right.

Republican editor William Allen White's advice to his party was . . . " don't. Whatever the instinctive Republican hunch is, it's wrong." What did the Republican party need? Republican Nicholas Murray Butler, president of Columbia University, supplied the obvious answer, " more votes." What should the Republican party do? Mark Sullivan, the syndicated columnist who was not unfriendly to the Republican party, offered this advice: " A party that will throw out all the reforms utterly gets nowhere. A party that promises to keep the reforms in principle but administer them capably, gets a hearing." [10]

Bruce Barton, New York advertising executive and Republican

---

[10] White, *Minneapolis Journal*, April 19, 1938; Butler, *ibid.*, July 21; Sullivan, *ibid.*, September 25.

member of the House, keynoted the Indiana State Republican Convention in 1938. The mass feeling of faith in President Roosevelt, he said, is the controlling political influence of the day. This faith, the Republican party must capture away from the Democrats. Republicans would be blind to ignore Roosevelt's popular appeal, and " to inveigh against it is political insanity." Condemn equally the reactionary employer and the labor racketeer. Accept the New Deal reforms as sound, Barton continued, but call for putting the administration of them into the hands of a Republican party " cleansed, chastened, re-dedicated to service." [11]

The same year the Republican National Committee officially took steps to examine the Republican appeal. A progress committee under the chairmanship of Dr. Glenn Frank, former president of the University of Wisconsin, set out to conduct an open-minded search for Republican policies by auditing the New Deal and restating Republican philosophy in the light of current conditions. Round-table discussions on social security, labor, and agricultural legislation were conducted with the help of recognized authorities in each of the fields. The committee's report on agricultural policy was indicative of what might be a new Republican middle road — be critical of the Agricultural Adjustment Administration and of scarcity economics, but favor the land-use program, the farm credit machinery, and the Rural Electrification Authority.

The Republican party, going into the general elections of 1938, had everything to gain and almost nothing to lose. Only 6 of the governors were Republicans. In the House, only 88 of the 435 members were Republicans; in the Senate, only 15 of the 96 senators were Republicans. After the election, the out-party had won a new lease on life — 15 instead of 6 governorships; 169 instead of 88 House seats; and 27 instead of 15 senators. No clear formula for rebuilding Republican party power, however, emerged. " McKinley reactionaries," in the words of Raymond Clapper, had been elected in Pennsylvania and Michigan.[12] Relatively traditional approaches elected Robert A. Taft to the Senate from Ohio and John W. Bricker to the governorship of that state. Harold Stassen had waged open war on the Minnesota Republican Old Guard and had been elected governor of Minnesota. Payne H. Ratner, one who advertised his sympathy for labor and social security programs, became Governor of Kansas. Thomas E.

---

[11] *Ibid.,* July 5.   [12] *St. Paul Pioneer Press,* February 27, 1939.

Dewey almost won the governorship of New York in a photo-finish with the Democratic incumbent, Herbert Lehman. Leverett Saltonstall, one of the new Republican school, was elected Senator from Massachusetts. A combination of both New Guard and Old Guard appeals had swept the New England states and New Jersey, South Dakota, Colorado, Idaho, and Oregon, and significant gains were registered in Nebraska and Wisconsin.

After the election of 1938 Raymond Clapper saw the Democratic combination in a process of disintegration with President Roosevelt standing at his Valley Forge. But, wrote Clapper, " So cocky are the Republicans that they are rapidly pulling to the right to a position of no compromise, feeling that — as in 1920 — they can get by with anything." [13] If Roosevelt was at his Valley Forge, however, the winter was mild and short as Republican intraparty conflict raged over which type of front the party should present — a conflict continuing up and into the Eisenhower Administration and one which did not quiet until Eisenhower reached top rating on the Gallup popularity scale.

In 1940 with Willkie's bid for the nomination and his campaign, and in 1941 in the Congressional fights over lend lease and revision of the neutrality acts, the Republican split reached its deepest point of the twenty-year period. Willkie boasted of having been a " college socialist," had good words to say for Robert La Follette, Sr., generally backed President Roosevelt's foreign policy and the Hull Reciprocal Trade Agreements program, and had not long before his candidacy been a registered Democrat. The weight of the " regular " Republican organizations had been thrown against Willkie at the 1940 national convention, and 100 Republican congressmen jointly issued a statement calling upon the delegates to nominate someone more in tune with the Republican members of Congress.

The conflict continued under the surface throughout the campaign, and after November it broke out into the open. Generally, the bitter Willkie critics were those who belonged to a Republican school of thought which saw the party's road to power as a " peace " party opposed to the Democratic " war " party. Congressman Harold Knutson (R), Minnesota, ranking Republican member of the House Appropriations Committee and the man whom Pearson and Allen later credited with the statement, " The whole New Deal stinks," [14] main-

---

[13] *St. Paul Pioneer Press,* February 27, 1939.   [14] *Ibid.,* August 16, 1941.

tained that Willkie's " leaving " the Republican party would create " about as much void as would the withdrawal of a finger from a pail of water." [15] Some Republicans circulated rumors that Democrats were building Willkie up for a 1944 Democratic Presidential nomination. At the National Young Republican League Convention in Des Moines in January, 1941, a series of resolutions like the following were introduced:

> In the last campaign . . . the Republican party [was] deliberately sabotaged by a candidate of the Democratic faith on the Republican ticket, whose campaign was epitomized by two words, ' Me, too.' [16]

" God forgive me," moaned Missouri's Republican Congressman Dewey Short at the height of the Congressional debate over revision of the neutrality act, " for ever having supported such an impostor [Willkie]." [17]

From the other side came answers such as these. " It [the Republican party] has become hopelessly dedicated to opposition for opposition's sake," said Clare Boothe Luce. " It is acting almost entirely on the childish premise that everything the New Deal has done is wrong and the only question is, how wrong is it? " [18] " Presumptuous politicians," charged the Republican *St. Paul Pioneer Press*. " They were repudiated when Willkie was nominated. They are always sure the country is sick of Roosevelt, yet the country never is. Men with such a record should have becoming modesty about their own views. They have no right to say who can and who cannot stay in the party." [19] Such was the intensity of the Republican conflict in 1940 and 1941 and such was the party unity problem, eight years after 1932. It stood solidly in the way of developing a new and positive Republican appeal.

The turning from the 1930's into the 1940's marks a milestone in a trend which has tended to reverse the sectional characteristics of the elements of the Republican combination. Before the turn, progressive Republicans generally tended to come from the Midwest and West; the conservatives, from the East. Progressivism of the earlier period bracketed domestic economic reform with an isolationism aimed at preventing " Wall Street internationalists " from diverting the country's attention away from the problems which

---

15 *Ibid.,* February 20.
16 *Ibid.,* February 1.   18 *Ibid.,* February 13.
17 *Ibid.,* October 23.   19 *Ibid.,* August 9.

needed solving at home. Largely beginning in the early 1940's, the characteristics of the sectional components within the Republican party changed. East and West coasts now tend to lean more toward a position which combines moderate progressivism in domestic affairs with the internationalist's collective security outlook. After 1940 the staunchest conservatives and isolationists in the Republican party tended to come from the great American heartland away from the smoke of industrialism and away from ocean shore — until, at least, the rebellion of the farmers.

Republican Presidential nominees in 1944, 1948, and 1952 have, but not without bitter national convention fights, been men whose appeal was moderately progressive in domestic affairs and collective-security oriented in foreign affairs. On the other hand, many Republican members of Congress from safe Republican districts have appeared to continue to want to fight Franklin D. Roosevelt on Roosevelt's chosen battleground. Before the development of the Eisenhower program, perhaps the biggest impression of the nature of Republican appeal during the second era of Democratic supremacy was one of somewhat bewildering confusion.

QUALITY OF DEMOCRATIC AND REPUBLICAN FLEXIBILITY, UNITY, AND PRESIDENTIAL LEADERSHIP

References to the quality of major party flexibility, unity, and Presidential leadership have run through the above discussions of the nature of Democratic and Republican appeals during the 1932 to 1952 period. It remains to summarize and further point up the political significance of these " minor themes." Because the supreme major party of the period was so dominated by one man, Franklin D. Roosevelt, because the flexibility and unity of the Democratic party operated in direct relationship to what Roosevelt did and was, and because Republican lack of flexibility and unity over most of the period can be understood only in relation to Roosevelt's Presidential leadership, the themes of flexibility, unity, and Presidential leadership are treated together in this section.

Franklin D. Roosevelt, before he entered the White House, was not expected to make much of a mark. He had won the nomination in 1932 only after a bitter convention fight. " There is no disguising the fact that beating Lord Hoover . . . with Roosevelt Minor and the Texas Bearcat is not going to be easy," wrote H. L. Mencken after Roosevelt's nomination. The Democratic nominee, continued Mencken, enters the campaign with two liabilities — a split party and " his own limitations." " He is one of the most charming of men, but like many another very charming man he leaves . . . the impression that he is also somewhat shallow and futile. . . . Whatever the cause, the fact is patent that he fails somehow to measure up to the common concept of a first-rate man." [20] Walter Lippmann agreed. Roosevelt was " a pleasant man, who without any important qualifications for office would very much like to be President." [21] " Wilson, with all respect to Governor Roosevelt," said Paul H. Douglas, " was a far keener thinker and a more determined fighter than the latter . . . how can we hope for better things from Franklin Roosevelt? " [22]

Such were the reactions before Roosevelt took office, yet the then new Democratic President who was only a " pleasant fellow " was to go on to capture his party, subdue the voice of the opposition to a mere whisper, and win a political foothold in the minds of the electorate which made him stronger than his party and carried him through four unprecedented Presidential elections. So great was the change in attitude about Roosevelt that John T. Flynn could report on a conversation with a Republican businessman in July 1933: " He ended by saying that he had voted for Hoover but that he hoped God would forgive him and that he believed Franklin D. Roosevelt was the greatest leader since Jesus Christ." [23]

Never in time of peace had a President and a Congress working together established such a record for action as came out of the first 100 days of Roosevelt's first term of office. The President had the force of an Electoral College landslide behind him. Democrats controlled both houses of Congress by wide margins. Inability of the Hoover Administration to attack flexibly and vigorously the country's problems had made the country ready for almost any kind of action, no matter what it was. If it is necessary to burn down the White House, Will Rogers had exaggerated, do it, but at least do something! The nation had fallen over the edge of economic catas-

[20] *Making A President* (New York: Alfred A. Knopf, 1932), pp. 169–170.
[21] Quoted by Wilfred E. Binkley, *President and Congress* (New York: Alfred A. Knopf, 1947), p. 247.
[22] *The Coming of a New Party* (New York: Whittlesey House, McGraw-Hill Book Company, 1932), p. 171.
[23] " Other People's Money," *New Republic* (December 11, 1935), Vol. 85, No. 1097, p. 129.

trophe. These were some of the factors that gave Franklin D. Roosevelt an almost unlimited political leadership opportunity.

Republicans in Congress cooperated with the President. Even if they had wanted to do otherwise, there was no other alternative. In the words of House Republican floor leader, Bertram Snell of New York, on the day of the passage of the Emergency Banking Bill when the House was acting without printed copies of the proposed legislation: " The House is burning down and the President of the United States says this is the way to put out the fire. . . . I am going to give the President of the United States his way today. He is the man responsible and we must follow his lead." [24]

Democrats, even those fundamentally opposed to the New Deal from the start, cooperated too, and to make sure they did not stray from the new party line, Roosevelt utilized several highly successful persuasion techniques. His radio fireside chats produced mail to members of Congress in such quantity that, once the lesson was learned, Roosevelt had only to threaten to go again to the people to often win his point. The President established cordial relations with the corps of Washington newspapermen, and from the start had a favorable press which, in turn, operated to strengthen his position with Congress. Some 90,000 new patronage jobs were created by emergency legislation, but the President took his time in filling the positions and let it be known that loyalty to his program would be required from those who might expect to get their full share.

In his relations with Congress the President, however, did not rely exclusively on pressure tactics. He was cordial with Democrats in the House and Senate and cooperated closely with the leaders in both houses. In the best of Theodore Roosevelt tradition, he cleared and counseled with Democratic Congressional leaders before he acted. Often he compromised to take account of their objections. Informal but regular conferences of legislative and executive leaders were held in the White House. So powerful had the President's position become that as late as 1935, with the crisis moderating, he could still ask for almost a 5 billion dollar blank check for " relief and recovery " and get it without detailing the general plans for how the money was to be used.

In the 1934 Congressional elections Democrats met with unprece-

---

[24] 77 *Congressional Record* 76. Quoted by Stephen K. Bailey and Howard D. Samuel, *Congress at Work* (New York: Henry Holt and Company, 1952), p. 235.

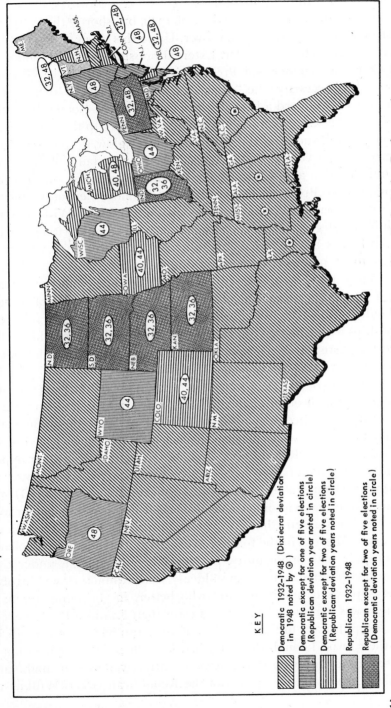

1932–1948 Composite Presidential Election Map Showing Party to Which States Gave Their Electoral Votes

KEY

Democratic 1932–1948 (Dixiecrat deviation in 1948 noted by ⊙)

Democratic except for one of five elections (Republican deviation year noted in circle)

Democratic except for two of five elections (Republican deviation years noted in circle)

Republican 1932–1948

Republican except for two of five elections (Democratic deviation years noted in circle)

Source: American Institute of Public Opinion, *The 1954 Pocket Almanac* (New York: Pocket Books, 1954), pp. 142–145.

dented success in building their Congressional majorities. Precedents were again broken in the elections of 1936, but shortly thereafter the honeymoon with Congress was over. Up to this point, Roosevelt had been a highly effective leader. External pressures pushing Democrats in Congress together and Presidential alternation of the " carrot " and, when necessary, the " stick " of sanctions within his power to apply, had produced a high degree of party unity. Roosevelt, to this point, had flexibly adapted himself and his party to the needs of the moment, and such was the politically bright glow in the eyes of the electorate the voters hardly noticed the glaring fault of Roosevelt Administration administrative confusion. Republicans, on the other hand, had no President to lead them, and almost their only unity in this period came when they supported the President. Without some minimum degree of unity, without leadership, and without being given breaks by the Democrats to exploit, Republican flexibility to adapt to the new environment was impossible.

From 1937 to 1940 Republicans had their first opportunity since 1932 to attempt to stage a comeback with some prospects of success. President Roosevelt was meeting with major reverses in his relationships with Congress, and with each succeeding setback his tactics became more harsh. Democratic Presidential leadership difficulties were also in part a result of the lessening of party unity as incongruous elements of the Democratic party remembered once again their differences with other elements, and each began to act on the basis of those differences. As disunity exerted its pull, the Democratic party's ability to adapt flexibly to each new situation tended to diminish. Had the Republicans been able to capitalize on their opportunity, they might have had a good chance to return to power in 1940. So serious, in fact, was the Republican threat that many Democrats feared that without Roosevelt as their nominee they might lose.

At this juncture, however, an uncontrollable — for Republicans — external event in the form of World War II tended to completely ruin their 1940 opportunity. By November Britain was under German bombardment, the war suddenly seemed much closer, involvement appeared imminent, and who better, in the minds of many voters, was there to lead in such a crisis than Franklin D. Roosevelt?

Republicans in the campaign of 1940 also had several liabilities of their own. Though the party had been flexible enough to nominate a candidate who would have an attractiveness that might lure independents and Democrats to the Republican ticket, Willkie, inexperienced as he was politically, committed major and damaging errors during the campaign. Willkie also imposed too great a strain on Republican unity at that time with the result that the party split into two camps almost as bitterly opposed as had been the Taft and Theodore Roosevelt factions in 1912.

After Pearl Harbor, though Congress accepted the President's leadership in international affairs, a coalition of conservative Democrats and Republicans blocked almost his every domestic move. Roosevelt responded by departing even further from his earlier and more happy methods of working with Congress. Overstepping the separation of powers boundary line by a very long step, the President in 1942 served up this ultimatum if the Congress failed to repeal the Emergency Price Control Act as he demanded: " In the event that Congress should fail to act adequately, I shall accept the responsibility and I will act." On this issue Congress gave him what he wanted. However, inserting anti-administration measures into legislative riders to important bills to circumvent Presidential vetoes, the Congress struck a number of direct blows at Roosevelt. When in February 1944, Roosevelt applied the first veto in history to a general revenue bill, Senate Democratic floor leader Alben Barkley resigned in protest and was immediately re-elected by the Senate Democratic caucus. The President was now needlessly driving the wedge between the factions of his own party, and even most pro-Roosevelt Democrats could only disavow such Presidential actions or brood in silence.

In the 1944 Presidential election the Republican threat was even more serious to Democratic power than it had been in 1940, and so the magic name of Roosevelt was again employed to pull his party through that election. The President's death on April 12, 1945, and Harry S. Truman's succession to the Presidency did not re-establish Democratic presidential leadership in domestic affairs nor Democratic party unity. Truman completely lost party control, with conservative Democrats and Republicans often meeting openly together to plan Congressional tactics, and in the Congressional elections of 1946 Republicans won control of the Eightieth Congress.

With each succeeding Presidential election Republican chances had appeared to be improving. Republicans in 1948 had again nominated Thomas E. Dewey, Governor of New York and a man whose record in that state had shown that he might be capable of retaining the good out of the New Deal, administering those programs capably and moving on to the solution of new problems in front of a fresh

1952 Presidential Election Map Showing Party to Which States Gave Their Electoral Votes

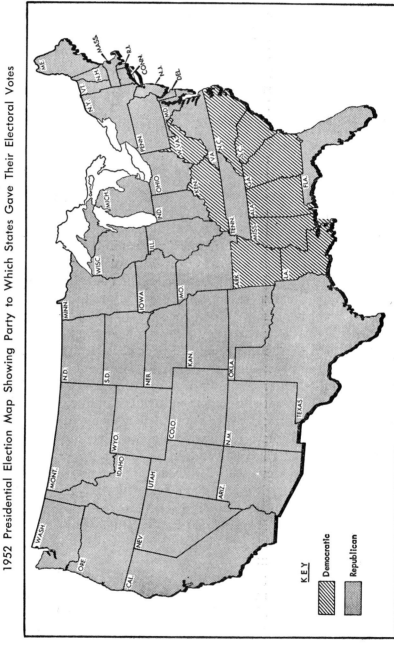

KEY

Democratic

Republican

Source: American Institute of Public Opinion, *The 1954 Pocket Almanac* (New York: Pocket Books, 1954), pp. 144–145.

364

and rededicated Republican party in control. Maneuvering in the limited area within which he could move, however, Harry S. Truman accomplished the political upset of the century. Dewey had tried to be the moderate conservative candidate, but so sure had he been of election and so mildly did he stress a vague call for " unity " that he could not counterbalance a popular impression that many Republicans in Congress had consistently given — that the Republican party would radically rip out all the works and ways of the Democratic administrations adopted since 1932 as soon as Republicans returned to power. The blunt Mr. Truman, in a very unconservative way, managed to steal the mantle of conservatism away from the Republican party.

For the Democrats, as disunity increased, both flexibility and Presidential leadership qualities of the party suffered. As Presidential leadership declined so did the degree of unity and the opportunity for adaptation. The interrelationships of these qualities is close, and all tended to narrow the broadness of Democratic party appeal. Democrats, however, were fortunate because the political health of the Republican party was generally below the lowest Democratic political-health level of the period.

For the Republicans, no nominee succeeded in election to the Presidency over the 1932 to 1952 period, and except for Presidential campaigns, whatever leadership the party had was split among the several wings of the party in Congress and various Republican governors. Though Republican national conventions and many Republican governors had learned the lessons taught by the Democrats from 1930 to 1936, the party's nominees for the Presidency were unable to generate a broad enough appeal to win. Not until after 1952 and well into the second year of the Eisenhower Administration did Republican unity approach the level it had generally held before 1932.

PART FOUR

Winning Elections:

PROBLEMS OF STRATEGY

INTRODUCTION

If a major party is to win Presidential elections, its nominee must command an absolute majority of electoral votes. If a major party is to win control of the United States House of Representatives, 218 or more of its nominees for House seats must win in their respective Congressional districts. If a major party is to organize the United States Senate, it must gain enough of the 32 seats up for election in any particular Congressional or Presidential election which, when added to that proportion of 64 seats not up for election that the major party holds, will produce a majority of 49 of the 96 Senate votes. Here, reduced to its most elemental terms, is the objective of the major party seeking to control the executive and legislative branches of the national government. Having formulated the problem, the major party next moves to consider its strategy — how can it develop a type of appeal broad enough to accomplish those three related objectives.

Chapter 14 is an attempt to develop a general theory of major party strategy, particularly as that strategy relates to the relatively differing problems of the supreme or " sun " and the minority or " moon " major parties. Chapter 15 is an analysis of the Democratic and Republican parties' problems in winning presidential elections, with the focus on the contemporary " political situation " in the large and doubtful pivot states and in the several distinguishable political sections of the United States. The politics of winning Congressional majorities is the subject of Chapter 16.

CHAPTER FOURTEEN

Some Elements of Major Party Strategy

Our political solar system . . . has been characterized not by two equally competing suns, but by a sun and a moon. It is within the majority party that the issues of any particular period are fought out; while the minority party shines in reflected radiance of the heat thus generated.

The essential strength or weakness of an American political party is not to be measured simply by the votes it commands, but by the timeliness *of the elements which compose the party's following. Thus, the rise of Jacksonian Democracy marked the coming-of-age of the western frontier and its alliance with the agrarian South against the commercial East. Within this Democratic party the issues of slavery were fought out. Not until the political heirs of Andrew Jackson split hopelessly was the emerging Republican party able to break through.*

In the period following the Civil War, the Republican party served as the arena in which the decisive conflicts of that era were battled out — all the issues of westward expansion, of the nationalizing of business and the growth of manufacturing interests under the protection of the tariff, of the struggle to bring the trusts under some measure of public control which would balance the older ideals of agrarian democracy against the new interests of a rising industrialism.

With the restoration of the South as a political force in 1876, a twenty-year period did ensue in which Democrats and Republicans tugged almost evenly, and indecisively, with neither party winning the Presidency

369

twice in succession and no President gaining a clear majority of the popular vote. Even through this period, however, the Republicans were the party moving forward into the future, while the Democrats instinctively pulled back toward the past.

The Southern Democrats could hardly avoid being a party of nostalgia — what could their program be but to yearn for a long past? In the North, the Democratic appeal was aimed primarily at those who were alarmed over the Republicans pressing too far and too fast, at those who felt themselves being ground under the rising money power or who were shocked by the corruption which accompanied the quadrupling of the federal bureaucracy and the distribution of the public domain to enterprising and greedy exploitation.

After 1896, when Bryan failed in his crusade to hold back the hands of the clock, Republican dominance became unquestioned. It was broken only by the Bull Moose split, until the depression and the revolt of the city brought a new majority party into existence.

Today it is within the Democratic Party that the issues of our times are being fought out, for better or worse. Civil rights, how to balance the interests of the newly emergent labor power against those of the rest of society, the yearning for security against another depression, the hunger for social status of the climbing urban masses — these are do-or-die problems for the elements of the Democratic coalition. They are not issues which agitate most strongly the Republican voting elements. These latter elements remain rooted in business interests, which suffered comparatively less in the depression. Their struggle for social and economic standing was fought out in terms of the agrarian frontier that has now passed.

This lack of timeliness in its voting elements is the basic reason for the " negative " Republican attitude to so many major problems. The G.O.P. dilemma does not arise out of a lack of " leaders " so-called, or " ideas " so-called, but out of the fact that the Republicans remain what the Southern Democrats were after the Civil War — essentially a party of nostalgia. There is one instinctive Republican program, in whose favor all doubts are resolved — to turn the clock back to an earlier era.

That does not mean the White House is out of Republican reach. On the contrary, as the party of the past, the Republicans are ideally situated to attract all voters who feel the Democratic majority is pushing too far, or who would evade the vexatious issues which wrack the Democrats. The problem of the Republicans . . . is whether — once they have won the presidency because of the excesses of the Democratic majority — they can hold it. Can the Republicans come to grips with the problems of our times? Or by ignoring them, will they restore the vigor and unity of the Democratic majority?

Samuel Lubell [1]

There is no one key with which a major party can unlock one Pandora's political strategy box to find one formula showing how the party should proceed to win any specific election. Instead, the major party strategist is faced with what appears to be a bewildering variety of many variables, all of differing weights and with the importance of each variable changing from time to time.

Studies clearly show an important relationship between economics and politics with the in-party advantaged by prosperity and disadvantaged by economic adversity. But the major party strategist must go beyond these. Sometimes moral issues assume great importance. Sometimes issues of foreign policy may in large part determine an election result. Character of a party's nominees for office may strengthen or weaken the party in any specific election. If the margin of victory is close, perhaps the personal appeal of the party candidate may be decisive.

The major party strategist must accurately judge the political nature of the elements making up his party, the quality of political cement that holds each element to the party, and the prospects for enlarging the party's power base. He must similarly be able to size up the opposition major party's strengths, weaknesses, and points of greatest political vulnerability. As if variables such as these were not complicating enough, he must be prepared to adapt to some other uncontrollable external events such as a sudden depression, some development in foreign affairs which might effect the outcome of an American election, or some unforeseen accident of a developing campaign. Such is the nature of the problem of the major party strategist as he seeks to formulate a strategic pattern which will make sense for the context of any particular campaign in any particular election year.

---

[1] *The Future of American Politics* (New York: Harper and Brothers, 1952), pp. 200–202. Reprinted by permission of Harper and Brothers.

At the same time he is engaged in planning a specific campaign, the scholar-political strategist will also be aware of several theories which imply that a party which is not in tune with long-term political cycles operating in American politics is not likely to win a specific election no matter what it does during the course of the campaign. One of these theories is that advanced by historian Arthur M. Schlesinger, Sr., of Harvard University. He sees the United States alternating between fairly regular periods of conservatism in which the rights of property receive first consideration and periods of liberalism in which property rights are less important than other human considerations. From 1841 to 1861, the United States, according to Schlesinger, was in the conservative half of a cycle (twelve years); and from 1861 to 1869 followed nine years of liberalism. From 1869 to 1901, the United States was again conservative (thirty-two years); and from 1901 to 1918 (eighteen years) it was liberal. From 1918 to 1931 (thirteen years) followed another conservative period, and Schlesinger, writing in 1939, estimated that the liberal era which began in 1931 would be replaced by a new conservative era in the late 1940's (approximately fifteen years). According to this thesis, based on liberal-conservative cycles as Schlesinger sees them from 1765 to 1939, each half of the cycle should last approximately fifteen or sixteen years.[2]

If the Schlesinger cycle theory is valid, then the major party which is most effectively conservative in a conservative era and most effectively liberal in a liberal era should have the best chance of winning elections. In the 1841 to 1861 period, the Democratic and Whig parties, until the latter's demise after the election of 1852, were both conservative and only the minor parties and finally the Republican party in 1856 dared to be liberal. In the 1861 to 1869 period the Republican party was liberal and the Democratic party conservative, and Republicans won. In the 1869 to 1901 period both major parties fought to represent the right blend of conservatism, and only minor parties, again, dared take the liberal position until the Democrats in 1896 switched " too far." In the 1901 to 1918 period the Republican party under Theodore Roosevelt was liberal, but when it split, the way was cleared for two liberal Wilson Democratic terms of office. In the 1918 to 1931 period both major parties tried to be conservative with the Republicans having the best of it. In the 1931 to late 1940

---

[2] Arthur M. Schlesinger, Sr., "Tides of American Politics," *Yale Review* (December, 1939), Vol. 29, pp. 217–230.

period Democrats were liberal, with the Presidential wing of the Republican party after 1936 attempting also to cast its party in the liberal role.

The real test of the Schlesinger theory, however, can only be made by comparing its projections for what might happen after 1939 with contemporary political developments. In 1946 conservative Republicans captured control of Congress at approximately the time Schlesinger predicted a change from a liberal to a conservative era. Truman's victory in 1948, however, would then be an aberration from what might otherwise have been expected to happen. Furthermore, if the reasons for the Democratic win in 1948 involved the contrast between the Truman campaign as distinguished from the Dewey-type campaign, the " farm scare " of the 1948 campaign or fear that Republicans would take away the economic gains of several of the economic groups making up what had been Franklin D. Roosevelt's coalition, then factors outside the liberal-conservative cycle theory must be taken into account. Or, perhaps, it might be argued that the liberal phase had not run its full course by 1948 but that it had by 1952. Yet in 1952 the principal issues determining the outcome of the Presidential election appeared to be the Korean war, fear of communism, discovered corruption among some officials in the Democratic administration, and the broad appeal of President Eisenhower. Here again, there are complicating " other factors."

Though Schlesinger can make a case for his liberal-conservative policy cycles over the past course of American political history, and even though a similar pattern should continue to unfold in the future, obviously the cycles do not tend to operate mechanistically and without relationship to other variables. Louis H. Bean, writing in 1948, states a more fundamental objection to the Schlesinger prediction that conservatism would be the probable trend of the immediate future. Says Bean:

> On the other hand, I project the political tide more specifically in terms of a two-party balance, which does not necessarily imply that conservatism will dominate in the 1950's. That balance will be determined by the success or failure attending the efforts of the party in power, Republican or Democratic, to smooth out the business cycle without creating unemployment and to establish peace.[3]

---

[3] Louis H. Bean, *How to Predict Elections* (New York: Alfred A. Knopf, 1948) , p. 162.

Instead of a new conservative era, Bean looks ahead to a long-term liberal era which would have as its principal driving force the demand for the maintenance of full employment — a demand which no party of the present or future could ignore. At the turn of the century " men made their way in political life with promises of a full dinner-pail but no promise that the dinner-pail would be full three hundred and sixty-five days of the year." Theodore Roosevelt's Square Deal for all the major economic groups followed, and it, in turn, was succeeded by Wilson's New Freedom " from trusts, monopolies and the money power." When Harding, Coolidge, and Hoover failed to continue in the same direction and when depression struck the American economy with violent force, the reaction came in Franklin D. Roosevelt's New Deal to restore full employment. With World War II that objective was achieved, and the over-riding political aspiration of the people for the immediate future and for years to come will be the desire to maintain prosperity — a force which would have to be classified as essentially liberal in character.[4]

Bean, instead of analyzing liberal and conservative cycles, is concerned with measuring the relative strength of the two major parties over the long run of political party history, particularly in the biennially elected United States House of Representatives. Though he sees shifts in party control as due to many complex factors, " the abrupt shifts that brought about the six periods (since 1858) of alternating Republican and Democratic control of Congress are traceable to one major cause — business depressions." [5] After the Buchanan depression in 1857 Republicans controlled the House until Grant's depression of 1873. After Cleveland's depression of 1893 Republicans again won House control until two years after the depression of 1908. Democratic House strength slipped after the depression of 1914 and gave way to a Republican House majority after the depression of 1920. After the 1929 crash Democratic House majorities replaced Republican majorities, but after the 1937 recession Democratic House strength again slipped as Republicans gained.[6]

Other studies charting the indices which economists use to denote prosperity and depression phases of the business cycle in relationship to political trends also tend to support Bean's general observations. " When booms turn to busts," concludes Bean, " and full

---

[4] From *ibid.*, pp. 172–173.
[5] *Ibid.*, p. 17.   [6] *Idem.*

employment to unemployment and misery, the party in power — be it Democratic or Republican — is usually turned out. *Greater economic stability in the future would mean greater political stability."* [7]

Franklin D. Roosevelt for the first time in American history mobilized the federal government for an all-out attack against depression. Democrats have stayed committed to that policy, and Republicans have also clearly committed themselves to it as well. The thermometer of the nation's economic health is watched by politicians of both major parties as closely as a crisis fever hospital case with around-the-clock private nursing care. With each little shift, orders flow out of Washington to reduce or increase credit margins in the stock exchanges, credit controls are aimed at expansion or contraction of general credit, farm aid programs are adjusted, and in general the party in office is determined to do all in its power to keep from the opposition a chance to effectively argue " economic depression " as a reason for political change.

Still another cyclical theory of party politics suggests that the length of tenure of a party in power depends primarily on the rapidity with which grievances mount against it to strengthen the out-party. As soon as the in-party is forced to make decisions, the elements of its combination, which feel those decisions are going against them, tend to break off and to associate with the out-major party. The in-party will have to continue to make " unity damaging " decisions on controversial questions. It may make political mistakes or move to extreme positions on issues — extreme by virtue of the fact that the party does not effectively sell its position and thus get the people to follow. Evidences of poor administration or corruption may develop. Perhaps the in-party will arrive at a point where Lubell suggests the Democrats were by 1952 — a point at which " *no new economic gains can be promised any group of Democrats today without threatening the gains of other Democrats."* [8] Perhaps a depression will strike. When grievances against the in-party, due to one or a combination of such factors accumulate to some breaking point, then the opposition major party is given its opportunity to control the machinery of the national government. Once the new in-party has assumed office, the same factors, according to the theory, begin to operate on it to eventually produce another change of party control.

---

[7] Bean, *op cit.*, pp. 17–18. Italics the author's.
[8] Lubell, *op. cit.*, p. 219. Italics Lubell's.

Some would suggest that this third theory of party cycles operates as mechanistically as Schlesinger seems to imply his liberal-conservative cycles do, or as others hold that economic cycles determine the outcome of election contests. There is, however, no justification for assuming that regardless of what a party does during the course of a

The Des Moines Register And Tribune

"Don't Complain To Me About Coffee Prices.
Talk To You-Know-Who."

campaign, regardless of who are its candidates, regardless of what has been its record and regardless of the virility of the opposition major party that the pendulum effect of some political or party cycle predetermines a certain result. Yet all three cycle theories, when their limitations are taken into account, are of value to the major party strategist. Drawing from the three theories and especially from the third, the following sections of this chapter will examine what appear to be major factors in determining whether or not there will be a turnover of major party control in any particular Presidential election.

THE MAJOR PARTY STRATEGIST'S TARGET — BROAD APPEAL

The Chief Justice of the United States Supreme Court, Earl Warren, was three times elected as a Republican to four-year terms as Governor of California. Simply stated, his analysis of the California electorate was this. Voters who were political extremists comprised, perhaps, some 30 percent of the electorate — 15 percent at the extreme left end of the political spectrum and 15 percent on the opposite and right end of the scale. In between, he saw a large 70 percent who would respond favorably to moderacy in the conduct of the affairs of the state. Warren, by conviction, by temperament, by the general impression he created, and by the programs he supported was ideally suited to convince a large proportion of that 70 percent " reasonable middle " of the electorate to support him. Here was a Republican who could consistently win elections and help carry others on the state Republican ticket into office — even though he ran his campaigns independently — in a state which was at the same time usually voting Democratic in Presidential elections and in which registered Democrats outnumbered registered Republicans in the approximate ratio of three to two.

Warren's first election to the office of governor had been made possible when California's first Democratic administration since the turn of the century had been identified from 1938 to 1942 in the public mind with extremism and administrative confusion, and had failed to successfully implement a California New Deal comparable to Franklin D. Roosevelt's program on the national level of government. On assuming office, two general alternative courses were available to Warren. First, he might have attempted to engage in a direct attack against the philosophy of New Deal " humanism " and have urged the adoption of state policies which were anti-New Deal in their intent. Second, Warren could move into middle ground by supplying his own Republican version of a New Deal for California, thus taking away from California Democrats the advantage which had been gained by the in-party Democrats in the national government. The latter plan was the one chosen, and it was successfully implemented.

Democrats had had an opportunity from 1938 to 1942 to establish a new power base in California, but had failed. Now as a price, because Republicans had occupied substantially the same political ground as Democrats would have had they been in power and operating with political effectiveness, Democrats as the out-party faced a dilemma. When their candidates appeared to be edging toward the extremist left edge of " reasonable middle," they were soundly defeated. To attempt to be more conservative than Warren was not a realistic alternative, and the few Democrats who tried met with a fate similar to those who went to the left.

Had Warren Republican administrations turned corrupt, shifted toward the extremist right edge of " reasonable middle," or been inefficient, then the Democrats might have been given another opportunity to show what they could do in governing the state. But none of those things happened. The out-party was thus left in a position of waiting for " breaks " which did not come or hoping that when Warren left office a less politically effective Republican governor might take his place to ease the Democratic way back into power. Warren's successor, Goodwin J. Knight, however, had no sooner taken office than he made it obvious that he would, in his own way, maintain the same type of appeal as his predecessor had done. As a result, even though there had been a change of leadership in the in-party, Democrats were still confronted with the same basic problem they had faced ever since the Warren appeal first began to fasten its hold on the California electorate.

A few other simple illustrations from state politics should be cited before moving to the major party's problem of developing broad appeal at the national level of government. Because Minnesota Republicans split and because of the developing depression, traditionally Republican Minnesota in 1930 elected Floyd B. Olson, a Farmer-Laborite, as governor. Olson was twice re-elected and through his version of New Deal as applied to Minnesota's problems, he appeared to have established a strong Farmer-Labor party power base. His Farmer-Labor successor, Elmer A. Benson, however, in the short space of two years from 1936 to 1938 moved so far to the left end of the political spectrum, made so many damaging political mistakes, and was such a politically unattractive candidate for his state that the Farmer-Labor party split and its strength was destroyed. Republican Governor Harold E. Stassen, elected for the first time in 1938, proceeded to implement his Republican version of a New Deal for

Minnesota and thus was able to establish a Republican tenure of power which lasted until 1954.

Governor Thomas E. Dewey of New York, once he gained office, was able to capitalize on the " New Deal orientation " of the New York electorate and to successfully maintain power because he pro-

'Will He Love Me In November, As He Does In July?'

duced a Republican state administration which responded to the needs of the " reasonable middle " in his state and was able to have translated into law the types of programs which could develop broad appeal. Likewise it is possible for a Democratic Governor like G. Mennen Williams to stay in office in a " safe " Republican state and to so effectively make his imprint on Michigan politics that that state now appears to be politically doubtful or " tending Democratic." This Williams was able to accomplish, in part, because he was able to capture support away from Republicans. How does a

Democratic Governor Frank J. Lausche continue to be elected in Ohio at the same time the voters of Ohio have generally been electing Republicans? The answer, in part again, is that Lausche has been getting votes which would otherwise have gone to a Republican nominee for governor.

Republican right-wing extremists would not have been able to accomplish what Warren did in California, what Dewey did in New York, or what Stassen did in Minnesota. Democratic left-wing extremists would likewise have been failures in Williams' Michigan or Lausche's Ohio. Each of these men skillfully determined what was the most broadly appealing political middle ground for his state and proceeded to occupy it. Though some of these men were Republicans and some Democrats, all developed substantially successful types of appeal.

For a Republican party strategist, the most vital decisions he will make are those through which he identifies between what would constitute right-wing extremism and what would appeal to the broad middle of the electorate in his constituency. For a Democratic party strategist, the decisions as to the line marking off left-wing extremism from the broad " reasonable middle " of his electorate are likely to be the most important decisions he makes. What will be broadly appealing may differ from constituency to constituency and from time to time, but the successful political strategist has got to find the right answer. If he does, his major party will prosper. If his estimate is not accurate, his major party will fail, provided, of course, that the calculations of the opposition are not just as bad or worse.

During the Federalist and Jeffersonian Republican periods, as the latter party was able to organize into a working opposition party and to clarify issues as it interpreted them, the " reasonable middle " of the electorate at that time could be described as follows. First, it would accept domestic policies which would take into account some kind of fair balance between the economic interests of the West, the South, and New England. Federalists failed to develop such a program when they responded almost entirely to the demands of New England and the coastal communities, whereas Jeffersonian Republicans did arrive at a balanced and generally acceptable compromise of the conflicting sectional interests. Second, the principal issues of foreign policy revolved around the conflict between France and England, with a numerical majority tending to side with the former country. The Jeffersonian Republicans were primarily French in their sympathies while Federalists tended to side with England. The Federalists were so extreme in their pro-British outlook, however, that even during the War of 1812 they continued to openly proclaim English attachments and thus laid themselves open to the charge of treason.

Third, the reaction against the Alien and Sedition Acts showed that the bulk of the electorate had a great respect for the free working of the democratic-representative system. This was the side on which the Jeffersonian Republicans stood, and, in fact, it had been they who formulated the theory with which Federalist attempts to stop the free flow of criticism were challenged. On all three of these general areas of program appeal the Jeffersonian Republican party tended to be the moderate party while the Federalist party tended toward extreme positions. The former party's appeal was further enhanced by the contrast between its leaders and Federalist leaders, with Jefferson a much more attractive political figure to the American electorate than either Hamilton or John Adams.

Once the Federalist party ceased to exist as effective competition to the Republican party, Republican mistakes, poor leadership, Madison's bungling of the conduct of the War of 1812, a postwar depression — all these accumulating grievances did not damage the Republican party because there was no acceptable alternative to which the electorate could turn. Only when the Republican party became so all embracing that it included all interest groups and when the desires of one set of groups could not be satisfied without dissatisfying others, did the break-up come with Adams men on one side and Jackson men on the other. As the ox carts had transported migrants into the area west of the Appalachians, a gradual shift of political power to enhance the political strength of the West and South had taken place. The broad middle of the changed electorate of the late 1820's required a new type of political appeal.

From 1828 to 1860 two-party competition existed throughout the period. Though Henry Clay devised complicated domestic programs in an attempt to develop broad National Republican and later Whig support, Jackson was able to galvanize the " common man " into action against the " monied interests." Old Hickory would have been an extremist in the early 1800's, but in the 1830's he was well within the limits of the " reasonable middle " having a balance of power in the electorate. Deflecting groups allied themselves with the Whig party and after Van Buren's depression and the nomination of

William Henry Harrison, a national hero running without a platform, Whigs for the first time won the White House. However, Harrison's death, the Congressional repudiation of Tyler, and confusion
made impossible the development of a broad-appeal Whig program.
During their second opportunity from 1844 to 1848 Whigs were little
more successful. For the remainder of the period the Democratic combination continued to control until the depression of 1857, the
break-up of the Democratic party, and a shift of the political climate
in the North on the slavery question to make possible the election
of Lincoln as a Republican.

From 1861 to 1896, although Republicans controlled the Presidency for all but eight years of the period, none of its Presidents were
able to develop a truly solid base of support. The South was lost
through what, for the time, were extremist reconstruction policies.
Grant had had an opportunity in the North to blend patriotism and
a fairly balanced East-West sectional economic Republican foundation, but in this he was not as successful as he could have been. His
failure, corruption in his administrations, and the depression of 1873
completed the destruction of the Republican opportunity at that
time. Democrats, however, as the disunited party of " nostalgia "
were hardly a more attractive alternative, and Cleveland through his
two separated administrations was unable to substantially enlarge the
Democratic power base. Then, again, with the depression of 1893
and eastern and business community fright at the prospect of Bryan
and " free silver," Republicans were presented with a new chance to
solidify and enlarge their power position.

From the turn into this century until the present time the " reasonable middle " of the electorate has tended more and more to demand that the party to which control of the federal government is
entrusted should meet two major tests. First, the major party is expected to have abandoned the doctrine of *laissez faire* for a position
which includes some level of government intervention in domestic
economic affairs. Second, the major party is expected to have abandoned the doctrine of isolationism for one of collective security in
order to meet the new problems imposed on this country by developments in international affairs.

Theodore Roosevelt took the first systematic steps to regulate
some of the most flagrant abuses of a previously unregulated business
economy. Though some Republicans tried to hold back the tide, he
was enthusiastically supported by a majority of the electorate. The

Republican split in 1912 produced an even more systematic attempt at regulation of business practices under President Wilson, and now the federal government also began to intervene to enhance the bargaining position of labor in its relationships with management. Under Franklin D. Roosevelt regulation and labor legislation were carried further, and now the federal government also committed itself to parity programs to underwrite the agricultural economy of the United States, to social security programs to underwrite a minimum income level under all economically unfortunate persons, and to economic controls to attempt to smooth out boom and bust phases of business cycles. Presidential election results, Congressional and Senatorial election results in doubtful districts and states in which political forces similar to those which operate in Presidential elections exist,[9] and public-opinion poll results revealed that what might be termed the New Deal philosophy of the role of government had been accepted and was demanded by the vast majority of the American electorate.

Though the trend toward the collective security position developed more slowly and haltingly, and though for a time in the 1920's it appeared that the trend was reversing itself, developments in and after World War II have made it clear that the broad middle of the electorate wants federal government collective security policies just as surely as it requires the philosophy of the New Deal in major party domestic platform planks and government programs. Both trends have been a result of attempts to find solutions to the most pressing problems facing the United States in the modern world. Both trends have so solidly captured the political imagination of a vast majority of the electorate that there is little possibility that they will or can be reversed.

Party cycles will continue to operate as they have in the past with alternating periods of Democratic and Republican control, provided no one of the two major parties refuses to adapt itself to each new expectation level of the American electorate. The new party battle, if battle there is to be, will find both major parties accepting both the idea of collective security and the underlying philosophy of the New Deal in domestic economic affairs. Yet there will still be much to disagree and fight about. Extremism from time to time in either right or left directions will be one subject for dispute. Administrative in-

[9] See Chapter 15.

competence, corruption, depressions or recessions, different theories as to how a policy of collective security should be implemented, political mistakes — all of these issues will continue to test the mettle of the in-party as it tries to hold and enlarge its base of support, and will test the mettle of the out-party as it seeks to exploit the weaknesses of the in-party in its efforts to return to power.

With Republican Presidents McKinley and Theodore Roosevelt in the White House, the electorate was generally satisfied and supported the in-party. There had been the depression of 1908, Taft allowed himself to be maneuvered into appearing to be an extremist, he lacked the personal political appeal of his two Republican predecessors, his party split — cumulative grievances such as these brought Wilson's opportunity. Postwar disillusionment, the breakdown of Wilson's health, the depression of 1920–1921 — cumulative grievances such as these brought another Republican opportunity. The inability to solve the farm crisis that lasted over the whole decade of the 1920's, failure of Hoover to alleviate the effects of the depression, " weak " Presidents, the crash of 1929 and its depression aftermath — cumulative grievances such as these brought Franklin D. Roosevelt his opportunity.

No one of these shifts from one party to another was predetermined to happen at the particular time it did. Rather, the in-party was unable to prevent the grievance-accumulating process against it from reaching a party-turnover point. And at the same time, the out-party could present itself as an alternative to which the electorate could turn. Both the manner in which the in-party conducts itself and the manner in which the out-party conducts itself are factors which may play an important role in determining when the in-party is turned out.

PROBLEMS OF IN–PARTY STRATEGY

When the major party which has been the out-party gains control of the White House and Congress by replacing the in-party, it is important that the winner examine the nature of its victory. First, the mere fact of winning after a series of defeats does not mean the new in-party has once again developed a new national majority. It has not, but rather is being given an opportunity to try and do so. The electorate at the stage preliminary to the start of the new administration is likely to have been just temporarily disgusted or distrustful of the party which had been in power, but that fact does not mean the electorate might not quickly reverse itself at the next election. Whether the new in-party stays in power or not will in part depend upon the kind of record it can make in its first years of office. The new in-party's power curve might, because of the record it establishes, sweep up as it did for Jefferson in 1804, for Jackson in 1832, for McKinley in 1900 or for Franklin D. Roosevelt in 1936. Or, it might fall as in the classic cases of the Whig administrations in 1844 and 1852.

Second, the new in-party's ability to continue to win elections will be dependent, in part, on the ability of the opposition major party to come back from its defeat to present an alternative attractive enough to allow the electorate once again to think of making a change. The electorate did not have such an alternative with the Federalists after 1800, with the National Republicans in 1832, with the Democrats from 1864 through 1872 or from 1900 through 1908 or from 1924 through 1928, or with Republicans through much of the Franklin D. Roosevelt era. While the Whigs were briefly in power, however, the Democratic opposition was always a ready alternative. Both major parties were similarly alternatives whenever they were out of power from 1876 to 1896. If the defeated party is weak, the new in-party's margin of safety is greater than if the defeated party was beaten in a close election and the defeated party remains strong and is priced within the existing political market range.

Third, the new in-party may ride in on a tidal wave where the " reasonable middle " of the electorate has drastically shifted as was the case in the victories of Jefferson in 1800, Jackson in 1828, Harding in 1920 and Franklin D. Roosevelt in 1932. Or, the new in-party may have been carried to power on a gentle wave which reflects indecision on the part of the electorate and a choosing between two almost equally bad or good alternatives. The latter type of election result immediately serves warning that at the next election the decision may very easily go the other way. The " 50–50 " elections from 1876 through 1888 are examples of one " little wave " type. The 1952 election where, though Eisenhower won the Presidency by a convincing margin, the Republicans did not correspondingly gain in Congressional strength is another example. If the election is the result of a political tidal wave, the opportunity for the new in-party is greater and more easy to exploit than is the lesser opportunity presented by the " little wave " election result.

Perhaps, except for the Jeffersonian Republicans in 1800, no out-party has ever become an in-party under more favorable circumstances in which to enlarge its power base than the Democrats in 1932. The Democratic party proceeded to capitalize on its tidal wave mandate and the disorganized state of the opposition Republican party in a manner which developed for President Franklin D. Roosevelt and Democratic Congresses a more all-embracing national political strength than any other major party had attained since the Jeffersonian Republicans were without opposition. So strong did the Democratic party become that even the accumulation of grievances against it did not have the effect they would ordinarily have had on a less strong in-party.

The Liability of Administrative Weakness. Although there was much administrative confusion in the Franklin D. Roosevelt administrations, and particularly in the first four years, the deficiency went almost unnoticed. Roosevelt himself, it is alleged, said he could have employed a more effective strategy against the Democratic party in 1936 than Republicans did by attacking the New Deal at its weakest point — namely, its poor quality of administration.[10] If an in-party does not have such a reservoir of power constantly being refilled from other well-springs of political appeal as was the case in the early years of the New Deal, administrative weakness can become a major political liability. When administrative weakness degenerates to its worst form — corruption — it is always a major political liability.

The Liability of Extremism. Decisions on controversial questions which will tend to drive elements of an in-party to the out-party to gradually enhance the power of the latter are inevitable. However, policies which represent such an extreme that the " reasonable middle " of the electorate is not ready to accept them or policies so extreme that they will never meet with acceptance are not inevitable, and ordinarily the result of extremism is an immediate party change. Perhaps it is a Cleveland in 1887 coming out so strongly for a radical tariff reduction when the question was such a delicate one and his Democratic party power base was so even with that of Republicans that he tips the balance to the opposition party's Presidential nomi-

---

[10] Wilfred E. Binkley, *President and Congress* (New York: Alfred A. Knopf, 1947) , p. 236.

nee the next year. Perhaps it is a Hoover standing so firmly against federal intervention in the economy in a crisis depression that he finds himself appealing only to extremists and he is out of touch with the " reasonable middle " of the then existing electorate. Perhaps it is a Franklin D. Roosevelt's " court-packing " plan which seems to threaten one of the most reverently regarded of American institutions. Had not the Franklin D. Roosevelt power base been so strong and had not international events turned to Roosevelt's advantage in domestic politics by the Presidential election of 1940, this extreme action might have been a major cause for a Democratic defeat then.

For the in-party to be moderate and not extreme does not mean that the in-party should not act and act positively. It does mean, however, that if the policies of the in-party are regarded by the " reasonable middle " of the electorate as extreme rather than moderate, either the in-party will have to convince the voter before the next election that he is wrong or perhaps that party will find itself removed from office. Where administrative confusion may often be overlooked by the electorate, extremism tends to be regarded as a more serious offense and usually results in major damage to the in-party — provided the out-party is not also extremist in outlook.

The Liability of Economic Depression. Also in the " major damage " category, at least in the past, have been economic depressions. Only Monroe of the American Presidents has survived a depression to be re-elected to another term in the White House, and that was at a time when there was no major party opposition to the Jeffersonian Republicans. This fact makes Franklin D. Roosevelt's survival after the recession which began in 1937 another significant measurement of the very great power which Roosevelt had developed since 1932. The 1937 recession did contribute to Republican gains in the Congressional election year of 1938, but it was not enough to topple Democrats from control of the Presidency and Congress. By 1940 the state of world affairs tended to relegate the recession of 1937 to the position of a secondary issue. As soon as the United States became actively involved in supplying the Allied forces, the prosperity curve began a rise which was to lead to new heights. Furthermore, in 1940 even though a recession had occurred during President Roosevelt's second term of office, the people had not far to look back and remember Roosevelt's efforts to promote economic recovery from the depression of the early 1930's and Hoover's earlier apparent failure to act.

Although depressions alone have been cause enough to produce the overthrow of the party in power at the time the depression occurred, there are indications that in the party cycles of the future this factor may not play as much a part in producing turnover of parties as it has in the past. Before the New Deal the parties in power when depression struck had tended to more or less helplessly stand by to allow economic depression to run its course. After the New Deal with its commitment and later with the Republican party's commitment to governmental intervention to attempt to smooth out the extreme high and low phases of the business cycle, the in-party may be able to prevent severe depressions and by its actions to alleviate the distress of recessions. If the in-party is able to do these things, it may be able to remain in power at a time when, in the past, the " law of the business cycle " would have operated to throw the in-party out. Even in 1930, 1931, and 1932, if Hoover had vigorously and with political skill attempted a Republican " new deal " to restore the nation's economic health, it is not impossible that Republicans

—Conrad, in the Denver Post

"... Then Some Darn Fool Moves the Ladder Up! ..."

might have maintained a balance of power. Or, if defeated in 1932, at least the defeat might not have been a rout to be followed by twenty-year consequences.

The Liability of Assorted Political Mistakes. Political mistakes of many different varieties other than miscalculations of the political effect of substantive policy decisions constitute another source of grievances accumulating against an in-party. Perhaps it is a Cleveland " illegally ordering the return to the Southern states of the captured Confederate flags and . . . going fishing on Decoration Day." [11] Perhaps it is a Truman taking pen in hand to give expression to a personal pique against a music critic's appraisal of daughter Margaret's concert singing. Perhaps it is the Radical Republicans of the reconstruction era trying to win the South for the Republican party and, by the methods employed, creating the Solid Democratic South. Perhaps it is a Franklin D. Roosevelt presenting a Nazi iron cross to a persistent columnist critic of his administration.

An in-party will inevitably make political mistakes. If they are few and minor and the party's power base is strong, the destructive effects may not be great. If, however, the mistakes are numerous and serious and the major parties are in relatively even balance, the " accumulated-grievance " result may produce significant damage to the in-party.

The Liability or Advantage of War. Involvement in war is a factor which might operate either to the political advantage or disadvantage of the in-party depending on several considerations, but it is not the unmixed political blessing that sometimes it appears to be. The in-party must successfully direct the war effort, and if it does do so, the feeling of patriotism and national unity will tend, at least temporarily, to enhance the in-party's position. Also, with a war economy, the business cycle turns sharply toward prosperity. But the long-range hazards of war to the in-party are also great. A depression has followed every major war in which America has been involved except World War II, and as a direct result of such depressions, the in-party lost control of Congress and the Presidency.

During a major war it is necessary that there be a high degree of concentration of power — almost dictatorial power — in the hands of the in-party's President. Generally after the war there has been a reaction. After the Civil War, although Republicans retained power, there was such a reaction against Presidential leadership and Grant went to such an opposite extreme that he forfeited for his party the

---

[11] Binkley, *American Political Parties,* p. 311.

opportunity to establish a solid and winning Republican party power base. Wilson's exercise of broad powers during World War I and his seeming slowness in being willing to relinquish those powers was a major issue in the campaign against the Democrats in 1920 and was a factor in Harding's victory. Only after World War II was there no such intense reaction against Presidential use of wartime powers.

Only for Lincoln in 1864 and for Franklin D. Roosevelt in 1944 when the country was at war during a Presidential election campaign has the " don't change administrations in the middle of a war " argument been an important factor in a Presidential election campaign. After a war comes the difficult problem of negotiating a peace which will live up to the expectations of those who have had to sacrifice so much during the fighting. Failure to achieve success in peacemaking may become a major grievance against the in-party as was the case with Wilson's second administration.

Wars have another political implication for the in-party because out of them generals establish reputations as national heroes and thus become " available " as Presidential nominees for the major parties. William Henry Harrison and Zachary Taylor established hero status under Democratic administrations and went on to become Whig Presidential nominees. Eisenhower made his reputation under a Democratic administration. On the other hand, the reputations of leaders of the in-party have also been developed or strengthened in the same manner, e.g., Grant in the Civil War (though at the time of his military success he was still nominally a Buchanan Democrat) and Theodore Roosevelt in the Spanish American War.

The Difficulty of Maintaining Quality of Political Leadership. The ability of an in-party to choose a broad-appeal Presidential nominee to replace a successful President is another factor that may directly affect that party's chance to longer perpetuate itself in power. Jefferson chose a Madison, Jackson a Van Buren, Theodore Roosevelt a Taft. Madison, Van Buren, and Taft had been able administrators and when functioning in an advisory capacity, appeared to have the necessary political talents. Yet when they themselves had to assume control, they so lacked their predecessors' popular leadership qualities that the contrast tended to operate against the in-party. In Madison's case, it is true, failure as a President did not serve as a bar to re-election with the opposition Federalists already all but defunct, but neither Van Buren nor Taft could win re-election.

If the in-party does not select an intimate of the President, the man will tend to be a compromise between several factions of the party such as was Harry S. Truman. In such a case, if the new leader is one who can develop into a popular leader, generally that result is an accident because his acceptability to factions within the party was more important in his selection than his then-known ability to develop broad inter-party appeal.

Only Franklin D. Roosevelt has sought and won re-election to a third and fourth term of office, and the adoption of the " two-term " Twenty-second Amendment will in the future limit the in-party's successful Presidents to eight years in office. Generally the successors to truly popular Presidents tend to be less popular, and succeeding administrations of the same party under different Presidents tend to lose the full head of steam under which the in-party once traveled. At this point, if the out-party can present an attractive alternative, perhaps in the form of some military hero or successful governor, the in-party becomes vulnerable.

Assuming the in-party has able Presidential leadership and a unity level which permits it to adapt to the needs of the American people at the time that it is in power, the in-party has the very great advantage of initiative over the out-party. If the in-party successfully straddles wide over the " reasonable middle " of the electorate, the out-party is barred from going around either extreme of left or right and is thus forced to wait its turn. How long the in-party will be able to maintain its initiative and broad appeal will then depend on the length of time it can keep the electorate from feeling that it is " time for a change." If the in-party's level of administration is efficient, if it is moderate and not extremist, if it can manage the economy to prevent depression without stifling the private forces which help make the economy dynamic, if it can avoid unnecessary and serious political mistakes or keep them small in number, if it can stay out of war or if war is necessary successfully conduct the war effort and negotiate the peace, if it can continue to elevate to its top position politically able and appealing leaders — if the in-party can do all these things, then theoretically it might stay in power for an unlimited period.

No in-party in the past, however, has been able to stop indefinitely the accumulation of grievances before they reach the " time for a change " stage. Jeffersonian Republicans lasted from 1800 until the break-up in 1824, but much of that tenure in power was without benefit of an organized opposition major party. Lincoln, Grant, Hayes, Garfield, and Arthur represent a twenty-four-year Republican period of White House control, but for a time under Lincoln it was the Union party, from 1874 Republicans generally did not control Congress, and from 1876 Presidential victory margins were extremely close. Franklin D. Roosevelt and Truman Democratic White House years numbered twenty. During those years Democrats lost control of Congress from 1946 to 1948; on other occasions the margins of Democratic Congressional control were close; and for much of the time after 1938 conservative Democrats worked with Republicans to block Administration domestic measures. The McKinley-Theodore Roosevelt-Taft combination held office for sixteen years before the 1912 split. Jackson and Van Buren from 1828 to 1840 and Harding, Coolidge, and Hoover from 1920 to 1932 represent twelve-year periods of control of the Presidency.

A twenty-year era of uninterrupted in-party power is a rare exception. So is a sixteen-year in-party tenure. An in-party generally begins its decline in its first Congress. Often at the end of its first four-year term it may be in trouble. If it does succeed in winning a second term, perhaps then during the next four years grievances will have accumulated to bring a change in party control. If the first eight years of an in-party's power have been dominated by a highly successful President, that party is likely to win another four-year term and then go down to defeat. Such has been the in-party mortality average of the past.

Where the in-party has exceeded its normal life expectancy, one of the reasons why it has been able to do so is that it has succeeded in slowing down the process by which grievances accumulate against it. Just as surely, however, its above-average uninterrupted tenure in power has been made possible because of the deficiencies of the out-party.

PROBLEMS OF OUT–PARTY STRATEGY

Table 1 in the introduction to Part Three of this book outlines the principal eras in American political party history. As that table suggests and as the development of party history in this country makes clear, except for the 1876 to 1896 period of even balance between the two major parties, the supreme or " sun " party of a period is in a more advantageous political position than the " moon " or minority major party. If the out-party is a " sun " party, its strategy problem is relatively simple by comparison with the out-party's problem if it is a " moon " party.

The " sun " party, by definition is the larger and more powerful of the two major parties. Perhaps it has lost an election because during a long tenure in office the party gradually ran down and needed, in the electorate's opinion, a four-year respite in which figuratively to recharge its batteries. Perhaps its last President was not a happy choice. Perhaps there had been a depression to produce the turnover in parties. Regardless of what the reason for the defeat — short of the end of one era and the beginning of the next — the " sun " party when it is out of office has a very good chance of returning to power at the next election. Such was the position of the Democratic party from 1840 to 1844 and from 1848 to 1852. Such was also the position of the Republican party from 1912 to 1920. Or, if the two major parties are evenly balanced as they were from 1876 to 1896, the out-party at any particular time similarly can entertain the realistic hope that after the next election it will again be the in-party.

In situations such as these, the elements of the out-party are " in phase " or at least not likely to be far " out of phase " with the " reasonable middle " of the electorate. In some such situations, all the out-party has to do is wait for the in-party to proceed to make the mistakes and quickly accumulate the opposition it inevitably will because its elements, as Lubell suggests in the introductory quotation for this chapter, lack " timeliness." During the two four-year Whig terms before the Civil War, for example, certainly the Democrats could not have devised more effective strategy against the Whigs than to allow the latter party to destroy with consummate effectiveness its own opportunities for re-election.

In the first Cleveland Administration the President's 1887 tariff-reduction message was undoubtedly more damaging to the in-party than anything the Republicans did in opposition. Likewise, during the second Cleveland Administration, the panic of 1893 did more damage than any punishment the then out-party Republicans could have inflicted. In neither of the Cleveland administrations was the Democratic party able to approach the building of a combination which would constitute a substantial threat to the then existing Republican power base. Even though Wilson in his first term was generally considered an effective President leading a surprisingly effective Democratic party to an almost monumental program accomplishment, Republicans missed electing Hughes in 1916 by less than 5,000 votes in California. In 1918, after Wilson had successfully conducted the war, Democrats lost control of Congress.

This is not to suggest that the " sun " out-party should not oppose the " moon " in-party by keeping the pressure on it. It is rather to say that the out-party in such a situation is so close to returning to power that it should choose that which it would oppose and the methods by which it would oppose with great care lest in extremist opposition it drive away votes that it would otherwise receive. For the " sun " party when it is out of office, a record of " responsible opposition " plus the nomination of a broad-appeal candidate for President is generally enough to insure a return to power. Even with relatively unknown presidential nominees like Polk, Pierce, Benjamin Harrison, and Harding, " sun " parties have returned to power after only four years out of office, or eight years out of office as was the case before Harding's 1920 election.

Far more difficult is the strategy problem of the " moon " party as it searches for a means of gaining power. Its record has been written by its members of Congress acting as an opposition to the " sun " party. In the compiling of that record there has always been the tendency to oppose for opposition's sake. If the " sun " party has built a winning base of support, the " moon " party's members in Congress are put in the position — if they are indiscriminate obstructionists — of opposing the very things the " reasonable middle " of the electorate has been voting for. The out-party has no leader, but several different Congressional leaders competing among themselves in an attempt to secure their party's next Presidential nomination or to secure it for someone who is their respective party faction's choice.

Even after such an out-party's national conventions select Presidential nominees who are in tune with the political environment of the era, the Congressional wing of the party tends to be grudging in its support of that nominee if support is given at all. Always in such a situation there is the charge of " me tooism " leveled against those who would attempt to adapt the " moon " party by making it face squarely its current political problem and act again as though it seriously wants to win Presidential elections.

Here is in essence the story of the Federalist party after 1800. So helpless was it in opposition that many of its members crossed over into the camp of the enemy and soon its power base was entirely

gone. Federalists could not hear the voices of the present, to say nothing of the voices of the immediate future. That party was tuned to a
long-gone electorate of the past and never did change, consequently
it tended generally to be extremist. Here too are the National Republicans and Whigs — not as helpless as the Federalists, but neither the
National Republicans nor the Whigs were resilient enough to long
survive. Finally the Whig national conventions discovered the technique of the national-hero Presidential nominee, but as soon as he
was elected, the Whigs in Congress refused or were incapable of taking the next adaptation step. Though some Whig state administrations attempted and succeeded in stealing the " champion of the
people " mantle from the Democratic party, the movement did not
succeed within the party on the national level of government.

Here too are the Democrats from 1860 to 1876 refighting the
Civil War and the battles of the Thirteenth, Fourteenth, and Fifteenth Amendments to the Constitution. But the Democratic party
was able somehow to continue to exist until the grievances against
the Republican party had mounted to the point that the Democratic
party became the equal of the Republican party. Here too are the
Democrats from 1896 to 1912 and again from 1920 to 1932 — often
very weak but still a major party hoping that Republicans would
someday need replacing. And here too is the Republican party from
1932 to 1952. Because this last example is the most recent and because it as clearly as any other reveals in bold outline the " moon "
party's problem when it is out of office, it will be examined in greater
detail.

The principal Republican problem from 1932 to 1952 was to
maintain itself as an alternative which the electorate could easily
turn to when grievances against the Democrats had accumulated to
a point where there would be a general demand for a change. Republicans were divided on the manner in which the party could best
maneuver itself into such a position. Republicans in Congress, often
allied with conservative Democrats, had written a record which
tended to give the impression that the Republican party wanted to
return to the days of the 1920's as though the New Deal and later
World War II had never happened. Starting at the 1940 Republican
National Convention, Republican Presidential nominees tended to
be men who accepted both the general principles behind the New
Deal and collective security in international affairs.

Where the Congressional wing would in effect make its stand

against the philosophy of the Roosevelt administrations in both domestic and international affairs, the Presidential wing of the Republican party tended to accept the " sun " party's basic philosophy. The
Republican Presidential wing's battleground was one on which Democrats could be charged with failure to adequately execute their theories. The implication was that if the Republican party were again
entrusted with the control of the national government, it would do
a better job than the Democrats were doing and that it could moderate some of the excesses of Democratic administrations. To support
the political practicality of such an approach, the Presidential wing
of the Republican party could point to several Republican state administrations which had successfully captured the initiative from
Democrats and which were successfully maintaining themselves in
power with Republican versions of what Democrats were trying to
do on the national level of government.

Congressional Republicans tended to the opinion that Republican Presidential nominees were embracing " me tooism " and that
if the Republican party did not stand up to be counted behind its
" party principles " there would be no cause for the electorate to
turn to a Republican administration. Furthermore, this group argued
that " me tooism " was so repulsive to good Republican voters that
they were refusing to turn out at election time because they were
given no alternative through which to express their hatred of Democratic policies. Presidential Republicans countered with the idea
that the Republican object should be to present an impression that,
if elected to office, the Republican party would not be radical in the
sense that it would wipe out the accomplishments of the Roosevelt
administrations but rather that it would be conservative in continuing the good policies, administering them well, and moving on then
to other new problems. At each successive national convention after
1936, this issue was refought, and each time the Presidential wing of
the party won. The Congressional wing, however, continued in its
actions on legislative questions to operate on its own and different
premises.

Because of this basic conflict within the Republican party, the
independent and Democratic voter who might tend to vote Republican could never be quite sure of what he would be getting if Republicans were returned to power. Not until 1952, after a literal mountain of grievances had accumulated against the Democratic in-party,
was the Republican party voted back into the White House. Yet,

though the 1952 election did give Republicans enough seats in the House and the Senate to organize both houses of Congress, those margins of control were so thin they did not represent working majorities. In 1954 even that minimum level of Republican Congressional control was lost. Whether the Congressional wing of the Republican party has now moved far enough in the direction of the position of the party's Presidential wing as a result of President Eisenhower's leadership only the future can tell.

CHAPTER FIFTEEN

The Politics of the Electoral College

The executive Power shall be vested in a President of the United States of America. He shall hold his Office during the Term of four Years, and, together with the Vice President, chosen for the same Term, be elected, as follows.

Each state shall appoint, in such Manner as the Legislature thereof may direct, a Number of Electors, equal to the whole Number of Senators and Representatives to which the State may be entitled in the Congress. . . .

The Electors shall meet in their respective states, and vote by ballot for President and Vice President, one of whom, at least, shall not be an inhabitant of the same state with themselves; they shall name in their ballots the person voted for as President, and in distinct ballots the person voted for as Vice President, and they shall make distinct lists of all persons voted for as President, and of all persons voted for as Vice President, and of the number of votes for each, which lists they shall sign and certify, and transmit sealed to the seat of the government of the United States, directed to the President of the Senate; — The President of the Senate shall, in the presence of the Senate and House of Representatives, open all the certificates and the votes shall then be counted; — The person having the greatest number of votes for President, shall be the President, if such number be a majority of the whole number of Electors appointed; and if no person have such a majority, then from the persons having the highest numbers not exceeding three on the list of those voted for as President, the House of Representatives shall choose immediately, by ballot, the

398

President. But in choosing the President, the votes shall be taken by states,
the representation from each state having one vote. . . .

From the Constitution of the United States, Article II,
Section 1, as amended by the 12th Amendment [1]

Several alternative methods of selecting men to fill the office of
President of the United States were considered by the delegates to
the Constitutional Convention before they settled on the procedure
set down in Article II, Section 1. One was to have the chief executive
chosen by the Congress. If the framers of the Constitution wanted a
separation of powers system, however, this first alternative was hardly
satisfactory. To make the President dependent upon and an agent of
the Congress would strengthen too much the legislative branch at the
expense of executive power. Although legislative supremacy had been
popular immediately after the break with England, by 1787 " radical " and " inflationist-minded " state governments with strong legislatures and weak governors had frightened the groups which were
most strongly in favor of a new national constitution.

Also discussed was the possibility of electing the President by
direct popular vote. To this proposal many objections were also
raised. One was the fear of " democratic passions." Another came
from small state delegates who tended to feel that large states would
cast such a great proportion of the total popular Presidential votes
that the small states would have almost no voice in selecting the chief
executive. A third proposal — to have the President elected by the
governors of the states — was objected to by the large states because,
in the opinion of large-state delegates, small states would have a
greater voice in the Presidential selection process than their populations warranted. And as the principle of separation of powers worked
against establishing a system through which Congress chose the President, so also the principle of federalism worked against giving governors that power. If power was to be counterbalanced with power,
the governors should not be able to control the President any more
than Congress should be able to control him.

The method of electing the President incorporated into Article
II, Section 1, was a compromise. For those who did not want election
by governors or by Congress and those who were afraid of direct

---

[1] The first two paragraphs above are from the original Article II, Section 1,
and the third paragraph is from the Twelfth Amendment.

popular election, there would be electors in each state, chosen in the manner prescribed by the respective state legislatures, who would function as deliberative bodies to vote for their choice. For the small states which wanted a larger voice in the Presidential selection process than they would be entitled to if the President were elected by popular votes, each state's representation in the Electoral College would be equal to the sum of the state's Senators and Representatives in Congress. Should no candidate receive an absolute majority of electoral votes, the decision would be made by the United States House of Representatives. But as a further concession to the small states, if the selection of a President did devolve on the House, each state's delegation in that body would have only one vote regardless of its population.

To the provisions of Article II, Section 1, must also be added three extraconstitutional developments which have tended to make the Presidential selection procedure what it is today.

(1) The first of these was the development of political parties. The intention of those who drafted the Constitution was that the electors chosen in each state would be able men of public affairs who would be named to exercise their independent judgment on the qualifications of the several candidates for the office of President. Yet within a few years political parties formed, the parties developed processes of agreeing upon a party ticket, and electors were committed at the time of their selection by the party to vote for the party nominee for President and Vice President. It is true that even today electors are not legally barred from exercising an independent judgment and that on occasion individual electors have not voted for the nominee to which they by party ties were bound, but so exceptional is the practice that it has been unimportant. A Republican elector is morally bound to vote the Republican ticket and a Democratic elector is likewise morally bound to vote for his party's nominees for President and Vice President. A Presidential election is, therefore, a contest between major parties to see which can obtain an absolute majority of electoral votes.

(2) Article II, Section 1, left the manner in which Presidential electors should be chosen up to the discretion of the several state legislatures. Until 1820 state legislatures generally performed this function themselves. During the next decade, however, the trend was away from legislative election toward popular election.[2] The latter is

---

[2] See page 245.

the universal practice today. The appeal of the political party is, therefore, directed to the several state electorates — a problem quite different from that of the period when electors were chosen by state legislators.

(3) A third extraconstitutional development which has great significance for the parties in their attempts to elect a President is the general practice in the states of awarding all the electoral votes in any state to the party ticket which polls the greatest number of popular votes in a Presidential election. Though major party strength in a state may be split 50.1 percent to 49.9 percent, the winner takes all. If a state is large and doubtful like New York with its block of 45 electoral votes, the prize of victory or the consequence of defeat in such a state becomes so significant to the major parties that they must devote their maximum efforts toward winning them.

In a close Presidential election the entire result may pivot on a few votes in a big state. Such was the case in the classic example of the New York campaign between James G. Blaine (Maine), the Republican nominee for President in 1884, and Grover Cleveland (New York), Blaine's opponent. Although Blaine had lost an unknown number of Republican Mugwumps who had bolted their party when he was nominated, as the campaign developed it appeared that the Mugwump defection would be more than offset by what seemed to be a shift of the traditionally Democratic Irish swinging away from Cleveland to Blaine. The Republican nominee was part Irish. His mother was a Catholic. Blaine as Secretary of State had pleased the Irish by twisting the British lion's tail.

However, a week before the election a freakish political incident removed the hand of destiny from Blaine's shoulder. By chance, late afternoon on October 29, 1884, a delegation of Protestant clergymen called at the Fifth Avenue Hotel where the Republican nominee was staying. The tired Mr. Blaine, standing at the head of the lobby stairs, received the group. By chance, the speech of the Reverend Dr. Samuel D. Burchard, a Presbyterian minister, contained these words: " We are Republicans and don't propose to leave our party and identify ourselves with the party whose antecedents have been rum, Romanism, and rebellion. We are loyal to our party, we are loyal to you." By chance a reporter caught and realized the significance of those two sentences. By chance Blaine was thinking of other things and did not hear or choose to repudiate them.[3] With the publication

[3] From Charles Edward Russell, *Blaine of Maine* (New York: Cosmopolitan Book Corporation, 1932), pp. 399–402.

of the next morning's papers the damage had been done. Catholics turned back to the Democratic nominee. Cleveland carried New York by a narrow 1,040 votes; the Presidential election did pivot on New York; and Cleveland was elected.

In 1916 Republican nominee for the Presidency Charles Evans Hughes lost California by a 4,000-vote margin, perhaps because of his alleged slighting of Hiram Johnson, California's popular Progressive Republican Governor. With California going for Wilson, Hughes lost the election.[4] Most Presidential elections are not as close as those of 1884 and 1916 nor do their outcomes turn so sharply on one or a few connected incidents. Always, however, the total electoral votes of several big and doubtful states like New York, California, Illinois, Ohio, and Indiana can determine the outcome. With them all, a nominee is likely to win; with none of them he almost certainly loses. Only when the pivot states are split among themselves in the nominee they support will the issue be decided by combinations of smaller doubtful states.

The concern of the major parties for the pivot states is in part shown in the number of Presidential and Vice Presidential nominations which go to men from such states. Forty-two of the 52 Presidential and Vice Presidential candidates nominated by the two major parties have, in the 13 elections since 1901, come from 11 states which have had 15 or more electoral votes. New York has alone accounted for 15 of the 42, and Ohio and Indiana each for 6 more. Rare indeed is the Presidential election campaign that does not have a New Yorker participating as a nominee for President or Vice President. In 1904, 1940, and 1944 both Democratic and Republican nominees for the Presidency were from New York. California, Illinois, Kansas, Massachusetts, Missouri, Nebraska, New Jersey, and Alabama have contributed the rest of the nominees since 1900. Over the same period, the 11 most populous states have received over two thirds of all Cabinet appointments and over one half of the appointments to the United States Supreme Court.

No major party dare neglect the large and politically doubtful states. They are the principal key to understanding Presidential politics. To this key, however, must be added one other — the sectional characteristics of American voting behavior. Though the influence

---

[4] See Frederick M. Davenport, "Did Hughes Snub Johnson? — An Inside Story," *American Political Science Review* (April, 1949), Vol. 43, pp. 321–332.

of sectionalism in Presidential elections appears today to be declining, politics is not yet so nationalized that sectional clusters of electoral votes can be ignored. The sectional factor in Presidential elections will be discussed in a following section of this chapter after a state by state analysis of the major parties' Presidential election problems.

MILEAGE MAP TO THE WHITE HOUSE

Summarizing, the basic rules of Presidential election mathematics are these. First, Presidents are not elected by popular vote. Two of them, Rutherford Hayes in 1876 and Benjamin Harrison in 1888 got to the White House even though their popular vote totals were less than those of their opponents. Chief executives are elected by the Electoral College. Second, the number of electors allotted to each state is the sum of its Senators and Representatives in the Congress. Third, the Presidential nominee receiving the largest number of popular votes in a state, no matter how close is his margin of victory, wins all that state's electoral votes. Fourth, of the 531 electoral votes, a nominee needs an absolute majority of 266 for election.

Having noted the rules, the next step is to rank all the states in the order of their electoral vote power. A state's electoral votes will vary from decade to decade, depending upon the number of Congressmen assigned to it. The number of Congressmen, in turn, is based on the proportion of the nation's population residing in each state. Since 1912 Pennsylvania has lost six Congressmen and thus six electoral votes. On the opposite extreme, California over the same period has gained nineteen Congressmen and thus nineteen electoral votes. For the decade of the 1950's, each state's electoral votes are as shown in Figure 18 on page 404.

Note from Figure 18 that winning New York's 45 electoral votes is more important than the 44 vote combined total of the 12 smallest states of Nevada, Wyoming, Delaware, Vermont, New Hampshire, Idaho, Montana, North Dakota, South Dakota, New Mexico, Utah, and Arizona. To win California's 32 electoral votes is more necessary than the 27 vote combined total of the 5 next smallest states — Rhode Island, Maine, Colorado, Nebraska, and Oregon. Pennsylvania's 32 votes balance the 32 vote total of Kansas, Arkansas, West Virginia, and Connecticut. A nominee for the Presidency could gain a majority of 266 electoral votes, with 11 to spare, by capturing only the 12 largest of the 48 states.

Figure 18. Electoral Votes by States for Decade of 1950's

State	Electoral Votes		
N.Y.	45	---	
Calif.	32	-------------------------------	
Penna.	32	-------------------------------	
Ill.	27	--------------------------	
Ohio	25	------------------------	
Tex.	24	-----------------------	277 electoral votes
Mich.	20	--------------------	
N.J.	16	----------------	
Mass.	16	----------------	
N.C.	14	--------------	
Mo.	13	-------------	
Ind.	13	-------------	
Ga.	12	------------	
Wis.	12	------------	
Va.	12	------------	
Tenn.	11	-----------	
Ala.	11	-----------	
Minn.	11	-----------	
Ky.	10	----------	
La.	10	----------	
Fla.	10	----------	
Iowa	10	----------	
Wash.	9	---------	
Md.	9	---------	254 electoral votes
Okla.	8	--------	
Miss.	8	--------	
S.C.	8	--------	
Conn.	8	--------	
W.Va.	8	--------	
Ark.	8	--------	32 electoral votes
Kan.	8	--------	
Ore.	6	------	
Neb.	6	------	
Colo.	6	------	27 electoral votes
Me.	5	-----	
R.I.	4	----	
Ariz.	4	----	
Utah	4	----	
N.M.	4	----	
S.D.	4	----	
N.D.	4	----	
Mont.	4	----	44 electoral votes
Ida.	4	----	
N.H.	4	----	
Vt.	3	---	
Del.	3	---	
Wyo.	3	---	
Nev.	3	---	

Unless there is a Democratic landslide, however, after a mere listing of the 12 states with 13 or more electoral votes — New York, California, Pennsylvania, Illinois, Ohio, Texas, Michigan, New Jersey, Massachusetts, North Carolina, Missouri, and Indiana — it is readily apparent that their records in the past suggest they are not likely to all give their electoral votes to the same Presidential nominee. Here is a fact which leads the major party strategist to still another analysis step in which he examines the voting records of the states and classifies them into " safe Democratic," " tending Democratic," " doubtful," " tending Republican," and " safe Republican " categories. Figure 19 adds a political dimension to the mileage map to the White House, and working from the table it is possible to still further narrow down the Presidential election problems of the major parties. (See page 406.)

The ten states at the top of Figure 19 make up the Solid Democratic South. Only twice since federal troops were withdrawn from the Confederacy has the Republican party been able to penetrate this Democratic heartland. The first Republican success in 1928 was clearly transitory. When the Protestant and dry South was faced in that year with the alternative of voting for the Catholic and wet Alfred E. Smith or deserting the Democratic tradition of its fathers, Florida, North Carolina, Texas, and Virginia chose the latter course. In 1932 with the Protestant Franklin D. Roosevelt the South could overlook his wet orientation, and immediately the Democratic curtain was drawn tightly to shut out the Republicans again.

Except for 1928, the only other Republican success in the South was in 1952. Eisenhower duplicated Hoover's southern state electoral vote feat and captured Florida, Texas, and Virginia. The penetration elsewhere in the South was deep. In South Carolina the Republican nominee received 49 percent of the two-party vote; in Louisiana, 47 percent; in Arkansas, 44 percent; and in Mississippi, 40 percent. How surprising was this showing may be seen by contrasting the Solid Democratic South Republican percentage of the two-party vote for the 1900 through 1948 period with the percentage in 1952 in Figure 19, and in none of the southern states is this shift of votes more dramatically illustrated than in Mississippi and South Carolina.

Can Republicans hold their 1952 level of strength in the South when a man such as Dwight D. Eisenhower is no longer the Republican nominee? Here is a question which no politician can today an-

Figure 19. Average Republican Percentage of the Two-Party Vote by States in Presidential Elections, 1900–1952

State	Electoral Votes	1900–1948	1932–1948	1952	
Miss.	8	8	3	40	
S.C.	8	12	3	49	
La.	10	18	14	47	
Ga.	12	20	13	30	
Tex.	24	23	17	54	Safe Democratic
Ala.	11	24	16	36	117 electoral votes
Fla.	10	29	28	55	
Ark.	8	30	21	44	
Va.	12	37	34	57	
N.C.	14	37	30	54	
Ariz.	4	41	36	58	
Tenn.	11	42	35	50	Tending Democratic
Okla.	8	43	37	58	36 electoral votes
Nev.	3	45	38	60	
Ky.	10	46	42	50	
N.M.	4	47	41	56	
Md.	9	47	43	56	
Mo.	13	47	42	51	Doubtful Democratic
Mont.	4	48	39	60	42 electoral votes
W.Va.	8	49	43	48	
Utah	4	49	39	56	
Colo.	6	51	47	61	
Calif.	32	51	41	57	
Ind.	13	51	48	59	Doubtful Republican
Del.	3	52	47	52	128 electoral votes
R.I.	4	52	43	51	
N.Y.	45	53	45	57	
Ohio	25	53	47	57	
Ida.	4	54	43	66	
Neb.	6	54	49	69	
Minn.	11	54	41	56	80 electoral votes
N.J.	16	54	48	58	
Mass.	16	54	46	54	
Ill.	27	54	46	55	
N.H.	4	55	49	69	Tending Republican
Ore.	6	55	43	60	200 electoral votes
Wash.	9	55	39	55	
Wyo.	3	55	45	63	
Conn.	8	55	47	56	68 electoral votes
S.D.	4	55	49	69	
Wis.	12	55	43	62	
Ia.	10	56	48	65	
Kan.	8	57	53	70	
N.D.	4	57	49	71	
Penna.	32	58	48	53	52 electoral votes
Mich.	20	59	47	56	
Me.	5	59	55	66	Safe Republican
Vt.	3	56	58	71	8 electoral votes

Note: Arranged in the order of Republican percentage of the two-party vote averaged over the 1900 through 1948 period. Vermont at bottom is placed out of order for classification with Maine.

swer. Great economic and social changes are taking place in this section which to Republicans in the past has been forbidden land. Sometime in the future, no doubt, the South may become a two-party area, but how fast such a development will take place can only be a matter of speculation. Though Republicans in 1952 showed surprising strength in the Presidential election, the penetration has not been great in elections for other partisan offices. The political effects of the United States Supreme Court's school desegregation decision are still to be measured. Under " ordinary " circumstances and with " ordinary " candidates, for the immediate future realistic Republican Presidential campaign planners still have no sound basis for assuming the Republicans can in 1956 and 1960 make significant inroads into the Solid Democratic South's block of 117 electoral votes.[5]

Looking to the opposite end of the Figure 19 scale, " safe " Republican states are notable not for their numbers or their electoral votes, but only because there are almost no " safe " Republican states left. Only Maine and Vermont, with 8 electoral votes between them, have steadfastly stood by Republican nominees in Presidential elections. Once all 6 New England states — Connecticut, Maine, Massachusetts, New Hampshire, Rhode Island, and Vermont with a total of 40 electoral votes — were solidly Republican, but the Republican spell over that section was broken in 1928 when Massachusetts and Rhode Island were the first to desert to Alfred E. Smith.

Though in 1952 all the New England states gave their electoral votes to Eisenhower, Massachusetts and Rhode Island went Democratic in the 5 Presidential elections from 1928 through 1948 and Connecticut and New Hampshire went Democratic in 1936, 1940, and 1944. In 1954 even Maine exhibited a tendency in the Democratic direction with the election of a Democratic governor and with substantial reductions from the previous elections in the margins by which 2 of its 3 Republican Congressmen were re-elected. On the basis of the 1900 to 1952 record, however, both Maine and Vermont must still be classified as " safe " Republican states in Presidential elections.

Assuming a strong tendency for the Solid Democratic South with

---

[5] See Alexander Heard, *A Two Party South?* (Chapel Hill, N. C.: The University of North Carolina Press, 1952) ; V. O. Key, Jr., *Southern Politics* (New York: Alfred A. Knopf, Inc., 1949) ; J. B. Shannon, *Toward a New Politics in the South* (Knoxville, Tenn.: University of Tennessee Press, 1949) ; and numerous articles on the subject.

its 117 electoral votes to go Democratic and for Maine and Vermont
with their 8 electoral votes to go Republican, the battleground for
the two major parties lies in the 36 states with 406 electoral votes
lying between the two " safe " Democratic and Republican extremes.

The Chicago Sun-Times

'Margaret—Thank God YOU'RE Safe!'

Republicans, to win a majority in the Electoral College, need 258
of those votes; Democrats, only 147.

If the remaining states which have over the 1900–1948 period
given Republicans less than 50 percent of the two-party vote — Arizona, Tennessee, Oklahoma, Nevada, Kentucky, New Mexico, Maryland, Missouri, Montana, West Virginia, and Utah — go Democratic,
the Democratic nominee gains an extra 78 electoral votes to swell his

total to 195. He then would need only 71 more electoral votes for his Electoral College majority, and New York and California alone with their combined total of 77 electoral votes would insure his victory. Such are the heavy odds stacked against a Republican Presidential nominee before he begins his campaign — provided the " tending Democratic " and " doubtful Democratic " states do vote Democratic.

Of the 5 states classified as " tending Democratic " in Figure 19, for the 1900 through 1948 period, Oklahoma went Democratic in Presidential elections except for 1920 and 1928; Tennessee, except for 1920 and 1948; Kentucky, except for 1924 and 1928; Arizona (participating in its first Presidential election in 1912), except for 1920, 1924, and 1928; and Nevada, except for the same years as Arizona. Eisenhower carried Arizona, Oklahoma, and Nevada in 1952 by substantial margins, and he won a close contest in Tennessee and lost a close contest in Kentucky. Except for 1952, however, the tendency of these 5 states in Presidential elections has been Democratic.

All of the 5 states except Nevada have Democratic governors.[6] Both United States Senators in Kentucky, Nevada, Oklahoma, and Tennessee are Democratic. In the United States House of Representatives all 9 of Tennessee's Congressmen, 6 of Oklahoma's 7 Congressmen, and 7 of Kentucky's 8 Congressmen are Democratic. Except for Nevada, where the state senate is Republican and the assembly Democratic, the other 5 state legislatures are overwhelmingly Democratic. Though Arizona elected a Republican governor in 1952, a Democrat replaced him in 1954, and further increased were the already very large Democratic majorities in both houses of the Arizona legislature. Only Nevada of the 5 " tending Democratic " states appears moving toward the Republican party with a Republican governor, a Republican state senate, one Republican United States Senator and its one Congressman a Republican. Except for Nevada's 3 electoral votes of the " tending Democratic " 36 electoral vote total, the Democratic nominee for President can be assumed to start with a very substantial advantage.

---

[6] Where in this section a state is said to have Republican or Democratic governors, United States Senators, Congressmen, and state legislatures, the date for which the statement is made is for January, 1955. Principal source of these data, and particularly for statistics showing Republican and Democratic gains or losses in state legislatures in 1954, was the *Congressional Quarterly Weekly Report,* March 18, 1955, pp. 268–272. See also *The Book Of The States Supplement January, 1955* (Chicago: The Council of State Governments, 1955).

Of the 6 states classified as " doubtful Democratic " in Figure 19 — New Mexico, Maryland, Missouri, Montana, West Virginia, and Utah — all went Republican in 1920, 1924, and 1928, and likewise all went Democratic from 1932 through 1948. Eisenhower carried all but West Virginia in 1952. Here in these states Republican prospects in Presidential elections are brighter than in the " tending Democratic " states and much brighter than in the " safe Democratic " states. When one examines the party affiliation of other partisanly elected officials in these states, however, there is relatively little comfort in the result for Republicans.

West Virginia which voted for Stevenson in 1952 has a Democratic governor, Democratic United States Senators, its entire House delegation of 6 is Democratic, both houses of the state legislature are overwhelmingly Democratic, and in 1954 Democrats gained 9 state lower house seats and 1 state senate seat. New Mexico is in a similar category except that it has only 2 House seats. In 1954 in the New Mexico legislature, Democrats reduced Republican strength in the lower house from 28 to 4, out of a total of 55 seats. Missouri has a Democratic governor, Democratic United States Senators and 9 of 11 House seats are Democratic. The lower house of its state legislature has 61 Republicans and 96 Democrats, a Democratic increase of 24 seats over 1953, and 15 Republican and 19 Democratic state senate seats. Montana has a Republican governor and 1 of its 2 Congressmen is Republican, but its United States Senators are Democratic. In 1954 Democrats gained 17 lower house seats in the Montana legislature to win a majority, and 3 seats in a still Republican-controlled state senate (33 to 23).

As Nevada was the Democratic soft spot in the " tending Democratic " states, so Maryland and Utah are soft Democratic spots in the " doubtful Democratic " states. Together they account for 13 of the 42 " doubtful Democratic " state electoral votes. Both Maryland and Utah have Republican governors and United States Senators. Utah's 2 Congressmen are Republicans and 3 of Maryland's 7 Congressmen are Republicans. Republicans control both houses of the Utah state legislature, though that party's margin in the lower house is only 32 to 28, and Democrats gained 6 seats and Republicans lost 6 in 1954. Democrats are overwhelmingly in control of Maryland's legislature, and that party took from Republicans 11 lower house and 4 upper house seats in 1954.

Of particular significance in these 6 states in the 1954 elections is the fact that Democrats won a total of 71 lower house seats from Republicans. Democrats also captured 8 state senators from Republicans. Only Republican state legislative gain was a single state senate seat in Utah.

Proceed on Figure 19 now from the states which have from 1900 through 1948 given the Republican Presidential nominee less than 50 percent of the two-party vote to an examination of the " tending Republican " and " doubtful Republican " states. After Maine and Vermont, which states can the Republican nominee feel quite sure might go his way in a Presidential election? The figure shows that he might have a right to expect to count on both Michigan and Pennsylvania with their very sizable combined total of 52 electoral votes. Michigan ranks with Maine in the percentage of the two-party vote which it has given to Republican nominees from 1900 through 1948. Pennsylvania, it should also be noted, is only 1 percentage point behind Maine and Michigan and is 2 percentage points ahead of Vermont. Yet it may also be significant that Michigan and Pennsylvania were 2 of the 3 states in which the 1952 Republican percentage of the two-party Presidential vote was less than the average Republican percentage support from 1900 through 1948.

Recent political developments not evident in Figure 19 suggest that both Michigan and Pennsylvania may be undergoing a rapid change from what was once almost " safe Republican " status to a very doubtful type of political complexion which may henceforth make them pivot states. In 1954 Democrats, in a major upset, captured the governor's office in Pennsylvania; and in just as much of an upset, a United States Senate seat from Michigan's Homer Ferguson, chairman of the Senate Republican Policy Committee in the Eighty-third Congress.

Not even at the height of the Franklin D. Roosevelt tide in the early 1930's had Democrats come as close to capturing the entire Pennsylvania state government as they did in 1954. With the Democratic governor came a gain of 14 seats in the Pennsylvania legislature's lower house to give Democrats control (112 to 98). Five Republican state senate seats were also lost to Democrats to bring the Republican majority in the upper house down to a close 27 to 23 differential. Democrats gained 3 Congressmen to bring their total in the 30-man House delegation to 9. Three years before Democrats had broken a 67-year Republican succession of Philadelphia mayors.

In Michigan in 1954 Governor G. Mennen Williams won his

fourth term with a solid 55.6 percent of the two-party vote. One of the 14 outstate Republican Congressmen was replaced by a Democrat, and all 6 Congressmen from Wayne County (Detroit) are Democrats. In the lower house of the Michigan state legislature, the Republican margin of control was down to 59 to 51. The Democrats had captured 17 seats from the Republicans. Although Republican control of the state senate is 23 to 11, Democrats increased their strength here by 3 in 1954. In 1955 Democrats made striking gains in judicial and minor state office contests.

Even though recent political trends in Michigan and Pennsylvania make their classification as almost " safe Republican " states perhaps an incorrect one, assume for the purposes of developing the Republican problem that they do give their electoral votes to the Republican nominee for President. The Republican party would then have a total, including Maine and Vermont, of 60 electoral votes, with 206 yet to go for an Electoral College majority.

Sixty-eight of those 206 electoral votes still necessary for a Republican nominee might come from the group of 10 relatively small " tending Republican " states of North Dakota, Kansas, Iowa, Wisconsin, South Dakota, Connecticut, Wyoming, Washington, Oregon, and New Hampshire. Of the 10, North Dakota, Kansas and South Dakota, representing a total of 16 electoral votes, are the most strongly Republican. Except for 1932 and 1936, these states have voted for Republican Presidential nominees since 1920. The United States Senators and Congressmen from them are Republicans. They have Republican governors and large Republican state legislative majorities. However, even in these states, Democrats gained 22 state legislative seats in South Dakota, 16 lower house seats in Kansas with no state senate election in 1954, and 2 legislative seats in North Dakota.

Next strongest in their Republican affiliation of these 10 states are New Hampshire and Iowa, representing 14 electoral votes. Their United States Senators, Congressmen, governors, and both houses of their state legislatures are Republican. Disquieting to Republicans as they contemplate Iowa, however, are the facts that this traditionally Republican state went Democratic in the Presidential election of 1948, Iowa's Republican governor was elected in 1954 by only a 51.4 percent of the two-party vote, and Democrats picked up 17 state legislative seats in the latter year.

Further graduating the Republican quality of these 10 states,

Wisconsin and Wyoming with their combined total of 15 electoral votes might be ranked in a category third removed from North Dakota, Kansas, and South Dakota. Both states have been Republican in Presidential elections since 1920 except for 1932, 1936, 1940, and 1948. Both states have Republican governors, though in 1954 Wisconsin's was elected with 51.5 percent of the two-party vote and Wyoming's with 50.5 percent. The 7 Wisconsin Congressmen are Republicans as is Wyoming's lone Congressman. Though Republican state legislative majorities in both states are large, Democrats gained 13 legislative seats in Wisconsin and 15 in Wyoming in 1954.

Least Republican in tendency of these 10 states are Connecticut, Washington, and Oregon, representing 25 electoral votes. All voted for Democratic Presidential nominees from 1932 through 1944, and Washington went Democratic also in 1948. Connecticut's governor is a Democrat, and Oregon's and Washington's United States Senators are Democrats. Republicans have all except 1 of the Congressmen from each of the 3 states. Of the 3 states, only Oregon's state legislature has Republican control in both houses, but even here in 1954 Democrats gained 14 lower house seats and 2 state senate seats from Republicans. Washington's lower house has 50 Democrats and 49 Republicans, with 9 of the Democratic seats picked up in 1954; and its state senate has 24 Republicans and 22 Democrats, with 2 Democrats gained in 1954. Connecticut's upper house has 20 Democrats and 16 Republicans, with 6 Democratic seats won from Republicans in 1954; and though Republican control of the lower house is substantial, 36 seats were taken from Republicans in 1954.

In a closely contested Presidential election at least Connecticut, Washington, and Oregon of these 10 " tending Republican " states might now be doubtful. Assume, however, that all do return Republican Presidential majorities and 68 electoral votes are added to the Republican column. The Republican nominee's cumulative total of electoral votes would now be 128, with 138 more needed to reach the 266 mark. He will, before reaching this point, have already had to work to win those 128 electoral votes — only 11 more than the Solid Democratic South's 117 electoral vote gift to the Democratic nominee at the time of the latter's nomination. From now on, however, the Republican road to the White House becomes a steeper grade.

Still in the " tending Republican " classification of states in Figure 19, proceed now to Illinois, Massachusetts, New Jersey, Minnesota, Nebraska, and Idaho. Here are 6 states which together have 80 electoral votes, and of particular importance to the Republican party are the first 4 which have 11 or more electoral votes. Of this group of 6 states, Nebraska and Idaho (total of 10 electoral votes) are the strongest Republican. The former cast its electoral votes for Franklin D. Roosevelt only in 1932 and 1936, and the latter from 1932 through 1940. The United States Senators from the 2 states are Republican, as are the governors. Nebraska's 4 Congressmen are Republican and 1 of Idaho's 2 Congressmen is a Republican. Nebraska's state legislature is nonpartisan. Idaho's state senate has 24 Republicans and 20 Democrats, with 9 of those Democratic seats gained in 1954; and its lower house has 36 Republicans to 23 Democrats, with 9 of the Democratic seats also added in 1954.

Republican prospects in Illinois, Massachusetts, New Jersey, and Minnesota are much less bright. With the exception of New Jersey's going Republican in the Presidential election of 1948, the 4 states voted 4 times for Franklin D. Roosevelt and once for Truman. All 4 had been almost solidly Republican in Presidential elections before 1932. Although New Jersey has 2 Republican United States Senators, 6 of its 14 Congressmen are Democratic, and it has a Democratic governor. Both houses of the New Jersey legislature are strongly Republican, and there were no state legislative elections in 1954. The Illinois United States Senate delegation has 1 Republican and 1 Democrat, 12 of its 25 Congressmen are Democratic. Its state legislature is Republican, though the margin of control in the lower house is only 78 to 74. Democrats in 1954 gained 7 lower house seats and 6 state senate seats. Although Massachusetts has a Republican governor, 1 of its United States Senators and 7 of its 14 Congressmen are Democrats. The lower house of the Massachusetts state legislature has 127 Democrats and 112 Republicans, with Democrats gaining 10 seats in 1954; and its upper house has 21 Republicans and 19 Democrats, with Democrats adding 4 seats in 1954. Minnesota's United States Senate delegation is also split; it has a Democratic governor; 5 of its 9 Congressmen are Democrats and in its nonpartisan state legislature the Democratic caucus in the lower house has organized that body in 1955 for the first time since 1937.

In Illinois, Massachusetts, New Jersey, and Minnesota with their total of 70 electoral votes, recent political trends make it appear that Republican Presidential nominees might have a difficult time in capturing them. Should all give their electoral votes to the Republican nominee, however, he would now have accumulated a total of

208 electoral votes. Fifty-eight more would be necessary to reach his Electoral College minimum target of 266 electoral votes.

Continuing the analysis from Figure 19, the Republican Presidential election problem is further developed by examining the 7 states in the " doubtful Republican " category. They are Ohio, New York, Rhode Island, Delaware, Indiana, California, and Colorado. Three of these states — Rhode Island, Delaware, and Colorado — are small and together have only 13 of the 7 states' 128 electoral votes. Rhode Island has voted Democratic in Presidential elections since 1932, except for 1948 and 1952; Delaware, Democratic since 1936, except for the same 2 years; and Colorado, Democratic since 1932, except for 1940 and 1952. Rhode Island's governor, 2 Congressmen, United States Senators and lower house of the state legislature are Democratic, while its state senate balances on a 22 to 22 major party tie. Democrats in 1954 gained 13 Rhode Island state legislative seats from Republicans. Though Delaware has a Republican governor, its United States Senate delegation is split, its sole Congressman is a Democrat and both houses of the state legislature are strongly Democratic. Delaware Democrats in 1954 gained 13 state legislative seats from Republicans. Colorado appears more hopeful to Republicans with its United States Senators, 2 of 4 Congressmen and both houses of the state legislature Republican. However, it has a Democratic governor and Democrats won 11 state legislative seats in 1954.

Should all the " safe Republican " and " tending Republican " states and Rhode Island, Delaware, and Colorado go Republican in a Presidential election, the Republican nominee would now need 45 more electoral votes from New York or some combination of Ohio, California, and Indiana. Of these large and doubtful states, Indiana with its 13 electoral votes might be the most likely Republican prospect. Except for casting its electoral votes for Theodore Roosevelt in 1912 and for Franklin D. Roosevelt in 1932 and 1936, it has been Republican in Presidential elections since 1900. Its United States Senators, 9 of 11 Congressmen, governor, and both houses of the state legislature are Republican. Democrats, however, did take 22 state legislative seats from Indiana Republicans in 1954.

California would appear the next most favorable state to a Republican nominee, and with its 32 electoral votes added to the 13 of Indiana the Republican party would have its 266 necessary electoral votes. Except for 1912 and 1916, California was Republican in Presidential elections from 1900 through 1928, and has been Democratic from 1932 through 1948. Its United States Senators, 19 of 30 Congressmen, governor, and both houses of the state legislature are Republican. California's party registration is 3 to 2 Democratic, however, and in 1954 Democrats gained 13 state legislative seats from Republicans.

Of the " doubtful Republican " states, Ohio with its 25 electoral votes and New York with its 45 electoral votes would, if they too went Republican, be enough to counterbalance Democratic wins in several of the smaller states which have from 1900 through 1948 given the Republican nominee 51 percent or more of the two-party vote. Ohio and New York are both doubtful and pivot states, and their position here suggests why both have been " mother of Presidential nominee " states. Except for 1912 and 1916, Ohio went Republican from 1900 through 1928, and it has been Democratic from 1932 except for 1944 — with Ohio's Bricker the Republican Vice Presidential nominee — and 1952. New York was Republican from 1900 through 1928 except for 1912, and has been Democratic since, except for 1948 and 1952. Both states have Democratic governors and Republican-controlled state legislatures. Seventeen of Ohio's 23 Congressmen and its United States Senators are Republican, and 26 of New York's 43 Congressmen and 1 of its United States Senators are Republican. In 1954 Democrats gained 15 seats in the Ohio legislature and 13 in the New York legislature.

Short of a radical realignment of Democratic and Republican party strength with Republicans winning states which have been " doubtful," " tending," or " safe " Democratic, the above outline of the respective Presidential election problems of the two major parties will continue to be substantially valid. Following are three of the most important summary observations from the analysis of Figure 19.

(1) Of the states giving the Republican party *less* than 50 percent of the two-party vote from 1900 to 1948, those with the most electoral votes are " safe Democratic " and those with the least electoral votes are " tending Democratic " or " doubtful Democratic." Of the states giving the Republican party *more* than 50 percent of the two-party vote for the same period, the most strongly Republican states are weak in electoral vote strength while the largest " tending Republican " and the large " doubtful Republican " states have great Electoral College power. Here is a Democratic advantage and a Republican disadvantage.

(2) Since 1932 the Democratic party has very substantially undermined Republican strength in many states which once qualified for the title of " Republican states." Recent political developments appear to be a continuation of a rising Democratic power curve in spite of the Eisenhower victory in 1952. Of special significance may be the evidences of Democratic trends in the 1954 state legislative elections. In only 3 state senates that year did Republicans capture a single seat from Democrats; while Democrats won 106 state senate seats from Republicans; in only 2 state lower houses did Republicans gain a single seat, while Democrats won 439 lower house seats from Republicans. Should the Democratic successes in state legislative elections continue in such a proportion to give that party control of many previously Republican-controlled state legislatures by the 1961 reapportionment of United States House of Representative seats, Democrats could destroy many an incumbent Republican Congressman or his district by a Democratic rather than a Republican redrawing of Congressional districts.

(3) The large and doubtful states of New York, California, Indiana, Ohio, Illinois, New Jersey, Massachusetts, Missouri, Minnesota, and perhaps Pennsylvania and Michigan are important to the Democratic party but they are absolutely essential to the Republican party. The Democratic nominee may reach the White House with only a few of these states if the Democratic state voting patterns on Figure 19 continue to hold in the future. The Republican nominee's road to the White House, however, cannot detour around but has to go through these large and doubtful states.

THE PIVOT STATES MORE CLOSELY EXAMINED

Because of the importance of the eleven large and politically doubtful states listed in the preceding paragraph, several of their political characteristics should be further developed and examined with the states placed in relation to one another. Figure 20 shows how the 11 states reacted to the political appeal of Franklin D. Roosevelt and Harry S. Truman and contrasts that political behavior with their 1952 and pre-1932 voting in Presidential elections. California, Illinois, Massachusetts, Missouri, and Minnesota gave their electoral votes 5 times in the 5 elections from 1932 through 1948 to the Democratic nominee; New York and Ohio, 4 times; and Pennsylvania and Michigan, 3 times. Only Indiana reverted to its Republican ways in

1940 with Hoosier Wendell Willkie as the Republican nominee and has been Republican since.

All 11 states voted for Eisenhower in 1952. Five also went for Dewey in 1948. Do these facts signify that the 11 states have cast off the Democratic habits they learned during the New Deal era and are ready to support a new era of Republican supremacy?

Though President Eisenhower won an Electoral College landslide in 1952, Republicans gained control of the Eighty-third Congress by a margin of only one seat in the United States Senate and

Figure 20. Political Behavior of Eleven Large and Doubtful States in Presidential Elections from 1900 through 1952

State	Electoral Votes	1900	'04	'08	'12	'16	'20	'24	'28	'32	'36	'40	'44	'48	'52
N.Y.	45	–––––––––				–––––––––									–––
Calif.	32	–––––––––		(P)		–––––––––									–––
Penna.	32	–––––––––		(P)		–––––––––––––––									–––
Ill.	27	–––––––––				–––––––––									–––
Ohio	25	–––––––––				–––––––––							–––		–––
Mich.	20	–––––––––		(P)		–––––––––						–––			–––
N.J.	16	–––––––––				–––––––––									–––
Mass.	16	–––––––––				––––––––									–––
Ind.	13	–––––––––				–––––––––						–––––––––––––			
Mo.	13	––––––				–––––––––									–––
Minn.	11	––––––––		(P)		–––––––––									–––

Note: (P) Theodore Roosevelt, Progressive.
Line means state went Republican; if blank, Democratic.

only 11 seats in the House. By the end of the Eighty-third Congress, the Senate Republican majority had evaporated and in the House it had fallen to 3 seats. In 1954 Republicans lost control of the Senate by 1 vote and the House by 29. The real significance of the Congressional elections of 1954 for both of the major parties, however, lies in the identification of the states in which Democrats registered their strongest advances — namely, in these 11 states.

There were United States Senate contests in 7 of the 11 states in 1954. Liberal Democrats Paul H. Douglas of Illinois and Hubert H. Humphrey of Minnesota were re-elected by large majorities. In Michigan, Democrat Patrick McNamara, literally a political unknown substituting for ex-United States Senator Blair Moody who died during the campaign, narrowly defeated Republican Senator Homer Ferguson. Ohio, New Jersey, and Massachusetts elected Republicans, but by close to extremely close margins. Only in California did the 1954 Republican United States Senate nominee gain election by a politically respectable majority. Of the 22 seats lost by Republicans in the United States House of Representatives in 1954, 16 of those losses came from these 11 states — 3 each in Pennsylvania and Illinois, 2 each in Massachusetts, Michigan, and Missouri, and 1 each in Indiana, New York, Ohio, and Minnesota.

Democrats won 8 governors' offices from Republicans in 1953 or 1954, and 4 of the 8 came from New York, Pennsylvania, New Jersey, and Minnesota. Democratic governors were re-elected in Ohio and Michigan. Seven of the 11 states now have Democratic governors. Excluding Minnesota and New Jersey, the 9 remaining of the 11 states contributed 119 of the Democrats' 439 state legislative lower house 1954 gains. Thirty-five of the Democrats' 106 state senate seat gains came from these 9 states. The Pennsylvania lower house changed from Republican to Democratic control, and so did the lower house of Minnesota's " nonpartisan " legislature.

Another standard against which the political character of the 11 large and doubtful states can be measured is the type of Republican or Democrat electable in their state-wide elections. A rough classification of two main types of Republicans might be developed around the two Republican principals in an incident which took place in the United States Senate chamber during the summer of 1954. Senator Herman Welker of Idaho contemptuously called Senator Edward Thye of Minnesota a " pseudo-New Dealer " in an exchange that was not good-natured banter.[7] Welker tends to be isolationist in foreign affairs and would perhaps, if he were in a position to make the decision, repeal almost every major item of domestic New Deal legislation passed since March, 1933. Thye is collective-security minded in foreign affairs and is a " moderate progressive " or " dynamic conservative " in domestic affairs. Nor was the Welker-Thye incident an isolated or purely personal conflict within Republican ranks.

Two more illustrations might be cited to further sharpen the Republican classification. Earl Warren, Republican Governor of California when he campaigned in his state's 1952 Presidential preference primary, was opposed by some Republicans on the grounds that he had abandoned Republicanism and had embraced the objectives of the New Deal and that he was a Republican by registration only and his " true political stripe " ought to be exposed. Or, to go to an even further extreme, here are the words of one of the speakers at a 1954 dinner in New York to honor Roy Cohen on his departure

---

[7] *The Los Angeles Mirror-News* (Drew Pearson), June 16, 1954.

from the position of counsel for the McCarthy Committee: " Roy
Cohen and Joe McCarthy will be redeemed when the people have
taken back their government from the criminal alliance of Communists, Socialists, New Dealers and Eisenhower-Dewey Republicans." [8]

Should the " Eisenhower-Dewey Republicans," the " Warren
Republicans," and the " Thye Republicans " — all essentially representing one school of Republican party thought — be read out of the
Republican party by " 100-percent Republicans " of one variety or
another, almost the entire Republican strength in New York, California, Pennsylvania, Illinois, Ohio, Michigan, New Jersey, Massachusetts, and Minnesota might be destroyed. Revealing is the analysis of Senatorial support for President Eisenhower on a selected list
of " Eisenhower issues " in the first session of the Eighty-third Congress by the Congressional Quarterly News Service. Of the 12 Republican Senators giving Eisenhower less than 70 percent support, only
2 — Jenner of Indiana and Bricker of Ohio — came from these 11
states. On the other hand, Pennsylvania's Duff was 100 percent in his
Eisenhower support; New York's Ives, 94 percent; Massachusetts'
Saltonstall, 94 percent; California's Kuchel and Knowland, 91 and 87
percent, respectively; New Jersey's Smith and Hendrickson, 91 and
84 percent, respectively; Michigan's Potter and Ferguson, 89 and 81
percent, respectively; Ohio's Taft, before his death, 86 percent; Minnesota's Thye, 85 percent; Illinois' Dirksen, 83 percent. The Republican senators from these 11 states, except for Jenner, Bricker, Cape-
hart (Indiana, 72 percent), and sometimes Martin (Pennsylvania, 75
percent), are generally collective-security minded in international
affairs and are moderates on domestic matters.

Though the Herman Welkers of Idaho (4 electoral votes) may
mirror the political complexion of their own constituencies, those
whom Welker might call Republican " pseudo-New Dealers " have
been elected from states with a combined total of 200 or more electoral votes. Likewise, though a Republican Governor J. Bracken Lee
of Utah (4 electoral votes) may be able to gain re-election by advocating the abolition of the social security program or refusing to pay
income taxes because federal receipts are used for foreign aid, the
Thomas Deweys and Earl Warrens tend to be representative of the
types of Republican governors electable in the large and doubtful
states.

---

[8] *Time* (August 9, 1954), Vol. LXIV, No. 6, p. 15.

Something about the political characteristics of these 11 large and doubtful states is also to be learned from the type of Democrats elected by their state-wide electorates. As has been noted, 7 of the 11 governors are Democrats. They include Averill Harriman of New York, George M. Leader of Pennsylvania, Frank J. Lausche of Ohio, G. Mennen Williams of Michigan, Robert B. Meyner of New Jersey, Phil M. Donnelly of Missouri, and Orville Freeman of Minnesota. Seven of the 22 United States Senators from these states are presently Democrats — Lehman of New York, Douglas of Illinois, Kennedy of Massachusetts, McNamara of Michigan, Humphrey of Minnesota and Hennings and Symington of Missouri. Although these names represent gradations on a progressive-conservative scale, all tend to stand for collective security when they are called upon to make judgments on foreign affairs questions and all stand on the basics of New Deal philosophy, though on the latter point some are more forward-New Deal in their opinions and actions than others. Essentially, however, as the Republicans elected by state-wide elections in these 11 states tend to be moderate in their Republicanism, so do these Democrats tend to be moderate in their northern Democracy, as befits the political climate of the states from which they come.

Why in each of these 11 states have both Democrats and Republicans assumed the political colorations they have — with those of one party tending toward a general political philosophy which is not essentially dissimilar from the governors and Senators of the opposition party? Why also is there a striking similarity between the governors and Senators of both parties in these widely geographically disbursed states? In part the answer may be found in the trend away from sectionalism in American politics and the trend toward a nationalization of political issues.

SECTIONALISM IN PRESIDENTIAL ELECTIONS [9]

Sectional factors operating in Presidential elections have been implicit in the foregoing state-by-state analysis of the major parties' Presidential election problems. The " safe Democratic " states in Figure 19 lie within the boundaries of the South as shown in Figure 21. These 10 states, since the end of the reconstruction period, have been Democratic except for the defection of 4 of them in 1928 and

---

[9] For sectionalism as it is revealed in the Congress, see Chapter 16.

1952. Furthermore, they have represented the most solid political section with Democratic percentages of the two-party vote up to 60 percent or more. The race relations problem with its social and economic implications has tended more than any other factor to condition the political behavior of the South in favor of the Democratic party.

Figure 21

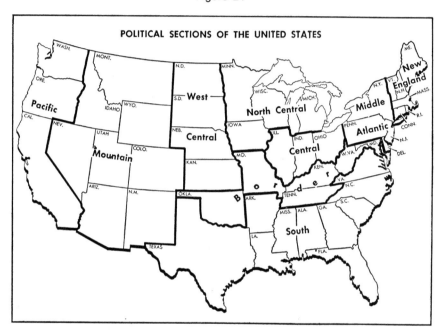

Almost as Democratic, and in large part for the same reasons, have been the 6 Border states. Tennessee, Oklahoma, and Kentucky of these 6 states are classified in Figure 19 as " tending Democratic; " and Maryland, Missouri, and West Virginia as " doubtful Democratic." The 5 remaining states which gave the Democratic party 51 percent or more of the two-party vote from 1900 through 1948 are Arizona, Nevada, New Mexico, Montana, and Utah — all Mountain states. Two factors contributing to these Mountain state Democratic tendencies are the following: (1), Arizona and New Mexico lie on the westward end of the South and have adopted many of the South's political thought patterns; and (2), Democrats with Bryan and their cry of " free silver " attracted the very substantial mining segments of the economies of these Mountain states.

The 10 states of the South, the 6 Border states and the above 5 Mountain states have been the states in which the Democrats since 1900 have been the strongest, and they do fit into a relatively compact sectional pattern. Except for the Mountain states, the primary interests of the Democratic states have been the following. First, there has been the desire to maintain white supremacy. Second, in order to maintain white supremacy and a share-cropping cotton agricultural economy, the South has stood for states' rights and against federal encroachment through regulation of elections or federal welfare programs. As industrialism in the South has increased and southern states have sought to lure northern industry by a cheaper labor market, there has also been the tendency to oppose federal government legislation sympathetic to organized labor. Third, the South has been a low-tariff section with its economy largely dependent on exports and without much manufacturing to protect.

How can the Democratic party continue to hold within its combination states with the interests of the South when Democratic administrations since 1932 have taken the lead in putting into effect or attempting to put into effect programs of the type which southerners tend to fear? Strains on the Democratic ties of the South were evident in 1948 when Louisiana, Mississippi, Alabama, and South Carolina voted for the Dixiecrat nominee, and again they were evident in 1952 with Eisenhower running only some 300,000 votes behind Stevenson in the Solid Democratic South states. On the other hand, Republicans have hardly scratched the surface of the Democratic power base in the South in state and local elections, nor have Republicans met with significant success in state and local elections in the Border states, with the exception of Maryland. Republican organizations in these states are still weak to nonexistent.

Perhaps the Republican party might hasten establishing itself in the South by attempting to go further in adapting its program to southern interests. Yet at some point in the making of concessions, the Republican party would find itself damaged in the remainder of the United States so no dramatic attempt of that party to cultivate the South at the expense of losing elsewhere seems worth the gamble.

If the South is to become a two-party section and if the Border states are to become doubtful to the extent that the Republican party has an equal chance with the Democratic party, the change is likely to be a long time in the coming. Alexander Heard in his *A Two-*

Party South? has given some of the reasons why this will be so. Young
voters are influenced by the traditional political affiliations of their
elders, and their elders have through their lifetimes been Democratic.
The economic and social changes now taking place which might pro-

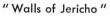

" Walls of Jericho "

duce a two-party South are yet only faintly discernible and are not
deeply felt. The entire southern political system has been constructed
to discourage building up the strength of a rival Republican party.
Republicans in southern state Republican organizations might lose
control of their patronage machines if the Republican party became
competitive with the Democratic party, and thus many such organization Republicans tend to resist a change. " Moreover, concern
about the social, economic, and political position of the Negro, the
twentieth-century form of the slavery issue, leads some southerners to

desire the maintenance of a political common front vis-a-vis the rest of the country." [10] Southern state Democratic members of Congress in powerful legislative positions and southern Senators with the filibuster can block national government programs even though a northern Democratic administration may be in control. Forces such as these suggest that the South and to a lesser degree perhaps the border states will tend to remain for the immediate future, at least, within the Democratic reservation.

Not as much can be said for the political stability of the once-strong Republican sections. The West Central section composed of North Dakota, South Dakota, Nebraska, and Kansas has been the only Republican sectional element as a whole to consistently vote for Republican nominees from 1940 through 1952. Once Republican New England is no longer a Republican sectional entity. The generally Republican North Central section of Minnesota, Wisconsin, Michigan, and Iowa has broken. Similarly has the political trend moved in the non-South and non-Border states. Where the South is one-party and much of Border state politics tends toward the one-party type, the old Republican sections now tend to be politically doubtful.

There remain sectional and subsectional interests, to be sure, but both major parties must compete in an attempt to work out appropriate balances between those interests. In the Pacific states, and particularly in Washington and Oregon, national resource, power, and reclamation policies tend to be very important. In the Mountain states mining, grazing, water, and federal land policies represent a sectional interest pattern. In the North Central, Central, and West Central sections there is a tendency for the rural elements in those states to judge a major party in large part on its farm programs and farm platform planks. In the Middle Atlantic section with its highly industrialized economic complexes in New York, Pennsylvania, New Jersey, and Delaware, and in all states where industrialism now represents a major proportion of economic activity, full employment, social security, and labor policies are the principal standards against which major parties are judged.

Arthur N. Holcombe, the foremost student of sectionalism in American politics, has concluded that sectional factors, though still important, are on the decline because the balance of political power in the United States outside the South has shifted from the country

---

[10] Heard, *op. cit.,* pp. 245–246.

to the cities and the interests of classes have become more significant to the voter than sectional interests. Where once the political parties would deal with states in sectional blocks in planning their Presidential campaigns, today the relatively uniform problems of the states with large urban populations have complicated the old and more simple type of sectional politics.[11]

Today it is becoming more important for the major parties to design program appeals which can reach across all sections — appeals directed to common problems in all sections. For the cities, full employment becomes the major domestic need; for the farms, a farm product price level to provide rural prosperity. Sometimes the city consumer and the farm producer will be in conflict, and when the friction produces political heat the major party's task will be to effect a more satisfactory compromise than the opposition major party. For both the city and the farm, in foreign affairs there is the need and desire for peace, and every test of majority opinion produces results which show that there is general agreement that peace can best be attained through collective security in military and economic foreign affairs policies.

Where the Democrats could win Presidential elections with that party's reservoir of southern state electoral votes plus a northern-city *or* perhaps even a northern-rural combination, the Republican party which is not yet competitive in the South needs both a northern-city *and* a northern-rural appeal, with the former becoming more important as the city balance of power becomes greater. Here is precisely the formula necessary for such states as New York, California, Pennsylvania, Illinois, Ohio, Michigan, New Jersey, Massachusetts, and Minnesota if the Republicans are to realistically entertain hopes of having a consistently good opportunity to win them. No longer can a state like Massachusetts be counted upon to vote Republican because of a New England sectional appeal as such, but rather its actions in Presidential elections will depend on how the major parties propose to solve Massachusetts' problems — problems similar with those of most of the larger states outside the South.

From 1860 to 1932 Republican power rested on a combination of West and East. Here was an alliance of the grain grower and manu-

---

[11] See Arthur N. Holcombe, *Our More Perfect Union* (Cambridge, Mass.: Harvard University Press, 1950), Chap. 3; *The Political Parties Today* (New York: Harper and Brothers, 1924); and *The New Party Politics* (New York: W. W. Norton and Company, 1933).

facturer, each selling primarily to a domestic market, and overlaying what both sections generally regarded as common economic interests was the memory of comradeship in arms in the fight to preserve the Union. Successful Republican Presidential nominees, who did not first gain the White House via the Vice Presidency by succeeding a President who died in office, came from the grain-growing states, with the tickets generally balanced by an eastern Vice Presidential nominee. In 1860 and 1864 it was Lincoln of Illinois; in 1868 and 1872, national hero Grant of Ohio; in 1876, Hayes of Ohio; in 1880, Benjamin Harrison of Indiana; in 1896 and 1900, McKinley of Ohio, to be succeeded by Vice President Theodore Roosevelt of New York; in 1908, Taft of Ohio; in 1920, Harding of Ohio, to be succeeded by Vice President Coolidge of Massachusetts; in 1928, Hoover of California, but born in Iowa; and in 1952, national hero Eisenhower of New York, but born in Texas and with roots in Kansas. Since 1940 it has been necessary for the Republican party to turn from midwest Republican organizations generally felt to represent Republican isolationism and often too strongly anti-New Deal to nominees from states like New York more in tune with the state-wide electorates of the large and doubtful states. Here is another measure of the transition which has taken place as a result of the rapidly increasing vote power of the large cities and the slippage from Republican status of a large percentage of farmers.

For the Democrats since the Civil War, the South has been the anchor sectional element along with the slightly less strong Democratic support given by the Border states. When Cleveland was able to win New York, New Jersey, and Connecticut in addition, Democrats won in 1884 and 1892. Bryan's appeal was primarily to the rural West and South, and at the time this combination proved inadequate to its purpose until the 1912 Republican split. During the 1920's, except for 1928, Democrats were driven back to the South. Beginning in 1928, that party began to show a majority — small at first — in the largest cities of the country. Democratic appeal since has been more class directed than sectional with only the South and sometimes the Border states retaining their sectional characteristics in the face of forces tending to lessen the old sectionalism elsewhere.

CHAPTER SIXTEEN

The Politics of Winning Congressional Majorities

Within the rims of at least one hundred congressional districts election hassles are so closely contested that they are actually decided — to use Pindar's apophthegm — " by the shade of a shadow." It is in these districts that we often find recounts and sometimes formally contested election cases that are ultimately decided by the House of Representatives. Here, again, we find the decisions being made at the ballot box that will entrust the legislative control of the Republic to one party or the other. For want of a better term, we may define these districts as marginal.

In general there are two schools of thought on the matter of a presidential candidate's influence over the success of his party's congressional ticket. One view — the so-called " coattail theory " — holds that the strong momentum generated by the presidential campaign along with the prestige of the presidential candidate helps to sweep into office a sizeable number of congressional candidates. Among the coattail clutchers opinion also divides. One group maintains that the additional interest accelerated by presidential campaigns is a more important element in the operation of the coattail theory than are the political appeal and interpersonal skills of the presidential candidate. At the other pole of coattail opinion we find those who stoutly proclaim that the number of congressmen who can ride into office on the President's coattails is dependent upon the personal charm of the presidential candidate.

Opposed to the coattail theory are the observers who feel that the presidential campaign has little to do with the number of congressmen elected by one party or the other. . . .

428

Another theory, though perhaps unlisted and one largely the concern of the practical politician, stresses the importance of minor candidates in helping the head of the ticket. Typical of the reasoning behind this theory is the reply of a Democratic candidate for the House of Representatives in New Jersey. Badly defeated and asked why he bothered to make the race in the first place, he said he had been beseeched to run by the state committee because it would help the presidential candidate, hence he had loyally submitted to the cause and filed his candidacy. And so the question of who helps whom seems to be a matter of endless debate.

Malcolm Moos [1]

Presidents are elected for four-year terms, Congressmen for two years and United States Senators for six. One third of the 96 Senate seats are regularly up for voter determination every two years. House members with the shortest terms are the most exposed to every political trend of the electorate. Only the more substantial and long-term trends can effect the over-all complexion of the Senate. Here was one of the forms through which the framers of the Constitution were able to insulate the elective organs of the national government from the " popular passions " of any particular election year.

For the entire House membership and the one third of Senators standing for election in a Presidential election year, national issues may have a direct bearing on all three types of contests. For Congressional election years when there is no Presidential campaign, local issues tend to be controlling.

A Presidential nominee must develop an appeal aimed at what he hopes will be a winning combination of sections and large and doubtful states. With this qualification, the Presidential nominee competes in a national election — the only national election. United States Senators have as their constituencies single states. Except for the few Congressmen elected at large, Congressmen have as their constituencies the even more homogeneous and smaller Congressional districts. The political pressure patterns which operate upon Presidential nominees are different from those operating on Senatorial or Congressional nominees. Likewise, the pressure patterns for the nominees in one state or Congressional district tend to be different from those of any other state or Congressional district.

---

[1] *Politics, Presidents and Coattails* (Baltimore: The Johns Hopkins Press, 1952), pp. 24 and 5–6. Reprinted by permission of The Johns Hopkins Press.

Figure 22. Democratic and Republican Margin of U. S. House of Representatives Control, 1861–1955

(In Number of Seats)

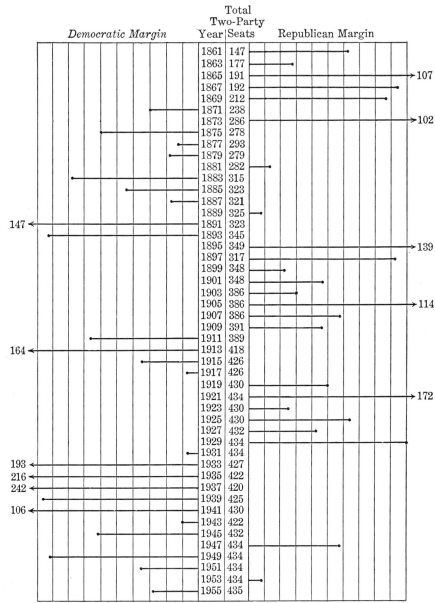

Source: U. S. Bureau of the Census, *Historical Statistics of the United States, 1789–1945* (Washington, D.C.: Government Printing Office, 1949), p. 293.

Though the problems of the major parties in winning Presidential elections are different from those in winning Congressional majorities, they are not unrelated. Here is one of the complexities which faces the major party strategist as he begins his Congressional campaign planning. Yet there are the results of researches available to make possible a generalized development of the Congressional election problem. What are the procedures followed by party strategists as they decide where to concentrate their campaign efforts and finances to win control of the House and Senate? What assistance does a Presidential nominee give to his Congressional ticket, or vice versa? It is questions such as these to which this chapter is directed.

Figure 22 illustrates the Democratic and Republican margin of United States House of Representatives control in number of seats in Congresses from 1861 through 1955. Several introductory observations may be made from that figure.

(1) Except for the post-Grant era and until McKinley, the party which has controlled the Presidency has generally controlled the House. In this period of even balance between the two major parties, though the Presidential election system worked to the advantage of Republicans, the sectional patterns influencing House elections advantaged the Democratic party. Whether party politics is today entering another such era, as some have suggested, only the results of future elections can tell.

(2) Except for 1878 and 1934, the party which controls the White House has lost seats in the Congressional election years when there was no Presidential contest. In 1870, 1882, 1890, 1894, 1910, 1918, 1930, 1946, and 1954 those in-party House seat losses were severe enough to throw the House to the opposition major party. Since 1900 and excepting 1934, the party with the President has lost an average of 45 seats in non-Presidential Congressional election years. The net decline of Republican House strength of sixteen seats in the 1954 election fit the trend pattern, though the Republican loss was the smallest suffered by the in-party in a non-Presidential election year since 1926.

(3) With two exceptions since 1888, the major party which has controlled the House in the biennium preceding a Presidential election has always elected its nominee for President. Those exceptions were 1948 and 1952. If the long-term trend holds in 1956, Democrats will win the Presidency. If it does not, another exception will be added to the 1948 and 1952 variations from the trend.

(4) Over the entire 1861 to 1955 period, Republican strength when that party has had a majority in the House has tended to decline, while Democratic strength when that party has been in the majority has tended to increase. Louis Bean's research has led him to this conclusion. Since the formation of the Republican party, that party has controlled the House over three extended periods of time — from the election of 1858 to the election of 1870, from 1894 to 1908, and from 1918 to 1930. Likewise, the Democratic party can point to three such periods — from 1870 to 1894, except for two brief two-year Republican interludes; from 1910 to 1918; and from 1930 to 1946.

The peak of Republican House strength when Republicans have been in control, Bean finds, measuring margin of control in percentages of total House membership, was in the beginning days of the party. The Democratic peak was as recent as 1936. In 1936 the Democratic peak exceeded the Republican peak of 1864 when the South was excluded from Congress and Republicans were a part of the Union party. The Democratic low point when it was in control of the House came in the 1870's whereas the Republican low point was in 1953. Bean, therefore, asks this question: " Shall we . . . conclude that from now on the Democrats normally will control about 60 per cent of the House, varying between 45 and 75 per cent, whereas in the 1860's and 1870's they normally elected about 45 per cent of the House members, varying between 30 and 60 per cent? " [2]

If such a trend continues to run, Republican prospects of controlling the House are not bright for the immediate future. If Republicans do control, the trend suggests it will be only for short periods and by slim margins. In searching for reasons for such a trend, Bean concludes the answer may lie in the continuously increasing proportion of population in the cities which in the past have been the major source of non-South Democratic strength. Where in 1860 20 percent of the population was urban, by 1940 the urban percentage had passed the 50-percent mark. Where Abraham Lincoln's Republican party had the support of a large proportion of the " labor vote," the Democratic party has attracted and the Republican party has lost this very important element of city voting strength.[3] If such be the case, if more Republican state legislatures become Democratic and if city populations receive a greater proportion of representa-

---

[2] Louis H. Bean, *How to Predict Elections* (New York: Alfred A. Knopf, 1948) , pp. 16–17.

[3] From *ibid.*, Chaps. 2 and 14.

Figure 23. Democratic and Republican Margin of U. S. Senate Control, 1861–1955

(In Number of Seats)

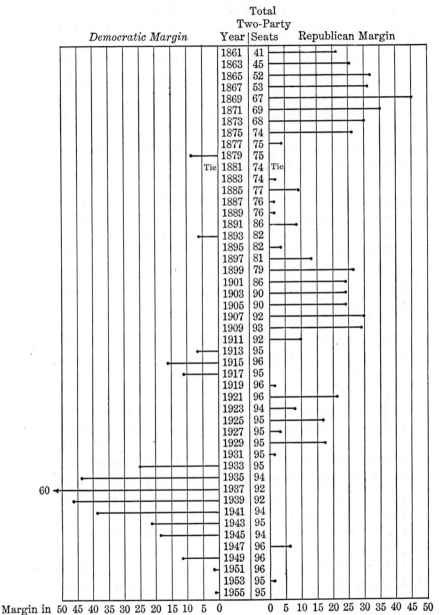

Source: U. S. Bureau of the Census, *Historical Statistics of the United States, 1789–1945* (Washington, D.C.: Government Printing Office, 1949), p. 293.

tion in the House through Democratic reapportionment of Congressional districts, the Republican party, unless it is able to adjust its appeal to city requirements, may be at a further disadvantage in winning House majorities.

(5) A fifth observation from Figure 22 and one which serves as introduction to the section which follows is the fact that in comparatively few Congresses has the margin of House control for either party exceeded 25 percent of the total membership of the House. From 1913 when the total two-party House membership has exceeded 400, in 4 of the 22 Congresses the margin of control was 10 seats or less; in 10 of the 22 Congresses it was 50 seats or less; and in 16 of the 22 Congresses it was 100 seats or less. In only 6 of those 22 Congresses has the House majority party had a margin of control exceeding 100 seats — Republicans once and Democrats five times. From this point one may proceed to the some 100 marginal House districts in which neither party loses by below 45 percent of the two-party vote nor wins by more than 55 percent. Selecting these districts is the first step in analyzing the major party's problem of winning House of Representatives majorities.

Figure 23 shows the Democratic and Republican margin of United States Senate control in number of seats in Congresses from 1861 through 1955. Introductory observations should also be made from this figure.

(1) In a comparison of Figures 22 and 23 it is immediately apparent that party control and margins of party control in the Senate are less subject to violent fluctuations than is the case in the House. Although Democrats controlled the House from 1871 to 1893 except for two Congresses, the situation was almost reversed in the Senate with all of these Senates controlled by Republicans except three. Not until Wilson and the Democratic Senates of 1913 through 1917 was the Republican power in the Senate cut into for as long as six years. Not until Franklin D. Roosevelt was the Republican hold on the Senate definitely broken.

Although the party which elects a President tends also to lose Senate strength in the next Congressional election, it does not happen as often nor are the losses as proportionately great as in the House. Furthermore, where a shift in party control in the House in a Congressional election has tended to mean that the Presidency will change party hands two years after, generally the Senate turnover does not come until the Presidential election, if it comes then.

(2) As Republican margins of Senate control over the 1861 through 1955 period have tended to decrease, conversely Democratic margins of control have tended to increase. Louis Bean's researches on Senate political tides have brought him to the same conclusion about increasingly favorable Democratic prospects in the Senate as in the House.[4] If projections from the data of the past are valid, either the Democrats might be expected in the immediate future to again take a commanding lead in the Senate or there will be another period in which Senate control margins will be very close.

(3) Generalization on some average number of Senate seats necessary to produce a change in party control of that body is more difficult than in the House. So much depends upon which one third of the seats are up for the determination of the voters in any particular election year. The problem of winning Senate majorities will, therefore, be illustrated by a particular case study of the Senatorial elections of 1954.

SAFE AND MARGINAL DISTRICTS — THE HOUSE

As Democratic and Republican Congressional campaign committees prepare for a Congressional election, their first step is to classify House districts on a safe-marginal-critical scale. Unless there is a political landslide, there is small chance that the out-party in a safe Congressional district is likely to be able to unseat the incumbent if he seeks re-election or the incumbent's party if he does not seek re-election. Campaign attention, then, will be directed to the marginal districts, and particularly to those marginal districts in which the margin of victory and defeat has been very close.

Malcolm Moos in his *Politics, Presidents and Coattails,* averaging Congressional election results from 1942 through 1950, found 105 marginal districts in which the victor won by receiving 50.01 to 55 percent of the two-party vote and the loser with from 45 to 49.99 percent of the two-party vote. Of these 105 districts, 60 were Republican and 45 Democratic. Within the marginal districts, Moos also set up a critical-marginal category where the issue was decided when the losers received not under 48.5 percent of the two-party vote and the winner got not over 51.5 percent. There were 42 such districts — 25 Republican and 17 Democratic.[5]

---

[4] Bean, *op. cit.,* pp. 16–17.   [5] Moos, *op. cit.,* pp. 24–25.

On the basis of the 1952 elections — the Eighty-third Congress — the *Congressional Quarterly Weekly Report* found 103 marginal districts. Of the 103, 39 were of a critical marginal nature — 27 Republican and 12 Democratic. For the elections of 1954, therefore, 65 Republicans and 38 Democrats were in districts that the opposition

"*I suppose we'll have to set this down as a doubtful district.*"

Reproduced by permission.
© *1948 The New Yorker
Magazine, Inc.*

party had a very good to fighting chance of unseating the incumbent.[6] In the 1954 Congressional elections, of the 21 Republican seats won by Democrats, 16 were Republican marginal in 1952. Of the 5 districts lost by Democrats to Republicans, 3 were Democratic marginal in 1952. These figures are but one illustration of the fact that generally the turnover in House seats from one party to another takes place within the marginal districts.

In the Eight-fourth Congress, using the same percentage classifications of two-party vote as does Moos, 200 House seats are safe

---

[6] September 10, 1954, p. 1146.

Democratic; 138, safe Republican; 31, marginal Democratic; and 66, marginal Republican. Of the 97 marginal districts, 23 are critical marginal, and of the latter, 17 are Republican-held seats and 6 are Democratic seats. Figure 24 provides the details by sections and by states.

As in Presidential elections, the greatest source of Democratic House strength comes from the Solid Democratic South. Of the 97 House districts in these 10 states, in 64 there were no Republican nominees in 1952. Of the 26 safe Democratic districts in which there was Republican opposition, in 16 of them the Republican candidate received less than 30 percent of the two-party vote. Over-all in the South, there are 90 safe Democratic districts, 2 safe Republican districts and only 5 districts which might, on the basis of the record, go either way in the elections of 1956. Democrats also hold a big advantage in the Border states with 30 Democrats and 6 Republicans safe, and with 7 of the 11 nonsafe seats held by Democrats.

The only comparable section in terms of Republican strength in the House is the West Central section. Republicans, however, do have distinct advantages in the North Central, Central, and Pacific sections. Except for the West Central and North Central states, should most of the marginal or critical Republican districts go Democratic, the latter party is within range of having a majority of the House seats from each sectional combination of states.

The advantage with which Democrats go into the House elections of 1956 is further revealed in a summary comparison of the percentages of the two-party vote which Democratic and Republican members of the Eighty-fourth Congress House won their seats. They are as follows:

Democrats — 232 seats		Republicans — 203 seats	
Unopposed	79	Unopposed	2
70% or more	44	70% or more	7
		65 to 70%	12
60 to 64.9%	51	60 to 64.9%	58
55 to 59.9%	27	55 to 59.9%	61
50.1 to 54.9%	31	50.1 to 54.9%	63 [7]

Note that the bulk of Democratic seats are toward the safe end of the two-party percentage of vote scale, where for the Republican party the concentration is even as sharply on the doubtful end of the scale.

[7] Republican National Committee, Research Staff, *The 1954 Elections: A Summary Report With Supporting Tables*, p. 7.

Figure 24. Democratic and Republican Safe, Marginal, and Critical House Districts by Section and by State in the Eighty-fourth Congress

Section and State	Number Seats	DEMOCRATIC				REPUBLICAN			
		No Republican Opposition	Safe	Marginal	Critical	Critical	Marginal	Safe	No Democratic Opposition
South									
Miss.	6	6							
S.C.	6	1	5						
La.	8	7	1						
Ga.	10	9	1						
Tex.	22	17	4				1		
Ala.	9	7	2						
Fla.	8	6	1			1			
Ark.	6	6							
Va.	10	3	4		1		1	1	
N.C.	12	2	8	1				1	
Subtotal	97	64	26	1	1	1	2	2	
Border									
Okla.	6	1	4					1	
Mo.	11		7	2			2		
Tenn.	9	4	3					2	
Ky.	8	3	3			1		1	
W. Va.	6		3	2	1				
Md.	7	1	1	2		1		2	
Subtotal	47	9	21	6	1	2	2	6	
West Central									
N.D.	2							2	
S.D.	2							2	
Neb.	4						1	3	
Kan.	6						3	3	
Subtotal	14						4	10	
North Central									
Minn.	9		3	1	1		1	3	
Ia.	8							8	
Wis.	10		2	1			2	5	
Mich.	18		5	1	1		3	8	
Subtotal	45		10	3	2		6	24	
Central									
Ill.	25		8	4		1	2	10	
Ind.	11		1	1		1	4	4	
Ohio	23		4	2			5	12	
Subtotal	59		13	7		2	11	26	
Middle									
Pa.	30		10	2	2	3	2	11	
N.Y.	43	1	15	1		3	3	20	
N.J.	14		6				3	5	
Del.	1			1					
Subtotal	88	1	31	3	2	6	8	37	

Section and State	Number Seats	DEMOCRATIC				REPUBLICAN			
		No Republican Opposition	Safe	Marginal	Critical	Critical	Marginal	Safe	No Democratic Opposition
New England									
Me.	3						2	1	
N.H.	2					1		1	
Vt.	1							1	
Conn.	6		1			2	2	1	
Mass.	14	3	3	1		1		5	1
R.I.	2		2						
Subtotal	28	3	6	1		4	4	9	1
Pacific									
Wash.	7		1				2	4	
Ore.	4			1			1	2	
Calif.	30	2	8	1		1	5	13	
Subtotal	41	2	9	2		1	8	19	
Mountain									
Ida.	2			1				1	
Mont.	2		1			1			
Wyo.	1							1	
Nev.	1						1		
Utah	2						1	1	
Colo.	4		1	1			1	1	
Ariz.	2		1				1		
N.M.	2		2						
Subtotal	16		5	2		1	4	4	
GRAND TOTAL	435	79	121	25	6	17	49	137	1

Notes: (1) Safe districts are those in which the Democratic or Republican nominee was elected by over 55 percent of the two-party vote.

(2) Marginal districts are those in which the winner received between 51.5 and 55 percent of the two-party vote and the loser between 45 and 48.5 percent.

(3) Critical districts are those in which the winner received between 50.01 and 51.5 percent of the two-party vote and the loser between 48.5 and 49.99 percent.

Source: Republican Congressional Campaign Committee, *1954 Congressional Vote Statistics.*

In the House elections of 1956 a major effort of the Democrats and Republicans will be directed toward the 6 Democratic critical districts — Virginia's *9th,* West Virginia's *4th,* Minnesota's *9th,* Michigan's *6th,* Pennsylvania's *11th* and *19th* — and to the 17 Republican critical districts — Florida's 1st, Kentucky's *3rd,* Maryland's *6th,* Illinois' 11th, Indiana's 3rd, Pennsylvania's 6th, 8th, and 10th, New York's 12th, 17th, and 25th, New Hampshire's 1st, Connecticut's 2nd and its at-large seat, Massachusetts' 10th, California's *6th,* and Montana's 1st. (The italicized critical districts changed party hands in 1954, with California's 6th and Florida's 1st won by Republicans from Democrats, and the remainder won by Democrats from Republicans.)

Next in importance will be the marginal districts. The Democratic party's 25 marginal seats in the House in the Eighty-fourth Congress are: North Carolina's 9th, Missouri's *4th* and *6th,* West Virginia's 1st and 2nd, Maryland's *5th* and 7th, Minnesota's 3rd, Wisconsin's *5th,* Michigan's 17th, Illinois' *3rd, 12th,* 21st, and *25th,* Indiana's *8th,* Ohio's 6th and 18th, Pennsylvania's 5th and *25th,* Delaware's *at-large seat,* Massachusetts' *8th,* Oregon's *3rd,* California's *12th,* Idaho's 1st, and Colorado's 4th. The Republicans' 49 marginal seats in the Eighty-fourth Congress are: Texas' *5th,* Virginia's 10th, Missouri's 2nd and 7th, Wisconsin's 1st and 2nd, Michigan's 7th, 11th, and 18th, Illinois' 4th and 23rd, Indiana's 5th, 6th, 9th, and 11th, Ohio's 3rd, 14th, *15th,* 16th, and 17th, Pennsylvania's 22nd and 24th, New York's 4th, 5th, and 15th, New Jersey's 1st, 8th, and 12th, Massachusetts' 1st and 2nd, Connecticut's 3rd and 5th, Washington's 1st and 2nd, Oregon's 2nd, California's 7th, 9th, 11th, 13th, and 18th, Nevada's at-large seat, Utah's 1st, Colorado's 3rd, and Arizona's 1st. (The italicized marginal districts changed party hands in 1954 with Kansas' 1st, Ohio's 15th, and Texas' 5th won by Republicans from Democrats, and the remainder won by Democrats from Republicans.)

Only one of the Congressional districts in which the party label of the Congressman changed in 1954 is not included in the Eighty-fourth Congress marginal or critical marginal lists. It was New York's 21st'district which elected a Republican in 1952 by 63.4 percent of the two-party vote and then in 1954 proceeded to elect a Democrat by a 67.8 percent margin. Changes such as this one are exceptional except in landslide years.

Though the distribution of critical and marginal districts is wide enough so that most readers of this chapter can examine one within their state or section, and though safe districts are close at hand for observation by almost everyone, it is necessary to add a qualitative dimension to the statistical classifications of district types to more fully understand the Congressional election problem for the major parties. Mississippi's 3rd district will illustrate the safe Democratic district in which there was no 1954 major party opposition nominee on the ballot. Tennessee's 1st district will illustrate a safe Republican district; and Ohio's 14th, a marginal Republican district. It is in districts like Ohio's 14th where House majorities are won, and a brief examination of the different district types suggests the reason why.

Mississippi's 3rd District.[8] Since reconstruction days no Republican has been elected to represent Mississippi's 3rd district in the United States House of Representatives. Its present Congressman is Frank E. Smith, elected for the first time, at the age of 33, in 1950. His predecessor had held the office for 26 consecutive years before retiring. Smith, if he avoids major political trouble, should be able to stay in office until he too wants to retire, and his chances of some day becoming a House standing committee chairman are very good.

The 3rd district is mostly Mississippi River delta land with cotton growing as its chief industry. It has a plantation economy largely dominated by a relatively few large planters with the remaining two principal economic groups being Negro laborers who work the land and the whites of the cities and towns who provide the legal, education, retail, and other services of the community. Seventy percent of the district's population is Negro, though only a handful vote.

There is general agreement on political objectives. The Negro should be kept in his place and thus there should be no federal meddling in the form of civil rights legislation. The interests of the cotton producer should be protected, whether the type of protection be a tariff structure to encourage exports or cotton price supports. Because the Mississippi River periodically overflows its banks, flood control becomes a major interest of the district's Congressman. Disenchanted in the early days with Franklin D. Roosevelt, the political leaders of the district tried in 1944 to swing Mississippi's Presidential electors away from voting for Roosevelt. During the Truman Administration the district was anti-Truman and, along with the rest of the state in 1948, voted Dixiecrat.

In 1950 the Republican nominee for Congress received 7.5 percent of the two-party vote; in 1952, 12.8 percent; and in 1954 there was no Republican nominee. Though Eisenhower won 49.9 percent of the two-party vote for President in 1952, the Presidential contest had little influence on the Congressional campaign. Democratic nominees for offices in the district do not bother to campaign in general elections because to campaign against a Republican might be construed as a sign that the Democrat felt his position to be abnormally weak. Here is a safe Democratic district which the Democratic Congressional Campaign Committee need not worry about losing and

[8] Based on Stephen K. Bailey and Howard D. Samuel, *Congress at Work* (New York: Henry Holt and Company, 1952), pp. 48–65.

MISSISSIPPI

6 Congressional Districts

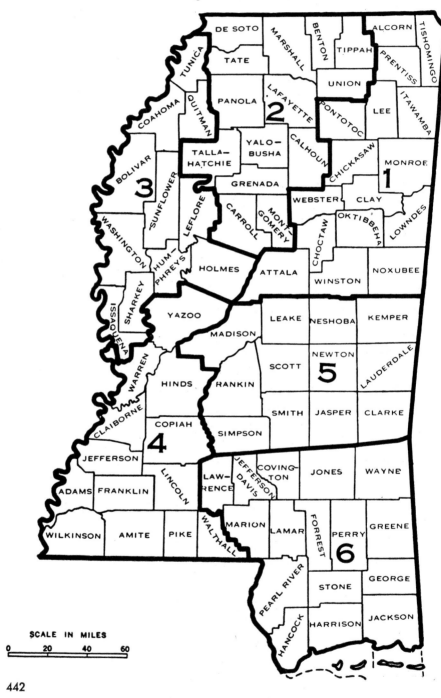

SCALE IN MILES

0   20   40   60

for which the Republican Congressional Campaign Committee should not expend money or effort in a useless attempt to win.

Whether the southern Congressional district is Mississippi's 3rd or nearly any other in the South, the following delightful article published in the *Los Angeles Times* of October 18, 1955, will illustrate the depth of the Democratic tradition which is found in that section. It was written by Alabama-born Dr. Leon Howard, English professor at the University of California at Los Angeles, and is entitled " The First One [Republican] I Saw."

Holmes Alexander [syndicated columnist with a southern Democratic background] has described the shaky, dry-mouthed feeling he experienced when he descended into the depths of his county courthouse, sought out the Supervisor of Elections, and changed his registration from Democratic to Republican.

Few of the fluctuating voters in the State of California, I suspect, can understand his feelings or even take his description of symptoms seriously. But I can. For one of the most vivid of my childhood recollections is the first time I saw a Republican.

I was nearly 7 years old at the time, on an early Saturday morning shortly before the Alabama election of 1910, and I had been disobedient the preceding night. I had remained in the dining room with my father and some masculine guests after the women and children had supposedly retired to another room.

The men were canvassing the probable vote of the neighborhood. I had curled up and almost gone to sleep when one exchange brought me to wide-awake attention.

" What about Mr. Parsons? " one of the guests asked.

" Oh, his vote won't count," responded my father. " He's a Republican."

I was thunderstruck. Although I was just learning about politics, I had known about Republicans since birth. And Mr. Parsons was my favorite neighbor! He was the only man in the whole region who would let me ride a plow, and I spent a fair part of my time haunting the small farm he worked alone.

I was up almost by daylight and down at the Parsons place as soon as I could gulp breakfast. My friend was at . . . work. I rested my chin on the middle rail of the fence and contemplated, with mixed emotions, my first Republican.

" Hey! " he called as he turned and saw me. " Want a ride? "

The panic I felt at that moment still makes my heart beat faster. It was the first time I had ever been spoken to by a man whose ballot I knew bore the mark of the elephant instead of the rooster. Nothing in my training had prepared me for such an emergency. My throat was paralyzed, but my legs weren't.

So I ran.

I ran as I had never run before. . . . I ran into the deepest woods on my father's place and didn't stop until I sank breathless to the ground.

Later I learned that my favorite uncle, by marriage, was One too, and I got better control over my reactions. But early conditioning is hard to overcome, and when the columnist from Maryland reviewed his background I recognized his symptoms and admired his courage. He has a stouter heart than I have.[9]

Tennessee's 1st District.[10] As Mississippi's 3rd district has been solidly Democratic, so has Tennessee's 1st district been almost as solidly Republican. Its present Congressman is B. Carroll Reece. First elected in 1920, he has served since except for two Congresses when other Republicans represented the district. From 1942 through 1948 there was no Democratic nominee for the Congressional seat. In 1952 Reece received 62.9 percent of the two-party vote, and in 1954, 62.5 percent. Republican Presidential nominees have won up to 90 percent of the two-party vote in the district, and have averaged from 75 to 85 percent.

Congressman Reece's district has a farm-based economy. Tobacco, wheat, corn, and potatoes are its primary crops. Its cities are relatively small and exist primarily to service the farm communities. Manufacturing is conducted on a small scale, but the type of commodities produced tend to be lumber, milk, and textile products. The district's principal political objectives are those of rural areas as yet not greatly affected by the industrial revolution.

As the tradition of Frank E. Smith's district has been Democratic,

---

9 Reprinted by permission of the *Los Angeles Times* and the author.
10 Based in part on Moos, *op. cit.,* pp. 88–89.

TENNESSEE

9 Congressional Districts

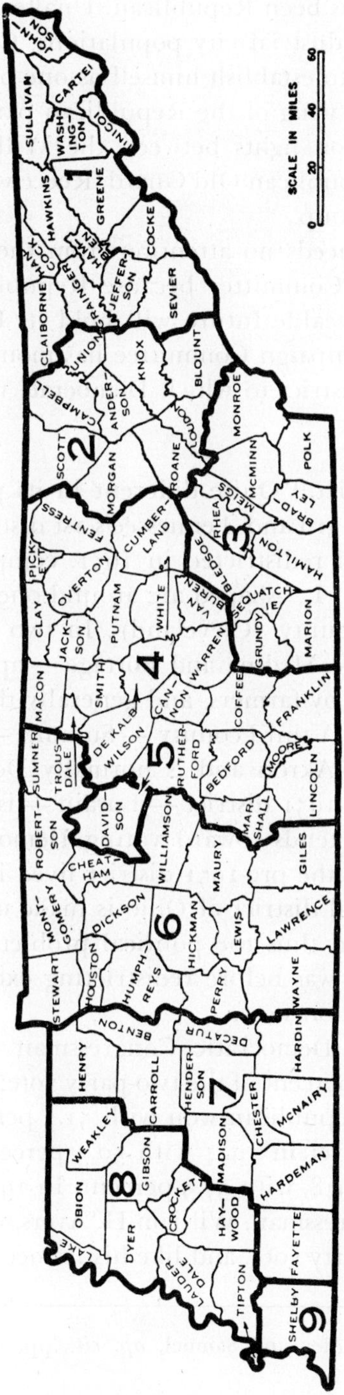

SCALE IN MILES

0   20   40   60

Tennessee's 1st has been Republican. Unaffected by the political demands of large industrial city populations, Congressman Reece has found it possible to establish himself as one of the leaders of the so-called Old Guard wing of the Republican party. In the Republican national convention fights between the Willkie-Dewey-Eisenhower forces and the Republican Old Guard, Reece was one of the inner circle of the latter group.

His district needs no attention from the Republican Congressional Campaign Committee because Republicans have safely held and for the foreseeable future will hold it. Unless the Democratic Congressional Campaign Committee has money to throw away, it is not the type of district to which Democrats will allocate nationally collected funds.

Ohio's 14th District.[11] Quite different in its political characteristics from Mississippi's 3rd and Tennessee's 1st districts is Ohio's 14th district. It was, until redistricted in 1951, composed of four counties which formed an " L "-shaped arc around one side and below populous Cuyahoga County (Cleveland). In two of the counties of the pre-1951 district — Medina and Portage — approximately one-third of the vote is cast by farmers, and generally these two counties have gone Republican. A third county — Summit — is the location of the industrial city of Akron and is normally Democratic. The fourth county of the pre-1951 district — Lorain — is mixed industrial and agricultural, and tends toward voting Democratic. Almost half of the population of the pre-1951 district lived in Akron. The present 14th Congressional district of Ohio is made up of Summit and Medina counties, and thus the political problem presented is in general much like it was before redistricting except that Akron needs even closer attention now.

In 1938 the Democratic Congressman from the district was elected with 53.3 percent of the two-party vote; in 1940, with 52.8 percent. In 1942 a Republican won with 51.3 percent. Democrats again captured the district in 1944 with 50.3 percent; in 1946, with 53.2 percent; and in 1948, with 57.5 percent. In 1950 the now incumbent Republican Congressman, William H. Ayers, was elected by 50.5 percent of the two-party vote, and like his immediate Democratic prede-

[11] Based on Bailey and Samuel, *op. cit.,* pp. 32–48, and Moos, *op. cit.,* p. 203.

OHIO

23 Congressional Districts

SCALE IN MILES

0   20   40   60

HAMILTON CO.

cessor, Ayers was able to consolidate his position to the extent of a 58.5-percent victory in 1952 and a 54.6-percent victory in 1954. In 1952, however, Eisenhower received only 50.5 percent of the two-party Presidential vote to run eight percentage points behind the Republican Congressional nominee.

Congressmen Smith of Mississippi and Reece of Tennessee have simple re-election problems because their districts are so homogeneous and one-party in nature. Ayers, on the other hand, is torn between the industrial pressure pattern of Akron and the farm pressure patterns of most of the rest of his district. Furthermore, the two main opposing forces in Ohio's 14th district are of relatively equal strength though more balanced in the old than the new district. Here Ayers, even though he had a Carroll Reece type of Republican outlook, could not stay long in office if he acted and voted politically as Reece does. Ayers can only be the type of Republican which his district permits him to be — moderately progressive in legislation which affects both industrial communities with their "labor vote" and farm communities with their "farm vote." If Republicans fail to satisfy those desires, there is no tradition in the district which would stand in the way of turning the in-party out.

Smith and Reece might be able to survive a few major political mistakes or votes which appeared contrary to the pattern desired by their districts. Ayers' district is so balanced between the major parties that he may not be able to overcome an occasional minor political misjudgment. As a Reece-type Republican appeal would tend to represent an unelectable political commodity in Ohio's 14th district, so for the Democratic party would a Mississippi type of Democratic appeal. Here is a politically doubtful Congressional district in a large and doubtful pivot state. It is to districts such as these in states such as these that Democrats and Republicans must be able to appeal in order to win Presidential elections. Likewise, it is in marginal Congressional districts such as Ohio's 14th, and not in Mississippi's 3rd or Tennessee's 1st districts, that House majorities are won or lost.

SAFE AND MARGINAL STATES — THE SENATE

To illustrate the problem of the Republican and Democratic Senatorial campaign committees in each Congressional election, the 1954 Senatorial contest will be developed as a case study. Through most of the Eighty-third Congress, the party alignment in the Senate was 48 Republicans, 47 Democrats, and Independent Wayne Morse of Oregon. If Morse had sided with the Democrats on the issue of organization of the Senate, so close was the Republican margin of control that it would have taken Vice President Nixon to break the tie.

Fifty-eight of the 96 Senators were not up for election in 1954. Thirty-three of these were Republicans and 25 were Democrats. Of the 38 seats to be decided in 1954, 16 were held by Republicans and 22 by Democrats in the Eighty-third Congress.

As in Presidential and House of Representative contests, Democrats and Republicans alike could look first at the South to establish the number of seats up for election which would surely return Democrats. Safe, therefore, were ten Democrats — Sparkman of Alabama, McClellan of Arkansas, Russell of Georgia, Ellender of Louisiana, Eastland of Mississippi, Ervin and Scott of North Carolina, Thurmond of South Carolina (elected by a write-in vote over the regular Democratic nominee) , Johnson of Texas, and Robertson of Virginia. Almost as sure of re-election were Kefauver of Tennessee and Kerr of Oklahoma, and on the basis of Rhode Island's political behavior since 1928, also apparently secure for the Democrats was Green of that state.

For the Republicans, Mundt of South Dakota, Curtis and Hruska of Nebraska, Schoeppel of Kansas, Smith of Maine, and Bridges and Cotton of New Hampshire appeared as the safe Republicans, with perhaps Dworshak of Idaho also in that category. To this point, the Democrats would have 13 and Republicans 8 of the 38 contested seats. The remaining 17 contested seats could be classified as doubtful to very doubtful, and it was in these states that the most intense Senatorial campaigns of 1954 took place.

Assuming that the party in control of the White House would lose strength in the off-presidential election year, attention would first focus on the eight doubtful Republican held seats. In California the Republican incumbent Senator up for re-election, Thomas H. Kuchel, had been appointed in December 1952 by Governor Warren to fill the vacancy created by the resignation of Vice President-elect Richard M. Nixon. Until after the election of 1954, however, Kuchel's Senatorial campaigning ability would be a question mark. In Kentucky, Republican John Sherman Cooper might have had a good chance to win over any other Democratic candidate than ex-Vice President Alban W. Barkley, but with the " Veep " as his opposition the seat was in doubt or tending Democratic. Massachusetts' highly unreliable recent political characteristics from a Republican point of view placed Leverett Saltonstall's seat in doubt. In that state in 1952 Republican Henry Cabot Lodge, Jr., had been narrowly defeated by a Democrat.

In Michigan, although Republican Senator Homer Ferguson was chairman of the Senate Republican Policy Committee and was a well-known national figure, the political climate had been rapidly changing from Republican to Democratic under the personable touch of Democratic Governor G. Mennen Williams. If there were no late 1954 increase in unemployment, however, Ferguson was given a slight edge in the race, particularly after the Democratic nominee, ex-Senator Blair Moody, died and the Democratic choice as Moody's successor, Patrick V. McNamara, was largely unknown.

In New Jersey, Republican Senator Hendrickson was retiring and the Republican nominee in 1954 was Clifford P. Case. Of all the Republican doubtful states, New Jersey appeared one of the most likely to go Democratic. Case was regarded by one faction of his party as too "New Dealish," and he had come out openly against McCarthyism. Furthermore, Democrats had elected a governor in 1953 and Democratic organizational effectiveness seemed to be increasing.

In Oregon, Republican Senator Guy Cordon appeared to be in difficulty, though Oregon had not elected a Democratic senator in 40 years. Richard Neuberger, his Democratic opponent, was regarded as a serious challenger, and the issue of alleged Republican " anti-public power " policies was calculated to produce a close election in public power conscious Oregon. In Wyoming, the Republican seat had been a result of a Republican governor's appointing a Republican to fill the vacancy created by the death of Democratic Senator Lester C. Hunt during the Eighty-third Congress. Likewise in Nevada, the Republican seat at stake was a Republican gubernatorial appointee to fill the vacancy caused by the death of Democratic Senator Pat Mc-Carran. Both Wyoming and Nevada might be expected to lean Democratic, but the Senatorial races were still regarded as doubtful.

These eight Republican seats had been classified as doubtful with good cause, as the election results of 1954 finally proved. Only Republicans of the group to be elected were Kuchel of California (53.2 percent of the two-party vote) , Saltonstall of Massachusetts (50.5 percent with the Democratic opposition split) , and Case of New Jersey (48.7 percent of the total vote representing a plurality of 3,370 out of approximately 1,720,000 votes cast) . Barkley took Cooper's

Kentucky seat with 54.5 percent of the two-party vote; McNamara, the Michign contest with 50.8 percent; Neuberger, the Oregon contest with 50.2 percent; O'Mahoney, the Wyoming contest with 51.5 percent; and Bible, the Nevada contest with 58.1 percent.

Of the nine apparently doubtful Democratic seats during the

" My program calls for a mammoth federal dam and a vast irrigation system that will convert this barren dust bowl into a veritable Eden of lush and prosperous farms, after which I shall press upon the Production and Marketing Administration the need for an adequate subsidy to purchase all the surplus farm produce of the entire area."

1954 campaign, the incumbents were re-elected in six cases. What had been expected to be a strong Republican challenge to Senator Clinton P. Anderson of New Mexico failed to materialize, and he won 57.3 percent of the two-party vote. J. Allan Frear of Delaware was next with 56.9 percent; Humphrey of Minnesota, with 56.4 percent; Neeley of West Virginia, with 54.8 percent; Douglas of Illinois, with 53.6 percent; and Murray of Montana, with 50.4 percent. The three Democratic seats to go Republican were Colorado's with Gordon Allott receiving 51.3 percent of the two-party vote; Thomas Martin of

Iowa, 52.2 percent; and George H. Bender of Ohio, 50.1 percent.

If the same percentage standards as were applied to define House marginal and critical districts are used as standards to judge these 1954 Senate contests, of the eight Republican seats believed to be doubtful during the campaign, none were safe Republican, three were marginal Republican, five were critical — of these Republicans lost three, and one became safe Democratic. Of the nine Democratic seats considered during the campaign to be doubtful, three became critical Republican, one critical Democratic, two marginal Democratic, and three safe Democratic. It was the turnover in these doubtful states which produced the final 1954 Senate election result of 49 Democrats and 47 Republicans to give the former party control of the Senate for the Eighty-fourth Congress.

Considering the fact that the Republicans controlled the White House in an off-Presidential election year, in the 1954 Senate election they did well to hold the Senate strength which they did. In 1954, however, the Republican party had only 16 Republican Senate seats up for election while 22 Democratic seats were decided. Projecting into the immediate future, however, it will be the Democratic party and not the Republican party which will have the fewest seats up for determination by the voters.

In 1956, 17 Republican and 15 Democratic seats will be on the election block. Seven of those 15 Democratic seats are in the South and 3 are from Border states which might be considered safely Democratic. That leaves, in effect, 5 Democrats whose re-election might be in doubt versus 17 Republicans, some of whom might be safe but more of whom are doubtful. With the political distress signals being sent up from Republican leaders in the Midwest farm states added to the doubtful states of which Republicans must win a good proportion of the Senators, the difficulties of the Republican Senatorial Campaign Committee in enhancing its party's Senate strength in 1956 will be great indeed.

Even more are the hazards in the way of Senate Republicans in 1958. Of the 32 seats which will regularly come up for decision in that year, 20 are Republican and 12 Democratic. Of the 12 Democratic seats, 4 are in the South and 3 appear to be safe in the Border states. That, in turn, would mean only 7 exposed Democratic seats to 20 more or less exposed Republican seats. If Republicans cannot make substantial gains in 1956, there is a strong possibility that that party will have no chance to control the Senate in January, 1959.

RELATIONSHIP OF A PARTY'S PRESIDENTIAL
NOMINEE TO ITS PROBLEM OF WINNING
CONGRESSIONAL MAJORITIES

In the introductory quotation to this chapter, Malcolm Moos suggests several theories about the influence of a Presidential nominee on the number of Congressmen and Senators of the nominee's party who will win election. Some contend that the number of legislators elected will vary directly with the political ability of the Presidential nominee. Others would say that the political ability of the nominees for Congress is important, but not as important a factor as the influence of the Presidential nominee. Still others suggest that the Presidential campaign has little bearing on the number of Representatives and Senators elected by each major party. A fourth school of thought is that Congressional candidates help the Presidential nominee of their party. There may be at least some validity to each of these theories, provided the problem of winning Congressional majorities is divided into several different types of problems rather than viewed as one problem.

For the approximately 79 House districts — most of them in the South — in which there is no Republican opposition to the Democratic nominee, regardless of whom the Democratic Presidential nominee may be, a Democratic Congressman will be elected. Even though the voters may support a Republican Presidential nominee, as four of those southern states did in 1928 and 1952, the effect of that action on the Congressional election will be zero or negligible in importance. In districts such as these the tendency since the 1930's has been for Democratic Congressional nominees to oppose the policies of Democratic Presidential nominees, and yet both are almost without exception elected.

In the approximately 250 safe Democratic and Republican House districts which tend to be one-party in nature even though there generally is an opposition major party nominee, the need of a Presidential coattail to clutch may be greater but seldom is it much greater. Congressmen from districts such as these tend to be elected and re-elected every two years, also regardless of the power of the respective major parties' Presidential nominees. In landslide Congressional elections, such as those of the early 1930's, it is true that many of the safe Republican House seats went Democratic, but the depression and factors other than the appeal of Franklin D. Roosevelt have to be taken into consideration in the assessment of those election results.

While a Presidential coattail may not be much of a factor in safe districts, its importance tends to increase for the approximately 100 House marginal districts. In those districts which are critical marginal, a good or poor Presidential coattail may make the difference between victory or defeat for a Congressional nominee. Here in the marginal district category, Presidential and Congressional nominees of the same party tend to receive about the same proportion of the two-party vote.[12] Furthermore, Louis H. Bean, from his analysis of Presidential and House voting tides during the New Deal era, finds that in Presidential election years approximately 6 to 7 percent more votes were cast for Democratic Congressional candidates than in the off-year Congressional elections. "In other words, about 26 to 30 Congressmen thus appear to have ridden into office on the President's coattail in 1932, 1936, 1940, and 1944. It may also be said that about as many Democratic Congressional candidates were defeated in each of the mid-term elections of 1930, 1934, 1938, and 1942 because they lacked Presidential support."[13]

Why might the appeal of the Presidential nominee tend to become a significant factor in elections in marginal House and Senate districts? During a Presidential campaign more interest tends to be focused on the big national contest where an Eisenhower battles with a Stevenson than on the less interesting activities in the smaller 435 House districts and 32 or more states where Senate seats are up for determination. The polls show that some 30 percent or more of the voters do not know the names of their Representatives in the Congress. Voting statistics show that more Presidential votes are cast than there are votes for lesser offices. In Congressional elections when there is no Presidential contest, voter participation drops sharply.

Moos, in his excellent monograph on the coattail influence, however, adds words of caution against an overestimation of Presidential nominee coattail effect. The Presidential nominee's pulling power, Moos writes, will vary depending upon local Congressional district factors and upon how well the Presidential and Congressional candidates are known to the voters.

At present, the presidential nominee is and may be increasingly in a better position to exercise a coattail influence. The accretion of many

---

[12] Moos, *op. cit.*, p. 107.   [13] Bean, *op. cit.*, p. 32.

advantages — the growing statute of presidential office, decline in the prestige of Congress, stronger financing of presidential candidates, and the increasing tendency to regard him as the spokesman of all the people — gives the presidential nominee the edge where he and his congressional candidates are making their *first* bids for their respective offices. But while the match is not equal, both because of the centrality of his position and by reason of his greater resources of finance, the problems of communication — the business of making meaningful appeals and becoming known to the electorate — are common to both. And, however upsetting it may be to the theory that champions the effectiveness of coattail influence, it must be said that *by and large* the success or failure of congressional candidates is not dependent upon the coattail pull of a presidential candidate.[14]

When the Presidential candidate is well-known and powerful and the Congressional candidate is in a marginal district running for office the first time, Moos would recognize the possibility that a good Presidential coattail might be a help. Generally there are an average of 75 new House members each Congress, and most of these will come from marginal districts. In other situations when a district is safe or when a Presidential nominee represents largely an unknown " presidential quantity," however, Moos suggests that local factors and the ability of the Congressional candidates themselves will tend to be determinative.

For any Congressional election, a strong Presidential nominee is not a substitute for a strong Congressional candidate. Nor is a strong Presidential nominee a substitute for a Congressional nominee who is not in tune with the political pressure group influence patterns of his district.

That Congressmen and Senators themselves do not put all of their faith in Presidential coattail hanging — provided they want reelection — is revealed in the choices they make in their Congressional voting. When they do follow the party, generally it is because the party position corresponds with what they and their district party organization regard as the interests of the district. If the party is controlled by those of a farm orientation and a metropolitan versus farm issue arises, regardless of party the metropolitan legislators will tend toward one position and the rural legislators toward another. If the issue is one revolving around a native versus foreign nationality

---

[14] Moos, *op. cit.,* p. 121. Italics the author's. Reprinted by permission.

group conflict, there is a tendency, regardless of party, for the legislator to vote his native or foreign district, whichever it may be. If there is a North-South sectional issue, the result will tend to be similar.[15]

The legislator who attempts to disregard party, his district's major interest groups, the major nationality and religious groups, and the sectional political climate of his district usually does not stay in office as long as the man who does not disregard them. Those who are able to develop a strong political appeal — to get themselves known and to give the impression that they are advancing the best interests of their districts and the country — tend to remain in office longer than those who cannot effectively so communicate. In short, the real key to a major party's winning Congressional majorities is in having the best nominees in the Congressional districts and states in which there are two-party contests.

Admittedly, in the House Democrats start with the advantage of approximately 100 seats from the South, and normally 25 to 30 more seats accrue to Democrats in the Border states. For a House majority, in addition to those 130 seats, the Democratic party needs but 88 more of the 278 seats in the West, Midwest, and East. Republicans, then, must be doubly effective outside the South and Border states — so effective, in fact, that a Republican average of 55 percent of the two-party vote in House contests in the West, Midwest, and East is necessary to give Republicans a narrow House majority.[16] There is the similar Republican disadvantage in the Senate, and there it is compounded by the fact that in 1956 and 1958 Republicans have more seats up for determination than Democrats.

On the basis of these facts, perhaps it might be said that Republicans more than Democrats need a good Presidential coattail for whatever benefits it will bring. A Presidential coattail in itself, however, is not enough — even for the Democratic party. There is no substitute for positive appeal.

---

[15] See Julius Turner, *Party and Constituency: Pressures on Congress* (Baltimore: The Johns Hopkins Press, 1951).

[16] Cortez A. M. Ewing, *Congressional Elections 1896–1944* (Norman: University of Oklahoma Press, 1947), p. 102.

█ PART FIVE

Winning Elections:

CAMPAIGN ORGANIZATION AND TACTICS

Part Four represents an attempt to outline the strategic problem of the major parties in winning Presidential elections and Congressional majorities and in elections in general. The problem, as it has been outlined, is essentially similar for both major parties. In Presidential elections there are a set of key states toward which both parties must direct their primary appeals, and for elections for state office in those key states the same type of appeal is necessary. United States House of Representatives majorities are won or lost in the some 100 marginal districts, and again the strategic problem in all of them tends to be roughly similar. And for all elections in any type of constituency the most fundamental objective of the major parties and their candidates has to be the development of broad appeal.

Part Five proceeds to the next step in the winning-elections process — the implementation of strategy decisions through campaign organization and tactics. Without sellable candidates no amount of quality in strategy decisions will bear fruit. Some of the elements which go into candidate selection are considered in Chapter Seventeen. Should strategy be sound and the candidate or candidates be able, the election effort may still fail if it is not well organized. Campaign organization is the subject of Chapter Eighteen.

If a party or candidate is to successfully devise strategy and communicate its appeal, decisions and actions need to be based on accurate information about both strategic and tactical problems. Chapter Nineteen on campaign research points up some of the subjects requiring research and some of the methods by which campaign research is done.

After strategy has been decided, candidates have been selected, the campaign organization has been set up, and research is being done, the party and its candidates must still be able to effectively communicate the message. Campaign propaganda is the subject of Chapter Nineteen. And last but not least in importance, the party and its candidates must have some minimum of campaign funds with which to finance the costs of organization, research, and communication. Here is the point, along with the effects of high-cost campaigns on the operation of our democratic-representative system, which is examined in Chapter Twenty-one on campaign finance.

CHAPTER SEVENTEEN

Candidates

----

*. . . [T]here has emerged the doctrine of " availability." The party needs
a candidate who, positively, will make the widest appeal and, negatively,
will offend the least proportion of the electorate. On the whole, he ought
to come from a doubtful state; a Democrat from New York is more " available " than one from the solid South because he is likely to win votes
which might otherwise be uninterested. It seems still to be true that it is
difficult to elect a Roman Catholic; half the solid South refused to vote
for Governor Smith in 1928. He must not be anti-religious; that would
offend the great vested interest of the churches. He must be sound on the
tariff; he must be against wild currency adventures; he must not be too
overtly internationalist in outlook. Administrative experience, like the
governorship of a state, is important. It is helpful if he is a self-made man;
the " log cabin to White House " tradition is still, despite the two Roosevelts, an influential one. He ought not to possess any nostrum which can
be represented as extreme. In the aftermath of a war period, it is important that he should have played his part in the army; from Jackson and
Taylor onwards, the military hero has had an immense appeal to the
electorate. It is undesirable that he should have too close an association
with the big interests, especially Wall Street; Wilson, in 1912, owed his
nomination to Mr. Bryan's famous pronouncement that he would not
support anyone under obligation to " Morgan, Ryan, Belmont, or any
other member of the privilege-seeking favor-hunting class." He must have
a sufficiently flexible mind to accept the implications of the trading necessary to build his majority. He must not be the kind of man whom it is*

460

obviously easy to ridicule in a campaign, either because he is "viewy,"
or for any other reason.

Harold J. Laski [1]

A political party may have enthusiasm, an illustrious record, adequate campaign funds, a smoothly working party organization, skilled
professional propagandists, but more than any of these things the
party must have good candidates for public office. The candidate is
the hub of the wheel around which all the other spokes revolve. If
the hub is sound, the wheel can perform its functions; if the hub is
not sound, the wheel is not sound. True it may be that the party is
bigger than the man, but the party is not bigger than the collectivity
of its candidates for public office. In the American political system
they are the party as it appears in the minds of those who make up the
electorate.

In previous chapters the methods by which the major parties select their nominees for public office have already been examined.
Where the convention system may be employed, the party organization may directly make its choice. Where the direct primary is in use
but official preprimary indorsing conventions are permitted, the
party organizations may also play a direct role in determining whom
nominees will be — provided the voters in the primary election heed
the preprimary convention's advice. Where the direct primary law
makes no provision for preprimary endorsements, then the party organization may only indirectly participate in the naming of its candidates for public office.

To these limitations on party in the nominee selection process
should be added still another which operates even in nominating conventions. Seldom is such a party gathering functioning as a deliberative body — whether bossed or theoretically democratic — free to
pick the most "available" candidate for a particular public office.
If there is an incumbent party member in that office and should he
desire renomination, whether he is the best possible nominee or not
he will almost without exception be in "control of the situation"
and thus be able to secure the renomination. Others in the party may
feel the incumbent has made a poor record, is slipping in strength in

---

[1] Harold J. Laski, *The American Presidency, An Interpretation* (New
York: Harper and Brothers, 1940), pp. 44–45. Reprinted by permission of Harper
and Brothers.

his constituency, or may be liable to go down to defeat in the general election, but party dynamics generally leave no alternative but to support the incumbent.

If the party has no incumbent or if one of its own who has held the office is retiring, even in a situation such as this what takes place at a nominating convention may hardly be called deliberation. Before the convention each candidate for a nomination will have been busily attempting to line up support. Perhaps one such candidate has enough promised votes to ensure nomination when the nominating body convenes. If he does not have a majority of delegates committed in his behalf, generally some large proportion of delegates is tied to one or another of the candidates. The contest then narrows to an attempt to win over those who are undecided and to make deals in order to shift whole blocks of delegates from one candidate to another.

Regardless of whether a party can directly select its nominees or whether the nomination process is deliberative or not, however, there are certain electability standards against which all candidates for party nominations are judged. It is to the elements which tend to determine " availability " rather than the mechanics or politics of candidate selection that this chapter is devoted. Because the Presidential nomination is the most important nomination within the power of the political party to bestow and because in the Presidential nominee selection process the operation of " availability " factors is reduced to language which is universal for the whole United States, the principal focus will be on candidates for nomination for the office of President of the United States.

" AVAILABILITY " FACTORS NOT CONSTANTS

Before examining some of the elements which tend to determine whether a candidate for a nomination is " available " or not, it should be noted that those elements and the weighting of the elements vary from time period to time period, from public office to public office, and from one section of the country to another. As David B. Truman has put it: " One whose personality and skills are appropriate to group leadership at one time may be completely inadequate at another. . . . One group situation may demand physical strength and courage, another oratorical skill, another intellectual acumen, another a facility at negotiation, and so on." [2]

---

[2] David B. Truman, *The Government Process* (New York: Alfred A. Knopf, 1951) , p. 190.

When a President is a candidate to succeed himself, he and his party are forced to stand on the record. He cannot very well be repudiated or the party will likewise risk repudiation by the admission that it has failed. The President has the weapons of patronage and other sanctions which he can apply to those within the party who would oppose his renomination. He will have in both his campaigns for renomination and re-election the advantage of being the President of the United States — the man who because of his position can draw attention and respect because of his office, if not through the power of his person. He also has the advantage of being a known quantity. Though he may have failed in many respects, he will tend to draw to his support all those who fear more an unknown quantity than the known quantity whose shortcomings can be taken into account. A President, when he seeks another term, generally is the most " available " candidate.

If the party has had control of the White House but its President is not a candidate for renomination, " availability " factors differ from those in situations where a President is a candidate. Now the " ideal " candidate tends to be one who can uphold the record of his party while in power and at the same time convey the impression that he will correct the errors which have been made and march ahead to an even better future. He has to accomplish this without, however, giving the appearance that he is critical of his party's immediate past.

If the party has been an out-party, its best nominee for President will tend to depend on what kind of opposition to the in-party would be most effective in that particular situation. Should the in-party have been successful in gaining broad public support for some of its projects, the out-party nominee should be one who can be counted upon to retain the good things and change the bad. Should the in-party not have been successful, the " ideal " out-party nominee may be one who is best equipped to slash the in-party's record to pieces.

These are only a few of the factors to be considered in different kinds of national convention situations. They are introduced to suggest that each time and in each type of situation the problem of the major party tends to be different in some respect from the problem it has faced at previous national conventions and different from the problem of the opposition major party. Yet, after taking cognizance of the fact that " availability " factors are not constants, there are still many generalizations on the basis of the past record which can be made to develop a descriptive definition of " availability."

WANTED: A MAN WHO IS A POLITICIAN

Raymond Moley in his *27 Masters of Politics* has used the famous " cave and shadow " parable of Plato's *Republic* to introduce a discussion of the manner in which a " political mind " functions. In the cave are individuals who, since birth, have been chained so that they may face only the wall opposite from the opening of the cave. All they can see of the outside world are the shadows which are cast upon the wall ahead of them. Those who manipulate the objects which are projected into shadows, therefore, " determine what the enchained human beings conceive to be the reality — the truth."

> Roughly translated into the terms of political behavior, the human beings are the public. The carriers of the objects are the politicians, considering not the substance of what they carry but the effect produced upon those who see the shadows.
>
> The politician creates illusions. His words must be selected not because they are the most forceful or descriptive in conveying exact facts and situations, but because they will produce in the minds of hearers or readers the reaction desired by the speaker or writer. . . .
>
> Ultimately, the considerations of a politician are not based upon truth or fact; they are based upon what the public will conceive to be truth or fact.
>
> This produces what is called a " political mind." It is an adaptation enforced by the necessities of environment and survival, just as is the fur of a polar bear or the coloration of a ground-hog. A sort of natural selection operates in the political environment which promotes the survival and success of minds capable of what some may call dissimulation and others call insincerity.[3]

What the politician does or says is not as important as what he appears to be doing or saying. Mere words or acts are not in themselves enough. The able politician must project himself in such a manner that he can see through the eyes of the people and hear through their ears what he and his acts look and sound like. Next, because he will succeed or fail depending upon the public support he

---

[3] Raymond Moley, *27 Masters of Politics* (New York: Funk and Wagnalls Company — Published for *Newsweek*, 1949) , pp. 42–43. Reprinted by permission of Raymond Moley.

can mobilize, the politician must be able to serve up his words and deeds in a manner which can inspire or educate to produce support.

Yet while the political party needs politicians who have " political minds," the selection process further narrows to those who have that quality but do not appear to have it. The fable of the major party " crusade " is that every word and campaign action is the result of a belief in a righteous cause the advancement of which is so important that the leaders of the crusade do not " stoop " to political techniques to accomplish their ends nor do they think of their political party's fortunes in the process. Many take such " crusades " at face value, but if they were in fact run on the basis of the theory, they would end as did John Brown with a noose around his neck.

It is the politicians like Abraham Lincoln and not the radicals like John Brown who reach political objectives whether it be a certain course of action or the winning of an election or a series of elections. Brown did not appear to have a " political mind " nor did he have one. His movement to create an army of slaves did not succeed.

Likewise, a politician with a " political mind " which appears to be a " political mind " immediately encounters solid resistance. The ideal major party candidate is an Abraham Lincoln type who has a " political mind " without giving the impression that his acts are political. With the prejudice against political manipulation so strong, both appearing not to be political and yet at the same time being politically able becomes perhaps the most important of a candidate's campaign assets.

How do men develop " political minds "? Some might be " born " with them, but generally the quality is developed through political experience. " To a philosopher, a scientist or a great lawyer," writes Moley, " the preoccupations of a politician seem to be the interests of a person too lazy to apply himself to serious things. This is a gross underestimation of the politician's job. For beneath the surface he is applying his mental faculties to exceedingly complex subject matter, and if he is to be successful, he must labor with incessant energy and meticulous care. For political genius is the capacity to give continuous, undivided and sedulous attention to matters that to most serious people seem too trivial to bother with." [4]

Only amateur politician Wendell Willkie can be classified as a businessman with no previous political or governmental background.

---

[4] *Ibid.,* p. 33.

" Despite the recurrent cry for ' business in government ' and against ' government in business,' our Presidents have always been chosen from among men who showed some talent for ' government in government.' " Nine have been Vice Presidents; 5, Secretaries of State; 3, Secretaries of War; 1, a Secretary of Commerce; 2, Assistant Secretaries of the Navy; 12, generals of the armies; 10, United States Senators; 14, governors; 12, members of the United States House of Representatives; 7, ambassadors; 12, state legislators; and 8 have had city government experience.[5]

Furthermore, most able politicians have been persons who systematically applied themselves to the learning of the ways of politics and politicians for a lifetime. Perhaps it is a Woodrow Wilson as a boy dreaming of being a United States Senator from Virginia and educating himself in politics. Perhaps it is a William Jennings Bryan at the age of 16 traveling from Nebraska to St. Louis to attend a national political convention and subsequently training himself for high political office.[6] Perhaps it is a Theodore Roosevelt, Franklin D. Roosevelt, or Calvin Coolidge systematically working his way up the rungs of the political ladder in his state. Politics, adds Moley, " is no profession to be taken up in later life, like golf or bridge, after success in business or a profession. It demands long experience, constant attention and, what is more important, a radical adaptation of mental processes. . . . It is a jealous art and can tolerate only slight time for other concerns." [7]

Perhaps a major party may select a Willkie with no previous governmental or political experience or an Eisenhower with only military experience, but when such a selection is made it is in its very nature a gamble where the man is chosen for qualities other than political ability in the hope that somehow the political ability may develop later. For every Eisenhower who may progress rapidly with his lessons in practical politics there is also a Grant who, though he attained the White House, never achieved the political touch or a Willkie who had too many lessons to master in too short a political lifetime.

---

[5] Sidney Hyman, *The American President* (New York: Harper and Brothers, 1954), p. 226.

[6] From Dayton David McKean, *Party and Pressure Politics* (Boston: Houghton Mifflin Company, 1949), p. 255.

[7] Moley, *op. cit.*, p. 31.

WANTED: A MAN WHO CAN COMMUNICATE

A President must, says Harold Laski, be a man of " common opinions." " But it is equally imperative that he be an ' uncommon man.' The public must see themselves in him, but they must, at the

" I was going to start off with an allusion to Plato's ' Republic,' but now I don't know."

same time, be confident that he is something bigger than themselves. They must see someone who compels respect. They must see someone who can say in the grand way what they half-articulately feel." [8]

The ability to communicate and thus be able to develop broad support depends not on verbal facility alone, but rather on the im-

---

[8] Laski, *op. cit.,* p. 38.

pact of the whole personality. An Abraham Lincoln can have an appearance which led some to liken him to a " baboon " and a Theodore Roosevelt can have a high-pitched voice which came out whistling through his teeth, but the impact of both a Lincoln at his time and a Theodore Roosevelt at his time can be greater than the highly polished appearance and voice of a Thomas E. Dewey at his time. Only once, in the opinion of Moley, was Dewey " thoroughly disheveled and completely informal " and that was in his primary fight with Harold E. Stassen in Oregon in 1948. " Somehow, in the fight his instincts got the better of his mind, and this revelation of Dewey the ' regular fellow ' won the state." [9] Yet there are times when a man too much the " regular fellow " cannot communicate either.

The candidate of today needs to be able to project himself on television, over the radio, in the press conference, and through any of the other numerous media available to him. There is, however, no set formula as to how he should use those media. The most effective communicator will be one who, given the setting in which he is placed and the psychology of the people at that time, can be an " uncommon man " of " common opinions." In short, he has to be able to establish contact — to first gain attention and having gained attention, to attract rather than repel or leave a neutral reaction, the product of which is passivity. And in politics which involve election to public office, the problem of communication is not to party alone but rather to those who hold the votes which will determine the outcome of the election.

WANTED: A MAN WHO CAN WORK WITH HIS PARTY

In making a nomination a major party desires that the nominee be a " party man " — " one who," in Frank R. Kent's words, " regardless of his party's sins and shortcomings, regardless of the character of its candidates, regardless of its record, regardless of its principles and policies, regardless of everything and everybody, with unvarying regularity and unshakable loyalty supports his party candidates after they are nominated and votes his party ticket on election day." [10] If the public office for which a nomination is being made has patronage at its disposal, the party wants a candidate who will, if

---

[9] Moley, op. cit., p. 58.
[10] Frank R. Kent, Political Behavior (New York: William Morrow and Company, 1928) , pp. 18–19.

elected, dispense the jobs to the party faithful. In the execution of public legislative and executive programs, the party wants a man who will always keep foremost in mind what those who control the party want in the way of governmental politics.

Though such a " party man " may be the type either major party would most like to nominate for all public offices, seldom for the more important offices is the political situation such that any old " party man " can win the election. Because winning elections is important to the major party, it is necessary to compromise from the type of nominee which the party as an interest group might most want and instead to accept a nominee who can win and be expected to work reasonably well with his party after he assumes office.

In 1920 when the Republican party appeared to have an excellent if not almost sure opportunity for regaining the White House, dark-horse United States Senator Warren G. Harding of Ohio could become an " available " candidate after the convention had deadlocked between Governor Lowden and General Wood. In 1916 the story of the Republican national convention had been a quite different one. In that year to win the Republican party needed a Presidential nominee with as much prestige as it could get. The party, therefore, turned to the United States Supreme Court in the person of Mr. Justice Charles Evans Hughes — one who had no close ties to those who controlled the Republican party, one who had fought with the controlling Republican machine in his home state of New York, and one who had a contempt for politicians which he was not always able to conceal.

Hughes was not liked by those who controlled the Republican party organization, but he did have two qualities in addition to his prestige which, as they were assessed by the party, made him an acceptable nominee. Although Hughes did hold the machine politician in contempt, he was not contemptuous of the Republican party. He was a Republican partisan, he was anti-Democratic party, and he had consistently voted the Republican ticket. Secondly, Hughes, it was felt, would work through the party organization on patronage matters.[11]

Different from both 1920 and 1916 was the 1940 Republican National Convention Presidential nomination action. Republicans, on the basis of Wendell Willkie's record, had no right to assume that

---

[11] From Kent, *op. cit.*, pp. 65–66.

Willkie was a Republican partisan in the Hughes sense, nor could they be sure of how Willkie would administer patronage. Furthermore, Willkie's prestige was a very recent development based largely on his colorful and dynamic personality — a prestige that might or might not last. Only an unresolvable deadlock between Robert A. Taft and Thomas Dewey permitted Willkie to become a serious contender. Once in contention, however, only the possibility that a man like Willkie could attract as no other man might the independent and Democratic voters who had been voting for Franklin D. Roosevelt brought the Republican delegates to what was an extraordinary decison.

If Willkie had had the ability to work with party and still retain his all-party appeal, he might very well have become President. Instead, however, the 1940 Republican nominee was lecturing his party in public instead of in private. The Willkie Clubs in many places appeared to be attempting to take over the Republican party during the campaign — something which they should not have tried to do, if that was their intention, until *after* Willkie's election. And in 1944 when Willkie staked almost his entire chance on the Wisconsin primary campaign, Republican leaders in that state very effectively made him pay the price for his past inability to work with the party.

It is not likely that either the Democratic or Republican parties will ever make such a nomination as the Republicans did in 1940. Dewey, though clearly of one wing of the Republican party, is a party man. Eisenhower, whose nomination campaign was managed by the Dewey organization, was a " calculated risk " for the Republican party, but the 1952 action was in no wise comparable to 1940. All the recent Democratic Presidential nominees have met the " ability to work with party " test.

As has been noted previously, the major parties both want and do not want Presidential candidates who can develop into " strong " Presidents. They do not want them because they would prefer a " safe " party man. They do want them when they feel they cannot win with a " safe " party man.

After a nominee becomes President, there are other forces which make it necessary for the party to pick the broad-appeal type of candidate. A President must draw a line on partisanship at some point short of the line over which extreme partisanship would preclude his symbolically becoming President of all the United States. Furthermore, each President, if he is to be politically successful, has to create a new *de facto* party broader in appeal than the party organization which nominated him.

Just as a mother who too possessively attempts to keep her growing child tied to her apron strings tends to limit the child's potential development, so does the political party which tries too possessively to dominate its Presidential nominees and Presidents restrict their opportunities for making the most of their political positions. However, neither does a political party want, nor should it be expected to nominate, a candidate who cannot work with the party. A compromise thus tends generally to be effected when nominations are made.

WANTED: A MAN FROM THE RIGHT STATE AND SECTION OF THE COUNTRY

In previous chapters the importance of pivot states such as New York, California, Ohio, and Illinois has been noted. The pivot state has a big proportion of the total national population and thus has a large number of electoral votes. It is also politically doubtful in that the strength of the two major parties is in relatively equal balance and Presidential elections in such a state will be close and might go either to the Democrats or Republicans. Consequently, the major parties have concluded that a Presidential or Vice Presidential nominee from such a state may pay big dividends in that he may make the difference between victory and defeat in a Presidential election.

But these are not the only reasons why most Presidential and Vice Presidential tickets are made up of men from certain of the large and doubtful states. In addition, the states which have produced the nominees have also been strategic in their geographical location. The reason for nominating a man from one such state is not only to win that state but also to attract votes in other states which are a part of that state's political section.

A first corollary to the pivot state-sectional principle has been the rule of the " balanced ticket." If the Presidential nominee comes from a pivot state in one section, the Vice Presidential nominee will be picked from a state — preferably a pivot state — in some other section of the country. When, for example, Ohioans were Republican Presidential nominees, that party tended to look first to New York for its Vice Presidential candidates. If Democrats selected a New Yorker as a Presidential nominee, they would tend to look to the Midwest to fill the second place on the ticket, or if necessary to hold the Border states, perhaps to a Border state. Only in 1952 did the Democratic party reach into the South for its Vice Presidential nominee.

The mention of the Stevenson-Sparkman 1952 Democratic ticket brings up the second major corollary to the pivot state-sectional principle followed by the major parties. Sparkman of Alabama was an exception to the rule that both major parties have usually excluded southerners from consideration for Presidential and Vice Presidential nominations. With the South solidly Democratic, certainly there was no reason for the Republican party to waste a nomination on that section in which there was no chance for success. Nor have the modern Democrats — with the Sparkman exception — gone to the South for their Presidential or Vice Presidential nominees. As long as the South remained safely Democratic, this section could be taken for granted by the Democratic party, and nominations could be placed in states and sections in which those nominations could cut into Republican strength.

Other factors in addition to the safe Democratic character of the South have operated to force the Democratic party in making nominations to ignore the section in which it had its strongest support. The South has only some 10 percent of the population of the United States. It has been primarily agricultural, while the other sections of the country have to varying degrees been an agricultural-commercial-industrial composite. In the North, as distinct from the South, as soon as a politician has begun to dream dreams of himself as a Presidential possibility, he has of necessity had to broaden his outlook from what it might otherwise have been if he were thinking only of winning his own state. In the South, with Democratic politicians having no chance at the political grand prize, there has not been the compulsion to break out of provincial thought patterns. Consequently the South has not produced many men of electable appeal to the whole country. Anti-Negro prejudices which southern society has produced in its politicians makes them unacceptable in the large and doubtful states of the other sections which have sizeable " civil rights " voting blocks.[12]

If the South tends to " slip " in its Democratic allegiance in Presidential elections, and if the economic and social characteristics of society there become more like those found in other sections of the

---

[12] From Hyman, *op. cit.,* pp. 198–200.

country, then the Democratic party will have to embark on a " care and nurture " program for the South which will include more Presidential nominations for Border state Democrats or more Vice Presidential nominations for southern Democrats. If Republicans become competitive with Democrats in the South, the Republican party too might begin to look to Border or southern states for Vice Presidential nominees. From the start of the Democratic solidification of the South until 1952, however, Presidential and Vice Presidential nominations have been reserved for men from non-southern states.

WANTED: A MAN WITH A PROTESTANT CHURCH AFFILIATION

Though a candidate for a Presidential nomination may be an able politician, though he can effectively communicate with the electorate, though he would be expected to work satisfactorily with his party, and though he comes from a pivot state with a politically ideal sectional location, the rules of Presidential and Vice Presidential nominee selection have dictated that he will not be chosen if he is a member of the Jewish religion, and, with one exception, that neither can he be a Catholic. Democrats may regularly select Catholics as national party chairmen. Catholics and Jews may occupy high positions in major party councils or in an administration. But members of either of the two religious groups are not considered politically sound choices for Presidential and Vice Presidential nominations.

The principal reason for such an unwritten rule lies in the fact that the major party needs candidates for the two highest offices in the land " who, positively, will make the widest appeal and, negatively, will offend the least proportion of the electorate." [13] Catholics and Jews are in a minority vote-power position in relation to Protestants, but that fact in itself has not produced the applied prohibition against these two religious groups. An Abraham Lincoln who was never a member of an organized church and an Eisenhower who was not a church member at the time of the 1952 Republican National Convention were in a minority position in relation to all organized religious denominations. Their lack of church membership was not held politically against them. The problem arises only when a candidate's affiliation is Catholic or Jewish, and then only because of the

---

[13] Laski, *op. cit.*, p. 44.

intensity of non-Catholic and non-Jewish opinion that the Presidency should not be placed in the hands of a member of either of these two faiths.

Either major party in selecting its Presidential ticket will attempt to designate as candidates men who will not unnecessarily arouse strong opposition. By refusing to nominate a Catholic or a Jew, the religious conflict is kept out of the campaign. By nominating a Catholic or a Jew, a major party invites a campaign in which religion might have more of a bearing on the outcome than any other issue.

In 1884, as soon as the newspaper reporter had heard and understood the significance of the Protestant minister's " rum, Romanism and rebellion " statement to Blaine, the political prospects for the Republican nominee darkened. As Catholics everywhere read the report or as they heard the words which Blaine had not effectively repudiated in sermons the following Sunday, they could feel that they had at least one reason for voting Democratic — one reason which had not existed prior to the incident.[14]

In 1928 the religious issue was Protestant-injected against the Catholic Alfred E. Smith. Hoover sought to reject the issue. However, it could not be ruled out of the campaign. True it is that no one knows whether, if Smith had not been a Catholic, the result on election day would have been different from what it was. Smith's religion, certainly made him to some degree politically weaker than he would otherwise have been. The mere injection of the explosive religious question was something which the Democratic party in 1928 could not afford — provided its object was winning that election.

As the major parties have tried to avoid unnecessarily arousing opposition by nominating Catholics or Jews for President or Vice President, so also has the unwritten prohibition tended to apply against men who have figured in divorce proceedings, regardless of whether a question is raised about their general moral standards. Where in the church-affiliation case the danger lies in Protestant reactions to Catholic or Jewish nominees, the question raised about a divorced candidate's electability is whether or not the fact of divorce will antagonize Catholics and perhaps some elements of Protestantism.

The Democratic party in 1952 broke precedent by nominating a divorced man — Adlai E. Stevenson. Whether Stevenson would

---

14 See page 401.

have fared materially better had he not been a divorced man is, like the Alfred E. Smith question, not certainly answerable. If the election of 1952 had been a very close one, however, political observers would no doubt have attributed Stevenson's defeat in part to this cause.

Today the fact that a candidate for a Presidential nomination has been divorced is not as much of an obstacle to him as would be Catholic or Jewish church membership. If other things are equal between candidates, however, the major party will tend to avoid potential trouble by refusing to nominate one who might arouse either the religion or the divorce issues.

WANTED: A MAN WITH THE RIGHT NATIONALITY BACKGROUND

Biographies of Presidents usually contain one or several chapters on family antecedents of the man, tracing the family tree as far back as records are available. The lineages of all but five Presidents are rooted in Great Britain. Sidney Hyman's explanation for the phenomenon is this: " Some 80,000,000 Americans trace their descent to the British Isles, to form the largest single ' interest ' in the nation. It is not spoken of as the ' English vote.' Nor does it act as a solid bloc. But it forms the cultural frame within which all other ' interests ' and ' blocs ' must make their adjustments." [15]

Not until three or four generations of assimilation with English-American stock does a nationality group acquire the kind of acceptance which makes it possible for one of its own to be seriously considered for the two highest offices in the land. Only in this century have major parties frequently nominated men with non-British family trees. By 1928 Alfred E. Smith's South Irish stock which had begun mass immigration to the United States before the Civil War was acceptable to the Democratic party. By 1940, a Willkie of Germanic stock identified with an immigration stream which also started before the Civil War was acceptable to the Republican party. Should one such as Chief Justice Earl Warren with Scandinavian roots receive a Presidential nomination, he would be the first descendant of the 1870–1880 wave of Scandinavian immigration to be so honored. Should these assimilation patterns continue to hold, Americans of

---

[15] Hyman, *op. cit.*, pp. 200–201.

southern European antecedents might not expect to be considered as Presidential timber for twenty-five or more years into the future.[16]

The rules of " availability " do not exclude whites of non-English national backgrounds from Presidential and Vice Presidential consideration. But when a non-English handicap is compounded by a racial difference, the political obstacle, at least for the immediate future, is insurmountable. Until all Negroes in the United States have the suffrage and the political power which would go with the right to vote, until assimilation of the Negro has proceeded much farther than it now has and until anti-Negro social prejudices have broken down, no Negro will be considered " available " for a Presidential or Vice Presidential nomination. For the man of oriental background, the " availability " potential is even less. Even though assimilation took place rapidly, he would have only a negligible nationality vote power behind him.

WANTED: A GENERAL OF THE ARMIES

An examination of the part which generals of the armies have played in national party conventions, Presidential campaigns, and in the White House must be divided into two distinct historical periods. The first was before 1900 when the military services had not yet become professionalized. During this era to have been a general was one of the principal routes to the establishment of prestige, and the major parties made much political use of the amateur military leader.

The second period, since the establishment of the General Staff, the development of huge military forces, and professionalization, has been one in which the full-time soldier does not often cross over the boundary line from his life work into active politics. Only Eisenhower since 1900 stands out as the conspicuous exception. For reasons different from those before 1900, however, the major parties are likely in the future to once again attempt to exploit generals for the special qualifications they can bring with them into political service.

Washington, Jackson, William Henry Harrison, Taylor, Pierce, Grant, Hayes, Garfield, Benjamin Harrison had all at one time in their careers been generals, and Johnson had been Military Governor of Tennessee during the Civil War and Arthur Quartermaster General of the New York militia. Of these, only Washington, Taylor,

---

[16] From *ibid.*, pp. 202–203.

and Grant came directly to the Presidency as a result of military service, and of the three, only Taylor had had an unbroken military career. Generals who won major party nominations for President but were defeated were Lewis Cass, Winfield Scott, John C. Frémont, George McClellan, and Winfield Scott Hancock.[17]

OUR ULYSSES
April 9, 1865 — A never-to-be-forgotten deed

Armies during the pre-1900 period were small. Appointment to high military position in many cases depended upon one's political power with the political officeholders in government. Or, as in the case of Jackson, the man became a major general in his state militia by virtue of his being elected by the field officers of his militia district. William Henry Harrison was also an elected general. Ambitious law-

[17] From Hyman, *op. cit.*, pp. 210–217.

yers like Hayes and Benjamin Harrison could organize a local military force and thus become soldier leaders. A teacher like Garfield who had translated a pamphlet by Frederick the Great could be regarded as qualified for command.[18]

How open were the doors for military advancement is revealed in the manner in which Grant, clerking in his father's leather store in Galena, Illinois, in 1861, resumed his soldiering. By chance he met the governor of Illinois who appointed him to the staff of the state adjutant general to muster volunteers. There, by chance, he met a brigadier general who had much political power. When President Lincoln asked the Illinois Congressional delegation to recommend some citizen from Illinois for the position of brigadier general, Grant — then a colonel — was surprised, because " my acquaintance with the Congressmen was very limited," to find his name first on the list.[19]

Here were men whom military activity had tended to make well known. But that fact did not necessarily assure the major parties that they had other qualities which might make them good Presidential nominees or Presidents. With a few exceptions, these men were selected not because they had been generals but for their prestige and general experience, and particularly experience in politics.

Eisenhower's " availability," however, was quite another matter. After World War II the United States had unequivocally committed itself to assume leadership in world affairs. The " cold war " made it necessary that the President of the United States thoroughly understand problems of foreign relations and problems of international leadership. Eisenhower had been commander in chief of the Allied forces in Europe during the war and was also in command of the European defense organization after the war. He had already had personal contact with the leaders of other countries with whom a President would have to deal in joint efforts to solve world affairs problems. " For the first time in American history," in the opinion of Sidney Hyman, " a man wholly divorced from domestic affairs nevertheless won the presidency on the grounds that his experience on the international scene gave him superior qualifications for the post." [20]

---

[18] From *ibid.*, pp. 212–213.
[19] From Dorothy Burne Goebel and Julius Goebel, Jr., *Generals in the White House* (Garden City, N.Y.: Doubleday, Doran and Company, 1945) , p. 39.
[20] Hyman, *op. cit.*, p. 4.

Today if a candidate for a Presidential nomination has not had the experience abroad of an Eisenhower, he quickly manages an assignment which will give such experience or embarks on the well-publicized grand tours which are designed both to gain an understanding of United States problems in international relations and to give the American people and his major party the impression that he does understand those problems. Where "availability" may once have consisted of elements which were exclusively or almost exclusively of a domestic character, now the man who would win a Presidential nomination must be regarded as competent in both domestic and international relations, with the latter quality more important in times of world crisis. American men who have held top international military or diplomatic positions are likely to be in political demand, and not alone for their prestige.

WANTED: A MAN IN GOOD HEALTH

Former Vice President John Nance Garner, as he shelled pecans in retirement in Uvalde, Texas, was reminded how close he had been to the Presidency. Wouldn't he have liked to have been President? " No," Garner replied, " I'd be dead by this time." [21]

The strains on a President are great. He is called upon to make decisions which may have national or international consequences for good or for bad. He must run the executive branch of the national government. He must establish and maintain relations with Congress. He must lead his party. He is a ceremonial chief — laying cornerstones, inspecting dams, and giving state dinners. Some of these activities can be delegated, but the ultimate responsibility is the President's. The pace of his life, therefore, is such that he needs to be in the best of health to meet day-to-day demands of routine and policy.

Since Vice Presidents are not chosen because they are expected to some day become Presidents, the party gambles that their Presidential candidate will live through the term for which he has been nominated and elected. Yet one quarter of the elected American Presidents have died in office. Of the seven Vice Presidents who have gained the White House by virtue of a Presidential death, only three have gone on to win re-election for themselves — Theodore Roosevelt, Coolidge, and Truman. In the other cases the accession of the

---

[21] Moley, *op. cit.*, p. 66.

Vice President to the office of Chief Executive has represented some degree of political disaster for the elements of the party which nominated the President.

Vice Presidential nominations are made to sectionally balance a ticket, to attempt to hold the wing of the party which loses the Presidential nomination, or for other reasons that are not always clear. Perhaps without exception, however, Vice Presidential nominees are not men whom the party would have selected had it been known that they would succeed the Presidential nominee.

Protesting against the New York Republican organization's desire to " get rid " of Theodore Roosevelt by nominating him for the Vice Presidency in 1900, Mark Hanna is reputed to have remarked: " Don't any of you realize that there is only one life between that madman Roosevelt and the Presidency? Platt and Quay are no better than idiots! What harm can Roosevelt do as Governor of New York compared to the damage he will do as President if McKinley should die? " [22]

If the Vice President who becomes President by virtue of a vacancy in the office is not politically able, the party's record and appeal will suffer. If he is from a wing of the party other than that of the President, if the latter should die, control of the party will tend to go to the wing which lost its fight at the preceding national convention. Likewise, if there are sectional rivalries based on strong differences between sections, death of a President upsets the sectional balance, and power in the White House rests with the section which came in second best in the nomination fight. Clearly, the major party has much at stake in its nominee for President, and so his health becomes not a personal but a party and public consideration.

In making its Presidential nomination decision the political party can only nominate someone it thinks to be in good health. Generally its only guide is the unreliable statistic of a candidate's age. Because Averill Harriman, for example, is a year older than President Eisenhower who had a heart attack, immediately Harriman's age becomes a major factor affecting his " availability." Yet, if a man is 65 years old or older and that fact constitutes a liability for his candidacy, might not also a man in his late 30's or early 40's lack the experience necessary to win election and to make a good record if elected? Again there is no certain answer.

---

[22] From Hyman, *op. cit.,* p. 189.

After weighing all the other " availability " factors and then relating them to the health or age factor, the major party in making its decision can only hope and pray that it has guessed correctly. With the Presidential office becoming more and more important in both foreign and domestic affairs and as the parties more clearly realize how greatly their future depends upon the man who occupies the White House, the major parties might be expected to move away from the old separate set of Vice Presidential " availability " factors to pick instead Vice Presidential nominees for the same reasons that Presidential nominees are selected.

WANTED: A MAN WITH MONEY

Campaigning for the Presidency is expensive. Throughout his attempts to win the nomination and election the candidate must have an income adequate to meet the needs of his family and himself. If he has to accept contributions for this purpose and the fact becomes known, he is immediately placed in a position of appearing to have engaged in an illegitimate transaction. Unless a man is personally wealthy or unless he can find financial supporters with ample resources, it is not likely that he can build himself up to the point where his party will consider him " available." Private wealth is not an absolute requirement, but a candidate with an independent income is in a more advantageous position than one without such income sources.

" AVAILABILITY " FACTORS APPLIED
TO OTHER OFFICES

" Availability " rules employed by the major parties in selecting nominees for the Presidency or Vice Presidency have general application to all types of offices, but they vary with the type of office to be filled and the nature of each constituency. For all types of nominations, able politicians who do not appear to be so " political " that they arouse anti-politician sentiments in the electorate are wanted. Likewise, for all offices the party desires a candidate who can work with party during the campaign and after election.

The ability to communicate is more important for the higher offices than for lower offices. This is particularly true when candidates for lower office run on a long ballot where the average voter cannot possibly know of or be informed about many of them. At the lower office levels a man might be able to be elected without any more communication ability than being able to get up and smile at a public meeting when his name is one of a long list of nominees who are introduced.

Where the candidate for a nomination lives is a consideration in any nomination contest, whether for high office or low. If the office is voted upon by a state-wide electorate and there is one particular city or county which has a major proportion of the population, usually a nominee who comes from such a city or county will be in a more advantageous position than one who does not. In states with several large cities or counties state-wide party tickets will be balanced to give nominee representation to each important population center. Likewise, within a city or county similar residence factors will tend to operate.

In national conventions Catholics and Jews do not meet " availability " tests. In a state-wide or smaller constituency where Catholics or Jews represent a significant proportion of the electorate, however, perhaps no one who is not a Catholic or Jew may be an " available " nominee. Even in states or districts where Protestants are in a majority, Catholics and Jews might be nominated and elected to state-wide office, depending upon the qualifications and abilities of the man himself. Below the offices of President and Vice President, though the religious factor still exists, it tends to be less important. As for divorce, in some constituencies a party would be foolhardy to nominate a divorced man and in others that fact would make no difference.

Though American Presidents have tended to come from English stock and each nationality group which is grafted onto the main English tree in America must undergo an extended period of assimilation before it becomes politically accepted, the national origin composition of each state or local constituency will determine what for each constitutes the most " available " nationality background. In a district in which Negro voters are in a majority, a Negro candidate is generally the most " available " for the nomination; in a strongly Irish district, an Irishman; and so on. Or when a constituency includes several major nationality background groups, party tickets will be balanced between them.

Physical health which is important when the delegates to a national convention evaluate Presidential candidates is less of a consideration for other offices — at least if health is measured in large part by age as is the case with the national conventions. Men in their seventies and even eighties might meet with no major objection provided the office they seek is not that of President of the United States. Similarly with the nonpresidential offices, youth is less of a handicap to the would-be party nominee.

For anyone who would be active in politics at any level above which campaigning for office becomes expensive beyond the average person's ability to finance himself, an independent income becomes a great advantage. The parties, if the several candidates' other qualities are relatively equal, like a nominee who can put his whole public office salary or more into the campaign. If politics is to be pursued over the years, only a financially secure man can afford the luxury of a political career without sacrifice for himself or his family — actual sacrifice when he is defeated or worry sacrifice for fear of what might happen should he be defeated.

——————

These are the kinds of factors which are considered by the major parties when they are in the process of determining their nominees for public office. All of the factors are related to the kind of a general election candidate the man will make, provided he gets the nomination. After the nomination questions are settled, the parties and their candidates next move on to the general election campaign. Now the concerns become campaign organization, research of the election problem, propaganda, and finance.

CHAPTER EIGHTEEN

Campaign Organization

A one-man business may involve many functions, many kinds of policy-making and execution. The same kind of business grown to require a thousand employees sees the operations enlarged and both policy-making and execution divided. The operations are not normally simply what they would be if there were a consolidation of a thousand one-man businesses. The thousand can do things acting together they could not do acting separately. The significance of the whole enterprise is in the division of labor, and labor is divided in two ways: operations producing the product are divided, and operations managing the undertaking as a whole are divided. In the organization of a thousand persons there are not only new opportunities, but there are also new problems of relating the parts of the operation, new problems of decision making. The thousand are not merely assembled, they are given form, organized. And the form in organizations of human beings is universally some form of hierarchy.

Paul H. Appleby [1]

A candidate for a seat in the lower house of a state legislature in a rural district in which political party organization is weak to non-existent may, like the " one-man business " of Paul Appleby's introductory quotation, perform every campaign function himself. He may do all his planning, with or without the advice of others. He may be the only person who gives speeches, attends meetings, or canvasses for votes in his own behalf. He may raise all his own campaign

----

[1] *Policy and Administration* (University, Alabama: University of Alabama Press, 1949) , p. 68. Reprinted by permission of the University of Alabama Press.

funds, or perhaps he will need no outside contributions. He may pre-pare his own ads for the village weekly newspapers of the district. In short, the candidate in such a situation is the campaign.

Consider in contrast another kind of election problem. Here there are a million or more voters to reach. There will be a party or-ganization which may run or play an important role in the campaign. The candidate may need professional political advice in planning his strategy. Even though he gives ten speeches a day, he will need other speakers to assist him. Any vote canvassing, because the candidate does not have time for door-to-door contacts, will have to be done by volunteers or paid workers. Rallies will have to be arranged. A full-time campaign manager may be necessary and perhaps a pub-licity agent and other specialists. The candidate will need large amounts of money, and perhaps he will hire professional fund rais-ers on a percentage fee basis.

At this level, campaign organization becomes a substantial un-dertaking. As the number of voters increases, as larger amounts of money must be raised and intelligently spent, as more specialized skills are required to effectively use mass media of communication, and as more volunteers need to be recruited and directed, the effi-ciency of the campaign organization generally becomes critical to the success of the campaign. No longer is the process a " one-man busi-ness." " The thousand," to return to the introductory quotation, " are not merely assembled, they are given form, organized."

Organization may be universal in any group effort; however, *good* organization is not universal. There may be no direct lines of authority and responsibility in the hierarchy. There may be a failure to co-ordinate the activities of different organizational units on the same hierarchical level or on different levels. There may be an in-ability to communicate between units and levels. The purpose at one level may be different from that at another. The quality of leadership may not be consistent, or it may be generally poor. These are some of the most common reasons for organizational inefficiency. Political campaign organizations by their very nature are particularly suscepti-ble to developing these weaknesses. In fact, the " big operation " po-litical campaign begins with at least some of these deficiencies already built into the organizational structure.

To more clearly understand difficulties standing in the way of efficient political campaign organization, look first at a simplified pic-ture of a corporation in Figure 25 on page 486.

At the top of the organization chart will be a board of directors. Here is where broad policy decisions will be made. Under the board will be a president responsible to the board for running the organization. Responsible to the president will be staff units, such as personnel and purchasing, performing through the president the housekeeping tasks of administration. Also under the president will be the

Figure 25

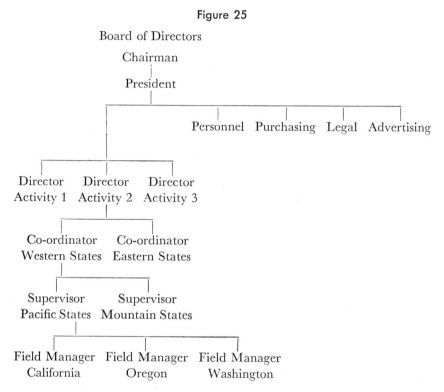

line departments charged with performing the functions for which the organization was formed.

From the lowest level field employee responsible to a field manager to the top of the organization there can be a direct line of responsibility, and from the top down there is a hierarchy of authority. This can be a tightly knit unitary system. Activities at each organizational level can be co-ordinated because each unit at each level is responsible to the same person at the level above. There can be two-way communication both up and down the hierarchy. The purpose of each organizational unit can hardly be inconsistent with the overall purpose of the corporation. Quality of leadership can be good because salaries adequate for attracting good men can be offered, and if a man is not performing as he should, there is authority to remove him. All members of the organization are paid and are full-time professionals. All in general have worked together for several years. Although the quality of organization varies greatly from one corporation to another, nevertheless, there are no inherent obstacles to efficient organization provided that those who run the corporation have the ability to organize effectively.

Now examine the vastly different type of organizational problem for a political party involved in a Presidential election campaign. Here a " simplified " organizational chart will look something like that in Figure 26 on page 488.

Although the chart appears to be complex, in fact the party organizational problem in Presidential campaigns is even more confusing than the drawing can show. Note first the few solid lines which connote an authority-responsibility relationship. Because the national chairman is selected by the Presidential nominee, the former is responsible to the latter, but even this line does not mean that all the members of the national committee will in whole or part support the Presidential nominee. When the governor is allowed by the state committee to select the state chairman, then also the latter will be responsible to the former, but again the governor is not necessarily assured of the support of all the members of the state committee. The solid lines linking the precinct captain to the ward chairman and the ward chairman, in turn, to the municipal chairman might or might not be justified depending upon what type of machine exists and what is the degree of control exercised in the municipal party hierarchy.

The dash lines connote what is generally at best a cooperative relationship, but not one based on authority. Question marks are inserted in the dash lines where most often cooperation may degenerate into passive or at worst antagonistic relationships. Perhaps, for example, a candidate for governor in a state and his state party organization will " sit out " the Presidential part of the campaign or openly oppose their Presidential nominee, as was the case in the Democratic party in Texas in 1952. Perhaps, as is usually true in California, nearly all candidates for partisan offices independently run their own campaigns, and often do their own fund raising. Perhaps the Citizens for Eisenhower or similar auxiliary party organizations are, in several states, at swords' point with the regular party organization.

Figure 26. Simplified Organization Chart for a Presidential Campaign

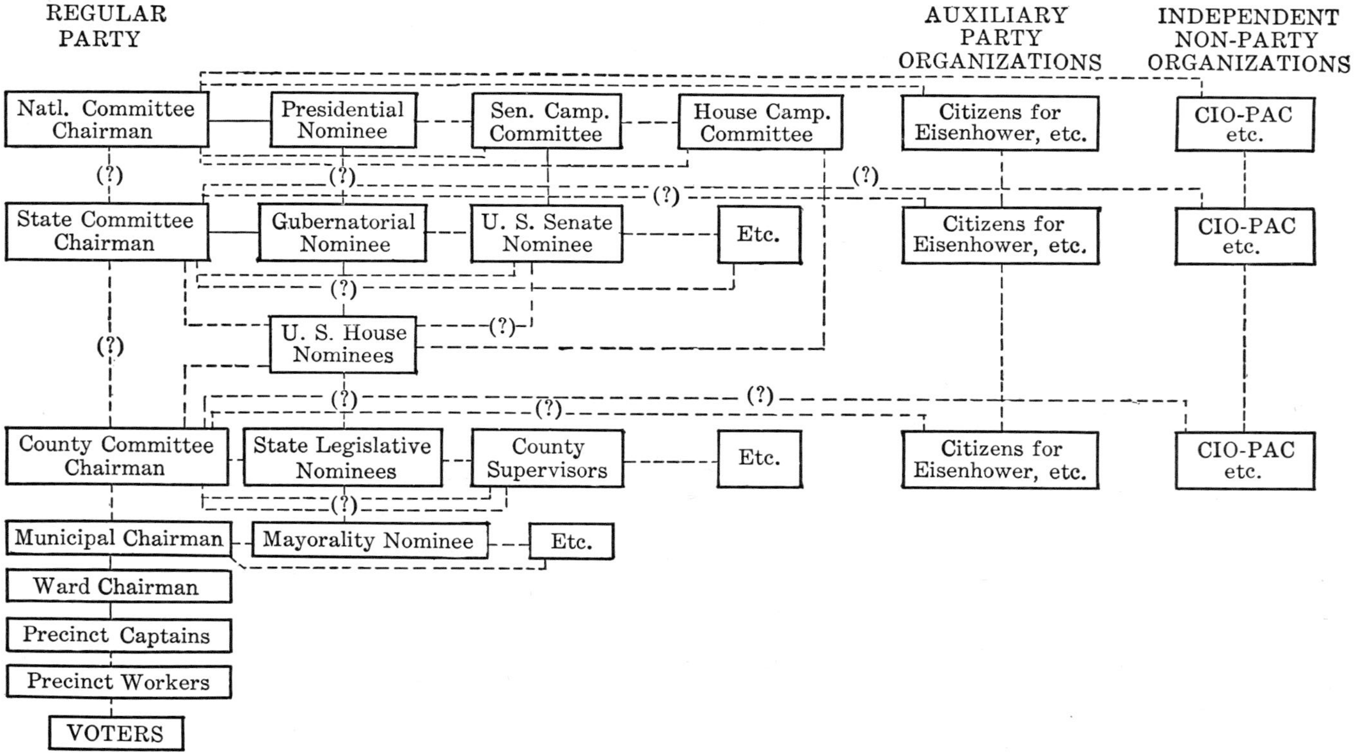

Perhaps the C.I.O.–P.A.C. or similar independent nonparty organizations stand in the same relationship to the state party of the Presidential nominee they are supporting. Perhaps, though the national unit of the American Federation of Labor's League for Political Education supports a Democrat, its state unit may support a Republican for state office and its local union components may officially reject their state organization's decision. These are some of the most obvious complexities, but there are more.

Assuming that all levels of organization and all party units, candidates, auxiliary party organizations, and independent nonparty organizations are willing to work together, the problem of co-ordination is still so great that the campaign effort can never approach the co-ordination attainable in a business corporation. Communication is difficult because units on the same organizational level and on different levels are independent of each other and each, if they want to, can go their own way. Leaders generally cannot be hired and fired for the same reason — they owe their offices to different groups. Except for candidates and the relatively few full-time professionals playing a part in a Presidential election year campaign effort, the stations on the organization chart are manned with part-time volunteers who have their own businesses to tend to and who can subvert or pull out of the joint effort any time they desire.

Furthermore, a large proportion of the volunteer personnel has enlisted only for the short period of the campaign, and from campaign to campaign there is a vast turnover of workers. By comparison with a business organization, the officers and workers in a campaign are almost unknown to each other. Consequently, during the campaign, relationships have to be established and qualifications judged in what amounts to the kind of preliminary preparation a football team gets in spring practice before the regular season's schedule. Only the campaign, in fact, is already the big game.

The foregoing comparison of a business organization with a major party's campaign effort in a Presidential year is not to suggest that the latter should be organized like the former. Obviously, this is neither possible nor desirable. The political party serves a different purpose than a business organization, and unless federalism, separation of powers, and other characteristics of the American political system are changed, the parties will probably remain what they are.

The organizational obstacles that a national party political campaign must overcome are similar for both major parties. The object of the organizational contest between the two major parties, then, is not to copy a business organization but rather to achieve the most efficient organization possible within political campaign limitations.

To make the subject of campaign organization manageable, the remainder of this chapter will concentrate on county campaign organization. This is the level where effective campaign organization pays off with the greatest dividends in terms of direct voter contacts. In using the county level as an illustration it is possible to show some of the most important relationships with the higher levels of party campaign organization. Also the county organizational problem is similar to that for any candidate for an office below the level of a Presidential or Vice Presidential nominee who would set up an independent campaign organization for his state or Congressional district.

CAMPAIGN ORGANIZATION AT THE COUNTY LEVEL

The functions involved in political campaigning might be classified into the four following separate but interrelated types. First is that of planning — sketching the main outlines of the kind of campaign which will be used, the kind of issues which will be stressed, and the techniques which will be employed to sell the party's candidates. Planning should not stop when the preliminary decisions have been made. Throughout, the campaign course which has been set should be flexible enough to enable the party to exploit opposition weaknesses and the party's newly found sources of strength which become more evident at each stage of the campaign's development.

The second and third types of functions also extend throughout the campaign. One of these is the utilization of every practical medium of communication to sell the party's candidates and whatever programs they are offering, and at the same time to directly or indirectly create in the voter's mind the impression that the party's product is better than that of the opposition. The third of these functions is the recruitment of volunteer workers and the collection of campaign funds — resources of which no well-managed campaign can ever get enough. When the volunteers have been integrated into the campaign organization, they too should be effective salesmen engaged in the party's selling process. Likewise the collected funds will be spent for the same purpose.

Fourth among the types of functions are the special election day

activities of the campaign organization — getting the " right " voters to the polls, providing poll watchers to challenge would-be voters
who might not be entitled to vote, and furnishing watchers to see that
no fraudulent practices are employed by the opposition when the
votes are being counted. As soon as the results are announced, the
party begins to arrange its interim activity program until the next
campaign, and throughout that interim the party will be planning to
hold at the next election what it has won or to gain from the opposition at the next election what it has lost.

Organizational forms set up to perform these functions vary
greatly from one county to another and from one party to another.
Nevertheless, there is a general pattern which can be outlined. And
for that information the student or politician must turn to the assortment of campaign manuals published by Democrats, Republicans,
party auxiliary organizations, and independent nonparty organizations.

The Importance of Organization As the Party Sees It. Campaign
manuals enthusiastically set down the virtues of good organization as
the parties hope it will be practiced in the counties. *A Guidebook
for County and Precinct Workers* (undated) published by the Democratic National Committee is entitled " The Key to DEMO-
CRATIC VICTORY," and as the reader turns to the first page he
finds " Organization — The Key to Victory." The third edition of
the Republican State Central Committee of South Dakota's *County
Workers' Campaign Manual* develops the point in more detail:

> *Team Work wins!* A number of South Dakota counties which for-
> merly yielded consistent majorities to the Democrats, now regularly
> return strong Republican majorities and elect their entire ticket of
> G.O.P. county candidates. WHY? A study of these counties, shows
> that trends were CHANGED because active, alert, organization-
> minded, TRAINED county workers had systematized their campaign-
> ing and their work on election day. They now have campaign " Com-
> bat Teams " that know what to do, where to do it, when and how.
>
> Effective political, community, or business leadership recognizes the
> importance of a careful division of labor. Set up SPECIAL COM-
> MITTEES to do SPECIFIC JOBS. *Fix responsibility.* Call for fre-
> quent progress reports. Follow through. When you (Mr. Chairman!)
> find that a job is not being done, have a personal visit with the people
> responsible for that work. If this fails to get results, assign the task

(opportunity for service) to somebody who WILL AGREE to do it. The victory must not be lost through failure to plug A FEW weak spots in the line! [2]

The Republican National Committee's *Republican Campaign Manual* (1951) puts it this way:

Organization in the political field has a single purpose — to SELL the Party's leaders and principles to the public. A political organization lacking in the ability to sell has little value. Organization is the first requirement for victory, for without effective political organization, it is difficult to sell the Party. The art of successful campaign management demands a thorough understanding of the principles of political organization.[3]

An Over-all View of a County Party Campaign Organization. Figure 27 is a composite of several existing and recommended party organization charts. Though no one county organization may divide functions exactly as shown here, some combination of division of labor devices such as these should be employed.

Several points about Figure 27 should be elaborated. First, it should be noted that the chart was drawn on the assumption that the campaigns within the county are being conducted by the county party organization. Though such an assumption makes the problem easier to illustrate, it is not necessarily accurate. Perhaps a candidate is operating his campaign independently of the county party organization. If that be the case, the candidate's organization chart might look somewhat as does that of Figure 27, except that the candidate and his campaign manager should go into the top center spaces where the county committee, its chairman, and executive secretary are now placed. Or perhaps the individual candidate has a smaller organization of his own and yet he relies on the county party organization for all of the services which it is able to provide for him. This is generally what the relationship between candidate and county party organization is likely to be.

Second, note that between the county committee and precinct captain there is a regional precinct co-ordinator. If the county is relatively small, precinct captains might deal directly with the county

---

[2] As quoted by Paul P. Van Riper, *Handbook of Practical Politics* (New York: Henry Holt and Company, 1952), p. 48.

[3] Page 7.

committee office staff or with the various county committee activity committee chairmen. When the county is large with several thousand precincts, however, such a relationship would be impossible. Here some kind of regional precinct co-ordinator over fifteen to twenty-five precincts becomes a necessity, and perhaps it is necessary to add

Figure 27. A Composite County Party Campaign Organization Chart

COUNTY COMMITTEE

County Committee
Chairman

Executive Secretary
Office Staff

Research Committee	Literature Committee	First Voters Committee	Speakers Committee	Publicity Committee	Finance Committee
Legal Committee	Special Services Committee			Rally Committee	Canvassing Committee

Regional Precinct
Co-ordinator

Precinct Captain — Election Day Precinct Committees
—Headquarters Committee
—Baby-Sitter Committee
Precinct Workers —Automobile Committee
—Poll Committee (check who voted)
VOTERS —Checking Committee (make lists of nonvoters to telephone)
—Telephone Committee
—Committee to Watch Vote Count

another co-ordinator level of organization between the regional precinct co-ordinator and the county committee. With highly organized big-city machines, a ward executive, district executive, and city boss might properly be inserted between the precinct captain and the county committee.

Third, note that the line upward from regional precinct co-ordinator extends only to the box around the county committee. This leaves much unsaid. If there are numerous county activity committees and numerous regional precinct co-ordinators, an administrative monstrosity would be the result if each co-ordinator worked directly with each activity committee chairman. Instead, regional coordinators would be likely to contact the executive secretary or members of his staff and they, in turn, would contact the activity committees. Or conversely, the activity committees would go to the regional precinct co-ordinators through the executive secretary.

Fourth, if the pattern of organization illustrated were followed, the county chairman, the executive secretary, and the chairmen of the county activity committees would, along with whichever candidates were asked to participate, serve as the executive board of the campaign. Here is where major policy decisions would be made and where co-ordination among the county activity committees would be achieved.

Fifth, in a large county generally the executive secretary and his office staff will be full-time paid employees of the county committee. If any of the activity committee chairmen are salaried employees, the nature of the publicity chairman's job is such that he would likely be the one if only one is paid. Next in terms of full-time demands on an individual is the position of chairman of the research committee. He too might be paid or paid for half time, provided some person with an independent income is not available and willing to volunteer.

Research Committee. The national committees of the two major parties maintain permanent research divisions which prepare " fact sheets " on current issues presenting pro and con arguments and the " party viewpoint," provided the party is not too badly split on the issue. They also conduct voting record studies of members of Congress and statistical studies of the party's prospects in the several political sections and states. Some state central committees also provide for a research facility. The county research committee chairman may, for the writing, obtain such materials from the research divisions of the national committee and state committee, if the state has one.

The research phase of county committee activity is generally one of the most underdeveloped of its functions, and yet if it is done well, the services which the research committee can provide should make it one of the most important of county party units. Information on political issues handed down to the county level often needs adapting for the county. A huge volume of political issue material may be clipped from magazines and from newspapers. Publications such as the *Congressional Quarterly Weekly Report* and that organization's annual *Almanac* should be available. All of these materials should be classified into a filing system in order to make them readily usable. They ought to be summarized into local issue campaign manuals or data sheets which can provide for the candidates, for the speakers' committee, for the publicity committee, for the literature committee, and for the rank and file party worker a useful tool with which he can keep himself informed in a partisan manner.

The county research committee should also engage in continuing analyses of county campaign problems by using voting statistics, United States Census Bureau and other organizations' information on population characteristics, and common sense observation. No candidate should have to do this kind of research work himself after he has been nominated and the campaign has begun. The data should have been gathered previously, interpreted, and used in the preliminary phases of campaign planning. The canvassing committee, if it is to operate effectively, should have reliable information on which areas are worth effort and which are not. Likewise the election day committee, the speakers committee, the rally committee and the literature committee will need such information, and for the same reason.

Still another function which may be performed by the county research committee, or a separate committee established for the specific purpose, is that of conducting public opinion polls. Though private polling organizations are often hired by the county party organization or by candidates to conduct opinion polls, the expense is considerable and thus local poll results with which the party can work are few. On questions where the accuracy level of a Roper or Gallup is unnecessary, the research or public opinion polling committee can design, interview, and interpret its own opinion research projects.

If some professional public opinion poller cannot be obtained by the county party organization for the chairmanship of such a committee, the young college graduate who has learned the basic polling techniques might be given an opportunity to enter party politics through this type of specialized activity. Or, perhaps there are numbered among the members of the party college professors who are specialists in opinion research. They may be induced to make their contribution to their party by providing expert advice or perhaps directing an opinion polling project committee.

Canvassing Committee. Functions of the canvassing committee are to see that every potential voter for the party is registered and gets out to vote on election day. Here is a function, unlike research, which must be decentralized into the precincts where person-to-person contacts with the voters can be made. In the canvassing operation the precinct captain becomes the key figure. With whatever volunteer workers he can assemble, he must know through personal acquaintance the 200 to 600 voters of this smallest election administration unit.

First, the precinct captain needs a map of his precinct. This, if the county canvassing committee is performing adequately, will be furnished to him. If it is necessary for the precinct captain to obtain the map himself, the county's registrar of voters will be able to supply it or give information as to where it can be obtained. Next, the precinct captain should make a list with names, addresses, and telephone numbers of all persons of voting age and set up a card for each person in a precinct file box. Such a list will have to be made by the precinct captain himself or the volunteer workers from the different blocks of the precinct.

Following that step, voter registration lists for the precinct should be checked and for those persons who are registered, party affiliation should be entered on the individual's file card. Should the county canvassing committee be unable to provide precinct registration sheets, the registrar of voters will again be the agency to which the precinct captain will have to turn.

Assuming that the precinct captain is taking over a precinct which has been unorganized by his party and there is time before the campaign to devote to an intensive registration drive, the captain should set his organization in motion to register all the unregistered qualified adults whom he has reason to hope would affiliate with his party. If registrations can only be taken at some public office of a deputy registrar, the unregistered persons will have to be persuaded to go to that place. If one of the party's precinct workers has been able to secure appointment as a deputy registrar of voters and can perform his registration functions anywhere, the man may personally call upon the unregistered persons in their homes.

For a political party, such a party-directed registration drive in the precinct is more politically effective than participation in general voter registration campaigns sponsored by nonpartisan organizations like the League of Women Voters — unless the nonpartisan registration campaign is in an area in which the party would expect to find a heavy concentration of unregistered persons who would affiliate with it. If a Democratic party organization is registering more Republicans than Democrats, for example, the organization is in fact working against itself.

Keeping the file of registered voters up to date is a continuing function of the precinct party organization. This is particularly important in precincts where the population is mobile. For each family which moves out of the precinct, their cards should be removed from the file and replaced by those of the members of the family which has moved in. If the qualified adults of the new family are not registered, the duty of the party organization is to make them qualified voters — provided, again, that they would not be on the opposite major political party side of the fence.

If the precinct file has been thoroughly prepared, the work of the party precinct organization can be systematic on election day. For all those registered with the party who will need baby-sitters to enable them to get away from home long enough to vote — a fact noted on the respective individual's file cards — the precinct baby-sitter committee can provide the service. Likewise, for those needing a ride to the polls, the precinct automobile committee can perform that service. From the file a list of all qualified voters in the precinct can be prepared for the poll committee members who may be stationed at the precinct polling place to challenge unqualified persons who might attempt to cast ballots. Perhaps it will be the same poll committee members who will be responsible for periodically checking the names of party registrants who have not yet voted. The latter type of information will then be relayed to precinct party headquarters where the checking committee can prepare lists of persons for the telephone committee to call to remind them to vote.

Such are the principal canvassing functions. The actual canvassing will be done by the precinct captain and his organization. The object is a mobilization of all the party's voters. The method is some form of personal contact with the voters. Co-ordination of the canvassing function over the entire county will be the responsibility of the party's county canvassing committee — preparing instructions on registration drives and election day activities, conducting schools for those who are doing the actual precinct front-line work, and mobilizing " floating " canvassing task forces for the precincts in which the party is not organized. As incentive for all those who take part in the canvassing operations, there are the many stories of the many elections which have been lost or won by the margin of *only* one vote in each precinct!

Speakers Committee. Functions of the speakers committee include the following: first, to exploit to maximum advantage the big-name party speakers with national reputations who make personal appearances in the county; second, to work with the rally committee in staging large campaign mass meetings or smaller rallies at which speakers will be required; third, to have available a stable of able speakers on specialized political subjects who can be assigned as requests for speakers are made to the committee; fourth, to operate a training course for the development of new speakers and the assessment of the speaking ability of any party speakers; fifth, to work with the research committee in developing resource material of such a type that it will have utility for political speech preparation; sixth, to work with the publicity committee to secure the best publicity for speakers and meetings; and seventh, to work with the literature committee in order to produce attractive and effective " fact sheets " or pamphlets for distribution to audiences which party speakers address.

For several reasons the county party needs some of its most tactful and politically sensitive members on the speakers committee. There always will be some party extremists preaching a doctrine of far-rightism if they are Republicans or far-leftism if they are Democrats who will represent themselves as official party speakers. In some manner, the speakers committee must let it be known that such individuals are not official party representatives and at the same time the committee should attempt to establish itself as the channel through which requests for speakers are routed.

The committee should also have a keen understanding of the types of speaking approaches that are best for different types of audiences. One who might appeal to a League of Women Voters gathering would tend to be different from one who might be most effective for a Pro-America chapter. The type best for a nonpartisan fraternal club might be a dismal failure at a strictly partisan party affair.

Only effective speakers should be sent by the speakers bureau to any kind of audience. In every county party there will be some who, though they want very much to be party speakers, should be tactfully eased into other assignments where they can help instead of do damage to the party cause. The tone of a political meeting is set by the principal speaker at that meeting. If he is effective, the meeting will tend to be a success. If he is not effective, the meeting will tend to be a failure. When all the speakers supplied by the speakers committee are able, the vitalization effect is felt throughout the party organization. If only some of those speakers are not able and they are allowed to keep themselves in circulation, the party may lose active members, fail to attract potential members, and party club meetings may degenerate into gatherings of officers or at most include only those who feel themselves duty bound to attend.

The speakers committee should also be recognized as perhaps the most fertile breeding ground for potential party nominees for public office. The party member who can effectively communicate from the speakers platform and over radio and television is the type who, if he has other " availability " qualifications, can rise most quickly as a public office prospect.

Literature Committee. During the course of a political campaign the average voter is likely to receive party pamphlets, newspaper or magazine format literature, or simple one-sheet fold-over cards. Perhaps the propaganda pieces reach him through the mail. Perhaps they are dropped at his front door or handed to him when he answers the doorbell. Perhaps they were given to him at a political rally or slipped into his hands by a campaign worker on the street. By whatever route the voter receives the material, the organization in charge of getting it to him is likely to be the party's county literature distribution committee.

Generally, the precinct workers are equipped with party literature to give to those individuals upon whom they make personal calls. If a party has efficient and well-distributed precinct organizations, this channel is one of the best means through which literature may reach the voter. Almost a necessity is this channel of distribution if the pamphlet is of such a weight that mailing costs would be prohibitive. In rural areas, because of the distances involved, systematic distribution of literature by canvassers tends to be almost impossible.

Should mailing be the method used and should the campaign propaganda piece be designed for all voters regardless of party affiliation, the blanket "Householder" post office service may be employed to cover every residence or apartment which has a mail box. More likely, however, the party will want to design special appeals to persons registered with that party and another type of appeal for the opposition party. In this case the literature committee may obtain the county list of registered voters from the registrar of voters and then mobilize a huge task force of volunteers to address the material. Only in counties of very stable populations is it possible to develop a file of addressograph plates of registered voters.

An efficient literature committee will have contacts with non-party groups, such as lawyers, veterans, labor union members, doctors, and ethnic groups. For each it will design a special appeal, preferably to go out under the signatures of respected members of each group. Perhaps the nonparty organization can be induced to assume the cost of distribution to its own members and also to contribute the labor.

The campaign posters the voter sees tacked on telephone poles or posted on bridge supports are likely to be where they are through the efforts of the literature committee. Sometimes the poster placing will be performed by the party precinct organization and at other times by specially organized poster-placing squads. So common has become the practice of tearing down opposition party posters that the poster-placing function might be divided into two parts — work by day putting your party's posters up and work by night removing all removable posters which have been put up by the opposition.

In addition to literature distribution, the literature committee — or sometimes a special publications committee — will be responsible for the designing and production of propaganda pieces. For the discharge of this function it is essential that professional advertising men as well as distribution experts be members of the committee.

Publicity Committee. So important is the publicity function to a political campaign that county publicity chairmen or newspapermen with political experience are one of the principal sources from which campaign managers are recruited. The voting public must be made aware of the party's candidates. Personal appearances are only a start toward this objective. In heavily populated areas they represent only a poor start. Campaign literature will help to make the candidate further known, and the publicity committee should also participate. Advertising, though it is necessary, is expensive. Publicity, however, is free, and the mass media of communication are always ready to accept and play up a newsworthy story. An able publicity committee can make good use of the publicity channel to keep its party's candidates in the public eye.

At least the chairman of the publicity committee should have had practical experience in the publicity field. He should have on file data sheets and pictures of any party candidates and leaders likely to make news. He should know the outlets for publicity — daily metropolitan newspapers, daily community newspapers, weekly newspapers in the smaller communities, throw-aways, foreign language newspapers, trade publications, and radio and television news commentators. He should have or should establish a personal contact with the editors, political editors, and political reporters. He should know the deadline requirements of all the publicity media and the requirements and slants of each which will govern the type of material they will accept. He must have imagination to recognize a good story and perhaps to set one up if none is available. If his party or candidates are receiving unfavorable publicity for any number of reasons, he should know how best to " put out the fire."

When no separate advertising committee exists, the publicity committee chairman should himself have also had advertising experience or have professional advertising men as members of his committee. If the services of advertising specialists are available on a volunteer basis, they should have the principal voice in determining what kind of advertising to buy, when to buy it, and how best to present the party's advertising message. To make sure that the publicity and advertising functions are performed well, in more populous county party organizations the practice may be to contract the publicity and advertising functions to professional publicity, advertising, or public relations firms.

Finance Committee. Functions of the finance committee include: first, raising as much money as possible by personally soliciting potential large contributors, managing campaigns for a large number of small contributions and organizing money-raising affairs such as dances, carnivals, and other entertainments; second, maintaining accurate financial records in accordance with the requirements of good business practice and the law; and third, participating directly with the county chairman in making budget decisions.

Sometimes the county committee treasurer will be the chairman of the finance committee, or if the record-keeping and fund-raising functions are separated, the treasurer will handle the former and the finance committee the latter. Finance committee members tend to be persons who themselves have substantial personal incomes and who have influence with others who might be persuaded to make large contributions.

Though most of the party personnel is volunteer, money is required for advertising, for literature, for the salaries of employees who are full time and cannot afford to work without pay, and for the hundreds of other activities which require expenditures. Finance committee members may not be as much in the party eye as the county chairman, party speakers, and candidates, but the large contributors and organizers of fund-raising activities are likely to be among the most influential when policy decisions are made. The greater the proportion of party funds which come from a few large contributors, the greater will be the party power of those from whom the money is obtained.

Rally Committee. Although rallies or mass meetings are less important to a political campaign today in the age of radio, television, and intensive competition from all fields of the entertainment industry than they were in William Henry Harrison's " log cabin and hard cider " campaign, nevertheless, there are a few campaign purposes which can only be served by a rally of some sort. The rally may serve as a setting for a radio or television program for state and local party candidates. Perhaps the party's nominee for President makes a speech in the county and a parade from the airport to the President's hotel is to be arranged as a build-up for an "all-out" mass meeting. It might be necessary to meet a national party figure or candidate at the airport or railroad station. Activities such as these which have to be planned and executed down to the last minor detail for maximum political effect are generally delegated to some group such as a rally committee.

Working with the rally committee in the production of rallies and parades should be the publicity committee. The rally or parade are in large part staged for the publicity they will bring. Also working with the rally committee should be the literature committee in order to use the occasion to distribute appropriate literature, the canvassing committee in order to assure maximum turnout, and the finance committee to both provide the funds or to use the occasion to raise more campaign funds.

First Voters Committee. In some counties the function of attempting to attract young persons who have just attained voting age to register as voters in your party and to volunteer as campaign workers may be the responsibility of the canvassing committee or the rally committee. In other counties a special first voters committee may be established to concentrate its full energies on the project.

First step in a first voters program is to discover who the first voters are. An efficient precinct organization will have assembled the information. If not, it may be necessary to go to automobile registration lists or the Bureau of Vital Statistics. College party clubs may be induced to gather such data, at least on the students of their college. After the cut-off date for registration for a particular election, information on who are the first voters may be obtained from the registrar of voters, but by that time the first voter will already have indicated a party preference if registration by party is required.

Ideally the precinct organizations should canvass all first voters. If that is not possible, special mailing lists should be prepared for letters from the candidates or special types of party propaganda. Annual or biennial first voters rallies may be held. Whether the contact is person to person, through a piece of literature, or in a rally situation, the party appeal should be designed for the interests of the age group it is attempting to reach.

Special Services Committee. One of the principal stocks in trade of the big-city party machine is the providing of special services for voters — responding to a wife's call to help get her husband out of jail, checking up to see why someone's garbage is not being regularly collected, or merely listening to complaints or advice in general. Though such services are not today as important an item of party business as they have been in the past, the party organization needs to be prepared for such activity.

If a request is made to a precinct worker and something can be done about the request by the precinct worker, he should show his concern by promptly providing the answer or service. If the request is of such a nature that the precinct organization cannot handle it, there should be some special services specialists on the county committee to whom the precinct captain can turn.

In county party headquarters during the course of a campaign at least a few special services requests will always be made. Perhaps a special service officer or a committee will do this job — a job which the other committees and officers concerned with other and more important things should not have to take time out to do. Also within the range of the special service function is the handling of those persons who appear at party headquarters with *the* right kind of advice on how to win the election or run the party. Again, those busy with other things should not be diverted, but rather a special unit should discharge the function. If the suggestions are good, they can be relayed to the proper people in the party hierarchy for their consideration. If the suggestions are poor, the suggester can be tactfully thanked and the matter closed at that point.

Legal Committee. Whether it be in the form of a committee or some individual, the county party organization should have volunteer lawyers on its staff who are experts on election and campaign law. Nominating petitions must meet legal requirements. If the opposition candidates have not complied with the law, the legal committee should advise as to how most effectively to exploit the mistake. Candidates should have experts to whom to refer questions on campaign expense reports. Campaign literature and posters must meet certain legal requirements. A legal committee can prepare a manual or conduct schools for the precinct workers whose function it will be to challenge voters or watch the vote count. A lawyer might be the best person to refer some types of requests which are made to the special services committe. If the opposition candidates resort to libelous tactics, again the lawyers will be necessary.

The County Chairman or Campaign Manager. Co-ordinating all the above activities is the county chairman, with perhaps a full-time paid executive secretary functioning for him if the county is a large one. If the political organization is a candidate's campaign organization, the candidate himself or his campaign manager does it. The function of the directing executive is not to do all these jobs himself, but rather to delegate so that each committee chairman and committee knows what it is supposed to do. The function is also to get all the organizational units working together when problems arise which involve interrelationships of the different committees.

Raymond Moley well illustrates the importance of co-ordinated campaign management in the following passage dealing with his work with Franklin D. Roosevelt from 1931 through Roosevelt's first term:

> In 1931 I came to be actively associated in the scheme of things and in early 1932 was designated to handle for him [Roosevelt] all matters

relating to the issues, speeches and statements of the national campaign — first for the nomination and then for the election.

It is astonishing that Roosevelt so ordered the various divisions of his political activity, so sharply delegated authority and so clearly maintained personal contact with each of us that there was never the semblance of conflict and never an overlapping of function. This was a mark of superb administrative ability in the political field.

I have known something of the administration of Republican campaigns in the four election years that have followed 1932. In every instance, even under the meticulous Dewey, there has been friction, jealousy and lost motion.

I can best illustrate Roosevelt's capacity for political administration through my own case. He made it clear that I was to gather the people necessary to the background and substance of his national policies and to be responsible for those people. I insisted on a promise that he would work through me exclusively in these matters. He so notified party leaders in the nation in writing. He never deviated from this in the four years that followed. I exercised arbitrary authority in my limited role, but only in that way could chaos be averted.[4]

The first test of the chief administrator's abilities will come in the appointment of the committee chairmen. He will generally have many more applicants than there are committee chairmanships. He must sift the applicants to strain out those who seek the position primarily to bask in the political limelight, the emotionally unbalanced who offer only their way of saving the party and who are likely to ruin anything which is delegated to them, the grafter who is in the campaign to slip into his pocket " loot " which he might sidetrack from fund-collecting drives, and the enthusiastic volunteer who without experience has no qualifications other than his enthusiasm to recommend him. Often the chief executive, if he is to have an efficiently functioning political organization, will have to go outside the ranks of those who offer themselves for the important positions to induce others who have not volunteered to give of some of their abilities which he needs. If the committee chairmen have been se-

---

[4] Raymond Moley, 27 *Masters of Politics* (New York: Funk and Wagnalls and Company — published for *Newsweek*, 1949), pp. 37–38. Reprinted by permission of Raymond Moley.

lected with care, the committee will usually be an effective committee — both because the chairman will, in turn, make his committee assignments well and know how to inspire the committee to produce on the job which has been assigned to it.

The second test of the chief administrator, after the committees have been set up, comes when he delegates authority. He must delegate, but how much and how far? If he delegates everything without maintaining contact with the committee chairmen, the organization will tend to split into competing suborganizations. If he does not delegate enough, he will be overworked and unable to perform any of his functions well, and committees will tend to become paper organizations because they do not have work to do. Obviously the chief administrator must be a man with both political and administrative experience. If he has learned his lessons and is a capable judge of men, he will know what, how, and how far to delegate authority.

The third test of the chief administrator is his ability to get all of the elements of his organization to work together. Here is the chief administrator's most difficult problem because most of his personnel is volunteer and much of that is inexperienced volunteer help, and because different wings of the party might be represented in the different positions. An ability to inspire confidence and respect, to plan and think ahead of his organization, and to lead will be the most important qualities which he can bring to the position he occupies. If he has those abilities, he will also know how to run the kind of staff conferences which are the next most important means of effecting coordination.

Should the chief executive meet these tests he will have produced an organization which can attract and hold volunteers. With such an organization he should also have been able to attract adequate campaign funds. At minimum such a political organization will wage a campaign that will frighten the opposition and, at best, win the election.

CHAPTER NINETEEN

Campaign Research

----

*There are several ways to analyze elections. Until relatively recently, offi-
cial vote records constituted the only available material on elections. They
were useful for the study of the geographical distribution of the political
temper of the people and not much else. Then a group of political scientists . . . introduced what might be called the ecological analysis of
voting. By examining vote records for small units of a city or state for
which a considerable number of background (census) data were available,
they were able to isolate to some extent the effects upon vote of such
factors as religion and nationality and gross economic status. Although
they worked under the handicap of dealing with voters in the large — e.g.,
not everyone living in a predominantly Irish district was an Irishman —
nevertheless they increased our understanding of some major determinants
of political decision.*

*Then came the opinion polls and they advanced our knowledge by relat-
ing political opinion to the characteristics of the individual voter and by
revealing vote intentions before the election itself. Thus they made much
more precise the study of certain determinants of vote and, to some extent,
they made possible the study of the development of vote during a political campaign.*

*But it was at this very point that further progress was needed. The full
effect of a campaign cannot be investigated through a sequence of polls
conducted with different people. They show only majority tendencies
which are actually the residual result of various sorts of changes — to or
from indecision and from one party to another. They conceal minor
changes which cancel out one another and even major changes if they are*

507

countered by opposing trends. And most of all, they do not show who is changing. They do not follow the vagaries of the individual voter along the path to his vote, to discover the relative effect of various influential factors upon his final vote.

Only by an investigation of the person's vote throughout a political campaign, from his pre-convention attitudes through his reactions to the barrage of propaganda which constitutes the campaign proper to his actual vote on Election Day, can we establish more closely the roles of the several influences upon vote (and other political attitudes), from both predispositions and stimuli.

Paul F. Lazarsfeld, Bernard Berelson, and
Hazel Gaudet [1]

As the scientific method has been applied to unlocking the secrets of physics, chemistry, or medicine, so also have attempts been made to systematically study politics. In the natural or physical science fields, data collection and experimentation can take place in a laboratory environment in which the subject of study can be examined under controlled conditions. An experiment involving man cannot be conducted under conditions in which the subject of study itself or all or most of the variables may be isolated. In the natural or physical science fields, the experimenter can make assumptions that substances of a certain type are generally uniform and permanent. When it comes to the study of man, however, the problem tends to be a quite different one. No two men are identical. Each individual is in a process of continuous change. No community of men is the same from one year to the next. A man in one geographical environment generally will be different than he would be if placed in another geographical environment.

Yet, in spite of the difficulties inherent in the study of man as a political animal, it is possible to discover relationships which tend to have validity and to arrive at some conclusions about the manner in which man politically behaves. The academic researcher in this process has as his basic concern the question of *why* men react as they do to political stimuli. The partisan researcher is concerned also with " why," but even more with *how* men might be moved to po-

---

[1] *The People's Choice* (New York: Columbia University Press, 1948), pp. 1–2. Reprinted by permission.

litical actions which will be favorable to the partisan group of which the researcher is a part.

This chapter will deal with the subject of campaign research under two main categories built around the academic as distinguished from the partisan researcher. The first part will include the most important conclusions developed by academic researchers which have

Pity The Poor Forecaster

a bearing upon political campaigning. The second part will include the research techniques which a partisan campaign organization can apply to its own particular election problem.

RESULTS OF ACADEMIC ELECTION RESEARCH — SOME GENERAL PROPOSITIONS

Significance of Party Affiliation in Voting Behavior. " There are around forty-five million voters in this country," said John Nance

Garner in 1938. " You've got a bedrock of around fifteen million in each party who will never scratch the party ticket and they serve a great purpose of stability. You have another fifteen million who swing often or occasionally, or go fishing or stay home on election days, and these fifteen million serve a great purpose too. That is where you get your changes." [2] Whether the Democrats, Republicans, and independents each comprised one third of the electorate in 1938 is a point which could not with sharp accuracy be determined, but some general relationship such as Garner suggests is borne out by the results of research. And in each party there is a hard core for which persistence of party affiliation in voting is high.

The political character of the hard-core partisan on either major party side is illustrated by the following responses to questions on party affiliation asked by the Survey Research Center of the University of Michigan in that organization's study of the 1952 Presidential election:

I. " All my ancestors all the way have always voted Democratic and I felt like it would have made my poor old daddy turn over in his grave if I voted any other way. He fought in the Civil War and went through too much."

II. " I'm a borned Republican, sister. We're Republicans from start to finish, clear back on the family tree. Hot Republicans all along. I'm not so much in favor of Eisenhower as the party he is on. I won't weaken my party by voting for a Democrat."

III. " I was just raised to believe in the Democrats and they have been good for the working man — that's good enough for me. The Republicans are a cheap outfit all the way around. I just don't like Republicans, my past experience with them has been all bad."

IV. " It's hard to explain, but I've always been a Republican and I just don't know why or anything about the reasons, issues, or such. I just think they're better than the Democrats in everything, nothing in particular." [3]

Not all Democratic and Republican partisans, however, are as strong in their partisanship as the four individuals quoted. In an at-

---

[2] Bascom N. Timmons, *Garner of Texas* (New York: Harper and Brothers, 1948), p. 236. As quoted by Malcolm Moos, *Politics, Presidents and Coattails* (Baltimore: The Johns Hopkins Press, 1952), p. 173.

[3] Angus Campbell, Gerald Gurin, and Warren E. Miller, *The Voter Decides* (White Plains, N. Y.: Row, Peterson and Company, 1954), pp. 91–92. Reprinted by permission.

tempt to determine what proportion of adults regarded themselves as Democrats, Republicans, or independents and how intensely they held their opinions, the Survey Research Center classified responses to their party affiliation questions as of October 1952 as follows:

			Region		Total
Party Identification	Northeast	Midwest	South	Far West	Sample
Strong Democrat	18%	17%	31%	22%	22%
Weak Democrat	18	25	32	24	25
Independent Democrat	13	9	8	10	10
Independent	8	7	2	7	5
Independent Republican	9	8	5	6	7
Weak Republican	18	15	8	13	14
Strong Republican	14	18	6	16	13
None, minor party, or not ascertained	2	1	8	2	4

Note there that approximately 47 percent of the sample considered themselves as Democrats (22 percent " strong " and 25 percent " weak " Democrats) and 27 percent as Republicans (13 percent " strong " and 14 percent " weak " Republicans) . Independents made up 22 percent of the sample.

For the election of 1952, the Survey Research Center states: " It is clear that both candidates . . . received the largest percentage of their support from their loyal partisans who had followed the party banner in 1948. This is the solid core which both parties depend on when they go into an election." Part of the statistical data upon which this conclusion was based are these: [4]

Of Those Who Voted for Eisenhower:	Of Those Who Voted for Stevenson:	
56%	3%	had voted for Dewey
24	74	had voted for Truman
1	1	had voted for minor candidates, or vote was not ascertained
13	16	had neglected to vote in 1948
5	5	were too young to vote in 1948
1	1	were people whose 1948 vote was not ascertained

[4] *Ibid.*, pp. 17 and 93.

Stevenson's loss was principally attributable to the fact that a large number of " weak " Democrats deserted their party affiliation to vote for Eisenhower.

In a study of the way in which counties voted in Presidential elections from 1896 through 1932, Ralph and Mildred Fletcher found that out of some 26,000 opportunities for counties to change from the Presidential nominee of one party to the nominee of the opposition major party, in 71 percent of those cases there was no change and in only 29 percent was there a change from one party to another. Measuring the strength of party attachment in Presidential elections for that period by sections of the country, the Fletchers found it to be most significant in the Democratic South and Republican New England and least significant in the states west of the Mississippi River.[5]

Other studies reach similar conclusions about the consistency of the " party vote." " It is probably not far wrong to estimate," writes V. O. Key, Jr., " that from 75 to 85 percent of persons voting in two consecutive presidential elections support the same party both times." [6]

For the major party, the existence of such a " party vote " pattern might lead the campaign strategist to these two seemingly contradictory assumptions: first, that it is more important to concentrate on getting out his party's vote than to aim broad appeals in the form of candidates and programs at the general electorate; and second, that it is more important to develop broad appeal by whatever means possible. Both propositions are valid *provided* they are applied to the proper elements of the electorate. The first is the most important rule when the party thinks of his own " hard-core vote " in relation to the " hard-core vote " of the opposition. The second rule is most important when it comes to the problem of holding your " weak " partisans and winning independents and " weak " opposition party partisans.

The campaign, then, must be divided into two interrelated phases. In getting out your already convinced " partisan vote," organization down to precinct level is the most effective tool. In attempting to win over those who are less strong in their political party

[5] Ralph and Mildred Fletcher, " Consistency in Party Voting from 1896 to 1932," *Social Forces,* 15 (1936), pp. 281–285.

[6] V. O. Key, Jr., *Politics, Parties, and Pressure Groups* (New York: Thomas Y. Crowell Company, 1953), p. 586.

ties, attractive candidates and propaganda are the most effective tools. No campaign is as effective as it should be if it ignores one of these two phases to the exclusion of the other.

Significance of Nonpolitical Party Group Affiliations. An individual's emotional attachment to the symbol of his political party is not

" I never thought that kind of people were Republicans."

Reproduced by permission.
© *1950 The New Yorker Magazine, Inc.*

the only factor which operates to make him the political man which he is. In addition, his nonparty group affiliations may operate to strengthen or weaken his identification to party. It is possible to at least roughly identify three major sets of such group influences which have political implications. They are, first, socio-economic status and age classifications; second, religious, racial and ethnic classifications; and third, regional and urban-rural classifications.

(1) *Occupation, Income, Education and Age.* In general the high and upper-middle socio-economic groups tend to associate themselves with the Republican party while the lower-middle and low socio-economic groups tend Democratic. One of the many studies on

which such a conclusion is based — an intensive survey of Erie County, Ohio, during the 1940 campaign — produced the following results: [7]

Socio-Economic Status *		Republican	Democrat
High	A	71%	29%
	B	68	32
	C+	56	44
	C—	46	54
Low	D	35	65

* Made up of occupation, education, and interviewer's opinion.

Although figures on party affiliation of members of different socio-economic groups will vary from place to place and from time to time, the over-all pattern usually remains much the same. Comparing the 1948 and 1952 Presidential elections, the Survey Research Center found the following party distribution of vote by occupation classes: [8]

Occupation of Head of Family	Voted 1952 Rep.	Dem.	Voted 1948 Rep.	Dem.	Nonvoters 1952	1948
Professional and managerial	59%	27%	58%	14%	12%	25%
Other white collar	52	28	38	38	19	19
Skilled and semiskilled	34	39	15	52	26	29
Unskilled	19	40	12	33	40	50
Farm operators	42	24	13	25	33	58

Making the same comparison by education levels, the results were these (continuing the columns above):

Education						
Grade school	31	30	16	35	38	45
High school	46	34	29	34	20	33
College	65	24	54	17	10	21

Making the same comparison by age levels, the results were these:

Age						
21–34	37	31	19	32	32	44
35–44	41	34	24	38	24	34
45–54	45	33	37	33	21	25
55 and over	48	27	31	27	23	37

[7] Lazarsfeld, et al., op. cit., p. 19.

[8] These data and the other tabular material on pages 515–517 are taken from Campbell, et al., op cit., pp. 70–73 and 77.

Of these groups, age and education groupings are mere categori-
zations of persons who happen to share a characteristic but do not
interact within an organization based on the characteristic. In the
occupations, exclusive of the white collar category, however, there is
organization. Although studies have not been made to determine how
membership in a managerial association will affect the manager's political outlook, studies have been made to compare organized and unorganized workers. The Survey Research Center's 1948 and 1952
Presidential elections surveys produced a significant difference in
political tendencies in the latter two groups:

Trade Union Affiliation of Head of Family	Voted 1952		Voted 1948		Nonvoters	
	Rep.	Dem.	Rep.	Dem.	1952	1948
Member	33%	43%	13%	55%	23%	27%
Nonmember	46	26	32	26	27	38

A more detailed study of this comparison of union and nonunion
members would be likely to produce the broader conclusions reached
in an intensive 1948 Presidential election study of Elmira, New York:

> Union members vote more Democratic than nonmembers (of the
> same occupation, class, education, age, religion, or selected attitude).

> The more that union members are committed to unionism, in gen-
> eral or in part, the more Democratic their vote.

> The more interaction with other union members (within a single
> plant), the more Democratic the vote, especially among (less inter-
> ested) women.[9]

To these conclusions should be added also the fact that a higher proportion of nonunion workers than unionized workers do not vote.

(2) *Religion, Race, and Ethnic Group.* The " Elmira Study "
and others like it have found a basically different political orientation
in white native-born Protestant voters and religious, racial, and
ethnic minorities. In Elmira in 1948, 81 percent of the white-native-
Protestant vote was Republican. Of Catholics, only 35 percent voted
Republican; of Jews, 33 percent; of Negroes, 19 percent; and of
Italian-Americans, 18 percent.[10]

---

[9] Bernard R. Berelson, Paul F. Lazarsfeld, and William N. McPhee, *Voting: A Study of Opinion Formation in a Presidential Campaign* (Chicago: The
University of Chicago Press, 1954), p. 53.

[10] *Ibid.,* p. 62.

Berelson, Lazarsfeld, and McPhee in their " Elmira Study " made a detailed analysis of the " Catholic vote." Regardless of the socioeconomic level, the proportion of Democratic and Republican votes among Catholics tended to remain substantially the same, and more likely to be determinative if the Catholic voted Republican was the fact that he had been a church member for a relatively short period of time. The longer the person had been a Catholic, the more likely he was to vote Democratic.[11] The authors conclude:

> . . . [T]he religious affiliation (and the ethnic differences it represents) appears to be a stronger influence upon vote than any other single factor. For example, on each socioeconomic level about half as many Catholics vote Republican as Protestants. Catholics of high status vote more Democratic than do Protestants of low status; thus Catholic affiliation is stronger than socioeconomic status in determining vote. In Elmira the Catholics have almost achieved the socioeconomic position of the Protestants, but this has not basically deflected their vote from the Democratic candidate.[12]

Substantially similar results are evident in the Survey Research Center's analysis of the 1948 and 1952 Presidential elections when comparisons of Catholic and Protestant and white and Negro voters are made:

Religion	Voted 1952 Rep.	Voted 1952 Dem.	Voted 1948 Rep.	Voted 1948 Dem.	Nonvoters 1952	Nonvoters 1948
Protestant	45%	26%	28%	25%	28%	42%
Catholic	41	43	25	49	15	21
Race						
White	47	31	29	33	21	34
Negro	6	26	10	18	67	64

Breaking the 1952 vote for President into the major ethnic groups of the electorate produced this result:

Voted for	Scandinavian	German	English-Scotch	Irish-Catholic	Italian	Polish
Eisenhower	59%	58%	55%	38%	38%	42%
Stevenson	24	20	25	55	49	40
Did not vote	17	20	19	5	11	13

[11] See *ibid.*, pp. 64–71.   [12] *Ibid.*, p. 65.

(3) *Sectional and Urban-Rural Orientation.* In previous chapters the influence of sections on political behavior has already been noted. The South is the most identifiable political section, and it has been solidly Democratic except for the Presidential elections of 1928 and 1952. New England was for a long period Republican. During the lean Republican years, principal sources of last-ditch Republican strength were farm states, and generally in the past the rural communities outside the South have tended to be Republican.

In the elections of 1948 and 1952 the Survey Research Center found the metropolitan-rural Presidential preference tendencies of its sample to be these:

Type of Community	Voted 1952 Rep.	Dem.	Voted 1948 Rep.	Dem.	Nonvoters 1952	1948
Metropolitan areas	44%	33%	32%	46%	21%	17%
Towns and cities	42	31	30	28	27	37
Rural areas	42	25	12	25	32	59

(4) Summarizing the political tendencies in nonparty groups, the higher socio-economic groups tend to be Republican and the lower Democratic; the " majority " religious, race, and ethnic groups tend to be Republican and the " minority " groups Democratic; and the rural areas have tended Republican while the cities since 1928 have tended Democratic. This does not mean that all the members of a particular group vote in the same way. The groups split, but in each there is a tendency to give a greater proportion of group votes to one of the two major parties.

In most of the groups there were evidences of a trend which gave the 1952 Republican Presidential nominee a greater proportion of the two-party vote in the group than Dewey received in 1948. Particularly was this true among the 21-34 age group, among Catholics, among the less educated, among the farm operators, among both union and nonunion workers, and in the rural areas. On the other hand, Negroes, those with a college education and the professional and managerial occupational group gave a slightly greater percentage of their respective group's votes to the Democratic nominee in 1952 than in 1948.

Several points of significance for the major party in its campaign planning flow from these data. First, by an examination of the statistics, the party may estimate with which groups its opportunities are poor and with which its opportunities are good or doubtful. It may then develop its appeals accordingly. Second, the many shifts within groups from Democratic to Republican from 1948 to 1952 show both major parties that an attractive program and/or candidate can cause the two-party proportion of the vote within a group to change significantly from one election to the next.

Significance of Voter Turnout. Turnout of estimated eligible voters in Presidential elections since 1920 has averaged between 50 and 60 percent. In 1952 it was 63 percent. Presidential election contests attract the highest proportion of voters. In Presidential election years the proportion of persons over 21 years of age who vote for state-wide offices is smaller than the proportion which participates in the Presidential election, and likewise, elections for offices below the state-wide level attract an even smaller proportion of the voters. In off-Presidential elections years, the turnout for state and local contests sharply declines from what it was for the same offices in the preceding Presidential election year. Primary elections tend to attract fewer voters than general elections.

If the proportion of those who did not vote was substantially the same for each major identifiable party and nonparty group, a low or a high turnout would have little or no effect on the final election result. Instead, there is a great variation in turnout from group to group, but the exact manner in which those variations affect the fortunes of the major parties is difficult to say.

In the immediately preceding section's tabulations of the political behavior of demographic groups in the 1948 and 1952 Presidential elections, the proportion of each group which did not vote in those two elections was included along with the Republican and Democratic distribution of vote within each group. Under occupation classes turnout of the very Republican professional and managerial classification is high while turnout among the strongly Democratic unskilled workers is low. Under education classes turnout among the college-educated group tending Republican is much higher than that of the grade school group which, at least through 1948, was strongly Democratic. On the other hand, Democratic advantages appear to exist in the religion classification with Catholic turnout rates higher than those of Protestants, in the type of community classification with metropolitan turnout higher than rural, and in the trade union classification with union member turnout higher than that of the nonunion member.

Does the over-all turnout rate work to the advantage of one major party over the other? There is no conclusive answer. During much of the 1940's it was felt that a higher election turnout would have worked to the Democratic party's benefit. Yet in 1948 Elmo Roper found the turnout rate among prosperous economic groups lower than in 1944 and among poorer economic groups higher than in 1944 — a situation in which Democrats were advantaged by the lower turnout.[13] V. O. Key, Jr., holds that the theory that a high turnout advantages the Democratic party is probably an exaggeration.[14]

Much further research need be done before the relation of turnout to partisan advantage can be understood. Even with such research, the political strategist could not use the data to predict that the turnout-partisan advantage pattern of the past would continue to operate in the future. A major party, therefore, can only work to get out the vote, being careful to as far as possible concentrate its major efforts on those persons who are registered with that party, those who the party might feel would be friendly even though registered with the opposition, and independents. If the party does not have an effective precinct organization which can make decisions as to who should be gotten to the polls, then rough estimates of the areas likely to produce majorities for that party will have to be made in order to decide where " get out the vote " work will be concentrated.

Significance of Candidate Appeal. The object of a major party in an election contest is to mobilize its own partisans, to attract those independents who are bound by no party ties and to cut into, at least for that election, partisans of the opposition major party. In 1948 the Survey Research Center concludes that Truman won because of " the considerable advantage enjoyed by the Democratic party in the number of people who had, during the previous sixteen years, been supporting it rather than the Republican party, and from the inability of the Republican party to attract any substantial number of these Democratic voters to their side." The fact that the 1948 Presidential election was close, the Center attributes to Truman's inability to attract to the polls a large number of persons who had voted for Franklin D. Roosevelt in 1944.[15]

---

[13] *New York Herald Tribune,* June 19, 1949. Cited by Key, *op. cit.,* p. 576.
[14] *Op. cit.,* p. 576.   [15] Campbell, *et al., op. cit.,* p. 165.

Viewing the outcome of the 1952 Presidential election, the same research organization suggests that the Eisenhower victory was produced in the following manner:

> . . . [O]ne of the decisive factors in the Republican victory . . . was the switching of a large number of former Democratic supporters to Eisenhower. With the Republican party having only a narrow margin over the Democrats in the total number of their party faithful that they were able to muster out to the polls, and with no major advantage gained by the Republican party in its ability to attract the new voters, it was the shift of almost one out of every four of the 1948 Truman Democrats to the Republican ranks which gave General Eisenhower his clear margin over Governor Stevenson.[16]

Eisenhower was an ideal Republican party candidate for 1952. He was well enough liked by Republicans to bring them out to the polls and at the same time he could attract large numbers of non-Republicans. Many of the latter who voted for Eisenhower did so even though they were opposed to what they thought were Republican positions on issues and without giving any indication that a vote for Eisenhower meant that they were changing their independent or Democratic status.[17] For the Democratic party an ideal candidate is one who can accomplish the " Eisenhower effect " in reverse.

If one is to ask which party most needs a Presidential candidate who can appeal to the opposition, the answer has to be the Republican party. The latter is still in the minority. If all Americans of voting age had to register today, George Gallup finds that 54.3 percent would register as Democrats, 34.3 percent as Republicans and 9.4 percent would be undecided.[18] The table on page 511 showed 22 percent of its sample as " strong " Democratic, 25 percent as " weak " Democratic (total 47 percent Democratic), and 13 percent " strong " Republican and 14 percent " weak " Republican (total 27 percent Republican). Twenty-two percent of the table's sample ranged from independent Democratic through independent to independent Republican. These data suggest that the Democratic party, if it can hold together, is likely to continue to be more successful in the immediate future than the Republican party.

---

[16] Campbell, *et al., op cit.,* p. 165.

[17] *Ibid.,* Chap. 12.

[18] As reported in *United States News and World Report* (October 7, 1955),
`. 44.

RESEARCH TECHNIQUES FOR CAMPAIGN
MANAGEMENT

In the above section of this chapter several products of academic research important to political campaigns have been cited. Our concern there was not with method but rather with result. For the analysis of the techniques used the reader will himself have to refer to the works from which the material was drawn and others cited in the bibliographical note for this chapter. Space and purpose limitations of this volume prevent their consideration here.

Research techniques which may be applied to specific problems of campaign management, however, are very directly within the scope of this chapter. Here the product sought from the research process is not the academic purpose of objective analysis in order to discover how or why the political system operates as it does, but rather the end is to use research techniques as a means toward the goal of winning elections. Though the latter goal is a biased one, the greater the degree of objectivity in the campaign research process the sounder will be the foundation of data upon which intelligent campaign decisions can be based.

At the start of a particular campaign, a party or a candidate will always begin with the participants having some level of political proficiency as it has been developed from practical experience. Also, at least with the party organization, there will be available the results of some research previously conducted that will be of value in a campaign. For development of the remainder of this chapter, however, it will be assumed that the party or candidate is " starting from scratch." Proceeding from that assumption, following are some of the things which the party or candidate in such a hypothetical situation will have to know or find out about and some of the means by which the research can be conducted.

Geography of the Constituency. The first step in any campaign is to obtain a map of the constituency in which the campaign is to be conducted. This is important for several reasons. If the campaign planner is an individual who is thinking of himself running for office, he will have to make sure that he lives within the boundaries of the district, and that he has lived there long enough to meet the residence requirements for officeholding as they exist in his state. If the campaign planners are party or nonparty group members who are considering the backing of one of several candidate possibilities, the same type of residence check will have to be made.

Although this step may seem too elementary to warrant inclusion under campaign research, it is a detail of major importance. Particularly in metropolitan districts, many have been the times when campaign planning has gone beyond the preliminary stage before the potential candidate or his backers have learned that he actually lives a block outside the district and is thus ineligible; or, if the candidate does live in the district, that he has not lived there long enough.

The geography of the constituency will also have a bearing on the type of campaign which is conducted. If the district is rural, has a relatively small population, and the voters are not too widely dispersed, perhaps the principal campaign technique will be one of personal contact with individual voters. If the district is rural and large, the population is widely scattered and if no media of mass communication like radio and television are available, the campaign will have to be built around personal contacts in the villages and small cities, advertising in the community newspapers, and direct mailings. If the district is of a populous and urban nature, opportunities for personal voter contact will be limited and mailings and utilization of mass media of communication might constitute the principal campaign selling devices.

Population concentrations, provided the district's people are not uniformly distributed, will also determine where the candidate or party will concentrate with the greatest proportion of energy and money. The voters will not come to the candidate. He will have to go to them. Because the candidate cannot seek out all voters, he will have to decide where the largest number can be most efficiently reached.

General Political Characteristics of the Constituency. Next, for the planning and execution of the hypothetical campaign, should come a detailed analysis of the political election problem in the constituency. The first step in this part of the campaign process is to compile voting record and party registration data. If registration and election returns show the district to be safe for one party and the prospective candidate is a member of the opposition party, perhaps his campaign planning will stop at this point as he decides that the odds against his winning are too great. Assume, however, that the candidate does proceed in the hope that he has a fighting to good chance to win.

A political map of the district should be prepared. Election and registration data included in the map ought to go back far enough and penetrate deeply enough in detail to show the voting habits of each significant geographical section. If the organization is down to the precinct level, there should be a political map for each precinct.

In the sections that have returned heavy majorities for the candidate's party in the past, the major campaign effort should be directed at getting the voters to the polls. In the sections that have gone heavily to the opposition party in the past, the campaign — unless it has a precinct organization which can pinpoint its partisans — may consist of the distribution of special types of literature designed to appeal to members of the opposition party. It is not likely that the candidate or party would want to conduct a general get-out-the-vote drive in such an area. The sections which have been politically doubtful will deserve the concentration of more intensive attention than either the pro or anti safe section types, provided that the party balance in the constituency is close enough to warrant an intensive campaign by both major party sides.

Wherever it is decided to work a section intensively, the campaign organization should go beyond election and registration data to ascertain also such information as occupation, income, education, and age levels. It should also ascertain what are the organized occupation, ethnic, religious, veteran, and other types of groups which, though they are " nonpolitical," nevertheless can have political implications. The reason why such data can be valuable in a campaign has already been suggested in the first section of this chapter.

After identifying the major nonparty groups which tend toward the support of one party or another, the next step is to supplement work through whatever party precinct organization is available with direct campaign headquarters contacts with such organized groups. Nonparty groups should be rated in terms of their vote power, and more attention be given to the more powerful rather than the less powerful. The political predispositions of the leaders of those groups should also be evaluated. If the candidate or party has access to the leaders of a group, then an attempt should be made to work through them. If the opposition candidate or party has access to the leaders and if the group is still politically doubtful and important enough to warrant attention, the approach will have to be one aimed at the rank and file of the group in the hope that they can be induced not to follow their leaders in this political campaign.

As it is necessary to understand the nonparty group structure of the constituency both for the channel of communication which organized groups can provide and because such information is necessary in the designing of a campaign appeal, so also should information be assembled on all other media of communication through which the campaign message might be sold. This knowledge the publicity and advertising men in a campaign should be able to furnish. There should be a list of all radio and television stations, newspapers, and other media. For each there should be information on advertising rates and the form in which publicity releases are acceptable. For publicity-obtaining purposes, the campaign organization should know the political " slant " — if there is such a " slant " — of those who control each news outlet.

From a study of back newspaper files or from interviews with those who have had a long acquaintance with the district, the campaign organization should find out what are the local political issues which evoke the strongest response among the people. Perhaps the district has an acute flooding problem during the rainy season and has long sought an adequate drainage system. Perhaps it is a coastal district in which property values would skyrocket if it obtained the small boat harbor which it has sought for ten to twenty years. Or, if there are no issues unique to the district itself, the district will always be a part of a larger section in which some one issue tends to be more important than any other — dairy price supports in a district in which dairy farming is the chief economic activity, for example.

Candidates who neglect the " local interest pattern " are not likely to get very far in an election campaign. In general, candidates who openly oppose the " local interest pattern " will not get as far as those who merely neglect them. A political campaign is not the time for an " educational campaign." It is too short for the seeds of education to take firm root, even though the people might someday be educated to another position. Even a Presidential candidate with the eyes of a whole nation focused on him dare not neglect the local appeal aspect of campaigning.

Classic is the illustration of Dewey, Truman, and the Midwest farmer in 1948. Both Dewey and Truman were invited to the National Plowing Contest in Dexter, Iowa. Truman accepted and firmly indicated his intention to maintain farm price supports while he charged that " the reactionary Republican answer is to let prices

The Miami Herald

"A Little Shadow That Goes In And Out With Me"

crash to the bottom." Dewey — leading in Iowa in the polls by 55 percent at the time — spoke two days later in Des Moines offering abstractions of a " unity of all interests." Truman carried Iowa and many Midwest states which early in the campaign only the most optimistic Democrat might have hoped would go Democratic.[19]

The Opposition Candidate and His Party. If the opposition candidate is an incumbent, he begins with the advantage of being better

---

[19] From Moos, *op. cit.,* p. 113.

known than his challenger and with the advantage of having had an opportunity to make a broadly appealing record. On the other hand, the incumbent may be at a disadvantage because his record in office is likely to have weak links — provided the challenger can find them through an intensive combing of the record.

When the contested office is a seat in the United States Congress, the challenger's campaign organization may obtain an analysis of the incumbent's voting record from the research facility of the challenger's national party committee. Beyond that the challenger should penetrate more deeply into what the incumbent has or has not been doing in Washington, D.C., by research in the *Congressional Record* — research pointed toward developing shortcomings which would carry particular weight in the district.

Perhaps the incumbent has " neglected " the " local interest pattern " in one or several of his official acts. Perhaps he has had a poor attendance record. Perhaps he has made statements recorded in the *Congressional Record* which have not in general stood the test of time or in particular the test of his district. Perhaps he has introduced only a few bills and one of these is ideally adaptable for the " ridicule treatment." Perhaps the challenger will see fit to attack the incumbent's entire voting record or to accuse him of being a " rubber stamp " for his President. If the challenger is to succeed in making the incumbent's legislative record look bad, the challenger will first have to know what that record is.

When the campaign fight is over a seat in a state legislature, similar research techniques may be applied. The principal sources will be the *Journal* of the house of which the incumbent was a member and perhaps the files of a newspaper which most thoroughly reports state legislative activities. Seldom will it be possible to obtain verbatim accounts of speeches on the floor. Regardless of what the type of office, however, a challenger can with research ingenuity construct the incumbent's record and then determine the points on which the latter is most vulnerable to attack.

Should the opposition candidate be running for the office for the first time, analysis of strong and weak points is a more difficult undertaking. If the opposition candidate has held other public offices, his record in them may be examined. If he has not, unless there are usable personal arguments against him — within " the rules of the game " — what he does and says as the campaign develops will have to be the principal source of his opponent's case-building information. And regardless of how much information has been unearthed from the record of the opposition candidate, during the campaign every available piece of information on what he says and does should systematically be gathered, placed on file and be available for use.

In case more arguments are needed by one candidate against the other than can be found in the record or campaign developments,

The Washington Evening. Star

As If They Weren't Falling Fast Enough!

perhaps the challenge will have to be made by linking the man with all the mistakes which have been made or with all the evils which have been committed by his party or other nominees of his party. Yet no matter what the charge, it must be based on accurate information. If it is not, the accusation may backfire to inflict more damage on the candidate who is doing the accusing than on the man against whom the charge is aimed.

Measurement of Public Opinion on Political Questions. Able politicians always appear to possess an ability to intuitively judge the temper of public opinion as it relates to political candidates and issues. Yet if one is to look behind the able politician's intuition, he will find some kind of effectively working intelligence service. James Farley, for example, could predict with great accuracy how a Presidential election would result. But he was not merely wetting his finger and putting it into the air to guess which way the political wind was blowing. Farley's opinion-gathering procedure was much more systematic. He had traveled widely and knew personally the general political climate of each state. He was continuously receiving reports from an organization nation-wide in scope, and his reporters were men of political experience who were collectively capable of making, at any time, highly educated estimates of the political situation in their area.

Until " scientific " public opinion polling techniques were applied to political problems in the middle 1930's, however, the politicians had to rely on impressionistic devices in order to ascertain political opinion. Stored in the politician's brain were impressions he had gained from talking to people, from the letters he received, from the newspapers he read, from condensations or digests of newspaper editorials all over the country, from audience reaction to speeches he had given, from reports up through his party's organization, and from reports of leaders of nonparty organized groups.

Impressionistic opinion research, for the politician who is able to evaluate effectively the information which he gathers, will always serve as a useful research tool, provided the limitations of the process are recognized and provided the interpreter is lucky enough to guess correctly when the voice of the people comes through only as an indecisive blur of sound. The possibility of major interpretive error is always very great.

In the era of the *Literary Digest,* politicians began to supplement their other sources of information on political opinion with polls conducted by mail. Many politicians today continue to use this device. The frequent inclusion of mail poll results in the appendix to the *Congressional Record* and the publicity given to Carmine De Sapio's use of the mail ballot in New York politics are indications of this fact. But accurate research results — if propaganda is not a prime reason for the mail poll — are possible only in special situations.

Should a state party chairman, for example, poll the membership of his state central committee, a postcard questionnaire may evoke responses from most or all of those questioned. To all, this would constitute an important item of business. Assuming the question or questions were understandable to all the members of the state central committee and assuming that they could easily follow instructions for marking down their answers, the result of the mail poll would be an accurate referendum of that public.

When a large public not bound together by a unity of purpose is to be polled, however, the problem of ascertaining opinion is quite different. Here the mail poll may be of value or be the best means of research only in cases such as the following: first, if accuracy is not too important; second, if funds are not available for a more scientific poll; third, if the poll must be conducted by only a very few individuals and cannot be done by a large organization; and fourth, if it is desired to reach individuals who would not be accessible to an interviewer calling in person.

Obviously, with a very large public, a mail referendum would take too long a period of time and would be too costly. If mail ballots are to go only to a sample of the entire public, how is the sample to be chosen? Telephone directories or automobile registration lists are inadequate. Not everyone has a telephone or an automobile, and the sample would be unrepresentative if taken from them. Neither do such lists provide a breakdown of the significant opinion segments of the universe to be polled such as economic group breakdowns, education group breakdowns, political party affiliation, and so forth. Voter registration lists could provide party affiliation, but they too would fail to supply other " breakdown information " and voter registration is not uniformly a requirement over the entire area of the United States. In short, the technical difficulties in constructing a scientific mail sample are insurmountable.

Even if it were possible to construct a sample which was a mirror of the universe for which public opinion readings were desired, the fact that interviewing is done by mail will distort results. Mail poll questions are answered by only a very small proportion of those asked the questions. Those who do answer will tend to be persons of a relatively high literacy level and persons who are interested in the questions. It is true that follow-ups might be made on those who do not reply to a first mail ballot request, but subsequent sets of replies would be made in time periods different from the time period of the first set of replies. Should an attempt be made to make the mail ballot procedure more accurate by personally interviewing a sample of those who did not reply, the mail ballot advantages of low cost and small organization will tend to dissipate or be cancelled out.

The *Literary Digest,* with a sample constructed from telephone directories and automobile registration lists and with the " literacy " and " interest " factors operating to further distort the sample, produced a mail poll result in 1936 which predicted a Landon victory over Franklin D. Roosevelt. That was the year in which Roosevelt won all but the eight electoral votes of Maine and Vermont. That was also the year when the Gallup, Roper, and Crossley polling organizations began to develop, for the political field, opinion research techniques vastly superior to those which had been in use prior to that time.

In recent times the public opinion poll has become one of the most valuable research tools for political campaign management. Politicians read and carefully weigh the results of Gallup and Roper polls. Perhaps a party organization will hire a public opinion polling firm to determine which of several candidates might most successfully run a general election campaign. Before he decides to enter the race, a potential candidate may conduct a poll to determine how much of a gamble he would be taking if he threw his hat into the political ring. Poll results are used to evaluate the types of issues and types of propaganda which might best be used in campaigns. Rare is the campaign for an important office in which public opinion polls are not used both for preliminary planning and throughout the course of the election fight.

When, for example, Jacob K. Javits, now Republican Attorney General of the State of New York, ran for the United States House of Representatives for the first time in 1946, he contracted with the Roper organization for a poll of his New York City district. One of the points developed out of that research was that only 8 percent of the sample knew the name of their Congressman. Javits decided to campaign on a " know your district, know your Congressman " theme. He unseated the Democratic incumbent and after two years in office another Roper survey revealed that now 30 percent of the sample in the district knew their Congressman's name. It might be added, parenthetically, that if 30 percent of the people knew Javits, the Congressman also thoroughly learned to know his district. Javits, until he ran for attorney general in 1954, was unbeatable in a district which would normally have been Democratic.[20]

Because " scientific " polling techniques are so widely employed

---

[20] From Moos, *op. cit.,* pp. 130–131.

in politics, an understanding of the methods used and polling problems becomes " must " information for any politician functioning at the candidate or campaign management level. If private polling organizations are retained, the politician must be able to set up the general specifications for the project and must have a background of general knowledge of the subject in order to interpret and make efficient use of the results. If a polling unit is set up within the campaign organization itself, an even more thorough understanding of the process will be required.

Discussion of polling methods and problems may be organized into four subtopics: sampling, or whom to question; interviewing, or how to ask questions; question construction, or what to ask; and interpretation, or how to weigh the raw poll data. The subject will be developed under these headings.

(1) *Sampling*. The assumption underlying the theory of the " scientific " public opinion poll is that it is possible to determine the opinion of a whole universe by determining the opinion of a relatively small cross-section sample of that universe. Critical, therefore, to the polling process is the selection of a representative sample which will be a miniature mirror of the entire population of the universe. Of the two principal sampling methods, one is known as *quota* or stratified sampling and the other as *area* or probability sampling.

If the quota method is employed and the universe is, as in the Javits poll, made up of all adults living in his district, the first step in establishing quotas will be to identify all the major groups of the universe between which opinions and interest levels on political questions might differ. The professional and managerial group, for example, tends to have different political opinions than organized workers. Likewise, the reactions of persons in the different income classifications and age, religious, education, urban-rural, sex, and political party classifications will differ in degree.

Relying upon United States Bureau of the Census data on characteristics of the population of the universe and on any other available source of such information, sample quotas for each major opinion segment will be established. The sample should contain the same proportion of men and women, the same proportion from each age bracket, from each education bracket, and so on for the other brackets, as does the universe. Because the groups with political characteristics peculiar to themselves are not always easy to identify and because, even after identification, it is difficult to determine the exact proportion of each group to the total population at any given time, there is the possibility of error at the point at which quotas are set.

Before sending instructions to interviewers, it is necessary for the headquarters of the polling organization to determine the size of the sample. Factors which will be evaluated in making this decision are the following. First, each additional interview will increase the cost of the project, so budgetary considerations may impose a limit. Second, if a high degree of accuracy is required, the sample will have to be larger than if accuracy requirements are not as exacting. Should accuracy be the principal objective, the sample will be enlarged to the saturation point beyond which additional interviews will no longer change the total results of the poll. Third, the degree of homogeneity of the universe will affect the size-of-sample decision. A heterogeneous universe will require more interviews than one which is more homogeneous. Fourth, if extensive use is to be made of the poll data for the different opinion segments of the universe, the sample will have to be larger than that of a poll in which no detailed analysis is to be made of the segments of the universe.

Having set the quotas and the size of the sample, the focus of the polling operation now shifts to the interviewers assigned to the several geographical areas of the universe. Each interviewer is instructed to interview a designated number of persons within each quota classification. The decision as to who those persons are to be rests with the interviewer.

Because interviewers are assigned to specific areas, the sectional and size-of-the-community (urban or rural) factors of the sample can be controlled. It is also possible to check the respondent's statement of his political party affiliation against voter registration lists where such lists are available. Respondents, however, tend to rate their socio-economic status and education status higher than they might actually be, and the age bracket assigned to the person being interviewed might not always be accurate. When interviewers misjudge, the sample will be distorted. Studies also show that a majority of interviewers belong to the middle class and often select too high a proportion of better-educated and white-collar and professional respondents. If the interviewer does not find a person at home, he will seek out someone else. Yet studies show that mothers with children and elderly persons are more apt to be at home and younger persons tend to spend more time away from home. Sample distortion may again result.

In an attempt to avoid possible sources of error because of the wide discretionary latitude of interviewers, the polling organizations have developed the area method of sampling to be used either as a check on quota sample results or sometimes, if a high degree of accuracy is necessary, the area method may be utilized exclusively. Under the area method, instead of dividing its universe into group segments and setting quotas for each, the polling organization selects an area or areas representative of the kind of population which it wants to interview. But rather than allowing the interviewer to select the respondents as under the quota method, the area procedure sharply reduces the latitude of interviewer discretion.

Everyone within the area should have an equal chance to be questioned, and therefore respondents are chosen at random — a person in every tenth or twentieth living unit within the area, for example; or if an alphabetical list of persons within the area can be obtained, then perhaps every tenth or twentieth person on the list. If the person or some adult at the address is not at home, the interviewer will be required to make follow-up calls, or perhaps, following a formula set by the polling organization's headquarters, the interviewer will mechanically select someone else. Even under the area method, however, interviewers will have to use some discretion in allocating persons to socio-economic or other groups for which group breakdown results are desired.

The area method tends to eliminate the possibilities for interviewer bias in selection of the persons to be interviewed. It is also more costly, but for the additional money expended, the research product tends to be more accurate than that of the quota method. On their most important polls, such as those used as the basis for predicting the outcome of Presidential elections, the Gallup and Roper organizations generally supplement their basic quota procedures with area sample checks.

The sample, by whichever method chosen, may be used for single interviews or repeat interviews over a period of time to study opinion trends. An example of panel reinterview research was the 1940 study of Erie County, Ohio, by Lazarsfeld, Berelson, and Gaudet.[21] In this case every fourth house in the county was visited in May and a total sample of approximately 3,000 persons representative of all the important opinion segments of the county was selected and interviewed.

---

[21] *The People's Choice* (New York: Columbia University Press, 1948).

The total sample, in turn, was broken down by the quota method into four subsamples of 600 persons each. One of the subsamples was reinterviewed every month from June through November. The other three subsamples served as " control groups " and were reinterviewed once each — one in July, one in August, and one in October.[22] The object here was, as stated in the introductory quotation for this chapter, to study " the development of the person's vote throughout a political campaign." If such be the objective — to study opinion trends and to penetrate into the qualitative aspects of opinion and opinion formation — the panel reinterview technique is necessary.

Reinterviewing of the same persons presents a new set of polling problems. The " control groups " of the Erie County study were designed to meet two of those problems — the possibility that as a person is reinterviewed he will tend to think of himself as a barometer of opinion and thus not be truly representative, and the possibility as interviewers come to know the respondents that the former will interpret the answers to questions in the light of what he as the interviewer has come to expect. A third and relatively minor problem is the fact that members of the sample will move or die, and thus the sample might be thrown out of adjustment.

Only by panel reinterview can intensive opinion studies be made. Costs in such a type of research are much greater than in a single-interview polling operation.

(2) *Interviewing.* Two of the functions of the public opinion poll interviewer have been discussed in the above paragraphs on sampling — selecting respondents under the quota method of sampling and, in both quota and area methods, classifying respondents into such universe segments as socio-economic or education level categories. Here the concern will be with a brief examination of the interviewer functions of asking questions and recording answers in what should be an " objective " interviewer-respondent relationship.

If all the interviewers of a polling organization were middle-class white women, the responses which they would get to questions would tend to be not as accurate as those which would be obtained if different types of interviewers were sent to different types of communities. Studies reveal, for example, that a white interviewer working in a Negro district usually will obtain a different type of answer than a Negro interviewer working the same area. Conversely, a Negro in-

---

[22] *Ibid.,* pp. 3–4.

terviewer in a white area would inject a distorting element into the interview situation. Neither should one who appears to embody the elements of the " management stereotype " interview in a wholly working class area, and so on.

Even if the interviewer is of the same general " type " as the respondent, the interviewer because he is a human being with human biases might consciously or unconsciously influence the result. At worst, an interviewer will attempt to actively sell his point of view. At best, he should attempt to be as unbiased as possible, leaving the respondent free to answer questions uninfluenced by what the latter might think the interviewer wants or expects. At all times the interviewer needs be on guard against the human tendency of hearing what he desires to hear and interpreting what he does hear in the light of his own expectations.

To reduce the influence of the interviewer on the respondent, experiments have been made in which the interviewer's function is limited to presenting written questions to which the respondent is asked to write replies and then place his answers in a secret ballot box. Though the interviewer's influence in such a situation is less than it might be in a verbal situation, studies show that the secret ballot does produce a distortion effect of its own. Particularly is this so when questions are asked which might affect the respondent's prestige. Where he feels limitations on his opportunity to exaggerate in the presence of an interviewer, a secret ballot imposes no such limits or checks on his reply. Furthermore, when the secret ballot is used, it is much more difficult to ask large numbers of questions or to attempt to measure intensity of opinion.

The best safeguard which a polling organization has against error in the interview situation is not a secret ballot technique but rather is a well-selected, well-trained, and well-instructed corps of interviewers. If the interviewer knows what he is supposed to do and is aware of the problems he can himself create in the conducting of interviews, he can do his best to minimize the distortion which he might otherwise unknowingly inject into his relationships with his respondents.

(3) *Question Construction.* In market research where the polling organization is desirous of learning reactions to such questions as " Do you like package ' X ' better than package ' Y '? " the problem of question construction is relatively simple. In polls in which attempts are made to measure the relative strength of two or more

candidates for a public office, the wording of questions is not difficult. But when a polling organization sets out to sample opinion on complicated political issues or to estimate intensity of feeling about an issue or a candidate, sound question construction is every bit as difficult as are the sampling and interviewing problems.

It goes without saying that questions should be clear and understandable, that wording should not be biased to lead the respondent in his answer, or that the impact of the question should not be so loaded with the "prestige factor" that the respondent is unduly tempted to exaggerate. Poll questions should be pretested to minimize the possibility of error for any of these reasons.

If the polling organization desires to go beyond a question which will only indicate which way a person's opinion leans on a candidate or an issue, a simple "yes or no" answer type is inadequate. In political research it is generally hoped to also gauge intensity of opinion and, if possible, to find out why the respondent takes the position he does.

Multiple-choice questions with several alternatives representing varying degrees of intensity may be employed to try to determine not only how a person might vote if he votes, but whether he feels strongly enough to take the trouble to vote. Or if both intensity and the "why" of an opinion are sought, perhaps the polling organization will permit the respondent to go beyond the confines of multiple choice alternatives and to answer an open or free question. As a variation of the latter type, there is the cross-examination in which the interviewer is trained to take the opposite side from the respondent's position in order to make possible an estimate of his intensity of feeling and the reasons he has for his reaction. Perhaps a filter question will be included early in the interview to find out whether the respondent is acquainted with the candidates or issues about which the poll is being conducted.

At best, intensity rating is a subjective process. A respondent's own rating of his intensity of feeling should be cross-checked by the interviewer's opinion of the respondent's judgment. The result even if both interviewer and respondent participate, however, can only provide a rough estimate.

One major additional question construction problem should be noted. When the respondent is confined to "yes or no" or to the selection of alternatives in a multiple choice question, the answers are easy to classify and tabulate. Classification and tabulation of answers to open questions is difficult. Here is a factor which must always be kept in mind. The use to which the research results are to be put will in large part determine whether limited or open types of questions will be employed.

(4) *Interpretation of Data.* If the sampling, interviewing, and question-construction stages of the polling process have been sound, further problems still arise in the interpretation of the research data. In pre-election polls to weigh the relative strength of candidates, for example, there will always have been some proportion of the sample which " didn't know " or would express no preference. What should be done with the " undecided vote "? Perhaps the pollster will be cautious and leave it as it is, but in an election which promises to be close then no prediction is in fact being made.

Generally the " undecided vote " is allocated to the candidates in the same proportion as the votes of those who expressed their preference. Although this rule had seemed adequate before 1948, it did not in that year prove to be the right one. Though Truman lagged behind Dewey among those who had early made up their minds, Truman actually won a greater proportion of the late-deciders than did Dewey.

What should be done about the voter turnout factor? Candidate polls are designed to gauge the opinions of eligible voters. Yet turnout for one office varies from election year to election year and there are great variations in turnout for different offices. The polling organization, in attempting to estimate turnout, must examine turnout rates among the various groups of the electorate and previous total turnout rates for the offices for which predictions are being made. In addition, it must maintain liaison with the weather bureau for the long-range weather forecast for election day. Balancing these factors and whatever intensity of opinion data the poll has developed, the polling organization must arrive at an estimate and weight its research results accordingly.

What should be done about shifts of voter opinion? Roper in 1948 committed the error early in the campaign of assuming that Republicans had the election " in the bag," made his prediction and turned to what he felt were more useful other pursuits. Gallup also erred when his last major test of sentiment fell several weeks before the election. During the closing days of the campaign a sharp trend in Truman's direction set in, and this the pollsters had missed. Perhaps this is why in 1952 polling activity continued to election day.

If an opinion trend runs uniformly over a long period and several poll results show the direction and rate, predictions might be made. However, there is no assurance that the same trend rate will continue. Therefore, the only antidote in a Presidential election poll effort is vigilance up to election day.

In an intensive study of the polls in the 1948 Presidential election conducted by Frederick Mosteller for the Social Science Research Council four major deficiencies were noted.[23] First, there had been quota sampling errors. Second, there were defects in the interviewing phase of the polling process. Third, the polling organizations had erred in their allocation of the " undecided vote." Fourth, proper precautions against late opinion shifts had not been taken.

With each success or mistake, however, new problems have been recognized or more has been learned about how to solve old problems. The public opinion poll as a research technique in politics is here to stay. No large political campaign organization can function efficiently without making use of the technique, though it should not do as did Dewey in 1948 and overlook the limitations of the technique.

---

[23] See Frederick Mosteller, *et al.*, *The Pre-Election Polls of 1948: Report to the Committee on Analysis of Pre-Election Polls and Forecasts* (New York: Social Science Research Council, Bulletin 60, 1949) .

CHAPTER TWENTY

Campaign Propaganda

In every age, the artifices of rhetoric have moved men to act — or to refrain from action. Techniques of persuasion are known to have a long history and they have, probably, a longer pre-history. But never before the present day has the quick persuasion of masses of people occurred on such a vast scale. The trivial and the large decisions alike are made the object of deliberate control. Large populations are brought to prefer a given brand of soap or hair tonic or laxative. Or, predisposed by their conditions of life, large masses are persuaded to follow a political leader who means many things to many men. Loyalties are captured and control of mass behavior temporarily ensured. Masses of men move in paths laid down for them by those who persuade.

Robert K. Merton [1]

But even if it is conceded that the propaganda approach to communication is a fruitless diversion of effort, a rather large question remains. . . . Why, even with the best of good will and a massive machinery to express it, are communication efforts so often misinterpreted? " If the people around you are spiteful and callous, and will not hear you," wrote Dostoevski in The Brothers Karamazov, *" fall down before them and beg their forgiveness; for in truth you are to blame for their not wanting to hear you." The counsel is a little extreme, perhaps, but there is a very good point to it.*

In our great new attention to techniques and methodology of communication we tended to forget one very simple but tremendous important

---

[1] *Mass Persuasion: The Social Psychology of a War Bond Drive* (New York: Harper and Brothers, 1946), p. 1. Reprinted by permission of Harper and Brothers.

matter: context. Who is saying it? And why? The point is almost plati-
tudinous, but it is for the oversight of it that the success of apparently
foolproof gimmicks and techniques . . . can be so extremely misleading.

This power of context — the importance of a congeniality between speaker
and audience — is a point easily proved. Here is the result of one in-
formal experiment — and it is of a type the reader can easily try out on
his friends. A cartoon chart of " The Four Goals of Labor " was clipped
from a C.I.O. newspaper and photostated. A new legend, however, was at-
tached at the bottom: " From June 3 N.A.M. Newsletter." Twenty C.I.O.
members were then shown the ad and asked if they thought it was a fair
presentation of labor's goals. Four grudgingly said it was and two couldn't
make up their minds. The remaining fourteen damned it as " patroniz-
ing," " loaded," " paternalistic," " makes me want to spit ". . . .

William H. Whyte, Jr.[2]

One of the best-documented case studies of the grand strategy of a particular political propaganda campaign was the successful 1935–1936 fight of California chain stores against a license tax on retail outlets based on the number of stores operated by the same owner. The larger the number of stores, the more steeply graduated would be the owner's tax. So well-conducted was the campaign of opposition to the tax that it has become a model for students of propaganda.[3]

In 1935 the California Legislature approved the chain store tax bill. In California, however, except for certain special classes of legislation, a law does not go into effect until 90 days after the adjournment of the session in which it has been passed, and then only if the opponents of the act have failed to secure enough signatures on a referendum petition to compel the secretary of state to place the measure on the ballot for a state-wide popular vote. In the case of the 1935 chain store tax, a referendum petition was successfully filed and the final decision was submitted to the voters of the state in the general election of 1936.

The fact that the chain stores won this second chance was no

---

[2] " Is Anybody Listening? " *Fortune* (September 1950). Copyright 1950 by Time, Inc. Reprinted by permission.

[3] Based on accounts in David B. Truman, *The Governmental Process* (New York: Alfred A. Knopf, 1951), pp. 234–235 and J. Handly Wright and Byron H. Christian, *Public Relations in Management* (New York: McGraw-Hill Book Company, 1949), pp. 116–119.

accident. In 1930 the National Chain Store Association had set up a public relations program with a budget of $115,000. Forty thousand of those dollars were allocated for the organization of speaking tours by such respected chain store executives as J. C. Penney, as well as for the development of procedures through which chain store budgets for civic and charitable contributions would be expanded and made more effective public relations tools. Seventy-five thousand dollars went into a war chest to fight discriminatory tax and anti-chain store legislation. Before the California threat, therefore, the chain stores were already organized on a national basis and ready to engage in political battle.

For the referendum campaign in California the Lord and Thomas Advertising Agency was retained. As a first step — with approximately a year and one half remaining to work before the referendum election — that advertising agency embarked on a research program to determine what was the real nature of its propaganda problem. A poll showed 60 percent of the adults in the state were in favor of the tax. Clippings of editorials from California newspapers indicated 85 percent of those newspapers appeared to be in agreement with the legislature on the tax bill. A series of special interviews with representatives of publics upon which the chain stores were particularly dependent tended to reveal similar attitudes of hostility. Especially strong were the anti-chain store feelings of the politically powerful farmers' groups.

In such a hostile environment the chain stores were in a position similar to that of the " Four Goals of Labor " advertisement with the National Association of Manufacturers label of the second introductory quotation for this chapter. Before the chain stores could successfully mount a full-scale propaganda offensive against the tax proposition, they first had to create a climate in which their message would be listened to. This was accomplished by several means.

A well-known and respected farm leader was hired to establish contact with farm groups and to quietly and logically show that farmer producers and chain store distributors of farm products had many interests in common. Similarly, a man who had access to labor organizations and could show what the chain stores contributed to lower prices for consumers was retained. Representatives of the chain stores called on newspaper editors to state the arguments against the tax and to develop the thought that chain stores were valuable assets to the community.

Also without reference to the tax proposition which they were not yet ready to openly fight, the chain stores embarked on a program to improve their employees' wages and working conditions. For the church publics and independent retailers who preferred closing on

Progress Of Politics . . . Former Presidents Didn't Have To Contend With Problems Of National Networks.

Sundays the chains offered to go on a six-day work week provided independent stores would also do so.

And fortunately for the outcome of the propaganda campaign, in the winter of 1935–1936 peaches were in such oversupply that canners and retail distribution at normal rates could dispose of but a small proportion of the supply. Facing huge losses if something were not done, peach growers organized a California Peach Stabilization Committee and appealed to the chain stores for help. This the chains wholeheartedly provided. So successful were their " buy peaches " drives that the producers' crisis was surmounted. Publicity on the chain stores' role in peach distribution came not from the chains but rather from the farmers' Peach Stabilization Committee.

Approximately a year after the first survey of attitudes toward the chain stores had been made, another survey was conducted. The degree of opinion change was startling. Where the state's newspapers had been about 85 percent anti-chain store a year before, now content analysis of the papers revealed some 79 percent of the papers were favorable. Attitudes of potential voters had just as dramatically been reversed.

Now, assured of a receptive audience for their message, the chain stores came out into the open with a massive propaganda campaign based on the slogan " 22 [Proposition 22] IS A TAX ON YOU. VOTE NO." The voters listened and made a decision favorable to the chains. In the general election of November, 1936, Proposition 22 lost in all but one of California's 58 counties. " Without giving the propaganda effort full credit for the outcome," writes David B. Truman, " one can agree that propaganda skill must have been of importance." [4]

THE PROPAGANDA SITUATION

The context of a propaganda situation involves several variables. One is the status or prestige position of the propagandizing organization as it is viewed by the public or publics which the propagandizer wants to reach. Another is the degree to which opinions have stabilized or are structured on the subject on which the propagandizer would exert influence. A third variable is the degree of cohesiveness of the propagandizing organization itself. And a fourth is the degree of access which the propagandizing organization has to the media of communication through which its message might be transmitted. The last of these four variables will be examined in the section which follows, and the first three are developed here.

Context: The Propagandizing Organization's Prestige. When the first set of surveys were taken in the 1935–1936 campaign of the California chain stores, the chain stores' prestige or status level was relatively low. Lord and Taylor suggested, therefore, that a propaganda campaign at that time might be useless or might actually do harm.

---

[4] Truman, *op. cit.*, p. 235.

The advice was heeded, and the chains worked first to build prestige. This was successfully done. Finally, when the propaganda message had a good chance of being sympathetically heard — and not until then — did the open propaganda drive begin.

No two competing propaganda campaigns begin the race from the same status starting line. If the propagandizer, for an extreme example, is the Communist party, in the U.S.S.R. it will have the field to itself but in the United States where the status of that party is very low the fact that it supports some particular objective is often almost enough in itself to defeat the proposal. Except for members of the American Communist party and a circle of fellow travelers, the Communist party label carries "the kiss of death." Here is the major reason why American Communists set up front organizations or seek to infiltrate noncommunist groups in order to acquire a prestige base from which to operate.

If, on the other hand, the propagandizer is a candidate of the majority party in a safe constituency, the mere fact of his party label provides for him a platform from which almost always success is assured. In most constituencies of the South a Republican candidate for any office under that of President of the United States will tend to be regarded as an " odd ball " or a joke. The Republican's chances of selling himself are about as great as his having to run a five-mile race course in less time than it would take for a Democratic candidate to sprint 50 yards. Only in politically doubtful areas do candidates from both parties stand an approximately equal chance to successfully propagandize in competition.

Nor does status affect only the possibilities of the propagandist's being heard. The financial rewards in our society are usually greater for members of high-status groups than low-status groups. The high-status propagandist will, therefore, have more money with which to conduct his campaign. Likewise, because of his high status he will more easily be able to attract contributions from other high-status persons who have the money to give. As propaganda campaigns become increasingly expensive, the financial advantage which prestige can bring is a not inconsiderable one.

Still another propaganda advantage for the high-status organization or candidate is the fact that it is easier to attract allies from among other groups in the community. The allying group can make its own internal communication channels available to the propagandist. Furthermore, the allied group may also throw its own propaganda machinery into the campaign. Where the low-status Communist party, for example, has to create its own fronts or attempt to infiltrate and capture other groups, the magnetism of the high-status organization or candidate will tend to attract useful allies almost automatically.

How vital to the propagandist are allied groups is suggested by the introductory quotation from William H. Whyte's *Is Anybody Listening?* If the " Four Goals of Labor " advertisement had been presented to the twenty C.I.O. members as a statement which had been issued by their labor organization's leaders, it is likely that all or almost all of those reactions would have been favorable. A member of any group tends more readily to be receptive to a message from one of his own group, particularly if it comes from a leader of his own group. If the propaganda comes from someone the individual does not know and who is outside his group, there follows a reaction which generally results either in refusing to hear or see or, if not that, the message will at best be regarded with skepticism. Here is the reason why a political party or candidate's campaign organization designs special appeals for veterans', women's, ethnic, religious, professional, labor, or other interest groups. And here also is the reason why the party or candidate attempts to work through leaders of an interest group when communicating with its members.

Status or prestige, then, may operate to give one side the only platform from which to sell its political product. Or if the advantage is not that great, at least one of two or more candidates and one of two or more parties will have a better platform than the others. Similar patterns of advantage-differentials will operate in the process of attracting the money necessary for propagandizing and the allies which make possible conducting the campaign on many fronts and through many voices.

Context: A Structured- or an Unstructured-Opinion Climate. A structured-opinion climate is one in which the members of a public are aware of an issue, feel they understand it, and have made up their respective minds about it. Opinion might be said to have already crystallized. An unstructured-opinion climate, on the other hand, is one in which the members of a public may not be aware of an issue, or if they are aware of it, they have not or cannot make up their minds. Perhaps in the latter case opinions are not yet set because the members of the public have not been aware of the issue long enough to have had a chance to decide, or perhaps the issue is so complicated and the alternatives are so confusing that structuring cannot take place.

Most advantageous for the propagandist is the type of situation in which opinion is already structured with a large majority on his side. One illustration might be a safe Democratic or Republican district in which the voters are following their traditional political pattern and no elements enter the campaign to cause them to seriously consider the possibility of altering their behavior. Another example, to return to the 1935–1936 California chain store campaign, was the favorable-to-the-chains opinion climate which existed after the second survey. This second case represents, however, a gradation once removed from the politically safe district. For the chain stores a propaganda campaign was necessary to clinch the result. In the safe district the candidate has only to go through the motions in a general election campaign.

Least advantageous for the propagandist is an opinion climate which is already structured, but with the large majority already decided against him. Under such a political handicap a minority party candidate in a safe district has almost no chance of success. His only hope is that the opinion already crystallized against him can be uncrystallized to the point where he has an opportunity to be heard. To accomplish this is always difficult and generally impossible. Seldom can the propagandist achieve the California chain stores' dramatic success in the course of a year to almost reverse the opinion climate from an unfavorable to a favorable crystallization.

Almost as undesirable to the politician-propagandist are the occasions on which an electorate splits into two sharply disagreeing groups of almost equal power. Take, for example, a district in which " wets " are evenly balanced with " drys " and both groups resist " education " by the other or by anyone who takes even a moderate position. Here the politician might best attempt no propaganda on the issue at all in the hope that the opposition will be less successful at fence-straddling or that the campaign result might then hinge on other factors. Perhaps the major sin of United States Senator Joseph McCarthy in the eyes of politicians of both major parties was that McCarthy was crystallizing the electorate into violently pro-and anti-McCarthy elements and then demanding that this be the issue on which all candidates be judged.

In American politics, if the politician-propagandist cannot have the advantage of a structured situation with a large majority favorable to him, the next most desirable is an opinion climate where those who are not strongly committed to either major party have unstructured opinions and where the unstructured element is large enough to swing the election either way by a mildly decisive margin. Propaganda from both sides can then be focused on this middle group with the most effective communicator having the best chance of success. It is at a time like this that the out-party will have a good chance to unseat the in-party, particularly if the indecision of the unstructured voters results from an environment of complicated crisis in which it is difficult to distinguish between logical alternatives.

Such was the condition in the Presidential campaign of 1952. The United States was involved in war in Korea, with much dispute over how that war should be conducted. China had been lost to Mao's Communists. The United States was involved in cold war everywhere with the U.S.S.R. The administration in power had permitted the opposition to successfully make a case with many voters that the incumbent party was not as concerned as it should have been about the danger of internal subversion. What was the best way out of peril? Even the technical experts seemed to disagree.

Then the Republicans nominated a man for the Presidency whose experience and personality seemed ideally to fit the crisis of that year. If anyone could make things better, that man would be General Eisenhower! Capitalizing on the ambiguous opinion climate, Eisenhower even promised to go personally to Korea if he were elected. Stevenson, on the other hand, did not have this unique set of qualifications. " Not only was there a highly charged foreign policy issue and a candidate of great appeal," write Campbell, Gurin, and Miller in *The Voter Decides,* " but, perhaps most significantly, for many of his supporters the Eisenhower appeal was very largely in terms of his presumed ability to handle this very problem of foreign policy, specifically the Korean War. . . . [T]he voters found it much easier to associate him favorably with their concern over the international crisis than they did Governor Stevenson. For a great many voters, it was a happy combination of the man and the hour." [5]

A more narrow interpretation of the terms " structured " and " unstructured " as related to public opinion is that the former ap-

---

[5] Angus Campbell, Gerald Gurin, and Warren E. Miller, *The Voter Decides* (White Plains, N. Y.: Row, Peterson and Company, 1954) , p. 176.

plies to persons who have adequate standards which they may critically apply in their judgment of propaganda, while the latter applies to persons who do not have such standards, are highly suggestible and easily swayed. The effect of Orson Welles' Mercury Theatre adaptation of H. G. Wells' *War of the Worlds* on the evening of October 20, 1938, is in point. The program, developed through a realistic-sounding newscasting technique, described an invasion of the United States by Martians against whom there seemed to be no possibility of offering resistance.

Newspapers the day after the broadcast described the " tidal wave of terror that swept the nation." [6] Though that was a gross exaggeration, nevertheless large numbers of those who heard the broadcast were panic stricken. Hadley Cantril in his *Invasion from Mars* records a not untypical reaction of a senior in a large eastern college:

> One of the first things I did was try to phone my girl in Poughkeepsie, but the lines were all busy, so that just confirmed my impression that the thing was true. We started driving back to Poughkeepsie. We had heard that Princeton was wiped out and gas was spreading over New Jersey and fire, so I figured there wasn't anything to do — we figured our friends and families were all dead. I made the 45 miles in 35 minutes and didn't even realize it. I drove right through Newburgh and never knew I went through it. I don't know why we weren't killed. My roommate was crying and praying. He was even more excited than I was — or more noisy about it anyway. . . .[7]

Such were the panic reactions of those who did not try to check the authenticity of the radio program or who failed in attempts to check and continued to believe the invasion story. They were highly suggestible and in the crisis lacked critical ability. The years of unsolved depression, the threat of war, frustrations of many sorts, and the thought of losing *everything* — family, home, and life in one cataclysmic blow — were enough to cause many to believe the fantasy.

Others analyzed the facts and came to the conclusion that this could not be real, or they checked to find out. Some recognized Orson Welles' voice. Some, with military experience, knew military forces could not have been moved around as quickly as the program had them moving. Some checked to see if the information was on other

---

[6] Hadley Cantril, *The Invasion from Mars* (Princeton: Princeton University Press, 1940) , p. 13.

[7] *Ibid.*, pp. 151–152. Reprinted by permission.

radio stations or called newspapers. Generally it was found that
" more highly educated people [whether formally or self-educated]
. . . were better able to relate . . . [the] event to a standard of judgment they *knew* was an appropriate referrant." [8]

The higher the suggestibility level of the public, the more sus-
ceptible it is to a propagandist's message. That a large proportion of
the public reacts in this way is the assumption made by those who
unscrupulously broadside a smear during a political campaign or on
the day before an election in the belief that enough voters will un-
critically take the propaganda at face value. Two defenses against
such tactics are available. One is a critical public able to judge the
facts and check them. The other is for the opposition to effectively
bring out the facts, or to offset a last-minute smear by warning repeatedly that such a smear may be forthcoming so that the voters are
put on guard.

The more chaotic an environment and the higher the suggestibility level, the more effective can be a Stalin or Hitler type of political propagandist. The more stable the environment and the higher
the critical ability of the public, the more effectively will a democratic-representative system of government operate.

Context: The Propagandizing Organization's Cohesion. The relation of the propagandizing organization's degree of cohesion and its
ability to effectively propagandize is a direct one because the degree
of agreement on an objective will determine the type of propaganda
message. If the cohesion factor is low, there is likely to be so little
upon which the organization's heterogeneous elements can agree that
no meaningful program can be formulated. Picture the position, for
example, of the publicity director of the Republican National Committee before Dwight D. Eisenhower became the Republican nominee for President. There were the so-called Taft and Dewey wings of
the party and each was more clearly identifiable than the party itself.
Each wing had subwings. Senator McCarthy had a wing of his own.

It is true that there could be unity on the subject that Democrats
ought to be replaced by Republicans in public offices, but before that
theme could be properly developed there had also to be agreement
on what was the best way of getting the Democrats out. The strictly
" oppositionist " school of thought within the Republican party

---

[8] *Ibid.,* p. 192.

would have liked to attack everything Democrats had done. Others wanted to develop propaganda which would distinguish the Democratic " good " from the Democratic " bad " and would make clear that the Republican party was not oppositionist for opposition's sake. McCarthy, if he had been able to have his way, would perhaps have had the propaganda machinery of his party develop the " 20 years of treason " theme.

Each potential candidate for the Presidential nomination was desirous of propaganda which might enhance his chances of being nominated to the high office he sought and would sharply criticize anything issued which could be interpreted as damaging to his candidacy. Furthermore, the party was a weak confederation of forty-eight state party organizations, many of which differed with others as to which approach should be employed. The publicity director in such a situation finds that he has to devote a major proportion of his time to avoiding trouble within his party. Because the unity level of the organization which he represents is low, his ability to devise a strong and positive propaganda program is severely limited.

After President Eisenhower became the undisputed leader of his party, the ability of that party to more effectively propagandize was greatly increased. Now there was a unity of purpose, and because of the new unity there was also flexibility to develop propaganda which could have greater impact.

A low level of organizational cohesion is not inevitably a characteristic of an out-party which operates to limit propaganda effectiveness. From 1930 until Franklin D. Roosevelt's nomination in 1932 while the Democrats had no party leader as such and while different candidates were maneuvering for that party's 1932 Presidential nomination, Charles Michelson, as publicity director of the Democratic National Committee, was given a relatively free hand to attack the Hoover Administration. In this situation, however, there was general Democratic agreement as to the kind of a case which should be built against Republicans. History has judged Michelson's work to have been devastatingly effective.

Because a candidate's campaign organization, when it is functioning independently from his political party organization, can be a cohesive unit with decision power in the hands of the candidate, a propaganda program is much more easily and effectively developed than for a heterogeneous party organization. A main theme may be selected which will most help the candidate's campaign. As " breaks " develop in the campaign, the candidate or his manager may quickly make decisions to capitalize on these opportunities. Here propaganda may be functionally adapted to the needs of the campaign.

MEDIA OF COMMUNICATION

The list of the media of communication available to the political party organization or candidates for public office is a long one. Two of the most important are the party organizations themselves and cooperating nonparty groups. In the chapter on campaign organization we have seen how both serve as channels for political propaganda. If the party organization is a strong one, the nonparty groups are auxiliary media. If the party organization is weak, perhaps the assistance which nonparty groups provide is more important than the propagandizing function carried on by the parties themselves.

Alfred DeGrazia has examined the party-nonparty group relationship in the western states in his *The Western Public,* and he arrives at this conclusion:

> Since the parties do not have generally effective party organizations, Republicans gain a strong initial advantage from their " natural " organization. By natural organization, it is meant that the Republicans number among their supporters by far the greater proportion of the business and professional groups who, without changing their way of life, engage in politics as a matter of course. There is no gentry in America, much less in the West, but the Republicans have a great many individual supporters who belong to real estate organizations, publishers' associations, insurance groups, Rotary, Kiwanis, and other fraternal organizations that function continually, and that, without breaking step with their routine operation, can convert themselves into political organizations. The transformation is often not a conscious one. Indeed it may not even be a transformation at all. But society is like a giant spider web of communication and contacts, and Republicans tend to be stationed at the centers of contacts and communications with the society at large. As spare-time politicians, such contact-controllers and opinion leaders can easily bring to bear upon the political process their strong influences and political leadership. In brief, the normal social structure provides an informal Republican Party organization.
>
> The Democrats in America and in the West have discovered and employed only two means for combating the Republicans' natural or-

ganization. One has been the bureaucracy of the local, state, and federal governments. But this has been foreclosed to politics by many laws against patronage and on behalf of merit systems and permanent tenure of nonelected officeholders. The second opportunity for natural organization has been afforded the Democrats through labor unions. But labor unions can only encompass a limited part of the public and they cause considerable antagonism among the balance of the public.

The third possibility is an organization founded upon disinterested spare-time politicians. It has always been a favorite doctrine among democratic theorists and even among the public, but it has never been shown to have succeeded elsewhere. . . . [T]he great possibilities of power inherent in maximum individual participation within a party should be emphasized, but such participation should not be looked upon as providing a political organization capable of disciplined work over a period of time.[9]

The above passage from DeGrazia is quoted at length because it is an excellent generalization of an aspect of party politics which has not received the attention which it deserves. Too often the thought is of the party organization and the mass media of communication as the only significant elements working in the campaign process. Yet in fact, the informal party organizations may well be more important channels of communication than party, and sometimes they may play a more determinative role in reaching voters than do the mass media of communication.

In constituencies where DeGrazia's analysis applies, Republicans start a campaign with a large initial advantage in access to the principal media of political communication. This does not, however, mean that Republicans will be able to exploit their initial advantage. If the Democratic candidate appeals strongly to the " natural " Republican organization, its effect may in large part be neutralized, particularly if the Republican candidate is not an attractive one. If the Republicans do not have a saleable political commodity, no matter what access advantages that party has through powerful community groups and leaders, the channel of communications may not do much good. A third factor will also determine how effectively the " natural " organization works. Even though the inclination might

---

[9] Alfred DeGrazia, *The Western Public 1952 and Beyond* (Stanford: Stanford University Press, 1954) , p. 185. Reprinted by permission.

be to help the Republican cause, the network cannot operate unless the party or principal candidates furnish intelligent leadership.

In constituencies where labor comprises a substantial proportion of the total vote and where labor organizations tend to become " natural " adjuncts to the Democratic party, the initial advantage of the Republican party will not be as great, or the Democratic party may have the initial advantage. For the future as labor organizations' political techniques improve and as the political potential of those organizations is further realized, such groups will surely become an element in the normal social structure to provide an informal Democratic party organization.

The mere fact that some Republicans today charge a " political conspiracy of organized labor " attests to the increasing effectiveness of labor unions in American politics. What the A.F.L.–C.I.O. merger will bring in the way of increased union political effectiveness only the future can tell. In campaigns such as those in Minnesota and Michigan in 1954, however, there is every reason to conclude that labor unions did more for the Democratic party than the " natural " Republican organization did for the Republican party.

Even if labor unions develop politically to the power position of the " natural " Republican organization, the Democratic party will have to meet tests similar to those that the Republican party must meet to hold and effectively use its allies. If the Republican candidate appeals to the " natural " Democratic organization, neutralization may at minimum be the result, particularly if the Democratic candidate is not attractive. Just as essential to the Democrats as to the Republicans will be leadership and a politically saleable product.

Both major parties face a real challenge in maintaining their party organizations down through the precinct level of organization for the media of communication purpose which they can serve. DeGrazia referred to the difficult if not impossible task of molding disinterested spare-time politicians into a political organization capable of disciplined work over a period of time. In the pre-civil service and the spoils era party organizations could consistently produce a machine vote of significant proportions in any election. It was not, however, a " disinterested " machine vote, and the machine was run by professionals.

With the reduction of patronage to a mere trickle and related developments, the major parties find it increasingly difficult to find the personnel to man the front party battle lines in political campaigns. "This decline of the big-city machines and the thinning of the ranks of the paid workers," notes the Republican National Committee's 1951 *Republican Campaign Manual,* "has brought a relative newcomer into politics — the *volunteer,* or average citizen recruited directly from the ranks of the public. Volunteers usually seek to work in practical politics because of idealism and an interest in the public welfare. When properly harnessed, they are very effective workers. . . ."[10]

Whether the major parties can make "idealism" and "an interest in the public welfare" enough of an inducement to rebuild party ranks is open to doubt. More likely the volunteers which do come to the party will be there not because of their interest in the party as such but by virtue of their affiliation with and devotion to the cause of some nonparty interest group. The groups allied with a party or potential allies, therefore, become doubly worth the party's attention: first, because the nonparty group is one of the most effective media of communication for party propaganda; and secondly, because the effectiveness of the geographical party organization down to the precinct level is likely to depend upon whether members of nonparty group allies are also willing to man the precinct lines.

Other advertising and publicity media of communication are television, radio, newspapers, books, magazines, motion pictures, exhibits, billboards, posters, pamphlets and cards, public speaking, word of mouth, parades, and so on. It is not the intention here to attempt to describe how media such as these should be used, but rather it is to develop the point that there are differentials in the opportunities of political parties and candidates to utilize them. Up to some saturation point, the side which has the most money has an advantage over an opposition which has less money. The side which has access to those who control the mass media has an advantage over the opposition which does not have such access.

First let us examine the "what money can buy" factor. Specially produced and distributed propaganda motion pictures, exhibits, posters, pamphlets, and cards are equally available to both sides, provided there are funds to pay for them. Likewise, advertising on television and radio and in newspapers is equally obtainable by both

---

[10] Pages 5–6.

sides, provided, again, that there is the money. The only limitation on party and candidate in these cases is adequacy of budget.

This does not mean, however, that the ability to propagandize always operates to the advantage of the side which is most affluent. There is such a thing as spending too much money for propaganda. If the opposition has small financial resources and is able to win underdog sympathy because of the fact that it is so relatively poor, the money advantage may in part be neutralized or turned into a disadvantage. If one side has a great deal of money and the other does not, the latter might successfully plant in the voter's mind the suspicion that money comes only for a price and that the rich party or candidate has had to make commitments which might be contrary to the general public interest. Another counterbalance to money for propaganda can be the ability of the poorer side to present candidates and an appeal with such an attraction that even though as much quantity of communication cannot be purchased the quality of message is superior enough to require less of the things money can buy.

Furthermore, research studies of the effect of propaganda from many different sources upon the voters tend to show concentration of effect on the few who are unusually interested. Berelson, Lazarsfeld, and McPhee in their 1948 Elmira Study found, for example:

(a) [T]here was an overlap through *time:* people who paid more attention to campaign matters in June were also paying more in October; (b) there was an overlap by *channel:* people who read more campaign material in the newspaper also read more in magazines and listened to more over the radio; and (c) there was an overlap in *events:* people who followed the Republican convention more closely also gave more attention to the Democratic convention. In fact, every one of fifteen cross-tabulations possible in our data between paired measures of political exposure to the mass media was positive. In no case is there a reversal or even the absence of a relationship. Beyond minimum exposure levels, there is a consistent and concentrated audience rather than a random and dispersed one.[11]

This should not be interpreted to mean that a party or candidate should not attempt to propagate its message by as many media and by as concentrated use of certain media as it can. The Elmira Study

---

[11] Bernard R. Berelson, Paul F. Lazarsfeld, and William N. McPhee, *Voting: A Study of Opinion Formation in a Presidential Campaign* (Chicago: The University of Chicago Press, 1954), p. 241. Reprinted by permission.

also produced these conclusions: first, the more a voter is exposed to propaganda through mass media, the more interested he becomes and the more strongly does he feel about his candidate; second, the greater the exposure, the less likely will it be for the voter to change his position; and third, the greater the exposure, the more likely will it be for the voter to have correct information and knowledge of where the candidates stand on issues.[12]

This point, therefore, can be made. Though adequate money is necessary in order to reach the voters, an enlarging money differential between competitors does not necessarily mean that with each enlargement progression the advantage of the richer side correspondingly increases. At some point the advantage curve will tend to level off regardless of how much more money is spent. And still another reason — one not yet noted — why this tends to be so is the availability to both sides of free channels of communication for publicity.

The overwhelming majority of newspapers in the United States are controlled by Republicans of some variety. Editorial policies clearly reflect this fact. However, publicity policies, though varying degrees of bias may be represented in them for different newspapers, do so to a much lesser degree. Seldom is a publicity blackout imposed against either side in a political campaign. Though one party or candidate may be advantaged by publicity policy, the advantage differential in publicity does not approach that of editorial policy. Broadly appealing candidates and skillful publicity management may often and in large part minimize, neutralize or counterbalance the effects of ownership bias.

PROPAGANDA TACTICS

One of the most revealing case studies of the techniques of a propaganda campaign in the United States is Robert K. Merton's *Mass Persuasion: The Social Psychology of a War Bond Drive.* The central figure is Kate Smith who, speaking 65 times at 15-minute intervals over a span of 18 hours on the Columbia Broadcasting System network on September 21, 1943, sold $39 million worth of war bond pledges. Twice before Miss Smith had conducted bond drives, and the first had netted $1 million and the second $2 million. Here are some of the reasons why the third campaign was so spectacularly suc-

---

[12] From *ibid.*, p. 252.

cessful, and in general they are just as significant to the study of political propaganda as to the propaganda of a war bond appeal.

First, Merton's survey revealed that Miss Smith ideally fitted the popular conception of what a war bond salesman should represent. "If you had to choose one well-known person to sell war bonds over the radio," went the interviewers' first question to a sample of approximately 1,000 in the New York area, "which one of these would be your first choice?" [13] Five alternatives were offered: Betty Grable and Frank Sinatra as "glamour personalities"; Martin Block, as a "radio salesman"; Wendell Willkie, as a national civic figure; and Kate Smith.

Miss Smith received 62 percent of the votes while Black was next with 13 percent. Why Kate Smith? Because people thought of war bond selling in a semisacred context and Miss Smith of the five seemed the most "sacred" person. Most often respondents listed her best qualification as sincerity. Ranking after sincerity in order of importance were: philanthropic, patriotic, "just plain folks," guide and mentor, motherly, virtuous, entertainer and "a success." "You know what she says is true," replied one of the respondents. "Next to God she comes when she tells it to you." In the sample, including both those who had heard the marathon broadcast and those who had not, 80 percent felt Miss Smith was "interested only in promoting bonds," and only 20 percent felt she was to some degree "interested in publicity for herself, as well." [14]

Second, the content of Miss Smith's talks struck deep to the roots of the emotional thought patterns of her listeners. There was the theme of sacrifice — "Could you say to . . . *Mrs. Viola Buckley whose son Donald was killed in action* . . . that you are . . . backing up her son to the limit of your abilities?" There was the theme of family love — "It's not as if those boys were strangers to us. *They are our sons . . . and our neighbors' sons."* There was the theme of participation — "We can do it together. . . . We can put this greatest of all war bond drives across." There was the personal theme — "*You* can help *me* send this war drive over the top." There was the theme of competition — "I was a little disappointed to discover that the good old town of *New York was behind Los Angeles* . . . now we're going to hold the switchboard open to give New Yorkers a chance to catch up. . . ." There was the facilitation theme to make

---

[13] Merton, *op. cit.*, p. 72.   [14] From *ibid.*, pp. 71–88.

the desired action easy — listen (to the telephone number in your locality), write (it down), call and order.[15]

Third, the program was developed in accordance with basic propaganda techniques of simplicity and repetition. Each sales talk ended with " Will you buy a bond? " Yet the body of each talk was a variation of one or several of her themes which " sought out a new vulnerability in some listeners." [16] The reactions of three of those listeners illustrate the effect:

> Listener A: " What struck me . . . was the way she kept saying, ' Won't you please buy a bond? ' The sort of tormenting way in which she did it. . . . She did a very good job — so good that she made me hock my wedding ring."
> Listener B: " What got me was that she never repeated herself. Each time she said something that broke your heart a little more.
> Listener C: " I felt I can't stand this longer. If I hadn't bought I'd have felt just like dying." [17]

Fourth, Kate Smith made the bond drive a special or even an extraordinary occasion. No one, it was suggested, had done anything quite like this before. It was the proudest day of her life. It was an entire Columbia Broadcasting System network effort. Regular business had been suspended so all the staff could answer telephones. It was a marathon. Once attracted to the program, as the theme developed and the focus centered on Kate Smith there was a compulsion to stay with it. " *We never left her that day,*" said one respondent. " *We stood by her side. I didn't go out all day, except to go shopping. Even then, I was anxious to get back and listen. Of course, my sister was holding down the post in the meantime and could tell me what had happened.*" [18]

Though political propaganda tactical problems may differ from this one, all the main elements of the propaganda process are to be found here. First, there must be the preliminary research to determine the social context into which the propaganda must go, and as a part of this step the propagandist must correctly judge existing attitudes, opinions, and emotional feelings which might bear on the objective and method of the propaganda. Next he must prepare his propaganda and then transmit it. If the campaign extends over a period which permits the evaluation, this would be the third phase.

---

[15] Merton, *op. cit.*, pp. 52–67.   [17] *Ibid.*, A and B, p. 36; and C, p. 37.
[16] *Ibid.*, p. 36.   [18] *Ibid.*, p. 27.

The concern of the remainder of this chapter will be primarily with propaganda preparation and dissemination.

Although there are several definitions of propaganda currently in use, the foregoing discussion has assumed the validity of a broad definition such as the one stated by Norman John Powell — " the spreading of ideas or attitudes that influence opinions or behavior or both." [19] Harold D. Lasswell, in speaking of propaganda as a technique of social control, defines the term as " the manipulation of collective attitudes by the use of significant symbols (words, pictures, and tunes) rather than violence, bribery, or boycott." [20] Such an interpretation would fall within the range of the Powell definition. It is added, however, because it places a greater emphasis on methods of propaganda. Another definition, this one by Leonard W. Doob, should be noted as an illustration of what has not been an assumption in this chapter — propaganda is " the attempt to affect the personalities and to control the behavior of individuals towards ends considered unscientific or of doubtful value in a society at a particular time." [21]

Further clarification of intent may be achieved by examining the difference between propaganda and education as the terms are used here. The latter is primarily an attempt to present facts and alternatives to the individual and to stimulate him to make as rational a choice between the alternatives as he can. Propaganda, on the other hand, presents one alternative and represents an attempt to positively sell it. To propagandize is to develop more of an emotional than a strictly logical or rational appeal.

The propagandist's aims are three in number. First, he wants to capture attention. Second, he must stimulate in the minds of those whose attention he receives pre-existing attitudes or emotions which are related to the propagandist's objective. Third, he seeks to produce a new or changed attitude that will move the individual to perform the act, whether it be to buy a certain brand of soap or to vote for a certain candidate, which the propagandist desires.[22]

---

[19] Norman J. Powell, *Anatomy of Public Opinion* (New York: Prentice-Hall, 1951), p. 7.

[20] Harold D. Lasswell, *Propaganda and Promotional Activities: An Annotated Bibliogtaphy* (Minneapolis University of Minnesota Press, 1935), p. 3.

[21] Leonard W. Doob, *Public Opinion and Propaganda* (New York: Henry Holt and Company, 1948), p. 240.

[22] See Truman, *op. cit.*, pp. 223–245.

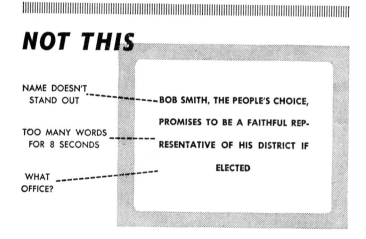

(1) *Capturing Attention.* Before a propaganda message can be transmitted, the propagandist must establish contact by gaining attention. The " hook " must be *simple* and if possible associated with the point of the propaganda. Perhaps the attention-getting device is a straight-forward emphasis on name and face as in the reproduced Democratic National Committee's suggested " TV 8 Second Spot " or " Large Newspaper Ad." Perhaps it is based on one of the emotion loaded three " B's " of publicity — beauties, beasts and babies — to bring out sex or love of animal or children emotions. Though politicians generally hold " cheesecake " attention-getting to a minimum, many " pull out all stops " for the beasts and the babies. When a baby

cried during a Huey Long speech, for example, Huey would pause, send one of his entourage to hold the child and then proceed to give advice on how to raise children and to extol the virtues of motherhood; or if a dog's barking presented an opportunity, a Long man would play with the dog and Huey would extemporize on his love for the animal kingdom.[23]

Perhaps the device is attention-getting primarily because of its *novelty*. There still lingers the symbol of Mayor " Little Flower " LaGuardia in his fireman's hat racing off to the scene of a conflagration. Harold Gauer in his *How To Win In Politics* provides another

---

[23] From Hugh A. Bone, *American Politics and The Party System* (New York: McGraw-Hill Book Company, 1955) , p. 457.

illustration. Gauer's political speaker is bemoaning high taxes, but no ordinary political speaker is he. Piled high beside his podium are large boxes labeled " TAXES." Throughout the speech he points to the " leaning tower of taxes " and tells what he would do about the deplorable incumbent's administration of office.

> Then the candidate comes to the end of his speech. He pauses significantly.

> " I'll show you how I propose to lower taxes in this community! " he shouts in a voice of raging thunder.

> Whereupon he marches over to the tower of tax boxes and, with one mighty blow of his fist, *smashes the whole works down into the front seats!*

> While the crowd screams in a frenzy of approval, astonishment and surprise, the candidate leaves the stage.[24]

Gauer's advice may be extreme, perhaps, but almost every day a sharp observer can see some politicians practicing some kind of variations on the novelty theme. Governor Eugene Talmadge of Georgia, for example, made his red suspenders a trademark. Governor James Folsom of Alabama has campaigned barefoot. Whether by accident or design, Governor Adlai Stevenson in the 1952 Presidential campaign obtained publicity as " a man with a hole in his shoe." Eisenhower exploited the novelty of a President's " going personally to Korea." Franklin D. Roosevelt had his long cigarette holder, and thus the list of novelty attention-attracting devices could proceed.

Repetition of simple novelty and emotion-loaded attention-attracters comes next in this stage of the propaganda dissemination process. It is based on the theory that the cumulative effect of the device will be compounded by each new use and that each time more persons will take notice. LaGuardia did not go to only one fire and Talmadge did not wear red suspenders only occasionally. They did it all the time. Action supplements action and words supplement billboards which supplement posters which supplement television

---

[24] Harold Gauer, *How To Win In Politics* (Boston: Bruce Humphries, 1946) , p. 163.

advertisements which supplement publicity. In its most blatant form repetition will be of the type described by Jon M. Jonkel as he used it as campaign manager in 1950 for United States Senator John Marshall Butler (R) of Maryland:

> . . . I don't think that the people you want to get at knew the name of Butler very well, so we would just give the name of Butler over and over again. I don't think that we could have put it over by saying. " This is Mr. Butler," and then having him say a few words.

> . . . We had one that we used pretty consistently and I guess it might have been a little irritating . . . but we set up a positive slogan for Butler, " Be for Butler."

> It did not have anything to do with being against Tydings. But we used that in little jingles, something like they use for Bromo-Seltzer, " Be for Butler, be for Butler, be for Butler, be for Butler, be for Butler, be for Butler," and then end up with, " Be for John Marshall Butler, United States candidate for United States Senate, Republican candidate for United States Senator.[25]

(2) *Arousing Pre-Existing Attitudes Related to the Propagandist's Objective.* When Kate Smith was applying the themes of sacrifice, family love, participation, and competition, the copy from which she was speaking had been prepared to touch the most significant pre-existing attitude complexes of the American radio-listening public as they related to the selling of war bonds. Other such general propaganda themes may be added to the list — fear, sex, prestige, being on the winning side, self-interest, " rules of the game." The aim of the propagandist here is to make such pre-existing attitudes do his work for him somewhat in the manner suggested by the following syllogism: " He says he's for Americanism and that his opponent is unAmerican; I am for Americanism; therefore, I am for him and against his opponent! "

Several of the more common techniques which the propagandist

---

[25] " Maryland Senatorial Election of 1950," Hearings before the Sub-Committee on Privileges and Elections of the Committee on Rules and Administration, Pursuant to Senate Resolution 250, Eighty-first Congress, 2nd session. As quoted in Henry A. Turner, *Politics in the United States* (New York: McGraw-Hill Book Company, 1955), p. 375.

uses to put pre-existing attitudes to work for him are the following.[26] First, there is *name-calling* or to associate something which is not accepted with the opposition candidate. The " unAmerican " element in the syllogism above is a case in point. Other examples are " Rock Age Republican," " Left Wing Democrat," " Bleeding Heart Liberal," twenty years of TREASON," " Fascist," " Reactionary Republican." The object is to get the individual to condemn an idea or person before he examines the facts.

Second, there is the *glittering generality* to gain acceptance by associating with a " virtue word " — " I am for *motherhood* " or " I am for *democracy*." Even Hitler and Stalin, for example, used the word " democracy " to describe what they were doing. Third, there is the process of *transfer* — to bring behind a candidate or an idea the force of some respected institution like a church. The photograph of the political candidate or public officeholder shaking hands with the minister after Sunday morning services, whether intended for transfer effect or not, accomplishes that purpose. Fourth, there is the *testimonial* through which the propagandist seeks to relate what some respected person has said to his side or what some person who is not respected has said to the side of the opposition — " My opponent's words sound very similar to something said last week by Earl Browder " or " This is the position taken by President Dwight D. Eisenhower," for example.

Fifth, there is the " plain-folks " technique to show that the propagandist is a " common man " — one of the people. Sixth, there is *card-stacking* in which facts, falsehoods, figures, or illustrations are manipulated in order to place the propagandist's case in the best possible light and the opposition's case in the worst possible light. Seventh, there is the *band wagon* which suggests that " everybody's doing it so why don't you." All these techniques are designed to win over the individual without his rationally weighing the facts and alternatives and then coming to his own decision.

Anyone attempting to communicate consciously or unconsciously utilizes propaganda devices such as these, whether he be an Abraham Lincoln delivering a Gettysburg address or a Huey Long performing on the front steps of a Louisiana county courthouse. Perhaps in no

---

[26] Based on Alfred McClung Lee and Elizabeth B. Lee, *The Fine Art of Propaganda* (New York: Harcourt Brace and Company, 1939). See also Clyde R. Miller, *The Process of Persuasion* (New York: Crown Publishers, 1946); and Doob, *op. cit.,* pp. 285–287.

type of propaganda, however, are these devices as clearly evident as in campaign comic-book format literature designed to appeal to the least politically sophisticated or educated segments of the public. The Democratic National Committee's *The Story of Harry S. Truman* (1948) provides an illustration of the comic-book type of appeal, and a brief summary follows.

The Truman story begins with 1945 battle scenes and next a family is pictured in shock and grief before a radio as news of Franklin D. Roosevelt's death is flashed to the nation. The family wonders what will happen now and how " anyone can ever take his place? " Truman is shown taking the oath of office " which fate had willed him," and then follows a series of flashbacks. Truman as a boy is shown up at 4 A.M. milking cows. Neighboring farmers watching the lad plowing observe that he plows the straightest furrow in the county. Then the young Truman is singing in his Independence church choir. Working as a bank clerk at $100 per month at the age of 22, Truman gives up the city to return to the farm where his family needs him. He works hard all day and becomes a progressive farmer studying far into the night. He courts his high school sweetheart with the " Missouri Waltz." He answers his country's call in World War I, and battle scenes lead him through a distinguished and cool-under-fire war record.

Back at home in Missouri he marries, opens a clothing store, and an out-of-business sign soon goes up with Truman and his partner observing: " You'd think the Republican administration would do something to help small businessmen." Later, returning home from an American Legion meeting, Truman tells his wife that the boys want him to run for county judge " AS A DEMOCRAT! " Then follows a public office record in which Truman appoints a Democrat *and* a Republican to determine where good roads should be routed and in which contracts are awarded to bidders who will do the best job. Observers comment, " Sure is an honest guy! "

In 1934 Truman is elected to the United States Senate " following the Hoover Administration's catastrophic depression." His distinguished work as Truman Committee chairman is shown, and he is credited with saving over a billion dollars by preventing inefficiency, waste, and graft. Then comes Pearl Harbor. Truman volunteers but is told he can best help in the Senate. In 1944 he is nominated for the Vice Presidency and there is a Roosevelt-Truman victory picture with the accent sharply on Roosevelt. Truman becomes President and leads wisely through the war, continuing Roosevelt's policies and using the atom bomb to save American lives and to prevent total devastation of Japan.

From this point Republicans receive more attention. Truman is pictured watching over " the highest national production, greatest profits, and biggest income in history " and expressing concern over inflation and high prices. Disreputable looking Republicans, " urged on by BIG BUSINESS," lift the control lid on prices and profits. The Taft-Hartley Act is passed over the President's veto. Republican " labor haters," a worker says, " have killed all the gains labor made under Roosevelt and the Democratic party." A family scene follows where the mother says they cannot afford meat and butter, junior wishes he could have milk at every meal, sister wants to know why they can't go to the movies, and father blames the Republican Congress. Big brother pounds the table as he says: " All the Republicans think of is BIG PROFITS for the BIG GUY! But we'll show them in the November elections! "

Then follow Truman's four goals: (1) human rights for all citizens; (2) protection of human resources by medical aid, aid for education, decent housing and a helping hand to veterans; (3) conservation and best use of natural resources; and (4) lifting the standards of living of other peoples who don't want communism. The pamphlet concludes with " REMEMBER IN NOVEMBER! "

Here we find examples of all seven of the propaganda techniques listed above. Examples from the comic book may also be used to illustrate two even more basic types of propaganda decisions which a campaigner must make. How many and on what issues should the candidate concentrate? If a propaganda campaign does not concentrate on one or a very few major points, generally it is felt that the message cannot be put across to the public. Each side chooses as the battlefield the ground which it feels will provide it with the most advantageous offensive advantages. The single greatest impact theme of the Truman pamphlet is that the Republican party is for " big business," with appropriate reminders of the " Hoover depression," while the Democratic party is for the common people. All subissues are directed toward that point. In recent years this has been perhaps the most basic Democratic tactic used against Republicans.

Republicans, on the other hand, have concentrated perhaps the most on attempting to push the Democratic party, in the minds of the people, off the left end of the political platform. For 1956 Republicans have chosen " peace and prosperity " as the issue they want to debate.

A second question which must be answered by the political propagandist is: " Should opposition charges be answered? " Again, the tactic will depend on the situation. If the charge is a grave one

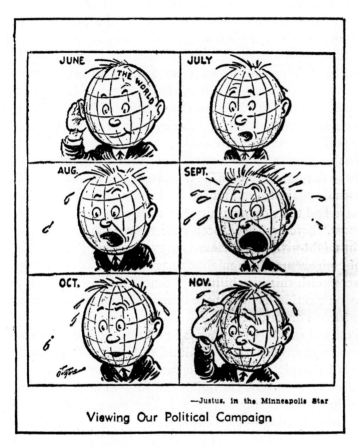

—Justus, in the Minneapolis Star

Viewing Our Political Campaign

which cannot be avoided, the only course is to meet it head-on and to perform the act so positively that initiative is gained rather than being forced into a defensive position. In the Truman pamphlet the flashbacks on his life are in part designed to answer the Republican charge that he must be a dishonest man because he rose in politics in a territory where Boss Pendergast was the dominant Democratic figure. The " Nixon Fund " episode of the 1952 campaign is an example of an even more direct answer to a more specific charge which could not be overlooked. The now famous Nixon dog Checkers and

Mrs. Nixon's cloth coat represent attempts to reach individuals through their emotions as well as through the presentation of a case.

(3) *Producing a New or Changed Attitude or Intensifying an Attitude That Will Move the Individual to Perform the Act Desired by the Propagandist.* Both stage 1 and stage 2 of the propaganda process have been directed toward the third and most important stage — getting the individual to do what the propagandist wants him to do. Here is the ultimate test of success or failure, and in political campaigns the test is administered on election day. To win, the political propagandist will have to have attracted attention, to have aroused pre-existing attitudes in his favor, to have had the staying power to hold and increase the strength of his position over the long course of a campaign, and finally to have caused the voter to go to the polls and vote his support.

In the interim between attraction of attention and voting, events may have developed to damage the propagandist's chances. Counter-propaganda against him and the other side's direct propaganda will also have had their opportunity to exercise an effect. The propagandist must, therefore, have been able to at least maintain whatever margin might give him a close victory or widen that margin in the face of both events which might damage him and counterpropaganda. To accomplish this his ability to " time " the campaign to reach its climax on election day will have been an important factor contributing to success or failure.

Political campaign history is replete with men who started too early and too strong, could not hold the pace and saw their power curve fall sharply off. The able candidate does not announce his candidacy prematurely. He builds carefully to keep his power curve ever rising, even if it means proceeding more slowly, toward that big day of reckoning — election day.

The fact that emotion appeals are used is not in itself undesirable, provided that the message is not designed only for the emotion and provided that the end is an acceptable one. Man is both an emotional and a rational creature, and perhaps he is more of the former than he is of the latter. Purely rational appeals, if there are such appeals, are not likely to gain a very large hearing audience.

This is not to say, however, that the moral implications implicit in the development of systematic propaganda techniques should not be of concern to both the propagandist and those who are the objects of his attention. To pose the moral question involved and to perhaps stimulate thinking about it, the following attempt by Charles A. Siepmann to distinguish between " good " and " bad " propaganda is reprinted here:

Bad propaganda is distinguished by a disregard for the welfare of those at whom it is directed. Such disregard either derives from or eventually results in a lack of proper reverence for individuality, for the private person and our relation to him. For " man " is substituted " mass," and the mass is manipulated for selfish purposes. Even when the propagandist (as with the reformist authoritarian) believes he is acting unselfishly and " in the interest " of the masses, this same fundamental disregard of personal integrity is involved. Its final outcome is always the same — a contempt for people.

Perhaps the supreme example of the degradation of outlook here involved is Hitler's definition of the means and ends of Nazi propaganda. " Mental confusion, contradiction of feeling, indecision, panic, play upon men's conflicting emotions and loyalties, undermine their faith and sense of purpose, and you get the crazed, lost, troubled soul in petrified search and desire of a savior." We know of no more diabolical prescription for the disintegration of human personality. Many, in our time, have thus been disintegrated — and carried to the cemetery; and the grave digger is still at work.

Good propaganda can be defined by reversing all of the directions in Hitler's prescription. It is rooted in reverence and concern for the individual. Its effect, if not its immediate or exclusive aim, should be to help clear the mind; to substitute straight for crooked thinking; to arouse the emotions in such a way as to induce harmony and to eliminate conflict; to create faith and a sense of purpose by raising " a standard to which the honest can repair "; to engender self-reliance and a confidence in others that subsequent experience will not prove to have been misplaced.

Good propaganda involves the deliberate avoidance of all casuistry and of the illegitimate devices. . . . No end, however virtuous, can truly justify their use. In so far as good propaganda operates upon us at the level of our weakness or disability, its intent must be to contribute a cure, not a sedative; inspiration, not an opiate; enlightenment, not accentuation of the darkness of our ignorance. The observance of such principles offers the propagandist no guarantee of immediate success. It may, indeed, involve retarded acceptance by the public. It insures only that we shall continue exempt from that degradation that comes upon the individual in a manipulated society. No short-term gain can outweigh this ultimate advantage.[27]

[27] Charles A. Siepmann, *Radio, Television, and Society* (New York: Oxford University Press, 1950) , pp. 197–199. Reprinted by permission.

Campaign Finance

*Since the days when Athenian candidates curried favor with voters by din-
ners and banquets, the problem of who pays our political bills, and why,
has risen to plague statesmen, politicians and political scientists. Sooner
or later in every age and type of civilization in which elections have been
held the question crops up and every modern democracy has attempted
some form of regulation of campaign funds. One modern writer has gone
so far as to characterize the financing of political campaigns as " the great
unsolved problem of democracy."*

Louise Overaker [1]

*The environmental factor most pertinent in an analysis of money in poli-
tics is the coloration given all phases of social behavior by the tenets of
trade, of competition, and of the profit system. Where so much of the
goods of society is for sale you never know the limits upon the power of
money until you dicker. If the talents of the artist can be bought in the
open market, why not those of the legislator? Where success is measured
by wealth, what rewards of a nonmonetary nature can attract the public
servant? Since questions of this sort can be raised, money in politics can
be seen to exercise an imponderable influence. It becomes one avenue for
the expression of social values. The influence of wealth permeates governmental as well as commercial relationships. Money is needed to run political parties, and the support of party politicians is often needed for
success in business.*

*In a society wherein money talks, its voice is bound to be heard in politics
whether or not we like its crude accent. Here is a language more universal*

---

[1] *Presidential Campaign Funds* (Boston: Boston University Press, 1946),
p. 3. Reprinted by permission.

than Esperanto and infinitely more eloquent. To use money in elections is to adopt the most common current means for defending or promoting subjective values in a society of materialistic standards. The danger to popular government lies not so much in the use of money itself as in the lack of balance between political groups of wealth and those of poverty. The use of money cannot be outlawed. Effective limitation of it is limited. As we achieve a more equitable social and economic balance within our society, money in elections will become of less importance.

Pendleton Herring [2]

In perhaps no area of American politics is there a greater tendency for the observer to tend toward either cynical or idealistic extremes of attitude than on the subject of money in politics. On the one side, and with by far the largest number of persons in agreement with him, a Charles Harris Garrigues can write:

> The basic device of corruption in modern politics is the campaign fund. This is true because, first, the collection of campaign funds serves to corrupt the official on whose behalf they are collected, and second, their expenditure is designed to corrupt either the intelligence or the integrity of the voter.[3]

And at the other extreme a Simeon Strunsky can conclude:

> The money will come from friends who like the man and believe in him; from executive individuals who like to have a finger in success; from politicians who think they can use the coming man in their business; from local pride in the home town boy; from sectional and regional pride; and, as he goes up, from the great mass of disinterested people who are drawn to a winner. The last of these factors is without doubt the greatest: it is the friendly unenvious American sense of democratic participation in individual good fortune. . . .[4]

Here are two views which no amount of interpretive legerdemain can bring together. Yet these are not the two only alternatives, and is there not a more sound position that can be taken which, if it were classified in relation to either Garrigues or Strunsky, would lie somewhere in-between?

---

[2] *The Politics of Democracy* (New York: Rinehart and Company, 1940), p. 341. Reprinted by permission.

[3] Charles H. Garrigues, *You're Paying For It! A Guide To Graft* (New York: Funk and Wagnalls Company, 1936), p. 63.

[4] Simeon Strunsky, *The Forum* (May, 1932), Vol. 87, No. 5, p. 264. Quoted by Herring, *op. cit.*, p. 339.

" Walt " Disney in his television dispensations of animal and human culture to young and old alike has at one time pictured a society of seals and, at another time, a primitive and nomadic society of several hundred Indians on a small and barren island off the coast of Baja California. Among the seals the chief objects in life appeared to be food, sleep, and mating; among the nomadic Indians, drinking water, food, and the hand-making of the other necessities of life. In neither society did money play a role. But civilized peoples have evolved, for better or for worse, from barter to money. No one can get along without some of it, and one of the standards of " success in life " is some minimum amount of income.

In the process of creation of governments in civilized societies, one of the institutions developed has been the political party and its political candidates. As ordinary people need money with which to buy the necessities of life, so the political parties and candidates need money for their attempt to win elections. As people in general can acquire money by fair or foul means and spend for fair or foul purposes, so can the political party or candidate acquire and dispense money in a manner which is " above or below the belt." The critical question in either personal or political financial ethics, then, becomes not whether money is necessary but: " At what level does the ' belt ' draw the line between what is ' good ' or ' bad '? "

Private business transactions are clearly on a *quid pro quo* basis. If an individual spends money, he rightly expects to make a direct and value-received return on his investment. If the same standards were to operate in relation to political contributions, the policies of government would go to the highest bidder and the result would be government by " wallet " rather than by " ballot." [5] Ours is not a government in which the wallet is more important than the ballot. Whether the different " belt line " in politics is determined by a different set of individual standards for private and public affairs or whether the risk of the investor is merely greater in public than in private affairs is a question which cannot be answered. But it is a fact that there are public as distinguished from private standards, and that the former do operate.

What can money invested in politics buy? In the first place, the " buyer " cannot be sure that the party or candidates in which he invests money will have control over governmental policies. Perhaps

---

[5] See Herring, *op. cit.*, p. 336.

the opposition party or candidates will win. Even though the " buyer's " side does capture the election, governmental power is so diffused through separation of powers, checks and balances and the federal system that no *quid pro quo* return is assured.

No " buyer " can " own " an entire political party, nor can he himself " own " a public officeholder. The party has in its constituency or the candidate in his constituency many different interests, and to win support there must be broad appeal. The power pattern in each constituency usually differs from that of another. Furthermore, once elected, the public officeholder, if he takes his oath of office seriously, must do more than give a passing thought to the public obligations which his office imposes upon him.

At best the " buyer " in a political campaign — whether he be one attempting to insure policies favorable to business, to labor, to agriculture, or to some similar interest or any of the subinterests within each group — can only hope that for what he invests there will be placed in public office men who are *in general* sympathetic to the pattern of interests which he espouses. And because public officers are human beings who have developed their way of looking at political questions before attaining office, such a result will follow whether money is invested in campaigns or not.

Political campaigns do require large sums of money. However, the " buyer " must know that it will take more than money to win the election. The media of communication cannot in general be dominated by one party or candidate to the exclusion of the other party or candidate. Thus money becomes only one of several elements which may determine the outcome. Some of the other elements are quality of candidates, political timeliness of program, and the size, at the time, of the respective " party votes." Paul W. Ward arrives at the same conclusion and adds another nonfinancial factor in campaigns:

> . . . [M]oney that counts is spent not on buying votes but on getting out the vote, and the rest is spent on propaganda. Enormous sums are spent on printing or broadcasting the output of the campaign committees' research and publicity divisions, and most of it is stupid, ineffectual stuff. At best the output of one division tends to do nothing more than cancel that of its rival; only the appeals to racial, religious, and class prejudice click in substantial fashion, and these must be handled not only gingerly but also subterraneously, for they cut both ways. The money that counts, the money spent on getting out the

vote, goes for hiring cars to take voters to the polls and for hiring runners to see that the cars are kept busy and filled. Some of this money, and no inconsiderable part, goes into the pockets of ward-heelers and other professionals whose chief stock in trade is their ability to make friends with a controlling minority of the residents of their bailiwicks, and much of that money is spent in turn on cultivating these friendships. . . .

The belief of those who lay out the dough in this manner is that the friendships so cultivated are transferable and that a substantial number of the citizenry who have enjoyed the hospitality and confidence of the precinct captain . . . will mark their ballots for the candidates whom they have heard praised by their friend and benefactor. Sometimes the belief is baseless; it is less likely to be so if the professional leader has been more than a jolly host. If he has been able to get parking tickets torn up, a street paved, an alley repaired, a son freed from police clutches, or jobs for the faithful, the loyalty and size of his following are many times the capacity of his till to buy.[6]

Ward, it is true, was writing in 1936 at a time when the big-city political machines were more effective as campaign organizations than they are today. As voter contact work on the precinct level has tended to decrease in efficiency, propaganda has become more important than it once was. But there is still much evidence that a great amount of the propaganda from both sides cancels itself out.

This is not to suggest that when one side has substantially more money than the other that the former does not have an advantage. It does, but the disadvantaged side may counterbalance that advantage — provided the media of communication are generally open to competing propaganda. In subsequent sections of this chapter we shall examine some of the steps which governments have taken to attempt to ensure for the voters the opportunity of getting campaign information from competing sources.

Garrigues characterized the campaign fund as the basic device of corruption in modern politics. By the statement he, in effect, labels all politics as corrupt. This is an untenable position because campaign funds are essential if there is to be democratic-representative government.

---

[6] Paul W. Ward, " Can the Presidency Be Bought? " *The Nation* (September 26, 1936) , Vol. 143, p. 354. Reprinted by permission. Quoted by Herring, *op. cit.,* p. 340.

At least one interpretation of the Strunsky statement permits the assumption that he does not feel campaign contributors make their contributions expecting *quid pro quo* returns of some sort. This is hardly more tenable than the " corruption concept." Private attempts to influence governmental policies will be made with money and by other means for as long as governments have the power to make decisions affecting the interests of private groups. The health level of a democratic-representative system depends on the ability of government and the people to keep the influence pressures, which are not in and of themselves corrupt or corrupting, within the limits which a democratic-representative system can tolerate.

MONEY AND CAMPAIGNS

Campaign Cost Data. According to the *Congressional Quarterly Weekly Report* the reported expenditures in the 1952 Presidential and Congressional campaigns totaled $23 million — $13.8 million by Republican national and special committees and Republican Congressional candidates, $6.2 million by Democratic groups and candidates, and $3 million by labor groups, minor parties, and politically unaffiliated groups. Of the Republican committees which reported, the five highest were: Republican National Committee, $2.9 million expended; Citizens for Eisenhower-Nixon (New York City), $1.5 million; Republican Finance Committee of Pennsylvania, $1.5 million; United Finance Committee of New York, $1.4 million; and Republican Finance Committee of Allegheny County (Pittsburgh), $588,000. Of the reporting Democratic committees, the five highest were: Democratic National Committee, $2.6 million; Stevenson-Sparkman Forum Committee, $800,000; National Volunteers for Stevenson, $791,000; 1952 Campaign Headquarters and Travel Committee, Stevenson Headquarters (Springfield, Illinois), $316,000; and Democratic Campaign Committee of Philadelphia, $307,000.

Included in the total expenditures by Democrats and Republicans, as shown above, was the sum of $5.6 million spent in United States House of Representatives and Senate contests — $4 million by Republicans and $1.2 million by Democrats. The average United States Senate candidate reported approximately $10,000 spent in the 1952 campaign. Senator Harry P. Cain, (R), of Washington, was the highest with $77,000, and he was defeated. The " lows " ranged down through Price Daniel (D), of Texas, at $3.01, to five Senators who spent nothing. In the five most expensive 1952 campaigns, as reported to the Clerk of the House, Democrats won three and Republicans two of the seats. Al Canwell (R), of Washington, reported $22,300 for the highest House contest expenditure, but he like Senator Cain was defeated. Of the ten most expensive House campaigns, Democrats won eight and Republicans two.[7]

In a similar analysis by the *Congressional Quarterly Weekly Report* of 1954 Congressional election spending, Republicans reported $7.3 million and Democrats $3.8 million. In addition, 41 labor organizations reported expenditures of $2 million, with most of the funds contributed to Democratic candidates. The five most expensive Senate campaigns, with the winner's name placed first, were:

1.	Rhode Island	Green (D) $14,000 — Sundlun (R) $105,000
2.	Oregon	Neuberger (D) $84,000 — Cordon (R) nothing
3.	Illinois	Douglas (D) $39,000 — Meek (R) $28,000
4.	New Jersey	Case (R) $39,000 — Howell (D) $25,000
5.	Michigan	McNamara (D) $37,000 — Ferguson (R) $21,000

The five most expensive House campaigns reported, with the winner's name placed first, were:

1.	New York — 6th District	Holtzman (D) $5,000 — Halpern (R) $34,000
2.	Maryland — 5th District	Lankford (D) $13,000 — Small (R) $22,000
3.	California — 13th District	Teague (R) $28,000 — O'Reilly (D) $7,000
4.	Washington — 1st District	Pelly (R) $15,000 — Mitchell (D) $16,000
5.	Washington — At Large	Magnuson (D) $12,000 — Canwell (R) $17,000 [8]

Two conclusions from these 1952 and 1954 expense data are immediately apparent. First, campaigns are expensive, and they are much more expensive than the above figures indicate. Second, Re-

---

[7] From "1952 Campaign Cost," *Congressional Quarterly Weekly Report* (July 17, 1953), Vol. 11, No. 29, pp. 915–940; and "Cost of Electing Congress," *ibid.*, (October 2, 1953), No. 40, pp. 1199–1208.

[8] From "Campaign Spending," *Congressional Quarterly Weekly Report* (April 15, 1955), Vol. 13, No. 15, pp. 369–404.

publicans in general have more money at their disposal than Democrats, but the Republican victory ratio does not vary directly with the amount of money expended.

(1) *Limitations on Reported Campaign Cost Records.* Although the figures for the 1952 and 1954 campaigns cited above are valuable — if only because they are the only official records available, they are not to be interpreted as reliable guides to a candidate's total campaign expenses. One of the reasons for this is revealed by an examination of a few of those expenditure reports. Guy Cordon in his contest with Richard L. Neuberger in Oregon in 1954 filed a federal report of "nothing" but indicated that the Cordon for United States Senate Committee had filed an Oregon state expenditure report. According to the Oregon report, thirty committees and four individuals for Cordon spent $141,000. Neuberger's state report was also not identical with his federal report — the former was some $4,000 more than the latter. Based on the Oregon expenditure records, the campaign had cost $228,000 and not $84,000 as the federal records showed. Senator Paul H. Douglas of Illinois reported $39,000 to the Clerk of the House, yet the Democratic Senatorial Campaign Committee listed $24,000 contributed to Douglas and eleven labor organizations together contributed $36,000 — $60,000 from these two sources.[9]

Not only are there wide variations between federal and state expenditure reporting requirements, where the latter exist, but the reporting laws themselves are so loosely worded as to permit a wide variety of interpretations as to what should or must be included. Nor do reported costs include amounts spent by private organizations which may indirectly be intended to influence political campaigns. It has been estimated that corporations spent $1.2 million for free-enterprise advertisements in Ohio that were "clearly timed for the election but did not mention the candidates at all" during Senator Robert A. Taft's 1950 Senatorial campaign.[10] Neither do these reported costs include campaign work donations which may be furnished by labor or other organizations or free publicity furnished by such media as newspapers be they city dailies or labor organs.

---

[9] From "Campaign Spending," *Congressional Quarterly Weekly Report* (April 15, 1955), Vol. 13, No. 15, p. 370.

[10] Ralph M. Goldman, "Political Conflict, Campaign Funds, and the Law," article in Henry A. Turner (ed.), *Politics in the United States* (New York: McGraw-Hill Book Company, 1955), p. 339.

In Presidential campaigns it is not necessary for political committees functioning exclusively within a state to report expenses to the Clerk of the House. Primary election campaign expenses likewise need not be federally reported, though sometimes candidates do report them as was the case with Walter I. Sundlun in the Rhode Island " most expensive " United States Senate contest in 1954. Limitations in campaign expense reporting such as these clearly lead to the conclusion that actual expenditures are substantially higher than the records indicate, and broad-based estimates for Presidential election years run from $39 million to as high as $75 million.

A survey of the things for which campaigners must pay tends to support the point. One of these items which is most difficult to estimate is the amount spent to hire election-day workers. Frank Kent says that in New York such costs have been as high as $500 per precinct.[11] In general, Kent, writing in 1928, has suggested that for a city of some 700,000 population, the amount would be $60 in precincts which need working. For a city with 600 precincts, that would mean $36,000 for this purpose alone.[12] Dayton McKean, developing the Kent estimates and attempting to bring them up to date, concludes that the total for election day workers " is about $17,500,000 for a national election, plus an amount for which a fair estimate cannot be made for primaries, local, and special elections." [13]

Advertising, particularly in campaigns in which television and radio are essential media, will take a substantial proportion of the campaign budget. For a small television station coverage — up to 50,000 population — one-minute spots will generally cost from $30 to $40, depending on daytime or nighttime rates, and a half-hour program from $90 to $120. For large market coverage — 250,000 to 750,000 population — the one-minute spot might cost from $70 to $150, and a half hour from $220 to $400. A coast-to-coast network, depending upon coverage, may vary from $50,000 to $100,000 for one half hour. One-minute radio spots may cost from $6 for a small market station to over $50 for a large market station; and thirty minutes from $40 with the small station to $175 for the large. For still

[11] Frank R. Kent, *The Great Game of Politics* (New York) : Doubleday, Doran and Company, 1923), p. 130.

[12] Frank R. Kent, *Political Behavior* (New York: William Morrow and Company, 1928), pp. 219–220.

[13] Dayton David McKean, *Party and Pressure Politics* (Boston: Houghton Mifflin Company, 1949), p. 342.

larger metropolitan area coverage both radio and television costs will be proportionately greater.[14] In the Presidential campaigns alone in 1952 over $3.5 million was spent for television and radio time.

A newspaper advertisement some 9 × 14 inches will average $90 in a small market newspaper and $530 for a 250,000 to 750,000 population center. Political rates for full-page newspaper advertisements in metropolitan newspapers may cost from $2,000 to $3,000, depending upon the paper's circulation. One-panel, unlighted billboards are likely to cost $18 per month, and if lighted, $43. For a large city transportation card advertisement average rates may be " 2,600 cards in 2,600 vehicles: $3,218." Sound trucks might be rented for $55 per day. One-inch diameter campaign buttons may cost $32 per thousand or $30 per thousand in lots of 5,000; wrapped unprinted soap samples, $14 per thousand.[15] Direct mailing printing costs vary greatly depending upon the locality and type of piece to be prepared, but postage cost is easily computed. At two cents per piece, only 5,000 items will bring the postage bill to $100. For a state with 1 million registered voters postage for one mailing would be $20,000.

Although publicity may not cost money in the same sense that advertising does, the outlays for professional services in getting out publicity are substantial. Breaking down the campaign dollar into the various purposes for which the combined Republican National, Senatorial, and Congressional campaign committees made expenditures in 1954, the results are in part: 20 percent for television and radio advertising, 19 percent for aid to candidates, and 13 percent for publicity.[16] How to get publicity is a refined art, and only the specialist can realize a maximum publicity potential. Few are the professional publicity specialists who are available for less than $800 per month. Perhaps, in addition, professional photographers will be employed. Perhaps some private public relations, publicity, or advertising firm will be retained to handle all mass media communication in a campaign, including the making and placing of advertising. Perhaps a

---

[14] Cost estimates from Democratic National Committee, *A Campaign Guide to Political Publicity* (Washington: The Democratic National Committee, Stephen A. Mitchell, Chairman, undated) , pp. 28 and 38.

[15] Cost estimates from *ibid.,* pp. 46 and 77–78.

[16] From Hugh A. Bone, *American Politics and the Party System* (New York: McGraw-Hill Book Company, 1955) , p. 494.

private polling organization will be contracted with to conduct public opinion polls. In addition to the outlay required for such specialist services, there is the cost of maintaining a headquarters and a head-quarters staff.

Obviously Senator Price Daniel of Texas, as one example, spent more than his federally reported \$3.01 — \$1.33 for postage and \$1.68 for stamps. His 1952 campaign is likely to have cost several hundred thousand dollars, including the primary election. Five hundred thousand dollars is not an unrealistic estimate for a hotly fought United States Senate campaign in a large and doubtful pivot state, and sometimes that amount might be spent by each side. Likewise, \$25,000 to \$50,000 is a realistic estimate for a contested United States House of Representatives seat, with many close contests going considerably higher. When one includes a Presidential election and gubernatorial, mayoralty, state legislature, and other contests the conclusion that expenditures are much in excess of reported campaign expenses becomes a fact.

(2) *Do the Large Spenders Win More Elections Because of Their Expenditures?* It has already been suggested that the prospects for an election victory do not increase, above some minimum, in proportion to the amount of campaign funds available. A few statistics will further illustrate the point. The *Congressional Quarterly Weekly Report* has compiled the following figures on 1950, 1952, and 1954 reported Congressional campaign expenditures and election results: [17]

	1950	1952	1954
Spending			
Republicans	\$4.7 million	\$4.1 million	\$7.2 million
Democrats	4.2	1.1	3.8
Labor			
Organizations	1.6	.3	2.1
Net Gain in			
Senate and			
House Seats	32 Republican	21 Republican	19 Democratic

From these data, and taking cognizance of the multitude of other factors influencing these campaigns, certainly no case can be made for a " money buys elections " thesis.

Neither does the information on Presidential elections establish

---

[17] (April 15, 1955), p. 371.

such a thesis, but rather it is on the negative side. In 1952, according to Campbell, Gurin, and Miller, before the national conventions 27 percent of the Eisenhower voters and 35 percent of the Stevenson voters had already made up their minds. During the conventions the Republican nominee added another 40 percent of his total and Stevenson, 27 percent of his total. During the campaign 28 percent of the Eisenhower voters made their decision and 31 percent of the Stevenson voters did the same.[18] From this it might be concluded that Stevenson, with less money to spend than his opposition, actually made a greater campaign impact than did Eisenhower.

Even more sharply at variance with the " money buys elections " thesis was the 1948 campaign. Twenty-eight percent of the Truman voters, according to the same study, made their decision after the convention while the corresponding figure for Dewey voters was 16 percent.[19] Berelson, Lazarsfeld, and McPhee, in their 1948 intensive survey in Elmira, New York, found that most voters remained constant in their decisions between the Presidential candidates — 81 percent of the Republicans and 50 percent of the Democrats. Half of Truman's vote, according to these findings, was developed during the campaign from those who wavered between parties or between the alternatives of Truman or not voting. Also, 75 percent of those who voted for Dewey had decided in June, but only 41 percent of Truman voters had decided by then. Truman picked up 22 percent of his vote in August; Dewey, 12 percent. In October Dewey added 7 percent of his total and Truman, 18 percent; and in November Dewey, 6 percent and Truman, 19 percent.[20]

Throughout the New Deal era from 1932 through 1948, Republicans generally spent more in campaigns than Democrats, but Democratic Presidents and Congresses were elected, except in 1946. Perhaps it might be said that Democrats would have done better in those years had they had more money, but such a proposition would be impossible to factually develop. Furthermore, it is an unlikely hypothesis.

Republicans and Democrats (though perhaps more of the latter)

---

[18] Angus Campbell, Gerald Gurin, and Warren E. Miller, *The Voter Decides* (White Plains, N.Y.: Row, Peterson and Company, 1954) , p. 18.

[19] *Idem.*

[20] Bernard R. Berelson, Paul F. Lazarsfeld, and William N. McPhee, *Voting: A Study of Opinion Formation in a Presidential Campaign* (Chicago: The University of Chicago Press, 1954) , pp. 17–18.

bemoan the fact that they do not have enough money to present their cases, and particularly is this likely to be heard from the camp of the defeated candidate after an election. Such reactions should often be viewed skeptically. In general, estimates of both major parties' expenditures in campaigns in modern times suggest that affluence differentials are not as great as they sometimes appear to be. Sometimes those who proclaim lack of funds as hurting their campaign chances are using the device as a propaganda technique. Other times that reason is given as a explanation for a defeat when often the person is overlooking or covering up what has in fact been an inability to make effective use of the funds that were available. The inability may have been the result of the inadequacy of the candidate himself or the record of his party, or perhaps the election result was determined by the nature of the constituency in which the campaign was conducted. On the other hand, lack of funds may in fact have been the determining factor.

Sources of Campaign Funds. In the Congressional elections of 1954 Republicans spent a reported $7.2 million, Democrats, $3.8 million and forty-one labor organizations, $2.1 million. Where did the money come from? Approximately 20 percent of the Republican total and 10 percent of the Democratic total was from persons or committees donating $1,000 or more. The " $1,000-or-More Club " dollar total for Republicans was $1,434,084 from 738 persons or committees and the Democrats' total was $418,900 from 244 persons or committees. A breakdown of these contributions compiled by the *Congressional Quarterly Weekly Report* is as follows: [21]

REPUBLICANS

Contributions	Size of Gift	Total
407	$1,000	$407,000
26	1,500	39,000
63	2,000	126,000
25	2,500	62,500
48	3,000	144,000
18	5,000	90,000
151	other amounts	565,584
738	Total	1,434,084

[21] (April 15, 1955), p. 376.

DEMOCRATS

Contributions	Size of Gift	Total
139	1,000	139,000
6	1,500	9,000
24	2,000	48,000
26	2,500	65,000
6	3,000	18,000
14	5,000	70,000
29	other amounts	69,000
244	Total	418,900

Largest contributors among recognized family names for Republicans were ten Rockefellers for $66,000; 14 du Ponts of Delaware for $51,000; the Mellons of Pittsburgh for $40,000; and the Pews of Philadelphia for $25,000. Democratic counterparts with a total of $10,000 from husband and wife were Senator and Mrs. Earle C. Clements of Kentucky, Senator and Mrs. Stuart Symington of Missouri, Mr. and Mrs. Clark Clifford, and Mr. and Mrs. Leslie Biffle. Clifford was counsel to President Truman, and Biffle served six years as Secretary of the Senate.[22]

A sampling of nationally recognizable names contributing between $1,000 and $4,000 from the California list adds to the picture of the " big contributors ":

1. To the Republican National Committee, Republican Senatorial or Congressional campaign committees, National Citizens' for Eisenhower Congressional Committee or other Republican groups: Leonard K. Firestone, Los Angeles, $1,000; Samuel Goldwyn, Los Angeles, $2,000; Paul Helms, Los Angeles, $1,000; Conrad N. Hilton, Los Angeles, $3,000; Paul Hoffman, Pasadena, $1,000; Louis B. Mayer, Los Angeles, $1,000; Mike Romanoff and three others, $5,000; Harry M. Warner, Burbank, $1,000. Also included are various California Republican committees with the largest committee contribution being that of the Republican State Central Committee, Los Angles — $47,856 — for the Republican National Committee.

2. To the Democratic National Committee or Democratic Senatorial or Congressional campaign committees: Lawrence A. Harvey, Torrance, $1,000; Edwin W. Pauley, Los Angeles, $3,000; Mrs. Edwin W.

---

[22] *Congressional Quarterly Weekly Report* (April 15, 1955), p. 371.

Pauley, Los Angeles, $2,000. Also included are Democratic committee contributions, the largest of which was the Stevenson Rally Committee, Los Angeles — $10,500 — for the Democratic National Committee.[23]

Twenty percent of the total reported spending for political activity by organizations in 1954, including Democratic and Republican committees, was done by forty-one labor organizations. Ranking first was the C.I.O. Political Action Committee with $351,886 from its individual contributions account and $339,991 from its educational account. Next were the A.F.L. Labor's League for Political Education with $485,081; the United Auto Workers (C.I.O.) Political Action Committee with $255,175; and the United Steelworkers of America (C.I.O.) Political Action Fund with $185,004 from its individual contributions account and $437 from its educational account.[24]

Why do individuals and groups contribute to political parties and candidates? To this question there is no simple answer. Contributions to labor organizations for political purposes may be obtained through systematic campaigns based on the premise that the Democratic party will be more friendly to labor than the Republican party, or on the premise that the union's leadership should have funds at its disposal to use as it sees fit to advance the organization's political objectives. In the relatively few cases where labor organizations have supported Republicans, the reason for that support has been that the Republican is friendly to labor or is at least a better risk, for a variety of possible reasons, than the Democrat.

Wealthy individuals or businessmen may contribute to the Republican party because they feel that if the government is in Republican control their interests would best be protected. Yet the Democratic party also has its wealthy or businessmen contributors, though not as many of them since 1932, and they may support the Democratic party for a set of reasons not dissimilar from those for which their Republican counterparts supported the Republican party.

Perhaps the individual contributes because he is an active member of a party organization, would like to be an active member, wants to improve his access to the leaders of his party, or wants someday to run for office as a party nominee. Perhaps there is a

---

[23] *Congressional Quarterly Weekly Report* (April 15, 1955), p. 397.
[24] *Ibid.*, p. 378.

thought that a contribution will place him in line for an important appointment, such as an ambassadorship. Perhaps he holds a patronage job and contributes for that reason. Perhaps he gives his gift — nondeductible for income tax purposes — because he is friendly with or has a great admiration for a particular candidate, or even more indirectly, because he feels a particular candidate is what the country or state needs. Perhaps there are idealistic reasons, and at the opposite extreme, perhaps the individual wants a very specific policy favor within the power of government to grant. Factors such as these and many more may enter into the contributor's decision. They do not in and of themselves connote corruption, though most do involve some kind of " influence " considerations.

Raising Campaign Funds. Methods of tapping sources of political campaign funds are many. For the large contributor — in many areas $100 constitutes a large contribution — party and candidate finance committees composed of the most financially influencial persons the party or candidate can enlist personally solicit those from whom large contributions might be obtained. Mailed personal letter appeals are aimed at large numbers of potential smaller contributors. Lincoln-Day, Jefferson-Jackson-Day or other $25 to $100 per plate dinner occasions are designed primarily for fund-raising purposes. Periodically parties experiment with dime-a-day clubs or their equivalent in an attempt to get large numbers of the less financially able to systematically save for party purposes in the manner of banks' Christmas lay-away accounts. Carnivals, dances, or other entertainments are organized to raise funds. When a person becomes a member of some party committee, it is sometimes understood that he should contribute a specified amount. Likewise, in some states to be selected as a delegate to a national party convention carries with it the moral obligation of a substantial campaign contribution. Nonparty organized groups are solicited by mail by a committee of their own members who are attached to a party or candidate. Here are techniques which are in general use throughout all the states.

In state or local units of government without effective civil service legislation it is a general practice for the party in power to assess each patronage jobholder a specified percentage of his income with the understanding that if he does not contribute he will not have a job. Also in such states the public treasury may be assessed indirectly by assigning public employees to full- or part-time campaign work.

One of the more common practices of this type is to enlarge the staff of the motor vehicle license plate inspectors during a campaign and to appoint to these positions men who are in fact supervising campaign activity. Thus party work is financed by state salaries, state expense accounts, and state cars. Another method of making the public treasury bear part of the campaign cost is the use, either by members of Congress or through members of Congress, of the Congressional franking privilege.

Nor is the public treasury the only tapable source for indirect campaign contributions. Business, labor, and other organizations often release employees from their jobs to work in campaigns while their regular salary checks continue to come. Commercial advertisers sometimes donate their regular billboards for campaign advertising purposes. Institutional advertising by private organizations may indirectly constitute political advertising.

The history of party politics shows that some other not so reputable or legal methods have been employed in campaign fund raising. At one time in some jurisdictions of government it was common practice to " sell " public utility franchises to large campaign contributors, and in more refined ways sometimes the practice is still employed. The shakedown, using the threat of adverse health, building inspection, or the police arm of government, is not unknown. On occasion underworld elements have bought political protection for their vice, gambling, and other illegal activities by campaign contributions.

For the legitimate campaign fund-raising operation several rules of financial administration have been developed. First of these is to exercise extreme care in selecting solicitors not only for their ability to attract contributions but also for their integrity. At no other organizational point in a campaign will persons be so tempted to try to " drain off " some money for themselves, or if graft is the individual's intention, here is the position in which he most wants to be placed. The wrong type of solicitor may injure the party or candidate in such ways as these. If graft money is being skimmed from contributions, the campaign will have less financial backing than it would otherwise have. If contributors learn that their gifts are not being properly handled, that fact will engender distrust or antagonism and may result in the source's drying up for future campaigns. If the solicitor is not careful of the " kind of money " he accepts, particularly if it is underworld money, and if the opposition is alert, sources of campaign funds may become a major issue in the campaign and place those who have accepted " questionable " contributions in an unfavorable defensive position.

A second rule of campaign financial administration is to meticulously maintain two sets of records. One of the sets should be the accounting-type record with procedures tight enough to minimize the possibility of graft, to identify the source of contributions, and to conform to statutory requirements. The second set of records is the one from which those in charge of personal and mail solicitation will obtain their lists of prospects. This latter list should be kept up to date with the continuous addition of new contributors and a never ceasing and systematic exploration of the field of potential contributors.

Whenever the internal dynamics of a party permit a united fund-raising effort in a particular area, centralized financial administration is more desirable than having many different party organizations and candidates all independently working the money field. This is a third rule of campaign financial administration. If there is not such centralization, co-ordination is difficult, and because the effort is not well organized, some potentially good sources of funds may be missed. If many different units are soliciting, it is easier for a grafter to set himself up as a party official and collect funds for himself using a fictitious or actual party organ's name. Contributors, if they are beset by requests for contributions from all sides may conclude that they are being imposed upon or that if the financial aspects of a campaign are being so badly managed the party's prospects are so poor that it does not deserve a contribution.

A fourth practice which is generally followed in campaigns is to set up the money-raising function in an organizational unit independent of the candidate. The theory is that the candidate is better off if he does not know the details of the financial operation. If this rule is followed and if questions about contributions or practices should be raised, the candidate can disclaim responsibility and repudiate whatever the trouble-causing act has been. If the candidate does not know financial details, he is in a better position to appeal for votes on the grounds that he would go into office " without any strings attached to him." Furthermore, legislation requiring financial reports for campaign receipts and expenditures places a premium on the candidate's not knowing any more than is absolutely essential about the campaign's financial affairs.

MONEY, CAMPAIGNS AND THE LAW

From 1883 until the present time numerous federal and state statutes have been enacted to regulate campaign contributions and expenditures. These laws are of interest to the student of party politics or to participants in political campaigns for two important reasons: first, the statutes are guideposts showing what the parties and candidates can and cannot do; and second, the statutes, in both their strengths and weaknesses, provide a means of gaining additional insight into the larger problems of campaign finance.

Prior to the passage of the Pendleton (Civil Service) Act in 1883, the major parties enlisted their campaign manpower and secured money contributions in large part from public officeholders or office-seekers. The theory of " to the victor belongs the spoils " was generally accepted and practiced. Those who helped a party win would get patronage appointments, and after taking office, would be required to maintain their position with their party through paying regular political assessments from their salaries. Those who had provided the same kind of assistance to the opposition major party found themselves either removed from jobs which they had held or not getting the jobs they wanted.

When Jackson became President, he brought his supporters into office with him. Adams men could not be expected to properly implement Jacksonian policies and Jackson workers had to be rewarded. The Whig party controlling the White House from 1840 to 1844, threw out Democrats and replaced them with good Whigs. The Democrats' turn again came from 1844 to 1848, and it was followed by another four-year Whig opportunity from 1848 to 1852. After the Democratic victory of 1852, Whigs were replaced by tried and true Democrats, and so the in-and-out political lottery continued.

By the end of Grant's first administration, spoils system abuses, much outright corruption, and a growing appreciation of the waste involved in such frequent turnover of federal employees led to a demand for a federal merit system. Garfield's assassination by a disappointed office-seeker proved to be the catalytic agent which, as a direct result, brought the Pendleton Act. That act, in part, made it illegal for any officer or employee of the federal government to solicit or receive any assessment, subscription or contribution for any political purpose from an officer or employee of the federal government. It also barred any person from soliciting for political purposes in any federal government building, and procedures were established to protect the federal officer or employee from demotion or dismissal for political reasons.

Although the establishment of civil service for federal employees did have the effect of removing the classified service one step away from political activity, several loopholes remained open. Party agents not in the federal service could solicit employees outside federal government buildings. There remained also more subtle means through which threats against the jobs of noncooperators might be enforced. Generally today, party fund raising within the federal government is confined to higher level officers.

That the problem had not been completely solved as late as 1939, however, is indicated by the Hatch Act's provision to forbid *any* federal employees except those on the policy level from taking an active part in political campaigns. The Pendleton Act had applied only to those in the "competitive classified service." Amendments to the Hatch Act in 1940 also expanded the employee political-neutralization attempt to state and local employees engaged in work on a project or in an agency financed wholly or in part by the federal government. In over half the states this 1940 provision is the only prohibition against political assessment of state employees by state parties. How important to state party financing is the state public employee is suggested by the estimate that in Pennsylvania alone there are some 58,000 state patronage jobs.[25]

Although some of the state legislatures were passing corrupt practices acts and although there was some agitation for further federal regulation of matters relating to campaign finance, from 1883 until the McKinley-Mark Hanna campaigns of 1896 and 1900 the pressures were not strong enough to bring Congress to action. Federal employees were being less of a factor in campaigns and at the same time the cost of campaigns was increasing, but both major parties with their "New York focused" appeals were attracting the money they needed. Both the Democratic and Republican parties appealed to those who had the big money to give.

Democrats spent as much as Republicans in 1876 and more in 1884 and 1892. In 1896, however, this balance was upset by the fright which soft-money and low-tariff man Bryan gave to the Eastern "monied interests" and by Hanna's efficiency in systematically mo-

---

[25] *Time* (November 15, 1954), Vol. 44, No. 20, p. 32.

bilizing corporation contributions for the Republican side. Where in the 1892 Presidential campaign Republicans spent $1.5 million, it has been estimated that in 1896 they collected some $10 to $15 million.[26] By 1904 the estimated differential between Democratic and Republican Presidential campaign spending was $700,000 for Parker and over $2 million for Theodore Roosevelt. Forty percent of the Republican money came from nine representatives of large corporations in gifts of $50,000 or more. Most of the Parker fund was contributed by two big businessmen.[27] Subsequent disclosure of these facts led to federal legislation to limit the sources of campaign contributions, to require the filing of receipt and expenditure statements, and to limit both expenditures and contributions.

Democratic nominee Alton B. Parker had charged in the 1904 campaign that Theodore Roosevelt was the beneficiary of large corporation contributions designed to secure governmental favors for the contributors. This Roosevelt denied, and he himself in both 1904 and 1905 recommended legislation to require public campaign finance reporting. In 1906 a National Campaign Publicity Association, which included the names of men like Samuel Gompers, Charles Evans Hughes, and William Jennings Bryan, had been organized to propagandize for federal publicity legislation. Congress in 1907 took a small step in the regulatory direction by denying the right of any national bank or corporation organized under law of Congress to contribute to any political campaign and by forbidding any corporation to contribute to a Presidential or Congressional campaign. The following year the Democratic National Convention included in its platform a plank calling for campaign fund publicity and pledged to report before the election the names of everyone who contributed $100 or more to the Democratic party. This it did. William Howard Taft, in his nomination acceptance speech, pledged that the Republican National Committee would report as required by New York law after the election. Here was the first Presidential campaign in which the parties, either before or after election, had systematically reported what previously had been " party secrets." [28]

This development was followed in 1910 by the first general Federal Corrupt Practices Act. A political committee attempting to

---

[26] From Howard R. Penniman, *Sait's American Parties and Elections* (New York: Appleton-Century-Crofts, 1952) , p. 468.

[27] From Overacker, *op. cit.*, p. 11.

[28] From *ibid.*, pp. 19–22.

influence in a campaign in which United States Senators or Representatives were chosen had to file within thirty days *after* the election a statement showing the names and addresses of persons who contributed $100 or more, the names and addresses of all to whom $10 or more was dispersed, and the purpose of the dispersement, and the total of all receipts and expenditures. Amendments in 1911 required statements *before* the election, required Congressional candidates to file like political committees, included primary elections as well as general elections, and limited Senate candidates to expenditures of $10,000 and House candidates to $5,000. Expenditures for travel, mail, and other personal items were specifically excluded from reporting or expenditure limit requirements.

After the United States Supreme Court held in Newberry *v.* United States, 256 U. S. 232 (1921), that the Congress did not have authority over primary elections, a new Corrupt Practices Act of 1925 was passed. It was based upon the 1910 act as amended, but applied only to general elections. Several other changes were made. First, to the limit of $10,000 for a Senate contest and a new $2,500 limit for a House contest was added the alternative of " an amount equal to the amount obtained by multiplying three cents by the total number of votes cast at the last general election for all candidates for the office which the candidate seeks," but in no case to exceed $25,000 for a Senate candidate or $5,000 for a House candidate. The broad exemptions for personal expenses, however, were retained. So broad are those exemptions that a candidate may, if he gives himself every benefit of interpretive doubt, succeed in including very little or none of his actual campaign expenses in his official reports.

Second, in addition to candidate statements of receipts and expenditures required both before and after election, the candidate must place on file any pledge he has made to any person of an appointment or recommendation for an appointment in order to secure that person's support in the campaign. This latter requirement has no meaning in that candidates do not directly make such commitments. If it is necessary to gain support by a promise of this nature, some member of the candidate's organization can in indirect ways convey a hint of what might be forthcoming after the election, but this can be done without implicating the candidate because he does not know of it.

A third change in 1925 broadened the definition of who, in addition to candidates, must submit campaign financial reports to the

Clerk of the House in March, June, September, twice before any general election, and on January 1 for the preceding year. A political committee within the terms of the act is one which accepts gifts or spends to influence Presidential or Congressional elections in two or more states, or any branch of a national political organization even if that branch operates within a single state. Furthermore, any person who spends to influence an election in two or more states must also report. In 1954 there were only four such persons, all from Houston, Texas.[29]

Such was the basic federal law in the field of corrupt practices from 1925 until 1940. Campaign finance scholar Louise Overacker summarizes the effect of this legislation and provides transition to the change in direction produced by the Hatch Act of 1940 as follows:

> Until 1940 we were moving slowly but steadily in the direction of effective publicity, and the voters were becoming increasingly aware of the extent to which they did and did not pay their own political bills. At the same time, the party national committees were assuming more responsibility for the collection and distribution of funds, a trend toward centralization which greatly facilitated the assembling of pertinent information. Our picture of the financing of presidential campaigns was still incomplete, but it was becoming steadily more complete and clear cut. With more experience, patience and imagination, the gaps in the legislation might have been filled in, and the defects remedied. Unfortunately, however, in 1940 we abandoned the path of Publicity for the characteristically American trail of Prohibition. Instead of tightening our publicity requirements we attempted to apply a very different formula — Prohibitions backed by criminal sanctions. . . . The result is a futile legislative gesture which has not limited expenditures and which lessens the effectiveness of publicity provisions.[30]

The 1940 Hatch Act imposed a campaign expenditure limit on the amount a party committee may expend in any year and a limit on individual contributions — limits which Overacker and most students of the subject feel have done much to make more difficult adequate publicity of campaign contributions and expenditures. The bill, as introduced by Senator Hatch, was designed to prohibit political activity of state employees paid from federal funds. Perhaps in an

---

[29] *Congressional Quarterly Weekly Report* (April 15, 1955), p. 371.

[30] *Louise Overacker, Presidential Campaign Funds* (Boston: Boston University Press, 1946), p. 24. Reprinted by permission.

attempt to kill the bill, an amendment to limit individual campaign contributions to $1,000 was offered, but failed. When the figure was raised to $5,000, it was narrowly accepted. Another successful amendment placed a $3-million limit on the expenditures of any political committee in any calendar year. Neither amendment killed the bill. Instead it sailed through the Senate and House and obtained the President's signature with little or no discussion of the implications of these provisions.[31]

Neither of the limits, however, was effective. Families like the duPonts or Marshall Fields could split up their contributions into $5,000 lots for each member of the family. Furthermore, each individual could give $5,000 to different party committees. The $3-million limitation on political committees did not apply to total expenses in a campaign, and consequently any number of committees could be formed and each could spend that amount. In short, the result has been to decentralize party finance and spread out giving and spending in such a manner as to make it more difficult to obtain a true picture of the over-all scope of campaign contributions and expenditures in any particular year.

In addition to these provisions, the 1940 Hatch Act contained language to outlaw an ingenious and successful fund-raising device developed by the Democrats in 1936. A *Book of the Democratic Convention of 1936* with articles, pictures, other political information, and advertising — $250,000 worth of advertising — was sold by the Democratic National Committee at prices ranging up to $100 per copy. After 1940 corporations have been barred from aiding candidates for federal office by buying advertising or goods of any kind.

Several other federal statutes regulating campaign finance should be noted. Three acts have elaborated on the 1907 prohibition against corporation contributions or have applied limitations to labor organizations. When public utility holding companies and their subsidiaries were placed under federal control in the Public Utility Holding Company Act of 1935, they were denied the right to contribute to any political campaigns. In 1943 Congress turned its attention to labor organization contributions. The Smith-Connally Act of that year provided that no labor organization could contribute to campaigns in connection with a Presidential or Congressional

---

[31] From *ibid.*, pp. 26–27.

election, but primary elections were not included. To meet the terms of the new law the C.I.O. Political Action Committee used union funds in the 1944 primary elections and then " froze " those funds and employed only money collected from individual union members in the general election. Direct " spending " in campaigns, it was held by the unions, did not constitute " contributing."

Provisions of the Taft-Hartley Act of 1947 were designed to further close loopholes for both corporations and labor unions. Under the act neither could " make a contribution or expenditure in connection with any election at which Presidential or Vice Presidential electors or a Senator or Representative . . . are to be voted for, or in connection with any primary election or political convention or caucus held to select candidates." [32] Exempt, however, are " educational " activities and trade associations or the political action committees of C.I.O. unions and the A.F.L. Labor's League for Political Education which are separate from the regular union or corporation organizations themselves. Also outside the federal prohibition are campaigns for state and local office.

State legislation on the subject of campaign finance varies so widely from state to state that the politician or student must make a separate study of the laws in each state in which he may be interested. In general, most of the states forbid in some manner corporation and labor organization campaign contributions, impose limits on campaign expenditures, and provide for some system of filing financial reports. In all states statutes of some type outlaw bribery and intimidation. In general, also, it may be stated that the loopholes for contributors, for parties, and for candidates in all states are numerous.

---

[32] The United States Supreme Court in United States v. Classic, 61 U. S. 1031 (1941) reversed the Newberry decision which appeared to bar federal government regulation of primary elections and primary election campaign activity.

PART SIX

The Parties and the Future

INTRODUCTION

In a sense the three chapters which follow in the last part of this volume are summary and conclusion to the preceding twenty-one chapters. Part One introduced the politician and the political institutions of the major party, the pressure group, and the minor party. It sketched the main outlines of their respective functions and posed some of the principal questions which their manner of operation has raised in the minds of all who would seek to improve upon the American party system and the parties. The chapters of Part Two developed major party organization and stated more of those questions. Parts Three, Four, and Five had as their primary concern the winning of elections, though here too additional questions about the effectiveness of the parties and the system were asked or implied.

In Part Six the whole emphasis is placed on evaluation of the American party system and the parties. There has been no attempt, however, to systematically summarize all that has gone before. The reader might with profit refer back to appropriate previous chapters for background detail and general information as arguments for or against the system or the parties are developed.

It is also desirable for the reader to carry his study of weaknesses and strengths of the system and parties beyond the confines of what is developed within the limitations of Part Six. Excellent books and articles are available for this purpose. For those who cannot do so, an attempt has been made to give some impression of the many different opinions and of the force or intensity with which they are held by the various disputants on the different sides of the issues around which arguments about the parties and the system proceed.

CHAPTER TWENTY–TWO

The Major Parties and the System: Weaknesses and Strengths — I

. . . [F]ormal party organization in its main features is still substantially what it was before the Civil War. Aside from adoption of the direct primary, organizational forms have not been overhauled for nearly a century. The result is that the parties are now probably the most archaic institutions in the United States.

Committee on Political Parties of the
American Political Science Association [1]

In the presence of resourceful executive leadership . . . congressional supremacy — that haunting ogre with its irresponsible habits which some critics charge to the failure of our party system — is more noisy than obstructionist in its over-all effect. And out of the healthy interaction of presidential leadership and congressional attitudes comes the gradualist tempo of change in public policy that has served us well. In fact it is through this blending of attitudes which the diversity of congressional representation and the party system inspires that we are spared the sharp wrenches over what direction public policy shall take.

Within this setting, no hierarchical centralized gadgetry to control party policy is indicated. National party councils or directorates and other proposals to standardize party policies not only raise serious practical considerations of workability, but beyond the operational sphere they threaten us in other directions. ". . . By pluralizing our power, we purge it of its

---

[1] *Toward a More Responsible Two-Party System,* a supplement to *The American Political Science Review* (September, 1950), Vol. 44, No. 3, Pt. 2, p. 25.

indigenous poison," writes philosopher T. V. Smith, reminding us again that formally delegating party control to a national hierarchy at the expense of invigorating local currents is not without its hazards.

As in all societies our individual citizens and various groups — organized as well as unorganized — are not uninfluenced by the tenderness of their own interests. And in our diverse society with its cultural differences and vast number of pressure groups ranging from bolt and nut manufacturers to cranberry producers, the party system has been hard-pressed to accommodate the representation of these interests and simultaneously uphold the national interest. Yet by reasonable standards of judgment it has managed with more than chance success, the delicate task of compromising our heterogeneous interest groups with the national interest.

It has managed this compromise so far with something of the political spectrum of America reproduced in each of the major parties. Neither party can lay claim to a monopoly of eminent leaders and neither party can be charged with a monopoly of the late hucksters. Thus the parties move somewhat together in a broad confluent action, the minority not radically dissimilar from the majority, each ever hoping that one more mighty heave will land it in the seat of power, while the followers of both along with the independents, are guided by the happy thought of Senator Ashurst: " That in a free Republic such as ours, it is the undoubted right of the people to change their servants, and to remove one and displace him with another at any time they choose, for a good reason, for a bad reason, or for no reason at all."

Malcolm Moos [2]

Political scientists and students of American politics have long debated the virtues and shortcomings of the American major parties. In the past five years, however, the intensity of discussion has sharply increased. Principally this has been a direct result of the publication of the American Political Science Association's Committee on Political Parties 1950 report, *Toward a More Responsible Two-Party System.* Because the report represents the most comprehensive recent attempt at critical analysis of American parties, the reader should examine it himself. For the same reason that report and its recommendations are used as the organizational framework around which is developed the assessment of the weaknesses and strengths of the major

---

[2] *Politics, Presidents and Coattails* (Baltimore: The Johns Hopkins Press, 1952), pp. 176–178. Reprinted by permission of The Johns Hopkins Press.

parties and the party system of these three concluding chapters of this volume. Before proceeding to an over-all evaluation, the contents of the Committee on Political Parties' report should be summarized.

"Who Do You Think You'll Vote Against?"

TOWARD A MORE RESPONSIBLE TWO–PARTY SYSTEM — A SUMMARY

The Need for Greater Party Responsibility. Political parties are, the report begins, indispensable instruments of government. They are necessary to provide the voter with a " proper range of choice between alternatives of action." An election is not just a contest between candidates but is rather one between public policies. Voters' choices are meaningful only in proportion to the manner in which they outline alternatives of policy. Discussion of public affairs for the most part makes sense only in policy terms.

With serious problems demanding solution, the parties must be able to decide upon and, if in office, must be able to implement party policy decisions. For the out-party the function is to act " as the critic of the party in power, developing, defining and presenting the policy alternatives which are necessary for a true choice in reaching policy decisions." The in-party should be responsible through the election process to the general public for management of the affairs of government. Leaders of the parties should be responsible to party members with control exercised by membership in primary elections, caucuses and conventions.

A majority within a party should be in a power position to compel local and state party organizations and leaders to " cooperate with the party as a whole " if the need for such compulsion arises. Today the emphasis in American politics is more and more on national issues. Yet the national organs of the parties are not well set up to deal with national questions. Party federal organizations are overbalanced in favor of state party units. At each organizational level there is " an excessive measure of internal separatism " between organs of the same party. Leadership of the party as a whole is vested in no single committee or person. Party membership is vague or meaningless. Little is done to make party membership something which will attract persons and bring the rank and file members into active participation in party affairs.

> *The expanding responsibilities of modern government have brought about so extensive an interlacing of governmental action with the country's economic and social life that the need for coordinated and coherent programs, legislative as well as administrative, has become paramount.* Formulating and executing such general programs involves more than technical knowledge. *In a democracy no general program can be adopted and carried out without wide political support.* Support must be strong enough and stable enough to guard the program as far as possible against such drives as come forth constantly from a multitude of special interests seeking their own ends. This kind of political support can be mobilized on a continuing basis only by stronger parties.[3]

Proposals for Party Responsibility. The Committee on Political Parties' major proposals for party responsibility are organized into four

---

[3] *Toward a More Responsible Two-Party System*, p. 31. Italics in this quotation and in subsequent quotations from the report, unless otherwise noted, are those of the Committee on Political Parties.

categories: national party organization, party platforms, party organization in Congress, and political participation. They will be developed in that order.

(1) *National Party Organization: The National Convention.* National party conventions are unrepresentative and are not truly deliberative bodies. Both major parties, it is true, have departed from the uniform representation formula of two delegates for each United States Senator and Congressman for determining convention representation from each state. Republicans allot two delegates at large for each Senator and each Representative elected at large, six delegates at large for a state which gave its electoral votes to the Republican nominee for President at the last Presidential election or which elected a Republican United States Senator or governor at the preceding election; and Republican voting strength in a Congressional district determines the number of delegates for each Congressman elected from a Congressional district. Democrats allot two delegates for each United States Senator and Representative uniformly, and since 1944 under the bonus rule four additional delegates have been allowed to each state which gave its electoral votes to the Democratic Presidential nominee at the preceding Presidential election. For the 1956 Democratic National Convention four bonus votes are also granted to states which have elected a Democratic governor or a Democratic United States Senator since 1952.

" But in either case," suggests the Committee on Political Parties, " the existing formula falls distinctly short of true representation of the party's grass roots strength in the individual states." [4] Both parties should go further than they have toward making their national conventions more representative.

To improve the deliberative ability of the national conventions, the Committee on Political Parties makes the following recommendations. First, the size of national conventions should be cut in half, down to a maximum of 500 to 600 delegates. Second, the methods of selecting delegates should be modified. Some 300 to 350 should be elected directly by party voters, and each of these delegates should represent approximately the same number of party members. Thus party strength in the various states would be recognized. Some 150 delegates to the convention should be ex-officio members — state party chairmen, national committeemen and committeewomen and

---

[4] *Ibid.,* p. 37.

party Congressional leaders. Some twenty-five delegate positions should be granted to prominent party leaders outside the party organizations. Third, national conventions should meet at least every two years instead of every four years, it should be easy to call special national conventions, and conventions when in session should function for longer periods of time than they now do.

Such a convention would, in the view of the Committee on Political Parties, achieve these objectives.

> It would provide a convention representative of the party voters and of the party organization, national and state. It would afford opportunity for expressing and harmonizing the views and interests of the different elements in the party. It would be small enough to make possible deliberation and action on program matters. And it would promote a more responsible consideration of the various programs before the party.[5]

National Party Organization: The National Committee. Because of the Presidential nominee's or the President's influence over the selection of the national committee chairman, the chief function of the national committee becomes the direction of Presidential campaigns. Even for this, however, it is not a truly national party organ. Although national conventions have the power to exercise authority over selection of members to the national committee, seldom is that authority used. Instead the matter is left to the state parties making their selections through the state central committee, state conventions, vote in primary elections, or through the state's delegation to the national convention. The Committee on Political Parties feels " *it is highly desirable for the National Convention to reassert its authority over the National Committee through a more active participation in the final selection of the committee membership.*" [6]

Furthermore, the national committees are not representative of relative party strength in the respective states. For both parties each state is entitled to a national committeeman and committeewoman, and Republicans in 1952 included also Republican state party chairmen for such states as went Republican in the last Presidential election, have a Republican governor or a majority of Republicans in that state's Congressional delegation. To make the national committees more representative of actual party strength in the states, the Com-

---

[5] The Committee on Political Parties, *op. cit.,* p. 38.   [6] *Ibid.,* p. 39.

mittee on Political Parties would apply a unit rule to weight the votes of national committee members on some proportionate basis which would relate party strength in each state to national party strength. Where New York and Nevada, for example, now have equal national committee power, vote weighting would increase New York's voice and decrease Nevada's voice in national committee affairs. Such a scheme, it is felt, would place a great inducement on each state party to build party strength within its state and would also make the national committee a more responsible body.

National Party Organization: The Party Council. At present no party organ is responsible for promoting understanding and harmony of action between the various elements of the party on the national, state, and local levels. Those who manage party affairs are different from those chosen by the party to carry out public policy if elected to public office. What is needed, the Committee on Political Parties suggests, is " a body that can meet frequently, consult easily with other party agencies, deal with current party problems, and become a source of continuing advice to the President or, in the case of the minority party, to some other recognized party leader." [7]

> *We therefore propose a Party Council of 50 members,* made up of representatives of five main groups: the National Committee (probably 5, chosen by the committee) ; the congressional party organization (5 from each house, chosen by the respective organization) ; the state committee (10, chosen on a regional basis by the regional groups, if any, otherwise by the National Convention) ; the party's governors (5, chosen by them) ; and other recognized party groups, such as the Young Republicans and Young Democrats, as well as the party following at large (20, with the majority chosen by the National Convention and the remainder by the particular groups) . The President and Vice-President, the nominees for these offices, the highest national party officials, and perhaps some Cabinet officers designated by the President ought to be considered ex-officio members and fully entitled to participate.[8]

The proposed functions of the party council — meeting regularly and often — would be these. It would link the party organization and President of the United States and his administration, if the party controlled the White House. " There must be sensible give-and-take between both, on the basis of a party program which will

---

[7] *Ibid.,* p. 42.   [8] *Ibid.,* p. 43.

have to be implemented by the Administration, Congress and the council." The council should, within the instructions of the national convention, " consider and settle the larger problems of party management." It should prepare a preliminary draft of the party platform for the national convention. It should interpret the platform in relation to current problems. It should choose the party leaders outside the party organs who would become national convention delegates. It should study and recommend who should be party Congressional nominees. It should recommend action to the national convention, national committee or other party organs " with respect to conspicuous departures from general party decisions by state and local party organizations." In Presidential election years, " the council would naturally become a place for the discussion of presidential candidates, and might well perform the useful function of screening these candidacies in a preliminary way." [9]

Functioning even more often, a smaller executive council might be developed within the party council to serve as adviser to the President or, if the party does not have the Presidency, as adviser to the party nominee for that office or recognized party leader. Members would include the permanent chairman of the national convention, the chairman of the national committee, the chairman of the party council, the chairman of a joint House-Senate party caucus, the party's House and Senate floor leaders, and the Vice President and Speaker of the House. " Such a group, if established, should have a prominent position in all other national party organs; at any rate it should have the right to appear, to speak, to consult and to be consulted." [10]

National Party Organization: Intraparty Relationships. The maze of party committees within a state is so confusing that lines of authority and relationships are unclear, boss rule is encouraged, party responsibility is seriously affected, national party officials are not certain as to which local party organization is the responsible one, local committees often fail to assist the state and national party tickets, the parties fail to " draft constructive policies for their nominees " and to inform the voters, and discipline over legislators is absent or relatively ineffective.[11]

---

[9] *Idem.*

[10] The Committee on Political Parties, *op. cit.,* p. 44.

[11] *Ibid.,* pp. 44–45. See George B. Galloway, *Congress and Parliament* (Washington, D.C.: National Planning Association, 1955) for British and American party contrasts.

*It is necessary for both parties to reexamine their purposes and func-
tions in the light of the present-day environment, state and local, in
which they operate.* Modernization of local party machinery in the
interest of effective performance in this environment is long overdue.
A reorientation of the leaders is needed from preoccupation with
patronage and control of offices to interest in local, state, regional and
national policies. Many country chairmen have failed to understand
the reasons for the creation of competitive party associations and for
the activities or organized labor's political action committees and such
groups as the local units of Americans for Democratic Action. One
of the main reasons is the dissatisfaction with the attitudes, purposes
and operation of the official party organization.[12]

State party organizations are independent of the national organizations, and state party organizations are also independent of one another. They may take different positions on public questions and
even employ different tactics.

The minor . . . parties are generally organized in such a way as to
ensure harmony within the party. They do not deny a measure of
state autonomy in respect to decision and action, but see to it that
decisions of the national bodies take precedence over conflicting state
decisions. There can therefore be only one kind of basic party doctrine and policy — that determined by the national organization. The
state and local organizations must conform to it.

Reorganization of the two major parties on the models of the minor
. . . parties in order to achieve the same ends appears neither desirable nor feasible. *Establishment of a Party Council . . . would do
much to coordinate the different party organizations, and should be
pressed with that objective in mind.*[13]

The parties have already taken some steps toward party co-
ordination. Area meetings of state chairmen and regional party meetings have been held. Regional party organizations should be encouraged. And on the local level loyalty to party and programs could be
enhanced by regular and frequent local meetings to discuss party
policy and make recommendations to the party council.[14]

When state party organizations are rebellious, the national committee may exclude or expel national committeemen and committeewomen from such a state, and national conventions may refuse to

---

[12] The Committee on Political Parties, *op. cit.,* p. 45.
[13] *Ibid.,* p. 46.   [14] *Ibid.,* p. 47

seat delegations from such a state. " Authoritative pronouncements " by the party council and public appeals to the party rank and file in the out-of-step states might be used. Party funds might be allocated to the function of replacing " the disloyal leadership " of some state organization. The party council might appoint temporary party officers for such a state. " One thing is entirely clear. It is contrary to the basic concept of our two-party system, destructive of party responsibility and disruptive of the party as a whole to permit organized disloyalty to continue." [15]

Another step which the parties have in part taken to strengthen the entire party structure is to develop full-time professional national committee staffs. After the Democratic defeat in 1928, that party set up its permanent staff, and Republicans followed suit after their 1936 debacle. More, however, needs to be done. Only with the help of professional staff workers can the party leadership hope to cope with the complexity of party strategy and tactics in our day.[16]

(2) *Party Platforms.* The party platform should be a statement of permanent party principles and the party's positions on immediate issues. It should offer a " coherent program " and provide voters with " a proper choice between the alternative policies and programs advanced by the two parties." Interpretation of the platform between national conventions would best be done by the party council. *" As a body representing the various parts of the party structure, the Party Council should be able to give authoritative and reasonably acceptable interpretations of the platform.* Perhaps it could occasionally even make more specific or reformulate the party principles in their application to current situations." [17]

When principles and policies of state party platforms are different from state to state and from those of the national platform, confusion for party candidates and the public is the result, and " Such divergencies . . . make nonsense of the party system." For better co-ordination, the national platform should be supreme on general principles and national issues. *" The Party Council would be the appropriate party agency to . . . determine the right position in case of conflict."* There is little likelihood that the party council would be " inconsiderate of arguable claims of state autonomy." [18]

Party platforms, when interpreted by the party council " by way

[15] The Committee on Political Parties, *op. cit.,* p. 48.
[16] *Ibid.,* p. 50.   [17] *Ibid.,* p. 51.   [18] *Ibid.,* pp. 51–52.

of authoritative and continuing statement," should be considered generally binding upon candidates, provided the platform was "responsibly formulated" and is one "reflecting ideas and promises behind which most of the party membership can line up." If there is conflict, the party council could establish the party line. "Of course, such implicit commitment by party candidates and office-holders is neither intended to produce dead uniformity of individual action nor is it in fact ever without bounds. It would allow defined reservations similar to those permitted under the Democratic House Caucus Rules." [19]

Party platforms should be adopted every two years to keep them up to date and to provide a guide in every election year, even when there is no Presidential election contest. National platforms should deal with general party principles and with national issues, and state platforms should conform to the national platform and emphasize state and local issues. The party council should prepare a platform draft well in advance of the national convention so that the convention platform committee may early be at work and the platform may be given the concentrated attention over a period of time which it deserves. Throughout the year local party meetings should discuss platform planks.[20]

(3) *Party Organization in Congress.* Development of a higher degree of party responsibility in Congress depends on the state of party organization both in and out of Congress. The cohesiveness of the national convention, national committee and President, if the party is in power, affects party cohesiveness inside Congress. Even more important for the party organization in Congress is what happens in the election process. If candidates of widely differing views on national issues and platform planks are elected under the same party label, then " little, if anything, can be done within Congress to heal the breach." Yet at a time when "there are signs on many fronts of a trend toward greater party responsibility," actions within Congress can accelerate the trend. Congressional party organizations should be tightened.[21]

Meetings of the President and the Big Four of Congress — floor leaders in both houses of Congress, Speaker, and Vice President — should continue and on occasion be expanded to include others. But

[19] *Ibid.*, p. 53.
[20] *Ibid.*, p. 56.   [21] *Ibid.*, p. 57.

because of the importance of the role played by the Big Four there should be " broad consultation throughout the national leadership of a party before a party leader is elected in either house." [22]

Party leadership committees — policy committees, steering committees, whatever type of committee or committees is used, and others — should be " consolidated into one truly effective and responsible leadership committee for each party," and at minimum, those committees should work closely together. Each of the leadership committees should be subjected to a confidence vote at least every two years. They should periodically meet together to plan program and strategy.[23]

Only if caucuses are frequently held can there be real rank-and-file participation of party members in House and Senate affairs. Caucus decisions should be binding on party principles and programs. " Such a decision should not be used merely to support the views of the President or of Congressional party leaders when their views do not rest on stated party policy, except in exigencies affecting the public record of the party." When party members abide by caucus decisions, they ought to be rewarded, and when party members are not loyal, they should expect to lose choice committee assignments or patronage because of their disloyalty to " party principles." [24]

Although the seniority rule should not be abolished, neither should it be applied absolutely. ". . . [I]t is not playing the game fairly for party members who oppose the commitments in their party's platform to rely on seniority to carry them into committee chairmanships. Party leaders have compelling reason to prevent such a member from becoming chairman — and they are entirely free to exert their influence." Such problems are not easy to solve, however, especially when the party dissidents hold a balance of power and might, if angered, throw control to the opposition party. " The task of party leaders, when confronted with revolt on the part of committee chairmen, is hence not easy. Obviously problems of this sort must be handled in the electoral process itself as well as in the congressional arena." [25]

Likewise, committee assignments should not be regarded as permanent prerogatives. Committee assignments should periodically

---

[22] The Committee on Political Parties, op. cit., pp. 58–59.
[23] Ibid., pp. 59–60.
[24] Ibid., pp. 60–61.
[25] Ibid., p. 62.

be re-examined. Furthermore, the practice of having the party ratio on committees parallel the party ratio in the House itself is not sound unless the party balance on the committee is wide enough to insure majority party control and thus prevents individual majority party members from having the opportunity to throw the decision to the minority side.[26]

Scheduling of legislative program is the function of the party leadership committee. The seniority-selected House Rules committee can undermine a party program in the House, and thus might well be abolished or procedures might be set up to bypass the Rules Committee when the need arises. In the Senate the cloture rule does not effectively shut off debate. A majority of the Senate should be able to impose cloture on all matters before the Senate.

(4) *Political Participation: Intraparty Democracy.* As a party member the voter may share in initiating the party's program, discussing issues, having a part in choosing party leaders or delegates to conventions, campaigning, or directly or indirectly participating in selecting party nominees for public office. As a citizen, the voter may vote in general elections. " When such participation is both free and widespread, parties are more fully responsive to popular preferences. *Widespread political participation* thus *fosters responsibility as well as democratic control in the conduct of party affairs and the pursuit of party policies. A more responsible party system is intimately linked with the general level as well as the forms of political participation.*" [27]

In some democratic countries party members pay dues, formally accept the party's principles, and may be disciplined if they publicly oppose their party's program. Such is not the basis of membership in American parties. Yet even in the United States " it is the hope of accomplishing common aims that leads people to act together." [28]

To justify its existence a party so conceived must demonstrate its capacity to direct the course of public policy in line with announced programs. This, in turn, means that those who speak for the party must follow a unified course of action. Unity among leaders, however, is difficult if they speak for members with entirely different objectives and fundamentally different ideas on public policy. The meaning of

---

[26] *Ibid.,* p. 63.
[27] *Ibid.,* p. 65.   [28] *Ibid.,* pp. 65–66.

membership itself suggests that those who identify themselves with
the group have something in common which they do not share with
those outside it.

Capacity for internal agreement, democratically arrived at, is a critical test for a party. It is a critical test because when there is no such
capacity, there is no capacity for positive action, and hence the party
becomes a hollow pretense. It is a test which can be met only if the
party machinery affords the membership an opportunity to set the
course of the party and to control those who speak for it. This test
can be met fully only when the membership accepts responsibility
for creative participation in shaping the party's program.[29]

Members of the same party, no matter what state they live in,
" should be able to appreciate their common concerns." They should
think not primarily in local terms but rather in national issue and
program terms. " In a party organized on democratic lines and with
a national point of view, cohesion springs naturally from willingness
to support aims which the member himself has helped to shape and
has come to accept. Such a party will seldom need to resort to the
artificial discipline of obligations declared binding." Such a party
would break down the patronage-nomination-election concept of
party. *" As stress is placed by the parties upon policy and the inter-
relationship of problems at various levels of government, association
with a party should become interesting and attractive to many who
hold aloof today."* [30]

National conventions should be nourished from below by local
party groups meeting frequently to discuss and initiate policy. The
local groups thus generating ideas would make it easier for the party
council to lead. Also, they would serve as channels through which
the party council " would inform the membership of action taken
or contemplated, and explain the reasons for it." [31]

Such local issue-oriented groups, as distinguished from the patronage-nomination-election orientation, could absorb much of the
" energy and interest which is now dissipated in writing letters to
individual congressmen and participating in numerous public-cause
groups." Regional party conferences would stimulate local group activity. So would formation of advisory councils to serve as liaison between a Congressman and his district. And the national party organi-

---

[29] The Committee on Political Parties, *op. cit.,* p. 66.
[30] *Ibid.,* pp. 66–67.   [31] *Ibid.,* p. 67.

zation should supply " challenging material " to " stimulate fruitful discussion " on the local level.[32]

While existing state legislation on primary elections defines party membership " in terms of support of party candidates rather than allegiance to a common program," it is possible to move to a different concept of party membership. " *The existence of a national program . . . should make a great difference. It would prompt those who identify themselves as Republicans or Democrats to think in terms of support of that program, rather than in terms of personalities, patronage and local matters.*" [33]

Political Participation: Nominating Procedures. For nominations for seats in Congress, forty-seven states now use the direct primary. Though it has imperfections the direct primary should be retained, and it " *probably can be adapted to the needs of parties unified in terms of national policy.*" Between open and closed primaries, however, the latter is more compatible with responsible parties. It tends " to support the concept of the party as an association of like-minded people. On the other hand, *the open primary tends to destroy the concept of membership as the basis of party organization.*" " Frequent attention to the party's national platform should underscore the program implications of nominations and alter the character of the primary contests." [34]

Cross-filing as practiced in California obscures program differences between the parties and destroys a feeling of party membership. Even worse is the Washington blanket or wide-open primary which permits voters to jump from party to party in the primary contests for the several offices. Development of preprimary endorsing meetings should be encouraged. The national council might also enter the primary process by encouraging the more able of its members to run for the United States Senate or House of Representatives.[35] For Presidential nominations it might someday be " feasible and desirable " to replace the national convention with a direct national Presidential primary election.[36]

Political Participation: Elections. Where the entire electoral vote of a state is given to the nominee who wins the largest number of popular votes in that state, the result tends to foster one-party monopoly in some states and concentration of party activity in pivot

---

[32] *Ibid.,* pp. 68–69.
[33] *Ibid.,* p. 69.
[34] *Ibid.,* p. 71.
[35] *Ibid.,* p. 72.
[36] *Ibid.,* p. 74.

states. " In various areas of the country . . . the one-party system shows itself the product of several causes, but among these the Electoral College in its existing form is perhaps the most important." In agitating for this change *" stress should be placed both upon giving all sections of the country a real voice in electing the President and the Vice President and upon developing a two-party system in present one-party areas."* Reduction of one-party areas would help the cause of party responsibility.[37]

United States House of Representative terms of office should be lengthened to four years to synchronize the terms of President and Congressmen. National issues would thus be emphasized in all House elections.[38]

In the field of campaign finance the Hatch Act limit of $3 million on political committee expenditures in any calendar year and the $5,000 limit on individual contributions should be repealed. The national bodies of the parties could then be more responsible for party finance. The federal government might also provide financial assistance to the parties through such devices as pamphlet distribution at public expense, free mailing, or, as in some countries, the furnishing of free television or radio time for each party, Also, if parties became more meaningful to voters, the parties' base of financial support would be broadened. " As the parties attract more members the time may be reached when they can depend largely if not entirely upon membership dues for their funds." [39]

There are wide disparities in population between Congressional districts. It is time to demand Congressional districts approximately equal in population. If districts were relatively equal, " the House of Representatives would reflect party strength much more fairly and accurately." [40]

Political Participation: Barriers to Voting. It is in elections that the greatest number of citizens can participate in politics. " To an important extent, the lack of adequate participation in the electoral process is the result of disappointment as well as inertia. More significant operation of the party system would create greater interest in voting." Other steps which might stimulate greater election participation would be these. First, permanent registration systems should replace those in which, to be eligible to vote, citizens must

---

[37] *Idem.*
[38] The Committee on Political Parties, *op. cit.,* p. 75.

[39] *Idem.*
[40] *Ibid.,* p. 76.

re-register periodically. Second, the government should attempt actively to register voters. Third, elections might be held on holidays or weekends, and voting hours might be extended earlier into the morning and later into the evening. Fourth, suffrage should be extended to the residents of the District of Columbia, and devices like poll-tax requirements designed to keep people from the polls should be " educated " and legislated out of existence. Fifth, instead of long ballots with many offices to be voted on, ballots should be short so the voter's burden will be reduced and he can concentrate *" on contests with program implications and thus shift his attention toward issues rather than personalities."* [41]

Summary. The thesis of the Committee on Political Parties' 1950 report is best summarized in the words of the authors of the work:

> And the *thesis?* It can be put quite briefly. Historical and other factors have caused the American two-party system to operate as two loose associations of state and local organizations, with very little national machinery and very little national cohesion. As a result, either major party, when in power, is ill-equipped to organize its members in the legislative and the executive branches into a government held together and guided by the party program. Party responsibility at the polls thus tends to vanish. This is a very serious matter, for it affects the very heartbeat of American democracy. It also poses grave problems of domestic and foreign policy in an era when it is no longer safe for the nation to deal piecemeal with issues that can be disposed of only on the basis of coherent programs.[42]

TOWARD A MORE RESPONSIBLE TWO–PARTY SYSTEM — A CRITIQUE

In the Foreword of *Toward a More Responsible Two-Party System* the authors state that their purpose is " to bring about a fuller public appreciation of a basic weakness in the American two-party system." In part they have achieved the purpose. That there are weaknesses in the American party system cannot be denied, and some of the Committee's recommendations have been well received. Furthermore, if one of the objects of the report was to stimulate thinking and discussion on the subject of American political parties,

---

[41] *Ibid.*, pp. 76–77.
[42] *Ibid.*, p. v.

that object, at least among those of the political science profession and among students of American party politics, has been realized. The controversy which has followed the publication of the report has been a vigorous, stimulating, and educational one.

If the purpose of the authors was primarily that quoted above, however, then perhaps reactions have been the opposite of what might have been expected. In several respects the Committee has failed " to bring about a fuller public appreciation of a basic weakness in the American two-party system." With many, the result has been precisely the opposite — to bring about a fuller appreciation of the strengths of the party system when they are balanced with the real or alleged weaknesses. Others have charged that the Committee has not gone far enough, and thus its arguments fail because there is no half-way method of achieving what the Committee apparently wants. And most of the critics have either stated or implied that the report makes broad assumptions about the manner in which its recommendations would work without adequately taking into account the obstacles which the " political realist " would see as blocking the path toward the Committee's goals.

Toward a More Responsible Two-Party System has been attacked on several grounds — for the assumptions it makes, for the proposals offered, and for the effect the proposals might have should they be implemented. In the remainder of this chapter and carrying on through the next two chapters, we shall examine these criticisms.

How Irresponsible Is Our Two-Party System? In answer to the question, the Committee on Political Parties takes the position that our two-party system is very irresponsible. The irresponsibility, it is suggested, has its effects on two levels. First, American major parties are not responsible because they do not give the voter " a true choice " between alternatives in elections and because the parties are not organized to be responsible for putting programs into effect once they are in power. Second, neither are party leaders internally responsible to the party membership. The first of the two types of irresponsibility identified by the Committee on Political Parties will be the concern of this section.

Julius Turner in his article " Responsible Parties: A Dissent from the Floor " [43] makes the most direct and systematic challenge

---

[43] *The American Political Science Review* (March, 1951), Vol. 45, No. 1, pp. 143–152.

to the assumption that the American major parties are very irresponsible to the electorate. The Committee, he suggests, has underestimated the quality of alternative choice which the Democratic and Republican parties provide for the voter. In comparing Democratic and Republican platforms, Turner holds that important differences between the parties do exist — differences which, if the Committee on Political Parties had conducted a detailed platform analysis study, would have led it to a different conclusion. Taking 1948 as an example, Democrats and Republicans differed on the Taft-Hartley Act, foreign aid, tax reduction, and the general question of federal versus state powers. The fact that platforms may not mean a great deal to the voters does not necessarily imply that no platform differences exist between the major parties, but may rather result because platforms are inadequately interpreted to the voter or because the voter may not in fact be very interested in party program.

On the basis of his extensive studies of party voting patterns in Congress, Turner concludes that here too there is enough party solidarity so that voters may distinguish between two points of view. In Congress there are few who vote with the opposition party more than their own party. And when party leaders are not followed, the member of Congress takes his step because in his mind it is necessary considering the political complexion of his district.

Only in some state and local elections where a party insurgent diverges consistently from his party outlook-pattern because of the views of his constituents is the " irresponsibility to the electorate " charge of the Committee in Political Parties valid. But for the political candidate in such a situation, his very political life depends on a modification of what appears to be his national party's policy. Except for the one-party South, where the lack of alternatives for the voter may be a serious problem, Turner sees no cause for alarm.[44]

Addressing himself to the second question implicit in a party's responsibility to the voter — " Is the program which received the support of a majority of voters put into effect? " — Turner arrives at a similar conclusion. Because the electoral college system of Presidential elections requires that primary attention be directed toward pivot states, platforms are not constructed as appeals toward all the voters in the country. Even so, much of the platform plank material of the winning party does find its way into law. From the 1948 plat-

---

[44] See *ibid.*, pp. 144–148.

form, Turner cites extension of the Marshall Plan, legislation to help Europe arm, changes in the Reciprocal Trade Agreements Act, increasing the minimum wage, expanding social security, and so on.

Though the Taft-Hartley Act was not repealed, federal aid to education was not adopted, and the civil rights declarations of the Democratic platform were not implemented, Turner suggests that those items which in fact had broad acceptance were successfully acted upon. To ask that all of the proposals stated in a party's platform and in its candidates' campaign speeches become law is hardly a fair standard. The need for reform is not great because voters, if they want to get the information, can distinguish between the positions of the Democrats and Republicans, and because most of the generally accepted parts of the majority party's program are enacted into law.[45]

Murray S. Stedman, Jr., and Herbert Sonthoff in their article "Party Responsibility — A Critical Inquiry"[46] also challenge the assumption of party irresponsibility, but on somewhat different grounds. Throughout American history majorities have been constructed by consensus through which different groups and individuals come to general agreement via compromise. Nor has the consensus process occurred exclusively within each major party, but rather it reaches across party lines. The Committee on Political Parties, Stedman and Sonthoff write, holds that consensus is an inadequate vehicle for translating popular wishes into governmental policy. Rather the system should be one of majority rule and the Committee on Political Parties identifies majority rule with majority party rule. Stedman and Sonthoff question the proposition that majority party rule would be better for the United States than its traditional consensus methods of arriving at compromise solutions.[47]

A better understanding of the point at issue here requires a brief review of the major contrasts between the British majority party rule system and the American consensus system. The British form of government is unitary with all legal power centralized in the national government. In the United States governmental power is divided under the Constitution between the federal government and the states with some powers delegated to the federal government,

---

[45] See Turner, *op. cit.,* p. 148.

[46] *The Western Political Quarterly* (September, 1951), Vol. 4, No. 3, pp. 454–468.

[47] See *ibid.,* pp. 454–455.

others reserved for state governments, some exercised concurrently, and some prohibited to both levels.

The British form of government is also parliamentary or cabinet as distinguished from the American presidential or separation of powers system. Parliament, in the former, is supreme, and within the Parliament the House of Commons is supreme. Legislation may not in fact be vetoed by the Crown. Neither is there a supreme court to review judicially and, if it desires, to void Parliament's decisions. In the American separation of powers system no one of the three branches is responsible to the other, and each can check the other.

Superimposed onto the institutional framework of both governments is a two-party political party system. As the British form of government is unitary, so are its two major parties unitary. The central offices of the parties manage the party organizations and the parties' leaders in the House of Commons determine party policy on issues. If a majority of Conservative party members, for example, is elected to the House of Commons, both the form of government and the centralization of power within the party make it possible for the Conservative party to accomplish in governmental programs whatever the party has committed itself to in the election campaign or whatever it wants to do.

A British election campaign is a contest between the two major parties with the candidates of each united on whatever may at that time be their respective party's line. All members of the House of Commons hold office for the same terms, and since a House of Commons election is the only election at which voters exercise a choice in selection of national government officers, the issues are national issues.

The British Conservative and Labour parties meet the responsibility tests to the electorate which *Toward a More Responsible Two-Party System* would apply to the Republicans and Democrats. At election time there are two relatively clear alternatives for the voter. After the election the majority party is so organized as to be able to deliver on whatever program it has pledged to implement.

The American party system presents a quite different organizational picture. As the American form of government is federal so are the parties federal. As the American form of government is separation of powers, so also is party power on either the national or state levels separated between the official party organization, the party's members in the legislative body, and the party member or members who hold elective office in the executive branch.

Those who feel that the American consensus method of arriving at governmental decisions is not adequate to the needs of government today prefer the British model majority party rule system. Among the persons who take such a position two identifiable subgroups are discernible. One of these, and the Committee on Political Parties is representative of its thinking, is of the opinion that we can arrive at a majority rule system without major constitutional changes in the federal and separation of powers features of American government.

The other subgroup of majority rule adherents makes the point that the nature of party organization is determined by the constitutional system in which the parties must operate. Austin Ranney's "Toward a More Responsible Two-Party System: A Commentary," [48] in taking this position, states that the Committee on Political Parties has placed the cart before the horse. Parties such as those the Committee appears to want cannot come before the obstacles in the way of making the majority will more articulate and unencumbered are removed. Ranney holds that it is necessary to make a choice between majority rule or minority rights, and that the choice has to be a decisive one because neither alternative is compatible with the other. The Committee on Political Parties, in Ranney's opinion, should have worked for the " whole package " of majority rule democracy.[49]

In summary, it may be stated that there is wide disagreement between those who feel the American party system is responsible enough to the electorate and those who feel it is not. Of those who take the latter position, one segment sees the need for substantial constitutional changes before parties can become " responsible " and the other segment sees the possibility for producing the change without constitutional revision.

Intraparty Democracy: Membership and Responsible Leadership. Much of the Committee on Political Parties' case for its recommended reformation of political parties rests on a new concept of democratic internal party organization. At the base of the party structure would be a mass membership composed of persons quite unlike the political man who presently is an active member of the Demo-

---

[48] *The American Political Science Review* (June, 1951), Vol. 45, No. 2, pp. 488–499.

[49] See *ibid.*, pp. 492–499.

cratic or Republican parties. The new party member would be primarily interested in governmental policies and not patronage, nominations, and winning elections. Members would be bound together by general agreement on common policy aims. There would be regular and frequent local party group meetings to discuss policy and forward the resolutions adopted upward in the party hierarchy. At the top level, national platforms and interpretations of the platform would be authoritatively expounded by the party council. Party rank-and-file members would hold party leaders accountable through caucuses, conventions, and primary elections. Party membership would thus become " interesting and attractive " to many of those who do not today participate in party affairs. If, the Committee on Political Parties seems to imply, intraparty processes were democratic, if party members participated in party business, if leaders would be held accountable — if these developments were brought about then the objects of both internal and external party responsibility would be served.

Austin Ranney, in the article cited above, takes issue with the Committee on Political Parties' " intraparty democracy " thesis. First, Ranney holds, one cannot talk about intraparty democracy and responsibility without carefully defining who shall be the party members to whom the party leaders should be held accountable. The Committee left unsolved the question of what should be standards for membership. At one point it noted that membership standards in parties in some other countries were the payment of dues, formal acceptance of party aims, and conformity to party decisions on party policy. At another point the Committee foresees the days when most of a party's finances might be raised from membership dues. Viewing the entire report, however, Ranney feels membership standards were not adequately defined. His interpretation was that the Committee intended that all those who voted for the national party ticket would be members of the party, and if such were the case, Ranny concluded, intraparty democracy as the Committee speaks of it would be impossible.

Secondly, Ranney takes issue with the Committee's assumption that probably the closed primary is an adequate institutional device through which responsibility of party leaders to members may be enforced. The history of the direct primary and its effects on the major parties hardly warrants the Committee's assumption.

In the third place, Ranney sees the Committee on Political

Parties' conception of democratic control as a confused one. For responsibility to the electorate the Committee seems to say that what is necessary is a true choice between alternatives. Intraparty democratic control, the Committee implies, will consist of two elements: first, choosing between alternatives at party caucuses, conventions, and primaries; and second, membership participation in the day-to-day conduct of party affairs. How, Ranney asks, can millions of " ticket voters " function at the participation level which the Committee on Political Parties envisions for them? [50]

Campbell, Gurin and Miller found in their analysis of the 1952 Presidential election that despite the substantial public interest in the campaign, " . . . the bulk of the political activity that went on . . . was concentrated in a fraction of perhaps one-tenth of the public. They were the meeting-goers, money-givers, party workers. Most people took the campaign much more casually, and approximately one person in three did not seem interested enough to care which party won." [51] Berelson, Lazarsfeld and McPhee in their study of the 1948 campaign in Elmira, New York, observed that the local party organizations functioned as " small bureaucracies on the edge of the great debate," but they did not politically guide the campaign. Older persons, answering questions as to whether local party activity had always been at this level, recalled the days some fifty years ago when local party units had been a real influence. Whether the decline in local party activity has come because much of the informing-the-voter function is now done through the mass media of communication, because the old social service function of the parties has been taken over by government, or because patronage opportunities have declined and private jobs have become more attractive — whatever the reason — local party units no longer are as active, strong or perform the political functions they once did.[52]

Perhaps it is desirable for a large proportion of citizens to participate in party affairs. Perhaps it is possible for the trend toward weaker and weaker party organizations on the local level to be reversed, but it seems hardly likely the suggestions of the Committee

[50] See Ranney, *op. cit.*, pp. 488–492.

[51] Angus Campbell, Gerald Gurin, and Warren E. Miller, *The Voter Decides* (White Plains, N. Y.: Row, Peterson and Company, 1954) , pp. 39–40.

[52] See Bernard R. Berelson, Paul F. Lazarsfeld, and William N. McPhee, *Voting: A Study of Opinion Formation in a Presidential Campaign* (Chicago: The University of Chicago Press, 1954) , pp. 178–179.

on Political Parties will accomplish such an effect. Party member-ship would be made interesting and meaningful, it is held, because the focus of the parties would be on policy questions and because party organization would be so democratic each individual could feel he was actively participating in decisions on party business.

Some day the time may come when large numbers of persons become so interested in public policy for public policy's sake that they would be drawn to party membership and participation for such a reason. If so, however, the time is beyond the foreseeable future. Present-day experience in local party organizations leads one to the conclusion that public policy, in the sense the term is used by the Committee on Political Parties, is one of the least sound bases upon which local party organizations can be built and maintained. Un-less there is an active social program, unless there are business ad-vantages to be gained from party activity, unless there is the prospect for power or party prestige, unless there is the thrill of nomination or election activity — unless there are the patronage-nomination-winning-elections inducements which the Committee on Political Parties disparages, local party organizations are little more than paper organizations.

Toward a More Responsible Two-Party System appears to en-vision parties made up of members like those in Americans for Demo-cratic Action or those who Harold E. Stassen in his campaign for the Republican Presidential nomination hoped would rush to join Re-publican political forum groups throughout the country. The Re-publican forum movement never did get much beyond the planning stage and the Americans for Democratic Action formula as a pat-tern for Democratic party organization can hardly be said to have fired the imagination of Democrats. In point here is Alfred De-Grazia's enumeration of methods by which the Democratic party might counteract the " natural organization " advantages which Republicans have with business and professional groups. First there is the possibility of utilizing the government bureaucracy, but merit laws have sharply limited the prospect. Second there are the labor unions. And third, quoting from DeGrazia, ". . . is an organization founded upon disinterested spare-time politicians. It has always been a favorite doctrine among democratic theorists and even among the public, but it has never been shown to have succeeded elsewhere." [53]

---

[53] Alfred DeGrazia, *The Western Public 1952 and Beyond* (Stanford: Stan-ford University Press, 1954) , p. 185.

Given the present context of American politics it is not likely either major party, even if it wanted to, could make public policy discussions so interesting as to provide an attractive and enduring inducement for participation.

Nor is it likely the major parties will become so democratic in their internal processes that the rank and file member can feel he personally plays an active role in helping chart his party's course on program and is in a position to hold at all times his party leaders accountable. Pressure groups, the Committee on Political Parties suggests, are not good examples of intragroup democracy at work. Yet oligarchic tendencies operate in any type of organization, and there is no reason to conclude political parties can be exempt from the rule. Particularly is this so if the principal membership control device is no more adequate to the purpose than is the direct primary, even if it is a closed primary.

Party members tend to cluster around party leaders and candidates to a much greater extent than around policy issues. Generally there are several leaders or candidates in competition for power. Power and not policy is the principal stake in the conflict. Once a leader or candidate gains power, if he is able, he will consolidate his position to the point that dissatisfaction against him has to mount to major proportions before it is likely he can be overthrown. The processes of membership control are slow, clumsy, and do not operate flexibly. Yet the assumption of the Committee on Political Parties appears to be quite the opposite with leaders and candidates regularly and frequently held to account for their leadership and with members exercising what, by comparison with present control standards, would constitute a delicate and almost " finger-tip " influence over their leaders. The standards for intraparty democracy which the Committee would have the American parties apply are standards which even the most visionary exponent of the British party system would not expect to find in the Conservative and Labour parties.

CHAPTER TWENTY–THREE

The Major Parties and the System: Weaknesses and Strengths — II

The argument for a stronger party system cannot be divorced from meas-
ures designed to make the parties more fully accountable to the public.
The fundamental requirement of *such* accountability is a two-party system in which the opposition party acts as the critic of the party in power,
developing, defining and presenting the policy alternatives which are
necessary for a true choice in reaching public decisions.

Committee on Political Parties of the
American Political Science Association [1]

Viewing the history of our political parties in a single glance, one is re-
minded of those giant-dwarf images at a carnival featuring concave and
convex mirrors. The liberal standing before the one sees the need to
shrink his claims in a bid to win or at least neutralize the conservative
opposition in and out of his party. The conservative standing before the
other sees the need to enlarge his political appeal in ways that might win
over or at least neutralize the liberal opposition. The optical distortion
can be a passing thing, or it can remake a party in its own image. Yet all
poles of political opinion are forced to exaggerate themselves — whether
by elongations or contractions — to foster a sense that they offer hospi-
tality to aims other than their own. And this is because no group in the
nation is big enough to form a majority of fifty percent plus one percent
all by itself. Indeed, on the single occasion when men neither could nor
would reach out for sources of political strength other than what they
themselves represented, all parties died, the government collapsed, and
we had our Civil War.

---

[1] *Toward a More Responsible Two-Party System*, a supplement to *The American Political Science Review* (September, 1950), Vol. 44, No. 3, Pt. 2, p. 18.

The idea of a " pure " conservative party and a " pure " liberal party in America, then, has the same air of unreality as a plan to have a mountain range without valleys or a river without banks. Of themselves, mountains imply valleys as rivers imply banks. And the same is true of our party life. So long as we don't want a welter of one-interest or ideological parties, by the very nature of our diversity each party will and must have a mixed character. In particular must this be true under our Federal arrangement where the legislative impulse is designed to come from below, and not from above as in England.

Sidney Hyman [2]

This chapter is a continuation of the preceding chapter. In the latter the most comprehensive recent attempt at critical analysis of American political parties — the American Political Science Association's Committee on Political Parties 1950 report, *Toward a More Responsible Two-Party System* — was summarized. The two concluding subsections of that chapter examined the topics: " How Responsible Is Our Two-Party System? " and " Intraparty Democracy: Membership and Responsible Leadership." The remainder of the critique on the Committee on Political Parties report follows.

HOW MUCH POLITICAL PARTY CENTRALIZATION DO WE WANT?

The question asked in the title of this section is the title of an article by T. William Goodman [3] in which he takes sharp issue with the Committee on Political Parties' 1950 report and suggests that the reforms which are recommended would call for replacing the presidential system with the parliamentary form of government, for replacing the federal system with a unitary form of government, and perhaps for replacing the two-party system with a multiparty system. Goodman's general answer to the question — " How much political party centralization do we want? " — is one which stops far short of the degree of centralization which the Committee on Political Parties would impose. And particularly is he concerned about the manner in which the proposed party council might operate were it given the

---

[2] *The American President* (New York: Harper and Brothers, 1954), pp. 176–177. Reprinted by permission.

[3] *The Journal of Politics* (November, 1951), Vol. 13, No. 4, pp. 536–561.

powers outlined for it in *Toward a More Responsible Two-Party System*.

Rejecting the assumptions that sectionalism in American politics is dead or can be eliminated by reorganization of the parties and

The Sioux City Journal

"Quit Stealing My Stuff!"

that party unity would be the consequence of intraparty discussion of issues, Goodman looks at the parties with their several respective factions as they exist today. As of 1951, for the Democratic in-party, Goodman estimates the fifty-member party council would have been composed in general as follows. President Truman would have been able to control the some four other ex-officio members chosen from among Cabinet officers and highest national party officers, and perhaps also the Vice President. Also, the five representatives of the Democratic National Committee would have been acceptable to the President because of his influence over that body. Likewise, if the Democratic National Convention of 1948 had selected ten members, it is likely they too would have had Presidential blessing. To this point the intraparty orientation of twenty of the fifty members of the council would tend to be Presidential. Next Goodman assumes that the council's five state governors, ten state committee representatives, and ten party members from Congress would reflect various shades of pro- or anti-New Deal viewpoints. Only the ex-officio members, however, would be a dependably cohesive group, and with such a complexion the council would proceed to compose its differences in order to present a united front.[4]

> It would be fascinating to see how the Democratic Party could accomplish this on such issues as the Brannan Farm plan, health insurance, and F.E.P.C. At once the Presidential designation of Cabinet members would become significant. Whether or not Secretary Brannan was chosen would ostensibly indicate the position of the President on the Brannan Farm plan — any timing involved in either designating or removing Secretary Brannan would be even more significant. In this particular case, agricultural policy may well create difficulties for Mr. Barkley, who campaigned in 1950 on the basis that the Party was not committed to the Brannan plan and at least inferred he was against it. What would happen if the President designated — as he undoubtedly could — Mr. Oscar Ewing for the purpose of advancing the administration health measure and Senator Lehman was a member of the Council? Since the Senator committed himself against this legislation during his 1949 campaign, he would either have to oppose Mr. Ewing or change his mind. There is no point belaboring the situation the Council would face in regard to F.E.P.C. if any southerners were represented as they almost certainly would be.[5]

Because the in-party's council would have to be led, the President would be the likely leader with the largest number of sanctions available to him to win support. This fact would lead, in Goodman's opinion, to overextending the Presidency even more than it now is — something the Committee on Political Parties wanted to counter-

---

[4] See *ibid.*, pp. 543–544.

[5] Goodman, *op. cit.*, p. 544. Reprinted by permission of *The Journal of Politics.*

act. No President could afford not to control his party council. The council's channels for propaganda could be used to further the President's purposes, and so could its sanctions. Through the party council the President would have to attempt to control the local party groups and have installed in the local offices men favorable to him.

Would not, Goodman asks, the parliamentary system be better than this? At least there the Prime Minister is theoretically responsible to the Parliament. Furthermore, since the Prime Minister's party has power to implement its program, he cannot campaign by making irresponsible promises to attract the votes of certain groups knowing that the legislative body or a supreme court might get him " off the hook " by defeating the proposals. The Committee on Political Parties would have the United States adopt some features of the parliamentary system without the protections against abuse of power to be found in either the presidential or parliamentary systems.[6]

For the out-party council, Goodman foresees a result such as the following — a result which no amount of tinkering with party machinery is likely to change.

> In the holocaust following their 1948 defeat, the Republicans presented an unusually intense picture of self-searching and recrimination. The year 1949 had hardly opened before Hugh D. Scott, Jr., the National Chairman, began talking about the virtues of convening a party policy conference; the suggestions immediately brought unfavorable reactions from Congress where some Republican members insisted that they would make the Party's policy. Variations on these arguments were repeated back and forth during the entire year, and the conference plan was dropped for the time being, some regional conferences being held instead. When the anti-Dewey forces finally ousted Scott and replaced him with Guy G. Gabrielson, the National Committee adopted a resolution empowering the new Chairman to create a committee to draft a Republican platform for the 1950 elections. Although the committee was supposed to include representatives from both Houses, from the National Committee and from the state committees, the actual text of the Statement of Principles and Objectives declared that it was adopted by the Republican members of Congress and " concurred in by the members of the Republican National Committee. . . ." However, some Republican members of

---

[6] See *ibid.*, p. 546.

Congress immediately took exception with all or parts of the Statement; e.g., Senators Lodge and Ives called the civil rights plank
" weasel words." The anti-Dewey significance of the Statement was
indicated both by the prominent position of Senator Taft in the
framing of the document and by the hostile reactions from Republicans in . . . New York. Almost with one accord, the Party indicated
by speech and by silence that the Statement had solved no problems.
The basic issues were not resolved, but there is no indication that
it is possible to resolve them so that all the Republican leaders will
be in agreement. However, if a Council had produced this Statement,
the dissenters would have been forced either to keep quiet or to risk
being expelled for party disloyalty. What this kind of situation would
mean in terms of the party system as a whole is incalculable, but
it would certainly make more difficult the moderating of extreme
positions within a party and would stifle those who were not able to
accept at face value and without qualms the existing party or-
thodoxy.[7]

For the out-party and for the in-party when its President could
not be a candidate to succeed himself, the party council would become the battleground for those seeking the next Presidential nomination. Only for the in-party with renomination possible for the
President could the party council " afford the luxury of settling down
to purely policy questions." [8] As soon as one element of the party
gained control of the party council, it would immediately be necessary for it to consolidate its position, using all the propaganda, patronage, finances, control over nominations and local party organizations, and other sanctions at its command. The locus of power would
be national and not state and local.[9] " It takes a brave man," concludes Goodman, " to allege that republican government is preserved
by providing a periodic choice between two oligarchical organizations." [10] " Quite possibly," write Stedman and Sonthoff, " because
of its widespread character the centralized type of bossism, even under the name of ' party government,' might be even more objectionable than the existing local bossism." [11]

---

[7] Goodman, *op. cit.*, pp. 545–546. Reprinted by permission of *The Journal
of Politics.*

[8] *Ibid.*, p. 546.

[9] See also Murray S. Stedman, Jr., and Herbert Sonthoff, " Party Responsibility — A Critical Inquiry," *The Western Political Quarterly* (September, 1951) ,
Vol. 4, No. 3, p. 546.

[10] Goodman, *op. cit.*, p. 561.   [11] Stedman and Sonthoff, *op. cit.*, p. 457.

In addition to estimates about the manner in which the centralized parties as envisioned by the Committee on Political Parties might work, many objections have been made to the results which the Committee's recommendations might produce. They may be classified under the following headings: (1) the number of one-party constituencies in the United States would be substantially increased; (2) self-destructive tendencies within the minority major party would more freely operate; (3) the direct primary election system in the states would be rendered superfluous or be destroyed; (4) parties would realign ideologically to produce either two extreme major parties or a multiparty system; (5) the new system would not be congenial to the type of choices the American voter wants to make; and (6) the breadth of our pluralistic political system would be reduced by greatly limiting the operation of pressure groups. Each of these anticipated results flowing from *Toward a More Responsible Two-Party System*'s recommendations will be examined in the following subsections.

Increase in Number of One-Party Constituencies. The Committee on Political Parties, though advocating " positive " means to obtain party unity, includes a large number of pressure devices for " last-resort " application should the need arise. A listing of such tools for discipline as set down in the various sections of the Committee's 1950 report brings one easily to the conclusion that any dominant group within a party, if it knew how to use the weapons at its command, might remake the party into a mirror of itself. The recommended weapons are: definition of membership; exclusion of rebellious state delegations from national conventions and national committees; utilization of national party funds against insurgent local party officers; appointment of temporary state officers to replace those locally in office; withholding patronage, committee chairmanships, and committee memberships from insurgent party members in Congress; recommendation by the party council of Congressional candidates; authority for the party council to screen candidates for the Presidential nomination and to interpret the national platform; and once the platform is interpreted, utilizing all these weapons to see that it is binding.[12]

---

[12] For itemization, see Julius Turner, " Responsible Parties: A Dissent from the Floor," *The American Political Science Review* (March, 1951), Vol. 45, No. 1, p. 149.

The purpose of disciplinary devices such as these would be to set and then hold a national party policy line. The dominant faction of a party would not have a choice of whether to use or not to use these weapons. It would have to use them were they available because if it did not do so someone else would. If each party actually set and held such a party line and if each party's program differed enough to give the voter " a true choice " between alternatives, then responsibility to the electorate, the Committee on Political Parties suggests, would be achieved. But would the process work that way?

Malcolm Moos warns: " Beset, therefore, by conditions that produce one-party areas . . . not only in the South but in all sections of the country, the risk of increasing the number of such areas is certainly not a prospect to be welcomed. Yet should we shift over to a system in which parties would require strict adherence to a nationally declared policy, it is almost a certainty that the effect would be to discourage minority party candidacies in still more congressional districts." [13] " The reforms which the Committee proposes would increase the tendency toward one-party districts," similarly writes Julius Turner. " If local parties and candidates cannot be insurgent, if they cannot express the basic desires of their constituencies, then those local parties can have no hope of success." [14]

Although the Committee on Political Parties deplores the existence of one-party areas, there is good reason to conclude that its recommendations, as Moos, Turner and others suggest, would only make worse an already existing defect in our party system. The large proportion of seats in the Congress which are safely Democratic or Republican has already been noted in Chapter Sixteen. These districts may be safe for several reasons. Perhaps the principal factor is a sectional characteristic based on race relations and related problems such as in the Solid Democratic South. Perhaps the safely northern Democratic city district is made up of an industrial, minority race and religion, and immigrant complex with which a Republican candidate has no chance. Perhaps the Republican safe district is rural, white, Protestant, and native. Perhaps either a Republican or a Democratic safe district has been brought to that " political security " level by an incumbent Congressman or Senator who has been popular and so solicitous of the district he has become an institution. But

---

[13] Malcolm Moos, *Politics, Presidents and Coattails* (Baltimore: The Johns Hopkins Press, 1952) , p. 168.
[14] Turner, *op. cit.*, p. 151.

whatever be the elements producing the safety factor, they vary from urban to rural areas and from one section of the country to another.

There has been a trend toward nationalization of issues in recent years with the economic interdependence of the different sections of the country becoming increasingly apparent. However, that fact does not mean that national issues are not viewed through sectional, state, and local colored glasses. Neither does that mean there still are not sectional, state, and local issues which might consistently or periodically take precedence in the local mind over the more broad general national issues. Even the party politician who today is considered a good follower of what may be his " national party line " makes adaptations and modifications in that line to suit the particular characteristics of his constituency. Though the party insurgent goes a step further in his deviation, he does so for a very good reason. His political life depends on it.

A Congressman Jacob Javits, if he had had to follow a course set by a Republican policy committee dominated by Senators Joseph McCarthy of Wisconsin or John Bricker of Ohio would never have been elected to Congress from his district in the first place. A Congressman James Roosevelt may be a great vote-getter in his relatively low-income, minority group 26th California district, but he would not even attempt to run for office in California's high-income, " majority group " 16th Congressional district of Santa Monica, Bel Aire, and Beverly Hills. If Democrats are to have a chance to win the latter, the Republican candidate would have to be highly unsatisfactory and the Democrat would have to be a " very moderate " Democrat; and if Republicans were to replace James Roosevelt, the Javits-type Republican candidate would be required. But at least there has been two-party competition in both the California Congressional districts cited as examples. A nationally imposed party line, if it were to encompass enough issues to be worthy of the title " party line," would tend to preclude the possibility of two-party opposition in such districts.

" To the extent that segments of the population can identify their political desires with the program of one party or the other," says Turner, " competition at the polls will be reduced in the United States, except in those fortunate constituencies where opposed groups are equally balanced." [15] Party responsibility to the electorate through

---

[15] Turner, *op. cit.*, p. 150.

the offering of alternatives to the voter, should the parties be cast in the mold prepared for them by the Committee on Political Parties, would in fact be reduced. In the increased number of one-party areas the possibility of two-party competition would tend to be eliminated. Unless the American federal system were abolished and all legal power over functions of government were vested in the national government, Turner adds, the enlargement of one-party areas would actually result in a lower level of popular control of government than presently exists.[16]

Self-destructive Tendencies in the Minority Major Party. The flexibility required of a major party if it is to remain politically virile is ably pointed up by Arthur N. Holcombe in a comparison of political parties with rivers of water:

> Parties are . . . like rivers or streams . . . now bearing upon their surface cargoes of goods and companies of men, now stopping in their flight to moisten a field, that agriculture may flourish, now rushing on to turn a wheel, that industry may prosper. Perchance the waters slacken and the stream falters in its course, or even dries up altogether, leaving only a waste, a sad reminder of former greatness; or again, a flood comes, and the mighty current carries all before it until its force is spent. So with the parties; they are bodies of men, urged on by the interests which move to action, now proceeding serenely in the channels which habit has fixed, now smashing the old order and building anew in response to the play of circumstances upon the dispositions and impulses which give them their character.[17]

Instead of following the flowing river downstream and out into the gulf, let us develop Holcombe's analogy one step further by looking back upstream. There will be a main source of water supply which might be likened to a party's hard core of support consisting of leaders and persons who will stand with the party through any adversity. There will also be other tributaries — smaller streams which flow into the main river channel. Whether the river maintains its " river " classification or dwindles down to a meandering stream will depend upon a continuous replenishing process. For the political parties the tributaries are the groups which can be attracted to sup-

---

[16] Turner, *op. cit.*, p. 157.
[17] Arthur N. Holcombe, *The Political Parties of Today* (New York: Harper and Brothers, 1924), p. 348. Reprinted by permission.

plement the strength of the " hard core's " support. And for the flood stage of Holcombe's figure — undesirable for those who live along-side the river but so desirable for the party if used to illustrate electoral success of landslide proportions — the main source and all the tributaries have to be producing at a maximum output rate.

If both major parties have an approximately equal chance of winning elections, both will tend to look very carefully to the channels through which tributary strength can flow into the party. If, however, one of the major parties is very much stronger than the other, the tendency for the minority major party is to narrow self-destructively its appeal to fit only those adherents who are left within its ranks. The " party principles " of such a minority major party tend to become narrower and narrower. The remaining leaders may even seek to dam up potential tributary strength sources in order to better control the organization and to have freedom to expound the ever contracting party doctrine. " This trend, unless interrupted," writes Turner who develops the point, " would lead to the suicide of the minority party." [18]

How have the minority major parties of the past — those surviving political adversity — been brought back to political health? As events have changed, new issues have been brought to the fore and grievances have accumulated against the in-party. And as a part of the new expansion process of the minority major party there has been an influx of new leaders and new groups ready to try out an alternative party to determine whether or not it is to their liking. By the " party principle " standards of the minority major party when it was at its low point, the recruits to its ranks qualify for definition as "insurgents." These the out-party badly needs, and the quantity of new blood necessary depends upon how wide is the political power gulf between the two major parties.

If the parties were highly centralized, the dominant group in control of the party machinery could and would tend to drive out insurgents from within and discourage attraction of " insurgents " from without. Here is a problem with which the Republican party, in minority or " moon " party status since 1932, has had to wrestle. The Republican party, however, was flexible enough to win in 1952 and was thus given the opportunity of attempting to build a new Republican majority. Had there been a Republican party council

---

[18] Turner, *op. cit.,* p. 152.

meeting the Committee on Political Parties' specifications, it is highly unlikely that an Eisenhower could have been nominated in 1952, or that any of the Republican nominees since 1940 would have won national convention majorities. " The party [Republican party]," wrote Turner in 1951, " is in great need of insurgents. The Committee might consequently devote its attention to the promotion of insurgency within the party rather than to reforms which will cement present groups in power." [19]

Centralized Parties and the Direct Primary. In Chapter Five the methods of nominating candidates to represent the political parties in general election campaigns were traced from the early legislative caucus through the convention system to the direct primary. The transition from conventions to direct primaries came as a result of an intentional movement to take away from a party's controlling oligarchy the right to make nominations. In the closed primary, nominating power was vested in the registered party voters; in the open primary, it was given to anyone who might choose to vote in a party's primary.

The Committee on Political Parties, in its only specific recommendation for machinery to hold party candidates responsible to party members, suggests that since no workable substitute has been found for the direct primary, it *" probably can be adapted to the needs of parties unified in terms of national policy."* [20] Between the alternatives of the closed or open primary, the Committee deems the former the more suitable for internal party responsibility. The closed primary, then, would be the device to select a party's nominees for partisan office in the states, and along with caucuses and conventions would also be used to hold party officers accountable. But given the type of political parties which the Committee on Political Parties wants, is its acceptance of the direct primary consistent with its general pattern of recommendations?

If the party council should be as strong and as responsible as the model proposed, it would have been more consistent with the overall plan to permit the party council to name party nominees for seats in the United States Senate and House of Representatives. If that was

---

[19] *Idem.* See also Moos, *op. cit.,* pp. 163–165.

[20] The Committee on Political Parties, *op. cit.,* p. 71. See also Austin Ranney, " Toward a More Responsible Two-Party System: A Commentary," *The American Political Science Review* (June, 1951), Vol. 45, No. 2, p. 491.

considered too radical an innovation, the next most logical proposal for the Committee on Political Parties might have been a return in the states to the convention system of making nominations. But the Committee recognized the obstacles in the way of changing constitutions and laws in the states and thus settled for the closed direct primary. In doing so the Committee has perhaps insured the unworkability of other features of its plan.

For the closed direct primary to operate in the manner which the Committee apparently hopes it would, a party's membership in a state would have to be so dedicated to the party's national program and national organization that it would follow en masse the recommendations of the national party for Congressional candidates. Furthermore, candidates not receiving the blessing of the national party, for the good of the party or because they were afraid of the sanctions which could be applied against them, would have to figuratively lie down without taking the fight to the voters in the primary election. When one views the present-day high quality of intraparty candidate fighting and the interest and motivational levels of the party electorates in the several states, he can find little evidence to assume that the direct primary system could ever be made to work as the Committee on Political Parties hopes it would function.

Party voters in a state have been notoriously touchy about " outside interference," whether in primary or general elections, but particularly in primary elections. Wilson failed badly when he openly tried to influence Democratic Congressional nomination contests in 1918. So did Franklin D. Roosevelt in 1938. Perhaps more subtle means of intervention could yield profitable results, but the recommendations for primary intervention of the Committee on Political Parties are not classifiable as " subtle." To envision a new feeling of national party identification which would override the traditional attitude in state primary elections is far-fetched indeed. Furthermore, the Committee on Political Parties sees program as so important that the candidate himself will become a relatively minor and secondary consideration. All the Committee is in effect asking, then, is an almost complete reversal of individual voter and party-worker motivational patterns by a transfer of the intraparty power struggle from a candidate and personality base to a program base.

The direct primary as a device for holding party officers responsible is even more ineffective, in the sense in which the Committee on Political Parties uses the word " responsible," than is its operation in the selection of nominees for public office. The party voter, particularly in large urban areas, knows little about candidates for party office and generally cares even less. A much smaller proportion of party voters vote in primaries for party officers than in primaries for nomination of candidates for public office. The possibilities of the dominant party group to perpetuate itself in office are virtually unlimited and will continue to be unless the average party member voting in a primary for party offices undergoes a miraculous transformation in his interest in party affairs.

Stedman and Sonthoff, in their examination of the assumption of the Committee on Political Parties that more responsible parties would require a highly centralized internal party structure, state that if nominations are to be determined by criteria set by the national party, ". . . it is difficult to see what, if any, purpose is served by retaining the direct primary." [21] The same authors see the Committee's recommendations as a threat to the direct primary — a control institution which they regard as valuable. Particularly would the consequences of the disappearance of the direct primary be serious in one-party areas. There the only meaningful choice on candidates and program which the voter has an opportunity to make comes in the primary, and not in the general election. "The net effect of the disappearance of primaries in such a situation," say Stedman and Sonthoff, " would be to take from the voter his only effective weapon for registering protest." [22]

Observers disagree on the merits of the open versus the closed primary and on the merits of the primary versus the convention system in two-party areas. Although the disappearance of the direct primary in two-party constituencies would not necessarily make the functioning of the American political system less effective, qualitative judgments as to which is the best nomination procedure are difficult to make. Some start from the premise, as does the Committee on Political Parties, that the most important standard against which nomination methods should be judged is the effect of those methods on party strength. Others, though they may feel parties are indispensable to the political process, look first to a " good government " standard. Thus there are Californians who will argue that a closed primary with cross-filing has produced good government, and other Californians who hold that the state's nominating procedures are

---

[21] Stedman and Sonthoff, *op. cit.,* p. 456.   [22] *Ibid.,* p. 457.

poor because they tend to weaken the political party organizations. Similar argument proceeds in any state and regardless of what type of nominating procedures are employed.

Of the stand which a majority takes on the question of nominating methods, however, this much can be said. There is no disposition to abolish the direct primary to return to a convention system or any other alternative. Perhaps one of the reasons for the widely differing viewpoints on this question is an underlying feeling that what is the best nominating procedure in one state is not necessarily the best in another. If the public were of the opinion that the Committee on Political Parties' plan would destroy direct primaries or would impose uniform nominating procedure on all the states, here would be one solid obstacle in the path of implementation of the Committee's general recommendations.

Perhaps even more surprising than the willingness of the Committee on Political Parties to retain the direct primary, considering the Committee's larger objectives, is its statement: *" In time it may be feasible and desirable to substitute a direct, national presidential primary for the indirect procedure of the convention."* [23] The point is not developed further beyond the notation that a constitutional amendment would be necessary before the proposal could go into effect.

If one speculates far enough into the future of time, all the assumptions made by the Committee may conceivably at some period be sound. Yet, considering again the Committee's larger objectives, the imagination has to be stretched beyond the limits of elasticity to see how a direct Presidential primary would fit in with the kind of party system outlined in *Toward a More Responsible Two-Party System*.

Those who urge the direct Presidential primary, and many distinguished persons have done so, would use the device to take the power of nominating a President away from a party's leaders and give it to the people. A major goal of the Committee's report is to strengthen the persuasive and disciplinary power of party leadership. Undoubtedly, if the party council was united on a particular candidate for the nomination, there might be little difficulty (if all the resources of the national party were thrown behind his national campaign in a Presidential primary) in getting that chosen candidate

---

[23] The Committee on Political Parties, *op. cit.,* p. 74.

nominated. Even so, however, a national convention nominating procedure would be easier for the party leadership to control.

Should there be several strong contenders in a Presidential primary, the party leadership would have to take the risk of matters getting completely " out of hand." At least in the convention system sound political considerations can be used as a guide to selecting the nominee most likely to win and most likely to make a good Presidential record. The average voter in a Presidential primary, though it were a closed primary in which only persons registered with that party could vote, might be swayed by quite different considerations. Furthermore, if state primaries can be raided by the opposition party, even in closed primaries, would not that possibility also exist in a Presidential primary?

Were the direct Presidential primary to supersede the convention system with the parties organized as they now are, some other very substantial criticisms against the proposal warrant substantial answers. Would it not be necessary, for example, for each candidate to build a separate state-wide campaign organization in each state? What might be the effect of that development on party unity and organization during and after Presidential primary campaigns? If numerous candidates were entered in each Presidential primary contest, would the candidate receiving the largest number of votes, even though not a majority, be the winner? If not, would there be a runoff primary? If there were a runoff primary, would that not mean three separate national Presidential campaigns in each Presidential election year and would that be desirable?

Who would select the Vice Presidential nominee? Might not potentially good Presidents be eliminated as possibilities because they would not, or, because of their positions, could not enter Presidential primary election campaigns? Would not intraparty dynamics in a Presidential primary operate to select men of a narrow party appeal without regard to the broad appeal requirements of winning general elections? Would it be possible for a man not well known and without the boost of a national convention nomination to have a chance to defeat competitors who already had had the advantage of national build-ups?

These are but some of the questions which have not yet been adequately studied or answered and which should be studied and answered before the direct Presidential primary deserves more serious consideration as a substitute for the national convention. Having made the recommendation it did, even if for some indefinite future time, the Committee on Political Parties should have attempted to examine such questions and to specify what purpose it thought the Presidential primary would serve for the reformed party system which the Committee proposes.

The Possibility of Extremist Major Parties or a Multi-party System. The Committee on Political Parties would continue the two-party system but centralize the parties and have them develop more specific party programs on the assumption that then the parties would present voters with " true choice " alternatives. More specific programs and parties such as those recommended, it is felt by the Committee, would not result in extremist major parties or disintegration of the two-party system. On the first of the two points, the Committee has this to say:

> *Needed clarification of party policy,* in itself *will not cause the parties to differ more fundamentally or more sharply than they have in the past.* The contrary is much more likely to be the case. The clarification of party policy may be expected to produce a more reasonable discussion of public affairs, more closely related to the political performance of the parties in their actions rather than their words. *Nor is it to be assumed that increasing concern with their programs will cause the parties to erect between themselves an ideological wall.* There is no real ideological division in the American electorate, and hence programs of action presented by responsible parties for the voter's support could hardly be expected to reflect or strive toward such division.[24]

On the second point, the Committee sees its program as a safeguard against the following dangers:

> *The . . . danger is that with growing public cynicism and continuing proof of the ineffectiveness of the party system the nation may eventually witness the disintegration of the two major parties. The . . . danger is that the incapacity of the two parties for consistent action based on meaningful programs may rally support for extremist parties poles apart, each fanatically bent on imposing on the country its particular panacea.*[25]

---

[24] The Committee on Political Parties, *op. cit.,* pp. 20–21.
[25] *Ibid.,* p. 92.

Both of the Committee's conclusions on these points are attacked by critics of its report. If the proposed parties are not " to differ more fundamentally or more sharply " than in the past, what is all the " hullabaloo " about, asks Goodman.[26] Throughout the Committee's report, however, it does ask that the parties differ more than they have in the past and asks also that they have consistent and discernible policies. Objections to the desirability of the development of the Committee's kind of " principled " parties are made on several grounds.

First, if party programs became more specific, would not the result generate intraparty disagreement rather than agreement, contrary to what the Committee suggests? [27] In the present parties, what degree of unity exists is in large part dependent on the parties' ability to postpone a stand on issues which might produce an internal explosion, to compromise on other points in order to satisfy competing groups enough to win or keep them within the party fold, and to take clear and specific stands only on the issues which are not, within the party, productive of internal controversy and disunity. If the parties are to produce more " meaningful " programs and make their decisions binding, will not they lose their resiliency qualities and become organizationally brittle? Vagueness in party program may be a weakness of American parties, but is it not also one of the principal sources of a major party's strength and of the party system's strength? And if vagueness is both a weakness and a strength, do not its strength advantages far outweigh its weakness liabilities?

James C. Charlesworth has well-stated what has been and still is the generally accepted view of an American major party's function:

> Since the principal parties in a two-party system are created to govern the country and not to carry torches, our established parties become institutionalized. Innocent observers exclaim because our principal parties avoid issues whenever possible, which is precisely what they must do if they are to remain principal parties. If we think of the party in power as being the government, which it is, it is easier for us to understand how the current custodian of power is less interested in changing the government than in operating it.[28]

---

[26] Goodman, *op. cit.*, p. 555.

[27] See *ibid.*, p. 554.

[28] James C. Charlesworth, " Is Our Party System Natural? " *The Annals* (September, 1948), Vol. 259, p. 9.

Should the parties attempt to develop the Committee's kind of " concrete " programs, might not the strong regional and sectional interests in American politics operate to destroy the parties at the national
level and replace them with narrowly oriented national and sectional
issue parties? The vagueness of Democrats and Republicans in the
past has in large part flowed from the assumption that this question
requires an affirmative answer. Appeals have been adapted to regions
and sections. Furthermore, if Democrats had a good thing, Republicans, if they were flexible enough, have sought to mount the bandwagon too with their own version of the product. Democrats have
acted likewise. Each party seeks to minimize its own weaknesses and
to accentuate the weaknesses of the opposition while it advertises its
own strengths. Even if the result is sometimes a blurred effect, to ask
the parties to differ for the sake of differing or because they might
become components in a " more responsible " two-party system is
not adequately to recognize the most basic function of the parties —
that of winning elections. Might not winning elections be incompatible with " responsibility " in the sense the word is applied by
the Committee on Political Parties?

Stedman and Sonthoff, in viewing European multiparty systems,
see the line between " specificness of policy " and developing a doctrinaire approach to political issues as a thin line. ". . . [A] glance
at those systems, warning examples of the erosion of the political
grass roots through political doctrine, indicates that the splitting of
the electorate into a multiplicity of parties which occurred through
the increasing radicalization of party programs, in turn was the logical result of what we might call competitive program specificness." [29]

The transition from a two-party to a multiparty system might
tend to evolve in this manner. As the two major parties become more
specific in developing their programs, those groups which lose out
on each issue decision may break away or be disciplined out of their
party. If the same process is not taking place within the opposition
party, perhaps the dissident groups will find a home there. If enough
groups are driven from the first to the second major party and the
first party does not itself acquire new adherents, the second major
party will soon become much stronger than its opposition. What would
be more likely, however, if both major parties fit the Committee on
Political Parties' model, would be the disintegration of both major

---

[29] Stedman and Sonthoff, *op. cit.*, p. 462.

parties at the same time. Those groups without a party home, seeking an outlet for the political expression of their objectives, would then tend to form their own party based on their own statement of objectives. Now party programs might be more "meaningful," but a multiparty system might be the end result.

Even if a multiparty system did not result from the Committee's type of parties, a second set of objections to the plan revolves around the possibility that the two major parties would tend to become more extreme. Bipartisan cooperation between the parties would, therefore, become more difficult.

Candidates of whichever party does not control the Presidency, when out on the campaign circuit, have maintained that the in-party is using bipartisanship in foreign affairs to its own advantage. Nevertheless, bipartisanship in this area has become a very real and constructive development in the conduct of foreign relations. On important questions in this policy area there has been a significant degree of cooperation. From the middle 1940's until 1952, when Democrats controlled the White House, many was the occasion when Republican votes made the difference between victory or defeat for a critical collective security measure. "Yet if the GOP minority in either House had been bound by policy strictures of the majority, nonpartisan cooperation on foreign policy would have floundered at the outset. Probably no more than a third of the minority members in either chamber during recent years were disposed to take a sufficiently broad view of the scope of American foreign policy to support actively a nonpartisan approach. . . ." [30] Had the dominant group within the Republican party been able to impose discipline to enforce a doctrinaire party line, the result would undoubtedly have been a quite different one, hurting not only the country but the future of the Republican party as well.

Even more critical to the stable functioning of the federal government has been the ability of one party to at least tolerate and at best cooperate with the other when control of both houses of Congress and the Presidency was not held by the same party. The Committee on Political Parties, suggest Stedman and Sonthoff, assumes in its plan that the White House and Congress will be held by the same party. But short of a constitutional amendment, of this there is no guarantee. ". . . [I]n the absence of cabinet responsibility under

[30] Moos, *op. cit.,* p. 158.

a parliamentary type of government, the prospect of a breakdown in democratic procedures would surely be aggravated rather than lessened by the existence of strongly disciplined and highly dedicated parties. If such a doctrinaire congressional-presidential impasse would be unfortunate in domestic affairs, it could conceivably be disastrous in the area of foreign policy." [31]

Although the Committee on Political Parties says it wants neither two extremist major parties nor a multiparty system, much of the language in its report is not compatible with the type of moderate parties we know today. A few examples will illustrate the tone. " The Party Council would be the appropriate party agency to interpret the respective platforms and determine *the right position* in case of conflict." [32] Democrats and Republicans today do not think in terms of *the* right position on a controversial issue. The vagueness of party policy lines and the general realization that controversial issues are highly complex admit and permit the possibility of several " right " positions.

The Committee on Political Parties seems to imply that relatively few national-state party issues would be matters for debate: " There is little likelihood indeed for the Party Council to be inconsiderate of *arguable claims* of state autonomy." [33] What state party claim, it might be asked in the light of past and present-day politics, if it is important enough to be a " state claim " would not be " arguable "?

" As a body representing the various parts of the party structure, the Party Council should be able to give *authoritative* and reasonably acceptable interpretations of the platform." [34] " It is contrary to the basic concept of our two-party system, destructive of party responsibility and disruptive of the party as a whole *to permit* organized disloyalty to continue." [35] Presently the terms " authoritative " and " to permit " are not much in evidence in the major party organizational vocabularies. To win elections the parties need broad support, and " authoritative " interpretations of platforms and " to permit " language in dealing with state parties is not regarded by politicians as the best approach toward winning and holding support.

---

[31] Stedman and Sonthoff, *op. cit.,* p. 467.
[32] The Committee on Political Parties, *op. cit.,* p. 52. Italics the author's.
[33] *Idem.* Italics the author's.
[34] *Ibid.,* p. 51. Italics the author's.
[35] *Ibid.,* p. 48. Italics the author's.

" In view of the independent position of the state party organizations, the state party platform may and frequently does state principles and policies quite different from those stated in the national platform. *Such divergencies* make things *confusing* both for the party candidates from the state and for the public, and make *nonsense* of the party system." [36] Seriously impeding " concerted party action," the Committee suggests, is the fact that the Republican party of California may differ on public questions and even on strategy with the Republican party of Iowa, that during the LaFollette period in Wisconsin Republican politics and the Nonpartisan League period in North Dakota the Republican organizations in those states differed with the national Republican organization, and that southern state Democratic organizations differ with the national Democratic party organization. The Committee next proceeds to note how minor parties require state and local party conformity and thus produce " concerted party organization." The minor party mold, however, is rejected as " neither desirable nor feasible," and the party council, it is said, " would do much to coordinate the different party organizations." [37] Although the minor party alternative is specifically discarded, yet the whole of the report leads to the conclusion that if the major parties should not be organized like minor parties, at least the hope is they should be organized in such a way as to produce the same type of discipline as in minor parties.

Homage is also paid at the altar of " consistency." " As a consciously defined and *consistently followed line of action* keeps individuals from losing themselves in irresponsible ventures, so a program-conscious party develops greater resistance against the inroads of pressure groups." [38] Even if party program consistency immunized against " inroads " of pressure groups, inconsistency on occasion may be the only politically or otherwise sound course of action. Should Raymond Clapper have remained " consistent " when on February 5, 1941, he wrote in his syndicated column: " This might be called the 'confession of an isolationist.' . . . I try to learn from events. Events are not consistent, therefore why should I be consistent? " [39]

Should the Republican party have resolved to bear an isolation-

---

[36] The Committee on Political Parties, *op. cit.,* p. 51. Italics the author's.

[37] *Ibid.,* p. 46.

[38] *Ibid.,* p. 19. Italics the author's.

[39] *St. Paul Pioneer Press.*

ist policy " cross " because the Democrats were in power when foreign policy shifted to a collective security orientation and because then the Republicans would be presenting the voters with a true choice between alternatives? With a Republican party policy committee to hand down " authoritative " pronouncements and discipline, the late Republican Senator Arthur Vandenburg, of Michigan, would have been an insurgent to be disciplined when he, during World War II, made his transition from an isolationist to a collective security position. The kind of consistency which the Committee on Political Parties implies it wants will generally be incompatible with the parties' need for flexibility.

A major party could quickly bring itself to the end of its rope if consistency behind " party principles " in the face of changing events and changing political situations is one of its political doctrines. Instead, the party must maintain a degree of flexibility sufficient to steal away and improve upon the opposition's most effective policies while, at the same time, the party discards " party principles " which if adhered to would be neither sound public or political policy.

If on most political questions there were a " clearly right " and a " clearly wrong " alternative, if the parties evolved with one having a monopoly of the " right " positions and the other was mostly " wrong," and if the parties were " consistent " in their stands, perhaps the voter might not be so " confused." American party history suggests, however, that if these are the developments which must take place before confusion ceases, then confusion will be with us for a long time to come.

Centralized Parties and the Voter. Is the voter confused? Is he dissatisfied with the party system as he finds it? If he is neither, the Committee on Political Parties would have him understand how poor are the alternative choices available to him in the present party system and would have him demand changes. In short, if the voter is not confused or dissatisfied, he should be. Critics of *Toward a More Responsible Two-Party System,* however, have argued for several reasons that the voter would be worse off with the Committee's type of parties than he is now.

We have already noted the suggestions that the voter does today have a realistic choice between alternatives, that if one-party areas were increased his range of choice in those constituencies would be reduced, that if the self-destructive tendencies in the minority major party are accentuated that party would become a less effective alternative, that if the direct primary were destroyed in one-party areas a channel through which voter protest can be registered would be lost, and that if a multiparty system were produced the voter would have no opportunity to select between alternatives as broad and national in scope as those available to him today.

These, however, are not the only points the critics of the Committee on Political Parties would have the voter think about before demanding new centralized and program-oriented parties. Goodman warns that " suggestions that everybody should choose up sides once and for all and never deviate in his devotion to the original party of his choice " should be resisted.[40] Independent voters, whether they represent one third, one fifth, or whatever proportion of the electorate, play an important part in the functioning of the American political system. The independent voter must be appealed to by both parties. In his hands he holds the weapon of a straight ticket for either side, or more generally he is expected to split his votes between candidates of both parties. Though the possibility of split-ticket voting may do violence to the theory of party responsibility, the practice, writes Goodman, is one of the most effective weapons voters have. A candidate will be judged not only by his party but on the basis of what he himself is, and a state party might win the approval of an independent voter even though the same party's national or local candidates do not receive it. " The knowledge that the whole party ticket can be elected, either through the preponderance of the party's following or the popularity of particular candidates [at the top of the ticket], can create as much irresponsibility among public officials as the decentralization of parties. Basically, it is the independence of voters that permits the bi-partisan system to operate." [41]

The Committee on Political Parties would have all voters shift their emphasis in vote decisions from candidate to party program. Were the voter to comply, however, might not he be discarding the most reliable reference point available to him in his vote-deciding process? Most issues of governmental policy, particularly on the national level, are highly technical questions about which even experts disagree. For the average voter to thoroughly understand even one major area in which governmental policy decisions must be made

---

[40] Goodman, *op. cit.*, p. 557.   [41] *Idem.*

is not likely. But every voter is an expert at judging other people. He does it every day in his regular activities. This ability the voter can easily transfer to the appraisal of candidates. Here the voter's competence level is high, even though he may know relatively little about details of issues.

In a federal and separation of powers system, even though a voter has a disposition toward voting a straight ticket, he generally does pause to consider the qualifications of the man who is running for each office. It is likely that the independent, the " weak " Democrat and the " weak " Republican will continue to perform in this way. By doing so, the major parties are forced to think in terms of both program appeal *and* candidate appeal and they can take no election contest for granted, other than those in one-party constituencies. This, in turn, makes it mandatory for both parties to appeal roughly to similar groups and neither may dare for long to close its ear to the peculiar political pulse sounds of any constituency.

Sometimes a vote may be cast for the man based on a sound appraisal of the candidate as an individual, and at other times for perhaps no better reason than liking or disliking the way in which he parts his hair. Personality has been and continues to be an important consideration in the voter's mind. Sometimes a vote may go for or against the " ins " depending upon the level of the business cycle at the time of election. Many may be the other reasons determining the way in which the ballot is marked, and generally party program is one of the less important of the considerations.[42] This has been and is the general mixed motivational pattern, if pattern it can be called. Most critics of the Committee on Political Parties' report are not of the opinion that it can be or necessarily should be changed.

Speaking of the disposition of the voter, Stedman and Sonthoff add a refinement to the advantages of the existing party system:

> That disposition of the average voter has made possible the present system of constituent-representative relations, which is one of remarkable closeness considering the size of the country and of the elec-

---

[42] See Stedman and Sonthoff, *op. cit.,* p. 464 and articles cited there. See also for general background on the points: Angus Campbell, Gerald Gurin, and Warren E. Miller, *The Voter Decides* (White Plains, N. Y.: Row, Peterson and Company, 1954) ; Paul F. Lazarsfeld, Bernard Berelson and Hazel Gaudet, *The People's Choice* (New York: Columbia University Press, 1948) ; and Berelson, Lazarsfeld, and William N. McPhee, *Voting: A Study of Opinion Formation in a Presidential Campaign* (Chicago: The University of Chicago Press, 1954) .

toral districts. It has kept the voter close to and interested in the Government. It is that disposition which has made for a more tangible basis of popular government in this country — for a more " personal " basis, in several senses of the word — that would not be possible by a system of increased party control.[43]

Centralized Parties and the Pressure Group. The existing relationships between the parties and pressure groups and the assessment of what would be the type of relationship between these two types of political institutions if the party system were highly centralized is deserving of attention in a chapter by itself and will be examined in the following and concluding chapter.

REFORM PROPOSALS ON WHICH THERE IS SUBSTANTIAL AGREEMENT

As has already been noted, some few critics of *Toward a More Responsible Two-Party System* are of the opinion the report did not go far enough. They would work for the long-range goal of constitutional change to alter the federal and separation of powers features of American government and replace them with forms adapted to the majority-rule concept of democracy. Such critics of both the constitutional system and the party system comprise only a small proportion of political scientists and observers of the American governmental process. Their proposals and the theory behind them are being vigorously challenged.

The Committee on Political Parties has held that centralized and program-oriented parties are possible within the existing constitutional framework. This too has been sharply criticized both in articles and panels at the annual conventions of the American Political Science Association — criticized for the assumption that no constitutional changes would be necessary and on the grounds of practicability and desirability. The principal arguments in this controversy have been developed in this chapter and the preceding one. It remains, however, to take note of some of the Committee's recommendations on points where there is general agreement or where at least the differences are not as sharp as those developed above.

---

[43] Stedman and Sonthoff, *op. cit.,* p. 465.

Reform of the National Convention. National conventions are too large to deliberate as effectively as they might. The number of delegates might be pared down to a more wieldy size, and likewise the parties might profit by selecting only some two thirds of the membership from the state parties and filling the other one third of seats with ex-officio members such as Congressional representatives and with a small group of prominent party figures outside the regular party organizations. From the parties, however, there come practical objections. The demand for delegate seats is so high that selection as a delegate to a national convention becomes an honor with which faithful party workers and contributors can be rewarded. Likewise, the question ceases to be academic when placed into the context of the quadrennial power struggle over the Presidential nomination contest. In a state where the governor controls the state party organization and the majority of the Congressional delegation are of a different party faction, for example, the governor would not want ex-officio Congressional representation and the other faction would want it. Considerations such as these stand in the way of radical and quick changes.

Perhaps the national conventions should meet every two years, but again there are practical considerations to be considered. Congressmen in general do not want to risk possible embarrassment in a Congressional campaign year with a platform without also the advantage possibilities of a Presidential coattail. Without a platform, each Congressional and Senatorial candidate can make his own, emphasizing and de-emphasizing issues depending upon the characteristics of the constituency in which the candidate seeks office.

Reform of the National Committee. The Republican party in 1952 attempted to make its national committee more representative of party strength in the states by providing that Republican state chairmen could be members if the state party met certain tests. Some system might be devised to weight state delegation votes on the national committee in relation to a party's strength in the respective states. Perhaps this would have been done long ago had the national committees had important party functions to perform. Politically, however, the only real power stake in the national committee, aside from the chairman's function as agent of the President or Presidential nominee, is the preliminary decision which it makes when preparing the temporary roll and list-of-officer suggestions for the national conventions. Proposals for radical representation changes away from the federal pattern on the national committee would immediately be assessed in relation to how such changes would effect the Presidential chances of nominees from particular states. With each faction seeking to prevent another faction from gaining an advantage, the *status quo* tends usually to be the easiest and safest answer.

The Committee on Political Parties would have the national convention take an active role in the selection of committee members. Again intraparty factional alignments within the states operate to block general implementation of the recommendation. The dominant group in each state wants no national convention majority telling it who should be its leaders.

Reform of Party Platforms. Few take issue with proposals to provide for longer study and deliberation in the platform-drafting process, though there are objections to a national platform every two years and violent objections to making the platform and its interpretation by a party council binding on the entire party and its candidates. This controversy has run through the criticisms of the main features of the Committee on Political Parties' report above.

Reform of Party Organization in Congress. Here more than in any major area the recommendations of the Committee on Political Parties meet with general acceptance among political scientists. Cooperation between President and party in Congress and between party in House and Senate is desirable. The functioning of the party leadership committees can be improved, but as soon as any leadership committee starts setting a party line or the suggestion is made that caucus decisions be binding the same opposing arguments as are developed in the major criticisms of the Committee's party reform proposals are heard again.

Absolute application of the seniority rule in selecting standing committee chairmen is not generally approved, except by members of Congress who are the only ones that can modify the application of the seniority rule. Likewise, periodic re-examination of committee assignments sounds reasonable to most observers, but again not to members of Congress. The Congressional argument, and one which is not without some grounds, is that intraparty factional fighting over chairmanships and committee assignments would be so severe there might not be much time for the affairs of state.

That the House Rules Committee, through its scheduling power, may throw the House majority into a tailspin is not questioned. In the Senate the lack of an effective cloture rule to shut off debate can on occasion place that body into an even more ridiculous posture. Rules changes and modifications of party organization in the Congress come, however, only through a gradual process of evolution. Public discussion and Congressional awareness of problems will continue to produce changes, and perhaps in the not too distant future it is not unrealistic to foresee the power of the Rules Committee clipped, though a workable cloture rule for the Senate appears much further away. And mighty will be Congressional opposition to binding caucuses, binding party leadership committee decisions, binding platforms interpreted by party councils, or institutionalization of devices through which a Presidential party line would be binding upon them.[44]

Reform of Elections. Proposed changes in the electoral college method of electing the President have been of several varieties. One, and the least radical, would merely make impossible the chance that an elector might vote for a candidate other than the one for whom he was chosen to vote. Another, and the most radical, would have the President elected by popular vote. Here, however, the small states object on the ground that their present advantage over the large states would be eliminated.

Most seriously considered, and the recommendation of the Committee on Political Parties, has been the proposal that the assignment of electoral votes to the states continue as before but that each Presidential candidate should get electoral votes in each state in proportion to the percentage of popular votes he polled in the state. The Lodge-Gossett amendment which included this provision obtained the necessary two-thirds majority in the Senate in 1950 but was defeated in the House.

Opposition to the Lodge-Gossett plan took these three forms, and

---

[44] See Norton E. Long, " Party Government and the United States," *The Journal of Politics* (May, 1951) , Vol. 13, No. 2, pp. 187–214. Long, in holding that leadership must come from the President, concludes on page 214 as follows: " Presidential government operating through a nationalizing bureaucracy with a Congress reduced to the role of critic may be far from the idea of party government we might desire. It still may be our only chance of successfully utilizing the expert knowledge and planning necessary to chart our way in the foul weather ahead."

all of them are examples of why it is so difficult to change political or governmental procedures once they have been set and vested interests develop around them. Senator Robert A. Taft led the Republican opposition on the ground a Republican's chances of election to the Presidency would be severely damaged. By winning close victories in northern pivot states, Republicans may capture such a state's entire block of electoral votes. In pivot states, if the winner did not take all, Republican strength might be cut as much as one half, with Democrats profiting. Republicans win by relatively close margins in all states in which they have a chance in Presidential elections. In the South, Republican prospects of winning a significant proportion of the two-party vote cannot yet be regularly and realistically regarded as good. Though a measure like the Lodge-Gossett amendment might help develop a two-party system in the South, some Republicans fear the transitional period would be too painful and the chance would be too great a one to take.

The Lodge-Gossett amendment was also opposed by some in the pivot states, particularly minority groups, who felt their influence in Presidential elections would be cut down because their " group vote " could no longer have the threat value of throwing all the pivot state's electoral votes one way or the other. A third opposition argument hinged on the theory that splitting a state's electoral votes might give undue encouragement to the development of minor parties.

Lengthening the term of members of the House of Representatives to four years was also proposed by the Committee on Political Parties. Sentiment for such a change has slowly and surely been developing and the possibility of its becoming a reality is relatively good. A major argument in its favor is, with Presidential and House elections fought out at the same time, that national issues will tend to receive as much emphasis as possible in all Congressional election campaigns and thus the electorates to which the President and House members are responsible would be made more similar.

In conclusion it should be observed that in general the reform proposals which are received with substantial agreement are those designed to improve the operation of the parties as they now exist. Opposition develops, however, as soon as an attempt is made to change the fundamental character of the parties.

CHAPTER TWENTY–FOUR

The Major Parties and the System: Weaknesses and Strengths — III

Pressure Groups and Parties

- -

A stronger party system is less likely to give cause for the deterioration and confusion of purposes which sometimes passes for compromise but is really an unjustifiable surrender to narrow interests. Compromise among interests is compatible with the aims of a free society only when the terms of reference reflect an openly acknowledged concept of the public interest.

Committee on Political Parties of the
American Political Science Association [1]

Lobbying is a dirty word. To those who have not looked critically at the issue, lobbyists are those who fight " the public interest " for " selfish " benefits. Politics is a " dirty game " because " weak " legislators " kowtow " to the " pressure boys " who " control " votes or money.

This stereotype is understandable, but it is accurate only if one is positive that he has a corner on the meaning of " the public interest." A trade unionist may see the National Association of Manufacturers as a " vicious lobby for selfish business interests." A businessman may see the C.I.O. as " an instrument of socialism exerting unconscionable pressure on Congress for the benefit of a few labor racketeers." But to the industrialist, the National Association of Manufacturers is the great bastion of defense against un-American ideas and social policies, and to many a trade unionist, his legislative representative is a protector of the legitimate interests of the workingman!

---

[1] *Toward a More Responsible Two-Party System,* a supplement to *The American Political Science Review* (September, 1950), Vol. 44, No. 3, Pt. 2, p. 20.

656 MAJOR PARTIES & SYSTEM: WEAKNESSES & STRENGTHS — III

Democratic government today is unthinkable without lobbyists. Lobbying is the participation of group interests in the governmental process. A summary outlawing of lobbying would immediately violate the right of petition which is guaranteed in the Bill of Rights. In a fundamental sense the electoral process in American politics is at times little more than an opportunity provided to the citizens to pass judgment on the particular amalgam of group interests which a legislator or political party has chosen to compound, qualify, and endorse.

To the busy legislator, lobbyists provide highly valued services. They indicate where the policy shoe pinches; they provide expert staff assistance in causes shared by legislators; they provide mechanisms for disseminating arguments and ideas to important and politically powerful segments of the public and to the press; they serve as whipping boys. In most important matters, however, it is impossible to separate the activities and influence of private lobbies from the temporary coalitions of power formed by Congressional, agency, and state and local government interests working toward specific goals, so inextricably are public and private groups woven in our governmental fabric.

Stephen K. Bailey and Howard D. Samuel [2]

Those who would abandon federalism and separation of powers for a majority-rule type of democracy and those who, though stopping short of constitutional change, would set up centralized, program-oriented and disciplined parties arrive at their conclusions through a reasoning process which proceeds generally in the following manner. First, serious problems in both domestic and foreign affairs confront the government of the United States.

Second, power within government on the national level is split between the several branches with no assurance that they will work together. Within the Congress the Senate is in a position to block the House, and within each house there are numerous power points in the hands of different individuals who are not necessarily cooperating among themselves. Power is also split between the national government and the states, and in many areas of domestic policy solutions to problems, because they depend on separate actions in the forty-eight states, cannot and are not uniformly applied throughout the country.

Third, the American two-party system, with Democratic and

---

[2] *Congress At Work* (New York: Henry Holt and Company, 1952), pp. 268–269.

Republican organizations decentralized and with party power diffused, is not adapted to provide national leadership and proper alternative policy choices for the voter. At this point comes the division of opinion between those asking for fundamental constitutional changes and those who do not. The former hold the party system cannot perform leadership and alternative functions given the nature of the governmental system. The latter at least imply that the parties, if properly organized and program-oriented, could bridge the gap between executive and legislative branches and between the national government and the states. Both groups, however, agree on the proposition that the gaps must be bridged more effectively than is now the case.

Fourth, where once the United States may have been able to afford the luxury of widely diffused governmental power and a piecemeal approach to solving problems, the critical nature of today's times and an increasingly critical prospect for the future demand a new approach to the solution of problems of government. Margins of permissible error are no longer as wide as they once were, and decisions of the United States of America, both when they are good and when they are bad, affect not only the fortunes of this country but those of the entire free world.

Fifth, if the parties do not provide a national and program-oriented leadership there is no other source from which it can come. And to the extent that parties abdicate the leadership function, to that degree will governmental policies be the result of compromises evolving out of the pressure group " war " as the various pressure groups seek to have government do what they want it to do in the field of their respective interests. This is undesirable because pressure groups advance their own particular claims on government from a point of view more concerned with their own group objectives than from an approach in which the chief concern is the " public interest." " The public interest may be described as the aggregate of common interests, including the common interest in seeing that there is fair play among private interests," writes E. E. Schattschneider. " The public interest is not the mere sum of the special interests, and it is certainly not the sum of the *organized* special interests. Nor is it an automatic consequence of the struggle of the special interests (a struggle in which everyone demands too much and feels entitled to it) ." [3]

---

[3] E. E. Schattschneider, " Political Parties and the Public Interest," *The Annals* (March, 1952) , Vol. 280, p. 22.

The following passages from Schattschneider, the chairman of the American Political Science Association's Committee on Political Parties which produced *Toward a More Responsible Two-Party System* and one of the most outspoken advocates of centralized, disciplined, and program-oriented parties as a defense against excessive localism and pressure group influence in national government decisions, illustrate the theory behind party reform proposals. To better provide background for an understanding of the problem posed in this chapter, Schattschneider is quoted at length.

I. Modern public policy involves general measures and general control of government at its highest levels. There is no *local* defense against inflation, and no special interest can find a special remedy for instability in the economy, just as no locality or interest can hope to survive untouched if the community as a whole is destroyed.[4]

II. The only satisfactory political base for general policies concerning the public interest is a majority. As long as politics was treated as a private matter, it was possible to conceive of the political process in the framework of concurrent majorities (in modern terms this means government by the unanimous consent of all special interests). But once it becomes necessary to make any great decisions, the community is forced to use the oldest and best-understood device for making decisions — the majority. The numerical majority has a role to play in modern government because we can no longer wait for the vegetative processes of an infinitely disintegrated system to solve our problems.

It follows that it is the function of political leaders to seek decisions on the greatest issues of public policy in terms that produce the majorities which alone can give any body of political leaders general control of the government and provide a stable base for public policy. The state of public affairs calls for the development of general alternatives by which the principle of majority rule can be exploited. At a time in which the nation needs to give direction to its affairs, a period in which public business must be discussed in terms of general policies, at a time when the greatest decisions must be made and broad policies require stable support, the failure to produce a numerical majority and the failure to use the principle of majority rule may be fatal to the survival of the whole regime.

Why is it impossible to create a majority by forming a combination of special interest groups? First, because the special interest groups

----

[4] Schattschneider, *op. cit.*, p. 24.

are usually very small and the accumulation of a majority by a process of trading with these groups one at a time would involve political leaders in an impossible task. This is doubly true because it is rarely possible to win the whole of any group by this process. Moreover, if the groups can be appealed to only on the grounds of their special interests, the complexities and conflicts within any possible majority become so great that it is inconceivable that the majority could ever take any decisive position on any question. . . .

Second, the *organized* special interests probably amount to substantially less than a majority of the people in the country, even if all of them could be brought into one combination.

There is no historical basis for the notion that anyone ever has produced a majority merely by forming a combination of special interests. Majorities are produced by general controversies about the public interest. . . .

As long as majoritarian politics is pursued in terms of controversies over the public interest, it may be carried on with great vigor without endangering the stability of the regime, because the public interest is best defended when competition for power is conducted on these terms. If the purpose is to exploit as fully and as effectively as possible the potentialities of general divisions about public interest, it follows that the form of political organization best adapted to this use is the political party. The parties are the only political organization established on a scale sufficiently extensive to mobilize a country-wide majority. However inadequate the traditional party structure may have been for these purposes, it is obvious that no other form of political organization can begin to compete successfully with it in a general conflict about broad policies for the control of the government at its highest level.[5]

INDISPENSABILITY OF POLITICAL PARTIES AND PRESSURE GROUPS

The Committee on Political Parties begins its 1950 report with this statement:

Throughout this report political parties are treated as indispensable instruments of government. That is to say, we proceed on the propo-

---

[5] E. E. Schattschneider, *op. cit.*, pp. 24–25. Reprinted by permission of *The Annals.*

sition that *popular government in a nation of more than 150 million people requires political parties which provide the electorate with a proper range of choice between alternatives of action.* The party system thus serves as the main device for bringing into continuing relationship those ideas about liberty, majority rule and leadership which Americans are largely taking for granted.[6]

The Committee does not say that pressure groups are not indispensable instruments of government, nor does it say pressure groups should be abolished. But throughout the report, by both statement and implication, the Committee assumes pressure groups are inferior to parties in both the manner in which the former operate and in the service to the public welfare which they perform. Furthermore, it is suggested, pressure groups have too large a voice in the determination of governmental policy.

What are the pressure groups? They, for our purposes, are the thousands of private associations in the United States organized to influence legislatures, executives, and even the courts, to propagandize with the object of gaining wide public acceptance and thus strengthen their position with public officials, and to " educate " almost anyone who will pause to listen to the arguments in support of their respective cases. In the field of business are found the United States Chamber of Commerce, the National Association of Manufacturers, and trade associations concerned with every phase of production, manufacturing, and distribution in every type of business activity. Individual corporations also lend themselves to a pressure group classification.

In the field of agriculture the best known Big Four are the American Farm Bureau Federation, the National Grange, National Farmers' Union, and National Council of Farmer Cooperatives. Also, paralleling somewhat the functional trade associations of business, there are organizations for every major commodity group such as corn, wool, cattle, and milk producers. In the field of labor the American Federation of Labor — Congress of Industrial Organizations receives the most attention, but the number of labor organizations operating independently or in part independently of the A.F.L.–C.I.O. number in the hundreds. Add to these the veterans, religious, ethnic group, professional group, reform, and other types of organizations. All are engaged in governmental relations to some

---

[6] *Op. cit.,* p. 15.

extent seeking at one time to have a policy adopted or at another time to prevent some action from being taken, or perhaps engaging in both types of activity at the same time. The pressure groups, as the second introductory quotation to this chapter points out, have become inextricably interwoven into our governmental fabric.

The pressure group in its relation with government is seeking to advance its own particular group objectives as distinguished from a political party which must mobilize a majority in a constituency in order to win elections. Though the pressure group may also interest itself directly or indirectly in elections, its purpose in doing so is not in winning elections *per se,* but in governmental policy. And conversely, though elements within a political party may earnestly be bent on changing or keeping certain governmental policies, this is only, for their party, a secondary concern.

The approach of the party is broad; that of pressure group leaders is narrowed to their group constituency and its support-building effort. The approach of the party is to hold down friction-creating issues in a search for a largest common denominator. For pressure group leaders in their relations with government, bringing up and pressing their issue positions is their principal business. With these distinctions again in mind, a few illustrative pressure group issue interests will further help place their function in the governmental process in perspective.

Business pressure groups in general are interested in tax and fiscal policies, government regulation of business, tariffs, and the Department of Commerce; farm pressure groups — in farm price support programs, other aids to agriculture including farm credit, tariffs, taxation, regulation of marketing channels, and the Department of Agriculture; labor pressure groups — in a favorable environment for collective bargaining, social security, full employment, housing, and the Department of Labor; veterans pressure groups — in bonuses and pensions, veterans' preference in civil service jobs, and the Veterans' Administration; religious pressure groups — in church and state relations, legislation with moral implications, and education; professional pressure groups — in licensing and standards applied to their profession and possible government interference with the environment in which the professions operate; and so on the long listing could be drawn out.

The interests of each type of pressure group are not narrowly confined to those items listed. Neither are the various groups within

business, agriculture, labor, religion, and other specialty areas necessarily in agreement with each other in general approach or on specific
issues. The pressure group " war " is a highly competitive one, both
between groups and between subgroups within the major groups.

Pressure groups are institutions without which the governmental
official and the system cannot get along. They inform public officials
and educate the public. They initiate policies. They provide a functional type of representation for the citizen in addition to the geographical base of representation afforded through the single-member
district system of electing public officials. They help build support
for governmental programs and their administration.

Though some pressure groups utilize illegal or unethical tactics,
though their internal organizations may not be as democratic as representative theory would like, though the organized group has a big
advantage in competition with the unorganized citizens — though
there may be shortcomings such as these when the pressure groups are
viewed as instruments in the governmental process, no one would
abolish them. Advocates of centralized and disciplined parties, however, would have the parties set a " national interest " policy line
and force the pressure groups to work through the parties rather than
around them and occasionally through them.

Critics of the Committee on Political Parties have held that
Toward a More Responsible Two-Party System should have said that
both pressure groups and parties are indispensable instruments of
government. " Indeed, the whole theory that the political party is
the primary agency for the enforcement of responsibility with respect to particular issues appears to be somewhat outmoded in contemporary America," says J. Roland Pennock. " When issues were
relatively few and simple, it made a great deal of sense. Half a century
ago, a few great but relatively simple questions such as those involving
tariffs and trusts, were predominant. It calls for no listing of the
issues that face Congress today to prove that the present situation is
very different." [7] So complex and so many are the issues of today and
so complex and many are the interests of the electorate that a dichoto-
mous two-party alternative statement of them cannot be made.[8]

Though we have logrolling, though alignments within a party
change from issue to issue and though there is competition with

---

[7] J. Roland Pennock, " Responsiveness, Responsibility, and Majority Rule,"
The American Political Science Review (September, 1952), Vol. 46, No. 3, p. 803.
[8] *Ibid.,* p. 804.

offers by parties and candidates to the different interest groups, centralized and disciplined parties are not likely to remove these things from American politics. " All of this," concludes Pennock, " does not mean that political parties are not important. They are one of the kinds of organization essential to the political process. They are indispensable; but without supplementation they would be woefully inadequate." [9] " Perhaps," say Stedman and Sonthoff, addressing themselves to the same point, " the central question is simply whether democracy is best realized through strong parties (' strong' meaning highly disciplined) or by a strong electorate organized in a variety of ways, including political parties." [10]

COMPROMISE AND A CONCEPT OF THE PUBLIC INTEREST

The 1950 report of the Committee on Political Parties states the need for a party system with greater resistance to pressure groups. This, it is felt, a program-conscious party would provide. Though pressure groups have a valuable function to perform, they cannot do the job of parties. " Indeed, it is only when a working formula of the public interest in its *general* character is made manifest by the parties in terms of coherent programs that the claims of interest groups can be adjusted on the basis of political responsibility." [11]

Interest groups, the Committee continues, cannot define public policy democratically. Nor do " coherent public policies " emerge as a result of the pressure group " war." " A stronger party system is less likely to give cause," to repeat the first introductory quotation for this chapter, " for the deterioration and confusion of purposes which sometimes passes for compromise but is really an unjustifiable surrender to narrow interests. *Compromise among interests is compatible with the aims of a free society only when the terms of reference reflect an openly acknowledged concept of the public interest.* There is every reason to insist that the parties be held accountable to the public for the compromises they accept." [12]

---

[9] *Ibid.,* p. 806.
[10] Murray S. Stedman, Jr., and Herbert Sonthoff, " Party Responsibility — A Critical Inquiry," *The Western Political Quarterly* (September, 1951), Vol. 4, No. 3, p. 461.
[11] The Committee on Political Parties, *op. cit.,* p. 19.
[12] *Ibid.,* p. 20.

It is one thing to say, as has Schattschneider in his many writings on the subject, that because pressure groups by virtue of their organization and objectives are not able to formulate a comprehensive public policy in the national interest, political parties should perform that function. It is quite another matter when the case is stated as narrowly as has been done in *Toward a More Responsible Two-Party System*. And perhaps the most extreme statement of the Committee is that setting down what should be the acceptable limits within which a party may compromise with pressure groups. A brief examination of the Committee's concept of " permissible compromise " will help illuminate the role of the pressure group and pressure group-political party relationship in the American system.

If " compromise among interests is compatible with the aims of a free society only when the terms of reference reflect an openly acknowledged concept of the public interest," one can only assume that the party must arrive at its " concept of the public interest " *before* any compromising is done. If not, there is no party standard against which to judge pressure group claims. If not, also, the " concept of the public interest " will be but a rationalization of a set of compromises which have already been made, and consequently the party's statement of public interest has already been watered down by private-interest considerations.

To carry the illustration to a ridiculous extreme, the party-platform makers and the party council in its interpretations of the platform would have to meet in an atmospheric vacuum environment purged of pressure groups and the latters' demands. Functioning thus, an initial task would be the formulation of a set of party principles about " liberty, majority rule, leadership " and other subjects. With the general principles worked out, next would come statements of what party positions should be on specific issues according to the party's conception of " public interest " at that time. Having done this, the party is now ready to puncture the pressure-purged vacuum, admit the pressure groups, listen to their competing claims, and then compromise if the party sees fit — but compromises made could only reflect " an openly acknowledged concept of the public interest."

Obviously this is not the way parties now work or ever could work. The major questions of public policy are so complicated that only experts in each field can supply the facts and opinions of what policy in each area should be, provided it is to conform to a " public-interest " standard. If more than one expert is called in, there will tend to be disagreement as to which of two or more courses of action are most in the " public interest." Neither will the experts be " pure " in the pressure-purged vacuum sense because they would bring with them their own interest attachments which they have inevitably acquired as they proceeded through the process of becoming an expert in some specialty field of public policy.

After expert opinions within a particular policy subject-matter area had been resolved into a " public-interest " answer satisfactory to the party policy body, the procedure would have to be repeated in attempting to bring into balance the " public-interest " findings from other areas. They might not necessarily agree where there is overlap. Only after attaining such a balance could a " comprehensive statement of public interest " be issued.

The hypothetical development of a party program such as is being done here ignores the most fundamental point of what the political parties actually are — loose combinations of different groups which very definitely know what they want in the way of public policy and groups which will tend to take everything the party will give them. Picture, for example, the Democratic party functioning in a labor-purged decision-making climate to evolve a plank on labor-management relations in order to live up to a nonlabor stated standard of what constitutes " public interest " in the labor-management field. Or stretch the imagination a little further to visualize the possibility of the Democratic party arriving at an " antilabor " program because it is in the " public interest " — a theoretical possibility if compromise is permissible only after the party has stated its " concept of public interest." Or, to turn the coin to the other side, visualize the Republican party making a decision on farm policy without reference to the farm pressure groups or on business policy without reference to business groups. Party officials are both party officials and pressure group members or officials, and they owe some proportion of their manner of thinking on public questions to both competing institutions.

Attempt to imagine a political party, the primary aim of which is winning elections and is not " being responsible " for responsibility's sake, evolving a program without reference to the " group-diplomacy " objective of amassing a majority big enough to win elections. As a filling station operator must sell good petroleum products, have a clean rest room, and hire attendants who provide service-plus in order to be successful in competition with other filling stations, so must the parties develop an appeal broad enough to bring the voters to the polls to vote for their candidates. If the parties know what the electorate wants, their appeals and the manner of appeal distribution is designed to take such knowledge into account;

HOG-CALLING CONTEST

MINNEAPOLIS STAR

if the parties do not know, they bend every effort to find out as accurately as they can.

It is not the intention to suggest that the Committee on Political Parties expects American political parties to enter vacuum chambers motivated only by party principles and good intentions of seeking out the "public interest" without reference to the world in which they must operate, although narrowly interpreted the statement being here developed might lead one to such a conclusion. Rather the purpose is to make the point that inevitably compromise with pressure groups and unorganized pressures known to exist is a part of the party policy decision-making process *during* the period in which the decisions are being made.

How then can the public interest be served? The first essential might be considered a recognition of the proposition that no such thing as an abstract " public interest " exists separate and apart from all private interests. Neither can the private interest be considered without reference to a wider community interest. The "public interest" and the " private interest" cannot be pulled apart. Recognizing the difficulty of definition formulation, what might be the duty of the political parties in relation to the demands of the pressure group?

It is not too much to ask of the political parties that they never think *only* in private terms. It is not too much to ask that they conscientiously strive to keep foremost in mind the greater public good while, at the same time, they keep their " feet on the ground " by understanding and compromising with what are felt to be legitimate pressure group or unorganized group desires. It is not too much to ask, in short, that public officials take their oaths of *public* office seriously and that parties consider themselves as agents not only of the groups clustered in party combination but also of the general public. It is, however, too much to ask the parties not to be political parties and the American system not to be the American system.

To V. O. Key, Jr.:

> . . . [T]he promotion of the public good cannot be accomplished apart from class or special interest. The public good is, after all, a relative matter. It rarely consists in yielding completely to the demands of one class or group in society. It more often consists in the elaboration of compromise between conflicting groups, in the yielding to one class at a time and to another at another, and sometimes in the mobilization of the support of the great unorganized general public to better down the demands of special interest.[13]

PRESSURE GROUPS AS AUXILIARIES OF POLITICAL PARTIES?

" Any tendency in the direction of a strengthened party," continues the Committee on Political Parties, " encourages the interest

---

[13] V. O. Key, Jr., *Politics, Parties, and Pressure Groups* (New York: Thomas Y. Crowell Company, 1953), p. 174.

groups to align themselves with one or the other of the major parties. Such a tendency is already at work. One of the noteworthy features of contemporary American politics is the fact that not a few interest groups have found it impossible to remain neutral toward both parties. To illustrate, the entry of organized labor upon the political scene has in turn impelled antagonistic special interests to coalesce in closer political alignments." Because pressure groups are organized and define their objectives on a national scale, power within the parties is moving in a centralizing direction to counteract and offset local interests. Particularly are large membership pressure groups attracted to parties " whose political commitments count." [14]

" *To a much greater extent than in the past, they* [the large member pressure groups] *operate as if they were auxiliary organizations of one or the other party."* [15] And, developing the point further, it is stated that:

> Thus the old local monopolies of the regular party organizations have been broken by new large-membership groups. To a very considerable extent the regular party organizations are now so yoked into a partnership with the newcomers that they have lost much of their old freedom of action. The successful political leader in the future is likely to be one who is skillful in maintaining a good working alliance between the older and the newer types of political organization. This applies partly even to conditions today.

> The emphasis of the new large-membership organizations is on national rather than sectional issues. What is no less significant, the interests of the membership are not identified with any single product or commodity. Workers must measure their pay against the level of prices as well as the value of social security. Hence the large membership groups are inevitably pushed into consideration of all the factors that affect the national well-being. How parties stand on programs designed to bring about stability and healthy expansion in the economy as a whole is therefore of great concern to most of the new groups in American politics.[16]

Several questions about the political party-pressure group relationship trend which the Committee observes and hopes will develop further might be asked. First, is there in fact such a trend? Second, if

---

[14] The Committee on Political Parties, *op. cit.*, p. 20.
[15] *Ibid.*, p. 34.
[16] *Ibid.*, pp. 34–35.

the trend does exist, is it desirable that it should continue on to produce a type of party-pressure group relationship such as the Committee desires?

(1) Addressing ourselves to the first of these questions — Does such a trend exist? — perhaps the answer is in the affirmative. But two qualifying counterquestions should follow immediately. Has the trend gone as far and are its effects as great as the Committee suggests? And will the trend continue to develop on a rising trend curve?

Over the course of the past two decades the membership strength of organized labor has jumped from about 5 million to approximately 15 million. During the same period labor has become active in politics and generally on the Democratic side, though Republican candidates have occasionally been endorsed and though the labor organizations have maintained they do not support nor are they a part of either major party. The first major labor move toward a new and intensified type of political activity came with the development of the C.I.O. Political Action Committee. The A.F.L. moved more cautiously from its traditional Samuel Gompers policy of " staying out of politics," but in 1948 made a fairly definite break from the past with the formation of Labor's League for Political Education. In 1955 the A.F.L. and C.I.O. merged. One of the reasons for the merger was to achieve a greater degree of effectiveness in political activity.

The role which organized labor, functioning as an auxiliary of the Democratic party, played in the 1954 elections in Michigan and Minnesota might serve to indicate how labor tends to operate in political campaigns and also how effective labor hopes it can politically be. The party-pressure group relationship trend observed by the Committee on Political Parties, as far as it applies to labor organizations, appears to have been validly interpreted. That labor is and will continue to be a major factor in Presidential campaigns, in many states, and in Congressional districts warrants classification as one of the political " facts of life " of modern American politics.

Farm pressure groups are mass membership organizations like the labor organizations; however, the evaluation of the farmer's role in politics must be different. First, the farmer organizations have not centralized to the point of labor organization centralization. Second, neither can the farm organizations be regarded as auxiliaries of the Democratic or Republican parties. Though the Grange and American Farm Bureau Federation might lean Republican on occasion or generally, they also might lean the other way. In general, the Farmers' Union stands alone among the farm organizations with a fairly solid Democratic party attachment. Third, farm organizations have not utilized their organizational structures and membership for political purposes to the same extent and in the same manner as have the labor organizations. Existing differences of political operation and outlook among the farm groups and between labor and farm groups, however, do not preclude the possibility that developing events and attitudes of the major parties might push the farm groups toward a labor-type approach toward political activity.

Political activity characteristics of business groups tend to differ from both farm and labor groups, though often there are farm group and business group alliances. Business organizations do not have the mass membership of their counterparts in the farm and labor fields. The advantages of business groups are the ability to more easily accumulate financial resources for political purposes and the strategic location of membership in the principal channels of communication in American society; the principal disadvantage is a relatively small mobilizable " organization vote." Business groups were in politics on an organized basis and were influential in major party politics long before either the farmer or the worker. Today, however, both of the latter groups have become or are fast becoming counterbalances to business influence in political affairs.

Should labor and a more centralized type of farm organization ally themselves with the same political party the implication of the Committee on Political Parties (though it does not directly say so) is that such a party might be able to muster a clear national majority for governing. Malcolm Moos, however, raises two points which might operate to prevent the maturation of the pressure-group-in-politics trend anticipated by the Committee. First, we do speak of a " labor vote " and a " farm vote," but the terms cannot mean what, on the surface, they appear to mean. In each of the groups there are loyalties overlapping into other groups. For example, it is true that organized labor tends to vote more Democratic than Republican, but there are Republicans here too. Republicans poll a much higher percentage of the unorganized workers, and in each of the major pressure group areas the organized groups to be found do not embrace all of the potentially organizable members. The pressure group leaders will have to dominate the political outlook of their members and potential members to a much greater extent than they do today in order

to produce cohesion of phalanx strength to be wielded as party auxiliaries in political campaigns.

Second, holds Moos, it is necessary to look beyond the recent
development of organized labor to its new level of political power.
Spectacularly growing is the so-called white-collar class. With the
coming of automation the ranks of the administrators, clerks, and
control-panel operators will continue to increase while the proportion of " laborers " in the total population will tend to decline. Furthermore, the white-collar proportion of the electorate can hardly
be described as a class because it is so highly diversified in its different occupational and other types of divisions. It has not yet been successfully organized around white collar objectives. It is not, unless
radical changes occur, likely to lend itself to organization such as in
the labor and farm fields.[17]

A third factor which is likely to level off the party-pressure group
trend line seen by the Committee on Political Parties, or to render
invalid some of the Committee's estimates, may be developed from
the Committee's assumption that the mass-based pressure groups are
developing a set of objectives in common with one another. Such
groups, suggests the Committee, will be concerned with " factors
that affect the national well-being " and will want " stability and
healthy expansion of the economy as a whole." Why, it might be
asked, are such concerns applied by the Committee only or primarily
to the so-called mass pressure groups? Why, it might also be asked,
have we the right to assume that different pressure groups, sections,
and local interests will not continue to have their own interpretations
of what will produce national well-being and what will keep the
economy healthy? And if nationalization of issues will tend to produce such unanimity of objective among groups competing in the
political arena, might we not expect to see the major parties move
even more closely together in their relative positions toward issues
than has been the case in the past?

Still another factor will have a direct bearing on the extent to
which mass pressure groups will tend to become auxiliaries of political parties, and that is the quality of flexibility which the parties
can bring to bear on their attempts to adapt to the modified political
environment in each stage of its progression from one type of pres-

---

[17] See Malcolm Moos, *Politics, Presidents and Coattails* (Baltimore: The
Johns Hopkins Press, 1952) , pp. 143–155.

sure group pattern to another. To the extent the Republican party becomes or allows itself to be labeled as an " antilabor " party, to that extent will labor leaders become more solid in their attachments to the Democratic party and be able to mobilize labor votes on the Democratic side. To the extent the Republican party becomes or allows itself to be labeled as an " antifarmer " party, to that extent will Democratic prospects for making farm groups Democratic auxiliaries be enhanced. If the major parties continue to be their old flexible selves, however, neither should permit crystallization of political components of the electorate as suggested by the Committee on Political Parties to take place. Only if either or both of the major parties became highly centralized and disciplined might one rightfully expect maturation of the apparent trend.

In point here was the controversy within the Republican party at the time of the A.F.L.–C.I.O. merger in December, 1955. Several highly placed Republicans held that the political arm of the new labor organization should have no right to endorse any Presidential candidate in 1956 because there would be infringements upon the rights of independent and Republican members of their organizations. Such an approach might be termed as negative, and if persisted in, Democratic designs on the " labor vote " would be helped along to realization by the Republican party. United States Senator Clifford Case (R), New Jersey, on the other hand, took issue and described some of the attacks against political activity on the part of labor organizations as " hysterical." Labor organizations, he said, have a clear right to encourage their members to exercise their franchise at the ballot box. And, Case continued: " Blanket attacks [by the labor organizations] on the Republican Party are unwarranted. The Republican Party must always respond to the needs of men and women in the ranks of labor just as it does to other segments of our population. I am confident that it will." [18]

(2) Would it be desirable for the mass membership pressure groups, or for all types of pressure groups for that matter, to become auxiliaries of one or the other of two major parties in a two-party system or for each major pressure group to form a party of its own in a multiparty system? Most observers are of the opinion either type of development would weaken instead of strengthen the American political system.

---

[18] *Los Angeles Times,* December 5, 1955.

Should the two-party system remain in spite of the pressure groups' choosing sides on a more or less permanent attachment basis, political conflict in the United States would become sharper and tend toward greater extremes of viewpoint than differentiate the Democrats and Republicans today. To produce political crystallization of American politics with the major parties representing a substantially clearer interest group pattern than is the case now, it would first be necessary for the leaders of the respective pressure groups to produce a much higher degree of concentration on group objectives to the exclusion of other overlapping interests of a group's membership. ". . . [T]he probability is that to the degree that groups succeed in monopolizing the loyalty of their members — in contrast with the situation in which individual loyalties are divided among many groups," writes V. O. Key, Jr., " to that extent intergroup cleavages are widened and deepened. . . . [T]he growth of stronger and stronger groups dedicated to the promotion of narrow group claims places greater strain on the social mechanisms for the settlement of group and class conflict." [19]

Might it not also be reasonable to expect that pressure group auxiliaries of political parties would demand and get, in return for the establishment or maintenance of auxiliary party status, a voice in proportion to their vote power and other resource strength in the management of party program and affairs. Election contests would then, more than is true today, become a battle between gigantic alliances of pressure groups for the satisfaction of pressure group claims. The contemporary Democratic and Republican parties are combinations of interests, it is true, but the combinations are loose and elastic. Furthermore, both parties must appeal roughly to the same groups and after elections most groups have some degree of access to the power points of government no matter which side the groups were on in the election campaign. Under the system envisioned by the Committee on Political Parties, the combinations of interest groups in a party alliance would be much more rigid, the parties would need less to appeal to the same groups for votes, and after elections access possibilities of the losing combination would be likely to be much smaller than they are today.

Stedman and Sonthoff, taking the view that the various organized pressure group interests and sectional and subsectional interests

---

[19] Key, *op. cit.*, pp. 179–180.

in the United States are so diverse they would not lend themselves to a two-party polarization, regard the Committee's concept of party-pressure group relations as possible only if there are many different political parties with each major pressure group becoming a minor party. This, however, would be the opposite of two strong parties. " The real choice [for the United States] is between a relatively weak two-party system with many outside interest groups or a very strong multi-party system with few nonpartisan interest groups." [20] If Stedman and Sonthoff's conclusion is warranted, the arguments against multiparty systems with all their instability characteristics are again in point.

One of the principal reasons why the Committee on Political Parties has recommended the type of party system it has is to establish parties more capable of formulating " public interest " programs. Yet, from its hope for pressure groups becoming auxiliaries for the major parties, might not the end product be a party system in which the parties are even less able to think in public interest terms than are the Democratic and Republican parties today?

CONCLUSION

Though the American party system and the major parties could undoubtedly function more effectively in the popular interest, has the system and have the parties failed so badly that either sweeping constitutional changes or a wholesale reorganization and realignment of the parties are necessary? A thesis in this volume has been that the answer to the question is in the negative. The American system has shown itself to be remarkably flexible in its ability to adapt to changing needs and problems. Though it might work more slowly than some systems, it can be made to function quickly if the nature of a crisis situation requires it. And the fact that the two major parties have survived for a century or more attests to their ability to react to political stimuli at a performance level which at least can be termed adequate but which perhaps warrants a much higher performance rating.

When, as will surely happen, modifications are made in the system or the parties do alter this procedure or that procedure or this approach or that approach, the change or alteration is likely to be

---

[20] Stedman and Sonthoff, *op. cit.,* p. 457.

gradual and, for the impatient, will appear imperceptible. The hazards inherent in moving too quickly when the nature of the times does not put a premium on speed, however, are certainly as dangerous as those of moving too slowly. Gradual progress, without standing still for the sake of standing still, is more likely to result in taking a sound forward step with at least one foot always planted on the ground.

There are many reasons of both a rational and irrational nature why the federal and separation of powers features of the American Constitution are likely to persist for a long time to come. Within this framework the two-party system, the pattern of party-pressure group relations, and the Democratic and Republican parties are likely, even in the quite distant future, to be recognizable in relation to what they are today. If the weakness of the system and the parties are not magnified in the mind to a point where their strengths are obscured, fundamentally both the system and the parties themselves are as adequate as any other democratic-representative alternative in sight for meeting whatever crises lie ahead.

Bibliographical Appendix

Although some of the important working materials on political parties, pressure groups, election laws, and party-in-government are cited in the footnotes of this volume, there are many other important sources which are not. For this reason and because it is advantageous to have assembled in one place the references to which one can go for a more intensive study of any of these subjects, a detailed bibliographical guide follows. Some of the sections are set up to parallel specific chapters of the book, and for parts where overlap of materials between chapters is heavy, the unit of organization is for an entire part of the book.

PART ONE: INTRODUCTION

Chapter One — The Politician

A series of recent books and articles on the general subject of ethics in government provides an excellent starting point for the development of an understanding of the politician, his functions and the environment in which he must operate. They include: Paul H. Appleby, *Morality and Administration* (1952); Marquis W. Childs, *Ethics in a Business Society* (1954); Paul H. Douglas, *Ethics in Government* (1952); George A. Graham, *Morality in American Politics* (1952); H. H. Wilson, *Congress: Corruption and Compromise* (1951); and the March, 1952, issue of *The Annals of the American Academy of Political and Social Science,* " Ethical Standards in American Public Life," Vol. 280.

If you want to approach the subject from the seamy side, there are many possibilities through which you may do so, such as Charles Harris Garrigues, *You're Paying for It! A Guide To Graft* (1936) or William P. Helm, *Washington Swindle Sheet* (1932). Or, if you would rather begin in writings designed to give the politician's viewpoint toward his role and functions, T. V. Smith's *The Legislative Way of Life* (1940), and the Frederick M. Davenport and Chester C. Maxey articles cited in Chapter One, and Claude G. Bowers, " In Defense of Politicians," *Virginia Quarterly Review* (Spring, 1943), Vol. 21, No. 2, pp. 219–233, will serve your purpose. See also F. S. Oliver, *Politics and Politicians* (1934).

The American political boss has received exhaustive attention. Some of the works on the boss are: Robert D. Bowden, *Boies Penrose* (1937); Edward J. Flynn's autobiographical *You're the Boss* (1947); H. F. Gosnell, *Boss Platt . . .* (1924) and *Machine Politics: Chicago Model*

(1937) ; Frank R. Kent, *The Great Game of Politics* (1923) ; Alfred H. Lewis, *Richard Croker* (1901) ; Denis T. Lynch, *Boss Tweed* (1927) ; Dayton D. McKean, *The Boss* (1940) , on Frank Hague of New Jersey; M. M. Milligan, *Missouri Waltz: The Inside Story of the Pendergast Machine* . . . (1948) ; Thomas C. Platt's *Autobiography of Thomas Collier Platt* (1910) ; W. L. Riordan, *Plunkitt of Tammany Hall* (1905) ; J. T. Salter, *Boss Rule* (1935) ; Charles Van Devanter, *The Big Bosses* (1944) ; and Harold Zink, *City Bosses in the United States* (1930) .

For very contemporary materials there are such books as Richard L. Neuberger, *Adventures in Politics* (1954) ; William S. White, *The* [Robert A.] *Taft Story* (1954) ; and the campaign biographies of almost any man who has been seriously considered as a Presidential possibility.

Chapter Two — The Major Party

Because Chapter Two is introductory in nature and because other sources on the character and functions of political parties will be cited in subsequent sections of this bibliography, only a few of the recent general works will be noted here. Maurice Duverger, *Political Parties: Their Organization and Activity in the Modern State* (1954) , is a comparative study of the party systems in several European countries and the United States. The most often used textbooks on American political parties all contain chapters on the role of the political party: Hugh A. Bone, *American Politics and the Party System* (1955) ; V. O. Key, Jr., *Politics, Parties and Pressure Groups* (1952) ; Dayton D. McKean, *Party and Pressure Politics* (1949) ; Peter H. Odegard and E. A. Helms, *American Politics* (1947) ; Howard R. Penniman, *Sait's American Parties and Elections* (1952) ; and Henry A. Turner's readings book, *Politics in the United States* (1955) .

Other works in which the role of political parties is the primary concern throughout are: Herbert Agar, *The Price of Union* (1950) ; D. W. Brogan, *Politics in America* (1954) ; Pendleton Herring, *The Politics of Democracy* (1940) ; Charles E. Merriam and H. F. Gosnell, *The American Party System* (1949) ; and E. E. Schattschneider, *Party Government* (1942) and *The Struggle for Party Government* (1948) . See also the bibliographical citations in the footnotes of Part Six for further development of the controversy about the adequacy of the parties and the system.

Chapter Three — The Pressure Group

One of the best brief developments of the role of the pressure group in American politics is Earl Latham, " The Group Basis of Politics: Notes for a Theory," *The American Political Science Review* (June, 1952) , Vol. 46, No. 2, pp. 376–397. Three general books on the subject systematically develop a group theory of politics. The earliest, written at a time when pressure groups were being largely overlooked by most political scientists, is Arthur F. Bentley, *The Process of Government* (1908, and now available in a 1949 edition). David B. Truman, *The Governmental Process* (1951) builds upon Bentley's work and represents an able analysis for the contemporary period, as does Bertram Gross, *The Legislative Struggle* (1953). Less theoretical but highly useful as systematic developments of pressure group-government relations are Pendleton Herring's *Group Representation Before Congress* (1929) and *Public Administration and the Public Interest* (1936); and parts of Avery Leiserson's *Administrative Regulation: A Study of Representation of Interests* (1942). The Herring and Schattschneider works cited under Chapter Two above also contain valuable materials in point here.

Other general works are: Donald C. Blaisdell, *Government under Pressure* (1942); Stuart Chase, *Democracy under Pressure* (1945); Kenneth G. Crawford, *The Pressure Boys: The Inside Story of Lobbying in America* (1939); John Dewey, *The Public and Its Problems* (1927); William B. Munro, *The Invisible Government* (1928); and Karl Schriftgieser, *The Lobbyists: The Art and Business of Influencing Lawmakers* (1951). James Burns, *Congress on Trial* (1949) has useful chapters on this subject.

Many studies of a monographic nature are available for the further study of specific pressure groups and their relations with government. For farm groups they include: Donald C. Blaisdell, *Government and Agriculture* (1940); Charles M. Hardin, *The Politics of Agriculture* (1952); Orville M. Kile, *The Farm Bureau Through Three Decades* (1948); Grant McConnell, *The Decline of Agrarian Democracy* (1953); and Wesley McCune, *The Farm Bloc* (1943). For labor groups they include: Fay Calkins, *The C.I.O. and the Democratic Party* (1952); Joseph Gaer, *The First Round: The Story of the C.I.O. Political Action Committee* (1944); Mathew Josephson, *Sidney Hillman* (1952); Lewis L. Lorwin, *The American Federation of Labor* (1933); and C. Wright Mills, *The New Men of Power* (1948). For business groups they include: R. A. Brady, *Business as a System of Power* (1943); John K. Galbraith, *American Capitalism: The Concept of Countervailing Power* (1952); Earl Latham, *The Group Basis of Politics: A Study of Basing Point Legislation* (1952); David Lilienthal, *Big Business* (1953); and Carl D. Thompson, *Confessions of the Power Trust* (1932). Books which overlap farm, labor, and business groups include: Harwood L. Childs, *Labor and Capital in National Politics* (1930); Thomas P. Jenkin, *Reactions of Major Groups to Positive Government in the United States 1930–1940* (1945); Stuart Rice, *Farmers and Workers in American Politics* (1924); and E. E. Schattschneider, *Politics, Pressures and the Tariff* (1935).

For other valuable pressure group materials see such works as: *The*

Annals . . . (May, 1935), Vol. 179, "Professional Associations"; (March, 1948), Vol. 256, "Organized Religion in the United States"; (November, 1946), Vol. 248, "Labor Relations and the Public"; and (March, 1951), Vol. 274, "Labor in the American Economy." See also: M. L. Rutherford, *The Influence of the American Bar Association on Public Opinion and Legislature* (1937); Oliver Garceau, *The Political Life of the American Medical Association* (1941); L. E. Ebersole, *Church Lobbying in the Nation's Capital* (1951); M. R. Dearing, *Veterans in Politics: The Story of the G.A.R.* (1952); Fred W. Riggs, *Pressures on Congress: A Study of the Repeal of Chinese Exclusion* (1950); Stephen K. Bailey, *Congress Makes A Law: The Story Behind the Employment Act of 1946* (1950); C. J. Culp, *The German-Americans in Politics* (1939); Peter H. Odegard, *Pressure Politics: The Story of the Anti-Saloon League* (1928); T. C. Kesselman, *The Social Politics of the FEPC* (1948); and Arthur Maas, *Muddy Waters: The Army Engineers and the Nation's Rivers* (1951). For a study of a group which has as yet proved unorganizable, see C. Wright Mills, *White Collar* (1952).

Two works which deal with the over-all pattern of pressure politics in particular states are Dayton D. McKean, *Pressures on the Legislature of New Jersey* (1938); and Belle Zeller, *Pressure Politics in New York* (1937).

Chapter Four — The Minor Party

William B. Hesseltine's *The Rise and Fall of Third Parties: From Anti-Masonry to Wallace* (1948) contains a valuable classified bibliography of works on minor parties. Specific minor party classifications included there are the Know-Nothing party, Anti-Masonic party, Equal Rights or Locofoco party, Free-Soil party, Populist party, labor and satellite parties, Communist party, Progressive parties of 1912 and 1924, Socialist party, Nonpartisan League, and the Granger, Greenback, and Wallace movements. Since the publication of Hesseltine's brief but interesting and valuable book, the principal general work on minor parties to appear has been Murray S. Stedman, Jr., and S. W. Stedman, *Discontent at the Polls: A Study of Farmer and Labor Parties, 1827–1948* (1950). See also biographies of minor party leaders.

One article warrants a special note — John D. Hicks, "The Third Party Tradition in American Politics," *The Mississippi Valley Historical Review* (June, 1933), Vol. 20, No. 1, pp. 3–28.

Paul H. Douglas' *The Coming of a New Party* (1932), the book around which much of Chapter Four was built, represents the most systematic attempt to analyze the relation of the minor party to the American political system with the object to show that minor parties can and should develop.

PART TWO: MAJOR PARTY ORGANIZATION

Chapter Five — State and Local Election Machinery

For early American suffrage requirements see A. E. McKinley, *The Suffrage Franchise in the Thirteen Colonies* (1905); and for a study of suffrage in the voting on the United States Constitution, Charles A. Beard, *An Economic Interpretation of the Constitution* (1921). Broader in its development of the historical background is Kirk H. Porter, *A History of Suffrage in the United States* (1918). Dudley O. McGovney, *The American Suffrage Medley* (1949), presents a recent and general study of the suffrage requirements in the several states. If the student desires a current check on the laws of the states, see the most up-to-date edition of the *Book of the States*.

On the woman suffrage movement the books include: C. C. Catt and N. R. Shuler, *Woman Suffrage and Politics* (1923); Ida H. Harper, *The History of Woman Suffrage* (1922); the National American Woman Suffrage Association, *Victory: How Woman Won It. A Centennial Symposium, 1840–1940* (1940); and Emmeline Pankhurst, *The Suffragette Movement* (1931). For the most detailed development of the movement see Elizabeth Cady Stanton and others, *History of Woman Suffrage* (1881–1902), in four volumes. On Negro suffrage the materials include: Ralph Bunche, *The Political Status of the Negro* (1940); C. S. Mangum, Jr., *The Legal Status of the Negro* (1940); Henry L. Moon, *Balance of Power: The Negro Vote* (1948); and for a foreigner's view of the problem, Gunnar Myrdal, *An American Dilemma* (1944).

On election administration and registration see Joseph P. Harris, *Registration of Voters in the United States* (1929) and *Election Administration in the United States* (1934); J. B. Johnson and J. J. Lewis, *Registration for Voting in the United States* (1946); G. F. Miller, *Absentee Voters and Suffrage Laws* (1949); the National Municipal League, *A Model Registration System* (1954); and James K. Pollock, *Absentee Voting and Registration* (1940). See also E. C. Evans, *A History of the Australian Ballot System in the United States* (1917). For detailed information about types of ballots consult Spencer D. Albright, *The American Ballot* (1942), and Carl O. Smith, *A Book of Ballots* (1938).

General works on the direct primary are: F. W. Dallinger, *Nominations for Elective Office in the United States* (1903); Arthur Harris and Carl Uhr, *Direct Primary Elections* (1941); the Illinois Legislative Council, *The Direct Primary Ballot* (1940); Charles E. Merriam and Louise Overacker, *Primary Elections* (1928); and E. C. Meyer, *Nomination Systems; Direct Primaries versus Conventions* (1902). See also Joseph P. Harris, *A Model Direct Primary Election System* (1951); and for two studies of the effect of the cross-filing in primary elections, see Robert W.

Binkley, Jr., *Double Filing in Primary Elections* (1945); and Evelyn Hazen, *Cross Filing in Primary Elections* (1951).

In addition to these over-all examinations of direct primary elections, there are numerous monographs for specific states. They include: Paul Beckett and W. L. McNutt, *The Direct Primary in New Mexico* (1947); R. D. Boots, *The Direct Primary in New Jersey* (1917); L. M. Holland, *The Direct Primary in Georgia* (1945); A. J. Lovejoy, *La-Follette and the Establishment of the Direct Primary in Wisconsin, 1890–1904* (1941); Boyd A. Martin, *The Direct Primary in Idaho* (1947); and James K. Pollock, *The Direct Primary in Michigan, 1909–1935* (1943). A very large number of articles on the operation of the direct primary in the respective states are also available in such publications as *The American Political Science Review*.

Chapter Six — State and Local Party Organization

Most of the written materials on state and local party organization are studies of specific boss-controlled party machines. See the citations on bosses under Chapter One. In addition, see also the following books which place all or a considerable part of their emphasis on organization: Sonya Forthal, *Cogwheels of Democracy, A Study of the Precinct Captain* (1946); Harold F. Gosnell, *Machine Politics: Chicago Model* (1937); Frank R. Kent, *The Great Game of Politics* (1923); V. O. Key, Jr., *Southern Politics* (1949); D. H. Kurtzman, *Methods of Controlling Votes in Philadelphia* (1935); and Roy V. Peel, *The Political Clubs of New York City* (1935). A study which concentrates its attention on local party personnel is Hugh A. Bone, *Grass Roots Party Leadership: A Case Study of Kings County, Washington* (1952). See also V. O. Key, Jr., *American State Politics* (1955).

Information on state and local party organization may also be obtained for many of the states from books or pamphlets describing the operation of state government and politics. Particularly valuable are manuals published by the state parties themselves describing their structure and functions. Ideally, however, no matter what the secondary sources available, the student should examine his own state's laws as they relate to party structure. Data on party-in-government may be found in state and local government books about specific states and in general state and local government textbooks. Harvey Walker, *The Legislative Process* (1948); and the recent report of the Committee on American Legislatures (Belle Zeller, chairman and editor), *American State Legislatures* (1954), are the principal general sources for party in the state legislatures. Up-to-date statistics on party complexion of state legislatures and state executive officers are included in the latest edition of the *Book of the States*.

Chapter Seven — National Party Organization: The National Convention

The most valuable source on national conventions is the five-volume set by Paul T. David, Malcolm Moos, and Ralph M. Goldman, *Presidential Nominating Politics in 1952* (1954). Here the student will find one volume devoted to a general survey of the conventions of that year and others to state by state accounts of the delegate selection process and delegation activities at the conventions. Older general works are: J. B. Bishop, *Presidential Nominations and Elections* (1916); and T. H. McKee (ed.), *The National Conventions and Platforms of All Political Parties, 1789–1905* (1906). For platforms see Kirk H. Porter (ed.), *National Party Platforms, 1840–1924* (1924).

For specific national conventions, the Democratic and Republican parties quadrennially prepare *Proceedings of the National Convention*. H. L. Mencken, *Making a President* (1932) is a brief and rather lurid account of the 1932 Democratic and Republican conventions. See also William Jennings Bryan, *A Tale of Two Conventions* (1912); and John Tweedy, *History of the Republican National Conventions* (1910). Likewise, accounts of specific national conventions may be found in autobiographies and biographies of men who have been candidates for Presidential nominations or other active participants. Some of the more recent of the latter type include: James A. Farley, *Behind the Ballots* (1938) and *Jim Farley's Story: The Roosevelt Years* (1948); Edward J. Flynn, *You're the Boss* (1947); and Charles Michelson, *The Ghost Talks* (1944). Studies of particular campaigns such as Roy V. Peel and T. C. Donnelly, *The 1928 Campaign* (1931) and *The 1932 Campaign* (1935) contain chapters on national conventions.

Chapter Eight — National Party Organization: National Committees and Party in Congress

Relatively few sources are available on the parties' national committees as organizations. G. S. P. Kleeberg, *The Formation of the Republican Party as a National Political Organization* (1911), deals with only one of the major parties and is out of date. The publicity function of the Democratic National Committee has received attention in Theodore M. Black, *Democratic Party Publicity in the 1940 Campaign* (1941), and in Thomas S. Barclay, "The Publicity Division of the Democratic Party, 1929–1930," *The American Political Science Review* (February, 1931), Vol. 25, No. 1, pp. 68–72. Otherwise the emphasis in studies has been on national party chairmen. For one such work see Ralph M. Goldman, *Party Chairmen and Party Factions, 1789–1900* (1951, University of Chicago PhD dissertation). The Farley, Flynn, and Michelson citations under

Chapter Seven above are good sources for this topic. See also Herbert Croly, *Marcus Alonza Hanna* (1912).

Materials on party organization in Congress are abundant. Some of the general books include: James M. Burns, *Congress on Trial* (1949); George B. Galloway, *The Legislative Process in Congress* (1953); Ernest Griffith, *Congress: Its Contemporary Role* (1951); Bertram M. Gross, *The Legislative Struggle: A Study in Social Combat* (1953); Joseph P. Harris, *The Advice and Consent of the Senate* (1953); Paul D. Hasbrouck, *Party Government in the House of Representatives* (1927); George H. Haynes, *The Senate of the United States* (1938); Estes Kefauver and Jack Levin, *A Twentieth-Century Congress* (1947); Floyd Riddick, *The United States Congress: Organization and Procedure* (1949); Lindsay Rogers, *The American Senate* (1926); and Roland A. Young, *This Is Congress* (1943).

Textbooks on legislatures which develop both state and Congressional organization and procedure are: Joseph P. Chamberlain, *Legislative Processes: National and State* (1936); Harvey Walker, *The Legislative Process* (1948); and W. F. Willoughby, *Principles of Legislative Organization and Administration* (1934). A monograph on a point vital to Senate party organization is Franklin L. Burdette, *Filibustering in the Senate* (1940). Woodrow Wilson's classic *Congressional Government: A Study in American Politics* (1885) is still a highly useful work. Stephen K. Bailey and Howard Samuel, *Congress at Work* (1952) contains a series of excellent case studies which do much to illuminate Congressional party organization workings. See also George B. Galloway, *Congress and Parliament: Their Organization and Operation in the U.S. and the U.K.* (1955).

Chapter Nine — National Party Organization: The President

The above works on the Congress and legislative process include sections or chapters on legislative-executive relationships. Books which view that relationship from the vantage point of the Presidency include: Pendleton Herring, *Presidential Leadership* (1940); Sidney Hyman, *The American President* (1954); Harold J. Laski, *The American Presidency* (1940); George F. Milton, *The Use of Presidential Power* (1944); and Norman J. Small, *Some Presidential Interpretations of the Presidency* (1932). For historical development of President-Congress relations see Wilfred E. Binkley, *The Powers of the President* (1937) and *President and Congress* (1947); and Edward Stanwood, *A History of the Presidency* (1928, in two volumes). For a more legal development of that office see Edward S. Corwin, *The President: Office and Powers* (1940). For a study of President-Congress relations on specific pieces of legislation over the 1890–1938 period see Lawrence H. Chamberlain, *The President, Congress, and Legislation* (1946).

PART THREE: WINNING ELECTIONS —
PARTY HISTORY THREADED ON FOUR THEMES

Works directly or indirectly concerned with American political party history are so many that only a relatively few guides for further study can be listed here. A condensed short-book account is to be found in Charles A. Beard, *The American Party Battle* (1928). Wilfred E. Binkley, *American Political Parties: Their Natural History* (1949) is the best available source and should be supplemented with the same author's *President and Congress* (1947). Both of the Binkley works are written in a very interesting style.

Other general party histories include: Herbert Agar, *Pursuit of Happiness: The Story of American Democracy* (1938); D. W. Brogan, *Politics in America* (1955); T. W. Couzens, *Politics and Political Organizations in America* (1942); W. C. Crandall, *Early History of the Republican Party* (1930); Francis Curtis, *The Republican Party, 1854–1904* (1904); Frank R. Kent, *History of the Democratic Party* (1928); W. S. Meyers, *History of the Republican Party* (1928); and Edgar E. Robinson, *The Evolution of American Parties* (1924). Two books which are primarily statistical and which show Presidential election votes by counties but which also contain descriptions of each Presidential election are: W. Dean Burnham, *Presidential Ballots, 1836–1892* (1955); and Edgar E. Robinson, *The Presidential Vote, 1896–1932* (1934). See also Henry A. Turner, "National Politics: Eras of One-party Control," *Social Science* (June, 1953), Vol. 28, No. 3, pp. 137–143.

For the Federalist-Jeffersonian Republican period see: Claude G. Bowers, *Jefferson and Hamilton* (1925); Stuart G. Brown, *The First Republicans* (1954); and Leonard D. White, *The Federalists* (1948) and *The Jeffersonians* (1951); and Manning Dauer, *The Adams Federalists* (1955).

For the Jacksonian Democratic-Whig period see: Claude G. Bowers, *The Party Battles of the Jacksonian Period* (1922); Arthur C. Cole, *The Whig Party in the South* (1913); Arthur M. Schlesinger, Jr., *The Age of Jackson* (1946); and Leonard D. White, *The Jacksonians* (1955).

For the Republican-Democratic period with emphasis on the years since 1900 see: Arthur N. Holcombe, *The Political Parties of Today* (1924); Herbert Croly, *Marcus Alonzo Hanna* (1912); William Jennings Bryan and M. E. Bryan, *The Memoirs of William Jennings Bryan* (1925); Henry F. Pringle, *Theodore Roosevelt* (1931); George Mowry, *Theodore Roosevelt and the Progressive Movement* (1946); Henry F. Pringle, *William Howard Taft* (1939, in two volumes); Kenneth W. Heckler, *Insurgency: Personalities and Politics of the Taft Era* (1940); L. B. Wehle, *Hidden Threads of History: Wilson Through Roosevelt* (1953);

Samuel H. Adams, *Incredible Era: The Life and Times of Warren Harding* (1939) ; M. E. Ravage, *The Story of Teapot Dome* (1924) ; William A. White, *A Puritan [Coolidge] in Babylon* (1938) ; Herbert Hoover, *The Memoirs of Herbert Hoover* (1952) ; W. S. Meyers and W. H. Newton, *The Hoover Administration: A Documented Narrative* (1936) ; and Ray L. Wilbur and Arthur Hyde, *The Hoover Policies* (1937).

For the Democratic-Republican period since 1932 see the Farley, Michelson, and Edward Flynn books cited under Chapter Seven and Arthur N. Holcombe, *The New Party Politics* (1933) ; Joseph Alsop and Turner Catledge, *The 168 Days* (1938) ; Frances Perkins, *The Roosevelt I Knew* (1946) ; Basil Rauch, *The History of the New Deal* (1944) ; Edgar E. Robinson, *They Voted for Roosevelt* (1947) ; Arthur M. Schlesinger, *New Deal in Action, 1933–1939* (1940) ; Robert E. Sherwood, *Roosevelt and Hopkins* (1948, in two volumes) ; and Schuyler C. Wallace, *The New Deal in Action* (1934). For a different viewpoint see: Alfred M. Landon: *America at the Crossroads* (1936) ; Norman Beasley, *Politics Has No Morals* (1949) ; and John T. Flynn, *Country Squire in the White House* (1940).

Other works primarily concerned with contemporary politics but which are historical as they relate to the years from 1932 to the present will be cited under Part Four.

PART FOUR: WINNING ELECTIONS — PROBLEMS OF STRATEGY

One of the most valuable tools for the politician or student of contemporary politics is the *Weekly Report* published by the Congressional Quarterly News Service. Much of the current data used in Chapters Fifteen and Sixteen is drawn from that source. In it also are analytical articles backgrounding every major political development in this country. The same organization annually publishes a *Congressional Quarterly Almanac* in which, among other things, can be found Congressional voting records on major items of legislation and a summary of the activities of Congress in such areas as agriculture, national defense, and so on. Current periodical literature includes, particularly in election years, much political analysis and every student of politics should attempt to examine at least the best of such articles as they appear.

Following are relatively recent books which have had as their central focus an interpretation of present-day American politics. General works include: Louis H. Bean, *How to Predict Elections* (1948) and *The Mid-Term Battle* (1950) ; Cortez A. M. Ewing, *Congressional Elections, 1896–1944* (1947) ; Louis Harris, *Is There a Republican Majority? Political Trends, 1952–1956* (1954) ; Samuel Lubell, *The Future of American*

Politics (1952); Malcolm Moos, *Politics, Presidents and Coattails* (1952); Roland Stromberg, *Republicanism Reappraised* (1952); and Charles H. Titus, *Voting Behavior in the United States: A Statistical Study* (1935).

Paul F. Lazarsfeld, Bernard Berelson, and Hazel Gaudet, *The People's Choice* (1948) is a study of the 1940 Presidential election in Erie County, Ohio. Angus Campbell and Robert L. Kahn, *The People Elect a President* (1952), analyze the 1948 Presidential election. Angus Campbell, Gerald Gurin, and Warren E. Miller, *The Voter Decides* (1954) analyze the 1952 Presidential election. Using the interview data for the western states as compiled by Campbell and associates, Alfred DeGrazia prepared his *The Western Public, 1952 and Beyond* (1954). Bernard R. Berelson, P. E. Lazarsfeld, and W. N. McPhee, *Voting: A Study of Opinion Formation in a Presidential Campaign* (1954), study the 1948 Presidential election in Elmira, New York, and in this book there is an appendix reference section starting on page 331 which summarizes the principal findings of recent books and articles on American political behavior. See also Samuel J. Eldersvelt, "The Influence of Metropolitan Party Pluralities in Presidential Elections," *The American Political Science Review* (December, 1949), Vol. 43, No. 6, pp. 1189–1206.

Three books on political developments in the South are: V. O. Key, Jr., *Southern Politics* (1949), which makes a comprehensive state by state survey; Alexander Heard, *A Two-Party South?* (1952); and J. B. Shannon, *Toward a New Politics in the South* (1949).

PART FIVE: WINNING ELECTIONS — CAMPAIGN ORGANIZATION AND TACTICS

Chapter Seventeen — Candidates

"Availability" factors in candidate selection are discussed in the Herring, Hyman, and Laski books on the President listed under Chapter Nine, and likewise they enter into the books on party history and bosses. Sidney Hyman, *The American President* (1954), Chapter Ten, is especially good. *The Great Game of Politics* (1923) and *Political Behavior* (1928) by Frank R. Kent present chapters which are highly realistic in their approach to the subject, particularly from the standpoint of what the political boss is looking for in the candidate selection process. Other useful works are: Harold Gosnell, *Champion Campaigner: Franklin D. Roosevelt* (1952); Charles E. Merriam, *Four American Party Leaders* (1926) and *Systematic Politics* (1945); Raymond Moley, *27 Masters of Politics* (1949); and J. T. Salter (ed.), *The American Politician* (1936) and *Public Men* (1946).

Representing broader approaches to the subject of political leadership are the following books: A. Barratt Brown, *Democratic Leadership*

(1938) ; A. W. Gouldner, *Studies in Leadership* (1950) ; Harold Laswell, *Power and Personality* (1948) ; William B. Munroe, *Personality in Politics* (1924) ; Ordway Tead, *The Art of Leadership* (1935) ; and Charles H. Titus, *The Processes of Leadership* (1950).

Chapter Eighteen — Campaign Organization

Materials, particularly analytical materials, on campaign organization as such are almost nonexistent in comparison with the other subject headings under which the study of party politics has been arranged. Information on local campaign organization may, with some purposeful effort, be gathered from several widely scattered sources. Both major party national committees prepare campaign organization manuals, and many of the state parties and sometimes county units of the parties do likewise. The student should, using his own devices, assemble a collection of such materials. Also, if the output of newspapers and magazines is watched during a campaign, one will occasionally find articles of value on campaign organization.

Paul P. Van Riper, *Handbook of Practical Politics: A nonpartisan guide to success in effective local political action* (1952) is perhaps the most comprehensive local campaign organization guide, and in it are to be found numerous passages from Democratic and Republican campaign organization manuals. Harold Gauer, *How to Win in Politics* (1946), is a breezy development of a campaign organization with particular emphasis on propaganda. Although not focusing on political party campaigning, John P. Keith, *Public Relations Program for a Citizen Committee* (1950), develops useful facets on organization for nonpartisan campaigns which may be applied for partisan purposes as well. Other works which to some degree develop political party campaign organization are: Oliver Carlson and A. Blake, *How to Get into Politics: The Art of Winning Elections* (1946) ; Lowell Mellett, *Handbook of Politics* (1946) ; and Hugh D. Scott, *How To Go into Politics* (1949).

Several works cited previously are of value for developing insight into campaign organizational problems, particularly as viewed from the Presidential campaign manager's viewpoint: T. M. Black, *Democratic Party Publicity in the 1940 Campaign* (1941) ; James A. Farley, *Behind the Ballots* (1938) and *Jim Farley's Story . . .* (1948) ; Edward Flynn, *You're the Boss* (1947) ; Frank R. Kent, *The Great Game of Politics* (1923) and *Political Behavior* (1928) ; Roy V. Peel and T. C. Donnelly, *The 1928 Campaign* (1931) and *The 1932 Campaign* (1935) ; and Charles Michelson, *The Ghost Talks* (1944).

Also useful as materials indirectly relating to party campaign organization are some of the books on pressure group politics. Of the studies of particular pressure groups and their campaign activities two of the best for this purpose are: Joseph Gaer, *The First Round: The Story of the*

C.I.O. Political Action Committee (1944); and Peter H. Odegard, *Pressure Politics: The Story of the Anti-Saloon League* (1928). See also David B. Truman, *The Governmental Process* (1951), Part II, for a general theoretical development of the relationship between organization and a group's public relations potential.

Chapter Nineteen — Campaign Research

Campaign research as such, like campaign organization as such, has been the object of almost no studies directly on the subject. Literature in the public relations field can, however, be applicable to the campaign research problem. Perhaps the most valuable of this type of work is Philip Lesly (ed.), *Public Relations Handbook* (1950), with Chapter 29 " Finding the Facts for Public Relations " and Chapter 31 " Fact-Finding for Public Relations Work." Of the public opinion and propaganda texts, the book which gives the most attention to " campaign research " in a broad sense is Norman J. Powell, *Anatomy of Public Opinion* (1951).

Materials on public opinion polling techniques are available in great number. Most comprehensive and practical and with an excellent bibliography is Mildred B. Parten, *Surveys, Polls, and Samples: Practical Procedures* (1950). An elementary and short book is George Gallup, *A Guide to Public Opinion Polls* (1944). See also Albert B. Blankenship, *Consumer and Opinion Research* (1943); Hadley Cantril, *Gauging Public Opinion* (1944); the National Opinion Research Center, *Interviewing for NORC* (1946); and Stanley L. Payne, *The Art of Asking Questions* (1951). *The Public Opinion Quarterly* is literally full of articles on every phase of the opinion polling process, and many others may be found in the political science, sociology, and psychology professional periodicals. Frederick Mosteller (*et al.*), *The Pre-Election Polls of 1948* (1949), is a systematic analysis of the major polling organizations' shortcomings in the ill-fated — from the pollsters' viewpoint — 1948 Presidential election. Lindsay Rogers, *The Pollsters* (1949), is an interesting general criticism of what the public opinion pollers think they can do.

Books which summarize or contain results of public opinion polls taken in the United States include: Jerome Bruner, *Mandate from the People* (1944); Hadley Cantril (ed.), *Public Opinion 1936–1946* (1951); and W. A. Lydgate, *What America Thinks* (1944). *The People's Choice, The People Elect a President, The Voter Decides, The Western Public 1952 and Beyond,* and *Voting* cited under Part Four above are all examples of studies which utilized polling techniques in analyzing election campaigns. They also include statements about methods.

Chapter Twenty — Campaign Propaganda

Materials in whole or in part devoted to political party propaganda include: Frederic C. Bartlett, *Political Propaganda* (1940); Theodore M.

Black, *Democratic Party Publicity in the 1940 Campaign* (1941); Hugh A. Bone, *"Smear" Politics* (1941); Ralph D. Casey, "Party Campaign Propaganda," *The Annals* (May, 1935), Vol. 179, pp. 96–105, and "Republican Propaganda in the 1936 Campaign," *Public Opinion Quarterly* (April, 1937), Vol. 1, No. 2, pp. 27–44; Joseph Gaer, *The First Round: The Story of the C.I.O. Political Action Committee* (1944), with illustrations of propaganda pieces used; Harold Gauer, *How to Win in Politics* (1946); Thomas B. Grandin, *The Political Use of Radio* (1939); Roy V. Peel and T. C. Donnelly, *The 1928 Campaign* (1931) and *The 1932 Campaign* (1935); and Charles W. Smith, Jr., "Campaign Communications Media," *The Annals* (September, 1948), Vol. 259, pp. 90–97; and pamphlets prepared by the parties such as Democratic National Committee, *A Campaign Guide to Political Publicity* (undated, Stephen A. Mitchell, chairman).

David B. Truman, *The Governmental Process* (1951), Chapter 8, is an excellent and condensed development of the propaganda process in general. See also the works cited in footnotes in Chapter Twenty. The principal bibliography in the field is B. L. Smith, H. D. Lasswell, and R. D. Casey, *Propaganda, Communication, and Public Opinion: A Comprehensive Reference Guide* (1946).

Chapter Twenty-one — Campaign Finance

Louise Overacker, in *Money and Elections* (1932), *Presidential Campaign Funds* (1946), and her periodic articles in *The American Political Science Review;* and James K. Pollock, *Party Campaign Funds* (1926), are the principal general works on political party finance. For corrupt practices legislation see S. S. Minault, *Corrupt Practices Legislation in the 48 States* (1942), and Earl R. Sikes, *State and Federal Corrupt Practices Legislation* (1928). *The Congressional Quarterly Weekly Report* analyzes campaign spending for each election. Congressional committee reports on the subject include *Report of the Special House Committee to Investigate Campaign Expenditures,* 2nd Session of the Eighty-second Congress, 1953, H. R. 2517. Isabella H. Hayes, *Financing Presidential Campaigns* (1953, University of Maryland, mimeo.) includes articles on 1952 campaign finance.

PART SIX: THE PARTIES AND THE FUTURE

The footnotes in Chapters Twenty-two, Twenty-three, and Twenty-four include the principal citations on the controversy over weaknesses and strengths of the American party system and the parties. They may also be supplemented by the works listed under Chapter Two.

Index